ScottForesman Spanish Program

PASO A PASO

Teacher's Edition

1

Myriam Met
Coordinator of Foreign Languages
Montgomery County Public Schools
Rockville, MD

Richard S. Sayers
Niwot High School
Longmont, CO

Carol Eubanks Wargin
Glen Crest Junior High School
Glen Ellyn, IL

ScottForesman
A Division of HarperCollins*Publishers*

Editorial Offices: Glenview, Illinois

Regional Offices: Sunnyvale, California • Atlanta, Georgia
Glenview, Illinois • Oakland, New Jersey • Dallas, Texas

ADDITIONAL WRITERS AND CONTRIBUTORS

The following individuals contributed their expertise and creativity in developing the many notes and features in this Teacher's Edition.

Lynn Andersen
Chattahoochee High School
Alpharetta, GA

Mary Louise Carey
Natick (MA) High School

JoAnn DiGiandomenico
Natick (MA) High School

Susan Dobinsky
Niles North High School
Skokie, IL

Gail Glover
Cheyenne Mountain
   Junior High School
Colorado Springs, CO

Marjorie Hall Haley, Ph. D.
George Mason University
Fairfax, VA

Thomasina Pagán Hannum
Albuquerque, NM

Lucía Nuñez
Stanford University
Stanford, CA

Bernadette M. Reynolds
Manual High School
Denver, CO

Luz Nuncio Schick
Naperville, IL

Judith B. Smith, Ed. D.
Baltimore City (MD)
   Public Schools

ISBN: 0-673-21672-1

Copyright © 1996

Scott, Foresman and Company, Glenview, Illinois

All Rights Reserved. Printed in the United States of America.

12345678910-RW-03020100999897969594

TABLE OF CONTENTS

PHILOSOPHY OF THE PROGRAM

Welcome to *PASO A PASO!*

This program is based on the belief that the purpose of learning Spanish is to communicate with the people who speak it and to understand their cultures. *PASO A PASO* is designed to help your students achieve that goal by getting them to communicate right from the start.

PASO A PASO reflects the most current thinking in the foreign language field. It reflects state-of-the-art research on how students learn languages and what teachers and materials need to do to help them become proficient language users, whether they are using their new language for oral or written communication.

Let's take a look at some basic premises about language and language learning, the components of *PASO A PASO,* and how each of these components contributes to developing language proficiency.

What is communication?

Communication is an authentic exchange of information for a real purpose between two or more people. By this we mean that people tell each other (through speech or writing) something the other person doesn't already know.

Communicating meaning has several aspects. Students need to learn to listen to and read Spanish in order to interpret intended meanings, to express meaning by conveying their own messages for a purpose and to a real audience, and to negotiate meaning through the natural give-and-take involved in understanding and in making oneself understood. Research tells us that classroom activities must provide students practice in interpreting, expressing, and negotiating meaning through extensive and frequent peer interactions, preferably in pairs or small groups.

Communication is driven not only by meaning, but also by purpose. In real life, people communicate to get things done. They may communicate to transact business, to get to know someone else, or to find out something they really need to

know. In authentic communication, people give and get new ideas or information. The information that one partner has and the other doesn't is often called an *information gap* or an *opinion gap.* How unlike the classrooms of old, where we typically asked students questions to which we (and everyone else) already knew the answer, questions such as, "Tom, what's your name?" and "Sally, are you a boy or a girl?" These questions are not heard in real life because they lack a communicative purpose: there is no information or opinion gap.

PASO A PASO is organized around the principle that just as meaning and purpose drive all language use, so too should they drive all language learning. Students are engaged in understanding messages, in sending their own messages, and thus in communicating on every page of every chapter. Because *PASO A PASO* structures almost all activities for pair or group interaction, students find themselves active participants in every lesson, every day. They communicate real ideas and real meanings for real purposes. Every component of *PASO A PASO* is designed with the goal of communication in mind.

Interpreting meaning

In the last decade we have learned more than ever before about how language is acquired. We know that students learn best when they have ample opportunities to internalize meanings before they have to produce them. That is, we know that comprehension precedes production. Many teachers will be familiar with the term "comprehensible input," first used by Stephen Krashen, who suggests that learners acquire language by understanding what they hear. Students need many opportunities to match what they hear with visual cues (pictures, video, or teacher pantomime) or experiences (physical actions) so that they can associate meanings with forms. This is as true for comprehending language structure and syntax as it is for vocabulary development.

In keeping with research on the importance of matching language with meaning, *PASO A PASO* gives students many opportunities to comprehend new language before producing it. The video allows students to hear native speakers using language in a contextualized format that makes the meanings of new words and structures clear. Students learn by matching what they hear with what they see. Numerous activities for providing comprehensible input are suggested in this Teacher's Edition, activities that involve visuals (transparencies and pictures) and that physically engage students as they acquire new language. Whenever possible, in the pupil's text, vocabulary is visualized, so that both video and print materials provide examples of language in context.

What kind of practice promotes communication skills?

The first and most critical step in the language development process is getting meaning—learning to understand by matching what is heard with what is seen or experienced. But by itself, understanding is not enough. Students also need to use their new knowledge.

Research tells us that students need extensive practice in using their new language to create and convey their own messages. While there may be a legitimate role for simply drilling new structures or vocabulary, the most valuable practice comes from using them to send messages that have meaning for the learner and serve a legitimate communicative purpose. When teachers (or texts) structure activities so there is only one right answer, clearly students are sending messages that convey someone else's thoughts, not their own, and are serving someone else's communicative purpose. In these kinds of activities students are *practicing* language, but they are not really *using* language to communicate.

In contrast, when the answers are determined by the students themselves—and are therefore unpredictable, with no single correct response—

students are involved in authentic communication. In these information- or opinion-gap activities, answers will vary. Research suggests that these types of activities are extremely important. After all, if the purpose of learning Spanish is to communicate, then students will need practice in doing just that! In contrast, if practice consists only (or mainly) of producing right answers determined by others, students will have difficulty spontaneously creating their own messages when needed. Thus language activities and tasks should not proceed from rote or de-contextualized to meaningful practice. All practice should be meaningful, with a predominance of activities that are truly communicative, activities in which students' answers will vary.

Research also tells us that pair and group language practice is far more effective than student-teacher practice alone. Cooperative learning and pair and group work both provide increased time for communicative language practice and promote the give-and-take necessary for negotiating meaning.

Working with a partner to make and share meaning lies at the heart of *PASO A PASO.* Everything students learn in each chapter is tied together in a meaningful way. The parts of language are taught and practiced (with a partner) within the context of the whole, with vocabulary and related grammar closely intertwined. Students use language in context to convey meaning and for a real purpose. All activities involve meaning, and most allow students to choose the meanings they want to convey. These are the kinds of information- and opinion-gap events that are characteristic of real-life communication. Even in structured activities designed to provide specific practice of forms and to elicit certain responses, teachers will find that students may still respond in ways that are personal and true for them. The activities are, however, focused, and you will often find "answers will vary, but look for correct use of . . ." in the answer keys.

To promote the development of communicative ability, *PASO A PASO* integrates vocabulary and grammar. They are then re-integrated continually, with gradually increasing complexity. In addition to the personalized and open-ended responses found in the vocabulary and grammar sections of the chapter, the *Todo junto* feature specifically focuses on weaving together newly learned material with material from previous chapters. It promotes the use of all the language students have learned to that point, in oral tasks and through reading and writing.

Teaching for understanding:
The whole is greater than the parts

In many academic disciplines today, instructional practices are based on constructivist theory, which suggests that learners are more likely to be successful when instruction focuses on making meaning, on students, pursuing their natural inclination to try to make sense of what they are experiencing, and on ensuring that the parts are carefully integrated. In foreign languages, we traditionally taught the parts (grammar rules, vocabulary, pronunciation) hoping that eventually students would have the opportunity and ability to integrate them into the "whole" of communicating their own ideas. Today, integration of the parts of language takes place right from the start. It has been suggested that the relationship between learning the parts vs. integration with the whole is like learning to play a musical instrument. The focus is always on making music, and from the outset, learners need to have many experiences producing it. But they can't learn to play an instrument without knowing something about how to produce sounds (e.g., use the violin bow or play scales) or without practice.

Just as students learn the specific skills they need to produce a piece of music in learning to play an instrument, in language-learning we proceed today by identifying the learner's communicative needs (that is, the "music" they want to be able to produce) and then identifying the vocabulary, structures, and cultural skills needed to accomplish their purpose. Vocabulary and grammar are thus taught in the context of the situations in which students will be communicating or the topics they will be communicating about. Everything ties together naturally.

All effective learning is rooted in a meaningful context. We know from research that information is most likely to be retained when it is connected to other information in a meaningful way. Thus, language learning is more successful and retention more likely when we present new language organized into topics or by situations. This also means that some things we have taught in the past may not get taught at the same point or in the same way. For example, students may need to learn the stem-changing verbs *jugar, perder,* and *querer* to describe leisure or sports activities. However, since *dormir, morir,* and *pedir* do not naturally fit with the theme of sports or leisure, they may not be introduced until another theme or situation arises that will logically involve the use of one or more of them.

PASO A PASO is organized into thematic chapters. All material—vocabulary, grammar, culture—is rooted in a context and used meaningfully. All the elements of a chapter tie together. Students learn the vocabulary related to the theme, the grammar they need to communicate about the theme, and the information that helps anchor language in its cultural context. The themes have been chosen to reflect what students want or need to talk about. And the end-of-chapter vocabulary list is organized to reflect how the new words are used to create and convey meaning.

Critical thinking:
Understanding and making meaning

We know from research that language learners are active makers of meaning. They learn by creating their own understandings, not by memorizing ours. This means that students are more likely to remember vocabulary when they have acquired it by figuring out its meaning in a logical context (video situation, visual, teacher pantomime). Grammar is most likely to be understood and rules applied when students have been guided to discover underlying patterns or have formulated the rules for themselves. In contrast, retention and applicability are greatly reduced when students simply memorize lists or rules without real understanding.

In order for students to construct their own understandings and generate rules of language usage, they need to be guided through interaction with teacher and text. Strategic questioning (in the text or by the teacher) plays an important role in this process, a process that is not at all the same as groping blindly to make a random discovery. Rather, through well-chosen examples and appropriate, inductive questioning, students can be led to make significant discoveries on their own, leading to a deep understanding that is much more likely to stay with them and be reflected in their own language use.

Understanding grammar

Understanding and critical thinking are reflected throughout *PASO A PASO*. This text is unique in its approach to the development of grammar skills, emphasizing as it does the critical roles that comprehensible input and student construction of knowledge play in language learning. New structures are foreshadowed through lexical presentation in the vocabulary section, and by the use of the *yo / tú* verb forms in vocabulary practice prior to the grammar presentation. Vocabulary activities familiarize students with new grammar before it is formally presented, allowing them to construct their own understanding.

To further facilitate grammar learning, students observe patterns of use in the comprehensible input that introduces the grammar section. This is done through a visualized context and strategic inductive questions. Through interaction with the teacher and the text, observation and analysis lead students to understand grammar, not merely to memorize formulas to be applied in rote fashion.

Understanding culture

Guided discovery is also an effective means of helping students construct an understanding of culture. Not only do we want our students to know about the cultures of the people who speak Spanish, we also want them to understand the cultural framework that determines what people say or do. In other words, we want students to understand the *why* of culture that determines the *what*. Whenever and wherever students may encounter speakers of Spanish, they will likely confront cultural practices and behaviors that are new to them. Cultural understanding begins with developing sensitivity to the possibility that people vary in how they think, live, and behave. Students must learn to observe other cultures without judging and to use what they see to help them discover the meanings that underlie cultural practices or behaviors. Specific information provides knowledge that aids in understanding the system of attitudes, values, and beliefs that frames cultural practices or behaviors. Students also need to understand other cultures in relation to their own, so that they may gain a deeper understanding of why they think, live, and behave as they do.

Background knowledge can serve as an important tool for the construction of meaning. It may be contextual (What normally happens in a restaurant?), topical (What are some typical leisure activities?), linguistic (What words do I already know that look like this new word?), or cultural (I know that interpersonal relationships are very important in Hispanic cultures, so that may be why people put so much value on greeting one another). This can serve to help students interpret new cultural information or contrast that information with values and practices common to their own culture. Students should be encouraged to understand the close relationship between language and culture. The social / cultural meanings of words (What does "friendship" mean in Hispanic cultures?) should be taught along with their dictionary meanings.

PASO A PASO develops important cultural understandings through a unique guided-discovery approach.

PASO A PASO provides students with a progression of activities that leads them from thoughtful observation to knowledge and understanding of Hispanic cultures and then to reflection on their own culture. A photo essay with strategic inductive questions leads them to reflect on what they are observing. An informative reading then provides cultural information or insights that expand upon the visual information and allows students to validate or reject the ideas they formulated at the beginning. They are then asked thought-provoking questions to lead to reflection upon their own culture and their own cultural perspectives.

Strategies for success

Effective learners not only construct their own understanding of new concepts, they also know how to help themselves be successful learners. One way they do this is by using specific problem-solving strategies. When confronted with unknown words in a reading passage, successful learners don't run for a dictionary or just give up. They know how to get around that obstacle.

PASO A PASO teaches students to use strategies to be effective listeners, readers, and writers. Each reading selection takes students through a multi-step process (Phillips, 1984). Before reading, they are encouraged to use their background knowledge to help them predict or anticipate information they are likely to encounter in the text. A first reading helps them focus on general ideas (gist) without getting mired in details or difficult expressions. Reading closely for specific information, with specific strategies for dealing with difficult aspects of a text, is a strategy frequently emphasized in the reading sections. Students are then encouraged to use what they have learned in the reading by applying it in a new way. Thus, from the start, students are empowered to deal with authentic print materials.

Effective writing is promoted through a process approach in *PASO A PASO*. In the pre-writing stage, students think about the topic, generate needed language, and organize their ideas. They then write a first draft. Reviewing this draft with a peer yields insights into needed revisions or clarification and results in a revision that may be published or placed in a portfolio. This approach is consistent with the ways in which many students are learning to write in their English classes. It also provides them with a strategy or model for independent writing.

Authenticity in language learning

Language teaching today places great value on authenticity. The content that students are expected to learn and how they practice it (objectives and tasks) should be authentic to the learner's interests and to real-life uses. Tasks should require an authentic exchange of meaning (an information or opinion gap) and should have an authentic purpose. Students should be taught authentic, not "textbook," language. Most important, information and, to the extent possible, materials should be culturally authentic.

PASO A PASO opens authentic avenues to communication and culture. Students continually engage in authentic communicative tasks. Pair and group activities in which students fill information or opinion gaps constitute the great majority of exercises. These activities allow students to express their own views on topics and questions of interest to them. The language presented is culturally accurate. Videos show native speakers engaged in real-life situations and experiences. Videos, photos, realia, and readings provide authentic contacts with the cultures of Spanish speakers.

PASO A PASO and the student

PASO A PASO is a learner-friendly series. It is friendly to the interests of students and provides extensive opportunities for them to talk about themselves, to explore with peers, and to be engaged, thoughtful learners. Each chapter opens with clearly stated communicative objectives that help focus on what students are expected to learn. Knowing what's expected of them makes students more comfortable.

Because we know that it is impossible for students to learn all the vocabulary related to a given theme at one time, and because we know that it is unusual for students to "master" the grammar the first time they are exposed to it, *PASO A PASO* reviews each Book 1 theme in Book 2. However, the review is not simply repetition, re-entry, or recycling. Rather, our approach is recursive: Each review allows students to expand to new levels of achievement, so that their language becomes more refined, more elaborate, and more complex. Students will find comfort in knowing that there is more than one chance to learn the material and that they don't need to know everything perfectly all at once. *PASO A PASO* is a program in which students are continually getting better at communicating in Spanish and are regularly made aware of their progress at specific points in every chapter.

The pupil's edition and tests convey a powerful message. Both emphasize knowledge in action. Students are asked to use what they know to communicate real messages to a real audience for a real purpose. Practice activities make it clear to students that they are expected to learn to communicate in the language. End-of-chapter tests reinforce the message, assessing students' ability to use what they have learned for receptive and productive purposes and allowing them to demonstrate their understanding of related aspects of Hispanic cultures.

We know more today than ever about how foreign languages are learned. Using that knowledge to help students become proficient communicators, and to acquire an understanding and appreciation of other cultures, can be facilitated by appropriate instructional materials. *PASO A PASO* is based on solid research on second-language acquisition, on accepted theories about the teaching of culture, and on sound pedagogical practices that are common to all disciplines. We are sure that you and your students will find this an exciting, engaging, and enormously successful approach to learning Spanish.

Bibliography

Adair-Hauck, Bonnie, Richard Donato and Philomena Cumo. 1994. "Using a Whole Language Approach to Teach Grammar," in Eileen Glisan and Judith Shrum, Eds. *Contextualized Language Instruction,* Boston: Heinle and Heinle Publishers. pp. 90–111.

Brooks, Jacqueline and Martin G. Brooks. 1993. *In Search of Understanding: The Case for Constructivist Classrooms.* Alexandria, VA: Association for Supervision and Curriculum Development.

Doughty, Catherine and Teresa Pica. 1986. "Information Gap Tasks: Do They Facilitate Second Language Acquisition?" *TESOL Quarterly.* 20:3, 305–325.

Ellis, Rod. 1993. "The Structural Syllabus and Second Language Acquisition." *TESOL Quarterly.* 27:1, 91–112.

Kagan, Spencer. 1992. *Cooperative Learning.* San Juan Capistrano, CA: Resource for Teachers Inc.

Krashen, Stephen. 1982. *Principles and Practice in Second Language Acquisition.* Oxford: Pergamon Press.

Nunan, D. 1991. "Communicative Tasks and the Language Curriculum." *TESOL Quarterly.* 25:2, 279–295.

Phillips, June K. "Practical Implication of Recent Research in Reading," *Foreign Language Annals* 17:4 (September 1984), pp. 285–299.

Resnick, Lauren B. 1989. *Knowing, Learning, and Instruction: Essays in Honor of Robert Glaser.* Hillsdale, New Jersey: Lawrence Erlbaum Associates, Publishers.

Swain, Merrill. 1985. "Communicative Competence: Some Roles of Comprehensible Input and Comprehensible Output in Its Development." In Susan Gass and Madden, C. (Eds.) *Input in Second Language Acquisition.* Rowley, Mass.: Newbury House.

COMPONENTS OF THE PROGRAM

PASO A PASO is a complete, three-level series with a full range of ancillary components that allow you to tailor the materials to the needs of your students and to your teaching style.

Pupil's Edition

Presentation material begins with maps of Spanish-speaking countries and *El primer paso,* a preliminary unit focusing on basic, high-frequency communication objectives. This is followed by fourteen thematic chapters and an appendix offering verb charts, a grammar index, and Spanish-English / English-Spanish vocabularies.

Teacher's Edition

This Teacher's Edition contains the student text in slightly reduced form, with answers, teaching suggestions, and cross references to ancillary materials. Each chapter presents an extensive array of Teacher Notes that includes:

- a scope and sequence chart with communicative, cultural, and grammar objectives

- an overview of components available for use in the chapter

- on-page cultural information for photos and realia

- on-page Learning Spanish Through Action notes (a modified version of Total Physical Response)

- on-page notes for Spanish-speaking students, students needing extra help, enrichment, cooperative learning, multicultural perspectives, cross-curricular activities, using the video, critical thinking, class starter reviews, reteach / review, and re-enter / recycle.

Ancillaries
Multisensory / Technology

 Overhead Transparencies: A package of 90 full-color overhead visuals that reproduce the vocabulary-teaching illustrations without labels or captions. Also included are maps, a pronoun chart, a clock, the realia from the *Gramática en contexto,* and additional teaching transparencies. Suggestions for use are provided in a separate booklet.

 Audio Cassettes / CDs: A set of ten 60-minute audio tapes on cassette or CD containing listening activities for each chapter and separate tapes for assessment, pronunciation and vocabulary, and songs. The primary focus is on developing listening comprehension, with secondary emphasis on supporting the beginning stages of speaking, including practice with pronunciation and some focused speaking opportunities.

 Vocabulary Art Blackline Masters for Hands-On Learning:
All teaching vocabulary art reproduced on blackline masters, ideal for making manipulatives or flashcards.

 Classroom Crossword: A wall-size crossword puzzle to be completed over the course of the school year.

 En vivo: A set of chapter-by-chapter videos taped on location in Miami, Guadalajara, and Madrid. Available on both tape and disc, the videos focus on culture, vocabulary, and real-life situational interactions. A Teacher's Guide is included with complete transcriptions, cultural information, teaching suggestions, and reduced reproductions of the Video Activities pages *(see next page)* with overprinted answers.

 Pasos vivos **CD-ROM:** Chapter-by-chapter real-world activities based on *En vivo* offer creative, interactive practice opportunities for listening, speaking, reading, and writing, while extending students' knowledge of Hispanic cultures.

Print

Practice Workbook: (with separate Teacher's Answer Key): Worksheets for basic, one-step writing practice for all vocabulary and grammar sections of the student text. Exercises include the support of learning strategies. Each chapter also has an Organizer that allows students to record and keep track of new vocabulary and structures.

Writing, Audio & Video Activities: Writing Activities provide chapter-by-chapter practice that is at the same or a slightly higher level than that in the student text. Audio Activities offer exercises necessary to focus attention on listening comprehension as students work with the audio tapes. Video Activities focus attention as students view the video. Follow-up activities verify and extend their understanding of what they have seen.

Teacher's Edition: Writing, Audio & Video Activities: Student material with overprinted answers and a complete tapescript of the audio tapes.

Communicative Activities Blackline Masters (Pair and Small-Group Activities with Situation Cards): Oral activities for pair and group practice.

Un paso más: Actividades para ampliar tu español: A worktext for Spanish-speaking students designed to supplement the textbook activities.

Assessment

Assessment Program: Blackline master quizzes *(Pruebas)* for each vocabulary section and each grammar topic in the student text; fourteen chapter quizzes *(Pruebas cumulativas);* fifteen chapter proficiency tests *(Exámenes de habilidades);* and a *Banco de ideas,* a set of cumulative proficiency sections for use in creating mid-term and special end-of-year tests to highlight teachers' own objectives or areas of concern. Suggestions for administering and scoring proficiency tests are included.

Test Generator: A multiple-choice test generator. Teachers can add their own questions to the question bank.

Teacher's Resource File: This convenient, desk-top organizer contains the Teacher's Edition of the Writing, Audio & Video Activities, the Assessment Program, and the Communicative Activities Blackline Masters.

CHAPTER ORGANIZATION

Organization of the Text

PASO A PASO 1 contains a preliminary chapter *(El primer paso)* and 14 thematically organized chapters in which students learn to communicate about their own lives and how to interact with Hispanic cultures. The 14 themes are:

CAPÍTULO 1   **Friendship**

CAPÍTULO 2   **School**

CAPÍTULO 3   **Sports and leisure activities**

CAPÍTULO 4   **Food**

CAPÍTULO 5   **Family**

CAPÍTULO 6   **Clothing**

CAPÍTULO 7   **Leisure and vacation**

CAPÍTULO 8   **Home**

CAPÍTULO 9   **Health**

CAPÍTULO 10   **Community**

CAPÍTULO 11   **Movies and TV**

CAPÍTULO 12   **Restaurants**

CAPÍTULO 13   **The environment**

CAPÍTULO 14   **Parties and celebrations**

Using *El primer paso*

El primer paso is designed as a 10-day teaching unit to give students a successful start in Spanish. In this chapter students will:

1 gain insight into the importance of Spanish in the global community, in the United States, and in their own community

2 recognize the importance of Spanish in the workplace

3 begin to communicate with their peers

4 develop successful learning strategies

5 understand the book's chapter organization

Chapter organization

The 14 chapters follow a consistent organization that increases student confidence while allowing for easy classroom management. Chapters are organized according to the latest research on how students learn a second language and follow a clear pedagogical model:

1 Introduce/Preview   **4** Apply

2 Present   **5** Summarize/Assess

3 Practice

CAPÍTULO 7

¿Adónde vas a ir de vacaciones?

OBJECTIVES
At the end of this chapter, you will be able to:
■ describe vacation choices and activities
■ talk about the weather
■ discuss what to take on a trip
■ talk about how teens in Chile spend their vacations

CAPÍTULO 1

Y tú, ¿cómo eres?

OBJECTIVES
At the end of this chapter, you will be able to:
■ describe yourself and tell about some of your likes and dislikes
■ find out what other people are like
■ compare your likes and dislikes with other people's
■ talk about teen activities and the concept of friendship in Spanish-speaking countries

Grupo de atletas de Esmeraldas, Ecuador

Each chapter follows this model:

Chapter Sections	Pedagogical Support
Objectives	Introduce
¡Piénsalo bien!	Preview

Vocabulario para conversar

• *Visualized vocabulary*	Present
• También necesitas ...	Present
• Empecemos a conversar	Practice
• Empecemos a escribir (y a leer)	Apply
• ¡Comuniquemos!	Practice
• ¿Qué sabes ahora?	Practice / Assess

Perspectiva cultural	Preview / Present
•La cultura desde tu perspectiva	Apply

Gramática en contexto	Preview / Present / Practice
•Ahora lo sabes	Practice / Assess

Todo junto

•Actividades	Apply
•¡Vamos a leer!	Apply
•¡Vamos a escribir!	Apply

¿Lo sabes bien?	Apply / Assess

Resumen del capítulo	Summarize

CAPÍTULO 1?

¡Vamos a un restauran
mexicano!

OBJECTIVES
At the end of this chapter, you will be able to
■ ask politely to have something brought to
■ order a meal
■ say what you ate or drank
■ compare family dinners in the Spanish-s
world and in the United States

Haciendo tortillas en el mercado de Chichicastenang

USING A CHAPTER

Chapter Opener *(Introduce)*

The chapter theme is introduced through a photograph and related communicative and cultural objectives.

Teaching ideas for the Chapter Opener

Wrap-around notes give many suggestions. Here are a few basic ideas for these two pages:

1 Prior to discussing the objectives, have students look at the photos and skim the chapter. Ask them to suggest objectives based upon what they have seen. Write these on the chalkboard and see if they compare with those listed.

2 Show additional pictures, posters, or slides that preview the chapter theme.

3 You may wish to use the first video segment to provide a broad cultural overview of the chapter theme. (See the Video Guide for further suggestions.)

Objectives:
Relate to real-life, purposeful communication and relevant cultural information. These will be referred to throughout the chapter so that students can monitor their own progress. Chapter assessment is based on the objectives.

CAPÍTULO 4

¿Qué prefieres comer?

OBJECTIVES

At the end of this chapter, you will be able to:

■ describe what you like and don't like to eat and drink

■ tell when you have meals

■ say whether you are hungry or thirsty

■ compare and contrast eating customs in Spanish-speaking countries and in the United States

Mercado al aire libre en Perú

119

¡**P**iénsalo bien! *(Preview)*

This section continues to preview the chapter theme. Students use their own experiences and background information to interact with the photographs.

Questions:
Students use critical thinking to answer inductive questions.

Teaching ideas for *¡Piénsalo bien!*

1 Ask students to study the photographs and to suggest as many words, phrases, or short sentences as they can about them.

2 Use the inductive questions to elicit the similarities and differences. Focus on the similarities.

3 If you haven't yet done so, use the first video segment to preview the cultural theme.

4 At the end of the chapter, return to these photos. See how extensively students can describe the pictures. Choose a photo and have students bring it to life by acting out the situation.

¡**P**iénsalo bien!

Look at the photos. How is the food similar to or different from what you might eat? Now look at the teens gathered at a fast-food place. How does this restaurant compare to a similar place in your community? What do you think *hamburguesa* means?

"Me gustaría una hamburguesa."

A la hora del almuerzo en la Ciudad de México

Un desayuno en un hotel de Asunción, Paraguay

120 Capítulo 4

En Navidad, una familia dominicana a la hora de la cena

121

Captions:
Easy-to-guess cognates and recycled vocabulary help build students' confidence. New vocabulary and structures are previewed.

Vocabulario para conversar (Present, Practice & Apply)

New vocabulary is presented in a visualized context in two short, manageable sections.

Teaching ideas

1 Use the Overhead Transparencies, the Vocabulary Audio Tape, the Vocabulary Art Blackline Masters, and / or the second video segment to introduce the new vocabulary.

2 Combine auditory, visual, and kinesthetic activities. Present the vocabulary using comprehensible input. Here are several suggestions:

> **Visualized vocabulary:**
> Research indicates that we learn best in logical sets or categories and through immediately associating words with objects.

A. Getting meaning from comprehensible input

The purpose of these activities is to allow students to match new language with its meaning.

- Using the Overhead Transparency, point to pictures as you simply and clearly name and talk about them in Spanish. Students should be able to understand new vocabulary from your body language and gestures. For example: *Es una manzana. La manzana es una fruta. Ésta es una manzana también. Tengo muchas manzanas.*

- You might also pantomime new vocabulary.

- As you progress through *PASO A PASO,* your descriptions will expand to include previously learned language.

¿Qué prefieres comer?

Vocabulario para conversar

¿Qué te gusta comer?
Here are some new words and expressions you will need to talk about mealtimes and foods you like and don't like to eat. Read them several times, then turn the page and practice with a partner.

El desayuno

el pan tostado   el cereal

el huevo   el jamón

El almuerzo

las frutas

las papas fritas

la hamburguesa

los sandwiches

el tomate

el queso

el sandwich de jamón y queso

122 Capítulo 4

La cena

el pan   la sopa de tomate   la sopa de pollo

la sopa de verduras   el bistec

el pescado

las papas al horno   el arroz

el pollo

También necesitas . . .

comer: (yo) como (tú) comes	to eat: I eat you eat	me encanta(n)	I love
la comida	meal	siempre	always
más o menos	more or less	nunca	never
¡Qué asco!	Yuk! That's disgusting!		
¿Por qué?	why?		
porque	because		
¿verdad?	isn't that so? right?		

¿Y qué quiere decir . . . ?
en el desayuno / el almuerzo / la cena
prefiero, prefieres

> **También necesitas . . . :**
> Non-visualizable vocabulary and lexical preview of grammar. Do not treat these *as grammar.* The more students can master without explanation, the more easily and thoroughly they will learn it.

> **¿Y qué quiere decir . . . ?:**
> Cognates and word families are the focus of this section.

Vocabulario para conversar 123

B. Demonstrating comprehension through physical response

The purpose of these activities is to allow students to demonstrate their comprehension non-verbally.

■ After presenting two or three pictures of new vocabulary, review by asking yes / no questions, e.g., *¿Es un plátano? ¿Es una naranja? ¿Te gusta comer naranjas?* Students may respond as a group with thumbs up / down (*sí / no*). Individuals may also be asked to respond in this way.

■ As students become more proficient, vocabulary from previous chapters can be used in these questions, e.g., *¿Necesitas beber leche en la cena?*

■ Continue alternating the steps in the first two paragraphs until all new vocabulary has been presented.

■ Distribute Vocabulary Art BLMs. As you name each new item, point to it on the transparency. Have students point to the corresponding picture. Tell students: *Señalen el plátano. Señalen la naranja.* This time, do not point to the picture on the transparency until students have pointed to it on their worksheet. Confirm student responses on the transparency.

■ Have students point to pictures on the Overhead Transparency as you describe the picture, e.g., *A Miguel le gusta comer zanahorias* (student points to picture of carrots).

■ Have students open their books and point to pictures you name or describe: *Señalen dos cosas que les gusta comer. Señalen dos cosas que no les gusta comer.*

■ Have students pantomime vocabulary.

■ Have students respond to commands: *Dale la hamburguesa a María. Muestra el sandwich a la clase.*

■ Provide each student with a worksheet from the Vocabulary Art BLMs. Direct them to cut out each picture. Have students move the pictures as you direct: *Pongan los guisantes a la derecha de las papas. Pongan la lechuga entre las uvas y las cebollas. Pongan las comidas en dos columnas: Comidas que me gustan y comidas que no me gustan.* Or students may use them to make your sentence true by arranging pictures to match your oral description, e.g., *Hay uvas y manzanas en la mesa.*

Each chapter provides suggestions for Learning Spanish Through Action (TPR).

C. Limited verbal response

Once students have had an opportunity to internalize meaning and to demonstrate comprehension of new language physically, they may respond verbally.

■ Ask yes / no or true / false questions, e.g., *¿Comes cereal en el desayuno? La lechuga es una fruta.*

■ Ask questions that require comprehension of new vocabulary but do not require using it in the answer. Responses will use language from previous chapters, e.g., *¿Prefieres ver la tele o ir al cine los fines de semana?*

■ Ask questions in which the correct answer is embedded: *¿Es una manzana o es una naranja? ¿Prefieres beber leche o té helado?*

■ Have students repeat after you for pronunciation practice.

3 On subsequent days, add details by recycling previously learned vocabulary. Retell an earlier narration without visual support. Ask students to draw their own visual representation of what has been said.

4 Have students re-view the video segment. Turn the sound off and let students provide their own narration.

Empecemos a conversar (Practice)

Students practice the new vocabulary in paired activities that provide models for real-life language.

Teaching ideas for *Empecemos a conversar*

1 Place students in pairs. (There are many ways of doing this.) You may want to pair students of different abilities. Assign "study buddies" for each week or chapter. They are not only pair-practice partners, but they also keep track of each other's papers and assignments. (Be sure they exchange phone numbers.) You might award extra credit for partners who work well together and show improvement.

2 Always model the pair practice. Quickly review the vocabulary so that students can be more successful.

3 Set a time limit. Finish an activity when approximately three fourths of the class have finished. Walk around the class, listening for areas of difficulty such as pronunciation or grammar. Focus on these at a later time.

4 Ask pairs of students to do selected items for the whole class.

5 Have students work in pairs to answer the questions, then with another group to compare responses. Ask individuals to write this section as homework. Use the more open-ended questions as one-on-one questions with students or as topics for class discussion.

6 See the list of ancillaries for additional resources to help students work with the new vocabulary.

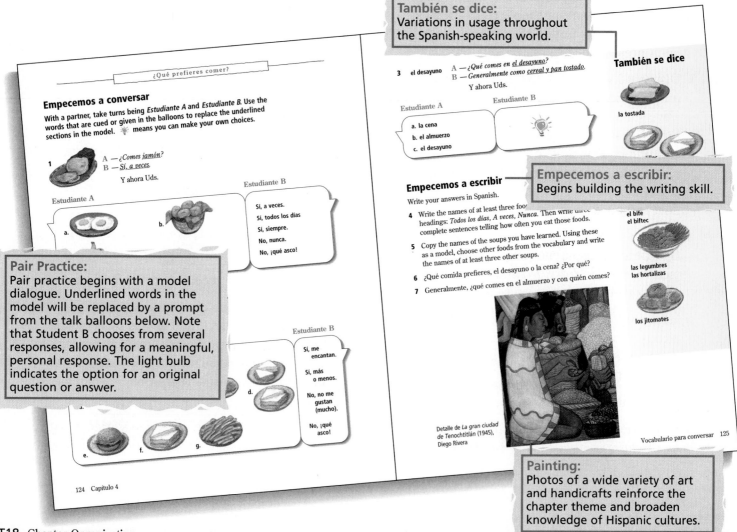

También se dice:
Variations in usage throughout the Spanish-speaking world.

Empecemos a escribir:
Begins building the writing skill.

Pair Practice:
Pair practice begins with a model dialogue. Underlined words in the model will be replaced by a prompt from the talk balloons below. Note that Student B chooses from several responses, allowing for a meaningful, personal response. The light bulb indicates the option for an original question or answer.

Painting:
Photos of a wide variety of art and handicrafts reinforce the chapter theme and broaden knowledge of Hispanic cultures.

¡ Comuniquemos! (*Practice*)

This section offers additional practice with the new vocabulary. The varied activities guide students to personalized communication.

Teaching ideas

Follow the guidelines for paired practice. At this point, students are familiar with the new vocabulary and the activities should go quickly, but choose from among them. Do not attempt to do them all.

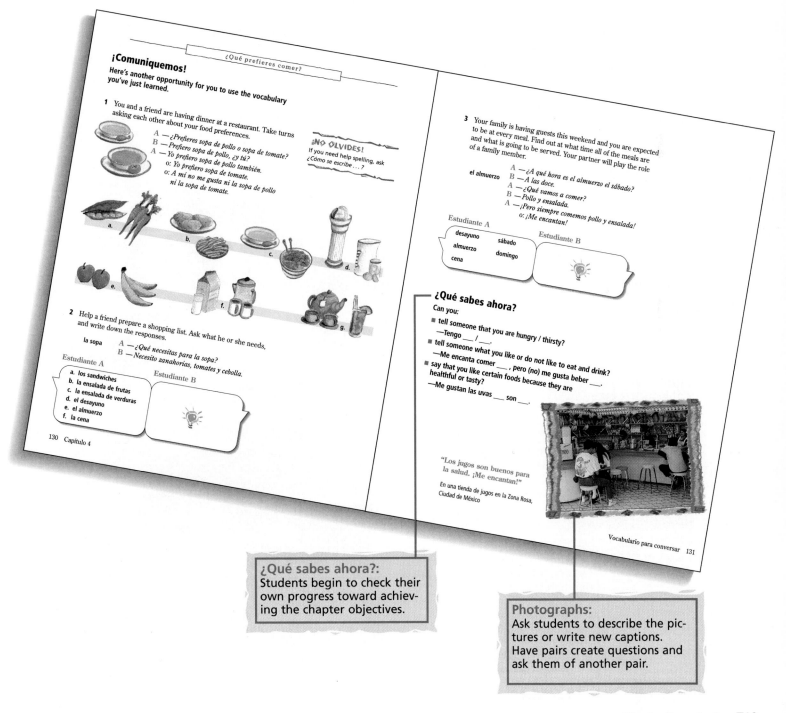

¡Comuniquemos!

¿Qué prefieres comer?

Here's another opportunity for you to use the vocabulary you've just learned.

1 You and a friend are having dinner at a restaurant. Take turns asking each other about your food preferences.

A —¿Prefieres sopa de pollo o sopa de tomate?
B —Prefiero sopa de pollo, ¿y tú?
A —Yo prefiero sopa de pollo también.
o: Yo prefiero sopa de tomate.
o: A mí no me gusta ni la sopa de pollo ni la sopa de tomate.

¡NO OLVIDES!
If you need help spelling, ask
¿Cómo se escribe . . . ?

a.
b.
c.
d.
e.
f.
g.

2 Help a friend prepare a shopping list. Ask what he or she needs, and write down the responses.

la sopa
A —¿Qué necesitas para la sopa?
B —Necesito zanahorias, tomates y cebolla.

Estudiante A
a. los sandwiches
b. la ensalada de frutas
c. la ensalada de verduras
d. el desayuno
e. el almuerzo
f. la cena

Estudiante B

130 Capítulo 4

3 Your family is having guests this weekend and you are expected to be at every meal. Find out at what time all of the meals are and what is going to be served. Your partner will play the role of a family member.

el almuerzo
A —¿A qué hora es el almuerzo el sábado?
B —A las doce.
A —¿Qué vamos a comer?
B —Pollo y ensalada.
A —¡Pero siempre comemos pollo y ensalada!
o: ¡Me encantan!

Estudiante A
desayuno   sábado
almuerzo   domingo
cena

Estudiante B

¿Qué sabes ahora?

Can you:

■ tell someone that you are hungry / thirsty?
—Tengo ___ / ___.

■ tell someone what you like or do not like to eat and drink?
—Me encanta comer ___, pero (no) me gusta beber ___.

■ say that you like certain foods because they are healthful or tasty?
—Me gustan las uvas ___ son ___.

"Los jugos son buenos para la salud. ¡Me encantan!"

En una tienda de jugos en la Zona Rosa, Ciudad de México

Vocabulario para conversar 131

¿Qué sabes ahora?:
Students begin to check their own progress toward achieving the chapter objectives.

Photographs:
Ask students to describe the pictures or write new captions. Have pairs create questions and ask them of another pair.

Perspectiva cultural (Preview, Present & Apply)

This section offers a unique perspective into understanding the richness of Hispanic cultures. Using a combination of a photographic and narrative essay, it asks students to think about culture in such a way as to develop real cross-cultural understanding and sensitivity.

Teaching ideas for the *Perspectiva cultural*

1 Have students answer the inductive questions as a whole-class or small-group activity. Write their responses on the board. This will activate background information, prompt and recycle related vocabulary, and show that, even in their own class, they will find a variety of customs and traditions.

2 Use the photographs to encourage students to make observations about Hispanic cultures. Describe the photos in Spanish, adding more information.

3 Add personal information or anecdotes. If any students have traveled to a Spanish-speaking country, let them share their experiences. Ask Spanish speakers to share family traditions.

4 In small groups or as a whole class, have students answer the questions in *La cultura desde tu perspectiva*. This is your best opportunity for helping students understand their own culture and the beliefs and attitudes they have formed.

5 You may want to ask how Spanish-speaking students coming to the U.S. might react to being in a culture with traditions such as those described by students when they answered the inductive questions.

Perspectiva cultural

¿A qué hora es el desayuno, el almuerzo y la cena en los Estados Unidos? ¿Qué comemos en el desayuno, por ejemplo? En las fotos, ¿a qué hora comen los hispanos?

Critical questioning:
A series of inductive questions focusing on students' background knowledge and on the photos.

7:00 and 8:30, is usually ... of coffee or *café con leche*, which is half coffee and half hot milk, and bread or rolls with butter and jam. Children and teenagers sometimes drink hot chocolate or chocolate milk instead of coffee.

El almuerzo (called *la comida* in Spain and Mexico) is the largest and most important meal of the day. It is eaten between noon and 3:00. Many businesses and schools close so that families can enjoy *el almuerzo* at home. Although this lengthy ... is still common, more and m... are adopting a *jornada continua ... continuado* (uninterrupted sch... working hours in the United S... leave time for employees to g...

Cultural reading:
Cultural information and insights that expand upon the information in the photos. Students validate or reject the ideas they formulated earlier.

La cena is the evening meal. It may start around 7:00 or much later, especially in countries that have a late midday meal. In Spain, *la cena* may start as late as 10:00 or 11:00, since most Spaniards enjoy going out after work or school and it is customary to wait until all family members are present before sitting down to eat. *La cena* is usually a light meal, and it may include leftovers from *el almuerzo*.

In some countries, there is also a late afternoon meal called *la merienda*. It may be like a *desayuno*, or it may resemble an English tea, with sandwiches, pastries, or rolls and *café con leche*, tea, or hot chocolate.

La cultura desde tu perspectiva

1 In what ways are mealtimes in Spanish-speaking countries similar to or different ... United States?

... afternoon snack probably ... someone from the United ... visiting a Spanish-speaking ... re any other times of day ... ight be needed?

La cultura desde tu perspectiva:
Students reflect upon and interact with new cultural information from the perspective of their own culture.

Unos amigos españoles a la hora del almuerzo

En México, a la hora de la merienda

Málaga, España

Ciudad de México, México

Santiago, Chile

12:30 PM

5:00 PM

9:30 PM

132 Capítulo 4

Perspectiva cultural 133

ramática en contexto *(Preview, Present & Practice)*

A realia-based reading provides comprehensible input for the new grammar. This gives students meaningful understanding of the structures by letting them intuit the rules. This inductive approach allows students to internalize and gain a deeper understanding of the grammar. Students were shown these structures in the vocabulary presentation and have practiced using them. They should not be uncomfortable with the structures themselves.

Teaching ideas for *Gramática en contexto*

1 Show the Overhead Transparency. Activate students' own experience by asking questions such as: How many students like cheese? What types of cheese? Ask what they might expect to find in an ad such as this. Have them skim the ad. Did they find what they expected?

2 Read the headline and ask what it means. Can students identify any of the flags? Read aloud the subhead. Can students tell you what it means? Have pairs of students read the ad and answer the questions. Let them verify their answers with another pair or as a whole-class activity.

3 As students generate an explanation, write it on the chalkboard along with examples from the reading.

Realia-based reading:
The reading combines cognates and previously learned vocabulary with the chapter's key grammar concepts.

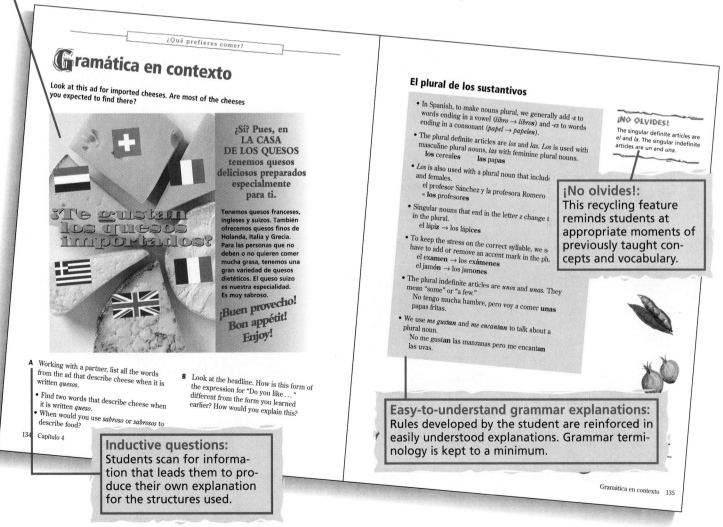

Inductive questions:
Students scan for information that leads them to produce their own explanation for the structures used.

¡No olvides!:
This recycling feature reminds students at appropriate moments of previously taught concepts and vocabulary.

Easy-to-understand grammar explanations:
Rules developed by the student are reinforced in easily understood explanations. Grammar terminology is kept to a minimum.

In a truly thematic approach, grammar is tied to the communicative objectives. What is not relevant is not presented. Here, for example, students work with three *-er* verbs appropriate to the theme: *deber, beber,* and *comer.* Additional *-er* verbs are, of course, taught in later chapters.

This thematic approach builds in regular review and recycling as students are reminded of the *-er* conjugation through the *¡No olvides!* feature. There are three to four grammar topics per chapter, each followed by a variety of activities.

Ahora lo sabes *(Assess):*
Students again assess their progress toward achieving the chapter objectives.

Ahora lo sabes

Can you:
- tell that you like or don't like certain food groups?
  —(No) _____ las frutas.
- describe groups of people or things?
  —Los huevos son _____, pero las verduras son _____.
- say what you eat or drink at different meals?
  —A ver . . . En el desayuno (nosotros) _____ cereal y _____ jugo de naranja.
- make clear to or about whom you are talking when more than one person is referred to?
  —Timoteo y tú _____ la televisión todos los días, ¿verdad?

¿Qué prefieres comer?

4 For each of these adjectives, name two famous people or p_
in your class or school whom the adjective fits.

Carl Herrera y Gabriela Sabatini son deportistas.

artístico, -a
deportista
atrevido, -a
callado, -a
desordenado, -a
gracioso, -a
sociable
ordenado, -a
serio, -a
trabajador, -a

Verbos que terminan en -er

You know the pattern of present-tense endings f_

- Another group of infinitives end in *-er.* Some
  beber, comer, leer, and *deber.*
- Here are the present-tense forms of the ve_
  this pattern differ from that of *-ar* verbs?

		(nosotro_
(yo)	como	(nosotra_
		(vosot_
(tú)	comes	(voso_
Ud.		Uds_
(él)	come	(ell
(ella)		(el_

- With *-er* verbs we use the vowel _
  Remember that *-ar* verbs use th_
- You also know the verb *ver.* It _
  which is *veo.*

1 Discuss with a partner wheth_
following foods.
A —¿Te gus_
B —Sí, me_
o: Sí, _
o: No, _

2 Now use the pictu_
like to eat those f_
A —¿Te gustaría_
B —¡Claro que _
o: No, no t_

138 Capítulo 4

141

Todo junto *(Apply)*

Todo junto is composed of three integrative sections: *Actividades, ¡Vamos a leer!,* and *¡Vamos a escribir!*

Teaching ideas for *Actividades*

1 To complement this section, use the third video segment in *En vivo.*

2 You may want to use different activities for different ability groupings. Better students might work together on Ex. 3 while others do either Ex. 1 or 2. Assess students on their effort, completion of the task, creativity, and ability to communicate rather than on accuracy.

Para decir más:
These optional vocabulary suggestions enable students to personalize the activities.

Actividades *(Apply):*
Pick and choose from among these activities.

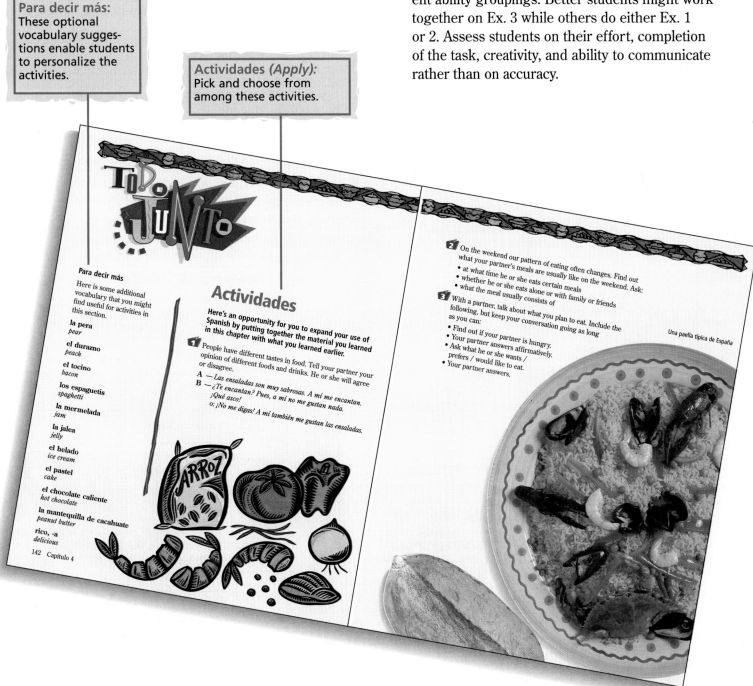

Para decir más

Here is some additional vocabulary that you might find useful for activities in this section.

la pera
pear

el durazno
peach

el tocino
bacon

los espaguetis
spaghetti

la mermelada
jam

la jalea
jelly

el helado
ice cream

el pastel
cake

el chocolate caliente
hot chocolate

la mantequilla de cacahuate
peanut butter

rico, -a
delicious

142   Capítulo 4

Actividades

Here's an opportunity for you to expand your use of Spanish by putting together the material you learned in this chapter with what you learned earlier.

1 People have different tastes in food. Tell your partner your opinion of different foods and drinks. He or she will agree or disagree.

A —*Las ensaladas son muy sabrosas. A mí me encantan.*
B —*¿Te encantan? Pues, a mí no me gustan nada. ¡Qué asco!*
o: *¡No me digas! A mí también me gustan las ensaladas.*

2 On the weekend our pattern of eating often changes. Find out what your partner's meals are usually like on the weekend. Ask:
• at what time he or she eats certain meals
• whether he or she eats alone or with family or friends
• what the meal usually consists of

3 With a partner, talk about what you plan to eat. Include the following, but keep your conversation going as long as you can:
• Find out if your partner is hungry.
• Your partner answers affirmatively.
• Ask what he or she wants / prefers / would like to eat.
• Your partner answers.

Una paella típica de España

¡ Vamos a leer! (Apply)

Students learn how to become efficient readers through a four-step process. Real comprehension is achieved through strategies, questions, and activities in the *Infórmate* and *Aplicación*. Students encounter unknown vocabulary, but gain confidence by realizing they don't need to know every word to read successfully.

Teaching ideas

1 *Antes de leer:* Use the maps in the textbook or on the Overhead Transparencies to point out where the Mayas and Aztecs lived. Use a world map to show the routes the Spaniards followed to reach Mexico. Ask students if they like chocolate and if anyone knows its origin.

2 *Mira la lectura:* Have students work in groups and report back to the class. Write the names of the products students mention on the chalkboard to reinforce the concept of cognates.

3 *Infórmate:* This can best be done as an individual task or as pair work.

4 *Aplicación:* Students will complete this activity successfully because of the careful structuring of the early steps in the reading process. You might have students compare their lists in pairs or small groups.

• Step 1
Antes de leer: Activates students' background knowledge to help them predict or anticipate.

• Step 2
Mira la lectura: Pre-reading section focusing on a specific reading strategy.

Todo junto

¡ Vamos a leer!

Antes de leer
STRATEGY ➤ Using prior knowledge

What you are about to read tells the history of chocolate, which was used by the Mayas and the Aztecs of Mexico over a thousand years ago. And they used it in a very different way! How do you think chocolate got to Europe and why did Europeans use it differently?

As you already know, you can use pictures and your own experience with certain kinds of reading materials to predict and understand the information you might find there.

Mira la lectura
STRATEGY ➤ Using cognates

As you read, try to use cognates (words that are similar to English words) to help you figure out the meaning.

1 What are some of the other products that the Europeans found when they came to America?

2 When did chocolate become one of the most popular drinks in Europe?

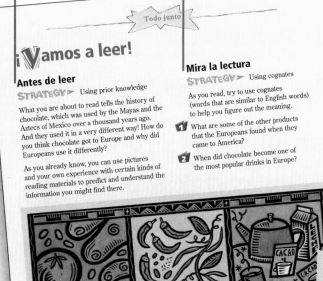

En el siglo XV los conquistadores llegan a América. Allí descubren muchos productos nuevos para la comida española y europea, por ejemplo: la papa, el tomate y el cacao. El cacao es uno de los ingredientes que los aztecas usan para hacer el *tchocolatl* (palabra azteca para chocolate).

Los aztecas preparan el *tchocolatl* con cacao, verduras y varios tipos de chiles. Es una bebida muy fuerte que los indios beben en sus ceremonias religiosas. Pero el *tchocolatl* azteca es muy diferente del chocolate que bebemos hoy.

En Europa, el *tchocolatl* se tran[ ] en una bebida más líquida y m[ ] á dulce. En los siglos XVI y XVII [ ] chocolate es una de las bebida[ ] populares de Europa. El choc[ ] caliente se hace con cacao y [ ] o leche. Hoy, en España, hay chocolaterías, lugares donde [ ] chocolate casi exclusivamente.

Infórmate
STRATEGY ➤ Using context to get meaning

Using context to get meaning is another useful strategy. When you are rea[ ]d you run across a word you don't [ ] look at the other words in the se[ ] See if knowing those words can [ ] understand the one you don't kn[ ]

Read this selection again. Mak[ ] words you don't understand. T[ ] guess their meaning by lookin[ ] surrounding words.

1 How and when was chocolate introduced in Europe?

2 How did the Aztecs prepare their *tchocolatl*? Was it an everyday drink or was it used on special occasions? Explain.

3 How was the chocolate the conquistadores brought to Europe different from the Aztecan *tchocolatl*?

Aplicación

List as many cognates as you can that you found in this reading.

• Step 4
Aplicación: Students use what they have learned by applying it in a different way.

• Step 3
Infórmate: Students read for specific information or details, using strategies for dealing with difficult aspects of the text. Questions help focus on key information.

¡Vamos a escribir! *(Apply)*

As with reading, students develop effective writing through a process approach consistent with the way they are learning to write in their English classes. It also provides a strategy or model for writing independently. Each writing task provides a creative, personalized opportunity to expand the chapter theme.

> **• Step 1**
> Pre-writing questions have students think about the topic, generate needed language, and organize their ideas. They then write the first draft.

> **• Steps 2 & 3**
> Through peer review students gain insights into needed revisions or clarifications for preparing the final draft.

Teaching ideas

1 This may be done in class or as homework. Students can work individually, in pairs, or in small groups to brainstorm the topic and needed vocabulary. They can jot down answers to the questions and share them with other students. They then use the questions and responses as a starting point for writing their first draft. You might have students skip lines on the first draft so that there is room for comments during the peer review.

2 Have students share their first draft with one or more partners. Peer reviewers should check for thoroughness and comprehensibility, as well as for errors in spelling, grammar, and punctuation. (You may want to make sure that each reviewer says at least one good thing about the writing sample.)

3 You might want to include final drafts in the students' writing portfolios.

Todo junto

¡Vamos a escribir!

Your health class is studying nutrition and the teacher wants you to think about what, when, and where you eat. Write a short paragraph about your favorite meal of the day. Follow these steps.

1 Answer these questions, then use the answers to write your paragraph.
- ¿A qué hora comes tu comida favorita?
- ¿Dónde comes: en la casa, en la escuela o en un restaurante?
- ¿Con quién comes?
- ¿Qué comes y qué bebes?

2 Show your paragraph to a partner. Does he or she have any ideas to suggest? Did you use the answers to all the questions in your paragraph? Think about any changes you may want to make, then write a second draft.

3 Check for correct spelling and punctuation. Did you use the *yo* form of the verbs? Did you use *me gusta(n)* or *me encanta(n)*? Does your partner have any further suggestions?

Write your final draft. Add the corrected paragraph to your writing portfolio.

grasa *(fat)*
azúcar *(sugar)*

146   Capítulo 4

¿**L**o sabes bien? *(Apply, Assess & Summarize)*

In this section students practice tasks similar to those they will encounter on the *Examen de habilidades.* They focus on the chapter objectives and show what they can do with the language.

Teaching ideas

1 Point out how this pre-test and the vocabulary on the following page prepare for the *Examen de habilidades.*

2 Do this as a whole-class activity or have pairs complete the section at home and then compare their responses with those of a partner. Or, with a partner, they can work through each section in class and then compare their answers with those of another pair.

3 Students who do well should feel confident about performing well on the test. Those having difficulty will know where they need to focus attention as they study for the test.

Resumen del capítulo *(Summarize)*

This section organizes the chapter vocabulary to reflect how it can be used to meet the communicative objectives. The objectives were stated in the chapter overview, and students have been given regular opportunities to assess their progress in the *¿Qué sabes ahora?, Ahora lo sabes,* and *¿Lo sabes bien?*

¿**L**o sabes bien?

This section will help you organize your studying for the proficiency test, where you will be asked to do similar, though not identical, tasks. There will not be any models on the test.

Listening
Can you understand when people talk about food? Listen as your teacher reads you a sample similar to what you will hear on the test. Which meal is Eugenio talking about?

Reading
Can you quickly read through this ad and use the context to guess any word or words that you might not know? Who is this product recommended for and why?

Writing
Can you write the order for the customers you are waiting on? Here is a sample:

Speaking
Can you discuss your food preferences with a partner? Do you like or dislike the same foods? For example:

A — *¿Te gusta el pescado?*
B — *No me gusta nada.*
   ¿Y a ti?
A — *No mucho. Mi madre siempre cocina pescado los viernes. Es horrible. ¿Te gustan las zanahorias?*
B — *Sí, pero prefiero las papas o las judías verdes. No me gustan nada las cebollas. ¡Qué asco!*
A — *Pues, a mí me encantan las cebollas. Son muy sabrosas.*

Culture
Can you describe the four meals that are typical of many Spanish-speaking countries?

La crema de cacao es un alimento especialmente indicado para adolescentes con una gran energía. Es un alimento nutritivo, ideal para la merienda.

"Me encantan los refrescos."

148   Capítulo 4

Teaching ideas

1 Have pairs review the vocabulary. They might make up a sentence or dialogue in each category. For example, *Tengo hambre ahora* or:
—*¿Qué bebes cuando tienes sed?*
—*Bebo agua.*

2 If students have created flashcards, have them organize these according to the communicative categories.

3 Have students quiz each other using the list in the book or their flashcards. Ask them to indicate any words their partner had trouble with by writing them on a sheet of paper or placing a check on the flashcard. This will focus their test preparation on problem areas.

Assessment options

1 The *Prueba cumulativa* is a prochievement instrument that focuses on students' knowledge of the chapter vocabulary and grammar in a communicative context.

2 The *Examen de habilidades* is a proficiency-oriented instrument that focuses on what students can do with the language in a real-world context.

3 The Test Generator provides a test bank of multiple-choice questions to which you can add your own questions.

Resumen del capítulo 4

e the vocabulary from this chapter to help you:
- describe what you like and don't like to eat and drink
- tell when you have meals
- say whether you are hungry or thirsty

indicate hunger or thirst
ner hambre / sed

describe meals
eber: (yo) bebo
(tú) bebes
omer: (yo) como
(tú) comes
a cena
a comida
el desayuno
en el desayuno / el almuerzo /
la cena

to talk about foods
el arroz
el bistec
el cereal
la ensalada
las frutas
  la manzana
  la naranja
  el plátano
  la uva
la hamburguesa
el huevo
el jamón
el pan
  el pan tostado
la papa
  las papas al horno
  las papas fritas
el pescado
el pollo

el queso
los sandwiches
  el sandwich de jamón y queso
la sopa de pollo / de tomate / de verduras
las verduras
  la cebolla
  los guisantes
  las judías verdes
  la lechuga
  el tomate
  la zanahoria

to talk about drinks
las bebidas
  el agua (f.)
  el café
  el jugo de naranja
  la leche
  la limonada
  el refresco
  el té
  el té helado

to describe foods
bueno, -a (para la salud)
horrible
malo, -a (para la salud)
sabroso, -a

to express likes or preferences
más o menos
me encanta(n)

me gusta(n)
preferir: (yo) prefiero
(tú) prefieres

to express an opinion
Creo que sí / no.
¡Qué asco!

to ask for an explanation
¿Por qué?

to give an explanation
porque

to elicit agreement
¿verdad?

to refer to obligation
deber: (yo) debo
(tú) debes

to indicate frequency
nunca
siempre

to refer to something you cannot name
algo

other useful words
son
unos, unas

Resumen   149

USING THE TEACHER'S EDITION

This Teacher's Edition provides all the support needed to work with the wide range of students in today's Spanish classes.

Each teacher chapter begins with a spread that provides organizational and cultural information for instructional planning.

Additional information and insight into the chapter's cultural theme

List of the chapter communication, culture, and grammar objectives

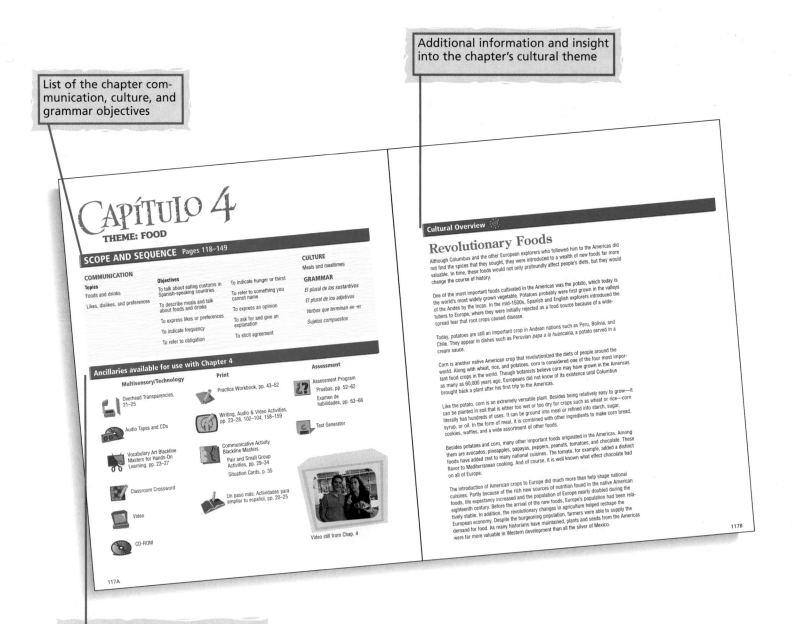

CAPÍTULO 4
THEME: FOOD

SCOPE AND SEQUENCE Pages 118–149

COMMUNICATION

Topics
Foods and drinks

Likes, dislikes, and preferences

Objectives
To talk about eating customs in Spanish-speaking countries

To describe meals and talk about foods and drinks

To express likes or preferences

To indicate frequency

To refer to obligation

To indicate hunger or thirst

To refer to something you cannot name

To express an opinion

To ask for and give an explanation

To elicit agreement

CULTURE
Meals and mealtimes

GRAMMAR
El plural de los sustantivos

El plural de los adjetivos

Verbos que terminan en -er

Sujetos compuestos

Ancillaries available for use with Chapter 4

Multisensory/Technology
- Overhead Transparencies, 21–25
- Audio Tapes and CDs
- Vocabulary Art Blackline Masters for Hands-On Learning, pp. 23–27
- Classroom Crossword
- Video
- CD-ROM

Print
- Practice Workbook, pp. 43–52
- Writing, Audio & Video Activities, pp. 23–28, 102–104, 158–159
- Communicative Activity Blackline Masters Pair and Small Group Activities, pp. 29–34 Situation Cards, p. 35
- Un paso más: Actividades para ampliar tu español, pp. 20–25

Assessment
- Assessment Program Pruebas, pp. 52–62 Examen de habilidades, pp. 63–66
- Test Generator

Video still from Chap. 4

117A

Cultural Overview

Revolutionary Foods

Although Columbus and the other European explorers who followed him to the Americas did not find the spices that they sought, they were introduced to a wealth of new foods far more valuable. In time, these foods would not only profoundly affect people's diets, but they would change the course of history.

One of the most important foods cultivated in the Americas was the potato, which today is the world's most widely grown vegetable. Potatoes probably were first grown in the valleys of the Andes by the Incas. In the mid-1500s, Spanish and English explorers introduced the tubers to Europe, where they were initially rejected as a food source because of a widespread fear that root crops caused disease.

Today, potatoes are still an important crop in Andean nations such as Peru, Bolivia, and Chile. They appear in dishes such as Peruvian papa a la huancaina, a potato served in a cream sauce.

Corn is another native American crop that revolutionized the diets of people around the world. Along with wheat, rice, and potatoes, corn is considered one of the four most important food crops in the world. Though botanists believe corn may have grown in the Americas as many as 60,000 years ago, Europeans did not know of its existence until Columbus brought back a plant after his first trip to the Americas.

Like the potato, corn is an extremely versatile plant. Besides being relatively easy to grow—it can be planted in soil that is either too wet or too dry for crops such as wheat or rice—corn literally has hundreds of uses. It can be ground into meal or refined into starch, sugar, syrup, or oil. In the form of meal, it is combined with other ingredients to make corn bread, cookies, waffles, and a wide assortment of other foods.

Besides potatoes and corn, many other important foods originated in the Americas. Among them are avocados, pineapples, papayas, peppers, peanuts, tomatoes, and chocolate. These foods have added zest to many national cuisines. The tomato, for example, added a distinct flavor to Mediterranean cooking. And of course, it is well known what effect chocolate had on all of Europe.

The introduction of American crops to Europe did much more than help shape national cuisines. Partly because of the rich new sources of nutrition found in the native American foods, life expectancy increased and the population of Europe nearly doubled during the eighteenth century. Before the arrival of the new foods, Europe's population had been relatively stable. In addition, the revolutionary changes in agriculture helped reshape the European economy. Despite the burgeoning population, farmers were able to supply the demand for food. As many historians have maintained, plants and seeds from the Americas were far more valuable in Western development than all the silver of Mexico.

117B

List of ancillaries available, each represented by an icon that will be shown at suggested point of use

This Teacher's Edition is organized to provide for maximum ease of use. The student page is slightly reduced. Teacher notes appear regularly in the same place on the page.

Sidenotes are organized around the five-step pedagogical model used throughout *PASO A PASO:*

- **Introduce / Preview**
- **Present**
- **Practice**
- **Apply**
- **Summarize / Assess**

Notes provide answers, teaching suggestions, ancillary cross-references, recycling references, and other useful information.

Previously taught vocabulary sets that are re-entered in the chapter

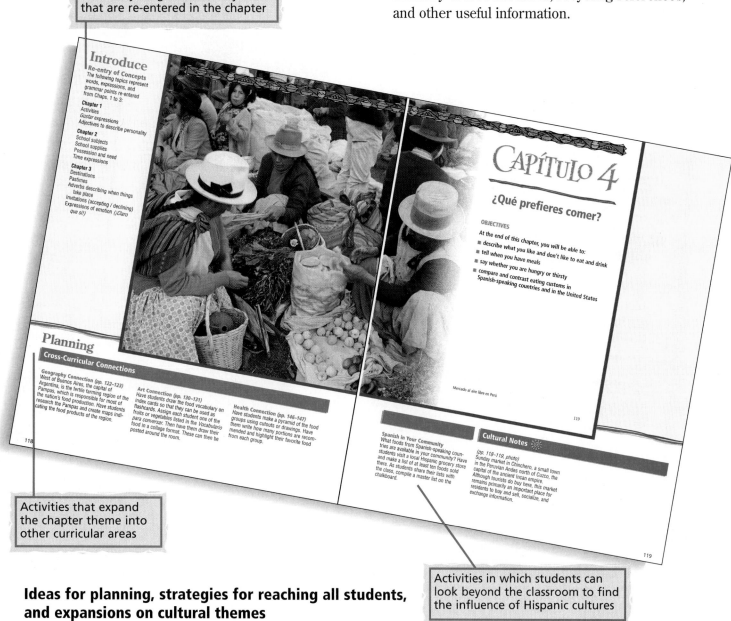

Introduce

Re-entry of Concepts
The following topics represent words, expressions, and grammar points re-entered from Chaps. 1 to 3:

Chapter 1
Activities
Gustar expressions
Adjectives to describe personality

Chapter 2
School subjects
School supplies
Possession and need
Time expressions

Chapter 3
Destinations
Pastimes
Adverbs describing when things take place
Invitations (accepting / declining)
Expressions of emotion (*¡Claro que sí!*)

Planning

Cross-Curricular Connections

Geography Connection (pp. 122–123)
West of Buenos Aires, the capital of Argentina, is the fertile farming region of the Pampas, which is responsible for most of the nation's food production. Have students research the Pampas and create maps indicating the food products of the region.

Art Connection (pp. 130–131)
Have students draw the food vocabulary on index cards so that they can be used as flashcards. Assign each student one of the fruits or vegetables listed in the *Vocabulario para conversar.* Then have them draw their food in a collage format. These can then be posted around the room.

Health Connection (pp. 146–147)
Have students make a pyramid of the food groups using cutouts or drawings. Have them write how many portions are recommended and highlight their favorite food from each group.

CAPÍTULO 4

¿Qué prefieres comer?

OBJECTIVES
At the end of this chapter, you will be able to:
- describe what you like and don't like to eat and drink
- tell when you have meals
- say whether you are hungry or thirsty
- compare and contrast eating customs in Spanish-speaking countries and in the United States

Mercado al aire libre en Perú

Spanish in Your Community
What foods from Spanish-speaking countries are available in your community? Have students visit a local Hispanic grocery store and make a list of at least ten foods sold there. As students share their lists with the class, compile a master list on the chalkboard.

Cultural Notes
(pp. 118–119, photo)
Sunday market in Chinchero, a small town in the Peruvian Andes north of Cuzco, the capital of the ancient Incan empire. Although tourists do buy here, this market remains primarily an important place for residents to buy and sell, socialize, and exchange information.

118   119

Activities that expand the chapter theme into other curricular areas

Activities in which students can look beyond the classroom to find the influence of Hispanic cultures

Ideas for planning, strategies for reaching all students, and expansions on cultural themes

References to help with planning and instruction

Chapter theme

Communicative objectives

Icons for ancillary references

Ideas for recycling previously taught material

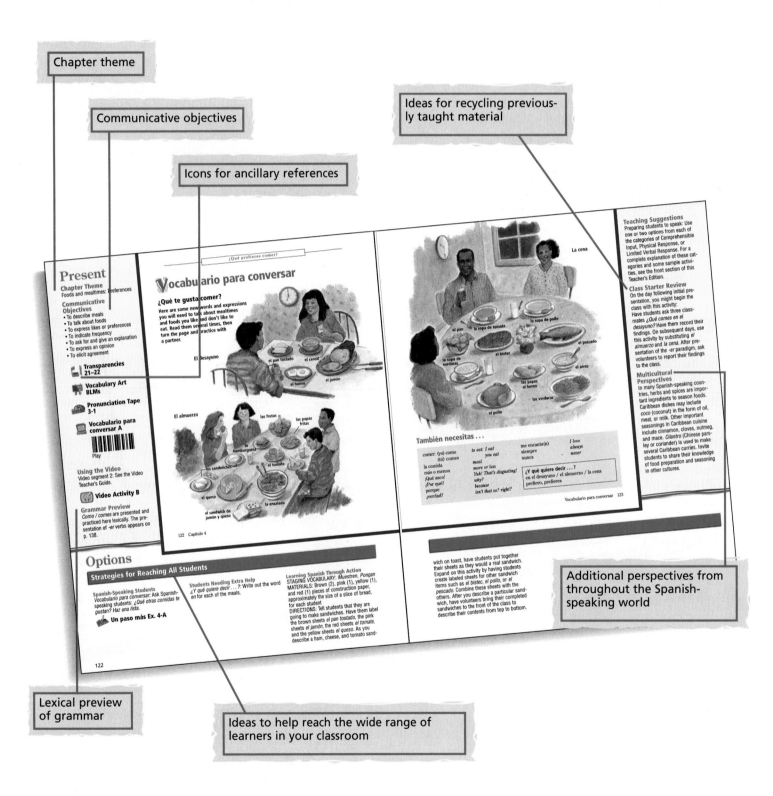

Lexical preview of grammar

Ideas to help reach the wide range of learners in your classroom

Additional perspectives from throughout the Spanish-speaking world

MANAGEMENT AND PACING

Management and pacing have frustrated many foreign language teachers in the past. Several factors affect pacing in a typical classroom:

1 Reduced or interrupted instructional time. The amount of class time for most teachers across the country varies from 38 to 60 minutes. Of that, time is lost due to the inevitable interruptions (assemblies, fire drills, announcements, etc.). In addition, flexible scheduling may change the amount of instructional time from day to day.

2 Wider range of students in the classroom. Many students are coming to the Spanish classroom with weak English skills and poor study skills. The pace of instruction must change to include more repetition and greater variety in teaching strategies.

3 Time for building proficiency. Our goals for language teaching today recognize the need for more time. Memorizing a conjugation is one thing. Gaining the ability to use it with some ease is another thing altogether. Pair and small-group practice—the most effective and long-lasting tool for learning a language—requires time. Though less material may be covered, what is learned is more likely to be retained.

4 Amount of content in textbooks. Many teachers are concerned that too much is presented in textbooks, especially in the first and second years. The combination of varying instructional time, the wide range of students, and more emphasis on communicative activities and proficiency contribute to a slower pace of instruction than in the past.

PASO A PASO 1 has been carefully developed to provide the instructional materials for one school year. The authors had as a goal the development of a realistically paced and easy-to-manage program that would relieve teacher and student frustration. There is flexibility and choice among the textbook activities and ancillaries. To help work with the wide variety of learners in your classroom, *PASO A PASO 1* offers unprecedented support on every page. We developed the Scope and Sequence to give students the tools needed to communicate about their interests. Thematic chapter organization allows for real integration of vocabulary, grammar, and culture, while avoiding unneeded grammatical content.

We present vocabulary in logical sets and, when possible, with visuals. Research shows that both of these approaches lead to more efficient and more permanent learning. Above all, lexical and contextual introduction of grammar allows students to learn structures in a truly natural way. *Fui* is not "the first-person singular preterite of the verb *ir*," but, quite simply, "I went"—a concept that presents no difficulty. (This is particularly true for students who neither know nor care that "I went" is a past-tense form of the verb "to go.")

We would urge you to allow this process to unfold. Avoid explanations in the vocabulary section. Allow students to use the words naturally. By the time they reach the explanations they will feel confident in their ability to use the language.

Pacing for *El primer paso*

Do **not** spend more than two weeks on *El primer paso*. While students will need to recognize the vocabulary through listening and reading, they will not need spelling mastery at this point. Use this chapter to let students learn the beginning communication tools, cultural insights, and learning strategies. All of the concepts presented will be recycled throughout the text.

Pacing for Chapters 1–14

We suggest that approximately 11–13 instructional days be spent on each chapter, including assessment. This time will vary based upon the amount of instructional time and the range of students in the class.

As you begin teaching with *PASO A PASO 1,* you will sense a rhythm, a flow within each chapter that helps students move smoothly and successfully. The thematic integration and spiraling within a chapter, the extensive use of context and comprehensible input for vocabulary and grammar, the inductive questioning that leads to real understanding, and the recycling of previously taught material are part of the carefully thought-out chapter design. You should be able to move quickly through the chapters in the suggested time period.

Bridging to *PASO A PASO 2*

As students move into *PASO A PASO 2,* it is expected that they will have completed at least the content in Chapters 1–12 of Book 1. The vocabulary and grammar in Chapters 13–14 of Book 1 are retaught in *PASO A PASO 2.*

Review and reteaching

As students move into *PASO A PASO 2,* they will continually be exposed to previously learned material from Book 1.

Thematic vocabulary and grammar from Book 1 are recycled in Book 2.

PASO A PASO 2 begins with a lively, communicative magazine-like section entitled *Paso doble.* This section reactivates the major vocabulary sets and structures of the early chapters of *PASO A PASO 1.*

The chart on the following page shows the reteaching and expansion of specific grammar points in *PASO A PASO 2* that students first learned in *PASO A PASO 1.* (For information on grammar re-entry in *PASO A PASO 3,* see the equivalent Front Matter pages in Book 2.)

rammar

Grammar	PASO A PASO 1	PASO A PASO 2
ser	1, **5***	*Repaso*, **4, 7**
adjectives	**1**, 3, **4, 5, 6, 7**, 8, **9**	*Repaso*, **1, 3**
negatives	**1, 2, 14**	**8**
regular *-ar* verbs	**2**	*Repaso*
tener	2, 4, **5**	*Repaso*, **1**
ir	**3**	*Repaso*
estar	**3**	*Repaso*, **8**
stem-changing verbs: *o→ue*	3, **7, 9**	**2**
stem-changing verbs: *e→ie*	3, 4, **7, 8**	**2**
regular *-er* verbs	**4**	*Repaso*
possessive adjectives	**5, 8**	**7**
demonstrative adjectives	**6**	**1, 3**
direct object pronouns	**6**, 10, **11**, 12, 13	**1**, 9
preterite	6, 7, 9, **10, 11, 12, 13**	**3, 4, 6, 9, 10**
salir	**7**	**1**
personal *a*	**7**	*Repaso*
regular *-ir* verbs	**8**	*Repaso*
hacer	**8**	*Repaso*
poner	**8**	**8**
indirect object pronouns	**9, 11, 12**	**2**, 3, 5, 9
dar	11, **14**	**6**
comparatives / superlatives	**11**	**1, 3**
stem-changing verbs: *e→i*	**12**	**2, 6**
traer	**12**	**1**, 9
saber	**13**	**4, 8**
decir	**13**	**7**
tú affirmative commands	**13**	**12**
conocer	**14**	**1, 5**
present progressive	**14**	**8, 9**

*Lightface numbers represent lexical introduction or quick review;
boldface numbers represent presentation of the grammar point.

ROLE OF THE VIDEO

Ever-increasing attention is being given to the important role that video can play in language learning. Today's teachers find video a highly effective tool in developing students' language proficiency and cultural understanding.

Video can provide access to new language and its meanings. In our native language we regularly acquire new vocabulary and grammar by hearing them used in meaningful contexts and surrounded by visual cues to meaning. That is, we figure out new meanings by our knowledge of the situation and what we observe people doing (think, for example, of how you learned what "to boot up" a computer means). Video provides the visual cue needed to match language with its meaning. It is a primary source of comprehensible input.

Video is also an important tool for preparing students for encounters with native speakers outside the classroom. Too often students lament that while they can ask questions they can't always understand the answers. That's because in classrooms there are limited opportunities to hear native speakers use the language in a natural way, without oversimplification of the content or a reduction of the rate of their speech. Video provides repeated opportunities for students to hear authentic language used in authentic situations by native speakers, thus gaining an increasing ability to understand the language in direct encounters outside the classroom.

Video can best be utilized when it is viewed several times, although each viewing may have a different purpose. A first viewing, perhaps with the sound off, allows students to understand the context, to draw on their background knowledge to anticipate what the segment will be about, and to anticipate what people might be saying. For example, a waiter holding a pad and pencil while talking to two people seated at a table will let students know that this is a restaurant. They may anticipate that he might be asking "What would you like to order?" A second viewing, with the sound on, might focus on getting the gist of what is happening and what people are saying. Repeated viewings might focus on specific meanings of words and then longer speech segments. With the picture off and the sound on, students may refine their ability to get meaning from spoken language because the visual supports are withdrawn. Conversely, with the picture on and the sound off, students can concentrate on the cultural information provided, whether it is of elements in the target culture environment (e.g., what one teenager's bedroom in Mexico looks like or what kinds of cars are most common in Spanish cities) or the body language used by native speakers when they interact.

En vivo is the video program that accompanies *PASO A PASO 1*. The program contains an integrated, three-segment video episode for each chapter in the text. The first segment is a mostly visual sequence that provides an overview of the chapter theme, allowing students to anticipate the situations they will see. This segment also provides a visual context for the language and cultural information they will be learning. In segment 2, students hear new language used by native speakers. The new language is presented in ways that help make the meanings clear (comprehensible input). In segment 3, which has been designed to be shown after all new chapter vocabulary and grammar have been presented and practiced, the new language is again used, but with fewer direct visual cues to meaning. This requires students to integrate and apply the newly learned material and to rely on the meanings they have acquired. An extensive Teacher's Guide accompanies *En vivo*. The Guide offers many suggestions for using the video program.

While it is certainly possible to teach *PASO A PASO 1* without using the video, teachers will find it a powerful tool in promoting the acquisition of new language, in developing the listening comprehension skills students need to function outside the sheltered environment of the classroom, and in bringing the cultures of the Spanish-speaking world into the classroom in a vivid and interesting way.

STRATEGIES FOR REACHING ALL STUDENTS

PASO A PASO 1 provides teachers the support and strategies needed to reach all students in the Spanish classroom. We offer an unprecedented commitment to providing materials that help meet the realities of today's classroom. This article focuses on strategies from *PASO A PASO 1* that will help you and all of your students enjoy a successful year learning Spanish . . . step by step!

1 Material that builds upon students' experiences

Language students learn best by using what they know, by building new knowledge on old, and by experiencing and doing. As you use the text, you will see that *PASO A PASO 1* provides for an authentic, meaningful experience for the learner. The fourteen chapter themes were developed by asking, "What do students want to talk about?" The vocabulary taught is high-frequency language that students want to learn. The grammar supports communication and is practiced communicatively. The cultural content provides a means toward understanding and a global perspective that will be meaningful to all students. The activities ask students to interact, to become active participants in the learning process, and to express real ideas and real meanings for real purposes.

2 A multisensory approach to learning

Each student enters the Spanish classroom with different learning styles and abilities. Some work best with an aural / oral approach; others need a strong visual approach. Many need to touch and be physically involved in learning. An approach that addresses the needs and strengths of each student lays the groundwork for reaching all.

PASO A PASO 1 provides a strong multisensory approach to language learning. Students have varied opportunities for success by working with activities that recognize different learning styles and employ more than one modality. Each chapter provides suggestions for incorporating TPR,

which we call Learning Spanish Through Action. The *Todo junto* offers activities that involve different learning skills and interests (creating a collage, preparing a skit, drawing a house).

The cornerstone of success in ScottForesman's foreign language programs has always been our strong visual approach. We have expanded this in *PASO A PASO 1*. Each chapter opens with culturally authentic photographs *(¡Piénsalo bien!)* that call upon students' background knowledge in discussing the chapter theme. Vocabulary presentation is facilitated by contextual visualization that is then recycled in the practice activities to reinforce learning. This approach is supported by the Overhead Transparencies and the Vocabulary Art Blackline Masters. We have enhanced the visual approach through a photo essay in the *Perspectiva cultural*. A new, realia-based approach offers students an opportunity to study grammar in a real-life context. And reading and writing practice are made more accessible through the strong use of visual cues.

The multisensory approach is further expanded through use of the chapter-by-chapter audio tapes, video, and the interactive multimedia CD-ROM. The video program brings the culture to students while providing support to the chapter's content. Language use is presented in an authentic context. The CD-ROM, *Pasos vivos,* provides opportunities for students to work at their own pace while engaging all learning styles.

3 Learning strategies

PASO A PASO 1 reinforces the strategies and skill-building techniques that students are using in their other classes. Some of these may be new to you but are easily implemented in the Spanish classroom. Strategies include building on background knowledge and experience, making lists or webs to organize their learning, inductive questioning, and consistent application of reading strategies and process writing.

4 Higher-order and inductive thinking

It sometimes seems that every day researchers are discovering new facts about the workings of the brain. We now know that information is stored in many areas of the brain and connected by a rich network of neurons. The goal of instruction should be to maximize the use of this network by helping students make connections and to learn information from a variety of perspectives and in a variety of ways. Activities aimed toward this goal are inherently interesting and motivating.

Students learn more successfully when they create their own understanding. Throughout *PASO A PASO 1* you will find activities that ask students to do just this. Inductive questions, for example, are the starting point of the following chapter features: *¡Piénsalo bien!, Perspectiva cultural, Gramática en contexto,* and *¡Vamos a leer!* Activities that engage students in higher-level thinking skills are the initial focus in each of these sections, as well as in the *Actividades* and *¡Vamos a escribir!* We sequence these activities so that all students can be successful.

Another important learning strategy, informed guessing, is embedded in the vocabulary section entitled *¿Y qué quiere decir . . . ?* and is focused on in the inductive questions about photographs, as well as in the process reading and writing sections of each chapter.

5 Multiple learning opportunities

We know that students will improve at different rates and will be stronger in some areas than in others. In addition, developing proficiency takes time for everyone, no matter how gifted. Therefore, instruction must provide multiple opportunities for learning and improvement.

PASO A PASO 1 offers these opportunities. New vocabulary is presented, practiced, and recycled throughout a chapter and in subsequent chapters. Students are first exposed to grammar lexi-

cally, use it as they practice, and have some degree of understanding and control of it before it is presented and practiced as grammar. It is presented in easy-to-deal-with increments. Direct object pronouns, for example, are first explained in Chapter 6, with reminders and / or additional information being presented in Chapters 10–13; similarly with the preterite, which is first presented lexically in Chapter 6, and later explained in Chapters 10–12. In addition, recursive themes from one level to the next allow for regular review, expansion, and elaboration.

Throughout the text you will find reminder notes to students entitled *¡No olvides!* These focus on previously learned concepts that students will need to do a particular exercise or to understand better an extension of a given structure. These reminders are not crutches, but rather important tools for mastery.

6 Additional opportunities for students who need them

A regular on-page feature of this Teacher's Edition entitled "Strategies for Reaching All Students" provides you support for working with:

- Spanish-speaking students
- those having difficulty learning
- the gifted

For working with Spanish speakers, there are suggestions throughout the text, as well as a specially written supplemental worktext, *Un paso más: Actividades para ampliar tu español.* Notes under the heading "Students Needing Extra Help" suggest adaptations of the textbook activities or grammar explanations for those with real learning difficulties. Enrichment suggestions allow students who are capable of doing so to move beyond the textbook. You will also find notes for cooperative learning, an excellent strategy for reaching all students.

Varied assessment options

Students will do better in assessment situations if they have a clear understanding of the objectives, of how they will be assessed, and if they are assessed in such a way as to focus on their strengths.

PASO A PASO 1 offers a variety of options. Besides the *Pruebas* and *Exámenes de habilidades* in the Assessment Program, the *Actividades* in the integrative *Todo junto* offer you different types of opportunities for assessment, asking students to draw upon auditory, visual, and kinesthetic strengths. The Communicative Activities Blackline Masters include Situation Cards that are ideal for use in assessing speaking proficiency. (For additional ideas, see the article on assessment, pp. T39–T44, and the Introduction to the Assessment Program itself.)

Through the clearly stated objectives at the beginning of each chapter and the mini-assessments within the chapter *(¿Qué sabes ahora?* and *Ahora lo sabes),* students are able to monitor their own progress. In addition, the end-of-chapter pretest *(¿Lo sabes bien?)* gives them a clear picture of how they will be assessed on the *Examen de habilidades.*

PASO A PASO 1 is committed to helping every teacher reach every student in the Spanish class. By providing materials that are strategy-based and that have built-in teacher support, we believe that we are enabling both you and your students to experience real enjoyment and unparalleled success.

SSESSMENT

Assessment in a communicative classroom can take many forms: informal daily assessments, short quizzes that check knowledge of vocabulary or grammar, longer end-of-chapter assessments that verify what students know and can do in Spanish, and student portfolios. To be most effective, assessment should be based on the following criteria: (1) clear objectives that allow for meaningful and purposeful communication; (2) student understanding of what is expected of them when assessed; (3) assessment that reflects what students have done in the chapter; and (4) varied assessment options that utilize the strengths of each student. *PASO A PASO 1* provides you a wide variety of assessment options.

At the beginning of each chapter, students see the objectives expressed as what they will be able to do by the end of the chapter. They have multiple opportunities to verify their progress toward achieving these objectives in the *¿Qué sabes ahora?, Ahora lo sabes,* and *¿Lo sabes bien?* sections. The end-of-chapter vocabulary list organizes vocabulary based upon the chapter objectives. Thus, students are told at the start what is expected of them, given opportunities to check their progress, and given a pre-test that models the *Examen de habilidades.*

Informal daily assessment

Class performance and homework are key elements in assessment. Throughout, the pupil's book offers a wide variety of daily assessment opportunities. Regular informal assessment builds self confidence, particularly for students who do not perform well in more formal or traditional testing situations. Encouraging creativity in activities and homework assignments often evokes rewarding results for the individual, the class, and the teacher.

At all stages of *PASO A PASO 1,* students participate in meaningful, purposeful activities that are ideal for informal assessment. The abundant ancillaries that accompany *PASO A PASO 1* also provide for flexibility and variety.

Expanding the textbook: Ideas for creative homework

The following are creative ideas for expanding on the various chapter sections.

Vocabulario para conversar

Students can:

- make collages of the vocabulary words and present them to the class

- make flashcards showing pictograms of the vocabulary

- create crossword puzzles, word searches, and scrambled word lists, including answer keys with new vocabulary; share these with a partner

- find and describe additional photographs related to the vocabulary theme; present descriptions to the class

- photograph or videotape people and objects representative of the chapter vocabulary; write captions for the photographs or narrate the video

- write expanded captions for the photographs in the textbook and explain them to a partner

- use a computer to create word games using chapter vocabulary

Empecemos a conversar

Students can:

- practice conversations on the phone and then present them to a small group or to the class

- produce videotapes with props and then present them to the class

- write new dialogues using pictures or talk bubbles and then present the dialogues in class

Empecemos a escribir
Empecemos a escribir y a leer

Students can:

- make up original questions and then interview a partner; the results of the interviews can be written up as interviews or as summaries of what they learned from one another

- create new questions or dialogues, including illustrations such as talk balloons or magazine cutouts; practice and then perform the dialogues in class

- interview a student or someone in the community who speaks Spanish; write out the interview and then report what was learned to the rest of the class

¿Qué sabes ahora? / Ahora lo sabes

Students can:

- illustrate the sentences or dialogues, including talk balloons that show what the characters are saying

- create collages representing the answers to the questions

- record the answers on an audio cassette

- create dialogues, practicing them with a partner on the telephone and then presenting them to a small group or to the class

Perspectiva cultural

Students can:

- make original posters that illustrate the main idea

- create travel brochures with illustrations and captions

- interview someone who is knowledgeable about the topic; make videos or audio cassettes of the interview; write illustrated summaries

- make posters showing similarities and differences between cultures

- find photographs that illustrate the cultural theme and write a caption or description

Gramática en contexto

Students can:

- write modified versions of the realia-based readings

- make charts illustrating one or more of the grammar rules presented, color-coding the essential points

- create mnemonic devices that will help them remember the grammar points

- compose simple lyrics or poems illustrating a grammar rule

¿Lo sabes bien?

Students can:

- create short listening passages with questions; have partners listen and then answer the questions, correcting one another whenever appropriate

- write advertisements, post cards, or conversations with questions; have partners read and then answer the questions

- make collages of the cultural topic, explaining them to the class or to partners

- create new dialogues using the one in the Speaking section as a model

There are several ways to evaluate student performance on informal assessment, including the above ideas for creative homework. You might want to evaluate some assignments or, at other times, let students evaluate each other's work or their own. There are several criteria you can use for informal assessment, including: completion of task, quantity of information, appropriateness, comprehensibility, originality, promptness, variety, quality above and beyond base expectations, individual improvement, accuracy, and fluency.

Formal assessment

Quizzes

PASO A PASO 1 provides blackline master quizzes, *Pruebas,* for each chapter vocabulary and grammar section. Feel free to use some or all of the quizzes based on the needs of your students.

End-of-chapter assessment

At the end of each chapter, you have several assessment options.

1 *Prueba cumulativa:* A contextualized, comprehensive chapter quiz that assesses student knowledge of vocabulary and grammar.

2 *Examen de habilidades:* A thematic, contextualized assessment of listening and reading comprehension, writing and speaking proficiency, and cultural knowledge. The vocabulary and grammar are fully integrated as opposed to being tested in isolation.

3 Test Generator (multiple-choice questions): A test generator provides a bank of questions per chapter. You can add your own questions to the test bank.

Final examinations

The Assessment Program offers you a *Banco de ideas,* a bank of test items that you can copy, cut, and paste to develop an end-of-semester/quarter or final exam.

See the introduction to the Assessment Program for a complete explanation of the formal assessment options.

Student portfolios

In addition to the informal and formal assessment, and the creative homework already described, another way to check student performance is through the use of student portfolios.

Portfolios in the second-language classroom

The portfolio should contain samples of a student's work collected over a period of time. This enables both you and the student to observe the progress being made. The portfolio should provide students the opportunity to examine and reflect upon what they have produced so that they become more involved in improving their work. The portfolio can be useful to determine grade / level placement.

Contents of the portfolio

- written work, such as short paragraphs, compositions, or journals
- audio and / or video cassettes of student performance
- quizzes and tests
- evidence of reading comprehension
- evidence of listening comprehension
- individual student projects
- pair or group projects
- art work
- cultural projects
- picture dictionaries
- story boards
- evidence that the language skills were practiced outside of the classroom
- evidence of contact with Hispanic cultures in the community
- original creative writing, such as poems, short stories, narratives, or explanations
- student-produced newspapers
- evidence of student reflection on his or her own writing or speaking

Introducing the portfolio

If the portfolio is to be used in the assessment of progress and proficiency in the language, then students must know that it is more than just a collection of materials. They need to know that it will be integrated with daily, weekly, or monthly activities. The following is one example of how to introduce the portfolio to your students:

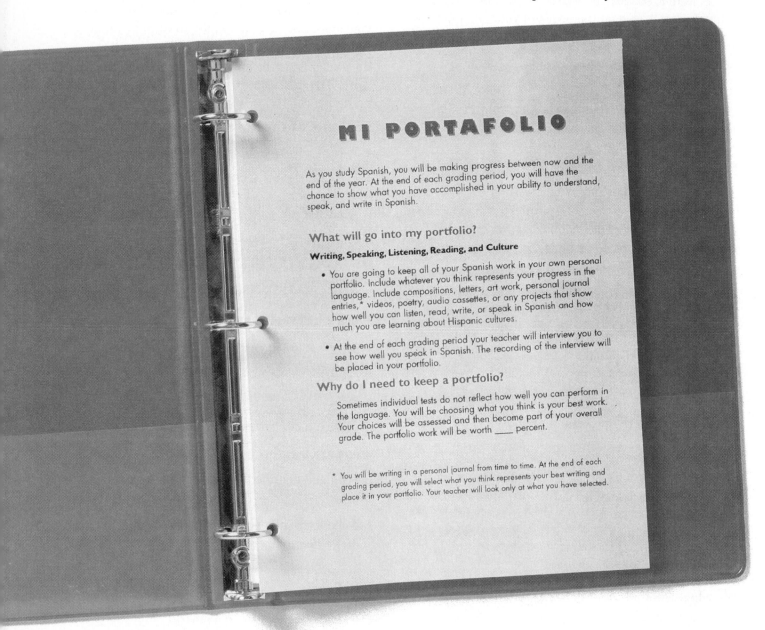

MI PORTAFOLIO

As you study Spanish, you will be making progress between now and the end of the year. At the end of each grading period, you will have the chance to show what you have accomplished in your ability to understand, speak, and write in Spanish.

What will go into my portfolio?

Writing, Speaking, Listening, Reading, and Culture

- You are going to keep all of your Spanish work in your own personal portfolio. Include whatever you think represents your progress in the language. Include compositions, letters, art work, personal journal entries,* videos, poetry, audio cassettes, or any projects that show how well you can listen, read, write, or speak in Spanish and how much you are learning about Hispanic cultures.

- At the end of each grading period your teacher will interview you to see how well you speak in Spanish. The recording of the interview will be placed in your portfolio.

Why do I need to keep a portfolio?

Sometimes individual tests do not reflect how well you can perform in the language. You will be choosing what you think is your best work. Your choices will be assessed and then become part of your overall grade. The portfolio work will be worth _____ percent.

* You will be writing in a personal journal from time to time. At the end of each grading period, you will select what you think represents your best writing and place it in your portfolio. Your teacher will look only at what you have selected.

Assessing the portfolio

The portfolio could be used as the sole means of assessing student progress, as an integral part of the overall grade, or only as a showcase of what students have accomplished. The following are some ways in which students could construct and edit the contents of their portfolio for eventual assessment by the teacher.

The students could:

- rewrite compositions after peer or teacher correction

- redo an oral performance such as an interview, summary, or dramatization

- reflect on their writing and speaking by writing an analysis of their work or by filling out a check list; this list could include columns to show what areas need improvement, those that have improved, and those showing real mastery

- provide written or spoken evidence that they have mastered the objectives of each chapter; this evidence could be assessed along with what they demonstrate on the tests

- select samples of work that illustrate their improvement, with the improvement being assigned a grade, but not the samples

- include notes taken in class as they learn vocabulary that is not a part of the text, or notes on cultural information; these can become a part of the assessment package

- include as evidence of improvement or mastery whatever they produce after working with a given chapter section

Informal assessment for Students Needing Extra Help

Because language production is a skill and involves considerable risk on the part of students as they try to perform well, it is important to encourage their participation and use a variety of assessment options whenever possible. Students should be acknowledged with positive remarks and by receiving credit for:

- doing activities outside of the classroom

- participating voluntarily in class activities

- trying to use Spanish rather than English

- completing assignments

- showing improvement

Acknowledgment of these efforts will help maintain students' enthusiasm.

Formal assessment

Students with learning problems have a particularly difficult time taking quizzes and tests. Apprehension, insecurity, lack of preparedness and / or mastery all serve to put the student in a less-than-desirable position prior to test time. Help students perform optimally by following these suggestions:

- provide a pre-quiz or pre-test practice opportunity that is identical in format to the actual quiz or test; be sure directions are also the same; this is adhered to in the *¿Lo sabes bien?* test preparation in the student text and the *Examen de habilidades* in the Assessment Program

- provide students with test-preparation guides that focus on what will be tested; tell them what they need to know and exactly how you will grade them

- allow extra time for quizzes and tests

- explain all directions on tests and give examples (in English if necessary)

- underline important words in directions and test items

- allow some students to take the test orally or to dictate answers to you

- if possible, tape record questions so that students can read and hear them simultaneously

- weight the scoring of the test to reflect individual strengths; do not require all students to do the entire test (allow them to do every other item or even skip certain sections)

- when appropriate, be lenient with spelling

- avoid unannounced quizzes and tests

- require a certain level of performance and retest if necessary

- be willing to accept projects or demonstrations as an alternative to a final test; give quizzes a cumulative grade

- use a grading system that rewards effort and participation

- allow students to write verb, pronoun, and other charts on their test papers so they don't have to rethink paradigms for each question

- before copying the quizzes and tests for your students, add models and cut and paste pictures and icons; in question-and-answer sections, add pronouns

Specific suggestions for the *Examen de habilidades*

1. Listening Comprehension
Play the tape more than once, or read the manuscript so that students hear a familiar voice. Remember that many students do not have auditory strengths.

2. Reading Comprehension
Read the questions first, or have students read one question and then look for the answer. The length of the reading may discourage some students.

3. Writing Proficiency
Determine specific learning objectives. If you are looking for students' ability to manipulate the language, allow them to use their Organizers. Alternatively, the writing section of the test could be a separate grade, scored in accordance with the fact that they can use their books and Organizers. You may want to prepare a form in which you have given the first few words of each sentence. Students then fill in the remainder.

4. Culture
Although students have taken notes, they may not remember to review them. Go over the notes in class or have students review their notes in pairs.

5. Speaking Proficiency
Choose the easiest of the topics. Offer extra credit if you elect to give both topics or the more difficult one. This section may be especially stressful for some students. Allow students to write some of their thoughts down and speak from notes. Allow students to use their Organizers.

INDEX OF CULTURAL REFERENCES

ScottForesman Spanish Program

PASO A PASO

1

Unas molas de San Blas, Panamá

These *molas* are hanging out to dry. *Molas* are decorative handsewn blouse inserts made and used by members of the Cuna Indians from the San Blas Islands, Panama. They are embroidered by reverse appliqué (a technique in which patterns are cut out and stitched over other fabrics, thus revealing the colors of the underlying fabrics). Their designs are traditionally abstract, often based on the patterns of coral in the local waters.

ScottForesman Spanish Program

PASO A PASO

1

Myriam Met
Coordinator of Foreign Languages
Montgomery County Public Schools
Rockville, MD

Richard S. Sayers
Niwot High School
Longmont, CO

Carol Eubanks Wargin
Glen Crest Junior High School
Glen Ellyn, IL

ScottForesman
A Division of HarperCollinsPublishers

Editorial Offices: Glenview, Illinois

Regional Offices: Sunnyvale, California • Atlanta, Georgia
Glenview, Illinois • Oakland, New Jersey • Dallas, Texas

ISBN: 0-673-21669-1

Copyright © 1996

Scott, Foresman and Company, Glenview, Illinois

All Rights Reserved. Printed in the United States of America.

For information regarding permission, write to:

Scott, Foresman and Company, 1900 East Lake Avenue, Glenview, Illinois 60025.

12345678910DQ03020100999897969594

Acknowledgments for illustrations appear on page 509. The acknowledgments section should be considered an extension of the copyright page.

Contributing Writers

Eduardo Aparicio
Miami, FL

Margaret Azevedo
Palo Alto Senior High School
Palo Alto, CA

Thomasina Pagán Hannum
Albuquerque, NM

Mary de López
University of Texas
El Paso, TX

Reader Consultants

The authors and editors would like to express our heartfelt thanks to the following team of reader consultants. Each of them read the manuscript, chapter by chapter, offering suggestions and providing encouragement. Their contribution has been invaluable.

Rosario Martínez-Cantú
Northside Health Careers High School
San Antonio, TX

Greg Duncan
InterPrep
Marietta, GA

Walter Kleinmann
Sewanhaka Central High School District
New Hyde Park, NY

Bernadette M. Reynolds
Manual High School
Denver, CO

Rudolf L. Schonfeld, Ph.D.
Brooklawn Middle School
Parsippany, NJ

Marcia Payne Wooten
Starmount High School
Boonville, NC

Tabla de materias

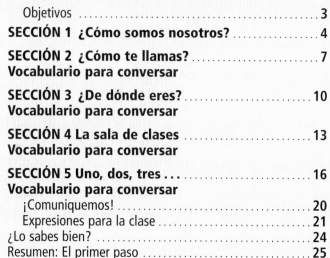

El Primer Paso

CAPÍTULO 3

Los pasatiempos

CAPÍTULO 4

¿Qué prefieres comer?

Capítulo 5

¿Cómo es tu familia?

Capítulo 6

¿Qué desea Ud.?

Capítulo 7

¿Adónde vas a ir de vacaciones?

Capítulo 8

¿Qué haces en tu casa?

CAPÍTULO 9

¿Cómo te sientes?

CAPÍTULO 10

¿Qué hiciste ayer?

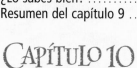

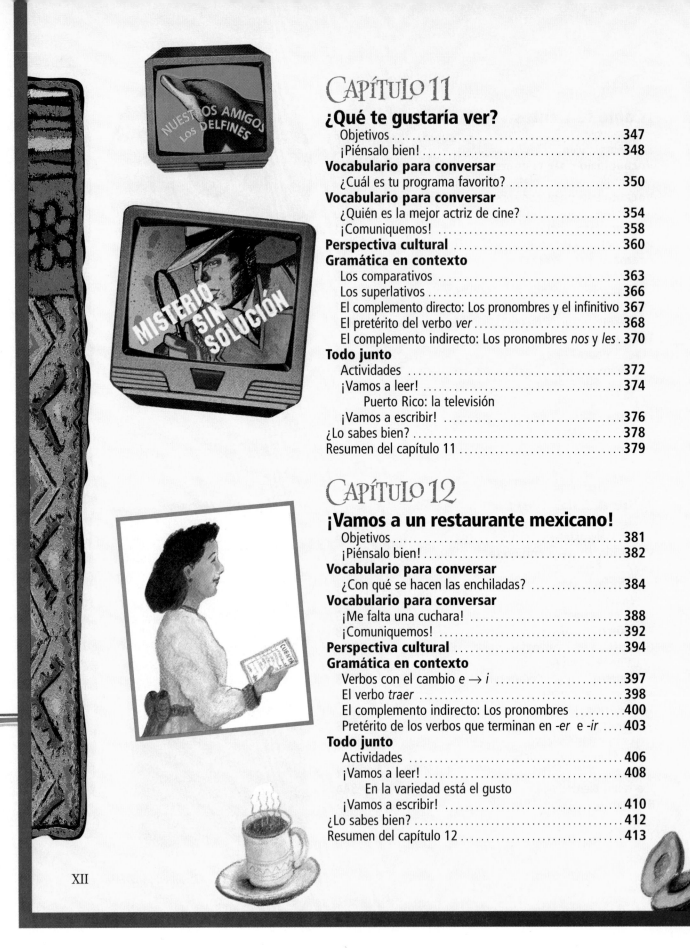

Capítulo 11
¿Qué te gustaría ver?

Capítulo 12
¡Vamos a un restaurante mexicano!

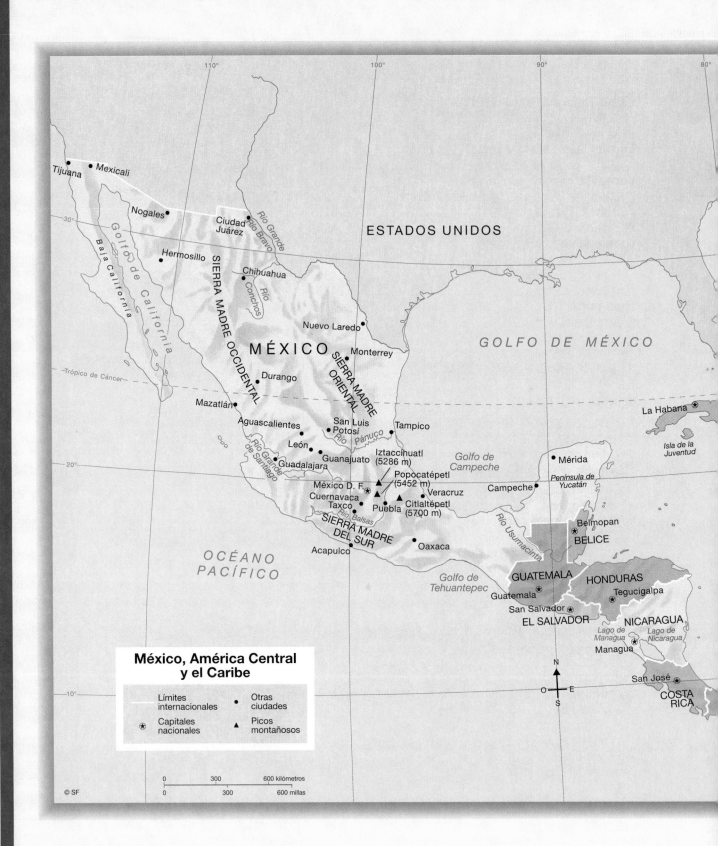

México, América Central y el Caribe

ESTADOS UNIDOS

GOLFO DE MÉXICO

MÉXICO

OCÉANO PACÍFICO

Golfo de California

Baja California

SIERRA MADRE OCCIDENTAL

SIERRA MADRE ORIENTAL

SIERRA MADRE DEL SUR

Golfo de Campeche

Península de Yucatán

Golfo de Tehuantepec

Tijuana
Mexicali
Nogales
Ciudad Juárez
Hermosillo
Chihuahua
Nuevo Laredo
Monterrey
Durango
Mazatlán
Aguascalientes
San Luis Potosí
Tampico
León
Guanajuato
Guadalajara
Iztaccíhuatl (5286 m)
Popocatépetl (5452 m)
México D. F.
Cuernavaca
Taxco
Puebla
Citlaltépetl (5700 m)
Veracruz
Acapulco
Oaxaca
Campeche
Mérida
La Habana
Isla de la Juventud
Belmopan
BELICE
GUATEMALA
HONDURAS
Guatemala
Tegucigalpa
San Salvador
EL SALVADOR
NICARAGUA
Managua
Lago de Managua
Lago de Nicaragua
San José
COSTA RICA

Río Grande
Río Bravo
Río Conchos
Río Pánuco
Río Grande de Santiago
Río Balsas
Río Usumacinta

Trópico de Cáncer

110° 100° 90° 80°
30°
20°
10°

N
O   E
S

México, América Central y el Caribe

Límites internacionales

Capitales nacionales

Otras ciudades

Picos montañosos

0   300   600 kilómetros
0   300   600 millas

© SF

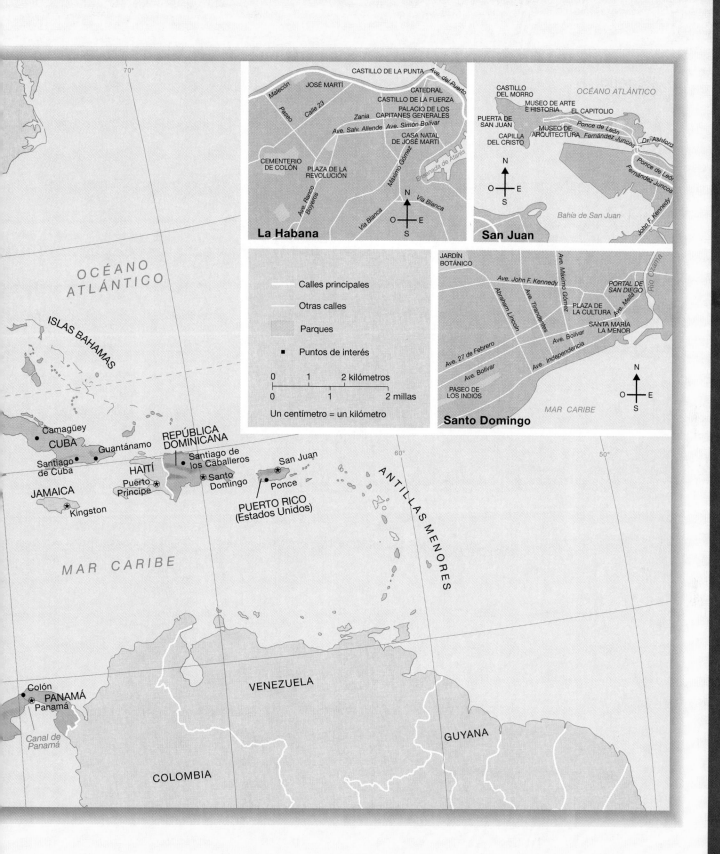

La Habana

CASTILLO DE LA PUNTA
Ave. del Puerto
JOSÉ MARTÍ
Malecón
CATEDRAL
CASTILLO DE LA FUERZA
Paseo
Calle 23
PALACIO DE LOS
CAPITANES GENERALES
Zanja
Ave. Salv. Allende
Ave. Simón Bolívar
CASA NATAL
DE JOSÉ MARTÍ
CEMENTERIO
DE COLÓN
PLAZA DE LA
REVOLUCIÓN
Máximo Gómez
Ensenada de Atarés
Ave. Rancio
Boyeros
N
Vía Blanca
O
E
Vía Blanca
S
Vía Blanca

San Juan

CASTILLO
DEL MORRO
OCÉANO ATLÁNTICO
MUSEO DE ARTE
E HISTORIA
EL CAPITOLIO
PUERTA DE
SAN JUAN
Ponce de León
Dr. Ashford
CAPILLA
DEL CRISTO
MUSEO DE
ARQUITECTURA
Fernández Juncos
Ponce de León
N
Fernández Juncos
O
E
S
John F. Kennedy
Bahía de San Juan

Calles principales
Otras calles
Parques
■ Puntos de interés

0   1   2 kilómetros
0   1   2 millas
Un centímetro = un kilómetro

Santo Domingo

JARDÍN
BOTÁNICO
Ave. John F. Kennedy
Ave. Máximo Gómez
PORTAL DE
SAN DIEGO
Río Ozama
Ave. Tiradentes
PLAZA DE
LA CULTURA
Abraham Lincoln
Ave. Mella
SANTA MARÍA
LA MENOR
Ave. 27 de Febrero
Ave. Bolívar
Ave. Independencia
Ave. Bolívar
PASEO DE
LOS INDIOS
MAR CARIBE
N
O
E
S

OCÉANO
ATLÁNTICO

ISLAS BAHAMAS

70°

Camagüey
CUBA
Guantánamo
Santiago
de Cuba
HAITÍ
Puerto
Príncipe
REPÚBLICA
DOMINICANA
Santiago de
los Caballeros
Santo
Domingo
San Juan
Ponce
JAMAICA
Kingston
PUERTO RICO
(Estados Unidos)

60°
50°

A
N
T
I
L
L
A
S
M
E
N
O
R
E
S

MAR CARIBE

Colón
PANAMÁ
Panamá
Canal de
Panamá

VENEZUELA

GUYANA

COLOMBIA

Mapas XV

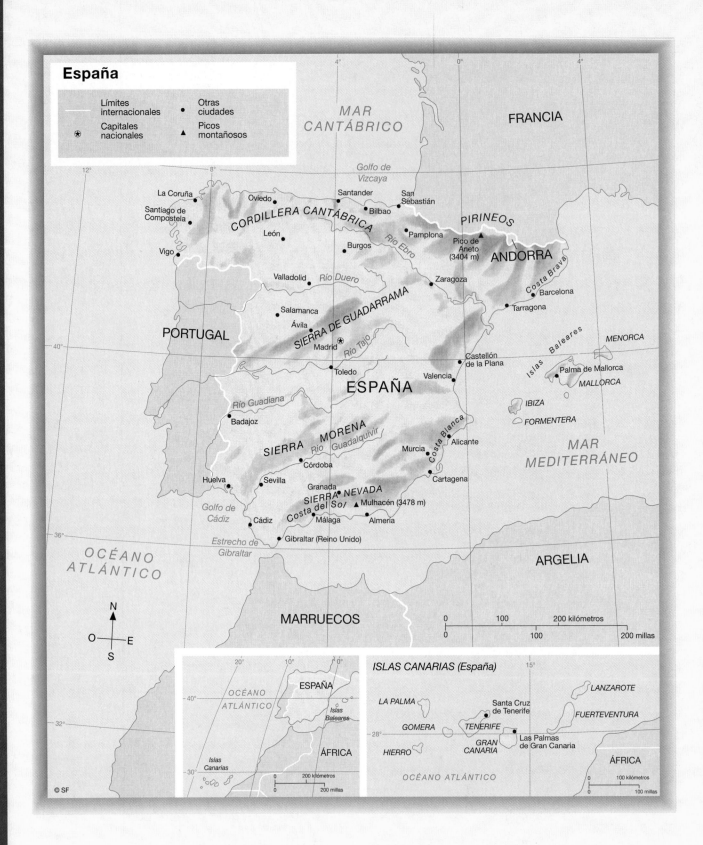

España

- Límites internacionales
- ✪ Capitales nacionales
- • Otras ciudades
- ▲ Picos montañosos

MAR CANTÁBRICO

FRANCIA

Golfo de Vizcaya

La Coruña
Santiago de Compostela
Oviedo
Santander
San Sebastián
Bilbao
CORDILLERA CANTÁBRICA
PIRINEOS
León
Pamplona
Burgos
Río Ebro
Pico de Aneto (3404 m)
ANDORRA
Vigo
Valladolid
Río Duero
Zaragoza
Costa Brava
Salamanca
Barcelona
Ávila
SIERRA DE GUADARRAMA
Tarragona
PORTUGAL
Madrid
Río Tajo
Castellón de la Plana
Islas Baleares
MENORCA
Toledo
Valencia
Palma de Mallorca
ESPAÑA
MALLORCA
Río Guadiana
IBIZA
Badajoz
FORMENTERA
SIERRA MORENA
Río Guadalquivir
Murcia
Costa Blanca
Alicante
MAR MEDITERRÁNEO
Huelva
Córdoba
Sevilla
Granada
Cartagena
SIERRA NEVADA
Mulhacén (3478 m)
Costa del Sol
Cádiz
Málaga
Almería
Golfo de Cádiz
Gibraltar (Reino Unido)
ARGELIA
Estrecho de Gibraltar
OCÉANO ATLÁNTICO

MARRUECOS

N
O — E
S

0   100   200 kilómetros
0   100   200 millas

OCÉANO ATLÁNTICO
ESPAÑA
Islas Baleares
ÁFRICA
Islas Canarias

0   200 kilómetros
0   200 millas

© SF

ISLAS CANARIAS (España)

LA PALMA
Santa Cruz de Tenerife
LANZAROTE
GOMERA
TENERIFE
FUERTEVENTURA
HIERRO
GRAN CANARIA
Las Palmas de Gran Canaria
ÁFRICA
OCÉANO ATLÁNTICO

0   100 kilómetros
0   100 millas

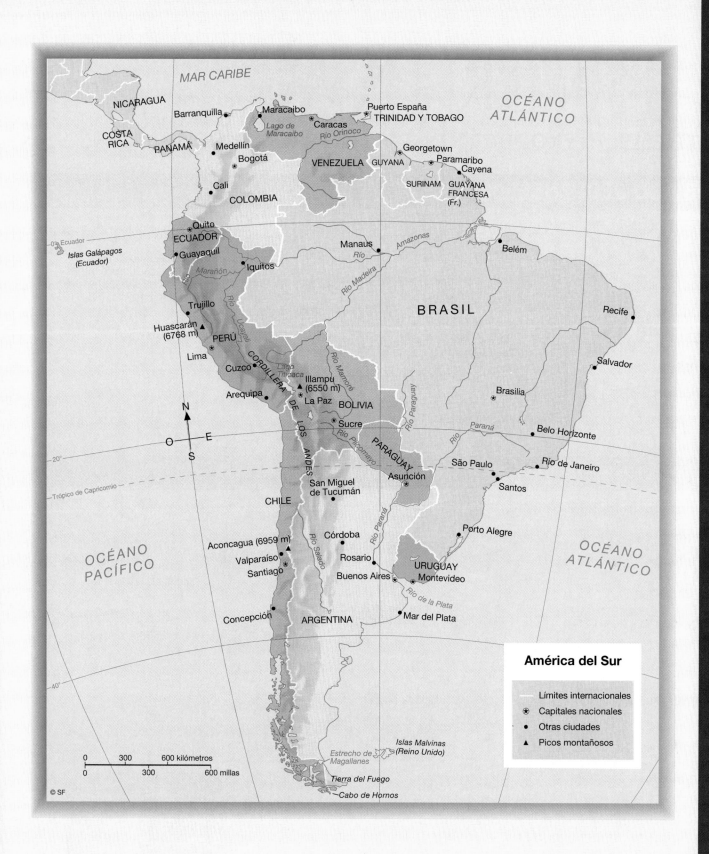

MAR CARIBE

OCÉANO ATLÁNTICO

NICARAGUA

Barranquilla
Maracaibo
Puerto España
TRINIDAD Y TOBAGO

COSTA RICA
PANAMÁ
Medellín
Lago de Maracaibo
Caracas
Río Orinoco

Bogotá
VENEZUELA
GUYANA
Georgetown
Paramaribo
Cayena

Cali
SURINAM
GUAYANA FRANCESA (Fr.)

COLOMBIA

Quito
ECUADOR
0° Ecuador
Islas Galápagos (Ecuador)
Guayaquil
Iquitos
Marañón
Manaus
Río Amazonas
Belém

Río Madeira

Trujillo
Río Ucayali
BRASIL
Recife

Huascarán (6768 m)
PERÚ
Lima
Río Marmoré
Salvador

Cuzco
Lago Titicaca
Illampu (6550 m)
La Paz
BOLIVIA
Brasilia

Arequipa
CORDILLERA DE LOS ANDES
Sucre
Río Pilcomayo
Río Paraguay

20°
Paraná
Belo Horizonte

Trópico de Capricornio
CHILE
San Miguel de Tucumán
PARAGUAY
Asunción
São Paulo
Río de Janeiro

Aconcagua (6959 m)
Río Salado
Córdoba
Río Paraná
Santos

OCÉANO PACÍFICO
Valparaíso
Santiago
Rosario
Buenos Aires
URUGUAY
Montevideo
Porto Alegre

OCÉANO ATLÁNTICO

Concepción
ARGENTINA
Río de la Plata
Mar del Plata

40°

América del Sur

——— Límites internacionales
✳ Capitales nacionales
● Otras ciudades
▲ Picos montañosos

0   300   600 kilómetros
0   300   600 millas

Islas Malvinas (Reino Unido)
Estrecho de Magallanes

© SF

Tierra del Fuego
Cabo de Hornos

N
O   E
S

EL PRIMER PASO

THEME: INTRODUCTION TO THE WORLD OF SPANISH

COMMUNICATION

Topics

Greetings and leavetakings

Names of countries

Professions

Classroom objects

Alphabet / Numbers 0–31

Classroom expressions

Objectives

To discuss the influence of Spanish language and culture

To greet people and say good-by

To tell how you feel

To ask someone's name and tell your name

To acknowledge introductions

To ask for and give information

To say when something takes place

To count or give dates

To say thank you

To talk about the classroom

CULTURE

Names and locations of Spanish-speaking countries

Spanish names

Ancillaries available for use with *El primer paso*

Multisensory/Technology

 Overhead Transparencies, 1–5

 Audio Tapes and CDs

 Vocabulary Art Blackline Masters for Hands-On Learning, pp. 3–7

 Classroom Crossword

 Video

CD-ROM

Print

 Practice Workbook, pp. 1–11

 Writing, Audio & Video Activities, pp. 1–4, 91–92, 151

 Communicative Activity Blackline Masters

 Pair and Small Group Activities, pp. 1–6

 Situation Cards, p. 7

Assessment

 Assessment Program

 Examen de habilidades, pp. 1–8

 Test Generator

Video still from *El primer paso*

The Richly Diverse Hispanic Americans

According to the 1990 census, 22,354,000 people (about 9 percent of the total population in the U.S.) classified themselves as being of Spanish or Hispanic descent. Out of that number, 17,268,000 indicated that they were of either Mexican, Puerto Rican, or Cuban descent. The remaining 5,086,000 people checked "Other Spanish / Hispanic" on their census question-naires. This broad category included people who came from or who had ancestral ties to other Spanish-speaking countries in the Caribbean, Central and South America, or Spain.

The nation's Hispanic population is growing at a tremendous rate. Between 1980 and 1990 it grew by an astounding 53 percent. In contrast, the nation as a whole expanded only 9.8 percent. The Census Bureau estimates that by 2080, people in the Spanish or Hispanic group will number almost 60 million and constitute more than 19 percent of the population. Collectively, the group would outnumber African Americans by that date.

The influence of the many diverse Hispanic cultures is everywhere. The Southwestern look, drawing on traditional Spanish architecture as well as contemporary influences, has emerged as an important design style. Ethnic groceries specializing in ingredients essential to many of the traditional dishes served in Hispanic cultures have sprung up across the country. The music of Celia Cruz, Gloria Estefan, Rubén Blades, and Los Lobos has introduced Spanish vocabulary into everyday English. Hispanic actors such as Raúl Julia and Rosie Pérez have earned great acclaim in recent years for their outstanding work. Motion pictures such as *La Bamba, Stand and Deliver,* and *Like Water for Chocolate* were hits at the box office.

Perhaps most important, Hispanic Americans have increased their political power in recent years. During the last several presidential administrations, Hispanics have been appointed to many major political posts. In 1988 President Reagan appointed Lauro F. Cavazos, a Mexican American, as Secretary of Education. He was the first Hispanic American appointed to the Cabinet. In 1990, Dr. Antonia Coello Novello, with roots in Puerto Rico, became the first woman and the first Hispanic American to become Surgeon General. Many other Hispanic Americans also achieved success in national, state, and local politics, and their numbers in the House of Representatives continue to increase.

Planning

Cross-Curricular Connections

Math Connection *(p. 4)*
Use the population figures to have students calculate the percentage of Spanish speakers from a certain city by comparing the information to all the cities or countries listed. For example, Buenos Aires represents 16.7 percent of Spanish speakers from all the listed cities, and 3.8 percent from all the countries.

Geography Connection *(p. 4)*
In pairs, have one student call out the different countries shown on the graph as the other locates them on the maps in the front of their books (pp. XIV–XVII). Then have them reverse roles where one student says a country and the other says the capital.

Language Arts Connection *(p. 10)*
Assign portions of the glossary in the back of the book to groups or pairs of students. Have them look for cognates and note the spelling differences between the Spanish and English. For example: *-ología* and *-ology; -dad* and *-ty; -mente* and *-ly.*

EL PRIMER PASO

You are about to embark on a wonderful journey through the Spanish-speaking world as you begin to learn the language. Think of the possibilities! By the end of this chapter, *El primer paso*, you will have experienced:

P resentations of some of the rich and varied aspects of Hispanic cultures

A cquisition of key vocabulary so that you can start speaking Spanish right away

S trategies and suggestions to help you learn more quickly and effectively and evaluate your progress—and have fun while doing it

O pportunities to increase your job and career choices, as well as improve your English-language skills and college entrance exam scores

1

Spanish in Your Community
How has Hispanic culture influenced your community? Have small groups of students brainstorm ideas and then develop lists of the various ways. If students have difficulty, you might suggest broad categories, such as politics or sports, under which students can supply specific examples. Groups can then share their findings with the class.

Introduce

 ¿Cómo somos nosotros?

Play

 **Video Activity A**

Using the Video

This chapter's video provides an overview of the video series and introduces the *En vivo* hosts: Alexander in Miami, Karina in Guadalajara, and Gracia and Jorge in Madrid. Alexander interviews Spanish-speaking patrons at Miami's Bayside Marketplace, asking them about their cultural backgrounds and interests.

Before students watch the video, ask them to predict what it will be about.

For future chapters, you may want to show the first segment of the video as an introduction to the chapter theme, the second segment as an introduction to chapter vocabulary, and the third segment as reinforcement.

Video segment 1: For more teaching suggestions, see the Video Teacher's Guide.

Options

Strategies for Reaching All Students

Students Needing Extra Help

Students who have had learning problems are often intimidated by a foreign language. This opening section gives you an opportunity to calm their fears with non threatening activities. Emphasize how very little Spanish they may know now and how much they will soon know.

EL PRIMER PASO

OBJECTIVES

At the end of this chapter, you will be able to:

- understand the widespread influence of the Spanish language and Hispanic cultures
- greet people and introduce yourself
- ask how someone is feeling and tell how you are feeling
- ask where someone's from and tell where you are from
- say good-by
- use the Spanish alphabet to spell
- use numbers to count and tell your age, your phone number, and the date
- ask questions and respond to requests in the classroom
- use your textbook to help you learn Spanish

3

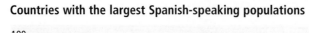
Present & Apply

Cultural Objective

• To discuss the influence of Spanish language and culture

 Vocabulario para conversar

Play

 Video Activity B

Using the Video

Video segment 2: See the Video Teacher's Guide.

Teaching Suggestions

The names of countries, Spanish names, Spanish alphabet, and classroom expressions presented in this chapter are for recognition only.

Current usage dictates the use of the country's name without a definite article *(Perú* rather than *el Perú,* for example). In this book, names of countries will appear without the definite article.

To enhance the discussion of Spanish-speaking populations in the U.S., bring in statistical information, such as population projections prepared by the Census Bureau, found in almanacs.

In this section you will learn about the widespread influence of the Spanish language and Hispanic cultures.

Countries with the largest Spanish-speaking populations

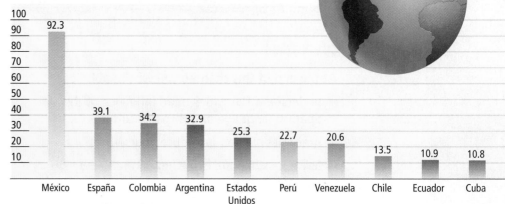

México 92.3, España 39.1, Colombia 34.2, Argentina 32.9, Estados Unidos 25.3, Perú 22.7, Venezuela 20.6, Chile 13.5, Ecuador 10.9, Cuba 10.8

Numbers shown in millions

Cities with the largest Spanish-speaking populations

Ciudad de México 20.8, Buenos Aires 11.6, Lima 6.8, Bogotá 5.9, Santiago de Chile 5.3, Madrid 4.5, Barcelona 4.2, Los Ángeles 3.9, Guadalajara 3.3, Caracas 3.2

Numbers shown in millions

4   El primer paso

Options

Strategies for Reaching All Students

Students Needing Extra Help
Review basic graph-reading skills, if necessary. Have students locate the countries listed in the top graph on p. 4 on the maps in the front of their books (pp. XIV–XVII) or on a wall map.
Ex. C: Most students are so used to these words that they don't realize that they are borrowed from another language.

Ex. D: Emphasize the word *cognate.* Tell students that a cognate is a tool for helping them understand the meaning of words. Say the Spanish words aloud so students can hear the difference in pronunciation from English.

Enrichment
As a written assignment, have students research a city or town near them that has a significant Spanish-speaking population. Ask them to include such census data as the estimated size, countries of origin, and average age of that population.

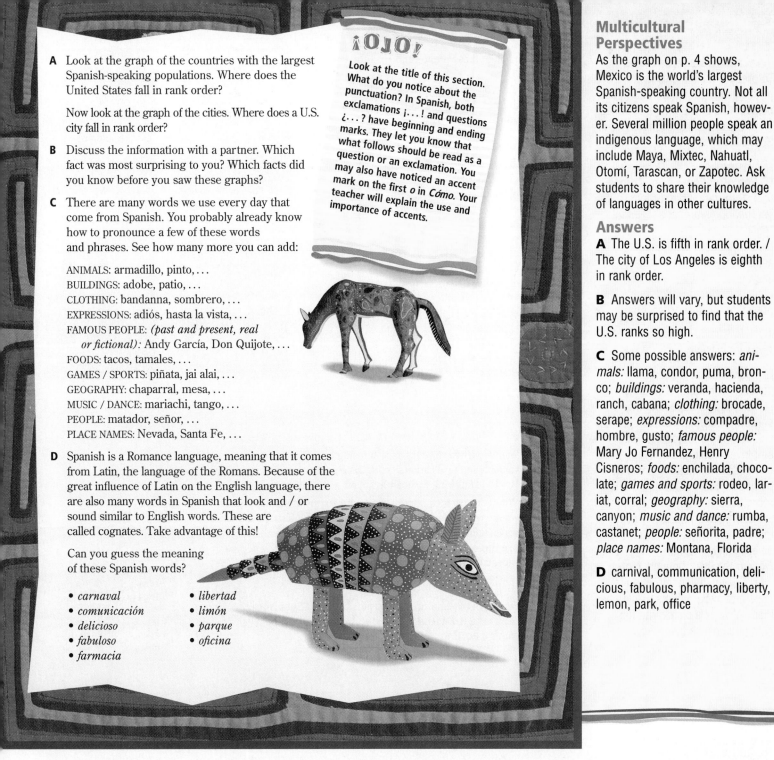

A Look at the graph of the countries with the largest Spanish-speaking populations. Where does the United States fall in rank order?

Now look at the graph of the cities. Where does a U.S. city fall in rank order?

B Discuss the information with a partner. Which fact was most surprising to you? Which facts did you know before you saw these graphs?

C There are many words we use every day that come from Spanish. You probably already know how to pronounce a few of these words and phrases. See how many more you can add:

ANIMALS: armadillo, pinto, . . .
BUILDINGS: adobe, patio, . . .
CLOTHING: bandanna, sombrero, . . .
EXPRESSIONS: adiós, hasta la vista, . . .
FAMOUS PEOPLE: *(past and present, real or fictional):* Andy García, Don Quijote, . . .
FOODS: tacos, tamales, . . .
GAMES / SPORTS: piñata, jai alai, . . .
GEOGRAPHY: chaparral, mesa, . . .
MUSIC / DANCE: mariachi, tango, . . .
PEOPLE: matador, señor, . . .
PLACE NAMES: Nevada, Santa Fe, . . .

D Spanish is a Romance language, meaning that it comes from Latin, the language of the Romans. Because of the great influence of Latin on the English language, there are also many words in Spanish that look and / or sound similar to English words. These are called cognates. Take advantage of this!

Can you guess the meaning of these Spanish words?

- *carnaval*
- *comunicación*
- *delicioso*
- *fabuloso*
- *farmacia*
- *libertad*
- *limón*
- *parque*
- *oficina*

¡OJO!

Look at the title of this section. What do you notice about the punctuation? In Spanish, both exclamations ¡ . . . ! and questions ¿ . . . ? have beginning and ending marks. They let you know that what follows should be read as a question or an exclamation. You may also have noticed an accent mark on the first *o* in *Cómo.* Your teacher will explain the use and importance of accents.

Cultural Notes ☼

5

Apply

Teaching Suggestions

To prepare for the discussion of professions, post pictures of people working at the jobs mentioned on this page. Label each picture in Spanish.

Answers

E Photo captions: *dentista* (dentist); *fotógrafa* (photographer); *veterinario* (veterinarian); *policía* (police officer)
List: actor, actress; architect; astronaut; banker; carpenter; chauffeur; scientist; engineer; mechanic; doctor; pilot; politician; president; professor; secretary; supervisor

Answers will vary.

Answers will vary, but might include: working at a clothing store or fast-food restaurant, delivering newpapers, babysitting, volunteering at a hospital. An employer would probably hire a teenager who spoke Spanish so he or she could communicate with more people. If any of these jobs are in a Spanish-speaking community, knowing Spanish would be especially helpful.
Explain the use of punctuation marks at the beginning of questions and exclamations. Elicit how these provide a clue about the type of sentence that follows.

E Look at these photos and read the captions.

Can you guess what these professions are in English? Here is an additional list for you to practice with:

el actor / la actriz
el arquitecto / la arquitecta
el / la astronauta
el banquero / la banquera
el carpintero / la carpintera
el / la chofer
el científico / la científica
el ingeniero / la ingeniera
el mecánico / la mecánica
el médico / la médica
el piloto / la pilota
el político / la política
el presidente / la presidenta
el profesor / la profesora
el secretario / la secretaria
el supervisor / la supervisora

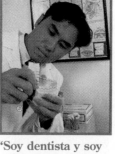

"Soy dentista y soy de Miami."

"Soy fotógrafa y soy de Costa Rica."

"Soy veterinario y soy de Ecuador."

"Soy policía y soy de la Ciudad de México."

- With a partner, discuss why knowing Spanish would be valuable in these careers. What career(s) are you considering? How will knowing Spanish help you with your goals?
- With your partner, make a list of the six most popular jobs or volunteer positions that students might have. If you were hiring a teenager, would you prefer one who spoke Spanish? Why? Are there summer jobs in which knowing Spanish would be especially helpful?

You have made a great decision to study Spanish. Let's take it *PASO A PASO*, step by step. You'll be communicating in Spanish very soon.

¡OJO!
Did you know that, according to research, high-school students with two years of a foreign language score up to 12% higher on the S.A.T. verbal exam—and their scores continue to rise by at least 5% for each additional year of foreign-language study?

6   El primer paso

Options

Strategies for Reaching All Students

Students Needing Extra Help
Help students pronounce the names of the occupations. With cognates, some students may be tempted to pronounce them as they know them in English.

Enrichment
Bring in photocopies of the classified ads page from a Spanish-language newspaper. Have students look for cognates.

Vocabulario para conversar

In the next four sections you will find some study notes to help you learn about the various parts of each chapter. Here are some words you will need to greet people and introduce yourself.

También necesitas . . .

Mucho gusto.	*Pleased / Nice to meet you.*
Igualmente.	*Likewise.*
Muy bien.	*Very well.*
Así, así.	*So-so.*

¡OJO!

You will need to learn the new words pictured in *Vocabulario para conversar* and the words in *También necesitas . . .* ("You also need . . ."). To learn them, you might want to keep a vocabulary section in your notebook by categories, or make flashcards with the Spanish word on one side and a picture or the English word on the other. Practice these from time to time with a classmate or family member. Maybe they can learn some Spanish too!

7

Present

Chapter Theme
Greetings

Communicative Objectives
• To greet people and say good-by
• To tell how you feel
• To ask someone's name and tell your name
• To acknowledge introductions

 Transparency 1

 Vocabulary Art BLMs

 Pronunciation Tape P-1

Teaching Suggestions
Preparing students to speak: Use one or two options from each of the categories of Comprehensible Input, Physical Response, or Limited Verbal Response. For a complete explanation of these categories and some sample activities, see the front section of this Teacher's Edition.

Explain the use of punctuation marks at the beginning of questions and exclamations. Elicit how these provide a clue about the type of sentence that follows.

Present & Practice

Class Starter Review

On the day after students have chosen the Spanish name they might use in class, have them ask three classmates their names. On a subsequent day, have students ask three classmates how they are feeling.

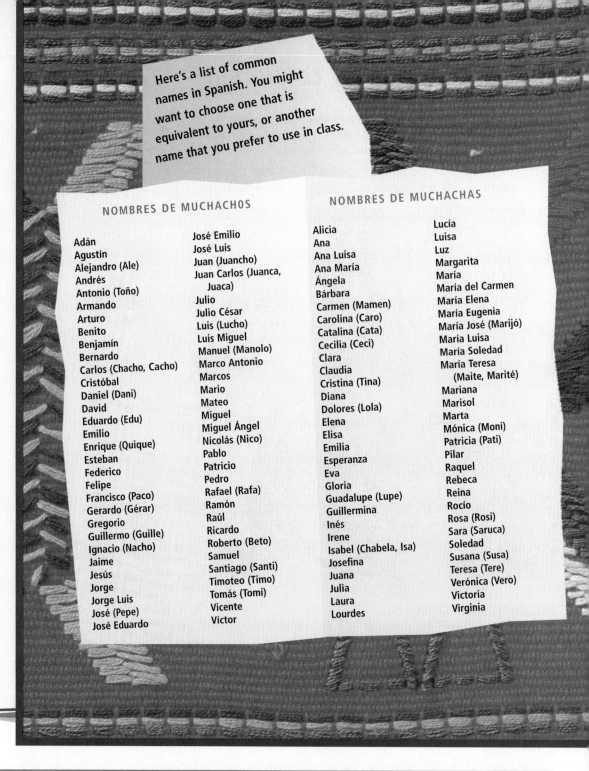

Here's a list of common names in Spanish. You might want to choose one that is equivalent to yours, or another name that you prefer to use in class.

NOMBRES DE MUCHACHOS

Adán
Agustín
Alejandro (Ale)
Andrés
Antonio (Toño)
Armando
Arturo
Benito
Benjamín
Bernardo
Carlos (Chacho, Cacho)
Cristóbal
Daniel (Dani)
David
Eduardo (Edu)
Emilio
Enrique (Quique)
Esteban
Federico
Felipe
Francisco (Paco)
Gerardo (Gérar)
Gregorio
Guillermo (Guille)
Ignacio (Nacho)
Jaime
Jesús
Jorge
Jorge Luis
José (Pepe)
José Eduardo

José Emilio
José Luis
Juan (Juancho)
Juan Carlos (Juanca, Juaca)
Julio
Julio César
Luis (Lucho)
Luis Miguel
Manuel (Manolo)
Marco Antonio
Marcos
Mario
Mateo
Miguel
Miguel Ángel
Nicolás (Nico)
Pablo
Patricio
Pedro
Rafael (Rafa)
Ramón
Raúl
Ricardo
Roberto (Beto)
Samuel
Santiago (Santi)
Timoteo (Timo)
Tomás (Tomi)
Vicente
Víctor

NOMBRES DE MUCHACHAS

Alicia
Ana
Ana Luisa
Ana María
Ángela
Bárbara
Carmen (Mamen)
Carolina (Caro)
Catalina (Cata)
Cecilia (Ceci)
Clara
Claudia
Cristina (Tina)
Diana
Dolores (Lola)
Elena
Elisa
Emilia
Esperanza
Eva
Gloria
Guadalupe (Lupe)
Guillermina
Inés
Irene
Isabel (Chabela, Isa)
Josefina
Juana
Julia
Laura
Lourdes

Lucía
Luisa
Luz
Margarita
María
María del Carmen
María Elena
María Eugenia
María José (Marijó)
María Luisa
María Soledad
María Teresa (Maite, Marité)
Mariana
Marisol
Marta
Mónica (Moni)
Patricia (Pati)
Pilar
Raquel
Rebeca
Reina
Rocío
Rosa (Rosi)
Sara (Saruca)
Soledad
Susana (Susa)
Teresa (Tere)
Verónica (Vero)
Victoria
Virginia

Options

Strategies for Reaching All Students

Spanish-Speaking Students

Have students add names to the list: *Haz una lista de otros nombres posibles. Empecemos a conversar:* Pair bilingual with non-bilingual students whenever possible for oral exercises. Bilingual students can model pronunciation.

Students Needing Extra Help

Every chapter in this book has an Organizer, found in the *Practice Workbook*. The purpose of the Organizer is to provide students with access to vocabulary and grammar points that, because of certain disabilities or learning styles, they may have difficulty recalling. It can be used as a type of clipboard sheet of important information they will be filling in so that they can perform the exercises and activities in the chapter.

Begin the vocabulary section of the Organizer.

Ex. 1: Choose a student to help you model the dialogue. This will make it clear from the beginning that the dialogues in the *Empecemos a conversar* throughout the text are active, involving two contributing students as partners. Point out the use of dashes before each line in the model dialogue. Explain that these markers indicate

Empecemos a conversar

In these exercises you will create conversations according to a model. With a partner, take turns at being *Estudiante A* and *Estudiante B*. Use the words that are cued or given in the balloons to replace the underlined sections in the model. means you can make your own choices for that item or exercise.

¡OJO!

You might want to scan the exercise first in order to get the gist of doing it. If you need help, review the *Vocabulario para conversar* or *También necesitas . . .* sections.

1   Estudiante A —¡Hola! Me llamo <u>María</u>. ¿Cómo te llamas?
    Estudiante B —Me llamo <u>Rafael</u>.
    Estudiante A —Mucho gusto, <u>Rafael</u>.
    Estudiante B —Igualmente, <u>María</u>.

    Y ahora Uds.

    (This is the cue for you and your partner to begin the exercise.)

Estudiante A   Estudiante B

Did you use your own name in the conversation? Now redo it with five other classmates. Play both roles. Your teacher may ask you to tell your classmates' names, so remember their answers.

2   A —*Buenos días. ¿Cómo estás, <u>Pilar</u>?*
    B —*Muy bien, gracias. ¿Y tú?*
    A —*Así, así.*

    Y ahora Uds.

Estudiante A   Estudiante B

Did you keep using the same answers for how you feel? Repeat this conversation with four other classmates and vary your answers.

El primer paso   9

Answers: Empecemos a conversar

1–2 Dialogues will vary.

Practice Wkbk. P-1

Writing Activity P-A

Comm. Act. BLM P-1

Cultural Notes

a dialogue exchange. Remind students to reverse roles with their partner as they work through the exercises. Encourage them to give logical responses when appropriate.

(p. 8, background photo)
Birds and vegetation are favorite subjects for Mayan weavers and embroiderers. Mayan textiles are crafted on the same kinds of backstrap looms that were used by their ancestors centuries ago. Ancient methods of extracting dyes from plants and insects are also still used to achieve the vibrant colors.

Present & Practice

Chapter Theme
Greetings, leavetakings, and introductions

Communicative Objectives
- To greet people and say good-by
- To tell how you feel
- To ask for and give information
- To say thank you

 Transparency 2

 Vocabulary Art BLMs

 Pronunciation Tape P-2

Teaching Suggestions
Preparing students to speak: Use one or two options from each of the categories of Comprehensible Input, Physical Response, or Limited Verbal Response. For a complete explanation of these categories and some sample activities, see the front section of this Teacher's Edition.

Vocabulario para conversar

Here are some more words and expressions you will need to greet people and tell where you are from.

¡OJO!
Do you remember ¿Y tú? and ¿Cómo estás? There is another way to say "How are you?" in Spanish. We use usted to show respect when speaking to an older person.

Buenas tardes, Señora García. ¿Cómo está Ud.?

Bien, gracias, ¿y tú?

Buenas noches. Me llamo Anita. ¿Qué tal?

Me llamo Miguel. Muy bien, gracias.

¡OJO!
Look at the words in the section titled ¿Y qué quiere decir...? You will see this section often. These are cognates, or are closely related to words you have already learned.

También necesitas . . .

¿De dónde eres (tú)?	*Where are you from?*
(Yo) soy de ___	*I am from ___*
¿Y usted?	*And you?*
Hasta luego.	*See you later.*

¿Y qué quiere decir . . . ?	
sí	o
no	Adiós.

10   El primer paso

Options

Strategies for Reaching All Students

Spanish-Speaking Students
Ask: ¿A quién le hablas de "Ud."? ¿A quién le hablas de "tú"?

Students Needing Extra Help
También necesitas . . . : Explain that the words in parentheses are optional.
Point out the two ways of saying "How are you?" and the concept of respect or formality in the Spanish language. This is presented later in Chap. 2.

Enrichment
Explain that the important distinction between "you" formal (usted) and "you" familiar (tú) still exists in many languages. In English, "one" is still used in place of the indefinite pronoun "you" in formal situations. For example, instead of saying "It's a good book, if *you* like sports," formal usage dictates saying "It's a good book, if *one* likes sports."

Empecemos a conversar

For Exercise 1, refer to the map below.

1 A — *¡Hola! Me llamo <u>Benito</u>. ¿Y tú?*
B — *Me llamo <u>Luisa</u>. ¿De dónde eres?*
A — *Soy de <u>Costa Rica</u>. ¿Y tú?*
B — *Soy de <u>Bolivia</u>.*

Y ahora Uds.

Estudiante A   Estudiante B

Did you use your own name and country? Now repeat this dialogue with three classmates. Pretend to be someone else, and use different names and countries.

2 Now repeat the conversation with five classmates, using a city name from page 4.

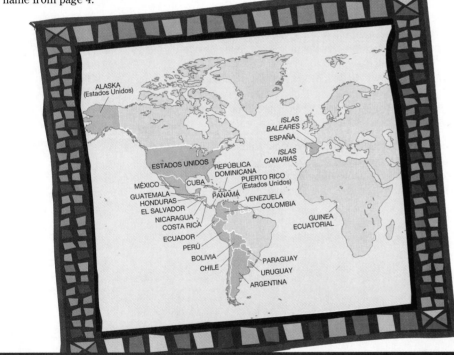

ALASKA
(Estados Unidos)

ISLAS
BALEARES
ESPAÑA

ISLAS
CANARIAS

ESTADOS UNIDOS
REPÚBLICA
DOMINICANA
PUERTO RICO
(Estados Unidos)

MÉXICO   CUBA
GUATEMALA   PANAMÁ
HONDURAS   VENEZUELA
EL SALVADOR   COLOMBIA
NICARAGUA
COSTA RICA

GUINEA
ECUATORIAL

ECUADOR
PERÚ
BOLIVIA
CHILE   PARAGUAY
            URUGUAY
            ARGENTINA

11

¿Y qué quiere decir...?
Explain that this section will appear from time to time in the *También necesitas* . . . to facilitate language learning through the use of cognates and word families. Use comprehensible input to introduce this new vocabulary without giving students an English equivalent.

Answers: Empecemos a conversar
1–2 Answers will vary. You may wish to use Transparencies 78–81 for the maps of Spanish-speaking countries with the Spanish names from the list on p. 8. Students can then choose their name and their country of origin at the same time.

Learning Spanish Through Action
Learning Spanish Through Action (LSTA), based on James Asher's Total Physical Response (TPR), is a strategy modeled on the way children acquire their native language. Through positive reinforcement, confidence building, and realia, students begin to comprehend, communicate, and even think in Spanish without native-language interference. See the front section of this Teacher's Edition for more information.

STAGING VOCABULARY: *Apunten, Señalen*
MATERIALS: transparency of a map of the Spanish-speaking world (Transparencies 78–81) or a wall map of the same areas
DIRECTIONS: Tell students to imagine that they are from the country you announce. Have them point to the country and ask: *¿De dónde eres?* They should respond orally.

Apply

Answers: Empecemos a escribir

3 Answers will vary, but may include: *buenos días, buenas tardes, buenas noches, ¿cómo está usted?, ¿cómo estás?, ¡hola!, ¿qué tal?*

4 *adiós, hasta luego*

5–7 Answers will vary.

Answers: Empecemos a escribir y a leer

8 Answers will vary, but look for the *usted* form: *Buenas tardes, señora. ¿Cómo está usted?*

9 a. *no;* b. *sí;* c. *sí;* d. *no*

 Practice Wkbk. P-2

 Audio Activity P.1

 Writing Activity P-B

Empecemos a escribir

Write your answers in Spanish.

3 List four ways to greet someone.

4 What are two ways to say "good-by"?

5 ¿Cómo te llamas?

6 ¿Cómo estás?

7 ¿De dónde eres?

Empecemos a escribir y a leer

In this section you will write your answers and also do some reading.

Write your answers in Spanish.

8 How do you greet an older person and ask how he or she is feeling?

9 Read the following conversation, then answer the questions with *sí* or *no*.

PROFESORA: Buenas tardes. Me llamo Señora Guzmán. ¿Y tú?
ESTUDIANTE: Me llamo Ana María Hernández. Mucho gusto.
PROFESORA: Igualmente. ¿De dónde eres? ¿De los Estados Unidos?
ESTUDIANTE: No, soy de Costa Rica. ¿Es usted de Argentina o de Chile?
PROFESORA: Soy de Uruguay. Adiós, Ana María. Hasta luego.
ESTUDIANTE: Adiós, profesora.

a. The people in the dialogue know each other.
b. The teacher is a woman.
c. We know the last names of both people.
d. The student is from the United States.

¡OJO!

In this section you will write your answers and ideas in Spanish. Above all, communicate the message. After you finish, you can refer to *Vocabulario para conversar* and *También necesitas . . .* or the *Resumen* at the end of the chapter to check your spelling.

¡OJO!

You might want to read the passage twice, once to get the general meaning, and a second time to try to figure out words you don't know. Many times you can guess the meaning of a word just by how it is used. YOU DON'T HAVE TO UNDERSTAND EVERY WORD TO GET THE OVERALL MEANING.

12   El primer paso

Options

Strategies for Reaching All Students

Spanish-Speaking Students
Empecemos a escribir: Ask students if they know other ways to say hello or good-by. *¿Sabes otras maneras de saludar a alguien o de despedirte? ¿Cuáles son? Escríbelas.*

Students Needing Extra Help
Empecemos a escribir: These sections serve as an opportunity to help develop students' writing skill. You may wish to use them as homework assignments throughout the chapters.
Emphasize the importance of keeping track of their progress.

Have students create a chart with four columns with headings: Greetings, Ways to ask how someone is, Responses, and Ways to end a conversation.
También necesitas . . . : Point out the gender differences in the vocabulary words. One way to help students remember gender is to color-code flashcards.

Vocabulario para conversar

la sala de clases

¿Cómo estás?

la pizarra

$\sqrt{64}$ $x \cdot y$

(+)/y=?

el profesor

la profesora

pl. los estudiantes

la estudiante

el estudiante

pl. los compañeros

el compañero

la compañera

el pupitre

la mesa

la hoja de papel

el libro

el bolígrafo

También necesitas . . .

¿Cómo se dice ___ en español?	*How do you say ___ in Spanish?*
¿Cómo se escribe ___?	*How do you spell ___?*
Se escribe ___.	*It's spelled ___.*

13

Present

Chapter Theme
The classroom

Communicative Objectives
• To ask for and give information
• To talk about the classroom

 Transparency 3

 Vocabulary Art BLMs

 Pronunciation Tape P-3

Teaching Suggestions
Preparing students to speak: Use one or two options from each of the categories of Comprehensible Input, Physical Response, or Limited Verbal Response. For a complete explanation of these categories and some sample activities, see the front section of this Teacher's Edition.

Class Starter Review
On the day following vocabulary presentation, you might begin the class with this activity:
In pairs, have students name three items in the classroom. A partner can then either touch the items or point to where they are.

Present

Teaching Suggestions

In April of 1994, the Association of Spanish Language Academies *(La Real Academia)* voted 17–1 to eliminate *ch* and *ll* as separate letters from the Spanish alphabet. The sole opposition came from Ecuador, while Panama, Nicaragua, and Uruguay abstained. The change was made primarily to simplify dictionaries and make the language more computer compatible. Spelling, pronunciation, and usage are not, of course, affected.

Some sources indicate that the *rr* is only a sound and not a distinct letter of the alphabet. We have opted to retain the *rr* as a letter and have listed it as so.

¡OJO!

Traditionally, there were two additional letters in Spanish: *ch* (che) and *ll* (elle). In 1994, however, the language academies of all Spanish-speaking nations voted to discontinue considering them as separate letters. *Ch* used to come after *c*. In many dictionaries you will find words beginning with *ch* in a separate section following the words that begin with *c*. The same applies to *ll*, which used to come after *l*.

EL ALFABETO

a (a)	k (ka)	s (ese)
b (be)	l (ele)	t (te)
c (ce)	m (eme)	u (u)
d (de)	n (ene)	v (ve *or* uve)
e (e)	ñ (eñe)	w (doble ve
f (efe)	o (o)	*or* doble u)
g (ge)	p (pe)	x (equis)
h (hache)	q (cu)	y (i griega *or* ye)
i (i)	r (ere)	z (zeta)
j (jota)	rr (erre)	

Options

Strategies for Reaching All Students

Enrichment

Tell students that when they are spelling aloud, they should say *acento* after a vowel that has an accent mark on it: *país se escribe pe-a-i acento-ese.* You might also have them say *mayúscula* after a capital letter: *Manolo se escribe eme mayúscula-a-ene-o-ele-o.*

Learning Spanish Through Action

STAGING VOCABULARY: *Digan, Levanten*
MATERIALS: sheets of paper labeled with the letters of the Spanish alphabet
DIRECTIONS: Pass a letter or letters to each student. As you recite the letters, have students raise their sheets, pronouncing the letters as they do so.

Empecemos a conversar

1 

A —*¿Cómo se dice* “table” *en español?*
B —*Mesa.*
Y ahora Uds.

Estudiante A | Estudiante B

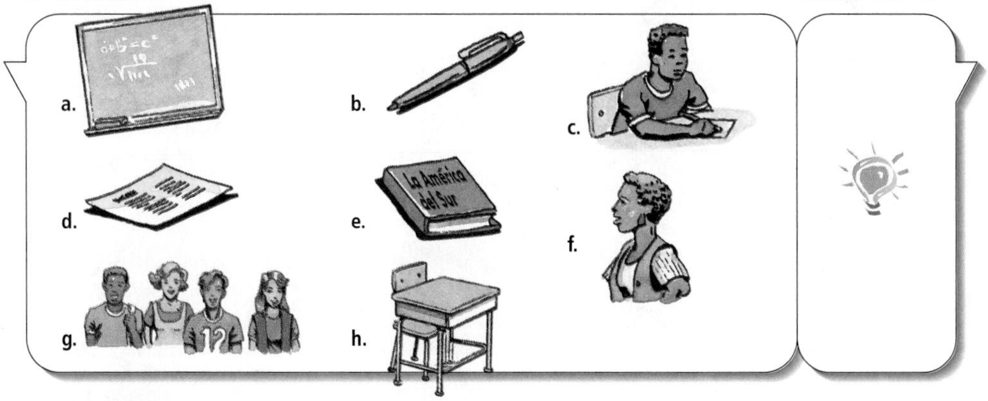

2 

A —*¿Cómo se escribe* *libro?*
B —*Se escribe* *ele-i-be-ere-o.*
Y ahora Uds.

Estudiante A | Estudiante B

Empecemos a escribir

Write your answers in Spanish.

3 Your teacher will spell some names. Listen carefully and write them down. Later, compare your paper with a partner’s.

Practice

Answers: Empecemos a conversar

1 ESTUDIANTE A

a. ¿Cómo se dice *chalkboard* en español?
b. . . . *pen* . . .
c. . . . *student (classmate)* . . .
d. . . . *paper* . . .
e. . . . *book* . . .
f. . . . *teacher* . . .
g. . . . *classmates (students)* . . .
h. . . . *student desk* . . .

ESTUDIANTE B

a. Pizarra.
b. Bolígrafo.
c. Estudiante (Compañero).
d. Hoja de papel.
e. Libro.
f. Profesora.
g. Compañeros (Estudiantes).
h. Pupitre.

2 ESTUDIANTE A

a. ¿Cómo se escribe *mesa?*
b. . . . *pizarra?*
c. . . . *pupitre?*
d. Questions will vary.

ESTUDIANTE B

a. Se escribe *eme-e-ese-a.*
b. . . . *pe-i-zeta-a-erre-a.*
c. . . . pe-u-pe-i-te-ere-e.
d. Answers will vary.

Answers: Empecemos a escribir

3 Answers will vary.

Practice Wkbk. P-3

Writing Activity P-C

Cultural Notes

(p. 14, background photo)
Mayan calendar glyphs on a limestone lintel from Yaxchilán, Mexico. The ancient Maya were fascinated with time. They devised a calendar as exact as the one we use today. Through rigorous and tenacious scholarship, Mayan scholars have determined that the combination of head forms and full figures in these glyphs represent a single date—February 11, 526 A.D. on our calendar.

Present

Chapter Theme
Calendar expressions and numbers 0–31

Communicative Objectives
- To ask for and give information
- To say when something takes place
- To count or give dates

 Transparencies 4–5

 Vocabulary Art BLMs

 Pronunciation Tape P-4

Teaching Suggestions
Preparing students to speak: Use one or two options from each of the categories of Comprehensible Input, Physical Response, or Limited Verbal Response. For a complete explanation of these categories and some sample activities, see the front section of this Teacher's Edition.

Vocabulario para conversar

¡OJO!
Spanish calendars begin the week with Monday *(lunes)* and end with Sunday *(domingo).*

* You will also see the numbers 16–19 spelled *diez y seis, diez y siete, diez y ocho, diez y nueve.* The numbers 20–29 may also be written *veinte y uno, veinte y dos,* and so on.

16   El primer paso

Options

Strategies for Reaching All Students

Students Needing Extra Help
Demonstrate on the chalkboard how *diez y seis* becomes *dieciséis.*
También necesitas . . . : Have students put these phrases in an organizer / notebook so that they will have them throughout the year for easy reference.

Learning Spanish Through Action
STAGING VOCABULARY: *Escriban, Pasen a la pizarra*
MATERIALS: cards with numbers 0–31 written on them
DIRECTIONS: Direct four to eight students to go to the chalkboard to write numbers. Show the class the card as you say the number while students at the chalkboard write the figure.

los meses

JUNIO
MAYO
ABRIL
MARZO
FEBRERO
ENERO

DICIEMBRE
NOVIEMBRE
OCTUBRE
SEPTIEMBRE
AGOSTO
JULIO

También necesitas . . .

¿Cuántos(as) ___ hay? *	*How many ___ are there?*
¿Cuántos años tienes?	*How old are you?*
Tengo ___ años.	*I'm ___ years old.*
el año	*year*
¿Cuál es tu número de teléfono?	*What's your phone number?*
¿Cuándo es ___?	*When is ___?*
¿Cuál es la fecha de hoy?	*What's the date today?*
Hoy es ___.	*Today is ___.*
Mañana es ____.	*Tomorrow is ___.*
¿Qué día es hoy?	*What day is today?*
Mi / Tu cumpleaños	*My / Your birthday*
el 6 de febrero	*the 6th of February / February 6*
el primero de mayo	*the first of May / May 1*

¡OJO!

We form dates using *el* + number + *de* + month. We use *primero* for "first," but we use the regular numbers for the rest of the dates. Notice, too, that the days of the week and the months of the year are not capitalized.

Hay	*There is / are*
Mi	*My*

¿Y qué quiere decir . . . ?
cero
en

* We use *cuántos* with masculine nouns and *cuántas* with feminine nouns.

17

Class Starter Review
On the day following vocabulary presentation, you might start the class with either of these activities:
1) Have students count to ten (and later to 20 and 30), forward and backward.
2) Have students share the date of their birthday with a partner. Partners should then be prepared to share the information with the class.

Multicultural Perspectives
Many Catholics in Latin America and Spain not only celebrate their birthday, but their *día santo* as well. Each day of the Catholic Church calendar is dedicated to one or more saints. Many people are named after their *día santo*. For example, a girl born on December 4 might be named Bárbara because this date is *el día de Santa Bárbara*. Ask students to find out if any of them share their names with a saint. Encourage them to find out how people in other cultures celebrate birthdays.

Practice & Apply

Empecemos a conversar

1 0, 2, 4, ...   A — *cero, dos, cuatro, ...*
          B — *seis, ocho, diez, ...*

          Y ahora Uds.

a. 5, 10, ...
b. 1, 3, 5, ...
c. 0, 3, 6, ...

2   A — *¿Cuántos bolígrafos hay?*
          B — *Hay tres bolígrafos.*

          Y ahora Uds.

Estudiante A   Estudiante B

Options

Strategies for Reaching All Students

Spanish-Speaking Students
Empecemos a conversar: Pair bilingual with non-bilingual students.
Empecemos a escribir y a leer: Ask: *¿Cuáles son otros días de fiesta hispanos que celebras con tu familia? ¿En qué fecha se celebran?*

Empecemos a escribir y a leer

Write your answers in Spanish.

3 Find out when these popular Hispanic holidays occur and write down the dates for each of them: *el Año Nuevo* (New Year's Day), *el Día de los Reyes* (Twelfth Night / Epiphany), *Cinco de Mayo, el Día de la Raza* (Columbus Day), *el Día de los Muertos* (Day of the Dead / All Souls' Day), *la Navidad* (Christmas).

4 Count the items listed below and write the answer in Spanish. Compare your answer with a partner's.

   a. books on your desk
   b. girls in the class
   c. countries in Latin America
   d. people wearing jeans
   e. letters in your teacher's last name

5 Read the following sentences and rewrite them, making the necessary corrections:

   a. Mi cumpleaños es el 15 de diciembre.
   b. El cumpleaños de Martin Luther King, Jr. es en octubre.
   c. El Día de San Patricio es el 14 de enero.
   d. El Día de San Valentín es en junio.
   e. Chanukah es en febrero.

6 ¿Cuál es la fecha de hoy? ¿Y de mañana?

7 ¿Cuándo es tu cumpleaños?

8 ¿Qué día es hoy? ¿Y mañana?

9 ¿Cuál es tu número de teléfono? ¿Y el número de teléfono de tu compañero(a) de clase?

19

3 El Año Nuevo: el primero de enero; el Día de los Reyes: el seis de enero; el Día de la Raza: el 12 de octubre; el Día de los Muertos: el primero de noviembre; la Navidad: el veinticinco de diciembre

4 Answers will vary. For item c., tell students to count the number of Spanish-speaking countries *(diecinueve)*.

5 a. Answers will vary.
   b. El cumpleaños de Martin Luther King, Jr. es en enero.
   c. El Día de San Patricio es el 17 de marzo.
   d. El Día de San Valentín es en febrero.
   e. Chanukah es en noviembre o diciembre.

6–9 Answers will vary.

 Practice Wkbk. P-4, P-5, P-6

 Writing Activities P-D, P-E, P-F

 Comm. Act. BLMs P-2, P-3

Cultural Notes ☼

(p. 19, top photo)
Mexican folk dancing at a *cinco de mayo* celebration in San Francisco. On May 5, 1862, invading French troops reached the city of Puebla, expecting little resistance on their way to Mexico City. At Puebla, however, they were overwhelmed by Mexican forces and forced to withdraw from battle. Although the French eventually established an empire in Mexico (1863–1867), this victory is commemorated as a national holiday.

(p. 19, bottom photo)
This is an example of *papel picado,* the product of a Mexican technique of cutting layers of fine paper to create delicate designs or scenes. When the paper cutting is finished, the layers are separated and strung along a cord and hung as a decoration. This craft has been practiced since pre-Columbian times. It reached its height during the 1800s, when artisans painstakingly created the effect of this delicate lace work around holy cards.

Practice

Answers:
¡Comuniquemos!
1–3 Dialogues will vary.

¡A conversar!

Play

Step

 Video Activity C

Using the Video
Video segment 3: See the Video
Teacher's Guide.

 Audio Activities
P.3, P.4

¡Comuniquemos!

**This is another opportunity for you to use
the vocabulary you've just learned.**

1 Find out when your classmates' birthdays are.
Then tally the results to find out which month
has the most birthdays.

A — *¿Cuándo es tu cumpleaños?*
B — *Es el cinco de julio.*

2 Role-play a conversation with a partner in
which you:

• greet each other
• find out each other's names
• ask and answer how you are
• say good-by

3 With a partner, role-play a meeting between
you and a new student in which you:

• greet each other and ask each
  other's names
• say that you are glad to meet each other
• ask each other your ages and where
  you are from
• ask for each other's phone numbers
• give the information and then say good-by

¡OJO!

In the *¡Comuniquemos!*
section, you are free to use
the language you already know.
Try to use different expressions
for the same ideas. Are you
aware that you are now REALLY
COMMUNICATING IN SPANISH?

Los cumpleaños

enero	febrero	marzo
₮₮₮		‖

abril	mayo	junio
	‖	

julio	agosto	septiembre
₮₮₮	‖‖	₮₮₮

octubre	noviembre	diciembre
	‖‖	

Options

Strategies for Reaching All Students

Spanish-Speaking Students
Ask students to mention any variations
they know for the list of requests and
instructions on pp. 21–23.

Cooperative Learning
Divide the class into groups of three.
Provide students with an index card and tell
them that they are going to assume the
identity of a Hispanic American by completing some sentences. On the chalkboard,
write *Me llamo ____.* Have students write
out the sentence and tell them to fill in a
name from the list on p. 8. After they write
the sentence, have them pass their cards to
the left. On the chalkboard, write *Tengo*

____ *años.* Have them write out the sentence, fill in the blank with a number, and
then pass their cards to the left. Finally,
write *Soy de ____.* Have them write out the
sentence and fill in the blank with the name
of a Spanish-speaking country. Call on individual students to read their "autobiogra-
phies." Ask if the information given could
correspond with the student reading the
card.

Expresiones para la clase

Por favor

Here is a list of requests and instructions. You will need to know what to do when your teacher says them, but you will **not** need to know how to say or write them.

Levántate, por favor.

Siéntate, por favor.

Pasa a la pizarra.

Trabajen con un compañero.

Saquen una hoja de papel.

Entreguen las hojas.

21

Teaching Suggestions
Present the classroom expressions from pp. 21–23 a few at a time, starting with four and adding one or two every day. (You may want to write these on strips of paper, have them laminated, and then display them around the classroom for reference.) Start with the most common commands. Review each time before presenting new ones. Act out each command so that students have a visual image.

Present

Teaching Suggestions

Have pairs of students play the roles of student and teacher. The student asks permission to do something and the teacher responds appropriately.

22   El primer paso

Options

Strategies for Reaching All Students

Students Needing Extra Help

Make sure students understand each class expression by having individuals act out or mimic the expressions.

Enrichment

Have pairs of students make a set of index cards, with each card bearing one of the questions and responses on p. 23. Students can practice the material by pulling a card from the deck, reading it aloud, and having their partner give appropriate responses.

Profesor(a), ¿puedo . . . ?

When you need to ask for permission to do something, you should ask in Spanish. Here are some questions that you may frequently ask in class, and some of the expected answers.

Profesor(a), ¿puedo ir al baño?

Profesor(a), ¿puedo ir a mi armario?

Profesor(a), ¿puedo ir a la oficina del director (de la directora)?

Profesor(a), ¿puedo sacarle punta a mi lápiz?

Profesor(a), ¿puedo abrir la ventana?

Profesor(a), ¿puedo cerrar la ventana?

Your teacher may respond to your requests in any of the following ways:

Sí / No.	*Yes / No.*
Sí, ve (al baño, a tu armario, etc.).	*Yes, go ahead (to ___).*
Sí, ábrela / ciérrala.	*Yes, open / close it.*
Claro.	*Of course.*
Ahora no.	*Not now.*
No, lo siento.	*No, I'm sorry.*

23

Multicultural Perspectives

In Spain, the federal government runs about two-thirds of all the primary and secondary schools. Approximately one out of every six students attends a school run by the Roman Catholic Church. (About 99 percent of Spain's population is Roman Catholic.) Spanish law requires that students attend school until they are 14. Ask students if they are familiar with the laws or regulations regarding school attendance in their area.

 Practice Wkbk. P-7, P-8, P-9

 Writing Activities P-G, P-H

 Comm. Act. BLMs P-4, P-5

Assess & Summarize

Test Preparation

You may want to assign parts of this section as homework or as an in-class writing activity prior to administering the *Examen de habilidades*.

Answers

Listening:
—Buenas tardes. ¿Cómo te llamas?
—Me llamo Luis.
—De dónde eres, Luis?
—Soy de Bogotá, Colombia.
—Tengo catorce años. Y tú, ¿cuántos años tienes?
—Quince. Claudia, ¿cuál es la fecha de hoy?
—El veintiséis de enero. ¡Es mi cumpleaños!

The students find out about their names, origin, age, and birthdays.

Reading: Yes, he has two friends or classmates that speak Spanish. / There are 29 students in his class. / He gives his name, origin, age, birthday, and teacher's origin.

Writing: Classroom objects: *bolígrafo, pizarra* / Months of the year: *agosto, enero* / Numbers: *cuatro, quince* / Greetings or Saying good-by: *Buenas noches, Hasta luego*

¿Lo sabes bien?

This section will help you organize your studying for the proficiency test, where you will be asked to do similar, though not identical, tasks. There will not be any models on the test.

Listening

Can you understand a brief conversation between two students who have just met? Listen as your teacher reads a sample similar to what you will hear on the test. What do the students find out about each other in this conversation?

Reading

Can you read a note and find out some information about that person? Read the following description about Arturo. Does he have any friends who speak Spanish? How many students are there in his class? What other information does he give?

> Me llamo Arturo. Soy de Boston, Massachusetts. Tengo dieciséis años. Mi cumpleaños es el 20 de noviembre. En mi sala de clases hay veintinueve estudiantes. El profesor es de la República Dominicana. En la sala de clases tengo dos compañeras de Venezuela.

Writing

Can you put the words in the list under the appropriate categories: Classroom objects, Months of the year, Numbers, and Greeting or Saying good-by?

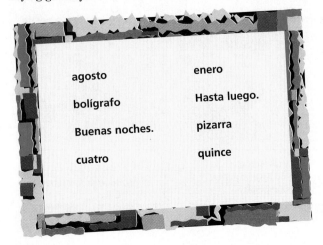

agosto   enero

bolígrafo   Hasta luego.

Buenas noches.   pizarra

cuatro   quince

Culture

What influences have the Spanish language and Hispanic cultures had on the United States? Can you give some examples?

Speaking

Can you and your partner play the roles of a teacher and a student greeting and introducing yourselves? Here is a sample dialogue:

A — *Buenos días. ¿Cómo está usted?*
B — *Muy bien, gracias. Y tú, ¿qué tal?*
A — *Así, así. Me llamo Miguel. ¿Y usted?*
B — *Me llamo Alfonso Beltrán.*
A — *Mucho gusto, Señor Beltrán.*

24

Options

Strategies for Reaching All Students

Students Needing Extra Help
Have students write out this section so they can keep track of what they have mastered. Emphasize that this is just a sample of what the actual test will be like.
Listening: Read the conversation more than once, if necessary. Review the types of questions that are asked when you first meet someone. Brainstorm for which words students should be listening and let them know how much information is required for an acceptable answer.

Reading / Writing: Have students use the Organizer.
Culture: In the culture sections for each chapter, students will be encouraged to take notes that they can later review for the *¿Lo sabes bien?* section in preparation for the chapter test. Have them reread pp. 5–6 for possible answers.
Speaking: Allow students to use the Organizer to prepare for this section. Limit the number of lines for the dialogue.

Resumen: El primer paso

Use the vocabulary from this chapter to help you:
- greet people and ask how they are feeling
- talk about classroom items
- use the Spanish alphabet to spell and tell numbers and dates

to greet people and say good-by
Buenos días.
Buenas tardes.
Buenas noches.
¿Cómo está usted?
¿Cómo estás?
¡Hola!
¿Qué tal?
Adiós.
Hasta luego.

to tell how you feel
Así, así.
(Muy) bien.

to ask someone's name and tell your name
¿Cómo te llamas?
(Yo) me llamo ___.

to acknowledge introductions
Mucho gusto.
Igualmente.

to ask for and give information
¿Cómo se dice ___ en español?
Se dice ___.
¿Cómo se escribe ___?
¿Cuál es la fecha de hoy?
Hoy es ___.
Mañana es ___.

¿Cuál es tu número de teléfono?
Mi / Tu (cumpleaños)
¿Cuándo es ___?
el año
¿Cuántos años tienes?
Tengo ___ años.
¿Cuántos, -as ___ hay?
Hay
¿De dónde eres?
(Yo) soy de ___.
¿Qué día es hoy?
es
¿Y tú?
¿Y usted?
no
sí
o

to say when something takes place
el día / el mes / la semana
en
el + *number* + de + *month*
lunes   viernes
martes   sábado
miércoles   domingo
jueves

enero   julio
febrero   agosto
marzo   septiembre
abril   octubre
mayo   noviembre
junio   diciembre

to count or give dates
el primero de
cero, uno, dos, tres, cuatro, cinco, seis, siete, ocho, nueve, diez
once, doce, trece, catorce, quince, dieciséis, diecisiete, dieciocho, diecinueve, veinte
veintiuno, veintidós, veintitrés, veinticuatro, veinticinco, veintiséis, veintisiete, veintiocho, veintinueve, treinta
treinta y uno

to say thank you
gracias

to talk about the classroom
el bolígrafo
el compañero, la compañera
    pl. los compañeros
el / la estudiante,
    pl. los estudiantes
la hoja de papel
el libro
la mesa
la pizarra
el profesor, la profesora
el pupitre
la sala de clases

Resumen   25

 Examen de habilidades

 Test Generator

CAPÍTULO 1

THEME: FRIENDSHIP

SCOPE AND SEQUENCE Pages 26–53

COMMUNICATION

Topics

Friendship

Likes and dislikes

Personality characteristics

Sports and leisure activities

Objectives

To talk about the concept of friendship in Spanish-speaking countries

To talk about activities

To say what you like and do not like

To ask someone what he or she likes

To ask if a statement is accurate

To say what you or someone else is like

To ask someone what he or she is like

To describe yourself or others

CULTURE

Concept of friendship

GRAMMAR

Los adjetivos

Ni...ni

Sí/tampoco

Ancillaries available for use with Chapter 1

Multisensory/Technology

 Overhead Transparencies, 6–10

 Audio Tapes and CDs

 Vocabulary Art Blackline Masters for Hands-On Learning, pp. 8–12

 Classroom Crossword

 Video

 CD-ROM

Print

 Practice Workbook, pp. 13–22

 Writing, Audio & Video Activities, pp. 5–10, 93–95, 152–153

 Communicative Activity Blackline Masters

    Pair and Small Group Activities, pp. 8–13

    Situation Cards, p. 14

 Un paso más: Actividades para ampliar tu español, pp. 1–6

Assessment

 Assessment Program

    Pruebas, pp. 9–18

    Examen de habilidades, pp. 19–22

 Test Generator

Video still from Chap. 1

25A

The Foundations of Friendship

Friendship has many components which include individual personality traits and cultural values. For example, when people of different Latin American nationalities meet, they may form friendships partly based on shared interests and personality traits and partly on common cultural values they share as Latin Americans.

Adriana and Ricardo are two teenagers who have recently immigrated to Chicago from Mexico and Argentina, respectively. They have become friends because they share a similar sense of humor and a great love of soccer, which is a favorite sport in Latin America. The former is a largely idiosyncratic trait, while the latter has much to do with their Latin American backgrounds.

For many young Latin Americans, two very strong influences in their lives are family and a close-knit group of friends. Adriana and Ricardo are part of a larger group of friends from diverse Hispanic nations, including Guatemala, Colombia, and El Salvador. There are several sets of brothers and sisters in the group and, as is common in Latin America, these siblings act as peers. For example, Adriana and her younger sister Rosalba are very close and share their social lives as well as their family life.

These friends spend free time and study time at each other's houses and all know each other's family members. Close friends, rather like extended family, are often included in family events and celebrations. Parties that Adriana and Ricardo attend commonly include several generations, from babies to grandparents.

Intimate friendship among Latin Americans is sometimes marked by *apodos,* or nicknames, denoting the special relationship. In Mexico, *primo(a), hermano(a),* or *cuate* (for males, meaning "pal" or, literally, "twin") are used. (Adriana can often be heard hailing Ricardo in the halls with *"¡Oye, primo!"*) Other terms, more frequently employed by Spanish-speaking adults, are *compadre* or *comadre* (godfather or godmother with respect to each other's child and, literally, "co-father, co-mother"), *maestro(a)* (master or teacher), *cuñado(a)* (in-law), or, in Venezuela, *poeta* (poet).

While friendship is a universal phenomenon, each friendship is unique. As the camaraderie between Adriana and Ricardo illustrates, the expression of friendship is a singular blending of personal affinities and shared culture.

Introduce

Planning

Cross-Curricular Connections

Career Connection *(pp. 34–35)*
Have students bring in pictures of people in various occupations. Ask them to name a personality characteristic that might contribute to success in that occupation.

Civics Connection *(pp. 42–43)*
Have pairs of students make illustrated posters for a person, real or imaginary, who is running for president of the U.S. Allow students creative latitude, but make sure posters include a list of the candidates' good characteristics.

Geography Connection *(pp. 48–49)*
Have students refer to a map of Mexico to locate and count the different states. Then have them refer to a map of the U.S. Invite students to make size comparisons between states in each nation.

CAPÍTULO 1

Y tú, ¿cómo eres?

OBJECTIVES

At the end of this chapter, you will be able to:

- describe yourself and tell about some of your likes and dislikes
- find out what other people are like
- compare your likes and dislikes with other people's
- talk about teen activities and the concept of friendship in Spanish-speaking countries

Grupo de atletas de Esmeraldas, Ecuador

27

Cultural Notes

Spanish in Your Community
How many students in your school came from or have parents who came from a Spanish-speaking country? Conduct a survey in class to get a rough idea of how many students there might be and the countries from which they came. Record the countries on the chalkboard. As you do so, have volunteers point to or flag each country on a world map.

(pp. 26–27, photo)
The faces of the members of this soccer team and of their friends reflect the racial makeup of inhabitants of Esmeraldas, Ecuador. The population of the seaport is composed mostly of descendants of African slaves. However, there is a mix in some faces of African, European, and indigenous traits. Esmeraldas, the first place in Ecuador where the Spanish *conquistadores* landed, now is a popular spot for tourists.

Preview

Cultural Objective
• To talk about teen activities and the concept of friendship in Spanish-speaking countries

Y tú, ¿cómo eres?

Play

 Video Activity A

Teaching Suggestions
Point out the use of quotation marks in the photo captions on pp. 28–29. Tell students that these indicate a statement from a person in the photo. Contrast this with a caption that gives an explanation of the photo content, as on p. 27.

Using the Video
This chapter's video focuses on friendship, what people are like, and what they like to do. Students will see our host in Miami interviewing several people and also talking about himself.
To prepare students for the video, first ask them to predict what this chapter's tape will be about. Then have students watch the segment several times. After the first time, you may wish to have them brainstorm possible vocabulary and expressions they will need to talk

¡Piénsalo bien!

Look at the photographs.
In the captions these teens tell us something about themselves.

"Soy de Madrid. Me gusta mucho estar con mis amigos."

What is this group of friends doing?

28   Capítulo 1

Options

Strategies for Reaching All Students

Spanish-Speaking Students
Ask individual students the following: *¿Eres como uno de estos chicos? ¿Quién es como tus amigos? ¿Te gustan estas actividades? ¿Por qué? Describe a las personas en las fotos.*

 Un paso más Ex. 1-A

Students Needing Extra Help
¡Piénsalo bien!: If your students correctly define *hablar,* emphasize how visual clues help us to learn. If they define *cine* correctly, ask them how they arrived at their answer. Show them how it resembles the English word cinema, and how this is a good technique for learning vocabulary.

"Soy de Barcelona. Me gusta hablar por teléfono con mis amigos."

What do you think the girl is saying in the caption?

"Me llamo Raúl y soy de Toluca, México. A mí me gusta ir al cine."

What do you think Raúl means when he talks about *cine*?

29

about what they saw on the video. Ask students to identify things they saw that looked familiar but were somewhat different from what they might see in their own community.

Video segment 1: For more teaching suggestions, see the Video Teacher's Guide.

Class Starter Review

Explain that because this chapter teaches ways to describe yourself and others, it is important to know your classmates' names. Have students ask the names of four classmates sitting near them. (Remind students that they saw *¿Cómo te llamas?* and *Me llamo ___* in *El primer paso*.)

Answers: ¡Piénsalo bien!

(p. 28) See if students can guess the meaning through visual context clues.

(p. 29, top photo) Have students use cognates *(teléfono)* and familiar vocabulary *(amigos)* to guess the meaning.

(p. 29, bottom photo) See if students can guess the meaning by associating the word with a cognate in English. Encourage students to look at the photo and see if they can recognize *multicinemas* as a cognate.

Cultural Notes

(p. 28, photo)
This group of friends has gathered at an outdoor café in Madrid's Plaza Mayor, one of the largest public squares in Europe. Designed by Juan de Herrera, architect to Felipe II, the Plaza Mayor has been the site of a wide variety of public events since its inauguration in 1620: the canonization of saints, royal weddings, coronations, bullfights, and masked balls.

(p. 29, top photo)
This Barcelona teenager is enjoying a privilege few of her peers are lucky enough to have—a telephone extension in her own bedroom. The Spanish telephone system is jointly run by government and private companies. In 1987, Spain, with a population of 40 million, had about 15.5 million telephones in use. In comparison, the U.S., with a population of 260 million, has roughly 134 million telephones in use.

(p. 29, bottom photo)
As this theater marquee in a shopping mall in Toluca suggests, American movies are popular in Mexico. Located 40 miles west of Mexico City, Toluca (the capital of the state of Mexico) has become a prosperous industrial center with its own symphony, university, and other cultural attractions. For example, the weekly outdoor market is one of the largest in the country.

Present

Chapter Theme
Friendship: Things friends do together

Communicative Objectives
• To talk about activities
• To say what you like and do not like
• To ask someone what he or she likes
• To ask if a statement is accurate

 Transparencies 6–7

 Vocabulary Art BLMs

 Pronunciation Tape 1-1

 Vocabulario para conversar A

Play

Using the Video
Video segment 2: See the Video Teacher's Guide.

 Video Activity B

Grammar Preview
Emphatic *sí* and *tampoco* are presented lexically. A brief explanation and practice exercise appear on p. 45.

Vocabulario para conversar

¿Qué te gusta hacer?

Here are some new words and expressions you will need to talk about your likes and dislikes. Read them several times, then turn the page and practice with a partner.

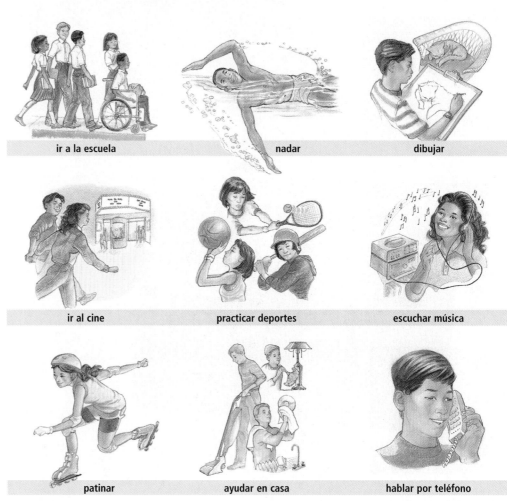

ir a la escuela · nadar · dibujar

ir al cine · practicar deportes · escuchar música

patinar · ayudar en casa · hablar por teléfono

30   Capítulo 1

Options

Strategies for Reaching All Students

Enrichment
También necesitas…: To reinforce *me gusta (más / mucho)* and *no me gusta (mucho / nada),* have students do a written assignment rating fast-food restaurants, entertainers, or TV programs, making sure to use each of the expressions at least once. Have students also conduct interviews in pairs and determine whether they like, dislike, or prefer any of the restaurants, entertainers, etc. Remind students to reverse roles.

Learning Spanish Through Action
STAGING VOCABULARY: *Señalen, Toquen*
MATERIALS: transparency of activities in the *Vocabulario para conversar* or pictures of similar activities from magazines
DIRECTIONS: Using the overhead or pictures placed along the chalkboard edge, ask students to touch or point to various activities you call out at random.

estudiar

ver la televisión (la tele)

cocinar

leer

tocar la guitarra

También necesitas . . .

¿Qué te gusta (hacer)?	*What do you like (to do)?*
¿Te gusta ___?	*Do you like ___?*
estar con amigos	*to be with friends*
(A mí) me gusta ___.	*I like ___.*
más ___.	*___ better. (I prefer.)*
mucho ___.	*___ a lot.*
¿Y a ti?	*And you?*
(A mí) sí me gusta ___.	*I do like ___.*
A mí también.	*I do (like it) too.*
(A mí) no me gusta ___.	*I don't like ___.*
mucho ___.	*___ very much.*
nada ___.	*___ at all.*
___ tampoco.	*___ either.*
¿De veras?	*Really?*
Pues	*Well . . .*
y	*and*

Practice & Apply

Answers: Empecemos a conversar

1 ESTUDIANTE A

a. ¿Qué te gusta hacer? ¿Te gusta patinar?

b. ...¿Te gusta escuchar música?

c. ...¿Te gusta dibujar?

d. ...¿Te gusta cocinar?

e. ...¿Te gusta estudiar?

f. Questions will vary, but look for *¿te gusta* + inf.? in second question.

ESTUDIANTE B

a.–f. Answers will vary according to selected choice.

2 ESTUDIANTE A

a. ¿Qué te gusta más, dibujar o leer?

b. ...ir a la escuela o ayudar en casa?

c. ...ir al cine o ver la tele(visión)?

d. ...escuchar música o tocar la guitarra?

e. Questions will vary, but look for *¿qué te gusta más?* + inf.

ESTUDIANTE B

a.–e. Answers will vary, but should include one of the infinitives suggested by *Estudiante A*.

3 Answers will vary. Encourage at least three exchanges.

Empecemos a conversar

With a partner, take turns being *Estudiante A* and *Estudiante B.* Use the words that are cued or given in the balloons to replace the underlined sections in the model. 💡 means you can make your own choices.

1   A —¿Qué te gusta hacer? ¿Te gusta *nadar*?
   B —*Sí, me gusta.*
      Y ahora Uds.

Estudiante A   Estudiante B

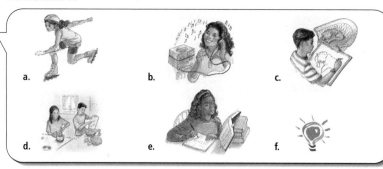

a.   b.   c.

d.   e.   f.

Sí, me gusta.

o: No, no me gusta.

o: No, no me gusta nada.

2   A —¿Qué te gusta más, *practicar deportes* o *hablar por teléfono*?
   B —*Pues, me gusta más hablar por teléfono.*
      Y ahora Uds.

Estudiante A   Estudiante B

a.   b.

c.   d.   e.

32   Capítulo 1

Options

Strategies for Reaching All Students

Spanish-Speaking Students
To model pronunciation, pair bilingual and non-bilingual students for Exs. 1–2. For more advanced practice, pair Spanish-speaking students with each other for Exs. 3–4.

 Un paso más Exs. 1-B, 1-C

Students Needing Extra Help
Have students fill in their Organizers (available in the *Practice Sheet Workbook)* before doing the exercises that require them to make choices. As students continue through the chapter, have them add to the Organizer whenever they are required to use newly presented vocabulary.
Ex. 1: Explain when to use each response. Do some examples aloud for those students who don't see the possible choices. Model at least one negative item.

Ex. 2: Review *pues.* Show what remains the same in the sentence when substitutions occur. Emphasize that *Estudiante B* creates his or her own answer when a situation is open ended.
Ex. 3: Model both possibilities for *Estudiante B.* Explain the use of the responses.
Ex. 4: Point out that *o:* indicates a choice. Have students use the Organizer for possible answers.

3 A — *No me gusta mucho <u>ver la televisión</u>.*
    B — <u>*A mí no me gusta tampoco.*</u>

      Y ahora Uds.

Estudiante A   Estudiante B

A mí no me gusta tampoco.

o: ¿De veras? A mí sí me gusta.

4 A — *A mí me gusta <u>tocar la guitarra</u>. ¿Y a ti?*
    B — *Pues, a mí me gusta <u>practicar deportes</u>.*
        o: *Pues, a mí también.*

      Y ahora Uds.

Estudiante A   Estudiante B

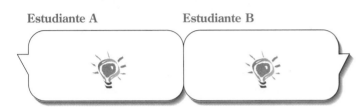

Empecemos a escribir

Write your answers in Spanish.

5 Categorize the activities on pages 30–31 either as entertainment or as duties. Make two lists. Put a check next to any duties you enjoy.

6 Make a list of all those activities that you do on a normal school day.

7 ¿Qué te gusta hacer?

8 ¿Qué no te gusta hacer?

9 ¿Qué te gusta más, leer o ver la tele?

También se dice

People in different English-speaking countries often use different words to refer to the same thing. For example, what we call an "apartment" the English call a "flat." Similarly, in various Spanish-speaking countries, there are sometimes different words for the same thing

mirar la televisión (la tele)

4 Answers will vary, but look for *a mí me gusta* + inf.

Answers: Empecemos a escribir
Note that Exs. 7–9 are directed to students in Spanish for further comprehension practice in the target language.

5–6 Answers will vary.

7–8 Answers will vary, but look for *me gusta* and *no me gusta* + inf.

9 Answers will vary.

También se dice
This feature offers examples of how Spanish vocabulary differs from region to region and discourages viewing vocabulary choice as a matter of right or wrong. These sections are for enrichment only. They point out to students that they might hear variant forms depending on the speaker's native country or region. Allow Spanish-speaking students who may use other words or expressions to add to this section.

 Practice Wkbk. 1-1, 1-2, 1-3

 Audio Activities 1.1, 1.2

 Writing Activities 1-A, 1-B

 Pruebas 1-1, 1-2

Exs. 5–6: To keep the possibilities orderly, have students create an organizer with three columns labeled "Entertainment," "Duties," and "School Activities."
Empecemos a escribir: For additional practice, have students categorize the activities from this vocabulary section as things they like to do, things they don't like to do much, and things they don't like to do at all.

Enrichment
Ex. 1: Encourage pairs of students to extend their dialogues by having *Estudiante B* ask *Estudiante A* what he or she likes: *¿Y a ti? ¿Qué te gusta hacer?*

Present

Chapter Theme
Friendship: Describing friends

Communicative Objectives
- To say what you or someone else is like
- To ask someone what he or she is like
- To describe yourself or others

 Transparencies 8–9

 Vocabulary Art BLMs

 Pronunciation Tape 1-2

 Vocabulario para conversar B

Play

Using the Video
Video segment 2: See the Video Teacher's Guide.

 Video Activity B

Vocabulario para conversar

¿Cómo eres?

Here's the rest of the vocabulary you will need to describe yourself and others.

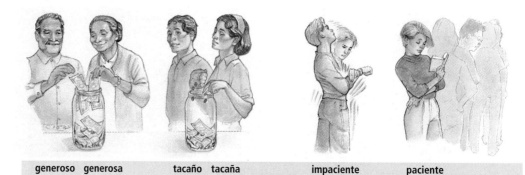

generoso generosa   tacaño tacaña   impaciente   paciente

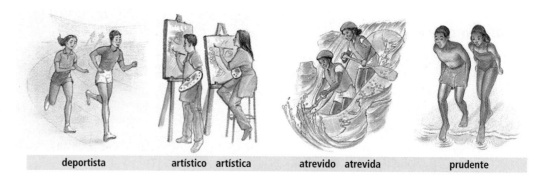

deportista   artístico artística   atrevido atrevida   prudente

34   Capítulo 1

Options

Strategies for Reaching All Students

Learning Spanish Through Action
STAGING VOCABULARY: *Señalen, Toquen*
MATERIALS: transparency of adjectives in the *Vocabulario para conversar* or magazine pictures of people in professions such as police officer, firefighter, judge, athlete, comedian, talk-show host, mime, stuntperson, artist, and chess player

DIRECTIONS: Have students touch or point to the appropriate overhead image or magazine picture as you call out various adjectives. If you do this activity with magazine pictures after presenting the grammar, have students listen carefully to masculine and feminine forms.

ordenado   ordenada   desordenado   desordenada

trabajador   trabajadora   perezoso   perezosa

gracioso   graciosa   serio   seria

También necesitas . . .

¿Cómo eres?	*What are you like?*	callado, -a	*quiet*
(Yo) soy ___.	*I am (I'm) ___.*	pero	*but*
(Tú) eres ___.	*You are (You're) ___.*	a veces	*sometimes, at times*
muy	*very*		
amable	*nice, kind*		

> **¿Y qué quiere decir . . . ?**
> sociable

Grammar Preview
Allow students to use these adjectives *before* presenting rules of agreement. The visuals will help them intuit the rule, making the understanding of grammar a natural outgrowth of its use and facilitating learning.

Teaching Suggestions
Preparing students to speak: Use one or two options from each of the categories of Comprehensible Input, Physical Response, or Limited Verbal Response. For a complete explanation of these categories and some sample activities, see the front section of this Teacher's Edition.

¿Y qué quiere decir…?: Remind students that the vocabulary in this section is either cognates or previously seen words or expressions.

Class Starter Review
On the day following initial presentation, you might begin the class with this activity:
Have students turn to a partner and describe themselves, using three adjectives. On the next day, have students do this same activity in written form.

Practice & Apply

Re-enter / Recycle
Ex. 16: greetings from *El primer paso*

Grammar Preview
The explanation of adjective agreement appears on p. 43. If students ask why it is *-o* in some cases, *-a* in others, encourage them to develop their own explanation. They will almost certainly decide on the right answer and teach themselves the grammar rule.

Answers: Empecemos a conversar
10 Model this carefully, alternating between male and female students.

ESTUDIANTE A
a. ¿Cómo eres, gracioso(a) o serio(a)?
b. ...atrevido(a) o prudente?
c. ...generoso(a) o tacaño(a)?
d. ...paciente o impaciente?
e. ...trabajador(a) o perezoso(a)?

ESTUDIANTE B
a.–e. Answers will vary, but look for correct adjective agreement.

11 Questions and answers will vary, but look for correct adjective agreement.

Empecemos a conversar

10  A —¿*Cómo eres, ordenado(a) o desordenado(a)?*
B —*Soy ordenado(a), pero a veces soy desordenado(a).*

Y ahora Uds.

Estudiante A

a.

b.

c.

d.

e.

Estudiante B

11 A —¿*Eres serio(a)?*
B —*Sí, y soy callado(a) también.*
o: *No, no soy serio(a).*

Y ahora Uds.

Estudiante A

Estudiante B

Options

Strategies for Reaching All Students

Spanish-Speaking Students
Have pairs of Spanish-speaking students write out at least three questions and answers for Ex. 10. With Ex. 11, have them write three short sentences describing themselves.

 Un paso más Ex. 1-D

Students Needing Extra Help
Have students add *tampoco* and *también* to their Organizers.
Ex. 14: Have students create an organizer with four columns for the exercise.
Exs. 15–16: Show students the number of tools (cognates, patterns, etc.) they have to help them, and the number of times they have already seen these words.

Enrichment
Ex. 10: Preview the grammar by asking students why there are two adjective endings. Ask what an adjective is and what it does.
Ex. 13: For each of the three words describing themselves, have students write a logical sentence telling what they like or dislike doing.

12

A —¿Te gusta *nadar*?
B —Sí, soy *deportista*.
   o: *No, no soy muy deportista.*

   Y ahora Uds.

Estudiante A

a.
b.
c.
d.

Estudiante B

Empecemos a escribir y a leer

Write your answers in Spanish.

13 Look at the vocabulary on pages 34–35 and write down three words that describe you.

14 Make a list of the words that you would use to describe:
   • the ideal student
   • the ideal teacher
   • the ideal parent
   • the ideal friend

15 ¿Cómo eres? ¿Eres amable? ¿Sociable? ¿Trabajador(a)?

16 ¡Hola! Me llamo Esteban. A mí me gusta nadar y patinar. También me gusta estar con mis amigos o hablar por teléfono. No me gusta ni cocinar ni ayudar en casa. ¿Cómo soy?

   Eres . . .

Vocabulario para conversar   37

12 Remind students that *Estudiante B* must make a logical response to *Estudiante A*.

ESTUDIANTE A
a. ¿Te gusta practicar deportes?
b. . . . dibujar?
c. . . . ayudar en casa?
d. . . . patinar?

ESTUDIANTE B
a. Sí, (No, no) soy muy deportista.
b. . . . artístico(a).
c. . . . trabajador(a).
d. . . . atrevido(a).

Answers: Empecemos a escribir y a leer

13–14 Answers will vary, but look for correct adjective agreement.

15 Answers will vary, but look for *soy* + correct adjective agreement.

16 Likely answers: *Eres deportista y sociable. No eres trabajador.*

 Practice Wkbk. 1-4

 Audio Activity 1.3

 Writing Activities 1-C, 1-D

 Pruebas 1-3, 1-4

Practice

Teaching Suggestions

The *¡Comuniquemos!* section allows for integrated practice of both vocabulary sections of the chapter.

Answers:
¡Comuniquemos!

1–2 Answers will vary, but look for the correct infinitive used:

a. practicar deportes
b. cocinar
c. hablar por teléfono
d. ver la tele(visión)
e. tocar la guitarra
f. dibujar
g. patinar
h. ir a la escuela
i. nadar
j. ayudar en casa
k. estudiar
l. ir al cine
m. leer

¡Comuniquemos!

Here's another opportunity for you to use the vocabulary you've just learned.

1 Find out how many of these activities both you and your partner enjoy. Take turns asking the questions. Be sure to choose only those activities you really like.

A —*A mí me gusta escuchar música. ¿Y a ti?*
B —*A mí me gusta también.*
   o: *A mí no me gusta.*

a.

b.

c.

d.

e.

f.

g.

h.

i.

j.

k.

l.

m.

Options

Strategies for Reaching All Students

Spanish-Speaking Students
For the *¡Comuniquemos!* section, have Spanish-speaking students describe themselves in four or five sentences, concentrating on telling what activities they like and do well.

Students Needing Extra Help
Exs. 1–2: Have students provide at least five examples of likes and dislikes. Remind them that *o:* indicates a choice.

Enrichment
For extra practice, begin by asking someone what he or she is like. That person should answer and then ask someone else the same question. Continue until everyone has participated. To save time, you may want to let each row or section do its own question-and-answer exercise. For example:
A —*Luis, ¿cómo eres?*
B —*Soy (muy) paciente y (muy) sociable también. Enrique, ¿cómo eres?*
C —*Pues, soy . . . .*

2 Now take turns finding out if you and your partner dislike the same things. Use the pictures in Exercise 1, and this time choose only those activities you <u>don't</u> like.

A — *No me gusta cocinar. ¿Y a ti?*
B — *A mí no me gusta tampoco.*
   o: *A mí sí me gusta.*

3 You are going to be an exchange student in Costa Rica and your host family wants to know what you are like. Write a few sentences telling them what you are like and some things you like to do. Then, with a partner, compare what you wrote about yourselves.

¿Qué sabes ahora?

Can you:

■ ask someone what he or she likes to do?
   —¿Qué ___ hacer?

■ tell someone what you like or do not like to do?
   — ___ ir a la escuela.

■ ask someone what he or she is like?
   —¿Cómo ___?

■ tell someone what you are like?
   —Soy ___.

Vocabulario para conversar   39

Present & Apply

Cultural Objective
• To talk about the concept of friendship in Spanish-speaking countries

Teaching Suggestions
In order to prepare students for a meaningful discussion about the similarities and differences between the concept of friendship in the U.S. and Spanish-speaking countries, you might wish to have them read the text the night before you present the lesson in class. Ask them to begin thinking about what friendship means to them.

Critical Thinking: Comparing and Contrasting
Although friendship is defined somewhat differently in the U.S. than it is in some Spanish-speaking countries, there are some aspects of friendship that would apply to both cultures. Ask students to suggest what some of these aspects might be and if some of them might be universally applicable.

Multicultural Perspectives
Have students list similarities, differences, and common interests of teens from a Spanish-speaking culture and of those from the U.S.

Perspectiva cultural

Te gusta estar con tus amigos, ¿no? ¿Qué te gusta hacer con tus amigos? ¿Les gusta ir al cine? ¿Hablar por teléfono? ¿Practicar deportes? Sí, probablemente. Pero, ¿qué quiere decir esa palabra mágica, "amigo"?

Muchachas y muchachos mexicanos en la escuela

Look at the people in the photos. How can you tell that they might be friends?

"Mike, this is my friend Luis." That is how my classmate introduced me to another boy in our class. It was my first day of school here. I was in the seventh grade. My family had come from El Salvador in July, so I had not met any English speakers my age. And here was someone introducing me as his friend when we had just met that morning! What a strange place I was in!

By the end of that year, I did have friends, friends in the Spanish sense. They are still my friends. I think that they will always be, because that is what we mean by *amigo,* a friend for life.

Where I came from, people didn't move around a lot. You would probably grow up in one neighborhood or town and might even live there your whole life. Yes, you might miss out on a few things, but you would form deep friendships and keep them. You would know people well, and would usually see your friends every day. You'd also get to know each other's families well.

And we share a lot. We share our true feelings and thoughts with our friends. We also share what we have. If a friend borrows money from me, I don't keep track or get an I.O.U. Or if I do a favor for a friend, I don't think any more about it. I know that my friend will always help me out. In the long run, it will probably turn out even.

Of course, we are warm and welcoming to people we don't know very well, people you might call friends but whom we would call *conocidos* (acquaintances). We may get along quite well, but they are not *amigos*. Perhaps some day they will be, but that takes time. An *amigo* is someone you can count on all your life.

La cultura desde tu perspectiva

1 What are some similarities and differences between who is considered a friend in a Spanish-speaking country and in the United States?

2 What could you expect to occur if you became friends with someone in a Spanish-speaking country?

40   Capítulo 1

Options

Strategies for Reaching All Students

Spanish-Speaking Students
After reading the text, ask Spanish-speaking students: *¿Te gusta salir con tus amigos? ¿Cuándo salen Uds. juntos? ¿Adónde van? ¿Salen los fines de semana? ¿Qué hacen?*

 Un paso más Ex. 1-E

Enrichment
Tell students that in Mexican Spanish, the word *cuate* is used to name a very special, trusted friend. Point out that the other meaning of this word is "twin." Ask students if they can think of any words in English that would be the equivalent for naming this kind of friend (buddy, pal, etc.).

"Soy de Chile. Me gusta tocar la guitarra."

Cultural Notes ☼

(p. 41, photo)
Students in Santiago, Chile. The guitar remains a popular instrument among students in most Spanish-speaking countries. Chileans place a high value on the arts, culture, and education. As a result of an intensive literacy campaign initiated in 1980, the rate of adult literacy rose from 89 percent in 1970 to 93.4 percent in 1990.

Preview

 Transparency 10

Teaching Suggestions

This poem serves as a summary of the structures students have been using and a preview of *ni…ni.* As they work through the poem and the questions, students will formulate for themselves the rules given on the following pages. *Encourage this to occur as students work with and examine the building blocks of the language.*

Answers

Answers will vary, but may include: adjectives or words that describe the author.

A Answers may include that the author is not extremely one way or another, that she is sometimes talkative and sometimes quiet, etc.

B The poet is female, since almost all of the adjectives end in *-a: callada, generosa, tacaña, atrevida, ordenada, desordenada.*

C See if students can guess the meaning from context.

D Answers will vary, but may include: Words ending in *-o* refer to males and words ending in *-a* refer to females. Yes; *amable, deportista, impaciente, paciente, prudente, trabajador, sociable.*

Gramática en contexto

Here is a descriptive poem entitled "Yo." What kind of information would you expect to find in such a poem?

Now read the poem.

Yo   Yo …
      Yo no …
      Yo no soy …
      ni sociable ni callada,
      ni generosa ni tacaña.
      Yo …
      Yo no …
      Yo no soy …
      ni atrevida ni prudente,
      ni ordenada ni desordenada;
      pero yo …
      Yo soy …
      Yo soy ¡YO!

A Think about the predictions you made before you read the poem. Did you find the information that you thought you would find in the poem? What did you find out about the person who wrote it?

B Is the poet male or female? How do you know? Find at least three words that give you that information.

C *Ni … ni* appears four times in the poem. What do you suppose it means?

D Think of a guideline that could help you decide whether to use the words *generoso* or *generosa* and *serio* or *seria* to describe a person. Are there any adjectives (descriptive words) on pages 34–35 that your rule does not cover? Which ones?

42   Capítulo 1

Options

Strategies for Reaching All Students

Students Needing Extra Help
For sections A–D, model aloud so that students hear everyone's responses. Write any responses on the board for visual learners. Ex. 1: Make sure students understand that they should choose words from the list. Ex. 2: Point out to students that they can start with a negative statement.

Enrichment
Ask for a male volunteer to read the poem aloud, making the necessary changes in adjective forms.
Ex. 1: Have students play a memory game in which they turn over cards with adjectives on them and try to match a feminine adjective with its masculine form (exclude adjectives ending in *-e*). Play with at least ten sets of adjectives (20 cards). A variation of this game is to have students match an adjective with its opposite. (This will be

more challenging if separate cards are made for masculine and feminine forms. For example, the correct match for *perezosa* has to be *trabajadora,* not *trabajador.)*

Los adjetivos

Words describing people and things are called adjectives.

- In Spanish, adjectives describing females usually end in *-a*.

- Adjectives describing males usually end in *-o*.

- Adjectives that end in *-e* can describe either females or males, for example: *amable.* However, there are some exceptions, such as *deportista,* which can describe both males and females.

1 Students are preparing a who's who that describes each member of the class. Ask your partner what he or she is like. Each of you should choose four or more words from the list on the right to describe yourselves.

A —*¿Cómo eres?*
B —*Soy graciosa, artística, paciente y sociable.*
    o: *Soy gracioso, artístico, paciente y sociable.*

2 How similar are you and your partner? For each of the following pictures, say whether you have that personality trait. Then find out whether your partner has it too.

A —*Yo soy deportista. ¿Y tú?*
B —*Yo soy deportista también.*
    o: *No, yo no soy deportista.*

o: A —*Yo no soy deportista. ¿Y tú?*
   B —*Yo no soy deportista tampoco.*
      o: *Yo soy (muy) deportista.*

a.　　　b.　　　c.　　　d.　　　e.

f.　　　g.　　　h.　　　i.

Here are the adjectives you already know:

amable	impaciente
artística	ordenada
artístico	ordenado
atrevida	paciente
atrevido	perezosa
callada	perezoso
callado	prudente
deportista	seria
desordenada	serio
desordenado	sociable
generosa	tacaña
generoso	tacaño
graciosa	trabajador
gracioso	trabajadora

Present & Practice

Class Starter Review

On the day following the presentation of adjectives, you might begin the class with this activity: Write these professions in English on the chalkboard: auto racer, politician, salesperson, sculptor, judge, comedian, baseball player, accountant. Ask students to choose adjectives that would describe the quality or qualities that a person wanting to enter one of these professions should have.

Answers

1–2 Answers will vary, but look for correct adjective agreement. In Ex. 2, the adjectives used will be:
a. impaciente
b. gracioso(a)
c. trabajador(a)
d. ordenado(a)
e. prudente
f. tacaño(a)
g. generoso(a)
h. serio(a)
i. artístico(a)

Practice Wkbk. 1-5, 1-6, 1-7

¿? Prueba 1-5

Present & Practice

Answers

3 a. Me gusta ir al cine y escuchar música, pero no me gusta ni nadar ni hablar por teléfono.
b. Me gusta leer y practicar deportes, pero no me gusta ni ver la tele(visión) ni ayudar en casa.
c. Me gusta nadar y tocar la guitarra, pero no me gusta ni estudiar ni ir a la escuela.
d. Me gusta cocinar y dibujar, pero no me gusta ni leer ni practicar deportes.

Ni . . . ni

- If you want to say that you do not like either of two choices, use *ni . . . ni* to mean "neither . . . nor" or "not . . . or."
  For example:
  No me gusta **ni** nadar **ni** dibujar.

- Use *ni . . . ni* to say that neither of two descriptions fits you.
  No soy **ni** deportista **ni** artístico.

3 Imagine that these are new students in your Spanish class. Tell what each person might say about his or her likes and dislikes.

María

Me gusta dibujar y tocar la guitarra, pero no me gusta ni cocinar ni patinar.

a. Pablo

b. Enrique

c. Elena

d. Isabel

44   Capítulo 1

Options

Strategies for Reaching All Students

Spanish-Speaking Students
Have Spanish-speaking students write out their responses to Ex. 3.

Students Needing Extra Help
Have students add *ni...ni* to their Organizers.
Ex. 4: Organize the four pairs of opposites in columns so that students can see a pattern. Reinforce and review the importance of gender in Spanish grammar.
Have students add *sí / tampoco* to their Organizers.

Ex. 5: Show what stays the same in the exercise and model both possibilities. If possible, use Spanish-speaking students to help model.

4 Take turns asking and answering questions to find out what your partner is like. Discuss whether your partner is *sociable* or *callado(a)*, *paciente* or *impaciente*, *prudente* or *atrevido(a)*, and *trabajador(a)* or *perezoso(a)*.

A — *¿Eres generoso(a) o tacaño(a)?*
B — *Soy (muy) generoso(a).*
　　o: *Soy tacaño(a).*
　　o: *No soy ni generoso(a) ni tacaño(a).*

Sí / Tampoco

> • Use *sí* + *me gusta* to contrast something you like with something you or someone else dislikes. For example:
> 　—A mí no me gusta hablar por teléfono. ¿Y a ti?
> 　—A mí **sí me gusta.**
>
> • Use *no me gusta* + *tampoco* to agree with someone who dislikes something. For example:
> 　—A mí no me gusta practicar deportes. ¿Y a ti?
> 　—A mí **no me gusta tampoco.**

5 You and your partner are discussing activities that you like and don't like. Choose some activities that you don't like, and find out whether or not your partner agrees.

A — *A mí no me gusta patinar. ¿Y a ti?*
B — *Pues, a mí sí me gusta.*
　　o: *A mí no me gusta tampoco.*

Ahora lo sabes

Can you:

- describe yourself or someone else?
  —Yo soy ___, pero tú eres ___.
- say that you do not like either of two choices?
  —No me gusta ___ ver la tele ___ ir al cine.
- say that neither of two descriptions fits you?
  —No soy ___ perezoso(a) ___ sociable.

- emphasize that you do like something?
  —¿No te gusta? ¡A mí ___!
- say that you do not like something either?
  —A mí ___.

Gramática en contexto　45

Apply

Pronunciation Tape 1-3

¡A conversar!

Play

Step

Using the Video
Video segment 3: See the Video Teacher's Guide.

🎙️ **Video Activity C**

Para decir más
These sections are for use with the *Actividades* and are not active vocabulary.

Answers: Actividades
You might assign Ex. 1 as written homework in preparation for doing either it or Ex. 2 orally in class for pair or small-group practice.

1 Answers will vary, but look for *soy* + correct adjective agreement and use of *me gusta* + inf.

Para decir más
Here is some additional vocabulary that you might find useful for activities in this section.

cariñoso, -a
affectionate

comprensivo, -a
understanding

dinámico, -a
energetic

estudioso, -a
studious

simpático, -a
nice, friendly

sincero, -a
sincere

cuidar niños
to baby-sit

jugar básquetbol
to play basketball

jugar videojuegos
to play video games

montar en bicicleta
to ride a bicycle

montar en monopatín
to skateboard

46   Capítulo 1

Actividades

Here's an opportunity for you to expand your use of Spanish by putting together the material you learned in this chapter.

 In order to get a job at a summer camp, you must convince the camp supervisor that you are the best person for the job. As part of your application, tell what you are like, and list some of the things you like to do.

Jugando básquetbol en San Miguel de Allende, México

Options

Strategies for Reaching All Students

Students Needing Extra Help
Exs. 1–3: Use the Organizer. For Ex. 3, have students base their chart on the model shown. Remind them that the verbs listed are examples, and that they should choose from all the verbs in the chapter.

Enrichment
Ex. 1: As a follow-up, you might have pairs of students act out a job interview in which the camp supervisor questions the applicant's qualities and the applicant must contradict him or her. For example:
—¿Eres impaciente?
—¡No! No soy impaciente. Soy paciente (y comprensivo).
Make sure students begin the interview with appropriate greetings and introductions (soy, me llamo, ¿cómo está Ud.?, etc.).

Ex. 3: Find out which activity is the class favorite by asking how many students ranked each activity number one. Keep track on the chalkboard. Repeat the procedure to rank the class's descending order of preference. Use ordinal numbers for comprehensible input.

Muchachas sacando fotos en Ambato, Ecuador

2 Answers should include *(no) soy* + adjective, *(no) me gusta* + inf., and correct adjective agreement.

3 Remind students to use *¿te gusta* + inf.? in their questions.

 Comm. Act. BLMs 1-4, 1-5

2 In four or more sentences, describe yourself, including your personality traits and interests. Your sentences should include:

- some words that describe you and some that do not
- some things you do and don't like to do
- contrasts of things you like to do with things you don't like to do

Músicos en Madrid

3 Take a poll to find out which activities your classmates like to do. On a sheet of paper, list across the top the activities mentioned in this chapter. In the left-hand column, write these words: *me gusta mucho, me gusta, no me gusta, no me gusta nada.* Then interview four classmates, asking about all the activities on the list. Mark the answers on your chart and total the number of votes for each activity under each heading.

	NADAR	PATINAR	VER LA TELE	IR AL CINE
ME GUSTA MUCHO	//			/
ME GUSTA		///		
NO ME GUSTA	/			//
NO ME GUSTA NADA	//	/	///	//

Actividades 47

Cultural Notes ☀

Cooperative Learning

Divide the class into groups of four or five students. Instruct each student to write his or her name at the top of an index card and then to pass the card to the left. Using an appropriate adjective, each student should write a compliment about the student named on the card. Cards should then be circulated until every student has written a complimentary description for each person in the group. Collect the cards and read the descriptions to the class.

(p. 47, top photo)

With a population of 140,000, Ambato is the fourth-largest city in Ecuador. It is about a two-and-a-half hour drive south of Quito on the scenic Pan American highway. In 1949 a major earthquake almost completely destroyed Ambato, which has been known since colonial times as *la ciudad de frutas y flores.* Ambato is famous for its *Fiesta de frutas y flores* every February and as a center for the production of distinctive Persian-knot rugs.

(p. 47, bottom photo)

Group of street musicians in Madrid. Young people in Spain, as in much of Latin America, enjoy a wide variety of music, from rock and roll (particularly from the 1950s and 60s) to the traditional folk music of their own country. The classic Spanish guitar, with its nylon or gut strings (derived from the Moorish *quitara,* a four-stringed version of the lute) is ever popular, particularly for street concerts.

Apply

Process Reading

Make sure students understand the four headings in this section and the tasks they represent:

- *Antes de leer:* pre-reading activity for activating prior knowledge; emphasis on one or more strategies for overcoming the tendency to read slowly, word by word, and instead to focus on receiving the message being communicated in the text.
- *Mira la lectura:* scanning / skimming for general ideas or information, looking for cognates, proper nouns, headings, numbered or bulleted items, familiar words, etc.
- *Infórmate:* reading for more detailed information
- *Aplicación:* post-reading activity

Critical Thinking: Classifying

Ask students to name the student or students from *Buscando amigos* who would most likely get along well with an American student who enjoys music as well as sports (Santiago).

Answers
Antes de leer

1 Age of the target readership.

2 Answers will vary, but may include names, addresses, ages, likes and dislikes, or hobbies.

Mira la lectura
Answers will vary.

¡Vamos a leer!

Antes de leer

STRATEGY ➤ Using prior knowledge

We usually make new friends through personal acquaintances, but sometimes we meet people through correspondence. For example, you might want to look through a pen pal column in a Spanish-language magazine to start a correspondence with someone from another country.

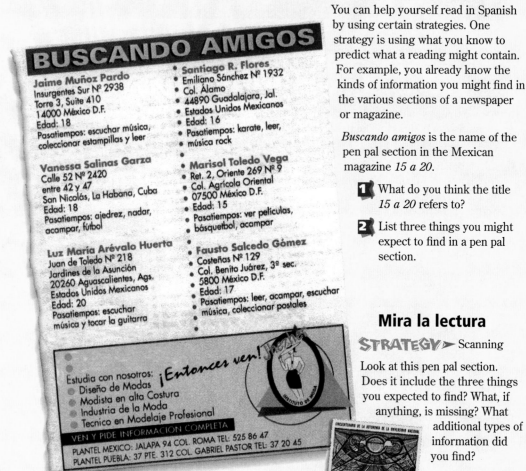

You can help yourself read in Spanish by using certain strategies. One strategy is using what you know to predict what a reading might contain. For example, you already know the kinds of information you might find in the various sections of a newspaper or magazine.

Buscando amigos is the name of the pen pal section in the Mexican magazine *15 a 20.*

1 What do you think the title *15 a 20* refers to?

2 List three things you might expect to find in a pen pal section.

Mira la lectura

STRATEGY ➤ Scanning

Look at this pen pal section. Does it include the three things you expected to find? What, if anything, is missing? What additional types of information did you find?

48   Capítulo 1

Options

Strategies for Reaching All Students

Spanish-Speaking Students

 Un paso más Ex. 1-F

Students Needing Extra Help
Do all the activities in *¡Vamos a leer!* as a class or in small groups. The latter might work better at first. Use the Organizer as needed.

Enrichment
Aplicación: You may want to have students create a bulletin-board display with their written responses. Encourage them to use photos.

Infórmate

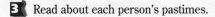

STRATEGY ➤ Scanning

Scanning is another strategy you can use. When you scan you only look for certain information. You do *not* have to read and understand every word.

1 Look at the first listing, for Jaime Muñoz Pardo. In what order does Jaime provide the following information?

address   age   hobbies   name

2 Look at the first names of the people seeking pen pals. On a separate sheet of paper, list them in the three categories shown below. How many are girls? How many are boys? What clue(s) did you use to help you decide?

Boys   Girls   Not sure

3 Read about each person's pastimes.

a. List the pastimes that two or more of them share.

b. List five pastimes that are not shared.

c. Are there any pastimes whose meaning you cannot guess? If so, you and a partner should choose two that you can't figure out. Each of you should find out the meaning of one of the words and share it with the class.

Muchacho ecuatoriano de Quito

Aplicación

Imagine that you are seeking a pen pal. Provide information about yourself that you think is important to share. You may want to use the following categories:

- Nombre
- Dirección
- Edad
- Pasatiempos

"Me gusta mucho leer y estudiar."

¡Vamos a leer! 49

Infórmate

1 Order is as follows:
a. name
b. address
c. age
d. hobbies

2 Boys: Jaime, Santiago, Fausto; Girls: Vanessa, Luz María, Marisol; Students might have used prior knowledge, what they now know about Hispanic names, or simple guesses.

3 a. acampar, escuchar música, leer
b. Answers will vary, but look for five of the following: *ajedrez, básquetbol, coleccionar estampillas / postales, fútbol, karate, la música rock, nadar, tocar la guitarra, ver películas.*
c. Tell students how reading for meaning is helpful. Encourage them to be inventive in finding out the meanings of words. How many use the dictionary? How many ask Spanish-speaking classmates?

Aplicación

Explain that, in Spanish, we usually write the street name first, then the number. Some abbreviations used in the reading are: *Col. (Colonia), Ret. (Retorno), sec. (sección), D.F. (Distrito Federal), Nº (Número).*

Cultural Notes

(p. 48, realia: top postage stamp)
The Tlaquepaque neighborhood southeast of downtown Guadalajara, Jalisco, was once a quiet, separate village where the city's wealthy families built spacious country retreats. Today these buildings are used as studios and shops by artists and artisans who produce some of the most prized works in all of Mexico. Tlaquepaque is particularly known for its exquisite blown-glass, an outstanding example of which appears on this stamp.

(p. 48, realia: bottom postage stamp)
The oldest university in the Americas, the Universidad Nacional Autónoma de México (UNAM) was founded in 1551 in Mexico City as the Royal and Pontifical University. It was run by the Roman Catholic church until 1867, when it was closed by the government. In 1910 the university re-opened as part of a new national school system. In 1929 it became autonomous, the occasion commemorated by this stamp.

(p. 49, realia: postage stamp)
Jalisco is one of many Mexican states known for its production of textiles handloomed from wool. Because handicrafts are central to culture and commerce in Mexico, the federal as well as many state governments fund artisans by providing them with training and places to show their work. Handicraft showrooms, such as FONART, subsidize artisans and assure shoppers that they are buying authentic, quality crafts.

Apply

Process Writing

Inform students in advance that their work will be kept in a portfolio of their writing. Explain that their portfolio will help them keep a record of their progress throughout the year.

Portfolios represent a systematic process involving both learner and teacher. They document progress toward specific standards by applying clearly stated criteria in selecting, monitoring, and evaluating significant products and performance. (For a more detailed explanation of portfolio writing and assessment, see the front section of this Teacher's Edition.)

In preparation for the writing assignment, you may wish to briefly review adjective agreement. For step 5, remind students about correct accent placement, question marks, and exclamation points. For spelling checks, tell students that they may always refer back to the vocabulary sections or the *Resumen del capítulo* at the end of the chapter.

¡Vamos a escribir!

Write a poem about yourself similar to the one on page 42. Follow these steps:

1 Read the poem on page 42 again.

2 Look at the vocabulary on pages 34–35 and write down five adjectives that apply to you and five that don't. Use the headings *Soy* and *No soy*.

Then, using the vocabulary on pages 30–31, write down at least three things that you like to do and three things that you don't like to do. Use the headings *Me gusta mucho* and *No me gusta nada*.

3 Write your poem based on the lists that you made. Focus on arranging your ideas in a way that you like.

4 Now show your poem to a partner. Ask which parts of the poem he or she likes and which ones might be changed. Decide whether or not you agree, then rewrite your poem, making any changes that you have decided on.

5 Check to make sure that everything is spelled correctly. Are capital letters used where they are needed? Are accents used correctly? Did you use question marks and exclamation points at the beginning and end of a sentence?

6 Now recopy your corrected poem. Add drawings or pictures if you like.

"¡Hola! Soy de Guatemala."

"Soy colombiano y soy muy amable."

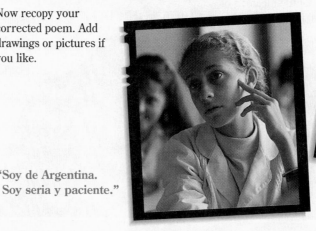

"Soy de Argentina. Soy seria y paciente."

50   Capítulo 1

Options

Strategies for Reaching All Students

Spanish-Speaking Students
Extend the assignment by having Spanish-speaking students write a poem describing their best friend or an ideal friend.

 Un paso más Ex. 1-G

Students Needing Extra Help
Step 2: Review the definition of an adjective, reminding students that it is a word that describes someone or something. Refer to the Organizer.
Step 5: Use the Organizer.

"A mí me gusta estar con mis amigos."

Cultural Notes

(p. 50, top photo)
This young weaver from Santiago Atitlán, Guatemala, is wearing a blouse that richly demonstrates the beauty of the hand-woven textiles for which her village is famous. Like other villages in the Maya highlands, Santiago Atitlán produces clothing that often tells a complex story of the local people and history through symbols, patterns, and colors.

(p. 51, photo)
Friendship in Spanish-speaking countries is characterized by much more physical contact than in the U.S. In Mexico, for example, teens and even adult women express their friendship by walking together in such a way that many Americans would consider excessive or an invasion of personal space—hand in hand or with their arms around each other's shoulders.

Assess & Summarize

Test Preparation

You may want to assign parts of this section as written homework or as an in-class writing activity prior to administering the *Examen de habilidades.*

Answers

Listening: *Soy callado. No me gusta hablar por teléfono. No me gusta ir al cine tampoco.* The person would be more likely to read at home.

Reading: The paragraph describes a boy who likes to skate and go to the movies. He is sometimes impatient, but nice and generous.

Speaking: Answers will vary.

Writing: Letters will vary.

Culture: Answers will vary, but students may say that, in a Spanish-speaking country, a friend is a person who grew up with you. Friendship involves sharing, trusting, knowing each other's families very well, and so on.

¿Lo sabes bien?

This section will help you organize your studying for the proficiency test, where you will be asked to do similar, though not identical, tasks. There will not be any models on the test.

Listening

Can you understand when someone talks about personality traits and interests? Listen as your teacher reads you a sample similar to what you will hear on the test. Would the person making the statements be more likely to participate in a school play or read at home?

Reading

Can you understand a written description of a person's traits and interests? Scan the paragraph below. What is the person like? Is it a description of a boy or a girl?

> Me gusta mucho patinar. También me gusta ir al cine. A veces soy impaciente, pero soy amable y generoso.

Writing

Can you write a letter describing your personality and interests? Here is an example of an appropriate letter.

> ¡Hola, Alfredo!
>
> Soy trabajador y me gusta ayudar en casa. También me gusta ir a la escuela y tocar la guitarra. No soy prudente. No soy callado tampoco. Y tú, ¿cómo eres?
>
> Saludos,
> Antonio

Culture

Can you explain what the word *amigo* might mean to a person from a Spanish-speaking country?

En Otavalo, Ecuador

Speaking

Can you describe yourself and tell what you like to do? Here is one example of a good response:

—*Pues, yo soy seria y callada, pero no soy ni deportista ni artística. Me gusta mucho leer y estar con amigos. No me gusta nada hablar por teléfono.*

52   Capítulo 1

Options

Strategies for Reaching All Students

Students Needing Extra Help
Have students write out this section so they can check off what they have mastered.

Resumen del capítulo 1

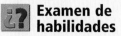

Use the vocabulary from this chapter to help you:
■ describe yourself and tell about some of your likes and dislikes
■ find out what other people are like
■ compare your likes and dislikes with other people's

to talk about activities
ayudar en casa
cocinar
dibujar
escuchar música
estar con amigos
estudiar
hablar por teléfono
   el teléfono
ir a la escuela
ir al cine
   el cine
leer
nadar
patinar
practicar deportes
tocar la guitarra
ver la televisión (la tele)

to say what you like
(A mí) me gusta ___.
              más ___.
              mucho ___.
(A mí) sí me gusta ___.
A mí también.

to say what you do not like
(A mí) no me
   gusta ___.
       mucho ___.
       nada ___.
       ___ tampoco.

to say what you or someone else is like
(Yo) soy ___.
(Tú) eres ___.

to ask someone what he or she likes
¿Qué te gusta (hacer)?
¿Te gusta ___?
¿Y a ti?

to ask someone what he or she is like
¿Cómo eres?
¿Eres (tú) ___?

to describe yourself or others
amable
artístico, -a
atrevido, -a
callado, -a
deportista
desordenado, -a
generoso, -a
gracioso, -a
impaciente
ordenado, -a
paciente
perezoso, -a
prudente
serio, -a
sociable
tacaño, -a
trabajador, -a

to ask if a statement is accurate
¿De veras?

other useful words and expressions
a veces
muy
ni . . . ni
pero
pues
también
tampoco
y

Resumen 53

Cultural Notes

(p. 52, photo)
The Saturday market in Otavalo is the most famous of the Ecuadorian Indian markets and one of the largest in South America. It dates to pre-Incan times, when the Cara Indians (ancestors of the modern *otavaleños*) prospered as traders with neighboring tribes. Today the market is best known for the textiles sold by the *otavaleños* who, like their ancestors, demonstrate remarkable weaving skills.

CAPÍTULO 2

THEME: SCHOOL

COMMUNICATION

Topics

School supplies

School subjects

Class schedules

Time-telling

Numbers 32–59

Objectives

To compare school systems in the U.S. and in Spanish-speaking countries

To talk about school subjects and supplies

To talk about what people need

To say what something is for

To express possession

To express quantity

To ask for information

To express regret / hesitation

To talk about location

To ask and tell when something takes place / To ask and tell the time

CULTURE

Mexican vs. U.S. school systems

Levels of speech: *tú/Ud./Uds.*

GRAMMAR

Los pronombres personales

Verbos que terminan en -ar

Los sustantivos

Ancillaries available for use with Chapter 2

Multisensory/Technology

 Overhead Transparencies, 11–15

 Audio Tapes and CDs

 Vocabulary Art Blackline Masters for Hands-On Learning, pp. 13–17

 Classroom Crossword

 Video

 CD-ROM

Print

 Practice Workbook, pp. 23–32

 Writing, Audio & Video Activities, pp. 11–16, 96–98, 154–155

 Communicative Activity Blackline Masters

Pair and Small Group Activities, pp. 15–20

Situation Cards, p. 21

Un paso más: Actividades para ampliar tu español, pp. 7–12

Assessment

 Assessment Program

Pruebas, pp. 23–33

Examen de habilidades, pp. 34–36

 Test Generator

Video still from Chap. 2

53A

Educational Traditions

Although educational goals in Spain, Latin America, and the U.S. are fundamentally the same—most educators, for example, want to develop good citizens—their educational traditions are quite distinct.

Many of the educational traditions of Latin America have their origin in Spanish traditions. The Spanish school system is divided into four different levels of education: 1) preschool, 2) *Educación General Básica* (EGB), which is primary education, 3) *Bachillerato Unificado y Polivalente* (BUP), which is a program of study aimed at university requirements, or *Curso de Orientación Universitaria* (COU), which is high-school-level training in technical fields, and 4) university study.

Children in Spain may enter free preschool programs. Primary schooling begins at age 6 and continues to age 16. *Educación General Básica* provides a background in languages, mathematics, social and natural sciences, and artistic expression. Children attend around 25 hours of instruction a week. Though school books are free in some special cases, Spanish families usually pay for books as well as school supplies, transportation, lunch service, and voluntary extracurricular activities. This is generally true throughout Latin America as well.

If students complete the EGB before age 16, they receive the certificate of *Graduado Escolar* and may choose to continue their education in either a secondary (BUP) or a technical-training school (COU). Those who do not complete their studies by age 16 receive a certificate of *Escolaridad* and are eligible only for technical training schools.

BUP is geared toward academics and COU is hands-on training in the areas of science and technology, health-care technology, or business. Evaluation in either option is through exams in each subject area. A final comprehensive exam is given twice a year. Students who wish to continue their studies must pass this exam.

Perhaps the most significant contrast between the U.S. and Spanish educational systems is the "tracking" of students for college. In the U.S., high-school graduates have theoretically received a general academic preparation enabling them to attend any of a variety of post-secondary educational institutions. In Spain, however, secondary education more specifically gears students to either university studies or further technical and business education.

Introduce

Re-entry of Concepts

The following list represents words, expressions, and grammar topics re-entered from *El primer paso* to Chap. 1:

El primer paso
School supplies
Numbers 0–31
Greetings
School vocabulary

Chapter 1
Activities
Gustar expressions
Adjectives describing personality

Planning

Cross-Curricular Connections

Math Connection *(p. 58)*
Explain the difference between ordinal and cardinal numbers. Have students be responsible for looking up words for 9th through 20th and then writing them on a poster or on the chalkboard. They may want to make a list for their notebooks.

Graphic Arts Connection *(pp. 58, 62–63)*
Have students plan a study schedule for the afternoon or evening based on the subjects that they study in school. Have them design and illustrate the time (beginning and ending) devoted to the study of each subject. Students could draw pictures to illustrate descriptions of activities.

Geography Connection *(pp. 80–81)*
Obtain two maps of Mexico from a travel agency or tourist office. Post one on the wall. From the second, cut out picture features, names of cities and sites, etc. Give pairs of students these cutouts and have them locate and pin them on the map. Continue by giving each pair a blank map and have them make a pictorial of the area. Have each pair pick one aspect or location and do a brief follow-up paragraph in English.

CAPÍTULO 2

¿Qué clases tienes?

OBJECTIVES

At the end of this chapter, you will be able to:

- describe your class schedule
- list some school supplies you use
- find out about someone else's schedule
- compare your school experience with that of a student in a Spanish-speaking country

Unos estudiantes delante de su escuela en Barcelona, España

55

Preview

Cultural Objective

• To compare your school experience with that of a student in a Spanish-speaking country

 ¿Qué clases tienes?

Play

 Video Activity A

Using the Video

This chapter's video focuses on school—classes, supplies, and schedules. Students will see our hosts in Madrid visiting a high school and interviewing students in class.

Since the videos for this chapter and for Chapters 3, 4, 6, 8, and 9 were filmed in Spain, students will hear the forms of *vosotros* being used. You may want to prepare your students by reviewing those verb forms.

To prepare students for the video, first ask them to predict what this chapter's tape will be about. Then have students watch the segment several times. After the first time, you may wish to have them brainstorm possible vocabulary and expressions they will need to talk about what they saw on the video. Ask students to identify: a) things they saw that looked familiar but

¡Piénsalo bien!

Look at the pictures.
In the captions these teens talk about school.

"A mí me gusta mucho jugar fútbol después de las clases."

What do you think *fútbol* means in this picture? What do you think the expression *fútbol americano* might mean? Which is more popular in your school: *fútbol* or *fútbol americano?*

En España

56   Capítulo 2

Options

Strategies for Reaching All Students

Spanish-Speaking Students

¡Piénsalo bien!: Ask Spanish-speaking students: *¿Qué clases tienes este semestre? ¿Qué necesitas para una clase de matemáticas? ¿Qué necesitas para tus otras clases?*

 Un paso más Ex. 2-A

"Los miércoles tengo inglés en la primera hora. La clase empieza a las siete y media."

Which of your classes is most like this *clase de inglés?*

"Los estudiantes de mi clase tienen un 10 . . ."

What do you think getting a grade of 10 in a Spanish-speaking school means?

En una escuela secundaria en México

57

were somewhat different from what they might see in their own school, and b) anything they saw that they probably would not see in their own school.

Video segment 1: For more teaching suggestions, see the Video Teacher's Guide.

Answers: ¡Piénsalo bien!
(p. 56, photo) Students should be able to guess that *fútbol* means soccer, and that *fútbol americano* is football. / Answers will vary for the question pertaining to which sport is more popular.

(p. 57, photos) Answers will vary. For the question pertaining to the bottom photo, most students would say this is equivalent to receiving an A or A+ in school.

Cultural Notes ☀

(p. 56, photo)
Soccer players in Spain. The first World Cup championship was held in 1930 in Uruguay, with only 13 participating teams. The World Cup, which is held every four years, has grown to be the world's most popular sporting event. The number of teams participating is now fixed at 24, culled from the "Dream Teams" of over 100 countries.

(p. 57, top photo)
English-language class in Málaga. For almost 40 years of General Francisco Franco's rule, foreign language instruction in Spain was either of very poor quality or nonexistent. Other indigenous languages of Spain, such as *catalán* and *vasco,* were forbidden to be taught. With Spain's entry into the European Community in 1992, however, Spaniards have hastened to study languages, particularly English, to keep pace commercially with the rest of the world.

Present

Chapter Theme
School subjects and supplies

Communicative Objectives
- To ask and tell when something takes place
- To talk about school subjects
- To talk about school supplies
- To talk about what people need
- To say what something is for
- To express possession
- To express quantity
- To ask for information
- To express regret
- To express hesitation
- To talk about location

 Transparencies 11–12

 Vocabulary Art BLMs

 Pronunciation Tape 2-1

 Vocabulario para conversar A

Play

Using the Video
Video segment 2: See the Video Teacher's Guide.

 Video Activity B

Vocabulario para conversar

¿Qué clases tienes?

Here are some new words and expressions you will need to talk about your class schedule and school supplies. Read them several times, then turn the page and practice with a partner.

Horario (m.)*		
	Primer semestre (m.)	Segundo semestre
(1ª) primera hora (f.)	matemáticas	inglés
(2ª) segunda hora	inglés	matemáticas
(3ª) tercera hora	educación física	ciencias de la salud
(4ª) cuarta hora	ciencias sociales	ciencias sociales
(5ª) quinta hora	almuerzo	almuerzo
(6ª) sexta hora	arte	música
(7ª) séptima hora	español	ciencias
(8ª) octava hora	ciencias	español

* The letters in parentheses indicate the gender of the noun: masculine *(m.)* or feminine *(f.)*.

58 Capítulo 2

Options

Strategies for Reaching All Students

Spanish-Speaking Students
Spanish-speaking students can make their own vocabulary lists with additional classes and supplies. If necessary, help students with spelling. (You may wish to label classroom supplies and objects around the room with note cards for the benefit of all students.)

Students Needing Extra Help
Have students start filling in their Organizers.

Enrichment
Enhance the vocabulary presentation by bringing in class schedules, course descriptions, etc., from schools in Spanish-speaking countries.
If students should ask: *novena hora* (ninth period / hour), *décima hora* (tenth period / hour).
Vocabulario para conversar: As a written assignment, have students use adjectives they've learned to describe their behavior in different classes, perhaps pointing out how

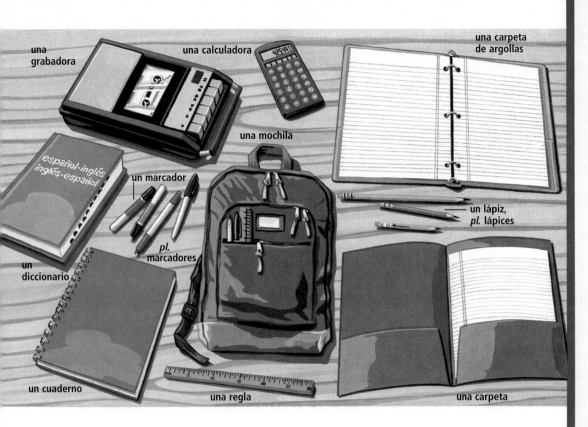

una grabadora

una calculadora

una carpeta de argollas

una mochila

un marcador

una carpeta de argollas

un lápiz, pl. lápices

español-inglés inglés-español

pl. marcadores

un diccionario

un cuaderno

una regla

una carpeta

También necesitas . . .

la clase de ____	____ *class*	tu	*your*
difícil	*difficult, hard*	¿Qué?	*What?*
fácil	*easy*	Lo siento.	*I'm sorry.*
la tarea	*homework*	A ver . . .	*Let's see . . .*
necesitar: (yo) necesito	*to need: I need*	Aquí / Allí está.	*Here / There it is.*
(tú) necesitas	*you need*		
tener: (yo) tengo	*to have: I have*		
(tú) tienes	*you have*		
para	*for*		

¿Y qué quiere decir . . . ?
mucho, -a

Vocabulario para conversar   59

Grammar Preview
Necesito and *necesitas* are presented lexically. The explanation of *-ar* verbs appears in the grammar section, along with nouns and articles, on pp. 71–76.

Teaching Suggestions
Preparing students to speak: Use one or two options from each of the categories of Comprehensible Input, Physical Response, or Limited Verbal Response. For a complete explanation of these categories and some sample activities, see the front section of this Teacher's Edition.

The indefinite articles *un* and *una* are used with school supplies for more natural language use in this vocabulary section. (The formal explanation of singular indefinite articles is on p. 76.)

Formation of plural nouns will be taught in Chap. 4. For now, students will use them, but they will not be expected to form them.

Class Starter Review
On the day following initial presentation, you might begin the class with this activity:
Name a class subject and have students signal *sí* or *no* as you mention school supplies that might be necessary for that class.

behavior may vary according to the class they're in. Example: *Soy perezoso(a) en la clase de matemáticas, pero muy trabajador(a) en la clase de ciencias.*

Learning Spanish Through Action
STAGING VOCABULARY: *Levanten, Muestren, Señalen, Toquen*
1) MATERIALS: transparency of school supplies in the *Vocabulario para conversar* or the actual items
DIRECTIONS: Using the transparency or actual school supplies, have pairs of students touch or point to the items that you mention. If the actual items are available, you may wish to have students raise the item, then ask them *¿Qué tienes?*

2) MATERIALS: transparency of school subjects in the *Vocabulario para conversar*
DIRECTIONS: Using the transparency, mention a class subject and have pairs of students touch or point at the appropriate illustration. Continue until each class subject is mentioned.

Practice & Apply

Re-enter / Recycle
Ex. 7: *gustar* expressions from Chap. 1

Critical Thinking: Classifying Information
As a written activity, have students use the *Vocabulario para conversar* to list the supplies they probably would *never* use in school. Then ask them to list the ones they would use in almost *every* class.

Answers: Empecemos a conversar

1 ESTUDIANTE A
a. ¿Tienes mucha tarea en tu clase de matemáticas?
b. ...ciencias de la salud?
c. ...ciencias sociales?
d. ...español?
e. ...inglés?

ESTUDIANTE B
a.–e. Answers will vary.

2 ESTUDIANTE A
Questions will vary, but should include school supplies. Encourage *Estudiante A* to ask at least three or four questions.

ESTUDIANTE B
Answers will vary depending on whether *Estudiante B* has the object mentioned. Ask students to show the object if they have it.

Empecemos a conversar

With a partner, take turns being *Estudiante A* and *Estudiante B*. Use the words that are cued or given in the balloons to replace the underlined sections in the model. means you can make your own choices.

1
A —¿Tienes mucha tarea en tu clase de <u>ciencias</u>?
B —Sí, tengo mucha tarea.
o: No, no tengo mucha tarea.

Y ahora Uds.

Estudiante A   Estudiante B

a.   b.   c.

d.   e.

2 A —¿Tienes <u>una calculadora</u>?
B —A ver... Sí, aquí está.
o: Sí, allí está.
o: A ver... No, lo siento.

Y ahora Uds.

Estudiante A   Estudiante B

60   Capítulo 2

Options

Strategies for Reaching All Students

Spanish-Speaking Students
Pair bilingual with non-bilingual students for Exs. 1 and 3. You may wish to have them write out Ex. 2, using at least three questions.

 Un paso más Exs. 2-B, 2-C

Students Needing Extra Help
Ex. 2: Explain the responses before moving ahead. Model with other school supplies.
Ex. 3: Explain that when we speak, we often repeat all or part of the question to be sure we understand what was asked. Model one or two examples in English.
Ex. 4: If students don't have supplies with them, have them list what they should have, including all classes in which they use those supplies.

Ex. 7: Remind students of *ni...ni.*
Empecemos a escribir: For additional practice, have students make a two-column chart. In the left column they should write the heading *Clase* and list their classes. In the right column, have them write the heading *Necesito* and list the school supplies they need next to each class.

3

A —¿Qué clase tienes en la *primera* hora?
B —¿En la *primera* hora? Pues, tengo *matemáticas*.

Y ahora Uds.

Estudiante A   **Estudiante B**

a. 2ª

b. 3ª

c. 4ª

d. 5ª

e. 6ª

f. 7ª

g. 8ª

Empecemos a escribir

Write your answers in Spanish.

4 List the school supplies you have with you right now. Next to each item, write the name of at least one class in which you use it.

5 In two columns, under the headings *Fácil* and *Difícil*, list the subjects you are taking this year.

6 ¿Qué necesitas para tu primera clase?

7 ¿Qué te gusta más, hacer la tarea de español o hablar con tus compañeros(as) en la clase de español?

8 ¿Qué tienes en tu mochila?

También se dice

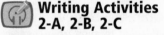

el lapicero
la pluma
el boli

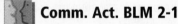

la carpeta de anillas
el archivador

Vocabulario para conversar   61

Present

Chapter Theme
School: Time-telling

Communicative Objectives
- To talk about school subjects
- To ask and tell when something takes place
- To ask and tell the time
- To tell who performs an action

 Transparencies 13–14

 Vocabulary Art BLMs

 Pronunciation Tape 2-2

 Vocabulario para conversar B

Play

Using the Video
Video segment 2: See the Video Teacher's Guide.

 Video Activity B

Grammar Preview
Enseña and *termina* are presented lexically here for communication skills. These will appear in the grammar explanation of *-ar* verbs on pp. 73–74.

Vocabulario para conversar

¿Qué hora es?

Here's the rest of the vocabulary you will need to talk about your class schedule.

Es la una.

Son las dos.

Son las tres.

Son las cuatro.

Son las cinco.

Son las seis.

Son las siete.

Son las ocho.

Son las nueve.

Son las diez.

Son las once.

Son las doce.

Son las dos y cinco.

Son las dos y cuarto. (Son las dos y quince.)

Son las dos y veinte.

Son las dos y media. (Son las dos y treinta.)

Son las dos y cuarenta y cinco.

Son las dos y cincuenta y ocho.

62 Capítulo 2

Options

Strategies for Reaching All Students

Learning Spanish Through Action
STAGING VOCABULARY: *Escriban, Muestren, Vayan*
1) MATERIALS: toy or student-made analog clocks (enough for the whole class or groups)
DIRECTIONS: Using a model clock, set a time and then say it out loud. Have a pair of students set the hands of their clocks to the proper positions. Ask students to show their clocks for verification and then show the correct time on your clock before proceeding to the next time.
2) MATERIALS: index cards with various times written on them
DIRECTIONS: Have volunteers go to the chalkboard to complete digital clocks. Say the time while showing the rest of the class the index card. Once the clocks are filled in, students can check their own work against the index cards.

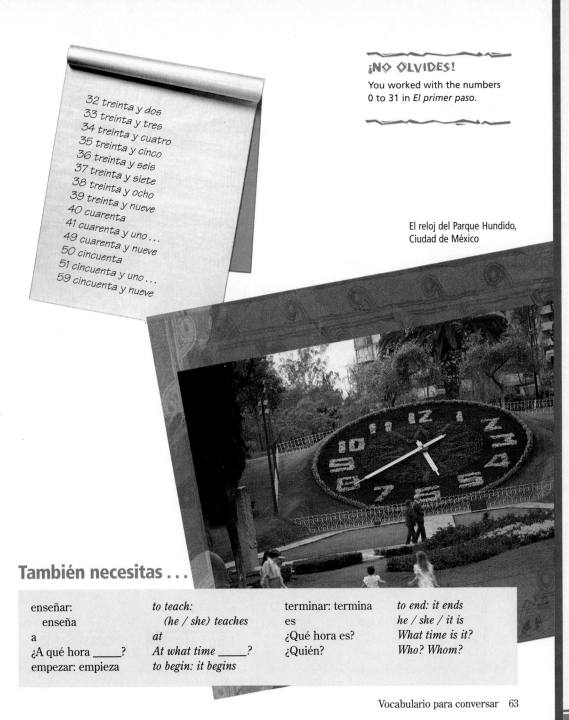

32 treinta y dos
33 treinta y tres
34 treinta y cuatro
35 treinta y cinco
36 treinta y seis
37 treinta y siete
38 treinta y ocho
39 treinta y nueve
40 cuarenta
41 cuarenta y uno...
49 cuarenta y nueve
50 cincuenta
51 cincuenta y uno...
59 cincuenta y nueve

¡NO OLVIDES!
You worked with the numbers
0 to 31 in *El primer paso.*

El reloj del Parque Hundido,
Ciudad de México

También necesitas . . .

enseñar:
  enseña
a
¿A qué hora _____?
empezar: empieza
	to teach:
	  (he / she) teaches
	at
	At what time _____?
	to begin: it begins
		terminar: termina
		es
		¿Qué hora es?
		¿Quién?
			to end: it ends
			he / she / it is
			What time is it?
			Who? Whom?

Vocabulario para conversar   63

Practice & Apply

Re-enter / Recycle

Exs. 9–14: numbers 0–31 from *El primer paso*
Ex. 15: *gustar* expressions and activities from Chap. 1

Answers: Empecemos a conversar

9 ESTUDIANTE A

a. ¿Qué hora es? ¿Son las once?
b. ...¿Son las doce y media (treinta)?
c. ...¿Son las diez?
d. ...¿Es la una y cuarto (quince)?

ESTUDIANTE B

a. No, son las once y veinticinco.
b. No, son las doce y cuarenta.
c. No, son las nueve y cincuenta y cinco.
d. No, es la una y treinta y cinco.

10 ESTUDIANTE A

a. ¿A qué hora empieza tu clase de ciencias?
b. ...ciencias de la salud?
c. ...matemáticas?
d. ...arte?

ESTUDIANTE B

a. ...las nueve ...las nueve y cincuenta.
b. Empieza a las dos y termina a las dos y cincuenta.
c. ...las diez ...las diez y cincuenta.
d. ...la una ...la una y cincuenta.

Empecemos a conversar

9

A — *¿Qué hora es? ¿Son las dos?*
B — *No, es la una y cuarenta y cinco.*
    Y ahora Uds.

Estudiante A   **Estudiante B**

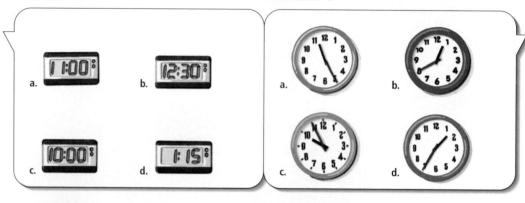

10

A — *¿A qué hora empieza tu clase de educación física?*
B — *Empieza a las diez y termina a las diez y cincuenta.*
    Y ahora Uds.

Estudiante A   **Estudiante B**

a.
b.
c.
d.

a. 9:00- 9:50   b. 2:00- 2:50
c. 10:00-10:50   d. 1:00- 1:50

64   Capítulo 2

Options

Strategies for Reaching All Students

Spanish-Speaking Students
Have Spanish-speaking students write out Ex. 9. Pairs of bilingual and non-bilingual students can write out Exs. 10–11. Encourage them to expand their answers, where possible.

 Un paso más Ex. 2-D

Students Needing Extra Help
Have students fill in their Organizers.
Exs. 9–11: Point out that these questions all ask about time, but in different ways.
Ex. 10: If students have difficulty, explain why *tu clase de educación física* is after the verb form in the model (inversion in questions). This explanation comes later in the chapter's grammar presentation of *-ar* verbs.

Ex. 11: Have students use their Organizers.
Ex. 12: Structure this activity for students and give them a model. Times should include minutes, and most students' schedules should have at least five classes.

11 A —*¿Cuándo tienes la clase de <u>ciencias</u>?*

   B —*A ver... A <u>las ocho y diez</u>.*

   A —*¿Quién es tu profesor(a)?*

   B —*<u>La profesora González</u>.*

   Y ahora Uds.

Estudiante A   Estudiante B

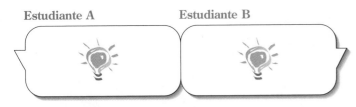

Empecemos a escribir y a leer

Write your answers in Spanish.

12 Redesign your school schedule. You decide when classes begin and end and how long each period lasts.

13 ¿A qué hora es el almuerzo? ¿Cuándo termina?

14 ¿Quién es tu profesor(a) favorito(a)? ¿Qué enseña? ¿A qué hora empieza la clase? ¿Cuándo termina?

15 Federico dice: "Yo soy artístico. Me gusta mucho dibujar," pero Ernesto responde: "A mí no me gusta nada dibujar, pero me gusta mucho practicar deportes, especialmente nadar y patinar." Ana dice: "A mí me gusta más leer libros de historia," pero Susana responde: "A mí no me gusta mucho leer, pero sí me gustan los números y los cálculos."

¿Quién dice...
a. "Mi clase favorita es matemáticas"?
b. "Mi clase favorita es educación física"?
c. "Mi clase favorita es arte"?

¡NO OLVIDES!

Remember that when using *señor(a)*, *profesor(a)* or any other title to talk about a person, we need to add the definite article to the title: *El señor López enseña inglés.* However, when addressing a person, we do not use the article: *¿Cómo está, señor López?*

11 ESTUDIANTE A
Questions will vary.
ESTUDIANTE B
Answers will vary, but look for appropriate times given.

Answers: Empecemos a escribir y a leer

12 Look for appropriate use of time-telling, names for school subjects, and class periods.

13–14 Answers will vary.

15 a. Susana, b. Ernesto, c. Federico

Multicultural Perspectives

With variances from one Spanish-speaking country to another, many schools have instruction from 9:00 A.M. to 1:30 P.M. before breaking for lunch. Students often go home for their midday meal where they are joined by other family members. The meal may last from 2:00 P.M. until 4:30 P.M. They then return for their afternoon classes, which may last until 7:00 P.M. or later. Ask students familiar with other cultures to share any information they know about school schedules.

 Practice Wkbk. 2-3, 2-4

 Audio Activity 2.2

 Writing Activity 2-D

 Pruebas 2-3, 2-4

Enrichment
Exs. 9–10: Encourage students to invent mini-dialogues naming other classes and times.

Practice

Re-enter / Recycle
Ex. 1: *gustar* expressions from Chap. 1

Answers:
¡Comuniquemos!

1 ESTUDIANTE A

a. ¿Qué clase te gusta más, arte o música?

b. ..., español o inglés?

c. ..., ciencias o matemáticas?

d. ..., ciencias de la salud o educación física?

e. ..., inglés o ciencias sociales?

ESTUDIANTE B

a.–e. Answers will vary.

2 ESTUDIANTE A

a. ¿Qué necesitas para tu clase de matemáticas?

b. ...arte?

c. ...ciencias de la salud?

d. ...ciencias?

ESTUDIANTE B

a.–d. A ver... Necesito...
(Answers will vary, but may include: una regla, una calculadora, un lápiz, un marcador, un cuaderno, un bolígrafo, una carpeta, una carpeta de argollas.*)*

¡Comuniquemos!

Here's another opportunity for you to use the vocabulary you've just learned.

¡NO OLVIDES!
To say that you don't like either of two things, use *ni . . . ni.*
See page 44.

1 Find out which classes your partner prefers.

A —*¿Qué clase te gusta más, ciencias o ciencias sociales?*
B —*Me gusta más la clase de ciencias.*

2 You are planning to go shopping for school supplies with a friend. Find out from each other what supplies you need for each class you are taking.

A —*¿Qué necesitas para tu clase de ciencias sociales?*
B —*A ver... Necesito un cuaderno y un bolígrafo.*

Estudiante A   Estudiante B

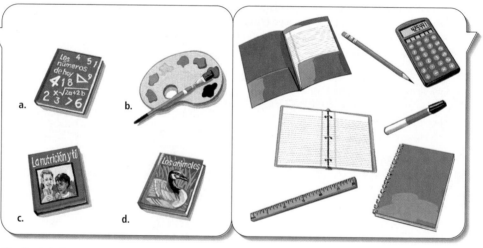

Options

Strategies for Reaching All Students

Spanish-Speaking Students
Ex. 1: Have Spanish-speaking students write out the questions they ask their partners about their preferences.

Students Needing Extra Help
Ex. 2: Use the Organizer.
¿Qué sabes ahora?: Have students write out this section to keep in their notebooks. Students will check off concepts as they are mastered.

Enrichment
Ex. 1: Have pairs of students vary and extend their dialogues by having *Estudiante A* express surprise, disagreement, or agreement with *Estudiante B*'s reply. Example: *¿De veras? Pues, a mí me gusta más la clase de . . .* or: *¿De veras? A mí también.*

¿Qué sabes ahora?

Can you:

- ask someone what he or she needs for a certain class?
  —¿Qué ___ para la clase de inglés?
- tell someone what you need for a class?
  —___ un bolígrafo o ___ lápiz y ___ cuaderno.
- ask someone what classes he or she has?
  —¿Qué clases ___ el primer semestre?
- tell someone what classes you have?
  —___ ciencias, español y matemáticas.

Cooperative Learning
Have groups of three or four students prepare a TV advertisement for a store offering school items for sale. The ad should have a poster display of items with prices clearly marked. Items should be discounted at different times during the day for special sales.

Once the display is ready, ask students to give pertinent details. For example: *A las ocho (tengo) carpetas. ¡25 pesos!* Students should be encouraged to include as many school vocabulary items as possible. At the end of the activity the class can select the store most likely to succeed.

Present & Apply

Cultural Objective
• To talk about similarities and differences between a Mexican and a U.S. high school

Teaching Suggestions
You might wish to prepare a list of additional discussion questions to ask students after they have read the material. Suggestions: Do you think American students spend more or less time on homework than Mexican students? How much time do you spend on homework each day? Do Mexican schools seem more or less structured than American schools? Do you think Mexican students or American students are more respectful of their teachers? Why?

If students ask: *Ciencias naturales,* Science; *Tecnología,* Computer or another technology-related class; *Receso,* Break; *Educación artística,* Art; *Orientación vocacional,* Career Counseling; *Libre,* Free period.

Perspectiva cultural

Los estudiantes en los países hispanos tienen muchas clases. Y tú, ¿qué clases tienes? ¿Qué clases te gustan más? ¿Qué clases no te gustan?

Look at the photo of public school students and the school schedule below. What do you notice that you didn't expect?

Although an *escuela secundaria* in Mexico City has a lot in common with a high school in the United States, there are some striking differences. And even though there are differences among Mexican schools, you might find that any or all of these things happen:

• In most schools, when a teacher enters the classroom, the students stand.
• The teacher probably calls the students by their last name.
• The students, on the other hand, are more likely to address their teacher simply as *maestro* or *maestra,* without a last name.
• The average amount of time students spend on homework ranges from 15 to 30 minutes per class.
• Teachers usually collect the homework the next day rather than reviewing it in class.

• The grading scale in Mexico ranges from a low of 1 to a high of 10, with 6 being the lowest passing grade. A grade of 6 or 7 is roughly equivalent to a C, 8 to a B, and 9 and 10 to an A.
• Grades are based much more on test results and homework than on class participation.
• Class time is generally spent with the teacher lecturing rather than with class discussion.
• Many public schools require uniforms at least four days a week.

La cultura desde tu perspectiva

1 If you attended school in Mexico City, what might you find that might be familiar to you? What would you have to adjust to?

2 Based on what you now know about schools in Mexico City, list five suggestions that might help an exchange student from Mexico City adjust to your school's system.

HORA	HORAS	LUNES	MARTES	MIÉRCOLES	JUEVES	VIERNES
1a	7:30 a 8:15	Ciencias naturales	Educación física	Inglés	Ciencias sociales	Ciencias naturales
2a	8:15 a 9:00	Ciencias naturales	Tecnología	Español	Ciencias sociales	Ciencias naturales
3a	9:00 a 9:45	Inglés	Tecnología	Ciencias sociales	Matemáticas	Español
4a	9:45 a 10:30	Ciencias sociales	Ciencias sociales	Ciencias sociales	Ciencias naturales	Matemáticas
	10:30 a 10:50			R E C E S O		
5a	10:50 a 11:35	Español	Ciencias sociales	Matemáticas	Ciencias naturales	Tecnología
6a	11:35 a 12:20	Matemáticas	Inglés	Ciencias naturales	Educación artística	Tecnología
7a	12:20 a 13:05	Tecnología	Educación artística	Tecnología	Educación física	Orientación vocacional
8a	13:05 a 13:50	Tecnología	Español	Tecnología	LIBRE	LIBRE

Estudiantes en la Ciudad de México

68 Capítulo 2

Options

Strategies for Reaching All Students

Spanish-Speaking Students
Ask Spanish-speaking students: *¿Te gustaría tener las clases que tiene este estudiante? ¿Qué clases te gustarían más? ¿Deben los estudiantes usar uniformes en la escuela? ¿Por qué?* Have students design a school uniform and describe it to the class.

 Un paso más Exs. 2-E, 2-F

Students Needing Extra Help
Have students use their Organizers for reading the schedule.

Enrichment
Elicit opinions from students regarding which kind of instruction they prefer: teacher lecture or class discussion. Ask them for reasons for their preference. Have students divide a sheet of paper in half and, by making two lists, compare or contrast Mexican and U.S. schools based on the information in the text.

Point out to students that there is no lunch break in the schedule, because most students would go home for lunch at 1:00 or 2:00. (Have them notice that they use the 24-hour clock system.) The class schedule varies from day to day, and there is no passing period, since the teachers move from room to room, not the students.

Answers

Possible answers to inductive question: Students may say that the class schedule varies from day to day with the student taking more classes than they do. There is no passing period. Some courses last for two class periods. Students should notice that they are wearing uniforms in the photo. Discuss your school's dress code policy (if any).

Answers: La cultura desde tu perspectiva

1 Answers will vary, but students may mention the following as similarities or differences: student-teacher relationships, amount of homework, grading system, and teaching methods.

2 Answers may include suggestions for the exchange student to be prepared to see possible relaxed rules or regulations for the classroom; changes in student-teacher relationships; different treatment of homework, grades, and testing; and differences in the school day with respect to number of courses, class length, and schedules.

Cultural Notes

(p. 69, photo)
Schoolgirls in Mexico City. While girls in Mexico nearly equal boys in enrollment in the lower primary grades, their numbers diminish progressively at the higher grades in primary and secondary levels. At the secondary-school level, the ratio is approximately four boys to every three girls.

Preview

Transparency 15

Critical Thinking: Identifying Evidence in the Text

Ask students what part or parts of the letter suggest that the teacher expects students to study at home (end of first paragraph).

Answers

Answers will vary, but may include an explanation of what the students can expect to learn in the course, course content, etc.

A *preparan, trabajan, necesitan /* Answers will vary, but see if students mention that the verb endings correspond to the subject (person) in the sentences.

B "we use"

Gramática en contexto

This is a letter that a science teacher sent home before school started. What information would you expect to find in a letter like this?

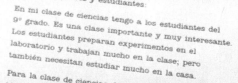

ESCUELA SECUNDARIA FEDERAL • FRANCISCO VILLA • VALLE NACIONAL Y JAZMINAL • CHIHUAHUA, CHIH.

28 de agosto

Estimados padres y estudiantes:

En mi clase de ciencias tengo a los estudiantes del 9° grado. Es una clase importante y muy interesante. Los estudiantes preparan experimentos en el laboratorio y trabajan mucho en la clase; pero también necesitan estudiar mucho en la casa.

Para la clase de ciencias, los estudiantes necesitan lápices, papel y una carpeta. También usamos frecuentemente una calculadora y una regla en la clase.

Si Uds. necesitan más información, favor de llamar al 222-89-67 durante la tercera hora, que empieza a las 10 y termina a las 10:50.

Atentamente,

A Find all the words in the letter that end in *-an*. Why do you think they end in those two letters? (Hint: *Necesito* and *tengo* both end in *-o*. Think about what the *o* might tell you. *Necesitas* and *tienes* also have similar endings. What might their *-s* ending tell you?)

B Now look at the word *usamos* in the second paragraph. Can you guess at the meaning of this word?

70   Capítulo 2

Options

Strategies for Reaching All Students

Students Needing Extra Help

Have students write out the letter so that they can highlight, underline, and so on. Or, use the transparency so that you can highlight for them. Point out that *estudiantes* is plural and that the corresponding verb ends in *-an.* Compare this to *necesito / necesitas* and *tengo / tienes* where the *-o* signals "I" and the *-as / -es* signal "you."

Show the subject pronoun chart by putting it on the chalkboard or overhead. Explain grammatical terms (pronouns, infinitives, etc.) to avoid discouraging students who have had difficulty with these in English.

Los pronombres personales

We often use people's names to tell who is doing an action.
We also use what we call subject pronouns.

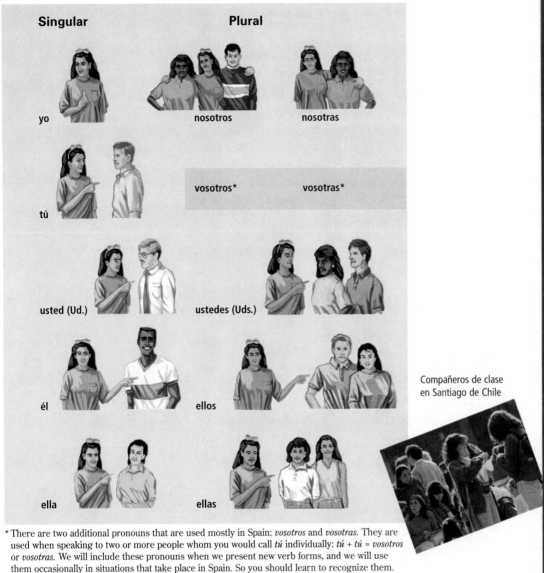

Singular	Plural	
yo	nosotros	nosotras
tú	vosotros*	vosotras*
usted (Ud.)	ustedes (Uds.)	
él	ellos	
ella	ellas	

Compañeros de clase
en Santiago de Chile

* There are two additional pronouns that are used mostly in Spain: *vosotros* and *vosotras*. They are
used when speaking to two or more people whom you would call *tú* individually: *tú + tú = vosotros*
or *vosotras*. We will include these pronouns when we present new verb forms, and we will use
them occasionally in situations that take place in Spain. So you should learn to recognize them.

Gramática en contexto   71

Present & Practice

Teaching Suggestions

Point out that a question in Spanish may omit the subject if it is clearly known. Example: *¿Cocina Juan en la clase de ciencias?* → *¿Cocina en la clase de ciencias?*

1 Answers

a. ella
b. Ud.
c. él
d. ellos
e. Uds.
f. tú
g. ellas
h. nosotras

• Yo means "I."

• *Tú, usted,* and *ustedes* mean "you."
  a. Use *tú* with family members, close friends, people around your age or younger, and anyone you call by a first name.
  b. Use *usted* with adults and anyone you would address with a title of respect, such as *señor, señora,* etc. *Usted* is usually written as *Ud.*
  c. Use *ustedes* when speaking to two or more people, even if you would call them *tú* individually. We usually write it as *Uds.*

• There are two forms for "we" in Spanish: *nosotras* for females, and *nosotros* for males or for a mixed group of males and females.

• There are also two forms for "they." *Ellos* refers to a group of males or to a mixed group of males and females. *Ellas* refers to a group of females only.

• In Spanish, subject pronouns may be omitted because most verb forms indicate who the subject is: ***Tengo*** *ciencias en la primera hora.*

• Subject pronouns are usually used for emphasis or contrast, or if the subject is not clear: ***Él*** *es trabajador, pero* ***ella*** *es perezosa.*

1 With your partner, take turns telling which subject pronouns Ana would use to speak to or about these people.

a.   b.   c.   d.

e.   f.   g.   h.

72   Capítulo 2

Options

Strategies for Reaching All Students

Students Needing Extra Help
Ex. 1: Have students turn to their Organizers to review subject pronouns.
Ex. 2: Use further examples from your school and community to show students the distinction between the three forms of "you."

Enrichment
Ex. 2: Ask students to name three people they would address as *tú* in Spanish, and three people they would address as *Ud.*

2 Now tell which form of "you" you would use if you were speaking to these people.

a. your father
b. the principal
c. the girl next door
d. your teacher
e. your mother and sister
f. your cousin
g. an older person sitting next to you on the bus
h. three classmates

Verbos que terminan en *-ar*

A verb usually names the action in a sentence. We call the verb form that ends in *-r* the infinitive. It is the form you would find in a Spanish dictionary. It means "to ___." On the right are some of the infinitives you already know. We call these *-ar* verbs.

ayudar	nadar
cocinar	necesitar
dibujar	patinar
enseñar	practicar
escuchar	terminar
estudiar	tocar
hablar	

• In Spanish, the last letter or letters of the verb tell you who does the action.

• To change an infinitive to a form that tells who is doing the action, remove the *-ar* and add the appropriate ending.

ESTUDIAR

Singular		Plural	
(yo)	estud**io**	(nosotros) (nosotras)	estudi**amos**
(tú)	estudi**as**	(vosotros) (vosotras)	estudi**áis***
Ud. (él) (ella)	estudi**a**	Uds. (ellos) (ellas)	estudi**an**

* Verb forms ending in *-áis*, such as *estudiáis*, are used mainly in Spain. We will use them occasionally and you should learn to recognize them.

Gramática en contexto   73

2 Answers
a. tú (Ud.)
b. Ud.
c. tú
d. Ud.
e. Uds.
f. tú
g. Ud.
h. Uds.

 Practice Wkbk. 2-5, 2-6

 Prueba 2-5

Class Starter Review
On the day following initial presentation of *-ar* verbs, you might begin the class with this activity: Prepare a sheet of paper with the personal pronoun icons or use the transparency of pronouns (no words), photocopy a class set, and cut into flashcards. (You may wish to mount these on index cards.) Call out an *-ar* verb. Have pairs of students take turns showing each other their personal pronoun flashcards and saying the correct verb form. Change verbs at regular intervals.

Present & Practice

Re-enter / Recycle
Ex. 3: activities from Chap. 1

Answers
3 b., c., g.

• The verb forms in the chart are in the present tense. They are the equivalent of both "I study, you study, he or she studies" and "I'm studying, you're studying, he's or she's studying," and so on.

• When you want to say that you do *not* do something, use *no* before the verb form.

 Yo **no cocino** en la clase de educación física.

• When we ask a question in Spanish, we usually put the subject after the verb or sometimes at the end of the sentence.

 ¿Cocina **Juan** en la clase de ciencias?
 ¿Estudia mucho **Paulina?**

3 Imagine that someone from Colombia has just arrived at your school. Which of these statements could you use to tell this student what you personally do and what you need at school?

 a. Necesitamos bolígrafos y marcadores.
 b. Hablo inglés.
 c. Practico deportes.
 d. Necesitan un cuaderno para la clase de español.
 e. Tocamos la guitarra en la clase de música.
 f. Habla inglés.
 g. Necesito una mochila.
 h. Estudian mucho para la clase de ciencias.
 i. Cocinamos en la clase de ciencias sociales.
 j. Dibuja en la clase de arte.
 k. Estudia inglés.
 l. Necesita un diccionario para la clase de inglés.
 m. Habla inglés y español.
 n. Nadamos en la clase de educación física.
 o. Escuchan música en la clase de inglés.

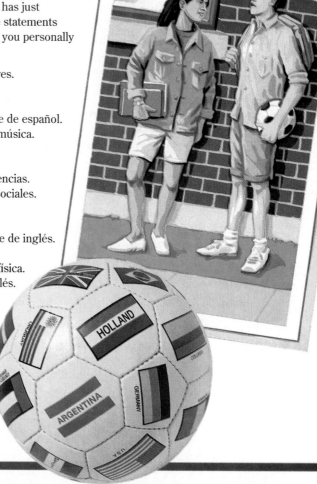

74 Capítulo 2

Options

Strategies for Reaching All Students

Spanish-Speaking Students
Ex. 6: Have Spanish-speaking students write out their answers and expand them where possible.

Students Needing Extra Help
Exs. 3–4: Have students fill in the verb chart in the Organizer so that they can refer to it when necessary.
Ex. 5: On the chalkboard or overhead, write the labels *Sandra y David, Carlos y yo, yo,* and *Norma.* Help students pair them with the correct verb forms. Have students use their Organizers.

Enrichment
Ex. 3: As a written exercise, have students group the sentences according to their verb endings. Then have them insert subjects into each of these sentences, using personal pronouns or proper nouns as required. They may also change each sentence by turning it either into a negative statement or into a question.

4 Which sentences in Exercise 3 could you use to tell about your friend Tomás? Which could you use to tell about Tomás and yourself? Which ones could you use to tell about two friends?

5 What school supplies do you and your classmates need for different classes? Talk about the students listed below.

a. what Sandra and David need
b. what Carlos and you need
c. what you need
d. what your friend Norma needs

6 Tell what these people are studying.

Ramón estudia matemáticas.

Ramón

a. Roberto

b. Max, Ana y yo

c. Samuel y Josefina

d. María y Linda

e. Ángela

f. Julia y yo

Practice Wkbk.
2-7, 2-8

Writing Activity 2-F

Prueba 2-6

Comm. Act. BLM 2-3

4 Tomás: f., j., k., l., m.
Tomás and yourself: a., e., i., n.
Two friends: d., h., o.

5 a. Necesitan . . . *(Answers will vary for school supplies.)*
b. Necesitamos . . .
c. Necesito . . .
d. Necesita . . .

6 a. Roberto estudia arte.
b. Max, Ana y yo estudiamos ciencias.
c. Samuel y Josefina estudian matemáticas.
d. María y Linda estudian inglés.
e. Ángela estudia música.
f. Julia y yo estudiamos español.

Ex. 6: Have students expand each answer by stating what school supplies they need as they study for each class.

Present & Practice

Re-enter / Recycle

Ex. 7: school supplies from
El primer paso

Answers

7 Be sure that students use indefinite articles in this exercise.

ESTUDIANTE A

a. ¿Tienes un lápiz?

b. ...una regla?

c. ...una carpeta de argollas?

d. ...un diccionario?

e. ...una calculadora?

f. ...un cuaderno?

g. ...una carpeta?

h. ...un marcador?

ESTUDIANTE B

a.–h. Sí, tengo. Aquí (allí) está. (No, lo siento.)

Los sustantivos

Nouns refer to people, animals, places, and things. In Spanish, nouns have gender. They are either masculine or feminine.

- Most nouns that end in *-o* are masculine. Most nouns that end in *-a* are feminine. For example:

  el libro   la calculadora

  There are a few exceptions. You know one: *el día*.

- Other Spanish nouns end in *-e* or a consonant. Some of these are masculine, and some are feminine. For example:

  el cine   el marcador
  la clase   la televisión

- A few nouns can be both masculine and feminine. For example: *el / la estudiante*.

- *El* and *la* are called definite articles and are the equivalent of "the" in English. We use *el* with masculine nouns, *la* with feminine nouns.

- *Un* and *una* are indefinite articles, like "a" and "an" in English. We use *un* with masculine nouns, *una* with feminine nouns.

It is a good idea to learn a noun with its definite article, *el* or *la*, because that will usually tell you the gender.

7 Take turns finding out which of these things you and your partner have with you right now.

A —*¿Tienes un libro?*
B —*Sí, tengo. Aquí está.*
   o: *Sí, tengo. Allí está.*
   o: *No, lo siento.*

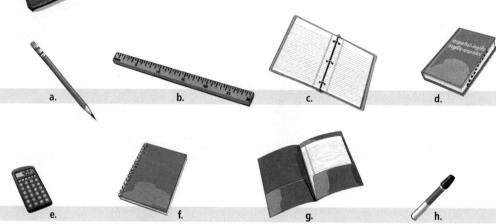

76   Capítulo 2

Options

Strategies for Reaching All Students

Students Needing Extra Help

Los sustantivos: Point out that the concept of masculine and feminine in Spanish deals with the spelling of the word, not with the actual definition in English of "masculine" and "feminine."

Ex. 7: If students don't have most of the school supplies with them, have them list what they should have brought to class.

Ahora lo sabes: Have students write out this section so that they can chart their progress.

76

Ahora lo sabes

Can you:

■ state who is doing an action without using people's names?

—¿Practican deportes Marta y Teresa?

—Sí, ___ nadan y patinan.

■ use the correct verb form to tell what you and others do regularly?

—¿Estudian Uds. para la clase de matemáticas?

—No, (nosotros) ___ para la clase de ciencias.

■ say that you do *not* do something?

—(Yo) ___ cocino en la clase de matemáticas.

■ use the appropriate subject pronouns when addressing someone?

—Miguel, ¿tocas ___ la guitarra?

—Señora, ¿habla ___ inglés?

—Jorge y Juan, ¿practican ___ deportes?

Gramática en contexto   77

Apply

 Pronunciation Tape 2-3

 ¡A conversar!

Play

Step

Using the Video
Video segment 3: See the Video Teacher's Guide.

 **Video Activity C**

Re-enter / Recycle
Ex. 1: numbers 0–31 from *El primer paso, gustar* expressions from Ch. 1
Ex. 2: *gustar* expressions from Chap. 1
Ex. 3: numbers 0–31 from *El primer paso*

Answers: Actividades
1 Dialogues will vary, but encourage students to use the full range of chapter vocabulary.

Para decir más

Here is some additional vocabulary that you might find useful for activities in this section.

la biología
biology

la computadora
computer

la historia
history

la literatura
literature

la química
chemistry

la física
physics

la economía doméstica
home economics

la geometría
geometry

la clase de computación
computer class

Actividades

Here's an opportunity for you to expand your use of Spanish by putting together the material you learned in this chapter with what you learned earlier.

1 Ask a partner:
• which classes he or she is taking
• who the teacher is
• what time each class begins
• when each class ends
• whether or not he or she likes the class

Afterward you can create a class schedule for each other, showing teachers' names and times.

Options

Strategies for Reaching All Students

Spanish-Speaking Students
Ex. 2: Have Spanish-speaking students expand their reasons why they like or don't like certain classes. You may wish to have them write out this exercise.

Students Needing Extra Help
Ex. 3: Give guidelines for when the Open House begins and ends. Work out the time schedule on the chalkboard to help speed time computations.

Enrichment
Para decir más: As a written assignment, students can list all the class subjects they now know in a chart with two columns: one with the heading *Me gusta la clase de . . .* and the other with *No me gusta la clase de . . . .*

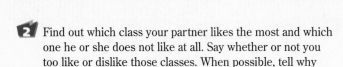

2 Find out which class your partner likes the most and which one he or she does not like at all. Say whether or not you too like or dislike those classes. When possible, tell why you like or dislike a given class.

A —¿Qué clase te gusta más?
B —Me gusta más la clase de ciencias.
A —A mí también. ¿Y qué clase no te gusta nada?
B —Pues, la clase de inglés. No me gusta mucho leer.
A —¿De veras? A mí sí me gusta.

3 Make a schedule in Spanish for a family member to follow at Open House at your school. Use your regular schedule, but make each period only 20 minutes long. Include the name of each class, who teaches it, which period, and when it begins and ends. When you have finished, compare your schedule with that of a partner.

2 Dialogues will vary, but look for logical reasons when possible.

3 Schedules will vary. Look for appropriate use of time-telling, names for school subjects, and class periods.

 Writing Activity 2-G

 Comm. Act. BLMs 2-4, 2-5

Muchachos y muchachas
jugando hockey sobre hierba

Actividades   79

Cultural Notes

Cooperative Learning
In groups of three or four, have students use Ex. 3 on p. 74 to list those activities that specifically apply to them during a normal school day. Ask one member from each group to tabulate everybody's responses, and then graph the results so that the information can be shared with the class or compiled to form a whole-class survey.

(p. 79, photo)
Most of Argentina's 33 million inhabitants are of European origin, primarily Spanish and Italian, as are these young field hockey players in Buenos Aires. The country's ties to Europe are markedly evident in the traditions, culture, and architecture of its big cities, particularly Buenos Aires, where approximately one third of Argentina's population is concentrated.

Apply

Process Reading
For a description of process reading, see p. 48.

Multicultural Perspectives
In most Spanish-speaking countries, students may take up to seven courses per school year. These may include: trigonometry, anatomy, history, geography, Spanish, English, French, physical education, and courses in fine arts. Ask students to compare their courses with those taken by their Spanish-speaking counterparts.

Answers

Antes de leer
Answers may include the student's name, class schedule, year in school, subjects, teachers' names, grades, comments, etc.

Mira la lectura
Answers will vary depending on what the student expected to find in the previous section.

¡Vamos a leer!

Antes de leer

STRATEGY ➤ Using prior knowledge

Depending on the kind of document we are reading, we can often predict the kind of information it will include. For example, in a menu we expect to find the names and prices of different dishes. In a bus schedule, we look for the time of arrival and departure of buses throughout the week, as well as ticket prices.

Here is a report card for a student in Mexico. Make a list of four things you might expect to find in a report card.

Mira la lectura

STRATEGY ➤ Scanning

Remember that scanning is a strategy to help you look for certain information.

Of the four things you listed, how many can you find on the report card shown here?

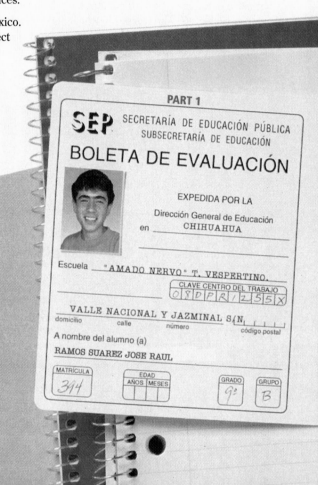

Options

Strategies for Reaching All Students

Students Needing Extra Help
Antes de leer: Have students brainstorm and list *all* possibilities, not just four.
Aplicación: Model a blank report card that your school uses. Use the Organizer to review the vocabulary for class subjects. You may wish to do this as a whole-class activity.

Infórmate

STRATEGY ➤ Scanning

As you read, match what you expected to find with the information given.

1 Study Part 1 of the *Boleta de evaluación.*

a. What is the name of the school?
b. Where is it located?
c. What is the name of the student?
d. What grade is he in? How old do you think he is?

2 Examine Part 2, *Resultados del aprendizaje.*

a. How many subjects did the student take?
b. How many grading periods were there during the school year?
c. Did the student's grades generally improve or decline during the year? In which subject(s) did he improve the most? In which was he most consistent? In which subject did he receive his lowest mark?
d. Using the scale explained in the *Escala de evaluación,* which words would you use to describe the student's overall academic work?

3 Read Part 3, *Asistencia.*

a. How many school days were there? How many days was the student absent?
b. In which month were there the fewest days of instruction?

4 Look at Part 4, *Resultado final.* Were you surprised by the student's final results for the year? Why or why not?

Aplicación

Design a report card in Spanish for your classes this year.

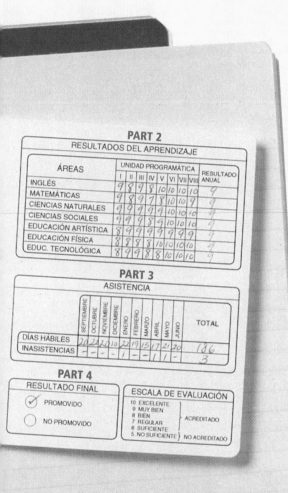

PART 2
RESULTADOS DEL APRENDIZAJE

ÁREAS	UNIDAD PROGRAMÁTICA								RESULTADO ANUAL
	I	II	III	IV	V	VI	VII	VIII	
INGLÉS	9	8	9	8	10	10	10	10	9
MATEMÁTICAS	9	8	9	7	8	10	10	9	9
CIENCIAS NATURALES	9	9	9	9	10	10	10		9
CIENCIAS SOCIALES	9	9	9	8	9	10	10	10	9
EDUCACIÓN ARTÍSTICA	8	9	9	9	9	9	9	9	
EDUCACIÓN FÍSICA	8	8	8	8	10	10	10	10	9
EDUC. TECNOLÓGICA	8	9	9	8	8	10	10	10	9

PART 3
ASISTENCIA

	SEPTIEMBRE	OCTUBRE	NOVIEMBRE	DICIEMBRE	ENERO	FEBRERO	MARZO	ABRIL	MAYO	JUNIO	TOTAL
DÍAS HÁBILES	20	22	20	10	22	19	15	17	21	20	186
INASISTENCIAS				1			1	1			3

PART 4

RESULTADO FINAL	ESCALA DE EVALUACIÓN
✓ PROMOVIDO	10 EXCELENTE 9 MUY BIEN 8 BIEN } ACREDITADO 7 REGULAR 6 SUFICIENTE 5 NO SUFICIENTE } NO ACREDITADO
○ NO PROMOVIDO	

Infórmate

Part 1:

a. Amado Nervo *(T. vespertino* means *turno vespertino.* This indicates that the student attends afternoon classes.)
b. Chihuahua, Mexico (Point out this state on a map.) Mention that the letters *S / N* in the student's home address stand for *sin número.* This means that he probably lives in a small village area where the street number is not required.
c. José Raúl Ramos Suárez
d. Ninth grade, around 13–14 years old

Part 2:

a. seven
b. eight
c. His grades generally improved. He improved the most in math and physical education. He was most consistent in art. His lowest mark was in math.
d. *muy bien*

Part 3:

a. 189, 3
b. December

Part 4:

Answers will vary, but most students should see that he was promoted to the next grade due to his good academic performance.

Aplicación

Guide this activity and show students a model.

Cultural Notes ☀

(pp. 80–81, realia)
As this report card from Mexico indicates, the grading system in most Mexican schools has traditionally been based on a scale of 1 to 10, with 10 being the highest grade and 6 or 7 the minimum passing grade. Letter grades similar to those in the U.S. are also used by some private secondary schools and institutions of higher education. The *Resultado final* of promotion or non-promotion is determined by the teacher's general evaluation of the student and not by any exam scores.

Apply

Process Writing
For information regarding developing a writing portfolio, see p. 50.

 Writing Activity 2-G

¡Vamos a escribir!

Write a letter to a Spanish-speaking friend about your school day. Follow these steps.

1 Write out your class schedule. Put a check mark beside those classes in which you have a lot of homework. Underline the classes that you like a lot.

2 Write your letter using the class schedule and the information you've added to it. On the right is an outline that will help you get started.

3 Now show your letter to a partner. Ask which parts might be changed. Decide whether or not you agree, then rewrite your letter, making any changes that you have decided on.

4 Check your letter for spelling and punctuation, including accents. Did you begin with the date and the greeting *Hola?* Did you end with a closing expression and your name?

5 Make any corrections and recopy. You might send your letter to:

- a new pen pal
- a student of Spanish in another school
- a student in another Spanish class at your school
- a student in your Spanish class

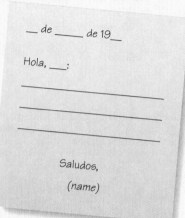

_ de _____ de 19_

Hola, ___:

_____

_____

_____

Saludos,

(name)

Options

Strategies for Reaching All Students

Spanish-Speaking Students
Have Spanish-speaking students answer the letter of one of the non-bilingual students. They can then compare classes and tell about a favorite class.

 Un paso más Exs. 2-G, 2-H

Students Needing Extra Help
Have students use their Organizers to check for spelling.

Enrichment
One organization through which you can arrange pen pals is: International Youth Service / PB 125 / SF-20101 / Turku, Finland.

"¡Hola! A mí me gustan muchas clases, pero me gusta más la clase de ciencias sociales."

Una estudiante prepara su tarea para las clases.

¡Vamos a escribir!   83

(p. 83, top photo)
This teenager is wearing a traditional outfit from the Colombian highlands: a straw hat known as a *jipijapa* and a *ruana* (a woolen cloak that measures about four square feet with an opening in the center for the head). Although traditional clothing is still common in rural Colombia, increasing numbers of people are adopting Western dress, which is now worn by nearly everyone in the cities.

You may want to assign parts of this section as written homework or as an in-class writing activity prior to administering the *Examen de habilidades*.

Answers

Listening: *Hoy tengo clase de ciencias sociales en la séptima hora y clase de arte a las 3:55.* He is talking about his afternoon schedule.

Reading: Mauricio has the following classes: English for first period, math for second, science for third, physical education for fourth, and lunch is fifth.

Writing: Lists will vary, but students should use the chapter vocabulary. Look for logical items. Remind them of *un / una* with masculine and feminine nouns.

Culture: Answers will vary, but may include: School uniforms, class schedules, length of school day, grades, homework, testing, student-teacher relationships, etc.

Speaking: Answers will vary, but look for expressions with *me / te gusta.* Encourage use of vocabulary from this chapter.

¿Lo sabes bien?

This section will help you organize your studying for the proficiency test, where you will be asked to do similar, though not identical, tasks. There will not be any models on the test.

Listening
Can you understand when people talk about their class schedules? Listen as your teacher reads you a sample similar to what you will hear on the test. Would you say the student making the statement is talking about his morning or afternoon schedule?

Reading
How well can you understand a person's written schedule? Scan the paragraph below. Can you chart out Mauricio's schedule based on this description?

Mauricio tiene muchas clases. En la primera hora tiene clase de inglés, su clase favorita. En la segunda hora tiene clase de matemáticas. La clase de ciencias es a las 10:00. La clase de educación física empieza a las 11:00 y termina a las 11:50. El almuerzo es a las 12:00.

Writing
Can you write a list of supplies you need for school? Your parents want to discuss the school supplies you need to buy. To prepare for the discussion, list under the headings provided below the supplies and the classes you need the supplies for. For example:

¿Qué?
regla

¿Para qué clases?
matemáticas, arte

Speaking
Ask a partner which classes he or she likes better, and which ones he or she doesn't like at all. Do you and your partner like and dislike the same classes? Here is a sample dialogue:

A —*¿Qué clase te gusta más?*
B —*Me gusta mucho la clase de música. También me gustan mucho la clase de ciencias y las matemáticas.*
A —*¿Qué clase no te gusta nada?*
B —*La clase de educación física. Yo soy muy perezosa. ¿Y tú?*

Culture
Can you list some possible differences between your school and one in Mexico City?

Options

Strategies for Reaching All Students

Students Needing Extra Help
You may wish to have students write out this section so that they can check off what they have mastered.

Resumen del capítulo 2

Use the vocabulary from this chapter to help you:

- describe your class schedule
- list some school supplies you use
- find out about someone else's schedule

to talk about school subjects
el almuerzo
el arte (f.)
las ciencias
las ciencias
   de la salud
las ciencias sociales
la clase de ___
la educación física
el español
el inglés
las matemáticas
la música
difícil
fácil
enseñar: enseña
la tarea

to talk about school supplies
la calculadora
la carpeta (de argollas)
el cuaderno
el diccionario
la grabadora
el horario
el lápiz, pl. los lápices
el marcador, pl. los marcadores
la mochila
la regla

to talk about what people need
necesitar: (yo) necesito
            (tú) necesitas

to say what something is for
para

to express possession
tener: (yo) tengo
       (tú) tienes
tu

to express quantity
mucho, -a
un, -a

to ask for information
¿Qué?

to ask and tell when something takes place
a
¿A qué hora ___?
empezar: empieza
terminar: termina
es
la hora
   la primera hora
   la segunda hora
   la tercera hora
   la cuarta hora
   la quinta hora
   la sexta hora
   la séptima hora
   la octava hora
el semestre
   el primer semestre
   el segundo semestre

to ask and tell the time
¿Qué hora es?
Es la una (y ___).
Son las ___ (y ___).

cuarto
media
treinta y dos
treinta y tres
treinta y cuatro ...
cuarenta
cuarenta y uno ...
cuarenta y nueve
cincuenta
cincuenta y uno ...
cincuenta y nueve

to express regret
Lo siento.

to express hesitation, to consider
A ver ...

to talk about location
aquí
   Aquí está.
allí
   Allí está.

to tell who performs an action
yo
tú
usted (Ud.)
él, ella
nosotros, -as
vosotros, -as
ustedes (Uds.)
ellos, -as
¿Quién?

Resumen   85

CAPÍTULO 3

THEME: SPORTS AND LEISURE ACTIVITIES

SCOPE AND SEQUENCE Pages 86–117

COMMUNICATION

Topics

Public buildings and places

Seasons

Sports and leisure activities

Objectives

To compare leisure-time activities in Spanish-speaking countries with those in the U.S.

To tell how someone feels or where someone is

To tell where someone is going

To talk about activities

To say when and with whom you do an activity

To express surprise, enthusiasm, or disappointment

To express possession

To extend, accept, or decline invitations

CULTURE

Leisure-time activities

Parks and *plazas*

GRAMMAR

El verbo ir

Ir + a + *infinitivo*

La preposición con

El verbo estar

Ancillaries available for use with Chapter 3

Multisensory/Technology

 Overhead Transparencies, 16–20

 Audio Tapes and CDs

 Vocabulary Art Blackline Masters for Hands-On Learning, pp. 18–22

 Classroom Crossword

 Video

CD-ROM

Print

 Practice Workbook, pp. 33–42

 Writing, Audio & Video Activities, pp. 17–22, 99–101, 156–157

 Communicative Activity Blackline Masters

Pair and Small Group Activities, pp. 22–27

Situation Cards, p. 28

 Un paso más: Actividades para ampliar tu español, pp. 13–19

Assessment

 Assessment Program

Pruebas, pp. 37–48

Examen de habilidades, pp. 49–51

 Test Generator

Video still from Chap. 3

85A

Teen Activities

Unlike in the U.S., where teen couples often go alone to a concert, movie, or a meal, young people in Latin America tend to socialize in groups until a couple's relationship is more serious. Generally, relationships are carefully scrutinized by parents, and family life has a strong influence on young people. Brothers and sisters often share the same group of friends and accompany each other on outings.

Night life in large Latin American cities such as Buenos Aires, Montevideo, Santiago de Chile, and Mexico City often begins late. During holidays, vacation, or on weekends, many teens often do not meet with friends until 10 P.M. or later. This late-night schedule is an inheritance from Mediterranean cultures where warm climates encouraged people to stay in during the heat of the day.

Besides going to movies, video arcades, and restaurants, teens in Latin America often meet at city parks. These parks, such as Chapultepec Park in Mexico City, attract pedestrians who stroll along the paths on their way to other destinations. Some rest for a while on park benches, chatting with friends or reading. Young couples may use the parks as meeting places where they can spend some time away from the scrutiny of family or friends.

Parks are lively places populated with many vendors who sell food, drinks, *paletas* (popsicles or ice cream bars), gum, small toys, and other treats. Some parks even include museums, small amusement parks, or zoos. Especially on weekends, parks have a very festive atmosphere and are a favorite destination for people of all ages.

Smaller towns are built around a *plaza,* which is a central square or public space where people meet to spend leisure time. *Cafés* and businesses surround the *plaza,* with concerts and other civic events held there. With trees and formal flower plantings, *plazas* are similar to our town squares and are comfortable spots for young people to gather and have fun.

Introduce

Re-entry of Concepts
The following list represents words, expressions, and grammar topics re-entered from *El primer paso* to Chap. 2:

El primer paso
Calendar expressions

Chapter 1
Activities
Gustar expressions
Adjectives describing personality

Chapter 2
School subjects
Time expressions
Possession
Personal pronouns

Planning

Cross-Curricular Connections

Geography Connection (pp. 90–91)
Have students create a map of North and South America and write in the current seasons above and below the equator. In pairs, they can select five states or countries from above and below the equator, and report on the current temperatures.

Business Education Connection (pp. 90–91)
Have students record on a daily basis the time and location of their activities for an entire week. Using this record as a personal profile, have them develop a time-management plan for the following week, including school and recreational activities.

Geography Connection (pp. 94–95)
In pairs, have students create a drawing of their ideal weekend vacation spot. Have them draw or cut out pictures to indicate featured activities and label each one. On the back, have them locate the vacation spot in a country or state, give the price for the trip, and provide some information on the weather in each season. Post these around the room and give points for the most creative or artistic.

CAPÍTULO 3

Los pasatiempos

OBJECTIVES

At the end of this chapter, you will be able to:

■ talk about some of your leisure-time activities

■ make plans with friends

■ extend, accept, or decline invitations

■ compare leisure-time activities in Spanish-speaking countries with those in the United States

En la piscina en Taxco, México

87

Preview

Cultural Objective

• To compare leisure-time activities in Spanish-speaking countries with those in the U.S.

 Los pasatiempos

Play

 Video Activity A

Teaching Suggestions

Bring several sports or leisure magazines or newspapers from Spanish-speaking countries to class. Share photos of the activities with your students, encouraging a discussion about how these activities compare with theirs.

Using the Video

This chapter's video focuses on sports and leisure activities. Students will see our hosts in Madrid visiting a famous park and interviewing athletes.
To prepare students for the video, first ask them to predict what this chapter's tape will be about. Then have students watch the segment several times. After the first time, you may wish to have them brainstorm possible vocabulary and expressions they will need to talk about what they saw on the video. Ask students to identify: a) things

¡Piénsalo bien!

Look at the photos and read the captions. How do the leisure activities of these teens compare to what you and your friends do? Which of these activities would you be most likely to do with your friends?

"Me encanta celebrar los días festivos y bailar flamenco."

What are these teens celebrating? By looking at the photo, how do teens participate in the celebration? Do you have similar festivals in your community?

En Sevilla, España

88   Capítulo 3

Options

Strategies for Reaching All Students

Spanish-Speaking Students
¡Piénsalo bien!: Ask students to describe what they see in the photos. In addition, you may want to ask: *¿Qué te gusta hacer con tus amigos? ¿Cuándo sales con tus amigos? ¿Cuándo vas a fiestas?*

Students Needing Extra Help
¡Piénsalo bien!: Discuss other activities that students are engaged in during weekends.

What do you think a "parque de diversiones" might be? And can you guess what the "montaña rusa" means?

"Me gusta mucho ir al parque de diversiones y montar la montaña rusa. ¡Pero a mi amiga Lupe no le gusta nada!"

"En el verano, me encanta ir a la playa y jugar vóleibol."

En Gijón, España

89

they saw that were familiar to them, and b) things they saw that they probably would not see in a park where they live.

Video segment 1: For more teaching suggestions, see the Video Teacher's Guide.

Multicultural Perspectives

In many urban Hispanic neighborhoods, *bodegas* (grocery stores) are an informal meeting place for people and for sharing news. Ask students, especially Spanish-speakers, if they know about any other types of informal meeting places from different cultures.

Answers: ¡Piénsalo bien!

Answers will vary to inductive questions.

(p. 88, photo) Students may say that they are celebrating some kind of festival. / They are together with friends. Some of them are dancing and wearing special outfits for the festival. / Answers will vary.

(p. 89, top photo) Students should be able to guess from context that a *parque de diversiones* means "amusement park." If students have difficulty with *montaña rusa* (roller coaster), tell them the literal translation ("Russian mountain"), and then see if they can guess the meaning.

Cultural Notes

(p. 88, photo)
The *sevillana,* a very popular kind of dance that originated in Sevilla, and is now well known in many other areas of Spain. Distinct from the *flamenco,* the *sevillana* is traditionally performed on three occasions: at *ferias* (town fairs), at spring parties known as *Cruces de mayo,* and on the annual pilgrimage to Nuestra Señora del Rocío.

(p. 89, bottom photo)
These teenagers are playing volleyball on San Lorenzo Beach in Gijón, a bustling city in Oviedo province, Spain. Situated on the Bay of Biscay in the region of Asturias, Gijón is a fishing port, a popular summer vacation resort, and a university town. In addition to the beach, Gijón offers folk festivals and many lively *cafés* and night spots for visitors.

Present

Chapter Theme
Leisure-time activities: Places to go

Communicative Objectives
- To tell where someone is going
- To say when and with whom you do an activity
- To talk about activities
- To express surprise, enthusiasm, or disappointment
- To express possession

 Transparencies 16–17

 Vocabulary Art BLMs

 Pronunciation Tape 3-1

 Vocabulario para conversar A

Play

Using the Video
Video segment 2: See the Video Teacher's Guide.

 Video Activity B

Vocabulario para conversar

¿Cuándo vas al parque?

Here are some new words and expressions you will need to talk about your leisure-time activities. Read them several times, then turn the page and practice with a partner.

Options

Strategies for Reaching All Students

Learning Spanish Through Action
STAGING VOCABULARY: *Señalen, Toquen*
MATERIALS: seasons from the Vocabulary Art BLMs or transparency
DIRECTIONS: Have students touch or point to one of the seasons. Then have them name an activity they like to do in that particular season.

las estaciones
(*sing.*, la estación)

la primavera

el verano

el otoño

el invierno

También necesitas . . .

a	here: *to*
a la, al *(a+el)*	*to the*
el pasatiempo	*hobby, pastime*
el lunes, el martes . . .	*on Monday, on Tuesday . . .*
los lunes, los martes . . .	*on Mondays, on Tuesdays . . .*
los fines de semana	*on the weekends*
después (de)	*after*
después de las clases	*after school*
(por) la mañana	*(in) the morning*
la tarde	*the afternoon*
la noche	*the evening*
generalmente	*usually, generally*
todos los días	*every day*
¡No me digas!	*Really? You don't say!*
mi, mis	*my*
tus	*your*

¿Y qué quiere decir . . . ?
¿Dónde?
ir: (yo) voy
   (tú) vas
con
el amigo, la amiga
la familia
solo, -a

Vocabulario para conversar 91

Grammar Preview
Voy / vas are previewed here. The complete paradigm of *ir* appears in the grammar section on p. 105.

Teaching Suggestions
Preparing students to speak: Use one or two options from each of the categories of Comprehensible Input, Physical Response, or Limited Verbal Response. For a complete explanation of these categories and some sample activities, see the front section of this Teacher's Edition.

Class Starter Review
On the day following initial presentation, you might begin the class with this activity:
Have students use *¿Cuándo tienes la clase de. . . ?* and *por la mañana / tarde* so that they can take turns asking for and giving information about their school schedules. Use visuals to elicit responses.

Practice & Apply

Reteach / Review: Vocabulary

Ex. 1: Expand this dialogue by having *Estudiante B* ask: *¿Y tú?* *Estudiante A* either gives the same answer using *también* or *tampoco,* or gives a different answer.
Ex. 2: Elicit another expression that can be used in place of *¡No me digas! (¿De veras?)*

Re-enter / Recycle

Ex. 2: *me / te gusta* from Chap. 1
Ex. 4: *me gusta* + activities from Chap. 1
Ex. 6: *me / te gusta* from Chap. 1

Answers: Empecemos a conversar

1 ESTUDIANTE A
a. ¿Cuándo vas al campo?
b. . . .a la piscina?
c. . . .al gimnasio?
d. . . .al centro comercial?
e. . . .al parque de diversiones?
f. . . .a la playa?
ESTUDIANTE B
a.–f. Answers will vary.

2 ESTUDIANTE A
a. ¿Qué te gusta hacer en la primavera?
b. . . .el verano?
c. . . .el otoño?
d. . . .el invierno?
ESTUDIANTE B
a.–d. Answers will vary. Look for *me gusta* + inf.

Empecemos a conversar

With a partner, take turns being *Estudiante A* and *Estudiante B.* Use the words that are cued or given in the balloons to replace the underlined sections in the model. 💡 means you can make your own choices.

¡NO OLVIDES!
a + el = al

1
A —*¿Cuándo vas al parque?*
B —*Voy los viernes.*
   o: *Pues, generalmente no voy.*
   Y ahora Uds.

Estudiante A   Estudiante B

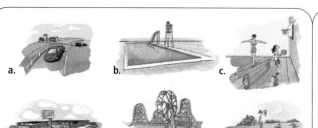

los lunes, los martes . . .

los fines de semana

todos los días

por la mañana / tarde / noche

después de las clases

2
A —*¿Qué te gusta hacer en el verano?*
B —*Me gusta nadar e* ir a la playa con mis amigos.*
A —*¡No me digas! A mí también.*
   Y ahora Uds.

Estudiante A   Estudiante B

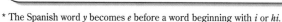

* The Spanish word *y* becomes *e* before a word beginning with *i* or *hi.*

92   Capítulo 3

Options

Strategies for Reaching All Students

Spanish-Speaking Students
In Ex. 4, Spanish-speaking students should mention at least five leisure activities.
In Ex. 7, also ask: *¿Por qué?*

 Un paso más Ex. 3-A

Students Needing Extra Help
Empecemos a conversar: Have students begin filling in their Organizers.
Exs. 1 and 3: Point out that *voy* and *vas* are used to state where someone is going. Explain why *vas* changes to *voy* in the response. Remind students that they need *a(l)* before the location. In Ex. 1, explain that *Estudiante B*'s responses are choices and are not to be used in the order given. Show the full verb chart to students who may need to see the pattern right away.

Ex. 5: Model on the chalkboard. Divide possibilities into interrogatives for people and places. Show students that they have practiced these questions in Exs. 1 and 3.
Empecemos a escribir: For additional practice, have students make four columns, labeling each one with a season. Using the vocabulary for places (p. 90), have them think about when they usually go there, and write the places in the appropriate columns.

3 A — ¿*Con quién vas al parque de diversiones?*

B — *Generalmente voy con mis amigos.*

o: *Generalmente voy solo(a).*

Y ahora Uds.

Estudiante A   Estudiante B

Empecemos a escribir

Write your answers in Spanish.

4 For each season write one activity that you enjoy doing.

5 Write questions to ask your partner about when and with whom he or she goes to three different places. Record your partner's answers.

6 ¿Te gusta más el verano o el invierno? ¿Qué estación no te gusta?

7 Generalmente, ¿adónde vas después de las clases? ¿Cuál es tu pasatiempo favorito?

También se dice

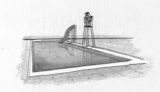

la alberca
la pileta

el parque de atracciones

3 Questions and answers will vary.

Answers: Empecemos a escribir

4 Answers will vary, but look for use of *me gusta* + inf.

5 Answers will vary. Look for *¿cuándo?* and *¿con quién?* along with use of *voy / vas.*

6 Answers will vary.

7 Answers will vary, but encourage students to use chapter vocabulary.

 Practice Wkbk. 3-1, 3-2

 Audio Activity 3.1

 Writing Activities 3-A, 3-B

 Pruebas 3-1, 3-2

 Comm. Act. BLM 3-1

Enrichment

Ex. 2: Students can prepare for this exercise by asking each other: ¿Qué te gusta más, la primavera, el verano, el otoño o el invierno?

Ex. 4: Students can also write about what they need to do in each season.

Ex. 7: Expand this exercise by having students tell with whom they go to that place.

Present

Chapter Theme
Leisure-time activities: Sports

Communicative Objectives
• To tell where someone is
• To talk about activities
• To extend, accept, or decline invitations
• To tell how someone feels
• To tell where someone is going
• To say when and with whom you do an activity
• To express surprise, enthusiasm, or disappointment

 Transparencies 18–19

 Vocabulary Art BLMs

 Pronunciation Tape 3-2

 Vocabulario para conversar B

Play

Using the Video
Video segment 2: See the Video Teacher's Guide.

 Video Activity B

Vocabulario para conversar

¿Te gustaría ir conmigo?

Here's the rest of the vocabulary you will need to talk about your leisure-time activities and to extend, accept, or decline invitations.

ir de compras

jugar básquetbol*

jugar fútbol

jugar vóleibol

jugar tenis

jugar béisbol

ir a una fiesta

jugar fútbol americano

ir de pesca

jugar videojuegos

* The names for the sports are all masculine, for example: *el básquetbol*.

94   Capítulo 3

Options

Strategies for Reaching All Students

Spanish-Speaking Students
Ask Spanish-speaking students to talk about their favorite leisure-time activities.

 Un paso más Exs. 3-B, 3-C

Enrichment
También necesitas. . . : Reinforce the difference between *mañana* and *por la mañana* by having students tell where they are going tomorrow morning. For example: *Mañana por la mañana voy al (a la). . . .*

Learning Spanish Through Action
STAGING VOCABULARY: *Señalen, Toquen*
MATERIALS: transparency of activities in the *Vocabulario para conversar* or pictures of similar activities from magazines
DIRECTIONS: Arrange the pictures on a bulletin board or use the transparency. Ask students to touch or point to one of the activities. You may wish to ask: ¿*Te gustaría (name of activity)?* Encourage students to use any appropriate response in *También necesitas. . .* for their answers.

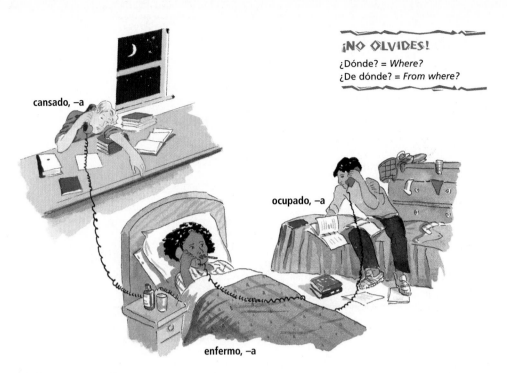

cansado, –a

ocupado, –a

enfermo, –a

¡NO OLVIDES!

¿Dónde? = Where?
¿De dónde? = From where?

También necesitas . . .

estar: (yo) estoy	to be: I am
(tú) estás	you are
¿Adónde?	(To) where?
conmigo, contigo	with me, with you
¿(A ti) te gustaría ___?	Would you like ___?
(A mí) me gustaría ___.	I would like ___.
poder: (yo) puedo	can: I can
(tú) puedes	you can
querer: (yo) quiero	to want: I want
(tú) quieres	you want
¡Claro que sí!	Of course!
¡Claro que no!	Of course not!
De nada.	You're welcome.
¡Genial!	Great! Wonderful!
¡Qué lástima!	That's too bad! That's a shame!

¿Y qué quiere decir . . . ?
Gracias.
hoy no
mañana*

* *Mañana* alone means "tomorrow"; *la mañana* means "morning."

Vocabulario para conversar 95

Grammar Preview
Estoy / estás are previewed here. The complete paradigm of estar appears in the grammar section on p. 108.

Teaching Suggestions
Preparing students to speak: Use one or two options from each of the categories of Comprehensible Input, Physical Response, or Limited Verbal Response. For a complete explanation of these categories and some sample activities, see the front section of this Teacher's Edition.

In current usage, native Spanish-speakers omit *a* + definite article after the verb *jugar*.

Class Starter Review
On the day following initial presentation, you might begin the class with this activity:
Call out each of the leisure-time activities. Have students signal (for example, thumbs up or thumbs down) if they like or don't like to do them. Have a volunteer keep a tally on the board of the activities that the class enjoys the most.

Practice

Re-enter / Recycle

Ex. 8: calendar expressions from *El primer paso*

Answers: Empecemos a conversar

8 ESTUDIANTE A

a. ¿Adónde vas el martes? / ¡No me digas! Yo también.

b. ...el miércoles? / ...

c. ...el jueves? / ...

d. ...el viernes? / ...

e. ...el sábado? / ...

f. ...el domingo? / ...

g. ...mañana? / ...

ESTUDIANTE B

a.–g. *Answers will vary.*
Suggested places include: Voy al centro comercial. / ...al campo. / ...al gimnasio. / ...a la playa. / ...al parque de diversiones.

9 ESTUDIANTE A

a. ¿Te gustaría jugar básquetbol conmigo?

b. ...ir de pesca...

c. ...jugar videojuegos...

d. ...ir de compras...

e. ...ir al cine...

f. ...jugar tenis...

ESTUDIANTE B

a.–f. Answers will vary.
Encourage students to select a different response each time.

Empecemos a conversar

8 el lunes

  A —¿*Adónde vas el lunes*?
  B —*Voy al parque.*
  A —¡*No me digas! Yo también.*
      Y ahora Uds.

Estudiante A   **Estudiante B**

a. el martes
b. el miércoles
c. el jueves
d. el viernes
e. el sábado
f. el domingo
g. mañana

9

  A —¿*Te gustaría ir a una fiesta conmigo*?
  B —¿*Contigo? Sí, me gustaría (mucho).*
      Y ahora Uds.

Estudiante A   **Estudiante B**

Pues, ¡claro que sí!

Lo siento, pero no puedo.

No puedo. Tengo mucha tarea.

¡Sí, genial! ¡Gracias!

¡Qué lástima! No puedo.

Sí, me gustaría (mucho).

96   Capítulo 3

Options

Strategies for Reaching All Students

Students Needing Extra Help

Empecemos a conversar: Have students continue filling in their Organizers.
Ex. 8: Remind *Estudiante B* to use *al* or *a la* before the pictured word.
Ex. 9: You may wish to explain responses for *Estudiante B.*

10
A —¿Puedes *ir al cine* conmigo?
B —*Hoy no; lo siento. Estoy ocupado(a).*
o: *¡Claro que no! Estoy enfermo(a).*

Y ahora Uds.

Estudiante A

Estudiante B

10 ESTUDIANTE A
a. ¿Puedes estudiar conmigo?
b. ... ir de pesca ...
c. ... ir de compras ...
d. ... jugar fútbol ...
e. ... jugar vóleibol ...
f. Questions will vary.
ESTUDIANTE B
a.–f. Answers will vary, but may include: ... *Estoy ocupado(a),* ... *cansado(a),* ... *enfermo(a).*

Practice & Apply

Reteach / Review: Vocabulary

Ex. 11: Students can do a variation of this exercise with *Estudiante A* asking *¿Te gustaría . . .?* and *Estudiante B* answering *Me gustaría, pero necesito . . . .*

Re-enter / Recycle

Ex. 11: activities from Chap. 1
Ex. 12: calendar expressions from *El primer paso*, time-telling from Chap. 2

Answers: Empecemos a conversar

11 Review activities vocabulary from Chap. 1.

ESTUDIANTE A
a. ¿Quieres ver la tele(visión)?
b. . . . escuchar música?
c. . . . jugar básquetbol?
d. . . . jugar béisbol?
e. . . . jugar fútbol americano?
f. . . . jugar fútbol?
g. . . . jugar vóleibol?

ESTUDIANTE B
a.–g. Answers will vary, but may include: . . . *Necesito ayudar en casa*, . . . *estudiar*, . . . *leer*, . . . *cocinar*.

11

A —*¿Quieres jugar videojuegos?*
B —*Quiero, pero no puedo. Necesito ir de compras.*
A —*¡Qué lástima!*

Y ahora Uds.

Estudiante A

a.
b.
c.
d.
e.
f.
g.

Estudiante B

98   Capítulo 3

Options

Strategies for Reaching All Students

Spanish-Speaking Students
Ex. 11: Pair bilingual and non-bilingual students. Have them write two or three more responses for *Estudiante B.*

 Un paso más Exs. 3-D, 3-E

Students Needing Extra Help
Exs. 12–16: Have students refer to their Organizers.

Enrichment
Ex. 15: Students can also write answers to *¿Qué no te gusta hacer los fines de semana?*

Empecemos a escribir y a leer

Write your answers in Spanish.

12 Write full sentences telling when you do any four of the following activities. You can mention the season, the day of the week, or time of day. For example:

En el otoño, voy a la playa los fines de semana.

or: *En la primavera, voy al campo los domingos.*

13 Write three excuses that you have learned how to say in this chapter.

14 ¿Qué te gustaría hacer hoy después de las clases?

15 ¿Qué quieres hacer el sábado por la noche?

16 ¿Es lógico o no?

"No soy nada atrevido. Al contrario, soy muy prudente. Generalmente voy al parque de diversiones cuando estoy cansado."

"¡Qué lástima! Estoy enferma hoy y no puedo ir de compras contigo."

"Soy paciente y me gusta estar sola. En el verano, cuando no estoy ocupada los fines de semana, me gusta mucho ir de pesca."

También se dice

jugar baloncesto

jugar balonvolea

Vocabulario para conversar   99

Answers: Empecemos a escribir y a leer

12 Suggested activities include: *ayudar en casa, ir a la escuela, ir de compras, ir de pesca, ir a la playa, ir al cine, practicar deportes, nadar, ir al gimnasio.*

13 Answers may include: *no puedo, estoy . . .; hoy no; me gustaría, pero . . . .*

14–15 Answers will vary.

16 No es lógico; Sí, es lógico; Sí, es lógico.

Practice Wkbk. 3-3, 3-4

Audio Activity 3.2

Writing Activities 3-C, 3-D

Pruebas 3-3, 3-4

Comm. Act. BLM 3-2

Practice

Re-enter / Recycle
Exs. 2–3: time-telling from Chap. 2

Answers:
¡Comuniquemos!

1 ESTUDIANTE A

a. ¿Quieres jugar básquetbol conmigo?

b ...jugar videojuegos ...

c. ...ir de pesca ...

d. ...estudiar ...

e. Questions will vary.

ESTUDIANTE B

a. Me gustaría, pero hoy voy al centro comercial con mi familia.

b. ...al campo ...

c. ...al parque de diversiones ...

d. ...al parque ...

e. Answers will vary.

2 Dialogues will vary. Places suggested for *Estudiante B* include *el centro comercial* and *el campo*.

¡Comuniquemos!

Here's another opportunity for you to use the vocabulary you've just learned.

1 Ask a partner to join you in an activity. He or she will refuse politely.

A— *¿Quieres patinar conmigo?*
B— *Me gustaría, pero hoy voy a la playa con mi familia.*

a.

b.

c.

d.

e.

Options

Strategies for Reaching All Students

Spanish-Speaking Students
Ex. 3: Have students write out the questions.

 Un paso más Exs. 3-F, 3-G

Students Needing Extra Help
Ex. 1: Help students see the pattern by pointing out the words that don't change.
Ex. 2: Review time-telling from Chap. 2.
Ex. 3: Model the exercise. Refer to time-telling in Chap. 2.
¿Qué sabes ahora?: Have students write out this section so that they can check off what they have mastered.

Enrichment
Ex. 1: As a written assignment, students can continue this dialogue with *Estudiante A* asking about another day to do the activity and the two of them settling on a time.
Ex. 2: Have students expand this dialogue with *Estudiante A* asking about another time *(¿Y el viernes a las tres?)* and *Estudiante B* either making another excuse or saying that he or she is free and then asking what *Estudiante A* would like to do.

2 Your partner wants to get together with you, but you are always busy.

A — *¿Estás ocupado(a) el sábado a las nueve?*
B — *Sí. Voy al parque para jugar béisbol.*
A — *¡Qué lástima!*

Estudiante A   **Estudiante B**

3 You're going to a party Friday night. Find out from a partner what time the party begins and with whom he or she is going. If your partner is going alone, ask if he or she would like to go with you.

¿Qué sabes ahora?

Can you:

■ say what you would like to do after class?

—___ ir al cine después de las clases.

■ say that you want to do an activity but cannot?

—___ ir a la playa, pero ___.

■ invite someone to do something with you?

—¿___ ir de compras conmigo?

■ accept or decline an invitation?

—¿Te gustaría ir al cine el sábado?

—Sí (No), ___.

3 Answers will vary, but encourage students to use the full range of chapter vocabulary.

Answers: ¿Qué sabes ahora?

• Me gustaría
• Quiero, no puedo
• Quieres
• gracias (no puedo, no quiero)

Multicultural Perspectives

Ball games similar to soccer were popular in the Americas long before the Spaniards arrived. The Mayas played a team game on large stone courts in which the players tried to hit a large rubber ball—with their elbows, hips, or knees—through vertical wood or stone rings placed about 20 feet above the ground. Such games had a religious significance to its participants. Some scholars believe the ball represented the sun and that the two teams fought a symbolic struggle between the forces of light and darkness, or life and death. Evidence suggests that the losing team was sometimes offered up as a sacrifice to the Mayan gods. Ask students to share with the class any information that they might have about games played by other cultures.

 Audio Activity 3.3

Strategies for Reaching All Students

Cooperative Learning
Supply each student with a blank index card. Divide the class into groups of three. First ask students to write down a season of the year, and to then pass their cards to the right. Next, have them write an activity they like to do, based on the season written on the card they have. Finally, have them pass the cards once more to the right. Tell them to write down an expression of frequency (for example: *todos los días, los sábados, por la mañana,* etc.). Ask a member from each group to summarize. Have the class compile all the information in a chart to find out which seasons, activities, or expressions of frequency were listed the most.

Present & Apply

Cultural Objective
• To talk about parks and leisure-time activities

Teaching Suggestions
Before they read the text, ask students to look at the photos and then discuss any similarities or differences between these parks and those in their neighborhood.

Critical Thinking: Identifying Evidence
After students have read the text, ask them: Which paragraphs provide information that parks in Spanish-speaking countries have a wide variety of family-oriented activities? (Paragraph two mentions an amusement park and a zoo. Paragraph four talks about a playground with vendors selling ice cream or balloons.)

Perspectiva cultural

Muchas personas, generalmente, van al parque los fines de semana. Van con la familia, con los amigos o van solas a practicar deportes, leer, visitar museos o a hacer un picnic y conversar.

Look at the photos. Why might a family often choose to spend time together in these places?

Mexico City's Chapultepec Park is one of the largest in the world. It has a castle, a zoo, a botanical garden, and a world-famous anthropological museum. It also contains an amusement park, which offers a variety of rides—*la montaña rusa* (roller coaster), *la rueda de feria* (Ferris wheel), *los carros locos* (bumper cars), and so on.

In the Retiro Park in Madrid you could visit the Crystal Palace, where numerous expositions are held, or row a boat in the *estanque* (lake).

However, most parks are not very big. In small cities and towns, the main outdoor gathering place would be a *plaza,* a small green area that usually includes a small playground. Like the park, the *plaza* is where people meet to exchange news and local gossip, and where vendors sell *paletas* (popsicles or ice cream bars) or *globos* (balloons). In many cities, the *plaza,* or town square, is truly the heart of town. Many families will often spend an entire Sunday afternoon in a *plaza* or a park.

La cultura desde tu perspectiva

1 In what ways are parks in Spanish-speaking countries similar to or different from parks that you know? Have you ever visited a park that has facilities similar to the ones in Chapultepec or El Retiro?

2 If you lived near El Retiro or Chapultepec, how often do you think you would go there? Why?

El parque del Retiro en Madrid, España

102   Capítulo 3

Options

Strategies for Reaching All Students

Spanish-Speaking Students
Ask: *¿Dónde está tu parque favorito? ¿Cómo es? ¿Con quién vas allí? ¿Cómo son los parques cerca de tu casa o tu escuela? ¿Qué te gustaría tener en un parque ideal? ¿Cómo sería tu parque ideal?* (Responses can be oral or written.)

 Un paso más Exs. 3-H, 3-I, 3-J

Enrichment
Additional questions for discussion: How have parks changed since you were a child? What do you think parks will be like in the future? What kinds of things do you like to do in parks? What would your ideal park be like?

Una plaza en San Juan, Puerto Rico

El parque de Chapultepec en la Ciudad de México

Perspectiva cultural 103

The area we now know as Chapultepec Park was developed by the Aztecs in the fourteenth century. In 1325, the Aztecs built the magnificent city of Tenochtitlán on the present-day site of Mexico City. The city, the capital of the Aztec Empire, had a population of around 100,000 in 1519, when the Spanish arrived. Although Chapultepec Park may be enjoyed by everyone today, its use originally was restricted to Aztec emperors. Ask students to share any information that they might have about the Aztecs.

Answers

Possible answers to inductive questions: Students may say that families might often choose to spend time together in parks, such as the ones in the photos, because they offer attractive, well-equipped facilities that appeal to people.

Answers: La cultura desde tu perspectiva

1 Answers will vary. Similarities may include: gardens, paths, lakes, fountains, monuments, etc. Differences may include: castles, zoos, restaurants, and amusement parks. / Answers will vary.

2 Answers will vary.

Cultural Notes ☀

(p. 102, photo)
El parque del Retiro in Madrid is a large, elegantly planned park. Dating to 1630, it was originally intended to be a *buen retiro* (nice retreat) for Felipe IV. Today it serves that function for the millions who go there to stroll, picnic, rent rowboats on its central lake (which is graced by a statue of Spain's twentieth-century monarch, Alfonso XII), and enjoy puppet theater, art exhibits, and concerts.

(p. 103, top photo)
Town square in Old San Juan, Puerto Rico. People in Hispanic countries generally spend a great deal more time outdoors than we do in the U.S. Parks, *plazas,* and *cafés* are so popular in Spain and Latin America that they tend to be very crowded, particularly in the evenings and on weekends, as residents take part in people-watching and engaging in conversation with family and friends.

(p. 103, bottom photo)
El parque de Chapultepec is the largest and most important park in Mexico City. The area is also a very old recreation spot, having been used by Aztec kings as a summer residence. Chapultepec is especially crowded on Sundays, when families come to stroll, picnic, and otherwise enjoy the many attractions the park has to offer. Among them are a world-famous zoo, an amusement park, fountains, lakes, museums, and art galleries.

Preview

 Transparency 20

Answers

Answers will vary, but may include location, facility information, activities, etc.

A *El Campamento Bella Vista está a dos kilómetros de la playa y es el lugar perfecto para sus vacaciones.* / *está* / three

B swimming, fishing, horseback riding, sunbathing, listening to music, playing sports (basketball) / *van* / *van* and *vamos*

C Students should be able to guess from meaning that the sentences read: "(you) are going to swim" and "(you) are going to listen to music." / Answers should include that we use a form of *ir* + *a* + inf. to tell what someone is going to do.

Gramática en contexto

Look at the brochure describing a family vacation camp. What kind of information would you expect to find in a brochure such as this?

¿Está Ud. cansado?
¿Necesita unas vacaciones?

El campamento Bella Vista está a su disposición.

Ud., su familia y sus amigos van a pasar unos días maravillosos con nosotros. El campamento Bella Vista está a dos kilómetros de la playa y es el lugar perfecto para sus vacaciones. Nosotros vamos a preparar un plan de actividades que les va a gustar.

Por la mañana van a nadar en la piscina olímpica o ir de pesca en la costa.

Por la tarde van a montar a caballo en el campo o tomar el sol en la playa.

Por la noche van a escuchar música o practicar deportes.

Para hacer reservas o para obtener más información, llame al 1-555-776-6181

A Find the sentence that tells where the camp is located. What verb is used? How many times does it appear in the brochure?

B What activities are planned for guests? What verb is used with each pair of activities? (HINT: You already know two forms of the verb *ir: voy* and *vas.*) What do you think the *ustedes* and *nosotros* forms of the verb *ir* might be?

C In the brochure, *van a* is always followed by a verb. What do you think *van a nadar* and *van a escuchar música* mean? Based on what you've seen here, could you create a rule for this?

104 Capítulo 3

Options

Strategies for Reaching All Students

Students Needing Extra Help
Have students fill in the *ir* chart in the grammar portion of the Organizer.
Ex. 1: Remind students that the verb form changes in some responses. Show how the *a* in *adónde* is shown again in the answers as *al* or *a la.*

El verbo *ir*

You know that verbs whose infinitives end in *-ar* follow a pattern. The endings show who is doing the action: *(yo) cocino (tú) cocinas,* and so on.

- Verbs that follow certain patterns are called regular verbs. Those that do not follow those patterns are called irregular. The verb *ir,* "to go," is irregular. It is often followed by the word *a: Voy al cine.* Here are its present-tense forms.

(yo)	**voy**	(nosotros) (nosotras)	**vamos**
(tú)	**vas**	(vosotros) (vosotras)	**vais**
Ud. (él) (ella)	**va**	Uds. (ellos) (ellas)	**van**

1 There is a teachers' meeting today and you have the day off from school. Everyone is going to a different place. With a partner, take turns asking and answering questions about where the following people are going.

A — *¿Adónde va Carlos?*
B — *Va al parque.*

Carlos

a. **Felipe y Ramón**
b. **Uds.**
c. **Anita**

d. **Isabel y Elena**
e. **Gustavo**
f. **tú**

Class Starter Review

On the day following the initial presentation of *ir,* you might begin the class with this activity:
Have pairs of students alternate giving subject pronouns and the correct form of the verb *ir.* As a variation, have students make up complete sentences rather than just stating the correct verb form. This activity may be done on the chalkboard or on a transparency.

Answers

1 ESTUDIANTE A
a. ¿Adónde van Felipe y Ramón?
b. . . . van Uds.?
c. . . . va Anita?
d. . . . van Isabel y Elena?
e. . . . va Gustavo?
f. . . . vas tú?

ESTUDIANTE B
a. (Felipe y Ramón) van al gimnasio.
b. (Nosotros, -as) vamos al campo.
c. (Anita) va al centro comercial.
d. (Isabel y Elena) van a la piscina.
e. (Gustavo) va a la playa.
f. Voy . . . .*(Answers will vary.)*

Practice Wkbk. 3-5

Writing Activity 3-E

Prueba 3-5

Present & Practice

Re-enter / Recycle

Exs. 2–5: activities from Chap. 1

Answers

2 a.–h. Look for correct use of *¿Vas a* + inf.? and *Sí (No), voy a* + inf.

3 Statements will vary, but look for correct use of *(No) va a* + inf.

 Practice Wkbk. 3-6

 Writing Activity 3-F

 Prueba 3-6

Ir + *a* + infinitivo

We also use a form of the verb *ir* + *a* + infinitive to tell what someone is going to do.

> Yo **voy a nadar**. Y tú, ¿**vas a jugar** fútbol?

2 With a partner, take turns asking and answering whether or not you're going to do these things tomorrow.

ir al cine
A —¿*Vas a ir al cine mañana por la tarde?*
B —*Sí, voy a ir.*
    o: *No, voy a ir al centro comercial.*

a. estudiar
b. ayudar en casa
c. ir al centro comercial
d. ir a una fiesta
e. jugar básquetbol
f. jugar fútbol americano
g. jugar vóleibol
h. jugar béisbol

3 Based on the answers your partner gave in Exercise 2, tell another student what your partner will and will not do tomorrow.

Niños paseando en bote en el estanque de la plaza de España, Sevilla

La preposición *con*

When you want to say that you do something with another person, use the word *con. Con* may be used with the names of people or in the following ways:

conmigo	**con nosotros / nosotras**
contigo	**con vosotros / vosotras**
con Ud. / él / ella	**con Uds. / ellos / ellas**

106   Capítulo 3

Options

Strategies for Reaching All Students

Spanish-Speaking Students
Ex. 2: Have students write five statements about themselves.
Ex. 3: Have them write five statements about their partners.

Students Needing Extra Help
Ex. 2: Model, emphasizing the *ir* + *a* + inf. construction. Point out that in c and d the infinitive is *ir*, as this may cause confusion. Have students write out responses in preparation for Ex. 3.
Ex. 3: Point out that *voy* in the responses for Ex. 2 becomes *va* when referring to another person.
La preposición con: Have students fill in this grammar portion of their Organizers.

Ex. 4: Remind students that *conmigo* is answered with *contigo.*
Ex. 5: Show students how a female name is replaced with *ella* and a male name with *él.* Students may need a model to see that *Uds.* becomes *nosotros (-as)* in the answer, and that *tú* will become *contigo* and will be answered with *conmigo.*

4 With a partner, take turns asking each other about doing these activities together.

estudiar

A —*¿Quieres estudiar conmigo después de las clases?*
B —*¿Contigo? ¡Claro que sí!*
  o: *¿Contigo? Me gustaría, pero no puedo.*

a. ver la tele

b. practicar deportes

c. ir al gimnasio

d. ir de compras

e. jugar videojuegos

f. jugar tenis

g. jugar fútbol

h.

5 Take turns asking a partner with whom he or she would like to do these activities.

A —*¿Con quién te gustaría ir al cine el sábado?*
B —*Con Alicia.*
A —*¿Con ella?*
B —*Sí, con ella.*

Alicia

a. Susana y Julia

b. Marcelo y Graciela

c. Uds.

d. Marcos

e. Ana María

f. tú

Gramática en contexto   107

4 ESTUDIANTE A
a. ¿Quieres ver la tele conmigo después de las clases?
b. . . . practicar deportes . . .
c. . . . ir al gimnasio . . .
d. . . . ir de compras . . .
e. . . . jugar videojuegos . . .
f. . . . jugar tenis . . .
g. . . . jugar fútbol . . .
h. Questions will vary.

ESTUDIANTE B
a.–h. Answers will vary.

5 ESTUDIANTE A
a. ¿Con quién te gustaría ir de compras el sábado? / ¿Con ellas?
b. . . . ir al parque de diversiones . . . / ¿Con ellos?
c. . . . ir a una fiesta . . . / ¿Con nosotros(as)?
d. . . . ir al gimnasio . . . / ¿Con él?
e. . . . patinar . . . / ¿Con ella?
f. . . . nadar . . . / ¿Conmigo?

ESTUDIANTE B
a. Con Susana y Julia. / Sí, con ellas.
b. Con Marcelo y Graciela. / Sí, con ellos.
c. Con Uds. / Sí, con Uds.
d. Con Marcos. / Sí, con él.
e. Con Ana María. / Sí, con ella.
f. Contigo. / Sí, contigo.

 Practice Wkbk. 3-7

 Writing Activity 3-G

 Prueba 3-7

Enrichment
Ex. 2: As a written assignment, students can tell what they are going to do on each day of the weekend, specifying whether they'll be doing it alone or with family or friends.

107

Present & Practice

Class Starter Review

On the day following the initial presentation of *estar*, you might begin the class with this activity: Use the Vocabulary Art BLMs showing the places in the *Vocabulario para conversar* and Transparency 76 (subject pronouns). Have pairs of students alternate saying where different people are.

Answers

6 ESTUDIANTE A

a. ¿Dónde está Rosa?

b. . . . está José Antonio?

c. . . . están Uds.?

d. . . . están Carolina y Lucía?

e. . . . está Silvia?

f. . . . estás (tú)?

ESTUDIANTE B

a. Está en el parque.

b. Está en el parque de diversiones.

c. Estamos en el centro comercial.

d. Están en el gimnasio.

e. Está en la piscina.

f. Answers will vary.

El verbo *estar*

Estar ("to be") is an irregular verb. We use it to tell how someone feels or where someone is. Here are its present-tense forms.

(yo)	**estoy**	(nosotros) (nosotras)	**estamos**
(tú)	**estás**	(vosotros) (vosotras)	**estáis**
Ud. (él) (ella)	**está**	Uds. (ellos) (ellas)	**están**

• In writing, be sure to use the accent mark on all forms except *estoy* and *estamos*.

6 With a partner, take turns asking and answering where these people are.

A — *¿Dónde está Alejandro?*
B — *Está en el campo.*

Alejandro

a. Rosa   b. José Antonio   c. Uds.

d. Carolina y Lucía   e. Silvia   f. tú

Options

Strategies for Reaching All Students

Students Needing Extra Help

Have students fill in the *estar* chart in the grammar portion of the Organizer.

Ex. 6: Have students use the Organizer.

Ahora lo sabes: Have students write out this section so that they can check off what they have mastered.

7 Find out from several classmates how they are feeling today. Take turns asking and answering using *bien*, *enfermo(a)*, *ocupado(a)*, or *cansado(a)*.

Ahora lo sabes

Can you:

- say where someone is going?
  —Mariana y yo ___ a la piscina.
- say what someone is going to do?
  —Alejandro y Marta ___ jugar básquetbol mañana.
- say who does an activity with you?
  —Mis amigos estudian ___ después de las clases.
- say how someone feels?
  —Felipe ___ muy cansado hoy.
- say where someone is?
  —José y Ana ___ aquí.

¡NO OLVIDES!

Many adjectives end in -o in the masculine and in -a in the feminine. Those ending in -e can describe either masculine or feminine nouns.

Juguando béisbol en la República Dominicana

Gramática en contexto   109

Cultural Notes

(p. 109, photo)
Baseball is by far the leading sport in the Dominican Republic. Fans avidly follow both U.S. and Caribbean major league teams. The port city of San Pedro Macorís is noted for producing more professional baseball players than any other place in the world. Juan Samuel and Joaquín Andujar are just two of the outstanding baseball players on U.S. major league teams who started their careers in San Pedro Macorís.

Apply

Pronunciation Tape 3-3

¡A conversar!

Play

Step

Using the Video
Video segment 3: See the Video Teacher's Guide.

Video Activity C

Re-enter / Recycle
Exs. 1–2: days of the week from *El primer paso*

Using Realia
Ask students to identify the information that gives the date and price of admission on the ticket from this page *(23 de junio, 10 pesos nuevos)*.

You may want to point out the difference in spelling for *folclórico* (on the ticket) and *folklórico* (in the photo caption). The former represents one way that this particular dance troupe wishes to individualize itself; the latter is a more traditional spelling for a

Para decir más
Here is some additional vocabulary that you might find useful for activities in this section.

jugar hockey
to play hockey

hacer gimnasia
to do gymnastics

ir a la iglesia
to go to church

ir al templo
to go to temple

ir a la mezquita
to go to the mosque

El ballet folklórico de México

110   Capítulo 3

Actividades
Here's an opportunity for you to expand your use of Spanish by putting together the material you learned in this chapter with what you learned earlier.

 Your teacher will designate certain parts of the room as favorite places to go when you are not in school. Choose your favorite place and go to that part of the room. With the other students who are there, discuss when you go to that place. Keep a tally of your group's responses.

A — *¿Cuándo vas a la playa?*
B — *Generalmente los sábados o los domingos.*

As a group, be prepared to report on the results of your poll.

A — *¿Cuándo van Uds. a la playa?*
B — *Tres estudiantes van a la playa los sábados.*
C — *Pablo y yo vamos a la playa en el verano.*

Options

Strategies for Reaching All Students

Spanish-Speaking Students
Pair bilingual and non-bilingual students for the activities in this section.

Students Needing Extra Help
Ex. 1: Brainstorm possibilities for places. (See Ex. 1, p. 92.)
Ex. 2: For extra practice, see if students can combine the two brief dialogues into one longer one.
Ex. 3: Model and have students use the Organizer.

Enrichment
Ex. 3: As a written assignment, students can modify the dialogue to include asking with whom their partner is going.

2 Tell your partner at least four things that you are going to do this weekend. Mention either when or with whom you are going to do the activities. Your partner will ask about the missing information.

A —*Voy a ir a la piscina el sábado.*
B —*¿Con quién?*
A —*Voy con Enrique.*
  o: *Voy solo(a).*

A —*Voy a ir a la piscina con Enrique.*
  o: *Voy a ir a la piscina solo(a).*
B —*¿Cuándo (vas a ir allí)?*
A —*El sábado.*

"Después de las clases,
voy a la playa con mis amigos."

3 With a partner, create a dialogue:
• find out where your partner is going
• ask if you can go with him or her
• your partner accepts
  or declines politely

"Cuando estoy sola,
me gusta leer."

ENCIENDA
SU
IMAGINACIÓN

LEER,
TAN DIVERTIDO
COMO VER
TELEVISIÓN

ES RICO LEER
PLAN NACIONAL DE LECTURA
PRESIDENCIA DE LA REPÚBLICA

Actividades   111

different troupe. *(See the Cultural Notes on the bottom of this page for more details.)*

Answers: Actividades
1 Questions and answers will vary, but look for correct use of *ir* forms. Places may include: *el centro comercial, el campo, la playa, el cine, el parque de diversiones, la piscina, el gimnasio, el parque.*

2 Dialogues will vary, but encourage students to use the full range of previously learned vocabulary.

3 Dialogues will vary, but look for correct use of ir forms, *puedo / puedes*, and *conmigo / contigo*. To decline an invitation, remind students that they can use expressions such as: *Tengo mucha tarea. / No me gusta ___. / Necesito ___.*

 Writing Activity 3-I

 Comm. Act. BLMs 3-4, 3-5

Cultural Notes ☀

Cooperative Learning
Divide the class into groups of four. Have each group brainstorm and prepare a list of activities that they and their friends are going to do this weekend. After a time limit of five minutes, have one member from each group share the results with the class.

(p. 110, photo / realia)
The Mexico City Ballet Folclórico Nacional Aztlán performs twice weekly in the elegant Teatro de la Ciudad, a stately, neoclassical building inaugurated in 1912. Tickets are less expensive and easier to obtain for performances of this newer, yet very distinguished troupe than for those of the world-famous Ballet Folklórico, whose spectacular repertoire of traditional dances is performed in the theater of the Palacio de Bellas Artes.

(p. 111, realia)
The Colombian government's commitment to increasing literacy is indicated by this ad promoting reading as an activity "as entertaining as watching television." In 1973 the rate of adult literacy was approximately 81 percent. A loan of $100 million from the World Bank in 1988 to improve primary education—plus continuing government measures—brought this figure to 86.7 percent by 1990.

Apply

Process Reading
For a description of process reading, see p. 48.

Teaching Suggestions
For sections 3–4 in *Infórmate,* emphasize the concepts rather than the content. For example, in Mexico, Spain, and South America, the 24-hour clock tends to be used in advertisements for events.

Explain that people from the U.S. making purchases in other countries will need to know the exchange rate and use a little math to calculate prices.

Answers
Antes de leer
Answers will vary, but may include activities along with their respective information for location, date, time, and price of admission.

Mira la lectura
1 Friday, Saturday, and Sunday

2 Saturday offers the greatest selection of activities with theater, sports (soccer), and music (concerts).

¡Vamos a leer!

Antes de leer

STRATEGY ➤ Using prior knowledge

Earlier you used your own experience with certain kinds of reading materials to predict the types of information you might find in a pen pal column or report card. If you are looking at a calendar of events, what types of information would you expect to find?

Remember that what you already know about a newspaper section like this in English can help you predict, look for, and even understand information in Spanish.

CALENDARIO

CIUDAD JUÁREZ

VIERNES 16

TEATRO.- Festival de Teatro de la UACJ Verano 93 presenta a su compañía con "Si algo te debo" en el Teatro del Centro de Convenciones Universitario en P.E. Calles y Hnas Escobar. Admisión N$10.00. Funciones a las 20:00 horas.

SÁBADO 17

TEATRO.- Festival de Teatro de la UACJ Verano 93 presenta a su compañía con "Si algo te debo" en el Teatro del Centro de Convenciones Universitario en P.E. Calles y Hnas Escobar.
Admisión N$10.00./20:00 horas.
FUTBOL con las Cobras en el inicio de temporada. Estadio Olímpico Benito Juárez a las 20:00 horas. Boletos en Superettes del Río.
MÚSICA: Grupo Liberación, en los Jardines Carta Blanca a las 20:00 horas, costo $30 pesos nuevos.
Little Joe y la Familia, La Peluza y los Ases del Norte en la explanada de la Feria Juárez, desde las 20:00 horas. Costo $25 pesos nuevos.

DOMINGO 18

TEATRO.- Festival de Teatro de la UACJ Verano 93 presenta a su compañía con "Si algo te debo" en el Teatro del Centro de Convensions Universitario en P.E. Calles y Hnas Escobar.
Admisión N$10.00. Funciones a las 20:00 horas.

ESTA VEZ VIENE CON SU PAPA

HARRISON FORD   SEAN CONNERY

INDIANA JONES
y LA ÚLTIMA CRUZADA

Distribuida por United International Pictures

Options

Strategies for Reaching All Students

Students Needing Extra Help
Some of your students may not be familiar with the newspaper format. Have one available for reference.
Infórmate: This would make a good small-group or whole-class activity. For section 4, explain the concept of money having different values in foreign countries. Bring in samples of foreign currency along with the exchange rate from the business pages of a newspaper.

Enrichment
Bring in calendars of events from local newspapers and discuss the cultural differences between the events listed there and in those in the text.
Ask students to pick an event to go to, tell a partner about it, and invite him or her to come along. The partner can accept or

decline, in the latter case giving a reason why he or she cannot go.
As an extension activity, have students make a newspaper listing for an activity taking place in their school or community this weekend. Follow the same format that is used in this section and provide the same kind of information.

Mira la lectura

STRATEGY ➤ Scanning

Look at the calendar of events, noting the title, format, illustrations, and boldface headings.

1 Which days of the week are featured?

2 Which day of the week offers the greatest selection of activities? What kinds of events are there?

3 Do you find the display ad effective? Does it contain all the information a reader would need to know? Did you find what you expected to find?

Aplicación

Take a poll to see which of the activities mentioned in the calendar of events would be the most popular among your classmates.

Infórmate

STRATEGY ➤ Scanning

Using the ad, make plans for Saturday night.

1 Look at the calendar of events and identify five places to go on Saturday, then choose the one you would like to go to.

2 Find the following information for the place you choose:

- Lugar (cine; concierto; partido de fútbol; teatro)
- Nombre de la película / del grupo musical / del equipo de fútbol / de la obra de teatro
- Dirección
- Hora
- Admisión

3 What seems unusual about some of the times given?
How else could you express 20:00?

The following movie times are based on the 24-hour clock. How would they read according to the 12-hour clock?

11:15   13:45   16:20   18:50   21:30

4 N$ means *nuevos pesos*. When the Mexican government revalued the peso in the spring of 1993, N$ 3 equaled US $1. Given this information, figure out the price of admission to the place you selected in United States dollars.

¡Vamos a leer!   113

3 Answers will vary. / Using a map or globe, ask students: Do you know in what country this city is located? (Mexico) Do you know what major U.S. city Ciudad Juárez borders on? (El Paso, Texas)

Infórmate

1–2 Answers will vary. As an extension activity, have students find this information for several different events.

3 The times given indicate the hour using numbers greater than 12. Explain the 24-hour clock and mention that the military uses this system. In most foreign countries, this system of telling time is widely used. Tell students that knowing this information is helpful when reading timetables, schedules, etc. / 20:00 = 8:00 / 11:15, 1:45, 4:20, 6:50, 9:30

4 Answers will vary, depending on the place selected. As an extension activity, have students calculate the price in U.S. dollars of a ticket for each of the events and compare them. Which is the most expensive? The least expensive? How do these prices compare with what you would expect to pay to attend a similar event in your city?

Aplicación
Compiled information will vary.

Cultural Notes

(p. 112, realia)
With a population of approximately 1 million, Ciudad Juárez, on the Mexico–U.S. border, is the largest city in the state of Chihuahua. Twin city to El Paso, Texas, Ciudad Juárez is the *maquiladora* (U.S.-owned factory) center of Mexico, with an estimated 65 percent of its working population employed in industry.
As in many cities in Mexico, Ciudad Juárez is strongly influenced by American culture just as El Paso, for example, is by Mexican culture.

113

Apply

Process Writing

For information regarding developing a writing portfolio, see p. 50.

Teaching Suggestions

If students ask why *estar* is used in the invitation (*¡La fiesta va a estar fantástica!*) instead of *ser,* tell them we often use *estar* for emphatic use in describing things in Spanish. (All the present-tense forms of *ser* will be taught in Chap. 5.)

Todo junto

¡Vamos a escribir!

You and a friend are giving a party. Plan your party and write the invitation you will send to your friends. Follow these steps.

1 Think about what you are going to do at the party. A checklist will help you plan. With a partner, write a list in Spanish of the activities and when each might begin. For example:

Actividad	Hora
Vamos a ...	a las ...

2 Next, write the invitation. Include the day and time, your names, the address, and what you are going to do. Here is a model blank invitation:

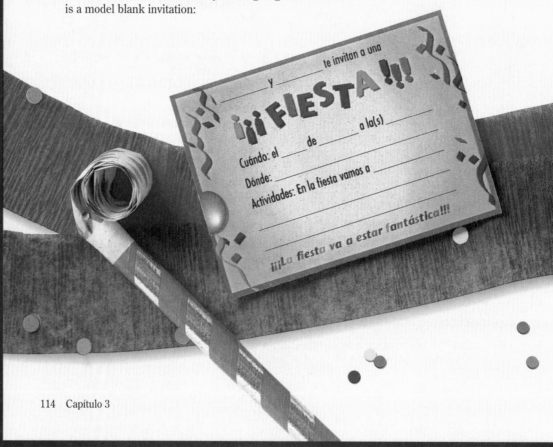

te invitan a una

_____ y _____ ¡¡¡FIESTA!!!

Cuándo: el _____ de _____ a la(s) _____

Dónde: _____

Actividades: En la fiesta vamos a _____

¡¡¡La fiesta va a estar fantástica!!!

Options

Strategies for Reaching All Students

Spanish-Speaking Students

Have students respond in writing to the invitation. If they cannot go to the party, they should express regrets and tell why.

 Un paso más Ex. 3-K

Students Needing Extra Help

If you elect to not use the model, brainstorm and develop an invitation. Give each student a copy or make one on the chalkboard or overhead. Have students use the Organizer for Chaps. 2 and 3.
Step 4: Have students use their Organizers.

Enrichment

Encourage students to be creative with their invitations, using different kinds of lettering, pictures, and layout to present the information. Students might also want to have sentences indicating acceptance or refusal with a blank space after them for invitees to check off.

3 Exchange invitations with another group and share any suggestions for improvement. Is there enough information, or should something be added?

4 Think about their suggestions and any other changes you may want to make. Rewrite your invitation. Check it for spelling and punctuation, including accents. Let the other group check it too. Ask them if you have included all the necessary information.

5 Now recopy your corrected invitation. You may want to file it in a writing portfolio.

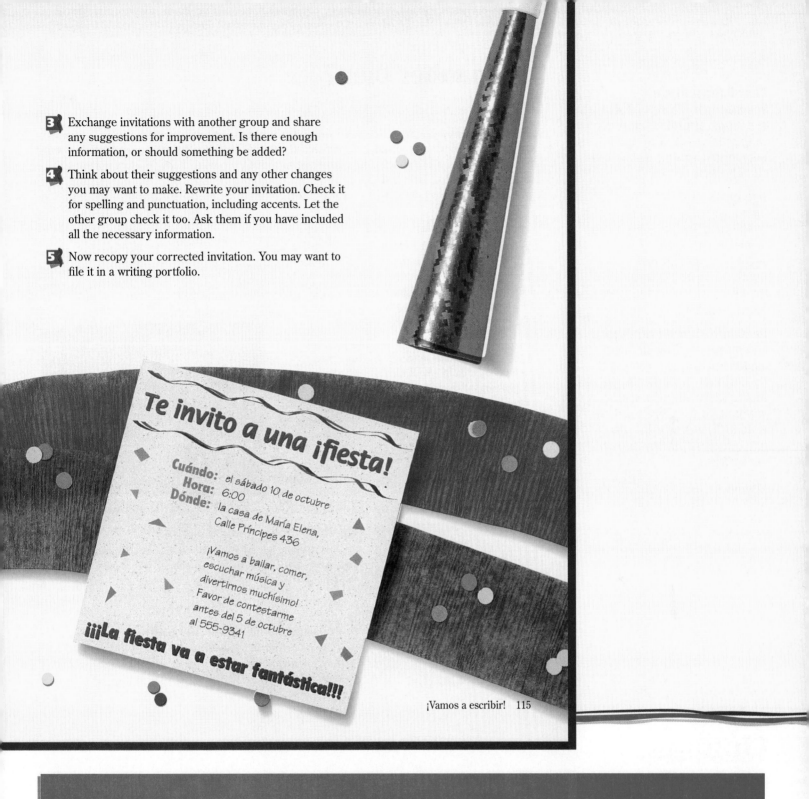

Te invito a una ¡fiesta!

Cuándo: el sábado 10 de octubre
Hora: 6:00
Dónde: la casa de María Elena,
Calle Príncipes 436

¡Vamos a bailar, comer,
escuchar música y
divertirnos muchísimo!
Favor de contestarme
antes del 5 de octubre
al 555-9341

¡¡¡La fiesta va a estar fantástica!!!

¡Vamos a escribir! 115

115

Assess & Summarize

Test Preparation
You may want to assign parts of this section as written homework or as an in-class writing activity prior to administering the *Examen de habilidades.*

Answers
Listening:
—*Margarita, ¿te gustaría ir al cine el domingo por la tarde?*
—*Claro que sí, Luis; pero no puedo. Tengo mucha tarea.*
No, Margarita is not going to the movies with Luis.

Reading: Ruth would like to go shopping Friday. Saturday morning she wants to go swimming at the beach and in the evening go skating with friends. On Sunday she needs to sleep, but would like to go to the movies in the afternoon. / She is spending the weekend in Miami.

Writing: Paragraphs will vary, but look for the use of *me / te gustaría, prefiero / prefieres, quiero / quieres,* and *puedo / puedes* + inf.

¿Lo sabes bien?

This section will help you organize your studying for the proficiency test, where you will be asked to do similar, though not identical, tasks. There will not be any models on the test.

Listening
Can you understand when people talk about their free-time activities? Listen as your teacher reads you a sample similar to what you will hear on the test. Is Margarita going to the movies with Luis or not?

Reading
Can you look at this letter and get an idea of how Ruth is planning to spend her weekend? In what city is Ruth spending the weekend?

> Querida Isabel:
> Voy a estar contigo tres días allí en Miami. El viernes me gustaría ir de compras todo el día. ¿Puedes ir conmigo? El sábado por la mañana quiero ir a la playa a nadar y por la noche quiero ir a patinar con mis amigos. El domingo necesito dormir. Soy muy perezosa, pero me gustaría ir al cine por la tarde. Y tú, ¿qué prefieres?
>
> Saludos,
> Ruth

116   Capítulo 3

Writing
Can you write a note to a classmate in which you decline an invitation and say why? You should also suggest other days when you are free and what you would like to do. Here is a sample:

> Rebeca:
> Me gustaría mucho ir de compras contigo el viernes, pero estoy ocupada. El sábado, claro que sí, no tengo ni clase ni tarea. Me gustaría ir a nadar por la mañana, y por la noche me gustaría ir al cine. También me gustaría ir contigo al campo el domingo. ¿Quieres ir?
>
> Cecilia

El parque del Retiro en Madrid

Culture
Can you compare a *plaza* to a park such as El Retiro or Chapultepec?

"¿Te gustaría ir al parque conmigo?"

Speaking
Can you invite your partner to do an activity with you? You and your partner should agree on what to do, where, and when. For example:

A —*¿Te gustaría jugar básquetbol?*
B —*Sí, pero prefiero ir a patinar.*
A —*¡Genial! ¿Adónde vamos? ¿Al parque?*
B —*Sí. ¿A qué hora? ¿Puedes ir a las 9:00?*
A —*No, necesito ir de compras con mi familia. ¿Y a las 11:00?*
B —*Sí, a las 11:00.*

Options

116

Resumen del capítulo 3

Use the vocabulary from this chapter to help you:
- talk about some of your leisure-time activities
- make plans with friends
- extend, accept, or decline invitations

to tell how someone feels or where someone is
¿Dónde?
estar: (yo) estoy
     (tú) estás

to tell where someone is going
¿Adónde?
ir: (yo) voy
    (tú) vas
a
a la, al *(a + el)*
el campo
el centro comercial
el gimnasio
el parque
el parque de diversiones
la piscina
la playa

to talk about activities
ir a una fiesta
ir de compras
ir de pesca
jugar básquetbol
jugar béisbol
jugar fútbol
jugar fútbol americano
jugar tenis
jugar videojuegos
jugar vóleibol
el pasatiempo

to say when you do an activity
la estación
    la primavera
    el verano
    el otoño
    el invierno
el lunes, el martes . . .
los lunes, los martes . . .
el fin (los fines) de semana
después de (las clases)
(por) la mañana
    la tarde
    la noche
generalmente
hoy no
mañana
todos los días

to say with whom you do an activity
con
conmigo, contigo
el amigo, la amiga
la familia
solo, -a

to extend, accept, or decline invitations
¿(A ti) te gustaría ___?
(A mí) me gustaría ___.
poder: (yo) puedo
    (tú) puedes
querer: (yo) quiero
    (tú) quieres
¡Claro que sí!
¡Claro que no!
Gracias.
De nada.
cansado, -a
enfermo, -a
ocupado, -a

to express surprise, enthusiasm, or disappointment
¡No me digas!
¡Genial!
¡Qué lástima!

to express possession
mi, mis
tus

CAPÍTULO 4
THEME: FOOD

COMMUNICATION

Topics

Foods and drinks

Likes, dislikes, and preferences

Objectives

To talk about eating customs in Spanish-speaking countries

To describe meals and talk about foods and drinks

To express likes or preferences

To indicate frequency

To refer to obligation

To indicate hunger or thirst

To refer to something you cannot name

To express an opinion

To ask for and give an explanation

To elicit agreement

CULTURE

Meals and mealtimes

GRAMMAR

El plural de los sustantivos

El plural de los adjetivos

Verbos que terminan en -er

Sujetos compuestos

Ancillaries available for use with Chapter 4

Multisensory/Technology

 Overhead Transparencies, 21–25

 Audio Tapes and CDs

 Vocabulary Art Blackline Masters for Hands-On Learning, pp. 23–27

 Classroom Crossword

 Video

 CD-ROM

Print

 Practice Workbook, pp. 43–52

 Writing, Audio & Video Activities, pp. 23–28, 102–104, 158–159

 Communicative Activity Blackline Masters

Pair and Small Group Activities, pp. 29–34

Situation Cards, p. 35

 Un paso más: Actividades para ampliar tu español, pp. 20–25

Assessment

 Assessment Program

Pruebas, pp. 52–62

Examen de habilidades, pp. 63–66

 Test Generator

Video still from Chap. 4

Revolutionary Foods

Although Columbus and the other European explorers who followed him to the Americas did not find the spices that they sought, they were introduced to a wealth of new foods far more valuable. In time, these foods would not only profoundly affect people's diets, but they would change the course of history.

One of the most important foods cultivated in the Americas was the potato, which today is the world's most widely grown vegetable. Potatoes probably were first grown in the valleys of the Andes by the Incas. In the mid-1500s, Spanish and English explorers introduced the tubers to Europe, where they were initially rejected as a food source because of a wide-spread fear that root crops caused disease.

Today, potatoes are still an important crop in Andean nations such as Peru, Bolivia, and Chile. They appear in dishes such as Peruvian *papa a la huancaina,* a potato served in a cream sauce.

Corn is another native American crop that revolutionized the diets of people around the world. Along with wheat, rice, and potatoes, corn is considered one of the four most important food crops in the world. Though botanists believe corn may have grown in the Americas as many as 60,000 years ago, Europeans did not know of its existence until Columbus brought back a plant after his first trip to the Americas.

Like the potato, corn is an extremely versatile plant. Besides being relatively easy to grow—it can be planted in soil that is either too wet or too dry for crops such as wheat or rice—corn literally has hundreds of uses. It can be ground into meal or refined into starch, sugar, syrup, or oil. In the form of meal, it is combined with other ingredients to make corn bread, cookies, waffles, and a wide assortment of other foods.

Besides potatoes and corn, many other important foods originated in the Americas. Among them are avocados, pineapples, papayas, peppers, peanuts, tomatoes, and chocolate. These foods have added zest to many national cuisines. The tomato, for example, added a distinct flavor to Mediterranean cooking. And of course, it is well known what effect chocolate had on all of Europe.

The introduction of American crops to Europe did much more than help shape national cuisines. Partly because of the rich new sources of nutrition found in the native American foods, life expectancy increased and the population of Europe nearly doubled during the eighteenth century. Before the arrival of the new foods, Europe's population had been relatively stable. In addition, the revolutionary changes in agriculture helped reshape the European economy. Despite the burgeoning population, farmers were able to supply the demand for food. As many historians have maintained, plants and seeds from the Americas were far more valuable in Western development than all the silver of Mexico.

Introduce

Re-entry of Concepts
The following topics represent words, expressions, and grammar points re-entered from Chaps. 1 to 3:

Chapter 1
Activities
Gustar expressions
Adjectives to describe personality

Chapter 2
School subjects
School supplies
Possession and need
Time expressions

Chapter 3
Destinations
Pastimes
Adverbs describing when things take place
Invitations (accepting / declining)
Expressions of emotion (*¡Claro que sí!*)

Planning

Cross-Curricular Connections

Geography Connection *(pp. 122–123)*
West of Buenos Aires, the capital of Argentina, is the fertile farming region of the Pampas, which is responsible for most of the nation's food production. Have students research the Pampas and create maps indicating the food products of the region.

Art Connection *(pp. 130–131)*
Have students draw the food vocabulary on index cards so that they can be used as flashcards. Assign each student one of the fruits or vegetables listed in the *Vocabulario para conversar*. Then have them draw their food in a collage format. These can then be posted around the room.

Health Connection *(pp. 146–147)*
Have students make a pyramid of the food groups using cutouts or drawings. Have them write how many portions are recommended and highlight their favorite food from each group.

CAPÍTULO 4

¿Qué prefieres comer?

OBJECTIVES

At the end of this chapter, you will be able to:

- describe what you like and don't like to eat and drink
- tell when you have meals
- say whether you are hungry or thirsty
- compare and contrast eating customs in Spanish-speaking countries and in the United States

Mercado al aire libre en Perú

119

Cultural Notes ☀

Spanish in Your Community
What foods from Spanish-speaking countries are available in your community? Have students visit a local Hispanic grocery store and make a list of at least ten foods sold there. As students share their lists with the class, compile a master list on the chalkboard.

(pp. 118–119, photo)
Sunday market in Chinchero, a small town in the Peruvian Andes north of Cuzco, the capital of the ancient Incan empire. Although tourists do buy here, this market remains primarily an important place for residents to buy and sell, socialize, and exchange information.

Preview

Cultural Objective

• To compare and contrast eating customs in Spanish-speaking countries and in the U.S.

¿Qué prefieres comer?

Play

 Video Activity A

Using the Video

This chapter's video focuses on food. Students will go with our hosts to the San Miguel Market in Madrid to discover the different types of food for sale there.

To prepare students for the video, first ask them to predict what this chapter's tape will be about. Then have students watch the segment several times. After the first time, you may wish to have them brainstorm possible vocabulary and expressions they will need to talk about what they saw on the video. Ask students to identify: a) things they saw that were familiar to them, and b) things they saw that they probably would not see in a market or grocery store where they live.

Video segment 1: For more teaching suggestions, see the Video Teacher's Guide.

¡Piénsalo bien!

Look at the photos. How is the food similar to or different from what you might eat? Now look at the teens gathered at a fast-food place. How does this restaurant compare to a similar place in your community? What do you think *hamburguesa* means?

"Me gustaría una hamburguesa."

A la hora del almuerzo en la Ciudad de México

Un desayuno en un hotel de Asunción, Paraguay

120   Capítulo 4

Options

Strategies for Reaching All Students

Spanish-Speaking Students

Ask Spanish-speaking students: *¿Qué comidas ves aquí? ¿Comes tú las mismas comidas? ¿A qué hora desayunas? ¿Cuándo almuerzas? ¿Con quién almuerzas?*

Students Needing Extra Help

Discuss the mealtimes of your students. Compare and contrast this information in a chart form, after presenting the *Perspectiva cultural.*

En Navidad, una familia dominicana a la hora de la cena

121

Present

Chapter Theme
Foods and mealtimes: Preferences

Communicative Objectives
- To describe meals
- To talk about foods
- To express likes or preferences
- To indicate frequency
- To ask for and give an explanation
- To express an opinion
- To elicit agreement

 Transparencies 21–22

 Vocabulary Art BLMs

 Pronunciation Tape 3-1

 Vocabulario para conversar A

Play

Using the Video
Video segment 2: See the Video Teacher's Guide.

 Video Activity B

Grammar Preview
Como / comes are presented and practiced here lexically. The presentation of *-er* verbs appears on p. 138.

Vocabulario para conversar

¿Qué te gusta comer?

Here are some new words and expressions you will need to talk about mealtimes and foods you like and don't like to eat. Read them several times, then turn the page and practice with a partner.

El desayuno

el pan tostado

el cereal

el huevo

el jamón

El almuerzo

las frutas

las papas fritas

la hamburguesa

los sandwiches

el tomate

el queso

el sandwich de jamón y queso

la ensalada

122   Capítulo 4

Options

Strategies for Reaching All Students

Spanish-Speaking Students
Vocabulario para conversar: Ask Spanish-speaking students: *¿Qué otras comidas te gustan? Haz una lista.*

 Un paso más Ex. 4-A

Students Needing Extra Help
¿Y qué quiere decir . . . ?: Write out the word *en* for each of the meals.

Learning Spanish Through Action
STAGING VOCABULARY: *Muestren, Pongan*
MATERIALS: Brown (2), pink (1), yellow (1), and red (1) pieces of construction paper, approximately the size of a slice of bread, for each student
DIRECTIONS: Tell students that they are going to make sandwiches. Have them label the brown sheets *el pan tostado,* the pink sheets *el jamón,* the red sheets *el tomate,* and the yellow sheets *el queso.* As you describe a ham, cheese, and tomato sand-

La cena

el pan   la sopa de tomate

la sopa de pollo

la sopa de verduras

el bistec

el pescado

el arroz

las papas al horno

las verduras

el pollo

También necesitas . . .

comer: (yo) como	*to eat: I eat*	me encanta(n)	*I love*
(tú) comes	*you eat*	siempre	*always*
la comida	*meal*	nunca	*never*
más o menos	*more or less*		
¡Qué asco!	*Yuk! That's disgusting!*		
¿Por qué?	*why?*		
porque	*because*		
¿verdad?	*isn't that so? right?*		

> **¿Y qué quiere decir . . . ?**
> en el desayuno / el almuerzo / la cena
> prefiero, prefieres

Vocabulario para conversar   123

Practice & Apply

Re-enter / Recycle

Ex. 2: *gustar* expressions from Chap. 1

Answers: Empecemos a conversar

1 ESTUDIANTE A
a. ¿Comes huevos?
b ...pan?
c. ...frutas?
d. Questions will vary.

ESTUDIANTE B
a.–d. Answers will vary depending on *Estudiante B*'s preferences.

2 ESTUDIANTE A
a. Te gustan las papas al horno, ¿verdad?
b. ...las verduras ...
c. ...los tomates ...
d. ...los sandwiches ...
e. ...las hamburguesas ...
f. ...los sandwiches de jamón y queso ...
g. ...las papas fritas ...

ESTUDIANTE B
a.–g. Answers will vary depending on *Estudiante B*'s preferences.

Empecemos a conversar

With a partner, take turns being *Estudiante A* and *Estudiante B.* Use the words that are cued or given in the balloons to replace the underlined sections in the model. 💡 means you can make your own choices.

1
A —¿Comes *jamón*?
B —*Sí, a veces.*

Y ahora Uds.

Estudiante A

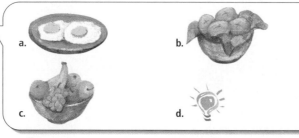
a.
b.
c.
d.

Estudiante B

Sí, a veces.

Sí, todos los días

Sí, siempre.

No, nunca.

No, ¡qué asco!

2
A —*Te gustan las ensaladas, ¿verdad?*
B —*Sí, me encantan.*

Y ahora Uds.

Estudiante A

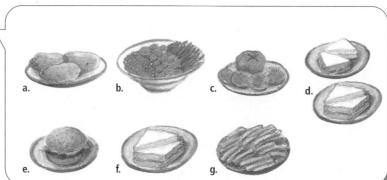
a.
b.
c.
d.
e.
f.
g.

Estudiante B

Sí, me encantan.

Sí, más o menos.

No, no me gustan (mucho).

No, ¡qué asco!

124   Capítulo 4

Options

Strategies for Reaching All Students

Spanish-Speaking Students
Try to pair bilingual students with non-bilingual students for Exs. 1–3. This will help both. The former will learn to speak clearly and carefully, and the latter will have good models.

 Un paso más Exs. 4-B, 4-C

Students Needing Extra Help
Have students begin to fill in their Organizers.
Exs. 1–2: Review the meanings of the responses. Point out that Column B contains choices and that it is not a linear match for answers.
Ex. 3: Have students write the names of the three meals in columns so as to organize them. Model a sentence.
Ex. 7: Remind students that they answered this type of question in Ex. 3.

Enrichment
Ex. 2: Do a similar exercise with you taking the place of *Estudiante A* and forming your questions using *te gusta* and singular nouns. Preview the grammar by asking students why you used *te gusta* instead of *te gustan* in your questions. Have them note the difference between *me / te gusta* + inf. and *me / te gusta(n)* + noun by contrasting these sentences: *Me gustan las ensaladas. Me gusta comer ensaladas.* Explain that *las* is not used here after the infinitive.

3 el desayuno A — *¿Qué comes en el desayuno?*
B — *Generalmente como cereal y pan tostado.*
Y ahora Uds.

Estudiante A

a. la cena
b. el almuerzo
c. el desayuno

Estudiante B

Empecemos a escribir

Write your answers in Spanish.

4 Write the names of at least three foods under each of these headings: *Todos los días, A veces, Nunca.* Then write three complete sentences telling how often you eat those foods.

5 Copy the names of the soups you have learned. Using these as a model, choose other foods from the vocabulary and write the names of at least three other soups.

6 *¿Qué comida prefieres, el desayuno o la cena? ¿Por qué?*

7 Generalmente, *¿qué comes en el almuerzo y con quién comes?*

Detalle de *La gran ciudad de Tenochtitlán* (1945), Diego Rivera

También se dice

la tostada

los bocadillos
los emparedados

el bife
el biftec

las legumbres
las hortalizas

los jitomates

Vocabulario para conversar   125

Cultural Notes

For an additional written assignment, ask small groups to rate the meals at three or four local restaurants with which they are familiar. Students can list the restaurants in one column and then put a check mark under columns with the headings: *Me encanta, Me gusta,* and *¡Qué asco!* or *No me gusta.* Another assignment could be about the time dinner begins and ends at home, with students answering these questions: *¿A qué hora, más o menos, empieza la cena en tu casa? ¿A qué hora termina?*

(p. 125, photo)
Detail from *La gran ciudad de Tenochtitlán* (c. 1945) by Diego Rivera. In this mural Rivera renders the bounty and bustle of the Aztec market held in Tenochtitlán's magnificent main square. When Cortés arrived in Mexico in 1519, the capital had a population of around 100,000, more than any Spanish city at that time. The present-day site is the *Zócalo,* Mexico City's main *plaza.*

Present

Chapter Theme
Foods: Fruits, vegetables, and beverages

Communicative Objectives
- To talk about foods and drinks
- To describe meals and foods
- To refer to obligation
- To indicate hunger or thirst
- To talk about something you cannot name
- To express an opinion

 Transparencies 23–24

 Vocabulary Art BLMs

 Pronunciation Tape 3-2

 Vocabulario para conversar B

Play

Using the Video
Video segment 2: See the Video Teacher's Guide.

 Video Activity B

Vocabulario para conversar

¿Tienes hambre?
Here's the rest of the vocabulary you will need to tell what you like and don't like to eat and drink and to say whether you are hungry or thirsty.

tener hambre

126   Capítulo 4

Options

Strategies for Reaching All Students

Spanish-Speaking Students
Ask: *¿Qué otras frutas y verduras puedes nombrar?*

 Un paso más Exs. 4-D, 4-E

Students Needing Extra Help
Have students continue to fill in their Organizers.

Enrichment
The names of many fruits and vegetables in Mexico are derived from *náhuatl*, a very ancient language spoken by the Aztecs in central Mexico and still spoken today in various dialects in Mexico and Central America. Words derived from *náhuatl* are distinguishable by their *-te* (formerly *-tl*) ending: *aguacate, chocolate, cacahuate, tomate, elote, ejote.*

tener sed

BEBIDAS

la leche

el café

el té

el agua (f.)*

la limonada   los refrescos   el jugo de naranja

el té helado

También necesitas . . .

beber: (yo) bebo, (tú) bebes	to drink: I drink you drink	deber: (yo) debo (tú) debes	ought to, should
bueno, -a (para la salud)	good (for your health)	son	(they) are
malo, -a (para la salud)	bad (for your health)	unos, unas	some
sabroso, -a	delicious, tasty		
Creo que sí.	I think so.		
Creo que no.	I don't think so.		
algo	something		

¿Y qué quiere decir . . . ?
horrible

*Note that *agua* is a feminine noun. However, we use the article *el* with feminine nouns beginning with stressed *a* or *ha*.

Grammar Preview
Bebo / bebes and *debo / debes* are presented here lexically. The explanation of *-er* verbs appears on p. 138.

Teaching Suggestions
Preparing students to speak: Use one or two options from each of the categories of Comprehensible Input, Physical Response, or Limited Verbal Response. For a complete explanation of these categories and some sample activities, see the front section of this Teacher's Edition.

Class Starter Review
On the day following initial presentation, you might begin the class with this activity:
As you call out the visualized items in this vocabulary section, ask students to categorize them as *frutas, verduras,* or *bebidas.*

Multicultural Perspectives
Aguas frescas, or flavored waters, are popular beverages in Mexican eating places. Among the selections are *agua de sandía, agua de limón, agua de tamarindo,* and *horchata* (made with rice flour). *Aguas frescas* are sold in restaurants, at market lunch counters, and with street vendors. Invite students to share their knowledge of popular beverages from other cultures.

Learning Spanish Through Action
STAGING VOCABULARY: *Den, Levántense, Muestren, Pongan*
MATERIALS: Three 8 1/2 X 11 sheets of paper labeled *frutas, verduras,* and *bebidas;* index cards with pictures of all the fruits, vegetables, and beverages in the *Vocabulario para conversar.* If possible, use plastic toys or magazine cutouts.
DIRECTIONS: Have three volunteers go to the front of the class. Give each volunteer one of the sheets, instructing him or her to hold it up for the class. Distribute the index cards to individuals in the class. As you recite each food or beverage, have the student who has the corresponding card for that item get up and give it to the appropriate volunteer. Continue until all of the foods and beverages are properly categorized.

Practice & Apply

Re-enter / Recycle

Ex. 8: *tengo / necesito* from Chap. 2, *¿te gustaría?* from Chap. 3

Answers: Empecemos a conversar

8 ESTUDIANTE A
Statements will vary. Make sure students correlate *hambre* with *comer* and *sed* with *beber*.

ESTUDIANTE B
¿Te gustaría una manzana?
. . . un plátano?
. . . una naranja?
. . . una zanahoria?
. . . una limonada?
. . . un té helado?
. . . un café?

9 Preview adjective agreement here by asking students to predict why *buenas* and *sabrosas* end in *-as*.

ESTUDIANTE A
a. Las ensaladas son buenas para la salud, ¿verdad?
b. Las cebollas . . .
c. Las papas fritas . . .
d. Las papas al horno . . .
e. Las zanahorias . . .
f. Las judías verdes . . .

ESTUDIANTE B
a.–f. Answers will vary depending on *Estudiante B*'s preferences.

Empecemos a conversar

8
A — *Tengo sed. Necesito beber algo.*
B — *¿Te gustaría un refresco?*

Y ahora Uds.

Estudiante A

Necesito beber algo.
Debo beber algo.

Necesito comer algo.
Debo comer algo.

Estudiante B

9
A — *Las verduras son buenas para la salud, ¿verdad?*
B — *Sí, y son sabrosas también.*

Y ahora Uds.

Estudiante A

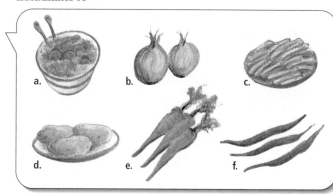

a. b. c.
d. e. f.

Estudiante B

Sí, y son sabrosas también.

Sí, pero no me gustan mucho.

Sí, pero no son sabrosas.

Sí, pero son horribles.

Creo que sí.

No, creo que no.

No, son malas para la salud.

Más o menos.

128   Capítulo 4

Options

Strategies for Reaching All Students

Spanish-Speaking Students
Exs. 8–9: Pair Spanish-speaking students. For Ex. 9, ask students to explain their answers.
Ex. 11: Ask Spanish-speaking students to find out about their classmates' beverage preferences for breakfast. Then have them write short paragraphs about their findings.

For example: *Pregúntales a tus compañeros qué beben en el desayuno. Luego escribe un párrafo sobre las bebidas más populares.* Guide students in their writing and provide further questions to be answered in paragraph form.

 Un paso más Exs. 4-F, 4-G

Students Needing Extra Help
Ex. 8: Show that *Estudiante A* has to construct two sentences. Emphasize that *hambre, comer,* and the foods go together and that *sed, beber,* and the beverages go together.
Ex. 10: Put a few choices on the chalkboard.
Exs. 11–13: Have students use their Organizers.
Empecemos a escribir y a leer: For additional practice, have students plan a dinner menu for some friends.

Empecemos a escribir y a leer

Write your answers in Spanish.

10 Imagine that you are waiting tables and need to write yourself a reminder. Write down what comes with the hamburgers, and at least four ingredients that are in the vegetable soup today.

11 ¿Qué bebida prefieres en el desayuno, en el almuerzo y en la cena? ¿Por qué?

12 ¿Qué verduras te gustan?

13 Unos animales hablan de lo que prefieren comer. ¿Qué dicen? *(What do they say?)*

el mono
el pato
el cerdo
la gallina
el conejo

¿Quién dice . . . ?

a. —A ver . . . Me encantan el pan y el agua. Sí, sí. Me gusta mucho beber agua, y como mucho pan en el parque.

b. —En el desayuno siempre como plátanos. En el almuerzo a veces como más plátanos. ¿Y en la cena? Pues . . . generalmente como plátanos también. Son muy buenos para la salud, ¿verdad?

c. —¿Comer huevos? ¡Ay, no! ¿Huevos? ¡Nunca!

d. —Como mucho todos los días. ¡Pero no puedo comer jamón! ¡Nunca voy a comer jamón!

e. —Yo como muchas zanahorias. ¡A mí me encantan las zanahorias! Me gustaría comer zanahorias en todas las comidas.

También se dice

las bananas
los guineos

las chinas

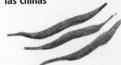

la chaucha *(sing.)*
las habichuelas verdes
los ejotes

las patatas

las arvejas
los chícharos

el zumo de naranja

Vocabulario para conversar   129

Answers: Empecemos a escribir y a leer

10 Answers will vary, but may include any vegetables that students learned in this chapter.

11–12 Answers will vary.

13 a. el pato
b. el mono
c. la gallina
d. el cerdo
e. el conejo

✏️ **Practice Wkbk. 4-3, 4-4**

🎧 **Audio Activity 4.2**

🎧 **Writing Activities 4-C, 4-D**

¿? **Pruebas 4-3, 4-4**

✂️ **Comm. Act. BLM 4-2**

Enrichment
Ex. 8: Have *Estudiante B* expand his or her answer by saying if the foods named are healthful.

Practice

Re-enter / Recycle

Ex. 2: *necesito / necesitas* from Chap. 2
Ex. 3: time-telling from Chap. 2, adverbs from Chap. 3

Answers:
¡Comuniquemos!

1 Remind students to include definite articles in their responses if they elect the last option for *Estudiante A.*

ESTUDIANTE A

a. ¿Prefieres guisantes o zanahorias?

b. ...papas al horno o papas fritas?

c. ...sopa o ensalada?

d. ...agua o limonada?

e. ...manzanas o plátanos?

f. ...leche o café?

g. ...té o té helado?

ESTUDIANTE B

a.–g. Answers will vary depending on *Estudiante B*'s preferences.

¡Comuniquemos!

Here's another opportunity for you to use the vocabulary you've just learned.

¡NO OLVIDES!

If you need help spelling, ask
¿Cómo se escribe . . . ?

1 You and a friend are having dinner at a restaurant. Take turns asking each other about your food preferences.

A — *¿Prefieres sopa de pollo o sopa de tomate?*
B — *Prefiero sopa de pollo, ¿y tú?*
A — *Yo prefiero sopa de pollo también.*
   o: *Yo prefiero sopa de tomate.*
   o: *A mí no me gusta ni la sopa de pollo
    ni la sopa de tomate.*

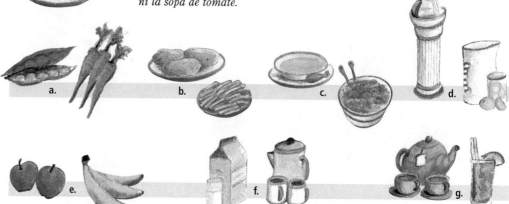

a.   b.   c.   d.

e.   f.   g.

2 Help a friend prepare a shopping list. Ask what he or she needs, and write down the responses.

la sopa   A — *¿Qué necesitas para la sopa?*
             B — *Necesito zanahorias, tomates y cebolla.*

Estudiante A

a. los sandwiches
b. la ensalada de frutas
c. la ensalada de verduras
d. el desayuno
e. el almuerzo
f. la cena

Estudiante B

130   Capítulo 4

Options

Strategies for Reaching All Students

Spanish-Speaking Students

Exs. 1–3: Pair bilingual and non-bilingual students.

Students Needing Extra Help

Ex. 2: Have students use their Organizers.
Ex. 3: Review time and days of the week. Have students use their Organizers. Explain the final *Estudiante A* response.
¿Qué sabes ahora?: Have students write out this section so they can check off what they have mastered. In item 1, repeat *tengo* for the second blank. In item 3, create a negative sentence also.

Enrichment

Ex. 3: As a written assignment, have students invent a dialogue in which they are responsible for fixing lunch on Saturday for the family and guests. Have them ask for help from a sibling who declines, perhaps giving an elaborate excuse why he or she can't help. Encourage students to be creative in their presentation, using as much known vocabulary as possible.

3 Your family is having guests this weekend and you are expected to be at every meal. Find out at what time all of the meals are and what is going to be served. Your partner will play the role of a family member.

el almuerzo

A —*¿A qué hora es el almuerzo el sábado?*
B —*A las doce.*
A —*¿Qué vamos a comer?*
B —*Pollo y ensalada.*
A —*¡Pero siempre comemos pollo y ensalada!*
 o: *¡Me encantan!*

Estudiante A

desayuno	sábado
almuerzo	domingo
cena	

Estudiante B

¿Qué sabes ahora?

Can you:

- **tell someone that you are hungry / thirsty?**
 —Tengo ___ / ___.

- **tell someone what you like or do not like to eat and drink?**
 —Me encanta comer ___ , pero (no) me gusta beber ___.

- **say that you like certain foods because they are healthful or tasty?**
 —Me gustan las uvas ___ son ___.

"Los jugos son buenos para la salud. ¡Me encantan!"

En una tienda de jugos en la Zona Rosa, Ciudad de México

Vocabulario para conversar   131

2 ESTUDIANTE A
a. ¿Qué necesitas para los sandwiches?
b. . . . la ensalada de frutas?
c. . . . la ensalada de verduras?
d. . . . el desayuno?
e. . . . el almuerzo?
f. . . . la cena?
ESTUDIANTE B
a–f. Answers will vary depending on what *Estudiante B* needs. Encourage students to use the full range of chapter vocabulary. Suggest that *Estudiante B* respond with at least three foods for each item.

 Audio Activity 4.3

3 ESTUDIANTE A
¿A qué hora es el desayuno (el almuerzo, la cena) el sábado (el domingo)?
ESTUDIANTE B
Dialogues will vary, but encourage students to use the full range of chapter vocabulary.

Answers: ¿Qué sabes ahora?
- hambre / sed
- Answers will vary.
- Answers will vary, but may include: . . . *porque / buenas para la salud (sabrosas)*

Strategies for Reaching All Students

Cooperative Learning
In groups of four or five, have students plan a complete lunch menu for each day of the school week. Each lunch should include an item from the dairy, meat, vegetable, bread, and fruit groups, a beverage, and some extras. Have a volunteer from each group write the menus on butcher paper, making sure to label each meal with the day on which it will be served. Post the menus on a bulletin board and discuss them. To extend the activity, have student "critics" rate the menus on a scale of 1–5.

Cultural Notes

(p. 131, photo)
These teenagers are enjoying fresh drinks at an establishment devoted to serving juice and juice-based beverages (such as *aguas* and *licuados*) in Mexico City's upscale shopping district, la Zona Rosa. Customers can choose a single flavor or a combination of flavors from fruits and vegetables such as papaya, banana, strawberry, grapefruit, melon, celery, carrot, and alfalfa.

131

Cultural Objective
• To compare and contrast eating customs in Spanish-speaking countries and in the U.S.

Critical Thinking: Making Hypotheses
After students read the text, have them speculate as to how the adoption of a *jornada continua* or *horario continuado* in some businesses in large Mexican cities will affect family traditions.

Multicultural Perspectives
In Colombia, for example, it is proper etiquette for someone who is eating to offer to share his or her food. Eating food while walking down the street is considered improper. Discuss these customs with students. Ask: How is eating and meal etiquette different in the U.S. and Colombia? How is it the same? Invite students to share information they have about food etiquette in other cultures.

Perspectiva cultural

¿A qué hora es el desayuno, el almuerzo y la cena en los Estados Unidos? ¿Qué comemos en el desayuno, por ejemplo? En las fotos, ¿a qué hora comen los hispanos?

Look at the mealtimes shown in the photos. Based on those times, do you think there might be another meal not pictured? Explain your answer.

In Spanish-speaking countries, as in the United States, there are three main meals—*el desayuno, el almuerzo,* and *la cena.*

El desayuno, which generally takes place between 7:00 and 8:30, is usually a light meal that consists of coffee or *café con leche,* which is half coffee and half hot milk, and bread or rolls with butter and jam. Children and teenagers sometimes drink hot chocolate or chocolate milk instead of coffee.

El almuerzo (called *la comida* in Spain and Mexico) is the largest and most important meal of the day. It is eaten between noon and 3:00. Many businesses and schools close so that families can enjoy *el almuerzo* together at home. Although this lengthy midday break is still common, more and more businesses are adopting a *jornada continua* or *horario continuado* (uninterrupted schedule) similar to working hours in the United States. This does not leave time for employees to go home for lunch.

La cena is the evening meal. It may start around 7:00 or much later, especially in countries that have a late midday meal. In Spain, *la cena* may start as late as 10:00 or 11:00, since most Spaniards enjoy going out after work or school and it is customary to wait until all family members are present before sitting down to eat. *La cena* is usually a light meal, and it may include leftovers from *el almuerzo.*

In some countries, there is also a late afternoon meal called *la merienda*. It may be like a *desayuno,* or it may resemble an English tea, with sandwiches, pastries, or rolls and *café con leche,* tea, or hot chocolate.

La cultura desde tu perspectiva

1 In what ways are mealtimes in Spanish-speaking countries similar to or different from those in the United States?

2 Why would a late-afternoon snack probably be necessary for someone from the United States who was visiting a Spanish-speaking country? Are there any other times of day when a snack might be needed?

Options

Strategies for Reaching All Students

Spanish-Speaking Students
Ask students: *¿Cuáles son tus comidas favoritas? ¿A qué hora cenas? ¿Cena toda la familia junta? ¿Comes algo entre el almuerzo y la cena? ¿Qué comes? ¿Vas con tus amigos a comer después de las clases?*

 Un paso más Ex. 4-H

Enrichment
Have students consult various up-to-date guidebooks in the library to do a brief written or oral report on fast-food restaurants in Spanish-speaking countries. For another assignment, ask students to watch any local television programs broadcast in Spanish and to take note of the content and format

of commercials from supermarket chains, small grocery stores, fast-food chains, and restaurants. Ask them to watch with these questions in mind: What's different about these commercials? What's the same? Are there any slogans? What are they? Do you think the same slogans would be effective in English?

12:30 PM — Málaga, España

Unos amigos españoles a la hora del almuerzo

Ciudad de México, México

5:00 PM

En México, a la hora de la merienda

Santiago, Chile

9:30 PM

En Chile, familiares y amigos empiezan a cenar.

Perspectiva cultural   133

Answers

Answers will vary: *a las 8:00, a las 12:00 y a las 6:00 / cereal, huevos, pan tostado, etc. / a las 12:30, 5:00 y 9:30*
Paragraph 1: Most students will probably say that breakfast is not pictured. Explanations will vary. Discuss students' mealtimes and compare them with the information provided in the text.

Answers: La cultura desde tu perspectiva

1 Students may say that midday meals are different because in some Spanish-speaking countries people go home for lunch. Lunch is eaten between noon and 2:00 and is usually a heavier meal. Other differences may include: *El desayuno* and *la cena* are lighter meals than in the U.S., and the afternoon *merienda* is a custom in some countries. Similarities include: Breakfast is eaten around the same time, and businesses in some countries are adopting an uninterrupted work schedule so that people no longer go home for lunch.

2 Answers will vary, but encourage student discussion by asking for reasons whenever possible.

Using Photos

Ask students, especially Spanish speakers, if they can identify any of the food items in the top and bottom photos on this page.

Cultural Notes ☼

(p. 133, top photo)
These diners in Málaga are enjoying a regional version of *paella,* the saffron-colored rice dish named for the shallow, two-handled pan in which it is cooked. *Paella* is considered by many to be the most typical Spanish dish. It is also one of the most varied. In Valencia, where it originated in the nineteenth century, it includes bits of seafood, chicken, and meat, with peas, crayfish, and strips of sweet red pimento placed on top.

(p. 133, center photo)
The floating gardens of Xochimilco, Mexico, have flourished since the thirteenth century, when the Chinampaneca Indians established themselves in this area about 13 miles west of what is today the center of Mexico City. A popular attraction for tourists and residents alike, the gardens can be viewed from gondolas like this one, called *trajineras.*

Preview

Transparency 25

Answers

Answers will vary. Discuss more common types of cheese that students may see or buy: American, cheddar, parmesan, Swiss, etc.

A *importados, deliciosos, preparados, franceses, ingleses, suizos, finos, dietéticos / suizo, sabroso* / Answers will vary, but look for explanations such as: You use *sabroso* when describing one item and *sabrosos* when describing more than one item.

B It ends in *-n*. Students may refer to the word as being plural.

Gramática en contexto

Look at this ad for imported cheeses. Are most of the cheeses you expected to find there?

¿Te gustan los quesos importados?

¿Sí? Pues, en **LA CASA DE LOS QUESOS** tenemos quesos deliciosos preparados especialmente para ti.

Tenemos quesos franceses, ingleses y suizos. También ofrecemos quesos finos de Holanda, Italia y Grecia. Para las personas que no deben o no quieren comer mucha grasa, tenemos una gran variedad de quesos dietéticos. El queso suizo es nuestra especialidad. Es muy sabroso.

¡Buen provecho! Bon appétit! Enjoy!

A Working with a partner, list all the words from the ad that describe cheese when it is written *quesos*.

- Find two words that describe cheese when it is written *queso*.
- When would you use *sabroso* or *sabrosos* to describe food?

B Look at the headline. How is this form of the expression for "Do you like ..." different from the form you learned earlier? How would you explain this?

134   Capítulo 4

Options

Strategies for Reaching All Students

Students Needing Extra Help
A: Review what students have already learned about the singular endings of adjectives. Have them use their Organizers from Chap. 3 to review other adjectives.
B: Write a *¿Te gustan ... ?* question, underlining the plural word.
El plural de los sustantivos: Have students fill in the first chart in the grammar portion of their Organizers.

134

El plural de los sustantivos

- In Spanish, to make nouns plural, we generally add -s to words ending in a vowel (*libro* → *libros*) and -es to words ending in a consonant (*papel* → *papeles*).

- The plural definite articles are *los* and *las*. *Los* is used with masculine plural nouns, *las* with feminine plural nouns.
   los cereal**es**   **las** pap**as**

- *Los* is also used with a plural noun that includes both males and females.
   el profesor Sánchez y la profesora Romero
   = **los** profesor**es**

- Singular nouns that end in the letter *z* change the *z* to *c* in the plural.
   el lápi**z** → los lápi**ces**

- To keep the stress on the correct syllable, we sometimes have to add or remove an accent mark in the plural.
   el ex**amen** → los ex**ámenes**
   el jam**ón** → los jam**ones**

- The plural indefinite articles are *unos* and *unas*. They mean "some" or "a few."
   No tengo mucha hambre, pero voy a comer **unas** papas fritas.

- We use *me gustan* and *me encantan* to talk about a plural noun.
   No me gust**an** las manzanas pero me encant**an** las uvas.

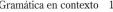
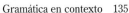

¡NO OLVIDES!

The singular definite articles are *el* and *la*. The singular indefinite articles are *un* and *una*.

Gramática en contexto   135

Present

Class Starter Review
On the day following initial presentation of the plural of nouns, you might begin the class with this activity:
In pairs, have students alternate asking and answering whether or not they like a particular food or beverage. Look for correct use of *me / te gusta(n)*.

Present & Practice

Re-enter / Recycle
Exs. 1–3: *gustar* expressions from Chap. 1
Ex. 2: invitations from Chap. 3

Reteach / Review: Definite & Indefinite Articles
Ex. 2: Contrast the use of indefinite and definite articles in this exercise to do a variation of Ex. 1: *¿Te gustaría comer unas papas al horno? / Sí, me encantan las papas al horno. / No, gracias. No me gustan las papas al horno.*

Answers
1 Explain that the definite article is used with foods when they occur with gusta(n).

ESTUDIANTE A
a. ¿Te gustan las papas fritas?
b. ...las verduras?
c. ...los guisantes?
d. ...las hamburguesas?
e. ...los plátanos?
f. ...los huevos?

ESTUDIANTE B
a.–f. Answers will vary depending on what *Estudiante B* likes or dislikes.

1 Discuss with a partner whether or not you like the following foods.

A —*¿Te gustan las zanahorias?*
B —*Sí, me gustan.*
   o: *Sí, me encantan.*
   o: *No, no me gustan nada.*

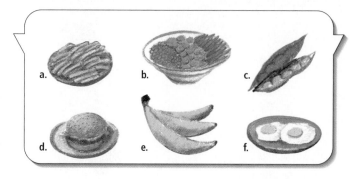

2 Now use the pictures in Exercise 1 to ask if your partner would like to eat those foods.

A —*¿Te gustaría comer unas zanahorias?*
B —*¡Claro que sí! A mí me encantan.*
   o: *No, no tengo hambre. Gracias.*

"Me encanta comer en un restaurante con mis amigos."

En un restaurante en la Ciudad de México

Options

Strategies for Reaching All Students

Spanish-Speaking Students
Ex. 2: Have Spanish-speaking students write questions such as those used by *Estudiante A* for each of the foods listed. Ask them to add four or five other foods.
Ex. 3: Pair bilingual and non-bilingual students for this exercise.

Students Needing Extra Help
Ex. 1: Explain the difference in degree between *me gustan* and *me encantan* and how both phrases include the idea of "them." (I like them. / I love them.)
Ex. 2: Review *te gusta* and *te gustaría.*
Ex. 3: Review possible responses *también* and *tampoco.*
El plural de los adjetivos: Have students continue to fill in the first chart (adjective endings) in the grammar portion of their Organizers.

Enrichment
Ex. 1: Have *Estudiante B* expand his or her answer by telling why he or she likes or dislikes the food named.

3 These foods might be served in your school cafeteria this week. Take turns with a partner telling whether you like them or not.

A — *Me gustan las papas al horno.*
B — *A mí también.*
   o: *A mí no.*

A — *No me gustan las papas al horno.*
B — *A mí tampoco.*
   o: *A mí sí.*

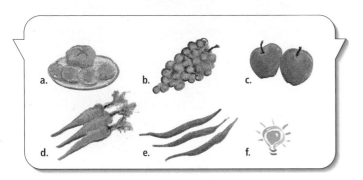

a.   b.   c.

d.   e.   f.

El plural de los adjetivos

You know that in Spanish most adjectives have different masculine and feminine singular forms: *La leche es sabrosa; el cereal es bueno para la salud.* If the noun is plural, the adjective too must be plural:

Las papas fritas son sabrosas pero no son buenas para la salud.
Los guisantes son buenos para la salud.

• To make adjectives plural, add -*s* to the final vowel. If the adjective ends in a consonant, add -*es*.
   horrible   horribles
   trabajador   trabajadores

• When an adjective describes both masculine and feminine nouns, use the masculine plural ending.
   Los plátanos y las manzanas son sabrosos.

Gramática en contexto   137

2 ESTUDIANTE A
a. ¿Te gustaría comer unas papas fritas?
b. ...unas verduras?
c. ...unos guisantes?
d. ...unas hamburguesas?
e. ...unos plátanos?
f. ...unos huevos?
ESTUDIANTE B
a.–f. Statements will vary.

3 ESTUDIANTE A
a. (No) me gustan los tomates.
b. ...las uvas.
c. ...las manzanas.
d. ...las zanahorias.
e. ...las judías verdes.
f. Statements will vary.
ESTUDIANTE B
a.–f. Statements will vary depending on *Estudiante B*'s preferences.

 Practice Wkbk. 4-5

 Prueba 4-5

Cultural Notes

(p. 136, photo)
These young people are in one of the many American-style restaurants in Mexico City. While some traditional Mexican dishes are available in these establishments, their main attraction for both residents and tourists is the American food they serve, such as hamburgers, French fries, and club sandwiches, in an American-restaurant setting.

Present & Practice

Re-enter / Recycle

Ex. 4: adjectives to describe personality from Chap. 1

Answers

4 Answers will vary. Make sure that students use correct adjective agreement.

 Practice Wkbk. 4-6

 Writing Activity 4-E

 Prueba 4-6

5 ESTUDIANTE A

a. ¿Qué bebe Anita en el desayuno?

b. ... beben Pilar y Pablo en el almuerzo?

c. ... beben Graciela y Juan en la cena?

d. ... bebe Carlitos en el desayuno?

e. ... beben Uds. en la cena?

f. ... bebes tú en el almuerzo?

ESTUDIANTE B

a. (Anita) bebe jugo de naranja.

b. (Pilar y Pablo) beben limonada.

c. (Graciela y Juan) beben agua.

d. (Carlitos) bebe leche.

e. Bebemos té helado.

f. Bebo ... *(Answers will vary.)*

---

4 For each of these adjectives, name two famous people or people in your class or school whom the adjective fits.

Carl Herrera y Gabriela Sabatini son deportistas.

artístico, -a
deportista
atrevido, -a
callado, -a
desordenado, -a
gracioso, -a
sociable
ordenado, -a
serio, -a
trabajador, -a

Verbos que terminan en *-er*

You know the pattern of present-tense endings for regular *-ar* verbs.

- Another group of infinitives end in *-er*. Some that you know are *beber, comer, leer,* and *deber.*

- Here are the present-tense forms of the verb *comer.* How does this pattern differ from that of *-ar* verbs?

(yo)	como	(nosotros) (nosotras)	com**emos**
(tú)	com**es**	(vosotros) (vosotras)	com**éis**
Ud. (él) (ella)	come	Uds. (ellos) (ellas)	com**en**

- With *-er* verbs we use the vowel *-e* in all forms except *yo.* Remember that *-ar* verbs use the vowel *-a* except in the *yo* form.

- You also know the verb *ver.* It is regular except in the *yo* form, which is *veo.*

138   Capítulo 4

Options

Strategies for Reaching All Students

Spanish-Speaking Students
Ex. 6: Have Spanish-speaking students write out the exercise, paying close attention to spelling and the use of accents.

Students Needing Extra Help
Verbos que terminan en -er: Have students fill in the verb chart in the grammar portion of their Organizers.
Ex. 6: Model some examples on the chalkboard. There are really three verbs involved in this exercise. Show how the verb in the first sentence becomes an infinitive in the second sentence.

5 With a partner, take turns asking and answering what the following people drink at different meals.

A — *¿Qué beben tus amigos en el almuerzo?*
B — *Beben refrescos.*

tus amigos / almuerzo

a. Anita / desayuno   b. Pilar y Pablo / almuerzo   c. Graciela y Juan / cena

d. Carlitos / desayuno   e. Uds. / cena   f. tú / almuerzo

6 These people do not eat certain foods. With your partner, discuss why they should eat them.

A — *Juan Carlos no come judías verdes.*
B — *¡Pero debe comer judías verdes!*
   Son buenas para la salud.

Juan Carlos

a. Víctor y Tomás   b. Inés   c. Raúl

d. Carmen y yo   e. Gloria y Victoria   f. yo

Gramática en contexto   139

6 Explain that the conjugated verb form of *deber* generally requires the infinitive to follow.

ESTUDIANTE A

a. Víctor y Tomás no comen tomates.

b. Inés no come naranjas.

c. Raúl no come papas al horno.

d. Carmen y yo no comemos verduras.

e. Gloria y Victoria no comen guisantes.

f. Yo no como . . . *(Statements will vary.)*

ESTUDIANTE B

a. ¡Pero deben comer tomates! Son buenos para la salud.

b. . . . debe comer naranjas! . . . buenas . . .

c. . . . debe comer papas al horno! . . . buenas . . .

d. . . . deben comer verduras! . . . buenas . . .

e. . . . deben comer guisantes! . . . buenos . . .

f. . . . debes comer . . . *(Statements will vary.)* . . . buenos(as) . . .

Practice Wkbk. 4-7, 4-8

Writing Activity 4-F

Prueba 4-7

Present & Practice

Re-enter / Recycle
Ex. 7: activities from Chap. 1; pastimes, destinations, expressions of emotion, and adverbs describing when things take place from Chap. 3

7 Answers
a. dibujamos
b. practican
c. hablan
d. ayudamos
e. comen
f. debemos
g. vamos
h. leemos
i. hablan
j. ven

Sujetos compuestos

- When you talk about yourself and someone else, you really mean "we." Therefore, you should use the *nosotros* form of the verb.
  Alejandro y yo (nosotros) estudi**amos** por la noche.
  Tú y yo (nosotros) com**emos** a las doce.

- When speaking to more than one person—even if you call one of them *tú*—use the *ustedes* form of the verb.
  Tú y Tomás (ustedes) practic**an** deportes.

- When you talk about more than one person or thing, use the *ellos / ellas* form of the verb.
  Marta y él (ellos) beb**en** jugo de uva.
  Marta y ella (ellas) escuch**an** música.

7 Imagine that these students are talking about activities they usually do or activities they are planning to do. Choose the correct verb form to complete each of the following sentences.

a. Mis amigos y yo *(dibujamos / dibujan)* en el parque.
b. ¡No me digas! Pablo y ella *(practican / practicamos)* deportes también.
c. Esteban y tú *(hablan / hablamos)* por teléfono todos los días, ¿verdad?
d. Juan va a cocinar hoy. Él y yo siempre *(ayudan / ayudamos)* en casa.
e. Él y ella *(comemos / comen)* en casa los fines de semana.
f. Tú y yo *(deben / debemos)* ir de compras mañana por la mañana.
g. ¡Qué lástima! Patricia y yo no *(vamos / van)* a ir de pesca en el verano.
h. Elena nunca lee, pero mis amigos y yo *(leen / leemos)* todos los días.
i. José y mis amigas siempre *(hablamos / hablan)* después de las clases.
j. No veo la tele por la tarde, pero Juanita y tú *(ves / ven)* la tele todos los días por la tarde.

140   Capítulo 4

Options

Strategies for Reaching All Students

Students Needing Extra Help
Ahora lo sabes: Have students write out this section so they can check off what they have mastered.

Enrichment
Ex. 7: As a written assignment, students may write sentences using the verb forms not used in this exercise, creating correct subjects for them, and any reasonable variations on the vocabulary in the original sentences.

Ahora lo sabes

Can you:

- tell that you like or don't like certain food groups?

  —(No) _____ las frutas.

- describe groups of people or things?

  —Los huevos son ___, pero las verduras son ___.

- say what you eat or drink at different meals?

  —A ver . . . En el desayuno (nosotros) ___ cereal y ___ jugo de naranja.

- make clear to or about whom you are talking when more than one person is referred to?

  —Timoteo y tú ___ la televisión todos los días, ¿verdad?

141

Apply

Play

Step

Using the Video
Video segment 3: See the Video Teacher's Guide.

 Video Activity C

Critical Thinking: Synthesizing
Actividades: Have small groups create an invitation to a dinner party that they will be hosting. Invitations should include a brief menu. Have other groups accept or decline the invitation. (Review Chap. 3 vocabulary related to accepting or declining invitations.)

Para decir más
Variants: peach, *el melocotón;* cake, *la torta, el bizcocho;* hot chocolate, *el chocolate hecho;* peanut butter, *mantequilla de cacahuete (de maní).* You or your students may be more familiar with one or another of the words given.

Para decir más

Here is some additional vocabulary that you might find useful for activities in this section.

la pera
pear

el durazno
peach

el tocino
bacon

los espaguetis
spaghetti

la mermelada
jam

la jalea
jelly

el helado
ice cream

el pastel
cake

el chocolate caliente
hot chocolate

la mantequilla de cacahuate
peanut butter

rico, -a
delicious

142   Capítulo 4

Actividades

Here's an opportunity for you to expand your use of Spanish by putting together the material you learned in this chapter with what you learned earlier.

 1 People have different tastes in food. Tell your partner your opinion of different foods and drinks. He or she will agree or disagree.

A — *Las ensaladas son muy sabrosas. A mí me encantan.*
B — *¿Te encantan? Pues, a mí no me gustan nada. ¡Qué asco!*
o: *¡No me digas! A mí también me gustan las ensaladas.*

Options

Strategies for Reaching All Students

Spanish-Speaking Students
Ex. 3: Have pairs of students write out the exercise. Then have them present the exercise orally.

Students Needing Extra Help
Exs. 1–3: Create some worksheets in which parts of a complete dialogue are missing, as in a cloze activity. For example, in the first dialogue a few words can be missing that the students will fill in. Then have a dialogue where *Estudiante B's* responses are missing. Finally, have the students create a complete dialogue. Build up to this carefully so as not to overwhelm.

Ex. 1: Have students use their Organizers. Talk through students' likes and dislikes of foods. Write some on the chalkboard.
Ex. 2: Review time-telling from Chap. 2. Have students use their Organizers.
Ex. 3: Review *te gustaría* along with the *yo* and *tú* forms of *tener hambre, querer,* and *preferir.* Model a complete dialogue.

2 On the weekend our pattern of eating often changes. Find out what your partner's meals are usually like on the weekend. Ask:

- at what time he or she eats certain meals
- whether he or she eats alone or with family or friends
- what the meal usually consists of

3 With a partner, talk about what you plan to eat. Include the following, but keep your conversation going as long as you can:

- Find out if your partner is hungry.
- Your partner answers affirmatively.
- Ask what he or she wants / prefers / would like to eat.
- Your partner answers.

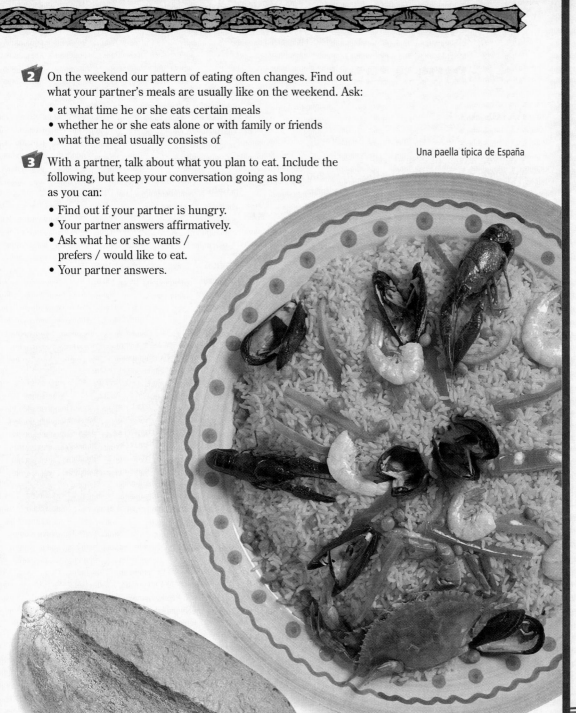
Una paella típica de España

Apply

Process Reading
For a description of process reading, see p. 48.

Answers
Antes de leer
Answers will vary.

Mira la lectura
Answers will vary.

1 potatoes, tomatoes, and cocoa

2 in the sixteenth and seventeenth centuries

¡Vamos a leer!

Antes de leer

STRATEGY › Using prior knowledge

What you are about to read tells the history of chocolate, which was used by the Mayas and the Aztecs of Mexico over a thousand years ago. And they used it in a very different way! How do you think chocolate got to Europe and why did Europeans use it differently?

As you already know, you can use pictures and your own experience with certain kinds of reading materials to predict and understand the information you might find there.

Mira la lectura

STRATEGY › Using cognates

As you read, try to use cognates (words that are similar to English words) to help you figure out the meaning.

1 What are some of the other products that the Europeans found when they came to America?

2 When did chocolate become one of the most popular drinks in Europe?

En el siglo XV los conquistadores llegan a América. Allí descubren muchos productos nuevos para la comida española y europea, por ejemplo: la papa, el tomate y el cacao. El cacao es uno de los ingredientes que los aztecas usan para hacer el *tchocolatl* (palabra azteca para chocolate).

Los aztecas preparan el *tchocolatl* con cacao, verduras y varios tipos de chiles. Es una bebida muy fuerte que los indios beben en sus ceremonias religiosas. Pero el *tchocolatl* azteca es muy diferente del chocolate que bebemos hoy.

En Europa, el *tchocolatl* se transforma en una bebida más líquida y más dulce. En los siglos XVI y XVII el chocolate es una de las bebidas más populares de Europa. El chocolate caliente se hace con cacao y agua o leche. Hoy, en España, hay chocolaterías, lugares donde sirven chocolate casi exclusivamente.

144   Capítulo 4

Options

Strategies for Reaching All Students

Spanish-Speaking Students
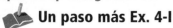 **Un paso más Ex. 4-I**

Students Needing Extra Help
Place the reading in context by reminding students that the chapter theme is food.
Antes de leer: Remind students to use context clues in the text along with the visuals to help them understand the reading.

Mira la lectura: You may wish to provide students with a brief overview of the history of the Mayas and Aztecs.
Infórmate: Go over the questions with students before you begin the reading. Emphasize that they don't need to know every word in order to understand the text.

Infórmate

STRATEGY ➤ Using context to get meaning

Using context to get meaning is another useful strategy. When you are reading and you run across a word you don't understand, look at the other words in the sentence. See if knowing those words can help you understand the one you don't know.

Read this selection again. Make a list of five words you don't understand. Then try to guess their meaning by looking at the surrounding words.

1 How and when was chocolate introduced in Europe?

2 How did the Aztecs prepare their *tchocolatl?* Was it an everyday drink or was it used on special occasions? Explain.

3 How was the chocolate the conquistadores brought to Europe different from the Aztecan *tchocolatl?*

Aplicación

List as many cognates as you can that you found in this reading.

¡Vamos a leer! 145

Infórmate
Lists will vary.

1 Chocolate was introduced in Europe in the sixteenth century as a sweeter and thinner liquid than its Aztec counterpart.

2 The Aztecs prepared *tchocolatl* with cocoa, vegetables, and different types of chiles. It was used in religious ceremonies.

3 Answers may vary, but may include that the chocolate differed in taste, appearance, and usage.

Aplicación
Lists will vary, but may include: *productos, cacao, ingredientes, aztecas, chocolate, preparan, tipos, chiles, indios, ceremonias religiosas, diferente, Europa, se transforma, líquida, populares, sirven, exclusivamente.*

Enrichment
Bring in a recipe for *mole* and show how it ties in with the Aztec recipe described in the text.

Apply

Process Writing
For information regarding developing a writing portfolio, see p. 50.

Multicultural Perspectives

With the influences and infusion of Hispanic cultures within the Americas, many restaurants cater to the varied tastes of their customers. Today, Hispanic cuisine can be classified as traditional or *nouveau,* vegetarian or *con carne,* Tex-Mex or Santa Fe, Salvadoran or Nicaraguan, and so on. Other establishments may feature only traditional Spanish dishes. Invite students to identify and describe other types of Hispanic cuisine.

Todo junto

¡Vamos a escribir!

Your health class is studying nutrition and the teacher wants you to think about what, when, and where you eat. Write a short paragraph about your favorite meal of the day. Follow these steps.

 Answer these questions, then use the answers to write your paragraph.
- ¿A qué hora comes tu comida favorita?
- ¿Dónde comes: en la casa, en la escuela o en un restaurante?
- ¿Con quién comes?
- ¿Qué comes y qué bebes?

146   Capítulo 4

Options

Strategies for Reaching All Students

Spanish-Speaking Students

 Un paso más Exs. 4-J, 4-K

Students Needing Extra Help
Step 1: Have students use their Organizers from earlier chapters to review time-telling, places, and *con.*
Step 3: Have students use their Organizers to check spelling.

Enrichment
If possible, bring in a poster of the food groups and have students make a poster showing similar items, but with the labels in Spanish. Students may wish to make original drawings or clip photographs from food magazines to make their posters more attractive.

146

2 Show your paragraph to a partner. Does he or she have any ideas to suggest? Did you use the answers to all the questions in your paragraph? Think about any changes you may want to make, then write a second draft.

3 Check for correct spelling and punctuation. Did you use the *yo* form of the verbs? Did you use *me gusta(n)* or *me encanta(n)*? Does your partner have any further suggestions?

Write your final draft. Add the corrected paragraph to your writing portfolio.

grasa *(fat)*
azúcar *(sugar)*

Assess & Summarize

Test Preparation

You may want to assign parts of this section as written homework or as an in-class writing activity prior to administering the *Examen de habilidades*.

Answers

Listening: *A esta hora siempre quiero comer cereal, huevos con jamón, pan tostado y café con leche. Prefiero comer frutas por la tarde.* Eugenio is talking about breakfast.

Reading: This product is recommended for physically active adolescents; it's a nutritious snack.

Writing: Writing samples will vary, but students should use the chapter vocabulary. Look for logical sentences.

Culture: Answers will vary, but may include: *El desayuno* is a light meal that consists of coffee and bread or rolls with butter and jam. *El almuerzo* or *la comida* is the largest and most important meal of the day. It is eaten between noon and 2:00. *La merienda* is a late afternoon meal that may resemble an English tea. *La cena* is the evening meal, which may be served around 7:00 or later.

¿Lo sabes bien?

This section will help you organize your studying for the proficiency test, where you will be asked to do similar, though not identical, tasks. There will not be any models on the test.

Listening

Can you understand when people talk about food? Listen as your teacher reads you a sample similar to what you will hear on the test. Which meal is Eugenio talking about?

Reading

Can you quickly read through this ad and use the context to guess any word or words that you might not know? Who is this product recommended for and why?

La crema de cacao es un alimento especialmente indicado para adolescentes con una gran energía. Es un alimento nutritivo, ideal para la merienda.

Writing

Can you write the order for the customers you are waiting on? Here is a sample:

Culture

Can you describe the four meals that are typical of many Spanish-speaking countries?

"Me encantan los refrescos."

Speaking

Can you discuss your food preferences with a partner? Do you like or dislike the same foods? For example:

A — *¿Te gusta el pescado?*
B — *No me gusta nada. ¿Y a ti?*
A — *No mucho. Mi madre siempre cocina pescado los viernes. Es horrible. ¿Te gustan las zanahorias?*
B — *Sí, pero prefiero las papas o las judías verdes. No me gustan nada las cebollas. ¡Qué asco!*
A — *Pues, a mí me encantan las cebollas. Son muy sabrosas.*

Options

Strategies for Reaching All Students

Students Needing Extra Help
Have students write out this section so they can check off what they have mastered.

Resumen del capítulo 4

Use the vocabulary from this chapter to help you:
- describe what you like and don't like to eat and drink
- tell when you have meals
- say whether you are hungry or thirsty

to indicate hunger or thirst
tener hambre / sed

to describe meals
beber: (yo) bebo
      (tú) bebes
comer: (yo) como
       (tú) comes
la cena
la comida
el desayuno
en el desayuno / el almuerzo /
   la cena

to talk about foods
el arroz
el bistec
el cereal
la ensalada
las frutas
   la manzana
   la naranja
   el plátano
   la uva
la hamburguesa
el huevo
el jamón
el pan
   el pan tostado
la papa
   las papas al horno
   las papas fritas
el pescado
el pollo

el queso
los sandwiches
   el sandwich de
   jamón y queso
la sopa de pollo / de tomate /
   de verduras
las verduras
   la cebolla
   los guisantes
   las judías verdes
   la lechuga
   el tomate
   la zanahoria

to talk about drinks
las bebidas
   el agua (f.)
   el café
   el jugo de naranja
   la leche
   la limonada
   el refresco
   el té
   el té helado

to describe foods
bueno, -a (para la salud)
horrible
malo, -a (para la salud)
sabroso, -a

to express likes or preferences
más o menos
me encanta(n)

me gusta(n)
preferir: (yo) prefiero
       (tú) prefieres

to express an opinion
Creo que sí / no.
¡Qué asco!

to ask for an explanation
¿Por qué?

to give an explanation
porque

to elicit agreement
¿verdad?

to refer to obligation
deber: (yo) debo
     (tú) debes

to indicate frequency
nunca
siempre

**to refer to something you
cannot name**
algo

other useful words
son
unos, unas

Resumen   149

 Prueba cumulativa

 Examen de habilidades

 Test Generator

CAPÍTULO 5

THEME: FAMILY

SCOPE AND SEQUENCE Pages 150–179

COMMUNICATION

Topics

Family members

Personal physical characteristics

Age

Numbers 60–100

Objectives

To explain how names are formed in Spanish-speaking countries

To talk about family members

To tell someone's name

To ask and tell how old someone is

To indicate possession

To talk about what someone likes

To indicate number

To talk about people

To describe people, animals, and things

To name animals

CULTURE

The family

Spanish last names

GRAMMAR

El verbo tener

El verbo ser

Los adjetivos posesivos

Ancillaries available for use with Chapter 5

Multisensory/Technology

 Overhead Transparencies, 26–30

 Audio Tapes and CDs

 Vocabulary Art Blackline Masters for Hands-On Learning, pp. 28–32

 Classroom Crossword

 Video

 CD-ROM

Print

 Practice Workbook, pp. 53–63

 Writing, Audio & Video Activities, pp. 29–34, 105–107, 160–161

 Communicative Activity Blackline Masters
  Pair and Small Group Activities, pp. 36–41
  Situation Cards, p. 42

 Un paso más: Actividades para ampliar tu español, pp. 26–31

Assessment

 Assessment Program
  Pruebas, pp. 67–76
  Examen de habilidades, pp. 77–80

 Test Generator

Video still from Chap. 5

Family Ties

Strong family ties and allegiances are central to the social structures of many Spanish-speaking countries. The structure of family surnames, which contain both the mother's and the father's family names, reflects the great importance of the family unit. For example, if Sr. David Ramírez Tejeda is married to Sra. Ángela Díaz Contreras, their children will use the surname Ramírez Díaz.

Although strict gender-defined roles are gradually disappearing, vestiges of a patriarchal family structure can still be found in the different treatment of young men and women within some families. In working-class families, it is often assumed that the girls will help with their younger brothers and sisters and do other domestic work. Boys are largely exempt from these expectations. Boys often receive more education than girls do and have greater independence at an earlier age.

Until recent years, divorce was illegal in several Latin American countries. Although divorce is now possible, it remains socially unacceptable in many places and is often granted with stipulations. In Mexico, for example, a divorce judgment may stipulate that one or both parties may not remarry for a year or more. The Mexican Civil Code specifies such a restriction because marriage is viewed as the foundation of the family and is not to be entered into lightly or abandoned easily.

In many Spanish-speaking countries, it is considered a duty to spend time with one's family. People would almost never consider missing an important family event such as a baptism, wedding, or birthday. Parties for such events span several generations with all family members attending. Everyone from babies to grandparents can be seen at a party on Saturday night.

Good friends are also included in many family events. In many cases, friends are considered part of the family. Friendship ties, like family bonds, are strong. Relatives and friends will help each other out and are regularly a part of the daily lives of each other's families.

Introduce

Re-entry of Concepts

The following list represents words, expressions, and grammar topics re-entered from *El primer paso* to Chap. 4:

El primer paso
Calendar expressions
Numbers 0–31
Greetings

Chapter 1
Activities
Gustar expressions
Adjectives describing personality

Chapter 2
School supplies
School subjects
Numbers 32–59
Possession and need

Chapter 3
Pastimes
Destinations
Adverbs describing when things take place

Chapter 4
Likes or preferences
Opinions
Adjective agreement

Planning

Cross-Curricular Connections

Drawing / Art Connection *(pp. 158–159)*
Have students draw an alien creature or monster as homework. The next day, pair students. As one student describes his or her creature in Spanish, the other student draws it. Pairs then compare drawings. Award a prize for the two drawings that are the most similar. Then have the pairs switch roles. Post some of the pairs of pictures on the walls and use for vocabulary warm-up questions.

Journalism Connection *(pp. 170–171)*
Have pairs of students each assume the identity of a famous person. Tell them that they will be interviewing each other for an article in the school newspaper. Give them several minutes to write a few appropriate questions before beginning their interviews. As homework, students can write out their interview and include a picture and headline.

Spanish in Your Community
Have students obtain a copy of a Spanish-language newspaper published in your community (if available). Ask them to look through the society section of this paper and find an announcement of a wedding, baptism, or funeral. Have them determine the family relationships mentioned in the article. As an alternative, have students look through the local phone book to see how many people in their community have common Spanish surnames such as González,

CAPÍTULO 5

¿Cómo es tu familia?

OBJECTIVES

At the end of this chapter, you will be able to:

- describe family members and friends
- tell what someone's age is
- say what other people like and do not like to do
- explain how names are formed in Spanish-speaking countries

Una familia mexicana

151

García, and Pérez. Have students discover more surnames as they look through the phone book. (You may also wish to bring in any phone directories printed in Spanish.)

Preview

 ¿Cómo es tu familia?

Play

 Video Activity A

Using the Video

This chapter's video focuses on family. Students will join our host in her own Guadalajara home and meet her family. Then they will accompany her to meet a family in nearby Tlaquepaque.

To prepare students for the video, first ask them to predict what this chapter's video will be about. Then have students watch the segment several times. After the first time, you may wish to have them brainstorm possible vocabulary and expressions they will need to talk about what they saw on the video. Ask students to identify:

a) ways in which the Mexican families were similar to their own family, and b) ways in which the families were different from their own family.

Video segment 1: For more teaching suggestions, see the Video Teacher's Guide.

¡Piénsalo bien!

Look at the two photos and compare the families to your own. How many people are in your family? Which family members do you think make up a family? Do you consider your grandparents, uncles, aunts, and cousins as your "family" or are they just "relatives"? Do you all get together sometimes?

"Aquí estoy con mis primos. Siempre voy a nadar con ellos."

En la República Dominicana

152   Capítulo 5

Options

Strategies for Reaching All Students

Spanish-Speaking Students

Ask Spanish-speaking students: *¿Qué es una familia? ¿Cómo es tu familia? ¿Es grande o pequeña? ¿Quiénes son?*

 Un paso más Ex. 5-A

Students Needing Extra Help

Be sensitive to the fact that many of your students' families may not be typical. Discuss what an American family today may look like: single parent, stepsisters and half brothers, and so on. Not all students will want to discuss this issue. Some may have neighbors or others with whom they feel close. Be open to these ideas. Imaginary families or the family they would like to have when they become adults are alternative topics.

"Me llamo Maricarmen y estoy con mi familia para celebrar el cumpleaños de mi abuelo. Tiene 67 años."

Who did you think the "abuelo" is? How did you know?

Una familia en Santiago, Chile

153

Present

Chapter Theme
Identifying family members

Communicative Objectives
• To talk about family members
• To tell someone's name
• To ask and tell how old someone is
• To indicate possession
• To talk about what someone likes
• To indicate number

Transparencies 26–27

Vocabulary Art BLMs

Pronunciation Tape 5-1

Vocabulario para conversar A

Play

Using the Video
Video segment 2: See the Video Teacher's Guide.

Video Activity B

Grammar Preview
Su and *de* are presented here lexically. The explanation of possessive adjectives appears in the grammar section on p. 170.

Vocabulario para conversar

¿Cómo se llama tu hermano?

Here are some new words and expressions you will need to talk about your family, to tell what someone's age is, and to say what other people like and do not like to do. Read them several times, then turn the page and practice with a partner.

mis abuelos

mi abuelo
Pedro, 80 años

mi abuela
Carmen, 75 años

mis padres

mis tíos

mi madre
María, 46 años

mi padre
Luis, 52 años

mi tía
Verónica, 50 años

mi tío
Tomás, 48 años

mis hermanos*

mis primos

mi hermano
José, 19 años

mi hermana
Gabriela, 23 años

yo
Mariana, 15 años

mi primo
Carlos, 16 años

mi prima
Ana, 18 años

* *Hermanos* can mean either "brothers" or "brothers and sisters."

154   Capítulo 5

Options

Strategies for Reaching All Students

Students Needing Extra Help
Have students start to fill in the Organizer. Students often have difficulty reading a family tree, especially the reference to *yo*. Show them how the relationships change when *yo* becomes another person. For example, if Ana becomes *yo*, then Verónica becomes *la madre* and María becomes *la tía,* and so on.

Point out the similarities between *abuelo / abuela, tío / tía,* etc.
También necesitas . . . : Point out that *único(a)* is used with nouns and age is expressed with *tener*—to "have" so many years.

Enrichment
También necesitas. . . : Elicit from students the English word for which *único(a)* might be a cognate. Explain that *único(a)* has two meanings in Spanish: "only," as in *hijo(a) único(a)* and "unique," as in *¡Eres único(a)!*

60 sesenta
61 sesenta y uno . . .

70 setenta
71 setenta y uno . . .

80 ochenta
81 ochenta y uno . . .

90 noventa
91 noventa y uno . . .

100 cien

También necesitas . . .

el hijo / la hija	*son / daughter*
el hijo único / la hija única	*only child (m.) / only child (f.)*
¿Cómo se llama?	*What is his / her name?*
¿Cómo se llaman?	*What are their names?*
Se llama(n) ___.	*His / her (their) name(s) is (are) ___.*
¿Cuántos años tiene ___?	*How old is ___?*
Tiene ___ años.	*He / she is ___ years old.*
su	*his, her*
de	*of*
(A + *person*) le gusta(n) / le encanta(n) ___.	*(He / she) likes / loves ___.*
¿Cuántos, -as?	*How many?*
sólo	*only*

┌─────────────────────────────┐
│ **¿Y qué quiere decir . . . ?** │
│ los hijos   │
└─────────────────────────────┘

Vocabulario para conversar   155

Teaching Suggestions
Preparing students to speak: Use one or two options from each of the categories of Comprehensible Input, Physical Response, or Limited Verbal Response. For a complete explanation of these categories and some sample activities, see the front section of this Teacher's Edition.

Point out that after *ser*, the article *el / la* is not used with *hijo(a) único(a)*.

Class Starter Review
On the day following initial presentation, you might begin the class with one of these activities:
1) Use the transparency of a family tree with one person labeled *yo*. Point to other members of the family and ask individual students who these relatives are in relation to *yo*. On the following day, label a different person *yo*. On the third day, arrange pictures of famous people in a family tree on the chalkboard and do the same activity.
2) Have pairs of students find out the name of at least one member of each other's family.

Learning Spanish Through Action
STAGING VOCABULARY: *Nombren, Señalen*
MATERIALS: transparency of family tree in the *Vocabulario para conversar*
DIRECTIONS: Using the transparency, have pairs of students take the part of Mariana by pointing at the relative as you mention the relationship.

Practice & Apply

Re-enter / Recycle
Ex. 2: numbers 0–31 from *El primer paso*, numbers 32–59 from Chap. 1

Exs. 4–5: activities from Chap. 1

Ex. 6: numbers 0–31 from *El primer paso*, numbers 32–59 from Chap. 1

Reteach / Review: Definite & Indefinite Articles
Do a quick practice exercise to review definite articles by naming a noun and calling on individuals to give the correct definite or indefinite article.

Answers: Empecemos a conversar

1 ESTUDIANTE A
a. ¿Cómo se llama el tío de Mariana?
b. ...el hermano...
c. ...la hermana...
d. ...el primo...
e. ...la prima...
f. ...el abuelo...
g. Questions will vary.

ESTUDIANTE B
a. Se llama Tomás.
b. ...José.
c. ...Gabriela.
d. ...Carlos.
e. ...Ana.
f. ...Pedro.
g. Answers will vary.

Empecemos a conversar

With a partner, take turns being *Estudiante A* and *Estudiante B.* Use the words that are cued or given in the balloons to replace the underlined sections in the model. 💡 means you can make your own choices.

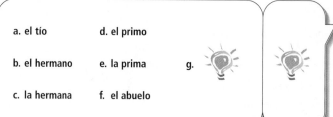

For Exercises 1 and 2, refer to the family tree on page 154.

1 la tía
A —¿Cómo se llama <u>la tía</u> de Mariana?
B —Se llama <u>Verónica</u>.
Y ahora Uds.

Estudiante A   **Estudiante B**

a. el tío   d. el primo

b. el hermano   e. la prima   g. 💡   💡

c. la hermana   f. el abuelo

2 José
A —¿Cuántos años tiene <u>José</u>?
B —Tiene <u>diecinueve</u> años.
Y ahora Uds.

Estudiante A   **Estudiante B**

a. el hijo de Verónica
b. la hija de Tomás
c. el padre de Mariana   g. 💡   💡
d. la madre de Ana
e. el hermano de Gabriela
f. Pedro

156   Capítulo 5

Options

Strategies for Reaching All Students

Spanish-Speaking Students
Try to pair bilingual and non-bilingual students for Exs. 1–4.
Empecemos a escribir: Spanish-speaking students can expand on answers, especially for Ex. 6. Have them tell why they like particular relatives. *(¿Por qué son tus favoritos?)*

 Un paso más Ex. 5-B

Students Needing Extra Help
Ex. 1: Some students may need a review for family relationship words in English. You may wish to go over these words before doing the exercise.
Empecemos a escribir: For additonal practice, have sudents write out how many family members they have in these categories: *tíos, primos, abuelos.*

Enrichment
Ex. 2: After completing this exercise, have pairs of students ask and tell each other their names and ages.
Ex. 5: To extend this exercise, students can write about three things that they and another family member *don't* like to do.

In Exercises 3 and 4, ask each other about your own family members or create ideal families to talk about.

3 A —¿*Tienes hermanos?*
   B —*Sí, tengo un hermano y una hermana.*
      o: *No, no tengo hermanos.*
      o: *No, no tengo. Soy hijo(a) único(a).*
   A —¿*Cómo se llama(n)?*
   B —*Mi hermano se llama Daniel y mi hermana se llama Laura.*

   Y ahora Uds.

Estudiante A   **Estudiante B**

4 A —¿*Qué le gusta hacer a tu primo?*
   B —*Le gusta dibujar.*
      o: *Le encanta dibujar.*

   Y ahora Uds.

Estudiante A   **Estudiante B**

Empecemos a escribir

Write your answers in Spanish.

5 Mention at least three interests you share with other family members. For example: *A mi hermana le gusta practicar deportes. A mí también.*

6 Give the name and age of your favorite relatives: *Mi tía favorita se llama Gloria. Tiene cuarenta años (más o menos).*

7 ¿Eres hijo(a) único(a)?

8 ¿Cuántos primos tienes?

Vocabulario para conversar   157

Present

Chapter Theme
Describing friends and family

Communicative Objectives
- To talk about family members
- To talk about people
- To describe people, animals, and things
- To name animals
- To indicate possession and number

 Transparencies 28–29

 Vocabulary Art BLMs

 Pronunciation Tape 5-2

 Vocabulario para conversar B

Play

Using the Video
Video segment 2: See the Video Teacher's Guide.

 Video Activity B

Grammar Preview
Tiene is presented here lexically. The complete paradigm of *tener* appears on p. 167.

Vocabulario para conversar

¿Cómo es tu abuelo?

Here's the rest of the vocabulary you will need to describe family members and friends.

el hombre — Juan
el pelo castaño
la mujer — Gloria
el pelo rubio
el muchacho — Marcos
la muchacha — Adela
baja
alto
pelirrojos
bonito
feo — el perro
los gemelos — Paco y Pepe

158   Capítulo 5

Options

Strategies for Reaching All Students

Students Needing Extra Help
One way of approaching this vocabulary is to categorize it in the Organizer under "Words That Describe People" according to eyes, hair, etc., or by opposites. *También necesitas. . . :* Have students continue filling in their Organizers.

Learning Spanish Through Action
STAGING VOCABULARY: *Dibujen, Señalen*
1) MATERIALS: transparency of people in the *Vocabulario para conversar* or pictures from magazines
DIRECTIONS: Using the transparency or magazine pictures, have students point to the person as you describe eye and hair color and other physical characteristics.

2) MATERIALS: colored chalk
DIRECTIONS: Have volunteers go to the chalkboard to draw people as you describe them. You may wish to use pictures of famous people as models for your descriptions.

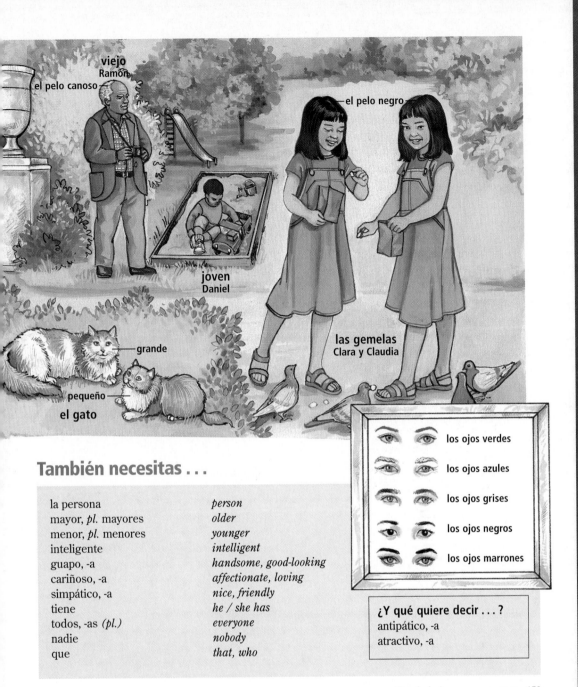

viejo
Ramón
el pelo canoso

el pelo negro

joven
Daniel

las gemelas
Clara y Claudia

grande

pequeño
el gato

los ojos verdes

los ojos azules

los ojos grises

los ojos negros

los ojos marrones

¿Y qué quiere decir . . . ?
antipático, -a
atractivo, -a

También necesitas . . .

la persona	*person*
mayor, *pl.* mayores	*older*
menor, *pl.* menores	*younger*
inteligente	*intelligent*
guapo, -a	*handsome, good-looking*
cariñoso, -a	*affectionate, loving*
simpático, -a	*nice, friendly*
tiene	*he / she has*
todos, -as *(pl.)*	*everyone*
nadie	*nobody*
que	*that, who*

Vocabulario para conversar 159

Practice & Apply

Reteach / Review: Adjectives

Do a quick drill in which you name an adjective and call on individual students to give you its plural form.

Answers: Empecemos a conversar

9 ESTUDIANTE A

a. ¿Cómo se llama la mujer que tiene el pelo rubio?

b. ...el hombre que tiene el pelo canoso?

c. ...la muchacha baja?

d. ...el joven que tiene el pelo negro?

e. ...el muchacho alto?

ESTUDIANTE B

a. Se llama Gloria.

b. ...Ramón.

c. ...Adela.

d. ...Daniel.

e. ...Marcos.

10 ESTUDIANTE A

a. En la clase, ¿quién tiene pelo...?

b. En la clase, ¿quién tiene ojos...?

ESTUDIANTE B

a.–b. Answers will vary.

Empecemos a conversar

For Exercise 9, refer to the pictures on pp. 158–159.

9
A —*¿Cómo se llama el hombre que tiene el pelo castaño?*
B —*Se llama Juan.*
Y ahora Uds.

Estudiante A      **Estudiante B**

10
A —*En la clase, ¿quién tiene ojos verdes?*
B —*Diana y Jeff.*
o: *Todos.*
o: *Nadie.*
Y ahora Uds.

Estudiante A **Estudiante B**

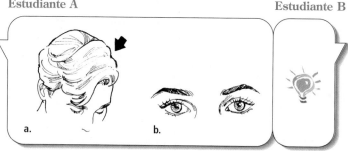

Options

Strategies for Reaching All Students

Spanish-Speaking Students

Ex. 14: Have Spanish-speaking students describe someone else in their family. (*¿Cómo son tus padres?*)

 Un paso más Exs. 5-C, 5-D, 5-E

Students Needing Extra Help

Ex. 9: Before students do this exercise, describe several possible combinations according to the model.

Ex. 10: Before doing this exercise, ask students similar questions about their families. Explain responses.

Ex. 11: Students may need your input to develop possibilities for *Estudiante A*.

Ex. 12: Before students do this exercise, have them describe each other. Then, to provide a model, describe for students someone in the family tree in the first *Vocabulario para conversar*. Finally, have students describe their family members. They should use their Organizers from previous chapters.

11

gemelos

A —¿Hay *gemelos* en la clase?
B —*Sí, James y John*.
   o: *No, no hay.*

Y ahora Uds.

Estudiante A

a. personas altas
b. personas rubias
c.

Estudiante B

In Exercise 12, you should ask you partner about his or her family members and pets.

12 A —¿*Cómo es tu hermana menor?*
B —*Es alta y simpática. Es pelirroja y tiene ojos verdes.*
   o: *No tengo hermana.*

Y ahora Uds.

Estudiante A

Estudiante B

Empecemos a escribir y a leer

Write your answers in Spanish.

13 You are going to the airport to meet someone you haven't seen before. How would you describe yourself to that person?

14 Now describe your best friend.

15 On a separate piece of paper, write *sí* or *no* in response to the statements about the following paragraph.

¡Hola! Me llamo Cristina. Soy la hermana mayor. Tengo pelo castaño y ojos marrones. Tengo dos hermanas gemelas. Son altas y tienen ojos verdes.

a. Cristina es hija única.
b. Ella es la hermana mayor.
c. Cristina tiene ojos verdes.
d. En la familia de Cristina hay gemelas.

Vocabulario para conversar   161

También se dice

güero, -a — los ojos de color café

la mamá   el papá

colorín, colorina

Practice

Answers:
¡Comuniquemos!

1 A —¿Cómo es George King?
B —Tiene ojos marrones y pelo castaño.
A —¡Ah! George es el número noventa y cuatro.

A —...Juan Enríquez?
B —...ojos azules y pelo negro.
A —...Juan ... cincuenta y cinco.

A —...John Green?
B —...ojos grises y pelo castaño.
A —...John ... ochenta y nueve.

A —...Hal Jensen?
B —...ojos azules y pelo rubio.
A —...Hal ... setenta y dos.

A —...Sean Morrow?
B —...ojos verdes y es pelirrojo.
A —...Sean ... setenta y ocho.

A —...Felipe del Castillo?
B —...ojos marrones y pelo negro.
A —...Felipe ... sesenta y siete.

A —...Matt Brown?
B —...ojos marrones y pelo rubio.
A —...Matt ... ochenta y dos.

¡Comuniquemos!

Here's another opportunity for you to use the vocabulary you've just learned.

1 These pictures of members of the football team are for the school yearbook. Before you can write the captions, you must identify the people in the pictures. Call the coach for help. Take turns with your partner playing the roles of the yearbook writer (A) and the coach (B).

Raja Patel

A —*¿Cómo es Raja Patel?*
B —*Tiene ojos negros y pelo negro.*
A —*¡Ah! Raja es el número sesenta y tres.*

a. George King   b. Juan Enríquez   c. John Green

d. Hal Jensen   e. Sean Morrow   f. Felipe del Castillo   g. Matt Brown

162   Capítulo 5

Options

Strategies for Reaching All Students

Spanish-Speaking Students
Ex. 1: Have pairs of Spanish-speaking students work together on this exercise and then present it to the whole class.
Ex. 2: Pair bilingual and non-bilingual students.
Ex. 3: Have students write out this exercise.

 Un paso más Exs. 5-F, 5-G

Students Needing Extra Help
Ex. 1: Model a second example. Put paper numbers on some students in class. Have the rest of the class describe them according to the example.
Ex. 2: Have pictures of dogs and cats available to describe with true statements. Then make up some false statements. Keep them separate at first.

Have students use their Organizers for *perezoso, prudente,* etc. (Chap. 1); *ir de pesca, la piscina,* etc. (Chap. 3); *hambre, sed, bistec, pescado,* etc. (Chap. 4). Model the responses.
¿Qué sabes ahora?: Have students write out this section so that they can keep track of their progress. You may wish to expand on these concepts.

2 Choose either the cat or the dog and describe him to your partner. To make sure your partner is listening, make two or three untrue statements. Your partner will correct you. Then your partner will describe the other animal to you. For example:

Se llama . . .   (No) es . . .   (No) le gusta . . .   Tiene . . .

Chispa

Michi

3 An exchange student from Ecuador is going to spend the next year with your family. Describe his or her family to your partner.

¿Qué sabes ahora?

Can you:

- describe what members of your family look like?
  —¿Es pelirrojo tu hermano mayor?
  —No, tiene pelo ___ y ojos ___ .
- describe the personalities of family members?
  —Mi abuela es ___ y ___ .
- tell how old people in your family are?
  —Mi primo ___ años.
- tell what members of your family like to do?
  —A mi tía ___ gusta ___ .

2 *Statements will vary, but may include:*
Se llama Chispa. Es grande (feo, marrón, inteligente, cariñoso, atrevido). No es prudente. Le gusta nadar (el bistec). Tiene ojos azules (hambre, dos años).

Se llama Michi. Es pequeño (bonito, guapo, negro, perezoso). No es inteligente. Le gusta el pescado. Tiene ojos verdes (cuatro años).

3 Statements will vary.

Answers: ¿Qué sabes ahora?
For item 1, a student who is an only child can select another family member to describe.
- Answers will vary for first two sets of questions, but look for correct adjective agreement.
- tiene / *(Numbers will vary.)*
- le / *(Activities will vary.)*

Audio Activity 5.3

Writing Activity 5-E

Enrichment
¿Qué sabes ahora?: As a written assignment, students can tell what each member of their family likes to do on the weekend, where they go to do it, and with whom they go.

Cooperative Learning
On poster board, have groups of three or four students develop family trees for a famous person. Have the groups discuss possible choices and then vote for their candidates. After students choose their personality, assign each group member a specific role. In groups of three, for example, the roles could be researcher, writer / artist, and presenter. Provide feedback as groups work independently. Have groups present their trees to the whole class.

Present & Apply

Cultural Objective
- To explain how names are formed in Spanish-speaking countries

Critical Thinking: Understanding Points of View

Tell students that married women in the U.S. were at one time almost exclusively formally addressed with the first name of their husbands (for example: Mrs. John Smith). Although some women may still prefer this form of address, this practice is deemed inappropriate to most women in the U.S. today. Discuss with students why most women would be offended if addressed by their husband's name.

Perspectiva cultural

Look at the names on the wedding invitation and the passport. In what ways do the names resemble or not resemble those you are used to? Can you identify the last names?

In Spanish-speaking countries a person's full name consists of a first name *(nombre),* a middle name, and two surnames—the father's family name *(apellido paterno)* followed by the mother's family name *(apellido materno).* Take, for example, the bride's mother's name on the wedding invitation:

> María Luisa González
> Prado de Enciso

González is her *apellido paterno.* Prado is her *apellido materno.* Enciso is her husband's last name. Now look at her husband's name. What are his *apellido paterno* and *apellido materno?*

Although a person's full name is used on all official documents, such as birth certificates, school records, passports, and identification cards, in daily life they usually use only one first name and one last name, most often the father's.

When a woman marries, she may keep her full name unchanged, or she may add her husband's last name to her own. For example, Gloria Luisa Enciso González may add *de* and her husband's last name, Ayala. Her *nombre completo* will then be Gloria Luisa Enciso González de Ayala. You would address her either as Señora Ayala or Señora Enciso de Ayala. But she would never be called Señora <u>Hugo</u> Ayala. Her children's last names will be Ayala Enciso.

La cultura desde tu perspectiva

1 Explain how names in Spanish-speaking countries are different from names in the United States. Based on the Spanish naming convention, what would your *nombre completo* be? Your father's? Your mother's?

2 You need to telephone *Ana Cristina Padilla Sánchez de Irujo.* Under what letter would you look in the phone book? When she answers the phone, how would you address her?

164   Capítulo 5

Options

Strategies for Reaching All Students

Spanish-Speaking Students
 Un paso más Ex. 5-H

Students Needing Extra Help
Students will need an extra visual to understand the concept of adding and dropping names. Either make an invitation on cardboard or on the chalkboard, color-coding the names that carry through or that are dropped.

Enrichment
Point out that in Spanish-speaking countries, a woman's widowhood is also indicated in her name. If the husband of Sra. Guerra de Olivas dies, she becomes Sra. Guerra, vda. *(viuda)* de Olivas.

En Pátzcuaro, México

Una boda en
Xochimilco, México

El Sr. Roberto Manuel Enciso Cuevas
y
la Sra. María Luisa González Prado de Enciso

El Sr. Antonio Miguel Ayala Arévalo
y
la Sra. Ana Clara Pérez Soler de Ayala

invitan cordialmente a la celebración del matrimonio de sus hijos
Gloria Luisa   y   Hugo Eduardo

Perspectiva cultural   165

Cultural Notes

(p. 165, photos)
Mexican weddings, like these in Pátzcuaro and Xochimilco, are often lavishly planned affairs, including as many family members and friends as possible. A very special role in Mexican weddings is played by the bride and groom's godparents, who drape a garland of beaded pearl leaves around the shoulders of the wedding couple, encircling them as they exchange vows. After the wedding mass the newlyweds bring a gift of roses and pray to the Virgen de Guadalupe, Mexico's patron saint.

Preview

Transparency 30

Answers

A 24 / In English, age is expressed as "being" so many years old. In Spanish, it is expressed as "having" so many years with *tener*.

B *somos*

C *Me gusta la comida de mi mamá.* / *de Sara, de telenovelas, de su madre* / *De* is used as a possessive here.

Teaching Suggestions

In a negative sentence, we generally don't use the indefinite article after the verb *tener* unless there is an adjective. *(No tengo lápiz. / No tengo un lápiz azul.)*

Class Starter Review

For the day after *tener* is presented: Give various classroom objects or school supplies to students. Then ask who has a specific item *(¿Quién tiene un(a) ... ? Miguel, ¿tienes un(a) ... ?* etc.). Remember to give a certain item to two students so that the plural forms are reviewed.

Re-enter / Recycle

Ex. 1: numbers 0–31 from *El primer paso*, classroom supplies from Chap. 2

Gramática en contexto

Look at this page from a Mexican magazine article about TV star Sara Sánchez. Now read the captions.

Sarita es muy seria y trabajadora. A veces es graciosa y perezosa, dice la madre de Sara, la señora María Sánchez.

Sara Sánchez, estrella de telenovelas mexicanas: Me gusta la comida de mi mamá. Sus enchiladas son deliciosas.

Tiene 24 años y hoy está en la casa de su madre: Me gusta estar aquí con mi mamá. Somos madre e hija, pero también somos muy buenas amigas.

A Sara's age is one fact that is given in the captions. How old is she? Look at the verb in the expression that tells her age. What is the difference between expressing age in English and in Spanish?

B You already know the verb forms *soy, eres, es,* and *son*. They are all forms of the verb *ser*. Using what you know about verb endings, read the captions and find the form of *ser* that we use with *nosotros*.

C Find the expression that tells about Sara's mother's cooking *(comida)*. Find two other places where an expression with *de* is used. What explanation can you give for this use of *de*?

166 Capítulo 5

Options

Strategies for Reaching All Students

Students Needing Extra Help
B: Put the verbs in chart form, using the pronouns. Then students can see that you have used all the forms except for "we." Remind them that they already know this setup from *-ar* verbs.
C: Discuss the English use of apostrophes to show ownership and how this concept is not used in Spanish. Give students a formula: object + *de* + person. Emphasize the word order: In Spanish the object is first, followed by the person. Give some examples.

El verbo tener: Ask students to identify what *tener* has in common with other *-er* verbs. What is different? Students may then complete the *tener* chart on their Organizers. Re-enter *¿Cuántos años tienes?* and *tengo / tienes, hambre / sed.*
Ex. 1: Model one or two more examples. Re-enter compound subjects and the verb forms they require.

El verbo *tener*

The verb *tener*, "to have," follows the pattern of other *-er* verbs. However, some forms of this verb are irregular. Here are all of its present-tense forms.

(yo)	**tengo**	(nosotros) (nosotras)	**tenemos**
(tú)	**tienes**	(vosotros) (vosotras)	**tenéis**
Ud. (él) (ella)	**tiene**	Uds. (ellos) (ellas)	**tienen**

You have already seen some of these verb forms. In what ways is *tener* irregular?

• As you know, *tener* is sometimes used where in English we use a form of the verb "to be": *tener sed / hambre / años.*

1 A class is getting ready to start a project. Several students have gathered the supplies they need. Find out who has them and how many they have.

carpetas de argollas

A —*¿Quién tiene las carpetas de argollas?*
B —*Miguel.*
A —*¿Cuántas carpetas de argollas tiene?*
B —*Cuatro.*

a. marcadores
b. reglas
c. diccionarios
d. cuadernos
e. lápices
f. carpetas
g. bolígrafos

Miguel (4) Marcos, Yo (16)

Carlos, Jorge (14)

Victoria (6)

Yo (3)

Anita (10)

Pilar, Sofia (8)

Andrés (5)

Gramática en contexto   167

1 Answers

a. A —¿Quién tiene los marcadores?
B —Anita.
A —¿Cuántos marcadores tiene?
B —Tiene diez.

b. A —. . . las reglas?
B —Andrés.
A —¿Cuántas reglas tiene?
B —Tiene cinco.

c. A —. . . los diccionarios?
B —Yo.
A —¿Cuántos diccionarios tienes?
B —Tengo tres.

d. A —. . . los cuadernos?
B —Pilar y Sofía.
A —¿Cuántos cuadernos tienen?
B —Tienen ocho.

e. A —. . . los lápices?
B —Marcos y yo.
A —¿Cuántos lápices tienen?
B—Tenemos dieciséis.

f. A —. . . las carpetas?
B —Victoria.
A —¿Cuántas carpetas tiene?
B —Tiene seis.

g. A —. . . los bolígrafos?
B —Carlos y Jorge.
A —¿Cuántos bolígrafos tienen?
B —Tienen catorce.

Present & Practice

Re-enter / Recycle

Exs. 2–3: singular and plural adjective agreement from Chaps. 1 and 4

Ex. 4: singular and plural adjective agreement from Chaps. 1 and 4, adjectives describing personality from Chap. 1

Answers

2–3 Answers will vary, but encourage students to use chapter vocabulary.

A follow-up activity might include one student standing and reading a statement such as, *Daniel y yo tenemos 15 años.* All other students about whom the statement is true also stand. Then all students sit down. Another student stands and reads: *Sara y yo no tenemos hermanos.* All students about whom the statement is true also stand. Continue with other statements.

Using Realia

Ask students if they get the gist of the phrase at the bottom of the ad ("Abdón and Lucas sofas are there when you need them.").

 Practice Wkbk. 5-5

 Writing Activity 5-F

 Prueba 5-5

---

2 Find out the ages and the number of family members of different students in your class. On a sheet of paper, copy the graph below. As you ask students the questions, write their names and the information you receive. While talking to them, observe their hair and eye color and write this information in the appropriate columns.

A — *¿Cuántos años tienes?*
B — *Tengo 15 años.*
A — *¿Cuántos primos tienes?*
B — *Tengo nueve primos.*
   o: *No tengo primos.*

Estudiante	Años	Familia	Ojos	Pelo
Daniel	15	9 primos	azules	rubio

3 Using the information from Exercise 2, compare yourself with your classmates. Write as many statements as you can about similarities in age, number of family members, and appearance. Then report to the class.

Daniel y yo tenemos 15 años.
Tenemos el pelo rubio.

168   Capítulo 5

Options

Strategies for Reaching All Students

Spanish-Speaking Students
Exs. 2 and 4: Have Spanish-speaking students write out these exercises.

Students Needing Extra Help
Ex. 2: You may wish to have students draw another vertical line between *Familia* and *Ojos* to remind them that the information to the right of the line pertains to the classmate, not to his or her family members.
Ex. 3: Model different combinations.
El verbo ser: Have students fill in the chart in the grammar portion of their Organizers.
Ex. 4: Model two more examples.

Enrichment
Ex. 2: As a written assignment, students can make up questions to interview a classmate regarding whether he or she has cats or dogs at home. Encourage students to be as thorough and creative in their questions as possible. For example, if the interviewee has no dogs or cats at home, students might turn their line of questioning to whether the interviewee likes cats or dogs, or whether they would like to have them but can't because another family member dislikes

168

El verbo *ser*

The verb *ser*, "to be," is also an irregular verb. We use *ser* with adjectives to tell what someone or something is like.

- You already know some forms of *ser*. Here are all of its present-tense forms.

(yo)	**soy**	(nosotros) (nosotras)	**somos**
(tú)	**eres**	(vosotros) (vosotras)	**sóis**
Ud. (él) (ella)	**es**	Uds. (ellos) (ellas)	**son**

¡NO OLVIDES!

Remember that adjectives agree in gender and number with the nouns they describe.

4 In each of these groups, two persons are alike in some way and the third is different. Describe their similarities and differences.

Ángela y Mónica son graciosas, pero Gregorio es serio.

Ángela y Mónica / Gregorio

a. José / Miguel y tú b. Carolina / yo y Luisa c. Juanito y David / tú d. Barrabás / Turquesa y Condesa

e. Claudia y Marisol / yo f. Jorge / Samuel y yo g. Coqui / Napoleón y Sultán

Gramática en contexto   169

Class Starter Review
For the day after *ser* is presented: Using adjectives that students have learned, ask *¿Quién (no) es . . . ? ¿Eres . . . ? ¿Son Uds. . . . ?* etc. Be aware of students' sensitivity to answering this type of question. You may wish to use the names of famous personalities instead of those of your students.

Reteach / Review: *Ser* with Adjective & Noun Agreement
To review agreement between adjectives and nouns as well as the verb forms of *ser*, call on individuals to answer questions about classmates or themselves.

Answers
4 Before beginning the activity, you may choose to practice making the adjectives agree in number and gender.
a. Miguel y tú son altos, pero José es bajo.
b. Luisa y yo somos deportistas, pero Carolina es artística.
c. Juanito y David son desordenados, pero tú eres ordenada.
d. Turquesa y Condesa son bonitas, pero Barrabás es feo.
e. Claudia y Marisol son tacañas, pero yo soy generoso.
f. Samuel y yo somos trabajadores, pero Jorge es perezoso.
g. Napoleón y Sultán son grandes, pero Coqui es pequeño.

them. If there are cats or dogs at home, students can ask how many of each there are, their names and ages, what the pets are like, and what they like to do.

Present & Practice

Re-enter / Recycle

Ex. 5: singular and plural adjective agreement from Chaps. 1 and 4, adjectives describing personality from Chap. 1.

Ex. 7: school supplies from Chap. 2

Answers

5 Questions and answers will vary, but look for correct adjective agreement.

 Practice Wkbk. 5-6, 5-7

 Writing Activity 5-G

 Prueba 5-6

---

5 Think of pairs of people in your class who are alike in at least one way. Your partner should tell you how these two classmates are alike. You may want to use the list on the right to help you.

A —¿Cómo son Pablo y Pedro?
B —Son altos.

Now ask your partner in what way you and various classmates are alike or different.

A —¿Cómo somos Ignacio y yo?
B —Uds. son trabajadores.
    o: Ignacio es trabajador, pero tú eres perezoso.

alto, -a	impaciente
amable	inteligente
artístico, -a	joven
atrevido, -a	ordenado, -a
bajo, -a	paciente
bonito, -a	perezoso, -a
callado, -a	prudente
cariñoso, -a	serio, -a
deportista	simpático, -a
desordenado, -a	sociable
generoso, -a	tacaño, -a
gracioso, -a	trabajador, -a
guapo, -a	viejo, -a

Los adjetivos posesivos

To tell what belongs to someone or to show relationships, we use *de* + noun. For example:

Tengo el cuaderno **de** Felipe.
La hermana **de** María es amable.

- Another way to tell what belongs to someone and to show relationships is to use possessive adjectives. You already know some of them.

mi hermano	**mis** hermanos
tu abuela	**tus** abuelas
su hijo	**sus** hijos

- The possessive adjective must be singular if the noun is singular and plural if the noun is plural.

Mi prima es alta.   Todas mi**s** prima**s** son alta**s**.

— ¿Son rubios los hermanos de Rafael?
— No, su**s** hermano**s** son pelirro**jos**.

170   Capítulo 5

Options

Strategies for Reaching All Students

Spanish-Speaking Students
Ex. 5: Pair bilingual and non-bilingual students.

Students Needing Extra Help
Ex. 5: Model, being careful to include students who might not otherwise be chosen for the comparison.
Los adjetivos posesivos: Have students fill in the grammar portion of their Organizers. Remind students of the information from Section C on p. 166. Discuss the idea of one owner, one thing; and one owner, two things. The *-s* in *mis, tus,* and *sus* automatically signals plural form. Give a few models.
Ex. 6: Have students do two true and one

false statement. First do all true statements. Then write false statements on the chalkboard. They may have to write these out to show how possessive adjectives work. In the example, show how *la* becomes *su,* and *de Mariana* disappears.
Ex. 7: Do two separate examples on the chalkboard, one for single items and one for plural.
Ahora lo sabes: Have students write out this section so they can check off what they have mastered. Add examples if necessary.

170

6 Using the family tree on page 154, make three true and false statements about Mariana's family to your partner. Your partner will look at the family tree and answer *sí* if a statement is correct. If a statement is incorrect, your partner will answer *no* and correct it.

A — *La hermana de Mariana tiene 23 años.*
B — *Sí, su hermana tiene 23 años.*
A — *Los abuelos de Mariana se llaman Pedro y Carolina.*
B — *No, sus abuelos se llaman Pedro y Carmen.*

7 Work in groups of three. Each of two students will choose three classroom items that they can "lose" for a moment. These students will turn their backs while their partner puts these objects out of sight. Then, when they turn around, one of them should ask where their things are.

A — *¿Dónde está mi carpeta?*
B — *¿Tu carpeta? Aquí está.*
A — *¿Dónde están sus libros?*
    o: *¿Dónde están los libros de Antonio?*
B — *¿Sus libros? Aquí están.*

Ahora lo sabes

Can you:

■ tell what someone has?

—Tomás y Mariana ___ doce libros.

■ tell what a person's age is?

—El abuelo de Celeste ___ 74 años.

■ tell what someone or something is like?

—Mi hermano ___ guapo.

■ tell what belongs to someone or show relationships?

—¿Dónde está el cuaderno ___ Luis?

—___ cuaderno está aquí.

El virrey José de Iturrigaray y su familia
(alrededor de 1805), (anónimo)

Answers
6 Statements will vary, but look for correct verb agreement.

7 Questions and answers will vary. Point out the plural form *aquí están.* (The singular form was introduced in Chap. 2.)

Answers: Ahora lo sabes
• tienen
• tiene
• es
• de, Su

 Practice Wkbk. 5-8, 5-9, 5-10

 Audio Activity 5.4

 Writing Activity 5-H

 Prueba 5-7

Comm. Act. BLM 5-3

Cultural Notes ☀

(p. 171, photo)
Between 1803 and 1808, José de Iturrigaray was one of the last viceroys of Nueva España (former Spanish possessions in the Americas). He and his family are portrayed in this painting, *El virrey José de Iturrigaray y su familia.* Painted by an unknown artist (c. 1805), the work is now part of the colonial-era collection in Mexico City's Museo Nacional de Historia, which is housed in the Castillo de Chapultepec.

Apply

**Pronunciation Tape
5-3**

¡A conversar!

Play

Step

Using the Video
Video segment 3: See the Video
Teacher's Guide.

Video Activity C

Para decir más
Other words your students may
want to know: *divorciado, -a*
(divorced); *casado, -a* (married);
soltero, -a (unmarried, single).

Para decir más

Here is some additional
vocabulary that you might
find useful for activities in
this section.

el esposo, la esposa
husband, wife

el nieto, la nieta
grandson, granddaughter

**el hermanastro,
la hermanastra**
stepbrother, stepsister

el padrastro, la madrastra
stepfather, stepmother

el padrino, la madrina
godfather, godmother

calvo, -a
bald

largo, -a
long (hair)

corto, -a
short (hair)

las pecas
freckles

las trenzas
braids

172   Capítulo 5

Actividades

Here's an opportunity for you to expand your use
of Spanish by putting together the material you
learned in this chapter with what you learned earlier.

 Write a brief description
of your ideal family,
including the number of
grandparents, parents,
aunts and uncles, cousins,
and brothers and sisters
that you have. Do not include their names.

> **¡NO OLVIDES!**
>
> Remember that *tú* with an accent
> means "you." *Tu* without an
> accent means "your."

*Tengo dos abuelos y dos padres. También tengo tres tíos.
Tengo una hermana.*

Exchange papers with your partner. Find out about the
members of your partner's ideal family by asking about
their names, ages, and appearance or personalities.
Write down the information you receive.

A —*¿Cómo se llaman tus abuelos?*
B —*Mi abuelo se llama Frank y mi abuela se llama
        Dorothy.*
A —*¿Cuántos años tienen?*
B —*Mi abuelo tiene 63 años y mi abuela tiene 59 años.*
A —*¿Cómo son?*
B —*Mi abuelo es muy alto y mi abuela también es alta.
        Él tiene pelo rubio y ojos azules, y ella es pelirroja y
        tiene ojos marrones. Mis abuelos son muy cariñosos.*

Options

Strategies for Reaching All Students

Spanish-Speaking Students

 Un paso más Exs. 5-I, 5-J

Students Needing Extra Help
Ex. 1: Make a chart that includes relationship, name, age, and description of relatives
for students to fill in before attempting the
conversation. Before working in pairs,
have a student carry on the conversation
with you.
Ex. 2: Have a paragraph similar to the one
presented here, but with blanks, so that students can fill in the new information and
report back.

Ex. 3: Have students use their Chap. 2
Organizers.
Ex. 4: This activity may pose a challenge for
some students. Ask for volunteers and write
their conversation on the chalkboard as a
model.

2 Report to your teacher the information you found out about your partner's ideal family.

Andrew tiene dos abuelos. Su abuelo se llama Frank. Tiene 63 años, es muy alto, es rubio y tiene ojos azules. Su abuela se llama Dorothy. Tiene 59 años, es alta, pelirroja y tiene ojos marrones. Sus abuelos son cariñosos.

Una familia a la hora de la cena en Santiago, Chile

Unos padres mexicanos

Unos abuelos en Madrid

3 Work in pairs to talk about each other's class schedules.

Write down the information you receive in order to report it later.

A —*¿Tienes matemáticas?*
B —*Sí, tengo. Empieza a las nueve y media y termina a las diez y media.*

A —*¿Cómo se llama tu profesora?*
B —*Mi profesora es la señora Pereda.*
A —*¿Y te gusta la clase?*
B —*Sí, me encanta.*

4 Now you and your partner should work with another pair of students. Take turns reporting to the other pair what you two found out. After each statement you make, a member of the other pair should tell how the information is similar to or different from his or her schedule. Keep the conversation flowing as long as you can.

A —*Alice tiene matemáticas a las doce y cuarto.*
B —*Yo también.*
o: *Yo no. Tengo matemáticas a las nueve y media.*

A —*Su profesora de matemáticas es la señora Rodríguez.*
B —*Mi profesora de matemáticas es la señora Rodríguez también.*

Actividades   173

Answers: Actividades
1–4 Answers will vary, but encourage students to use the full range of chapter vocabulary. Look for correct verb and adjective agreement.

The follow-up step for Ex. 4 can be done orally or in written form. You might prefer to have students report to small groups.

Multicultural Perspectives
Riddles and rhymes are an integral part of all cultures. They often are learned at home from parents or siblings and are passed from one generation to another. A rhyme common to many Hispanic families is one that is recited while preparing tortillas or gathering eggs:
*Tortillas de pan y de vino
pasa papá que viene en camino
Tortillitas de pan y de queso
pasa papá que va de regreso*
Some riddles reflect upon the wonders of nature and explain a natural occurrence or phenomenon. Invite students to share with the class a riddle or rhyme that has been in their families for many years.

Comm. Act. BLMs 5-4, 5-5

Cooperative Learning
Divide the class into groups of three or four students. Have each individual write the name of one sports or entertainment personality on a notecard. Students should not see each other's cards. Now, have each group play "Guess the Personality." Designate one student in each group to serve as the moderator. Taking turns, each student gets to ask the moderator one question about the celebrity on the moderator's card. For example: *¿Es un hombre? ¿Tiene pelo rubio?* After each question, the moderator answers either *sí* or *no.* Students record the information on a piece of paper. Students alternate asking questions. Play continues until someone guesses the celebrity. Assign a new moderator and personality for the next round.

Apply

Process Reading

For a description of process reading, see p. 48.

Teaching Suggestions

Elicit previously learned Spanish words: *(perros, gatos);* same as English *(hamsters);* sounds like English *(periquitos).*

Answers
Antes de leer

Compatibility of the personalities of the pet and the personalities and ages of family members; compatibility of the size of pet and the size of the house; indoor and outdoor needs of the pet; feeding, grooming, and medical care; affordability, etc. / Answers will vary.

Mira la lectura

1 Answers will vary. You may have to help students with the meaning of *mascota* (pet).

2 Four animals are listed: cats, dogs, hamsters, and parakeets.

¡Vamos a leer!

Antes de leer

STRATEGY ➤ Using prior knowledge

What are some important considerations when choosing a family pet? What kinds of information would you hope to find in an article offering advice about pet choices?

Mira la lectura

STRATEGY ➤ Using titles and context clues for meaning

1 Does the title give a good idea about the subject of the article?

2 Look at the listings in the column entitled *mascota.* How many animals are considered here?

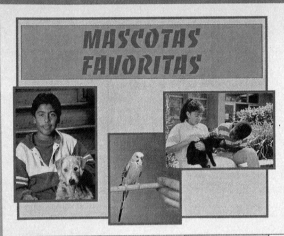

MI PRIMERA MASCOTA

MASCOTAS FAVORITAS

A los niños les gusta casi cualquier animal. Sin embargo, algunos animales no son recomendables para ellos. Es conveniente que los padres escojan una mascota de acuerdo a la edad de sus hijos. Los niños de entre cinco y diez años pueden tener un perro, por ejemplo, un pastor alemán, un dálmata o un collie. También pueden escoger otras clases de mascotas: gatos, conejos, periquitos, peces, tortugas, hámsters (ratoncillos domésticos), etc. Cuando escojan una mascota deben tener en consideración los siguientes aspectos: la longevidad, los cuidados y la alimentación.

Mascota	Gatos	Perros	Hámsters	Periquitos
Longevidad	15 años	15 años	2 años	5 años
Cuidados	Agua y comida todos los días. Vitaminas. Bañarlo con agua tibia una vez al mes.	Agua y comida todos los días. Vitaminas. Collar para pulgas. Bañarlo una vez a la semana.	Agua y comida especial todos los días. Limpiar la jaula cada cinco días.	Agua y comida todos los días. Lechuga, plátano y semillas. Limpiar la jaula una vez por semana.

Options

Strategies for Reaching All Students

Spanish-Speaking Students

Ask Spanish-speaking students to write about one or all of the following:
(1) ¿Tienes mascota? ¿Qué tienes? ¿Cómo es? (2) Describe la mascota ideal para ti. (3) Escribe un anuncio para vender un producto para una mascota. Puede ser una comida especial, un collar o un jabón, etc.

Students Needing Extra Help

Mira la lectura: Brainstorm as a class.
Infórmate #2: Remind students about the meaning of cognates. Give examples. Explain the term "longevity" in English.
Aplicación: Ask why these are good recommendations. Ask for specifics.
Have students explain why they would give certain jobs to certain family members.

Enrichment

As a written assignment, students can pretend that they are applying for a job at a pet-sitting service and name all of the characteristics that they have that would make them good for the job.

Infórmate

STRATEGY → Scanning

Column and row headings identify the main categories. We can scan the entries relating to them for the specific information we need.

Scanning, or reading for specific information, is useful because charts and tables offer an efficient way to condense information in order to make quick comparisons.

1 Scan the long paragraph and find the age range of children for whom these pets are recommended. Using what you know about cognates, can you identify the names of some of the dog breeds? From what you know, do you agree that these are good pets for children in this age range?

2 Turning to the table, scan the information in the row entitled *Longevidad*. Do you know an English equivalent for *longevidad?* Does this information correspond to your own experience with pets? What do you think the row next to *Cuidados* is about?

Dos hermanas con armadillos en Taxco, México

Aplicación

The recommendations given below are described in the table as necessary for the care of *los perros.* Can you figure out what these recommendations are? To which of these family members would you assign each of the first two tasks: *hijo mayor (10 años), hija menor (5 años), los padres?*

- bañarlo una vez a la semana
- comida y agua todos los días
- collar para pulgas
- vitaminas

¡Vamos a leer! 175

Infórmate

2 between 5 and 10 years old / German Shepherd, Dalmatian, Collie / Answers will vary.

longevity / Answers will vary. / care and feeding

Aplicación

Recommendations include: give it a bath once a week, food and water every day, flea collar, vitamins. / Answers will vary.

Cultural Notes ☼

(p. 175, photo)
These young girls holding armadillos live in Taxco, a town 104 miles southwest of Mexico City. Built on a hill where silver has been mined since pre-Columbian times, Taxco was founded in 1522 by Hernán Cortés. Today it is famous for its exquisitely crafted silver products and its eighteenth-century colonial architecture.

Apply

Process Writing

For information regarding developing a writing portfolio, see p. 50.

Teaching Suggestions

If this activity is done in class, you may want to begin by having partners ask and answer questions: *¿Tienes tíos? Sí, tengo cinco tíos que se llaman . . . y una tía que se llama . . . .*

You may wish to ask students to bring in family photos or photos of a TV family for which they may write captions. Later, the photos may be displayed as a class project.

Arrange with another class (Levels 1 & 2) to answer these letters. Try to participate in this activity and exchange letters. This can begin a dialogue journal to continue throughout the year.

Answers: ¡Vamos a escribir!

Look for correct use of adjectives and verbs in students' letters.

¡Vamos a escribir!

You have a new pen pal and you want to tell your new friend about your family. Write a letter about your family in which you are going to include 3 to 5 photos or drawings. Follow these steps.

1 Think about how you would describe the people in your photos or drawings: Who are they? What do they look like? What type of personality do they have? List your answers under each of these categories. Number your pictures so that you can refer to them easily.

2 Write a first draft of your letter describing three or four people in your family as completely as you can.

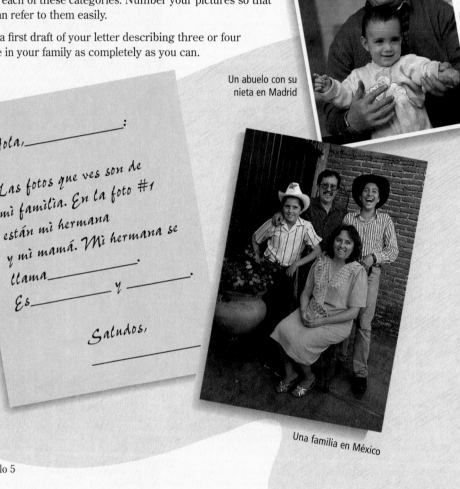

Un abuelo con su nieta en Madrid

Hola, _____:

Las fotos que ves son de mi familia. En la foto #1 están mi hermana y mi mamá. Mi hermana se llama _____. Es _____ y _____.

Saludos,

_____

Una familia en México

176   Capítulo 5

Options

Strategies for Reaching All Students

Spanish-Speaking Students

Have Spanish-speaking students answer one of the letters and compare his or her real, imaginary, or ideal family with the one in the letter. *Contesta la carta de un(a) compañero(a) de clase. Compara a tu familia con la de tu compañero(a).*

Students Needing Extra Help

Step 1: Some students might be very uncomfortable doing this activity with real family photos. Instead, let them create a family from magazine pictures or let them draw a family. Have students use their Organizers. Make a chart with the headings listed in the directions.

Step 2: Students have enough vocabulary so that they could expand on this example. Use a picture from a magazine and have the students do the exercise as a class.

Step 4: Have students use the Organizer.

3 Show your letter to a partner and ask if he or she would make any changes. Do you give enough information about each person? Think about any changes your partner suggests as well as others you may want to make. Then rewrite your letter.

4 Check for accuracy in spelling, accents, and punctuation. Did you use the correct forms of the adjectives? Does your partner have any further suggestions?

5 Make a clean copy of your letter and attach the pictures. Add the letter to your writing portfolio. You may send it to a "pen pal" in another Spanish class in your school.

En Cuernavaca, México

Con su mascota favorita

Hermanas en Guatemala

Cultural Notes

(p. 177, top photo)
As this photo of Mexican boys in football uniforms indicates, there is a strong American influence in Cuernavaca, the capital of the state of Morelos. Its cool climate and lush vegetation have made it an appealing home to Mexicans and foreigners since colonial times. Today Cuernavaca has a community of about 20,000 U.S. residents, and attracts many more *norteamericanos* with its numerous language schools.

(p. 177, bottom photo)
Descendants of the ancient Mayan civilization make up approximately half of Guatemala's 10.3 million people. The other half consists of *ladinos*—people of mixed Spanish and Indian ancestry.

Test Preparation
You may want to assign parts of this section as written homework or as an in-class writing activity prior to administering the *Examen de habilidades*.

Answers
Listening: *Me llamo Enrique. En mi familia somos cuatro: mi padre, mi madre, mi hermano Alberto y yo. Mi padre es muy alto. Tiene ojos marrones y pelo castaño. Mi madre y Alberto tienen ojos verdes y pelo castaño. Mis ojos son verdes también, pero soy pelirrojo.* Enrique's hair is red. No, nobody else in his family has his hair color.

Culture: Ana Ríos

Reading: The chart lists four people with their name, age, and hair and eye color. / The dominant color of eyes is green. / Answers will vary: gray or dark-colored eyes.

Writing: Ads will vary, but students should use the chapter vocabulary. Look for logical sentences.

Speaking: Dialogues will vary, but look for the correct forms of *tener* and *se llama(n)*. Encourage use of vocabulary from this chapter and from previous ones.

¿Lo sabes bien?

This section will help you organize your studying for the proficiency test, where you will be asked to do similar, though not identical, tasks. There will not be any models on the test.

Listening
Can you understand when someone describes family members and friends? Listen as your teacher reads you a sample similar to what you will hear on the test. What color is Enrique's hair? Does any other member of his family have the same color hair?

Culture
What version of her name would Ana Carmen most likely use to introduce herself to a new friend?

Reading
Can you quickly glance through this chart and get an idea of its content? Now look at the information under the column entitled *Color de ojos*. What is the dominant color of eyes? Is there any common color of eyes missing?

Nombre	Edad	Color de pelo	Color de ojos
Rosalba	19	castaño	marrones
José Miguel	18	pelirrojo	verdes
Carlos	21	castaño	verdes
Maribel	19	rubio	azules

178   Capítulo 5

Writing
Can you write an ad for actors for a school play? Here is a sample:

Necesito una mujer
50-60 años
alta
pelo canoso
_____
para representar
a la madre

Speaking
Can you talk with a partner about your families?
For example:

A — *Tengo tres hermanos mayores. ¿Y tú?*

B — *Yo tengo una hermana mayor y una hermana menor. Mariana tiene dieciocho años y Roxana cinco.*

A — *Mis hermanos se llaman Roberto, Ramiro y Rafael. Todos son muy deportistas.*

B — *Mis hermanas son pelirrojas y tienen ojos verdes. Son muy simpáticas.*

Options

Strategies for Reaching All Students

Students Needing Extra Help
Have students write out this section so they can check off what they have mastered.

Resumen del capítulo 5

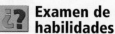

Use the vocabulary from this chapter to help you:
- describe family members and friends
- tell what someone's age is
- say what other people like and do not like to do

to talk about family members
los abuelos: el abuelo,
           la abuela
los hermanos: el hermano,
             la hermana
los hijos: el hijo,
       la hija
los padres: el padre,
         la madre
los primos: el primo,
         la prima
los tíos: el tío,
      la tía
el hijo único, la hija única
los gemelos, las gemelas

to tell someone's name
¿Cómo se llama(n) ___?
Se llama(n) ___.

to ask and tell how old someone is
¿Cuántos años tiene ___?
Tiene ___ años.
sesenta (sesenta y uno ...)
setenta (setenta y uno ...)
ochenta (ochenta y uno ...)
noventa (noventa y uno ...)
cien

to talk about people
el hombre
el muchacho, la muchacha
la mujer
la persona

to describe people, animals, and things
alto, -a
antipático, -a
atractivo, -a
bajo, -a
bonito, -a
cariñoso, -a
feo, -a
grande
guapo, -a
inteligente
joven
mayor, *pl.* mayores
menor, *pl.* menores
pequeño, -a
simpático, -a
viejo, -a
ser + *adjective*
el pelo: canoso
        castaño
        negro
        rubio
pelirrojo, -a

los ojos: azules
        grises
        marrones
        negros
        verdes

to name animals
el gato
el perro

to indicate possession
de
su, sus
tener

to talk about what someone likes
(A + *person*) le gusta(n) / le
    encanta(n)

to indicate number
¿Cuántos, -as?
nadie
sólo
todos, -as

other useful word
que

CAPÍTULO 6
THEME: CLOTHING

SCOPE AND SEQUENCE Pages 180–215

COMMUNICATION

Topics
Clothing
Colors
Prices
Numbers 101–199

Objectives
To compare where people shop for clothes in Spanish-speaking countries and in the U.S.

To talk about articles of clothing, colors, and prices

To describe clothes

To indicate a specific item or items

To assist customers in a store

To address people

To start a conversation

To talk about shopping and places to shop for clothing

To talk about when something happened

To indicate location

CULTURE
Shopping for clothes
Types of clothing stores

GRAMMAR
La posición de los adjetivos

Los adjetivos demostrativos

El complemento directo: Los pronombres

Ancillaries available for use with Chapter 6

Multisensory/Technology

 Overhead Transparencies, 31–35

 Audio Tapes and CDs

 Vocabulary Art Blackline Masters for Hands-On Learning, pp. 33–37

Classroom Crossword

Video

 CD-ROM

Print

 Practice Workbook, pp. 64–72

 Writing, Audio & Video Activities, pp. 35–40, 108–110, 162–163

 Communicative Activity Blackline Masters
  Pair and Small Group Activities, pp. 43–48
  Situation Cards, p. 49

 Un paso más: Actividades para ampliar tu español, pp. 32–37

Assessment

 Assessment Program
  Pruebas, pp. 81–90
  Examen de habilidades, pp. 91–94

 Test Generator

Video still from Chap. 6

Shopping

Throughout Latin America and Spain, people traditionally have shopped for clothing in small neighborhood specialty stores or at public marketplaces. These shopping habits are changing in many cities, however, as large department stores are becoming more commonplace.

Popular department stores include Colombia's San Andresito and Spain's El Corte Inglés, Galerías Preciados, and Galerías Primero. Shopping malls such as Mexico City's Perisur are also becoming more commonplace. Perisur, like malls in the U.S., features a variety of chain store branches *(sucursales)*. Among them are Liverpool, a fashionable clothing store, and Sanborn's, a department store and favorite lunch spot. Perisur has become a central place for friends to meet and spend time together as well as to shop. *Puntos de fábrica* (factory outlet stores) are becoming increasingly popular places to buy clothing.

Local indoor and outdoor markets still exist in many communities throughout Latin America. At El Mercado Oriental, a market that covers dozens of square blocks in Managua, Nicaragua, one can buy almost anything. In many smaller cities and towns in Mexico, *el día de plaza,* a once- or twice-weekly event, draws people from many surrounding communities. Vendors may travel from town to town depending on where the market will take place that day. Local residents rely on the market to supply them with clothes and other items. Customers can pay for their merchandise with cash or by credit without using a credit card. The merchant writes down the name of the client and how much she or he owes. For example, in Mexico, *botas de piel Alcalá* (fine leather boots) are very expensive. A person can put a down payment on the boots and take them home. Every week the customer pays off a portion of the debt until the boots have been paid for.

Another common way of shopping is to wait for the *mercado a ruedas* (market on wheels) and *vendedores ambulantes* (door-to-door salespeople) to make a stop on the block. Shoppers appreciate the convenience as well as the congenial, personal service from familiar vendors.

Introduce

Re-entry of Concepts

The following list represents words, expressions, and grammar topics re-entered from *El primer paso* to Chap. 5:

El primer paso
Numbers 0–31
Greetings
Calendar expressions

Chapter 1
Gustar expressions
Activities

Chapter 2
Numbers 32–59
School supplies
Time-telling
Expressing need

Chapter 3
Places and buildings
Seasons

Chapter 4
Food
Expressing likes and preferences
Adjective agreement

Chapter 5
Numbers 60–100
Family and friends
Adjectives describing physical
   characteristics
Possessive adjectives

Planning

Cross-Curricular Connections

Geography Connection *(pp. 184–185)*
Have students find out the name of the currency for a Spanish-speaking country by using a reference book or calling a currency exchange or bank. Have them copy or draw an example of one of the bills and attach it by tape or string to a large map. If you don't have any foreign currency, ask consulates or travel agencies to help you.

Economics Connection *(pp. 184–185)*
Have students find out today's value of a currency from a Spanish-speaking country and convert the prices on p. 184. Have students then compare amounts among the different currencies.

Business Connection *(p. 200)*
Have pairs of students create an ad for a shop in a Spanish-speaking country showing three or four featured items and the prices in that country's currency and in U.S. dollars. They should name the store and write any other pertinent advertising information. Display the ads around the room.

CAPÍTULO 6

¿Qué desea Ud.?

OBJECTIVES

At the end of this chapter, you will be able to:

- describe the color, fit, and price of clothes
- ask about and buy clothes
- tell where and when you bought clothes and how much you paid for them
- compare where people shop for clothes in Spanish-speaking countries and in the United States

Un muchacho buscando ropa en Chichicastenango, Guatemala

181

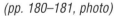

Preview

Cultural Objective

• To compare where people shop for clothes in Spanish-speaking countries and in the U.S.

 ¿Qué desea Ud.?

Play

 Video Activity A

Using the Video

This chapter's video focuses on shopping for clothing. Students will search for clothing bargains with our hosts in Madrid, visiting a major women's clothing store and a popular street market.
To prepare students for the video, first ask them to predict what this chapter's tape will be about. Then have students watch the segment several times. After the first time, you may wish to have them brainstorm possible vocabulary and expressions they will need to talk about what they saw on the video. Ask students to identify: a) things they saw that were familiar to them, and b) things they saw that they might not see in a clothing store in their home town or city. Video segment 1: For more teaching suggestions, see the Video Teacher's Guide.

¡Piénsalo bien!

Look at the photographs and read the captions.

"¡Qué bonito!"

En Buenos Aires

182   Capítulo 6

Options

Strategies for Reaching All Students

Spanish-Speaking Students

Ask Spanish-speaking students: *¿Tienen las mismas tiendas en el centro comercial por donde vives tú? ¿Cuánto cuestan los artículos que ves en las fotos? ¿Vas a los centros comerciales con tus amigos? ¿Qué hacen allí?*

 Un paso más Ex. 6-A

182

En la Ciudad de México

How do the stores in these pictures compare with those in a mall that you know?

"¡Me encanta la ropa de esta tienda!"

"¿Cuándo vas a las zapaterías?"

En España

183

Critical Thinking: Evaluating Information
Ask small groups of students to prepare lists of factors they consider when making a clothing purchase. Lists might include price, quality, style, and so on. After students have prepared their lists, have them rank the factors according to importance. Discuss the lists.

Answers: ¡Piénsalo bien!
Answers will vary, but students may say that some stores are the same as those in the U.S.

Cultural Notes

(p. 182, photo)
Shopping malls in Spain and Latin America can offer the same attractions found in U.S. malls, with the exception that many stores often emphasize a regional or national specialty. At Galería Pacífico, the Buenos Aires mall shown here, shoppers can find bargains for renowned Argentine merchandise, such as leather goods, wool clothing, and high-quality jewelry.

(p. 183, bottom photo)
Young Spaniards reviewing a selection of athletic shoes. Jogging is one of the most popular forms of exercise, especially in cities where access to large parks provide scenic running paths. Health clubs with well-equipped facilities for joggers are also flourishing.

Present

Chapter Theme
Clothing and colors

Communicative Objectives
- To talk about articles of clothing, colors, and prices
- To describe clothes
- To talk about shopping
- To indicate a specific item or items
- To assist customers in a store
- To address people
- To start a conversation

 Transparencies 31–32

 Vocabulary Art BLMs

 Pronunciation Tape 6-1

 Vocabulario para conversar A

Play

Using the Video
Video segment 2: See the Video Teacher's Guide.

 Video Activity B

¿Qué desea Ud.?

Vocabulario para conversar

¿Cuánto cuesta la camisa?

Here are some new words and expressions you will need to talk about clothes and colors. Read them several times, then turn the page and practice with a partner.

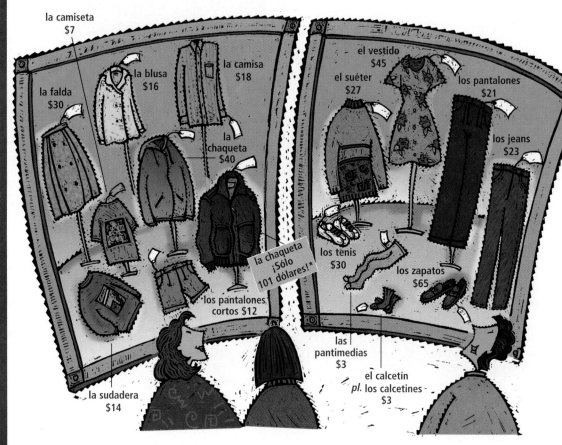

la camiseta $7
la falda $30
la blusa $16
la camisa $18
la chaqueta $40
los pantalones cortos $12
la sudadera $14
la chaqueta ¡Sólo 101 dólares!*
el vestido $45
el suéter $27
los pantalones $21
los jeans $23
los tenis $30
los zapatos $65
las pantimedias $3
el calcetín pl. los calcetines $3

* Note that the number 100, *cien*, becomes *ciento* when followed by another number: *cien dólares*, but *ciento un dólares*. If followed by a feminine noun, we use *ciento una: ciento una camisas*.

184   Capítulo 6

Options

Strategies for Reaching All Students

Enrichment
To reinforce the new vocabulary, bring in pictures of clothing from magazines and mail-order catalogues. Have individual students or small groups present pictures to the class, naming the item of clothing, its price, and color. As a follow-up conversation, elicit opinions about the items from individual students, asking questions such as: *¿Te gusta(n)...? ¿Qué te gusta más? ¿Qué no te gusta nada? ¿Cuesta(n) mucho o poco...?*

Learning Spanish Through Action
STAGING VOCABULARY: *Levántense, Siéntense, Señalen, Toquen*
1) MATERIALS: transparency of clothing from the *Vocabulario para conversar*
DIRECTIONS: Using the transparency, point to an article of clothing. Ask students who are wearing that item to stand. While students remain standing, state a color.

Students wearing that color may then sit down. Continue naming colors until all students are seated, and then repeat with another article of clothing.
2) MATERIALS: none
DIRECTIONS: Ask students to touch or point to articles in the room as you mention a color.

184

Los colores

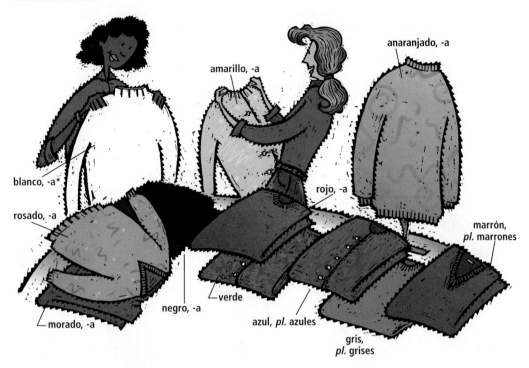

amarillo, -a

anaranjado, -a

blanco, -a*

rosado, -a

rojo, -a

marrón,
pl. marrones

morado, -a

negro, -a

verde

azul, *pl.* azules

gris,
pl. grises

También necesitas . . .

¿Cómo te queda(n)?	*How does it (do they) fit you?*	¿Cuánto?	*How much?*
Me queda(n) bien.	*It fits (They fit) me well.*	Cuesta(n) . . .	*It costs (They cost) . . .*
		¿Qué desea (Ud.)?	*May I help you?*
¿De qué color?	*What color?*	joven	*young man, sir, young lady*
buscar	*to look for*	perdón	*excuse me*
comprar	*to buy*		
llevar	*to wear*		
para mí / ti	*for me / you, to me / you*		
este, esta; ese, esa	*this; that*		
lo, la	*it*		
los, las	*them*		

¿Y qué quiere decir . . . ?

el dólar
señor
señora
señorita

* When talking about individual colors, we use the masculine definite article: *Me gustan el rojo y el amarillo.*

Vocabulario para conversar   185

Grammar Preview
Demonstrative adjectives and direct object pronouns are previewed here. The explanation appears in the grammar sections on pp. 202 and 204.

Teaching Suggestions
Preparing students to speak: Use one or two options from each of the categories of Comprehensible Input, Physical Response, or Limited Verbal Response. For a complete explanation of these categories and some sample activities, see the front section of this Teacher's Edition.

Point out that *marrón* does not change form in the feminine.

Remind students that they have seen *joven* as an adjective in Chap. 5. Explain that it can mean both "young man" and "young woman," and *jóvenes* can mean "young people," but as a form of address, *joven* is used mainly with males. *Señorita* is used when addressing a young, unmarried female.

Class Starter Review
On the day following initial presentation, you might begin the class with this activity:
Call out different items of clothing. Have individuals point to these items if they are wearing them. Make this activity more specific by describing the colors.

Practice

Reteach / Review: Vocabulary
Ex. 2: Have students review the vocabulary for family members by naming other relatives for whom they're shopping.

Re-enter / Recycle
Ex. 1: numbers 0–31 from *El primer paso*, numbers 32–59 from Chap. 2, numbers 60–100 from Chap. 5
Ex. 4: adjectives describing physical characteristics from Chap. 5

Answers: Empecemos a conversar

1 ESTUDIANTE A
a. Perdón, ¿cuánto cuesta el suéter?
b. . . . cuestan los jeans?
c. . . . cuesta el vestido?
d. . . . cuesta la chaqueta?
e. . . . cuesta la blusa?
f. . . . cuestan las pantimedias?

ESTUDIANTE B
a. Cuesta veintiséis dólares.
b. Cuestan veinticinco . . .
c. Cuesta cuarenta y tres . . .
d. Cuesta ciento veinticinco . . .
e. Cuesta dieciséis . . .
f. Cuestan cinco . . .

2 ESTUDIANTE A
a. ¿Qué desea, señor (señora / joven / señorita)? ¿Una camiseta?
b. . . . ¿Un suéter?
c. . . . ¿Una chaqueta?
d. . . . ¿Una camisa?

Empecemos a conversar

With a partner, take turns being *Estudiante A* and *Estudiante B.* Use the words that are cued or given in the balloons to replace the underlined sections in the model. 💡 means you can make your own choices.

1

A — *Perdón, ¿cuánto cuesta(n) <u>la(s) camisa(s)</u>?*
B — *Cuesta(n) <u>veintidós</u> dólares.*
  Y ahora Uds.

Estudiante A   Estudiante B

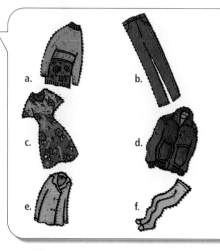   

2

A — *¿Qué desea, señor (señora / joven / señorita)? <u>¿Una camisa?</u>*
B — *Sí, busco <u>una camisa amarilla</u> para mí y <u>una camisa rosada</u> para mi hermana.*
  Y ahora Uds.

Estudiante A   Estudiante B

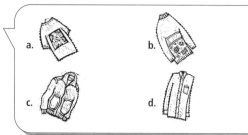   

186   Capítulo 6

Options

Strategies for Reaching All Students

Spanish-Speaking Students
Pair bilingual with non-bilingual students for Exs. 1–4.

 Un paso más Ex. 6-B

Students Needing Extra Help
Have students begin filling in their Organizers. Explain the difference between the definite articles and direct object pronoun use of *la, los,* and *las.*
Ex. 1: Show students that they have to search for the answer. The *Estudiante B* response is not directly across from the *Estudiante A* clue. Explain the use of *cuesta(n)* with singular and plural nouns.
Ex. 2: Do a few of these aloud.

Ex. 3: Point out that the first response will be used if the requested color is there, and the second response if it isn't. Remind students that they have to search for the answer as in Ex. 1.
Ex. 4: Isolate the two possible responses and show how they work with the pictures. Once students understand the process, you may want to add more pictures for further practice.

3

A —*Me encanta esa <u>camiseta</u> azul. ¿La tiene en amarillo?*
B —*¿Esta <u>camiseta</u>? Sí, aquí la tiene.*
   o: *No, no la tenemos en amarillo.*

   Y ahora Uds.

Estudiante A

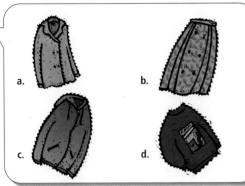

Estudiante B

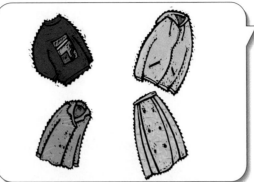

4

A —*¿Cómo te quedan <u>los zapatos</u>?*
B —*<u>Me quedan bien</u>. Los compro.*
   o: *No me quedan bien. Son muy grandes (pequeños).*

   Y ahora Uds.

Estudiante A

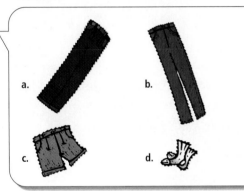

Estudiante B

ESTUDIANTE B
a. Sí, busco una camiseta azul para mí y una camiseta anaranjada para mi hermana.
b. ...un suéter rosado ...un suéter morado ...
c. ...una chaqueta marrón ... una chaqueta gris ...
d. ...una camisa blanca ...una camisa azul ...

3 In the model, note that the name of the color, *amarillo*, is a noun, and that there is no agreement: *¿La tiene en amarillo?*

ESTUDIANTE A
a. Me encanta esa blusa azul. ¿La tiene en amarillo?
b. ...esa falda azul ...
c. ...esa chaqueta azul ...
d. ...esa sudadera azul ...

ESTUDIANTE B
a. No, no la tenemos en amarillo.
b. Sí, aquí la tiene.
c. Sí, aquí la tiene.
d. No, no la tenemos en amarillo.

4 ESTUDIANTE A
a. ¿Cómo te quedan los pantalones?
b. ...los jeans?
c. ...los pantalones cortos?
d. ...los calcetines?

ESTUDIANTE B
a. No me quedan bien. Son muy grandes.
b. No me quedan bien. Son muy pequeños.
c. Me quedan bien. Los compro.
d. No me quedan bien. Son muy grandes.

Enrichment
Ex. 1: To practice *cien* and *ciento*, have students redo the entire exercise with prices ranging from $100 to $199.
Ex. 3: To preview the grammar, ask students the meaning of *esa*. You may want to make this preview more concrete by picking up pairs of objects and placing them so that you can touch one and point to the other to illustrate the difference between *esta / esa*, *este / ese*. Try not to place anything very far away so as to avoid *aquel(la)*.

Apply

Re-enter / Recycle

Ex. 5: seasons from Chap. 3
Ex 8: *gustar* expressions from Chap. 1

Answers: Empecemos a escribir

5–9 Answers will vary, but encourage students to use the chapter vocabulary. Look for correct adjective agreement.

Empecemos a escribir

Write your answers in Spanish.

5 The seasons affect how we dress. List a couple of clothing items you wear in each season of the year.

6 Choose three of the following items and say which colors you prefer for each one: *la chaqueta, los tenis, las medias, la sudadera, los jeans, los pantalones cortos.*

7 ¿Qué ropa vas a llevar mañana?

8 ¿Qué colores te gustan más?

9 ¿Qué ropa compras para ti?

Unos jóvenes chilenos en la playa

Unos jóvenes en una plaza en México

188   Capítulo 6

Options

Strategies for Reaching All Students

Spanish-Speaking Students

Ex. 7: Ask Spanish-speaking students: *¿Qué llevas los fines de semana?*

Students Needing Extra Help

Ex. 5: Review the seasons.
Ex. 6: Review colors and adjective endings for colors not ending in *-o.*
Empecemos a escribir: For additional practice, tell students that they have $100 to spend on clothes at the shopping mall. Ask them to write a sentence telling what items they would like to buy and their cost: *Me gustaría comprar . . . .*

Una zapatería en Madrid

En la Sierra Nevada en España

También se dice

el jersey
la chompa

el vaquero

la pollera

la remera
la franela
la playera

la chamarra
la campera

el short

las medias

las zapatillas (deportivas)
los zapatos de tenis

de color café

Vocabulario para conversar 189

Practice Wkbk. 6-1, 6-2

Audio Activity 6.1

Writing Activities 6-A, 6-B

Pruebas 6-1, 6-2

Comm. Act. BLM 6-1

Multicultural Perspectives

Latin American currencies tell much about the histories and cultures of the countries. The official currency of Venezuela, the *bolívar*, is named after Simón Bolívar, the great liberator who led the fight for independence in South America between 1810 and 1824. The *quetzal*—the official unit of money in Guatemala—is named after a rare, exotic bird found only in Central American rain forests. Ask students if they are familiar with other foreign currencies.

Cultural Notes

(p. 188, top photo)
The beach resort of Concón, Chile, lies north of Valparaíso, the country's principal port. The climate in this region is pleasant, with fresh breezes easing the summer heat and sunshine making the winters more tolerable. Swimming, fishing, camping, tennis, and horseback riding are some of the activities visitors enjoy there. An interesting wildlife attraction is a pelican colony near the beach.

(p. 189, top photo)
High-quality leather goods, like those shown in this store window in Madrid, are a specialty of Spain. Their manufacture is carried out by small firms located away from big cities and often employ only a handful of craftspeople. Firms as those in Ubrique, a small town in southern Spain, turn out fine leather work for prestigious fashion houses.

(p. 189, bottom photo)
Skiers at El Picacho de Veleta, in Spain's Sierra Nevada. At 11,190 feet, this mountain is one of the highest in Spain. The highest point in this area is Pico Mulhacén at 11,847 feet. Both mountains provide excellent skiing conditions from November to mid-May.

Present

Chapter Theme
Clothing stores

Communicative Objectives
- To talk about shopping and places to shop for clothing
- To talk about articles of clothing
- To describe clothes
- To indicate a specific item or items
- To talk about when something happened
- To indicate location

 Transparencies 33–34

 Vocabulary Art BLMs

 Pronunciation Tape 6-2

 Vocabulario para conversar B

Play

Using the Video
Video segment 2: See the Video Teacher's Guide.

 Video Activity B

Vocabulario para conversar

¿Cuánto pagaste por el suéter?

Here's the rest of the vocabulary you will need to talk about where and when you bought clothes.

el almacén

la tienda de ropa

la ropa

Options

Strategies for Reaching All Students

la tienda de descuentos

la zapatería

¡Gangas!

También necesitas...

la ganga	*bargain*	pagar:	*to pay:*
barato, -a	*inexpensive*	(yo) pagué	*I paid*
caro, -a	*expensive*	(tú) pagaste	*you paid*
nuevo, -a	*new*	por	*for*
¡Qué + *adjective!*	*How ___!*	estos, estas; esos, esas	*these; those*
comprar:	*to buy:*	otro, -a	*another, other*
(yo) compré	*I bought*	hace + *time expression*	*___ ago*
(tú) compraste	*you bought*	por aquí	*around here*

Vocabulario para conversar 191

Practice

Re-enter / Recycle

Ex. 11: numbers 0–31 from *El primer paso,* numbers 32–59 from Chap. 2, numbers 60–100 from Chap. 5

Reteach / Review: Spelling

Ex. 12: Stress the importance of the accent mark on *mí* by writing *mí / mi* on the chalkboard with these sentences: *Para mí esa camisa es muy cara. Yo compré mi camisa en un almacén.*

Answers: Empecemos a conversar

10 ESTUDIANTE A

a. ¿Dónde compraste esos pantalones cortos nuevos?

b. ...zapatos ...

c. ...jeans ...

d. ...calcetines ...

ESTUDIANTE B

a. Los compré en la tienda de ropa Ramírez y Hermanos.

b. ...en la zapatería El Calzado Elegante.

c. ...en la tienda de descuentos La Casa de las Gangas.

d. ...en el centro comercial Loma Verde.

Empecemos a conversar

10

Gómez y Caló

A —¿Dónde compraste esos *pantalones* nuevos?
B —Los compré en *el almacén Gómez y Caló*.
    Y ahora Uds.

Estudiante A   **Estudiante B**

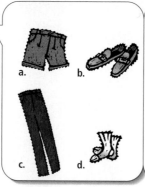

El Calzado Elegante

La Casa de las Gangas

Loma Verde

Ramírez y Hermanos

11

A —¿Cuánto pagaste por *el suéter*?
B —Pagué *veintiséis* dólares.
A —¡Qué caro!
   o: ¡Qué barato!
   Y ahora Uds.

Estudiante A   **Estudiante B**

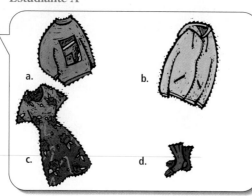

192   Capítulo 6

Options

Strategies for Reaching All Students

Spanish-Speaking Students

Pair bilingual with non-bilingual students for Exs. 10–13.

 Un paso más Ex. 6-C

Students Needing Extra Help

Ex. 10: Point out that *Estudiante B*'s response is not directly across from *Estudiante A*'s clue.

Ex. 11: Again, point out that the response is not directly across from the clue. Keep in mind that the responses *¡Qué caro!* or *¡Qué barato!* are subjective.

Ex. 12: Review the formation of plural nouns. Explain that because of the expense, the customer is looking for another store to see if the prices are better.

Enrichment

Ex. 11: Pairs of students can extend this dialogue by having *Estudiante A* contrast what he or she paid for the item in question. Example: *¡Qué caro (barato)! Pues, por mi suéter, yo pagué . . . . Estudiante B* can then ask where *Estudiante A* bought the item.

192

12

A — *Estos <u>calcetines</u> son caros, ¿verdad?*
B — *Sí, para mí son muy caros. ¿Hay otra <u>tienda de ropa</u> por aquí?*

Y ahora Uds.

Estudiante A

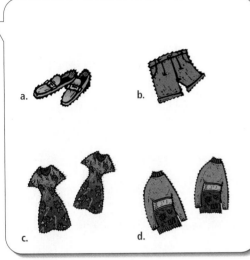

a.

b.

c.

d.

Estudiante B

13

A — *Esa <u>blusa</u> es muy bonita. ¿Es nueva?*
B — *Más o menos. La compré <u>hace dos días</u>.*

Y ahora Uds.

Estudiante A

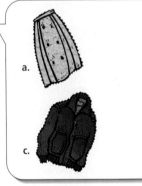

a.

b.

c.

d.

Estudiante B

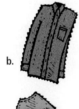

11 ESTUDIANTE A
a. ¿Cuánto pagaste por la sudadera? / ¡Qué cara (barata)!
b. ...la chaqueta? / ¡Qué cara (barata)!
c. ...el vestido? / ¡Qué caro (barato)!
d. ...los calcetines? / ¡Qué caros (baratos)!

ESTUDIANTE B
a. Pagué sesenta dólares.
b. ...doce dólares.
c. ...ciento cincuenta dólares.
d. ...dos dólares.

12 ESTUDIANTE A
a. Estos zapatos son caros, ¿verdad?
b. ...pantalones cortos ...
c. ...(dos) vestidos ...
d. ...(dos) suéteres ...

ESTUDIANTE B
a. Sí, para mí son muy caros. ¿Hay otra zapatería por aquí?
b. ...otro almacén ...
c. ...otra tienda de descuentos ...
d. ...otro centro comercial ...

13 ESTUDIANTE A
a. Esa falda es muy bonita. ¿Es nueva?
b. Esa camisa ...
c. Esa chaqueta ...
d. Esa camiseta ...

ESTUDIANTE B
a.–d. Más o menos. La compré hace ... *(Answers will vary.)*

Apply

Re-enter / Recycle
Ex. 17: calendar expressions from *El primer paso*
Ex. 18: *gustar* expressions from Chap. 1, adjectives describing physical characteristics from Chap. 5

Answers: Empecemos a escribir y a leer

14–17 Answers will vary, but encourage students to use the full range of chapter vocabulary.

18 Answers
a. Marta
b. Silvia
c. una tienda de descuentos
d. Answers will vary.

Empecemos a escribir y a leer

Write your answers in Spanish.

14 Choose three of your favorite clothing items, and tell in what kinds of stores you bought them.

15 Describe your three favorite items of clothing.

16 Cuando vas de compras, ¿buscas gangas o no?

17 ¿Compraste algo hace dos semanas? ¿Qué? ¿Y hace un mes?

"¿A qué tienda quieres ir ahora?"

Dos jóvenes en un centro comercial en México

194   Capítulo 6

Options

Strategies for Reaching All Students

Students Needing Extra Help
Ex. 14: Model one example.

Enrichment
Ex. 14: Have students also tell how long ago they bought each of their favorite clothing items.
Have pairs of students invent a dialogue in which they go shopping. Encourage students to use extensive vocabulary to describe their favorite shopping companion. If students don't shop with anyone or don't like to go shopping, have them say so and describe reasons as best they can for their shopping habits or preferences.

18 Lee este diálogo.

SILVIA   Hola, Marta. ¡Qué bonito tu vestido!
MARTA   ¿Te gusta?
SILVIA   Sí, me gusta mucho. ¿Es nuevo?
MARTA   Pues, lo compré hace una semana.
SILVIA   ¿Dónde lo compraste?
MARTA   En la tienda de descuentos Nosotras.
SILVIA   ¿Y cuánto pagaste?
MARTA   ¡Diez dólares!
SILVIA   ¡No me digas! ¡Qué ganga! Yo también necesito comprar un vestido nuevo. ¿Quieres ir de compras mañana?
MARTA   ¡Claro que sí!

a.   ¿Quién tiene un vestido nuevo?
b.   ¿Quién necesita un vestido nuevo?
c.   ¿Qué es "Nosotras"?
d.   En tu opinión, ¿la ropa en los almacenes es barata o cara? ¿Es necesario comprar ropa cara? ¿Por qué?

Vocabulario para conversar   195

Multicultural Perspectives

The indigenous people of Mexico and Central America may be seen wearing unique clothing. A *huipil* is an embroidered blouse. An *enredo* is a long, wrapped skirt. A *rebozo* is a shawl that can serve as a fashion accessory, as a head covering, or to cradle a baby. Men wear *sarapes* (ponchos), *huaraches de seis agujeros* (sandals with two rows of three eyelets, laced with leather cords) and *sombreros de palma* (straw hats). The patterns embroidered on the fabric of the clothing often contain information about community, marital status, or family affiliation. If you have students from other countries, ask them to share information about their traditional clothing.

 Practice Wkbk. 6-3, 6-4

 Audio Activity 6.2

 Writing Activity 6-C

 Pruebas 6-3, 6-4

Practice

Re-enter / Recycle

Ex. 1: activities from Chap. 1, places and buildings from Chap. 3
Ex. 2: numbers 0–31 from *El primer paso,* school supplies from Chap. 2

Answers:
¡Comuniquemos!

1 ESTUDIANTE A

a. ¿Qué ropa llevas cuando vas al cine?

b. ...al centro comercial?

c. ...a la escuela?

d. ...al parque de diversiones?

e. ...al campo?

f. ...a una fiesta?

ESTUDIANTE B

a.–f. Answers will vary.

2 ESTUDIANTE A

a. ¿Cuánto pagaste por tu mochila?

b. ...calculadora?

c. ...carpeta de argollas?

d. ...regla?

e. ...cuaderno?

f. ...carpeta?

g. ...grabadora?

h. ...marcador?

ESTUDIANTE B

(Answers may vary depending on whether *Estudiante B* uses real prices instead of the suggested ones.)

a. Pagué dieciséis dólares.

b. ...quince dólares.

c. ...siete dólares.

¡Comuniquemos!

Here's another opportunity for you to use the vocabulary you've just learned.

1 Find out what your partner wears to different places.

A — *¿Qué ropa llevas cuando vas al parque?*
B — *Generalmente llevo ...*
   o: *Nunca voy al parque.*

¡NO OLVIDES!
a + el = al

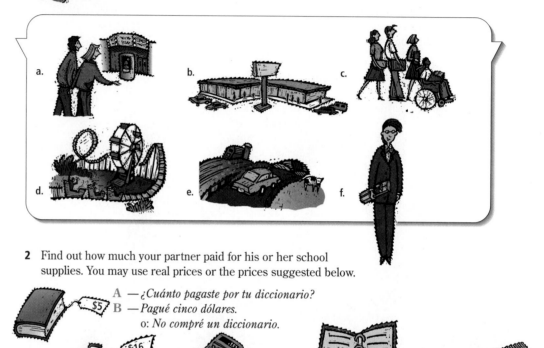

2 Find out how much your partner paid for his or her school supplies. You may use real prices or the prices suggested below.

A — *¿Cuánto pagaste por tu diccionario?*
B — *Pagué cinco dólares.*
   o: *No compré un diccionario.*

a. $16   b. $15   c. $7   d. $1
e. $4   f. $3   g. $25   h. $2

196   Capítulo 6

Options

Strategies for Reaching All Students

Spanish-Speaking Students

Ex. 1: Have Spanish-speaking students write out part of the exercise: *Escribe seis oraciones que describen lo que llevas a diferentes lugares.*

 Un paso más Ex. 6-D

Students Needing Extra Help

Ex. 1: Have students use their Organizers for this chapter and from Chap. 3 to review the places.
Ex. 2: Have students use their Organizers from Chap. 2 for school supplies.
Review Ex. 10 on p. 192 to show how *compraste* is answered with *compré.*
¿Qué sabes ahora?: Have students write out this section so they can track their progress.

Cooperative Learning

Divide the class into groups of three or four students. Using vocabulary from the *Vocabulario para conversar,* have each student prepare a list of the clothing they are wearing and their colors. Have one student in each group collect the lists and record the colors of one type (shoes, socks, etc.) of clothing. Have another student record colors for another type of clothing. Repeat until each type of clothing is recorded. Collect the responses and tally them. Before putting the

3 Plan your next shopping trip for clothes. Decide on three items you need and what colors they should be. Your partner will estimate how much money you will need.

A — *Necesito una blusa azul.*
B — *Vas a necesitar quince dólares.*

¿Qué sabes ahora?

Can you:

■ describe what clothes you wear?
  —Hoy llevo ___.

■ tell where you bought something?
  —___ mis jeans en ___.

■ tell how much you paid for something?
  —___ veinte dólares ___ la camisa.

■ ask how much something costs?
  —¿Cuánto ___ esa camisa?

Vocabulario para conversar 197

d. ...un dólar.
e. ...cuatro dólares.
f. ...tres dólares.
g. ...veinticinco dólares.
h. ...dos dólares.

3 Dialogues will vary, but encourage students to use the full range of chapter vocabulary.

Answers: ¿Qué sabes ahora?

• Answers will vary.
• Compré / *Answers will vary.*
• Pagué / por
• cuesta

Using Realia

Ask: *Describe la ropa que los muchachos llevan en la foto.*

 Audio Activity 6.3

Cultural Notes ☀

results on the chalkboard, ask students: What do you think is the most popular shoe color? The most popular color of jeans? and so on. (Combine some of the clothing categories for this exercise. For example, shoes / sneakers, pants / jeans.)

(p. 197, realia)
Ad for the Miami International Mall. Cubans make up Miami's oldest and largest Hispanic community. They first came to Miami in large numbers in 1960 as exiles from the government of Fidel Castro. Today, Miami has other large Hispanic groups, notably Nicaraguans, who like the first group of Cubans, fled political unrest in their homelands.

Perspectiva cultural

¿Te gusta ir de compras en los almacenes o los centros comerciales? ¿Qué compras?

Look at the photos on these pages. What kinds of stores do you think are shown here?

In big cities in Spanish-speaking countries, you can usually find a variety of malls or shopping centers. The idea of the shopping mall originated in the United States, and other countries have adopted the concept by creating malls of great beauty. However, there are also tailors and dressmaking stores where people can have their clothes custom-made at affordable prices.

Teenagers in Spanish-speaking countries like to window-shop at malls and clothing stores, just as they do here. And, just as in other countries, there is a wide variety of materials, styles, and fashions to choose from. Teens in Spanish-speaking countries tend to be fashion-conscious and stylish in the way they dress, and many like to wear custom-made formal clothes on special occasions.

La cultura desde tu perspectiva

1 What do you think are some of the advantages and disadvantages of shopping in a mall rather than in separate stores within several blocks?

2 Do you think you would be able to find some clothing brands that you are familiar with in the stores pictured? Why or why not?

Una joven en un centro comercial en Córdoba, Argentina

De compras en una tienda en Caracas, Venezuela

Tienda de ropa en la Ciudad de México

198   Capítulo 6

Options

Centro comercial en Zaragoza, España

Plaza de las Américas en San Juan, Puerto Rico

1 Answers will vary, but may include the fact that they carry a greater variety of items in a mall. You have the convenience of many stores grouped together, often under one roof. On the other hand, small stores may carry items that are hard to find in other places.

2 Answers will vary.

Multicultural Perspectives

Although bargaining once was a common practice in the U.S., this method of procuring goods and services is used on a much smaller scale today. In Latin America, however, it is a part of everyday life. In markets such as the one in Chichicastenango, both locals and tourists bargain with shop owners and vendors to establish prices. A unique aspect of these markets is that the sellers actually expect potential buyers to bargain. If they don't, the sellers may think that the buyer does not value the product! Ask students to think of examples of when they or someone in their family has used bargaining to buy something (flea markets, antique stores, etc.).

Cultural Notes

(pp. 198–199, photos)
Shopping malls are now commonplace in most Spanish-speaking countries. Not only do they have clothing stores, bookstores, and fast-food restaurants, many of them have supermarkets as well. At the Alcampo mall in Zaragoza, Spain, shoppers can eat in their favorite restaurant, look at the latest fashion designs, and buy their groceries, all without leaving the complex.

Preview

 Transparency 35

Teaching Suggestions

Ask students: What comparison can be made between a department store and a discount store in an ad like this? Find the place in the ad where the comparison is made (*¿Por qué pagar los precios altos . . .*).

Have students find these phrases from the ad: *precios altos, ropa espectacular*. Identify which of these words are nouns and which are adjectives. As a preview to the grammar, ask about the position of the adjectives in relation to the nouns.

Answers

Answers may include: name of the store, address, business hours, description of merchandise, prices, etc.

A *Esta* is used before *ropa* because it refers to a feminine, singular noun. *Este* refers to *mes* and is masculine. *Estas* would be used before *gangas* because it is feminine.

B *Las* refers to *camisas, blusas y faldas.* / *Ropa* determines the use of *la.* / If you were talking about a shirt, the phrase would be *la compro*, because *camisa* is feminine.

Gramática en contexto

Here is an ad for a store. What kinds of information would you expect to find in an ad for a discount clothing store?

A You know that *estos* and *estas* mean "these." Look at the ad. Which word is used before *ropa? Mes?* Which form of the word would be used before *gangas?* Can you explain the difference?

B You know that *lo* and *la* can mean "it," and *los* and *las* can mean "them." In the question that begins "*¿Por qué pagar los precios altos . . . cuando nosotros las tenemos . . . ,*" what does *las* refer to? In the sentence that begins "*La Tienda de Descuentos Bolívar tiene . . . y ahora Ud. la puede comprar . . . ,*" why do you think *la* is used, and not *lo?* If you were talking about a shirt *(camisa),* would you say *lo compro* or *la compro?*

200　Capítulo 6

Options

Strategies for Reaching All Students

Spanish-Speaking Students
Ex. 1: Have Spanish-speaking students write out part of the exercise. *Escribe oraciones para estos artículos (estas prendas). Incluye tus colores preferidos.*

Students Needing Extra Help
Remind students that *la, las,* and *los* are also the definite articles meaning "the." Explain that the context makes clear which use is meant.
Be sure students understand the difference between *esta* (demonstrative adjective) and *está* (third person singular form of *estar),* and *estas* (demonstrative adjective) and *estás* (second person singular form of *estar).*

A: Remind students of adjective endings. Going from "these" to "this" will be a leap for some students. Walk them through this comparison.
B: Direct students back to the paragraph or write the sentences on the chalkboard so they can find out what *las* represents.
La posición de los adjetivos: Have students start to fill in the grammar portion of their Organizers.

La posición de los adjetivos

In Spanish, adjectives usually come after the noun they describe.

Me gusta más la camisa **blanca.**

Tenemos un perro **grande y feo.**

1 You and your partner are going shopping for clothing. Look at the items pictured and tell your partner which you would like to buy. Your partner will respond with his or her choice.

A — *Me gustaría comprar una camiseta blanca.*
B — *A mí también.*
   o: *A mí no. Prefiero una camiseta roja.*

a.   b.   c.   d.

e.   f.   g.   h.

¡NO OLVIDES!

Adjectives agree in number (singular / plural) and gender (masculine / feminine) with the nouns they describe.

Gramática en contexto   201

Reteach / Review: Indefinite Articles
Ex. 1: Do a quick review of the indefinite articles and the gender of nouns by mentioning a noun and calling on a student to give the correct indefinite article.

Re-enter / Recycle
Ex. 1: gustar expressions from Chap. 1, adjective agreement from Chaps. 1 and 4

Answers
1 ESTUDIANTE A
a. Me gustaría comprar unos pantalones negros.
b. ...una chaqueta marrón.
c. ...una camisa azul.
d. ...unos calcetines azules.
e. ...unos zapatos rojos.
f. ...unos pantalones cortos grises.
g. ...un suéter rosado.
h. ...una sudadera anaranjada.
ESTUDIANTE B
a.–h. Statements will vary depending on *Estudiante B*'s preferences. Look for correct adjective agreement and placement.

Ex. 1: If *Estudiante B* chooses the second response, he or she will have to determine the color. Have students use the Organizer.
¡No olvides!: Emphasize the terms singular / plural, masculine / feminine, rather than number and gender.

Present & Practice

Answers

2 ESTUDIANTE A

a.–h. ¿Qué desea, señor (señora / joven / señorita)? / ¿Para Ud.?

ESTUDIANTE B

a. Busco un vestido verde. / *Statements will vary for* Estudiante B's *second part.*

b. . . . unos pantalones cortos grises.

c. . . . un suéter azul y blanco.

d. . . . una sudadera marrón.

e. . . . una camisa blanca y unos pantalones negros.

f. . . . una chaqueta negra.

g. . . . una camiseta roja y una camiseta amarilla.

h. Statements will vary.

 Practice Wkbk. 6-5

 Prueba 6-5

---

2 Take turns with your partner playing the roles of a salesperson and a customer. The salesperson should find out what item the customer is looking for and for whom. The items can be for a family member or a person of your choice.

A —*¿Qué desea, señor (señora / joven / señorita)?*
B —*Busco unos calcetines blancos.*
A —*¿Para Ud.?*
B —*Sí, para mí.*
    o: *No, para mi madre (padre).*

a. b. c. d.

e. f. g. h.

Los adjetivos demostrativos

We use demonstrative adjectives to point out people and things. You've already seen these forms: *este, esta, estos, estas* (this, these), and *ese, esa, esos,* and *esas* (that, those).

Demonstrative adjectives come before the noun. They have the same gender and number as the nouns that follow them.

SINGULAR	PLURAL
este vestido (**this** dress)	**estos** vestidos (**these** dresses)
esta blusa (**this** blouse)	**estas** blusas (**these** blouses)
ese suéter (**that** sweater)	**esos** suéteres (**those** sweaters)
esa sudadera (**that** sweatshirt)	**esas** sudaderas (**those** sweatshirts)

202   Capítulo 6

Options

Strategies for Reaching All Students

Spanish-Speaking Students
Pair bilingual with non-bilingual students for Exs. 2–4.

Students Needing Extra Help
Ex. 2: Point out the choices in the first line for *Estudiante A*. For the first *Estudiante B* response, review the indefinite articles. Model an example using a singular article of clothing.
Los adjetivos demostrativos: Have students fill in the chart in the grammar portion of their Organizers. The concept of "this,"

"that," "these," and "those" may be confusing for students. (Color-coding these words in sentences written on a transparency can help.) Associating the four letters in *este* with the four letters in "near" and the three letters in *ese* with the three in "far" also helps many students. Point out that the masculine, singular form of "this" and "that" end in *e*, not *o*, as students might expect.

3 You are at a party and you want to get to know the guests. Find out from your partner their names and ages.

Marta

A —¿Cómo se llama esa muchacha alta y rubia?
B —Marta.
A —¿Cuántos años tiene?
B —Quince.

Lucía, 28
Pilar y Conchita, 17
Carlitos, 9
Marta, 15
Javier, 35
Eva, 75
Miguel y Mateo, 14

4 While shopping with a friend, you pick up and look at several items. Ask if your partner likes them.

A —¿Te gusta este suéter azul?
B —Sí, me gusta mucho.
o: No, no me gusta nada.

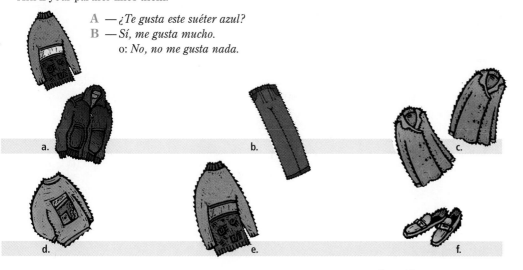

a.
b.
c.
d.
e.
f.

Gramática en contexto   203

3 Dialogues may vary.
A —¿Cómo se llama ese hombre bajo? / ¿Cuántos años tiene?
B —Javier. / Treinta y cinco.

A —. . . se llama ese muchacho alto? / . . . tiene?
B —Carlitos. / Nueve.

A —. . . se llama esa mujer vieja? / . . . tiene?
B —Eva. / Setenta y cinco.

A —. . . se llaman esos gemelos sociables? / . . . tienen?
B —Miguel y Mateo. / Catorce.

A —. . . se llaman esas muchachas rubias? / . . . tienen?
B —Pilar y Conchita. / Diecisiete.

A —. . . se llama esa mujer pelirroja? / . . . tiene?
B —Lucía. / Veintiocho.

4 ESTUDIANTE A
a. ¿Te gusta esta chaqueta marrón?
b. ¿Te gustan estos pantalones grises?
c. ¿Te gustan estas blusas anaranjadas?
d. ¿Te gusta esta sudadera rosada?
e. ¿Te gusta este suéter verde?
f. ¿Te gustan estos zapatos amarillos?

ESTUDIANTE B
Answers will vary.

Practice Wkbk. 6-6

Writing Activity 6-D

Prueba 6-6

Ex. 3: Have students use their Organizers from previous chapters. Review *se llama(n)* and how to talk about age.

Ex. 4: Remind students to use *gusta* with singular and *gustan* with plural nouns. This exercise may be made more realistic by bringing in actual items of clothing. This will help them visualize the difference between *este* and *ese.*

Enrichment
Ex. 4: Pairs of students can vary and extend this dialogue by having *Estudiante B* name an item that he or she prefers. Encourage students to specify *ese* as well as *este* along with colors when they name the preferred item. Example: *¿Te gusta este suéter azul? / No, prefiero esa sudadera roja.*

Present & Practice

Class Starter Review

On the day following the presentation of pronouns, you might begin the class with this activity:
Put ten objects representing nouns students know (classroom supplies, doll clothes, plastic food) on a table and have them choose one or more items. Ask: *¿Quién tiene . . . ?* Students should answer with the correct object pronoun *(Yo lo tengo)*. Repeat until all objects have been used.

El complemento directo: Los pronombres

A direct object tells who or what receives the action of the verb.

Quiero **esa falda.**

Compré **unos zapatos.**

To avoid repeating a direct object noun, we often replace it with a direct object pronoun ("it" or "them").

— ¿Cuándo compraste **la falda?**
— **La** compré hace cinco días.

— Isabel, ¿tienes **mi suéter?**
— No, no **lo** tengo.

	SINGULAR		PLURAL
lo	*it* (masculine)	**los**	*them* (masculine)
la	*it* (feminine)	**las**	*them* (feminine)

- The direct object pronoun usually comes right before the verb. If the verb is negative, the pronoun is placed between *no* and the verb.
  — ¿Compras **esos pantalones?**
  — No, no **los** compro.

- When we have a verb followed by an infinitive, the direct object pronoun is usually placed right before the main verb (not the infinitive).
  — ¿Quieres comprar **esa falda?**
  — Sí, **la** quiero comprar.

- Direct object pronouns have the same gender and number as the nouns they are replacing. When the pronoun replaces both a masculine and a feminine direct object noun, we use *los.*
  — ¿Cuándo compraste **la falda y el vestido?**
  — **Los** compré el sábado.

204   Capítulo 6

Options

Strategies for Reaching All Students

Students Needing Extra Help
El complemento directo: Los pronombres:
This may be another difficult concept for students. Break the explanation into these steps:
1. Discuss what they already know about direct objects from English. Most students have been taught that direct objects answer the question "who" or "what" of the verb, or receive the action of the verb.
2. Remind students that pronouns replace nouns. Emphasize that once we have stated

the noun, we usually replace it with "it" or "them."
3. Using Spanish nouns familiar to students, have them decide which object pronoun will replace each noun.
4. Using examples from the book and then creating others, have two students stand in front of the classroom, one holding a card that reads *Quiero* and the other *ese suéter.* The back of the *Quiero* card should read *quiero* and the back of the *ese suéter* card should read *Lo.* Read *Quiero ese suéter* and

its translation—"I want that sweater"—followed by "I want it." At this point the students should flip their cards. The second student moves to the other side of the first student, creating *Lo quiero.* This gives the class a memorable visual.
5. Repeat this process with variations, using sentences with *no* and a verb followed by an infinitive.
6. Delay the explanation of attaching the object pronoun to the infinitive. This will appear in Chap. 11.

204

5 Today is November 28 and you recently went shopping for clothes. Use the calendar to answer your partner's questions.

A — *Tu camisa es nueva, ¿no?*
B — *Sí, la compré hace tres semanas.*

Gramática en contexto   205

Re-enter / Recycle
Ex. 5: calendar expressions and numbers 0–31 from *El primer paso,* adjective agreement from Chaps. 1 and 4

Answers
5 Order of students' exchanges may vary.
A —Tu chaqueta es nueva, ¿no?
B —Sí, la compré hace dieciocho días.

A —Tus calcetines son nuevos . . .
B —. . . los compré . . . quince días.

A —Tu sudadera es nueva . . .
B —. . . la compré . . . dos semanas (catorce días).

A —Tus vestidos son nuevos . . .
B —. . . los compré . . . doce días.

A —Tus jeans son nuevos . . .
B —. . . los compré . . . ocho días.

A —Tu suéter y tu camiseta son nuevos . . .
B —. . . los compré . . . seis días.

7. Remind students that they already know how to replace and combine a masculine and feminine subject with the masculine plural form.
Ex. 5: Review adjective agreement and *hace* + time expression. Show students how to arrive at the number of days (subtracting the date from November 28). Be aware that some math errors may occur. Point out that, like the direct object pronoun, *nueva* will change depending on the clothing item.

Practice

Re-enter / Recycle

Ex. 6: school supplies, school subjects, and *necesito / necesitas* from Chap. 2
Ex. 7: school supplies from Chap. 2

Answers

6 Order of students' questions may vary.

ESTUDIANTE A
¿Necesitas los lápices?
...los cuadernos?
...la regla?
...las carpetas de argollas?
...los bolígrafos?
...las carpetas?
...la mochila?
...los marcadores?

ESTUDIANTE B
Answers will vary, but look for correct use of direct object pronouns.
¡Claro que sí! Los necesito para ... (No, no los necesito.)
...Los necesito ...
...La necesito ...
...Las necesito ...
...Los necesito ...
...Las necesito ...
...La necesito ...
...Los necesito ...

6 You're trying to help your partner clean out a messy locker. Ask whether or not he or she needs the objects pictured.

A — *¿Necesitas la calculadora?*
B — *¡Claro que sí! La necesito para mi clase de matemáticas.*
    o: *No, no la necesito.*

206   Capítulo 6

Options

Strategies for Reaching All Students

Spanish-Speaking Students
Pair Spanish-speaking students for Exs. 6–7.

Students Needing Extra Help
Ex. 6: Have students review their Chap. 2 Organizers for school supplies.
Remind students that they will be using direct object pronouns in the answers.
Ex. 7: Remind students that the direct object pronoun comes before the first verb in *Estudiante B's* question.
Ahora lo sabes: Have students write out this section so that they can chart their progress.

Enrichment
Ex. 7: Have pairs of students continue this dialogue with *Estudiante B* asking *Estudiante A* where he or she plans to buy the item.

7 It's the first day of class and you're talking to a friend about the supplies you need to buy. With a partner, take turns asking and answering based on the pictures from the previous exercise.

A —*Necesito comprar una calculadora.*
B —*¿Cuándo la quieres comprar?*
A —*Mañana.*

Ahora lo sabes

Can you:

■ **place adjectives in the correct position in a sentence?**
—Necesito un(a) ___.

■ **point out people and things?**
—¿Qué bolígrafo prefieres?
—Prefiero ___ bolígrafo.

■ **avoid reusing a noun by replacing it with** *lo, la, los,* **or** *las?*
—¿Tienes la calculadora y la regla?
—Sí, ___ tengo.

Gramática en contexto   207

7 Order of dialogue exchanges may vary. Make sure students use the correct indefinite articles and direct object pronouns. A sample dialogue is as follows:
A —Necesito comprar unos lápices.
B —¿Cuándo los quieres comprar?
A —Mañana.

Answers: Ahora lo sabes
• Answers will vary, but look for correct placement of adjectives.
• este (ese)
• las

 Practice Wkbk. 6-7, 6-8

 Audio Activity 6.4

 Writing Activities 6-E, 6-F

 Prueba 6-7

 Comm. Act. BLMs 6-2, 6-3

Apply

Using the Video
Video segment 3: See the Video Teacher's Guide.

 Video Activity C

Re-enter / Recycle
Ex. 1: numbers 0–31 from *El primer paso*, numbers 32–59 from Chap. 2, numbers 60–100 from Chap. 5
Ex. 2: food from Chap. 4
Ex. 3: adjective agreement from Chaps. 1 and 4

Para decir más

Here is some additional vocabulary that you might find useful for activities in this section.

el abrigo
overcoat

las botas
boots

el cinturón
belt

la gorra
cap

gastar
to spend

ahorrar
to save

el dinero
money

el sombrero
hat

208   Capítulo 6

Actividades

Here's an opportunity for you to expand your use of Spanish by putting together the material you learned in this chapter with what you learned earlier.

1 With your partner, play the roles of a store clerk and a customer who wants to buy an item of clothing:
- Get the clerk's attention
- The clerk will ask how he or she can help you
- Tell the clerk that you want to see an item
- The clerk will clarify which item you are talking about
- Find out the price of the item
- Find out if they have it in another color
- Tell the clerk whether you will buy it or not

Options

Strategies for Reaching All Students

Enrichment
Ex. 3: As a homework assignment, have students write a dialogue in which the parent wants the son or daughter to buy certain kinds or colors of clothes.

Cooperative Learning
Have students work in groups of three or four to role play fashion designers. Their assignment is to come up with the best-looking outfit design for today's teenager. Using pictures and text, have one student in each group be responsible for presenting and explaining the new design to the class. Allow the class to vote for the best one.

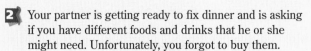

2 Your partner is getting ready to fix dinner and is asking if you have different foods and drinks that he or she might need. Unfortunately, you forgot to buy them.

A —*¿Tienes cebollas y tomates?*
B —*A ver... No, no los tengo.*
A —*¿Pero, no los compraste? ¿Y qué voy a cocinar para la cena?*
B —*Podemos comer un sandwich de...*

3 Role-play a scene in which you try to convince your parent(s) that you need to buy some new clothing. As the adult, your partner will try to convince you that you don't need the clothing. For example:

A —*Mamá, necesito una blusa nueva.*
B —*Pero, hija. Tienes tres blusas blancas y una blusa amarilla.*
A —*Ay, no, mamá. ¡Esas blusas son viejas!*
B —*¡Viejas! ¡Pero las compraste hace sólo un mes!*

209

Apply

Process Reading
For a description of process reading, see p. 48.

Answers
Antes de leer
Responses will vary. Students may mention that part of the story deals with clothing and someone's birthday.

Mira la lectura
a. He received two shirts as birthday gifts from his grandmother. He's invited to dinner at her place, and he doesn't know which shirt to wear.

b. He decides to wear the gray shirt.

c. She asks Juanito if he doesn't like the yellow one.

¡Vamos a leer!

Antes de leer

STRATEGY ➤ Using titles and pictures to predict

Look at the title and pictures to predict what the story is about.

Mira la lectura

STRATEGIES ➤ Skimming
Identifying the main idea

Skimming is another useful strategy. By quickly glancing through a reading selection, you can often get a general idea of the subject and content.

This story tells of a decision a boy has to make. Skim through it quickly to get the main ideas.

a. What is Juanito's problem?
b. What does he decide to do?
c. What is the grandmother's reaction?

EL PROBLEMA DE LAS DOS CAMISAS

Juanito es un muchacho amable y sociable. Para su cumpleaños, Juanito recibe muchos regalos y muchísima ropa de su familia. Le encanta la ropa, pero una semana después de su cumpleaños, recibe una invitación para ir a cenar a la casa de su abuela.

Ahora tiene un problema: Su abuela le regaló dos camisas, una gris y otra amarilla. ¿Cuál va a llevar? Habla con su mamá.

Juanito: Mamá, ¿qué voy a llevar? Tengo las dos camisas nuevas de la abuela.

La mamá: Bueno, hijo, ¿por qué no llevas la camisa que te gusta más?

Juanito: Es que no quiero ofender a la abuela. Ella es un poco difícil a veces.

La mamá: Pues, hijo, puedes llevar una de las camisas para esta cena, y otro día puedes llevar la otra camisa.

Juanito decide llevar la camisa gris. Cuando él entra en la casa, la abuela le dice: "Y, ¿qué pasa? No llevas la camisa amarilla. ¿No te gusta?"

La mamá le dice a Juanito: "No te preocupes. Es imposible contentarles a todos."

¡Feliz cumpleaños!

210 Capítulo 6

Options

Strategies for Reaching All Students

Students Needing Extra Help
Mira la lectura: Make sure students understand the nature of skimming. You may wish to have students work in pairs, where one student answers the questions and the other records the responses. Set a limited amount of time for this activity.

Infórmate: Remind students of the saying "You can't please all of the people all the time."
Aplicación: Brainstorm some situations as a class. For example: (Chap. 3) Two friends can't decide whether to go to the amusement park or the mall. (Chap. 4) Two friends talk about what they want to eat for dinner.

Infórmate

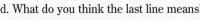 Using context to get meaning

Remember that when you are reading and you come across a word you don't understand, you should look at the other words in the sentence to see if they will help you understand.

As you read the story again, make a list of five words or phrases you don't understand.

a. What type of boy is Juanito? What words or phrases tell you that?

b. What do you think of the mother's advice? Would you have given the same advice? Why or why not?

c. What would you have done in Juanito's place?

d. What do you think the last line means?

Aplicación

Think of a similar situation where it seemed impossible to please someone. Create a short dialogue with a partner and end it with a solution that pleases both of you.

¡Vamos a leer! 211

Infórmate
Lists will vary.

a. Juanito is nice and outgoing, and he likes clothes. / *amable, sociable, le encanta la ropa*

b.–c. Answers will vary.

d. "Don't worry. It's impossible to please everyone."

Aplicación
Dialogues will vary.

211

Apply

Process Writing

Starting in this chapter, the revise and edit steps will appear in an abbreviated form.

For information regarding developing a writing portfolio, see p. 50.

Answers: ¡Vamos a escribir!

1–5 Look for correct use of adjectives and verbs. Encourage students to use all the vocabulary learned thus far.

Multicultural Perspectives

The fashion industry has been influenced by styles and designs typical of Spain and Latin America. (Two of the leading fashion designers in the world are from Latin America—Óscar de la Renta and Carolina Herrera.) *Gauchos* are the cowboys of the Pampas in Argentina. The word *gauchos* is also used to describe a type of women's baggy trousers that are often gathered at the ankles. Ask students to name other types of clothing from various cultures with which they are familiar.

¡Vamos a escribir!

Many teens love to shop. They read fashion magazines and browse in stores to learn about the newest fashions, styles, and colors. Create an ad for an article of clothing to appear in a teen magazine or catalog.

1 First, think about what might appeal to you and your friends. What article of clothing are you going to sell? What colors does it come in? Where can you buy it? How much does it cost? Write out the answers to these questions in Spanish.

2 Invent a brand name for your clothing. Use it and the answers to the questions in Part 1 to help you design your ad. Be sure to give all the information and arrange it in a way that will catch the eye.

3 Show your ad to a partner. Does he or she want to suggest changes or additions? Think about any changes you might want to make, and rewrite your ad.

4 Check the ad for spelling, accents, and punctuation. Did you use the correct forms of the adjectives? If necessary, make a clean copy and add drawings or magazine pictures to illustrate your ad.

5 You can file your ad in your writing portfolio, or the entire class can collect the ads into a catalog ("ROPA DE PRIMAVERA / VERANO / OTOÑO / INVIERNO 19__").

212   Capítulo 6

Options

Strategies for Reaching All Students

Spanish-Speaking Students

 Un paso más Exs. 6-F, 6-G, 6-H

Students Needing Extra Help
Step 1: Use the Organizer.
Step 2: If you elect to have students do this activity in groups, try to get an art-gifted student or visual learner in each one.
Step 4: Use Organizers from other chapters.

Enrichment
Groups of students might enjoy collaborating on a poster showing what clothes students will be wearing in the future. Encourage them to make up titles for their posters. Students should also label the clothes they display, indicating what they are and their color.

LOS NUEVOS PAREDES
¡ya están en las zapaterías!

Con éstos, de base de POLIURETANO
no sentirás el frío ni el calor, son ISOTÉRMICOS.
Su base es totalmente ANATÓMICA.
Caminar con ellos, es un auténtico placer.

...y, si te gusta cosido.

Ésta, es la nueva versión (mejorada)
del legendario modelo COMPETICIÓN

Su piel, es napa y está cosida a una estudiada
suela de caucho de gran agarre.
Se le ha incorporado una entresuela
de EVA para que amortigüe y absorba
los impactos que se producen en
el talón durante un partido
de tenis.

PAREDES la estrella

ZAPATOS

¿Buscas zapatos de tenis?

En la tienda Suárez, tenemos muchos colores
y estilos para ti. Tenemos también los colores
atractivos de este año: verde y rojo.

Los tenis de Suárez:

¡SÓLO $25!

Test Preparation

You may want to assign parts of this section as written homework or as an in-class writing activity prior to administering the *Examen de habilidades*.

Answers

Listening: *Este fin de semana voy a ir de compras. Necesito comprar un suéter, una sudadera, una chaqueta y dos camisetas, pero sólo tengo 120 dólares.* The person is planning to buy five items and spend approximately $120.

Reading: Inés prefers to go to shopping malls, because there are many types of stores and restaurants there.

Writing: Letters will vary, but students should use most of the chapter vocabulary. Look for logical sentences.

Culture: Answers will vary. Some students may say that they prefer a shopping center because of the convenience and variety of stores. Others may say that they would go to a tailor or dressmaker because of more personalized service.

Speaking: Answers will vary, but students should use the chapter vocabulary. Encourage use of vocabulary from previous chapters.

¿Lo sabes bien?

This section will help you organize your studying for the proficiency test, where you will be asked to do similar, though not identical tasks. There will not be any models on the test.

Listening

Can you understand when people talk about clothes? Listen as your teacher reads a sample similar to what you will hear on the test. How many items is the person planning to buy? Approximately how much money is he or she going to spend?

Reading

Can you understand a description about shopping and clothes? Read through this paragraph to get the main idea. What kind of store does Inés prefer to go to, and why?

"A mí me gusta ir de compras en todas partes, pero lo que más me gusta es ir a los centros comerciales. Es agradable también ir a los almacenes, y a veces puedes comprar ropa buena y barata en las tiendas de descuentos. Pero hay muchas tiendas de todo tipo en los centros comerciales. También hay restaurantes allí, y si estás cansada puedes ir a beber un refresco y descansar."

214   Capítulo 6

Writing

Can you write a letter to your parents similar to the one an exchange student might write home asking for money to buy school clothes? Here is an example:

Queridos papá y mamá:

Necesito comprar ropa nueva. Me gustaría comprar tres o cuatro camisetas. Hay camisetas muy bonitas y baratas. Sólo cuestan 10 dólares. No tengo pantalones cortos ni tenis. Necesito también unos pantalones y dos camisas. Los necesito para ir a fiestas. La ropa aquí es muy barata. Voy a necesitar sólo . . . 150 dólares.

Su hijo,
Luis

Culture

If you were visiting a Spanish-speaking country, would you prefer to buy clothes at a shopping center or go to a tailor or dressmaker? Why?

Centro comercial en Buenos Aires, Argentina

Speaking

Can you and a partner play the roles of a salesperson and a customer in a store? For example:

A — *¿Qué desea, señora (joven / señor / señorita)?*

B — *Busco un suéter blanco.*

A — *Sí, señora. Tenemos unos suéteres muy bonitos.*

B — *¿Cuánto cuestan?*

A — *Sólo 165 dólares.*

B — *¿Sólo 165 dólares? Perdón, señor . . . ¿hay otra tienda de ropa por aquí?*

Options

Strategies for Reaching All Students

Students Needing Extra Help

Writing: Use the Organizer. Point out key phrases in the example or have students write out the paragraph so they can highlight their own copies.

Culture: Have students review the *Perspectiva cultural*.

Resumen del capítulo 6

Use the vocabulary from this chapter to help you:
- describe the color, fit, and price of clothes
- ask about and buy clothes
- tell where and when you bought clothes and how much you paid for them

to talk about articles of clothing
la blusa
el calcetín, *pl.* los calcetines
la camisa
la camiseta
la chaqueta
la falda

los jeans
los pantalones (cortos)
las pantimedias
la ropa
la sudadera
el suéter
los tenis
el vestido
los zapatos

to describe clothes
la ganga
barato, -a
caro, -a
nuevo, -a
¿Cómo te queda(n)?
Me queda(n) bien.
¡Qué + *adjective!*

to talk about colors
el color
¿De qué color?
amarillo, -a
anaranjado, -a
azul, *pl.* azules
blanco, -a
gris, *pl.* grises
marrón, *pl.* marrones
morado, -a
negro, -a
rojo, -a
rosado, -a
verde

to talk about places to shop for clothing
el almacén
la tienda de descuentos
la tienda de ropa
la zapatería

to talk about shopping
buscar
comprar: (yo) compré
       (tú) compraste
llevar
pagar: (yo) pagué
    (tú) pagaste
para mí / ti
por

to indicate a specific item or items
ese, -a, esos, -as
este, -a, estos, -as
lo, la, los, las
otro, -a

to talk about prices
ciento un(o), una . . .
¿Cuánto?
Cuesta(n) . . .
el dólar, *pl.* los dólares

to assist customers in a store
¿Qué desea (Ud.)?

to address people
joven
señor / señora / señorita

to start a conversation
perdón

to talk about when something happened
hace + *time expression*

to indicate location
por aquí

Resumen 215

Cultural Notes

(p. 214, photo)
The Unicentro shopping center in Buenos Aires gives shoppers yet another locale for finding the same goods available in the shops along the city's downtown Calle Florida. Shoppers in Buenos Aires can also enjoy numerous Sunday markets, where souvenirs, antiques, clothes, books, and stamps are sold at bargain prices.

CAPÍTULO 7

THEME: LEISURE AND VACATION TIME

SCOPE AND SEQUENCE Pages 216–247

COMMUNICATION

Topics
Nature

Travel

Weather

Clothing

Objectives
To talk about how teens in Chile spend their vacations

To talk about vacation and planning a vacation

To talk about places to visit and things to do on vacation

To say that you want or would like something

To say where you went

To say when events occur

To name items to take on vacation

To ask about or describe weather

To express amazement or satisfaction

CULTURE
Leisure and vacation time

GRAMMAR
El verbo poder

Para + *infinitivo*

Los verbos querer *y* pensar

La a personal

Ancillaries available for use with Chapter 7

Multisensory/Technology

 Overhead Transparencies, 36–40

 Audio Tapes and CDs

 Vocabulary Art Blackline Masters for Hands-On Learning, pp. 38–42

 Classroom Crossword

 Video

 CD-ROM

Print

 Practice Workbook, pp. 73–83

 Writing, Audio & Video Activities, pp. 41–46, 111–113, 164–165

 Communicative Activity Blackline Masters

Pair and Small Group Activities, pp. 50–55

Situation Cards, p. 56

 Un paso más: Actividades para ampliar tu español, pp. 38–43

Assessment

 Assessment Program

Pruebas, pp. 95–106

Examen de habilidades, pp. 107–110

 Test Generator

Video still from Chap. 7

Vacations and Holidays

Many countries of the Spanish-speaking world are favorite international vacation spots. Many northern Europeans escape their winters by vacationing on the beaches of Spain, especially along the Costa del Sol. Many Canadians spend several weeks out of every year in one of several small fishing villages near Acapulco, Mexico. Countless others flock to sites such as Lake Titicaca, Bolivia.

People who live in the Spanish-speaking world may often vacation within the boundaries of their own country. In Argentina, for example, professionals and businesspeople commonly own small *pisos* (apartments) in coastal towns such as Mar del Plata, south of Buenos Aires. They use the *pisos* during vacations and sometimes on weekends. Middle-class families in Spain also share this custom of having a small country house for vacations.

In both Europe and in some Spanish-speaking countries, such as El Salvador, many people take vacations during August. Many private businesses as well as government offices shut down for two weeks. At this time of the year, el Lago Atitlán, in Guatemala, is a popular destination for Salvadorans. It becomes nearly impossible to find an empty hotel room in the small towns surrounding the lake.

Not everyone in Latin America and Spain may have a great amount of vacation time. Workers often receive days off only during holidays and festivals. In Mexico, for example, the Christmas-time *posadas* are a nine-day celebration ending on Christmas Eve. A different family hosts the *posada* for each of the nine nights, as people form a candlelight procession through the streets to reenact the travels of Mary and Joseph seeking shelter.

In addition to the *posada*, a number of other one- or two-day celebrations provide vacation time for the general public. For example, many towns celebrate the day of their local patron saint. Processions are held that day, the town square becomes the site of a general celebration, and fireworks illuminate the evening skies.

Introduce

Re-entry of Concepts

The following list represents words, expressions, and grammar topics re-entered from *El primer paso* to Chap. 6:

El primer paso
Calendar expressions

Chapter 1
Gustar expressions
Activities

Chapter 2
Time-telling

Chapter 3
Places and buildings
Seasons
Leisure-time activities

Chapter 4
Food
Expressing likes and preferences

Chapter 5
Family and friends
Possessive adjectives

Chapter 6
Clothing

Planning

Cross-Curricular Connections

Geography Connection *(pp. 218–219)*
Have small groups or pairs of students choose one of the countries mentioned in the chapter introduction. Have them use library resources to find out the special features, cultural sites, important products, and famous tourist or natural sites to create a pictorial map. When finished, ask them to share their work with the class. Display their work around the classroom.

Science / Geography Connection *(pp. 224–225)*
Have students prepare a weather chart for a city or region in a Spanish-speaking country of their choice for one month of each season. Charts should include average temperatures, average precipitation, and other facts. Encourage students to add pictures or drawings that illustrate various activities appropriate to each season.

Business Education / Advertising Connection *(pp. 232–233)*
Have small groups prepare tourist brochures for a Spanish-speaking country of their choice. Encourage the use of pictures or original drawings. On the back of their brochures, have students create a list of names of fictitious hotels with prices for various packages. Students should use the country's currency, give approximate equivalents in dollars, and include a phone number and address.

CAPÍTULO 7

¿Adónde vas a ir de vacaciones?

OBJECTIVES

At the end of this chapter, you will be able to:

- describe vacation choices and activities
- talk about the weather
- discuss what to take on a trip
- talk about how teens in Chile spend their vacations

Pirámide maya en Uxmal, México

217

Cultural Notes

Spanish in Your Community
Have small groups look through the travel sections of newspapers for advertisements or articles dealing with vacations in Spanish-speaking countries. (Can they also find ads directed toward Spanish speakers?) Using learned vocabulary, students could then summarize the articles or ads for the class.

(pp. 216–217, photo)
The Mayan ruins at Uxmal differ from those of neighboring Chichén Itzá in that they are in the Puuc architectural style, which features complex geometric patterns of mosaics running along the upper façades of the buildings. The Pyramid of the Magician, shown here, stands 40 meters high. First occupied around 600 A.D., Uxmal was abandoned approximately 300 years later, possibly due to severe droughts.

Preview

- To talk about vacation and places to visit

¿Adónde vas a ir de vacaciones?

Play

Video Activity A

Using the Video

This chapter's video focuses on travel and vacations. Host Karina Romera takes viewers to her favorite places in and around Guadalajara, including a cathedral, a rodeo, a mariachi performance, and a waterfall. At various locations she interviews residents of Guadalajara about their vacation plans and preferences.

To prepare students for the video, ask them to predict what this chapter's tape will be about. Then have students watch the segment several times. After the first time, you may wish to have them brainstorm possible vocabulary and expressions they will need to talk about what they saw on the video. Ask students to identify: a) how a vacation in Guadalajara is similar to vacations they have taken, and b) anything they saw which they had not seen before.

¡Piénsalo bien!

Look at these photographs of four vacation destinations in Mexico, Colombia, Ecuador, and Uruguay. Which place would you most like to visit? Why?

"Quisiera ver la cancha de juego de Chichén Itzá en Yucatán . . .

In what ways is this playing field like or different from a football field or a basketball court that you know?

218   Capítulo 7

Options

Strategies for Reaching All Students

Spanish-Speaking Students
Ask Spanish-speaking students: *¿Has estado en algún lugar como éstos? ¿Cómo se llama? ¿Cuál de estos lugares te gustaría visitar? ¿Por qué? ¿Qué te gusta hacer en las vacaciones?*

 Un paso más Ex. 7-A

Students Needing Extra Help
Students may know very little about the Mayas and Mayan ruins. Provide information from reference books and show them the geographical area of this civilization on the map in the front of their books (p. XIV).

Cultural Notes

(p. 218, photo)
The Mayan ruins at Chichén Itzá are the most extensive and renowned in Mexico's Yucatán peninsula. The ball court shown, the largest of the city's eight courts, was the site of games in which athletes tried to maneuver a ball through one of the stone hoops on the walls without using their hands. Carvings on the court's walls indicate that the losers were most likely decapitated in sacrificial rituals.

. . . o visitar el Museo del Oro
en Bogotá, Colombia . . .

. . . o explorar las islas Galápagos en Ecuador. . .

The Galápagos Islands are located off the coast of Ecuador. What do you know about these islands? Do you know the name of a famous British scientist who visited the islands in the nineteenth century?

. . . o descansar en las playas de Punta del Este, Uruguay."

219

Video segment 1: For more teaching suggestions, see the Video Teacher's Guide.

Teaching Suggestions

Bring to class a variety of pictures of the four vacation destinations. Travel brochures and encyclopedias are good sources. If you've traveled to any of these places, bring in any slides, photographs, or realia.

Answers: ¡Piénsalo bien!

Answers will vary.

(p. 218, photo) Answers will vary, but may include the size and shape of the field.

(p. 219, center photo) Answers will vary. / The scientist was Charles Darwin.

(p. 219, top photo)
This is one of the many treasure displays in the Museo del Oro in Bogotá. The museum is world famous for its unique collection of over 30,000 gold pieces. The collection includes earrings, rings, bracelets, masks, scepters, and various delicately wrought figures from a dozen pre-Columbian cultures, in addition to jewel-encrusted gold crosses from the colonial period.

(p. 219, center photo)
Ecuador's 400 Galápagos Islands, of which only five are inhabited, were declared a national park by the government in 1959. The islands are of volcanic origin and range in size from barren scraps of rock to larger islands filled with exotic animal and plant life whose adaptation Charles Darwin studied in 1835. This photo of the largest island, Isabela, shows one of the several thousand Galápagos tortoises that live on the slopes of Alcedo volcano.

(p. 219, bottom photo)
Uruguay's most glamorous beach resort is Punta del Este, a narrow peninsula with two beach areas: Playa Mansa, on the bay side for swimmers, and Playa Brava, on the Atlantic side for surfers. Punta del Este is a favorite spot among Argentines and other foreign tourists.

Present

Chapter Theme
Vacation time

Communicative Objectives
- To talk about vacation
- To talk about places to visit and things to do on vacation
- To say that you want or would like something
- To say where you went
- To say when events occur
- To indicate use or purpose

 Transparencies 36–37

 Vocabulary Art BLMs

 Pronunciation Tape 7-1

 Vocabulario para conversar A

Play

Using the Video
Video segment 2: See the Video Teacher's Guide.

 Video Activity B

Grammar Preview
Para + inf. is presented here lexically. The complete presentation is in the grammar section on p. 235.

Vocabulario para conversar

¿Qué puedes hacer en México?

Here are some new words and expressions you will need to talk about vacation choices and activities. Read them several times, then turn the page and practice with a partner.

la selva tropical

explorar la selva

pasear en bote

el bote

el lago

los recuerdos

el museo

las montañas

sacar fotos

la foto

esquiar

220   Capítulo 7

Options

Strategies for Reaching All Students

Spanish-Speaking Students
 Un paso más Ex. 7-B

Students Needing Extra Help
Have students start filling in their Organizers.
También necesitas . . . : Point out that *quisiera* is a more formal or polite expression than *quiero*.

Learning Spanish Through Action
STAGING VOCABULARY: *Pongan, Señalen*
MATERIALS: large map of Spanish-speaking countries placed in front of the classroom; enlarged photocopies of the pictures in the *Vocabulario para conversar* from the transparency or Vocabulary Art BLMs; thumbtacks or tape
DIRECTIONS: Direct students to point to the countries as you mention them. Then ask them to place a picture on the correct location on the map as you call out a country.

220

las cataratas

la pirámide
subir la pirámide

tomar el sol

las ruinas

la catedral

bucear

la playa

el mar

También necesitas . . .

la ciudad	*city*
el país	*country*
los lugares de interés	*places of interest*
descansar	*to rest*
quisiera	*I'd like*
ir: (yo) fui	*to go: I went*
(tú) fuiste	*you went*
pasado, -a	*last (year, month, week)*
ninguna parte	*nowhere, not anywhere*
para + *inf.*	here: *in order to*

¿Y qué quiere decir . . . ?
cuando*
las vacaciones *(pl.)*
ir de vacaciones
visitar

* When question words are used as conjunctions to join two parts of a sentence, we do not use
the accent mark: *¿Cuándo?* → *cuando, ¿Cómo?* → *como,* etc.

Vocabulario para conversar   221

Practice & Apply

Reteach / Review: Vocabulary

Ex. 2: Pairs of students can extend this dialogue by having *Estudiante A* ask *Estudiante B* with whom he or she went. Encourage students to use vocabulary for family members.

Re-enter / Recycle

Ex. 1: activities from Chap. 1
Ex. 2: calendar expressions from *El primer paso*, seasons from Chap. 3
Ex. 3: activities from Chap. 1, seasons from Chap. 3
Ex. 5: calendar expressions from *El primer paso*, places and buildings from Chap. 3

Answers: Empecemos a conversar

1 ESTUDIANTE A
a. Cuando voy de vacaciones a la selva tropical, ¿qué puedo hacer?
b. ...al mar, ...
c. ...a la playa, ...
d. Questions will vary.

ESTUDIANTE B
a.–d. Puedes ... *(Answers will vary.)*

Empecemos a conversar

With a partner, take turns being *Estudiante A* and *Estudiante B.* Use the words that are cued or given in the balloons to replace the underlined sections in the model. 💡 means you can make your own choices.

1
A — *Cuando voy de vacaciones a <u>las montañas</u>, <u>¿qué puedo hacer?</u>*
B — *Puedes <u>esquiar.</u> (También puedes ...)*
Y ahora Uds.

Estudiante A   **Estudiante B**

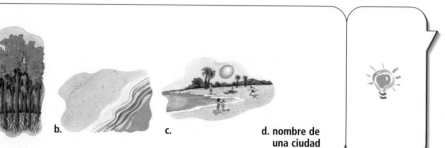

a.   b.   c.   d. nombre de una ciudad

2 el verano pasado
A — *¿Adónde fuiste <u>el verano pasado</u>?*
B — *Fui a <u>Los Ángeles.</u>*
o: *No fui a ninguna parte.*
Y ahora Uds.

Estudiante A   **Estudiante B**

a. el año pasado
b. el mes pasado
c. la semana pasada
d. el invierno pasado
e. el fin de semana pasado

222   Capítulo 7

Options

Strategies for Reaching All Students

Spanish-Speaking Students

 Un paso más Ex. 7-C

Students Needing Extra Help

Ex. 2: To ensure varied responses, give students a minute to think about their answers.
Ex. 3: Remind students that *primavera* is a feminine noun and will require *esta.*
Ex. 5: Have students refer back to Ex. 2.
Ex. 6: Have students brainstorm by using their Organizers from previous chapters.

Empecemos a escribir: For additional practice, tell students to imagine that they've just won a trip to any location of their choice. Ask them to write a sentence telling where they would like to go and what they would like to do there.

3

A — *¿Qué quieres hacer este verano?*
B — *Quisiera ir a la playa para tomar el sol.*

Y ahora Uds.

Estudiante A

a.

b.

c.

d.

Estudiante B

Empecemos a escribir

Write your answers in Spanish.

4 List three things you have never done on vacation that you would like to do.

5 Using *fui,* name a place you went to last week, one you went to last month, and one you went to last year.

6 ¿Qué puedes hacer en tu ciudad?

También se dice

los suvenires

tomar fotos

Vocabulario para conversar   223

223

Present

Chapter Theme
Weather and vacation time

Communicative Objectives
- To talk about planning a vacation
- To name items to take on vacation
- To ask about or describe weather
- To express amazement or satisfaction

 Transparencies 38–39

 Vocabulary Art BLMs

 Pronunciation Tape 7-2

 Vocabulario para conversar B

Play

Using the Video
Video segment 2: See the Video Teacher's Guide.

 Video Activity B

Grammar Preview
Pienso / piensas are presented lexically. The complete paradigm of *pensar* appears in the grammar section on p. 236.

Vocabulario para conversar

¿Qué tiempo hace?

Here's the rest of the vocabulary you will need to talk about the weather and to discuss what to take on a trip.

la lluvia

el viento

Llueve.

Hace viento.

Hace fresco.

el abrigo

el gorro

la bufanda

la nieve

los guantes

las botas

Hace frío.

Nieva.

224   Capítulo 7

Options

Strategies for Reaching All Students

Students Needing Extra Help
Have students continue to fill in their Organizers.
También necesitas . . . : Have students practice *pensar* + inf. in isolation. Ask how they would say "I plan to study."
Have them also practice *menos mal que* in isolation. Ask them to look at their previous Organizers to help them develop statements such as *Menos mal que tengo mi cuaderno.*

Enrichment
As a review of the months and to reinforce weather expressions, write this poem on the chalkboard or a transparency. (You may need to explain *neblina* and *tronar.*)
Los meses del año
En enero hace frío,
En febrero también.
En marzo hace viento,
En abril está bien.
En mayo hay flores,
En junio el amor.

En julio vacaciones,
En agosto el calor.
En septiembre hay neblina,
En octubre el tronar.
Noviembre trae lluvia,
Y diciembre el nevar.

el traje de baño

los anteojos de sol

el bronceador

Hace calor.

Hace mal tiempo.

Hace sol.

el sol

Hace buen tiempo.

la maleta

el paraguas

el impermeable

También necesitas . . .

llevar	here: *to take, to carry along*
salir*	*to leave*
regresar	*to come back, to return*
pensar + *inf.*: (yo) pienso	*to plan: I plan*
(tú) piensas	*you plan*
¿Qué tiempo hace?	*What's the weather like?*
¡Vaya!	*My goodness! Gee! Wow!*
Menos mal que ___.	*It's a good thing that ___.*

¿Y qué quiere decir . . . ?
la cámara
fantástico, -a
el pasaporte

*Salir has an irregular *yo* form: *salgo.*

Vocabulario para conversar   225

Practice & Apply

Re-enter / Recycle

Ex. 7: calendar expressions from *El primer paso*
Ex. 8: possessive adjectives from Chap. 5, clothing from Chap. 6
Ex. 10: seasons from Chap. 3
Ex. 11: activities from Chap. 1
Ex. 13: clothing from Chap. 6

Answers: Empecemos a conversar

7 ESTUDIANTE A

a. ¿Qué tiempo hace en Miami en julio?
b. ... en Denver en enero?
c. ... en San Francisco en noviembre?
d. ... en Chicago en octubre?
e. ... en Washington, D.C., en abril?
f. Questions will vary.

ESTUDIANTE B

a. *(First part of responses will vary.)* ... Hace calor.
b. ... Hace frío.
c. ... Hace mal tiempo.
d. ... Hace viento.
e. ... Hace fresco.
f. Answers will vary.

8 ESTUDIANTE A

a. ¡Vaya! Hace sol (buen tiempo) hoy.
b. ... Llueve ...
c. ... Nieva ...
d. Statements will vary.

Empecemos a conversar

7

San Antonio / noviembre

A — ¿*Qué tiempo hace en* San Antonio *en* noviembre?
B — *Un tiempo fantástico. Hace sol.*
     Y ahora Uds.

Estudiante A

a. Miami / julio
b. Denver / enero
c. San Francisco / noviembre
d. Chicago / octubre
e. Washington, D.C. / abril
f.

Estudiante B

Miami   San Francisco   Washington, D.C.

Denver   Chicago

8

A — *¡Vaya! Hace frío hoy.*
B — *Menos mal que tienes tu abrigo.*
     Y ahora Uds.

Estudiante A

a.   b.
c.   d.

Estudiante B

226   Capítulo 7

Options

Strategies for Reaching All Students

Spanish-Speaking Students

 Un paso más Ex. 7-D

Students Needing Extra Help

Exs. 7–8: Remind students that the responses depicted by art for *Estudiante B* are not in sequential order with the phrases for *Estudiante A*.
Ex. 9: Have students brainstorm and use their Organizers.
Ex. 11: Have students use their Organizers from Chaps. 1 and 3.

Enrichment

Ex. 11: Students can also name activities they *don't* like to do in each type of weather.

9

A —¿Qué piensas llevar <u>a la playa</u>?
B —Pienso llevar <u>el bronceador y una cámara</u>.

Y ahora Uds.

Estudiante A   **Estudiante B**

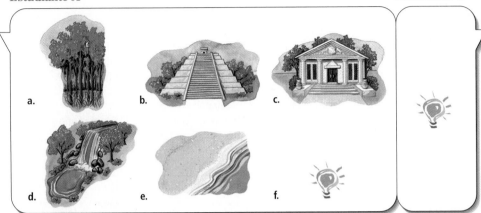

a.   b.   c.

d.   e.   f.

Empecemos a escribir y a leer

Write your answers in Spanish.

10 Describe what the weather is like in your community in all four seasons. *En el invierno . . .*

11 Choose three types of weather and tell one activity you like to do in each one. *Cuando hace mal tiempo, . . .*

12 ¿Vas a ir de vacaciones este año? ¿Cuándo piensas salir? ¿Y regresar?

13 Cuando una persona va a esquiar, ¿qué ropa lleva en su maleta?

14 ¿Es lógico o no?

¡Vaya! Hace frío hoy. Me gustaría ir a la playa para tomar el sol.

¿Piensas ir a Argentina? Debes llevar tu pasaporte y una cámara para sacar fotos de los lugares de interés.

El año pasado no fui a ninguna parte. Este año voy a ir a la selva tropical para pasear en bote.

También se dice

la loción bronceadora
la crema para el sol

las gafas de sol
los lentes de sol

la máquina fotográfica

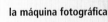

el bañador
la malla
la trusa
la ropa de baño

Vocabulario para conversar   227

Practice

Re-enter / Recycle
Ex. 1: possessive adjectives from Chap. 5, clothing from Chap. 6
Ex. 2: *gustar* expressions and activities from Chap. 1

Reteach / Review: Vocabulary
Ex. 3: Students can continue this dialogue by taking turns asking and answering what clothes or other items they need to buy for their vacations.

Answers:
¡Comuniquemos!
1 a. Menos mal que tienes tu impermeable.
b. . . . fuiste a Cancún el año pasado.
c. . . . no hace mucho sol.
d. . . . no nieva mucho.
e. . . . tienes tu pasaporte.
f. . . . compraste un traje de baño la semana pasada.

2 **ESTUDIANTE A**
a. ¿Qué te gusta hacer cuando hace frío?
b. . . . hace sol (buen tiempo)?
c. . . . hace viento?
d. . . . hace calor?
e. . . . nieva?
f. . . . hace fresco?
g. . . . llueve?
h. Questions will vary.
ESTUDIANTE B
a.–h. Answers will vary.

¡Comuniquemos!

Here's another opportunity for you to use the vocabulary you've just learned.

1 Read the sentences in the first column. Your partner will give you the appropriate response from the second column.

a. ¡Vaya! no tengo paraguas.
b. No voy a tener vacaciones este año.
c. No llevo mis anteojos de sol.
d. No tengo botas.
e. Necesito ir a Colombia en dos semanas.
f. Vamos a ir a la playa esta tarde.

Menos mal que no hace mucho sol.
Menos mal que no nieva mucho.
Menos mal que tienes tu impermeable.
Menos mal que compraste un traje de baño la semana pasada.
Menos mal que fuiste a Cancún el año pasado.
Menos mal que tienes tu pasaporte.

2 With a partner, take turns asking and telling what activities you like to do in different kinds of weather. The list of verbs on the right will help you answer.

A —¿Qué te gusta hacer cuando llueve?
B —Pues, me gusta leer o ver la televisión.

bucear	esquiar	leer	practicar
comer	estar	nadar	sacar
descansar	hablar	pasear	ver
escuchar	ir	patinar	visitar

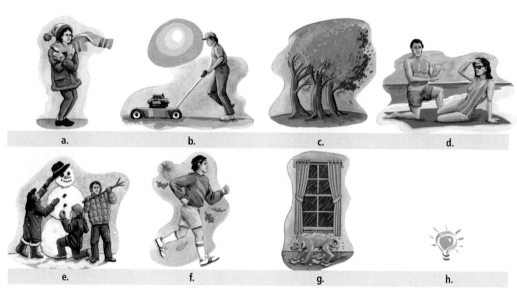

a. b. c. d.

e. f. g. h.

228 Capítulo 7

Options

Strategies for Reaching All Students

Spanish-Speaking Students
Have Spanish-speaking students write a paragraph: *Escribe un párrafo acerca de tus vacaciones ideales. ¿Adónde te gustaría ir? ¿En qué estación del año te gustaría ir? ¿Qué puedes hacer allí? ¿Con quién te gustaría ir?*

Students Needing Extra Help
Ex. 2: Review the suggested verbs, especially *estar, ir,* and *ver,* since students will need to add an object or prepositional phrase. Model a few possibilities.
Ex. 3: Review interrogatives, then have students review Exs. 1–6 on pp. 222–223 to help them create a model.
¿Qué sabes ahora?: Have students write out this section so that they can record their progress.

Enrichment
Ex. 3: As a written assignment, students can describe what they like to do or what they would like to do during summer and winter vacations.

3 You and your partner are planning your vacations. Take turns asking and answering where and with whom you would like to go, and what activities you would like to do there. Don't forget to say when you are leaving and when you are planning to come back.

¿Qué sabes ahora?

Can you:

- tell what you can see or do on a vacation?
  —En México puedo ___.
- tell what you plan to do on a vacation?
  —En las vacaciones ___ visitar museos.
- tell what you will take on your vacation?
  —Pienso llevar ___ a España.
- describe the weather at your vacation destination?
  —___ en San Antonio en el invierno.

BIENVENIDO

EL TIEMPO EN MONTERREY

	HOY	MAÑANA	MARTES
		Máx. 21°	Máx. 22°
		Mín. 8°	Mín. 9°
		Hum. 45%	Hum. 45%
Máxima:	18°		
Mínima:	5°		
Humedad relativa:	25%		

HOY	Máx.	Mín.
REYNOSA	19°	11°
MATAMOROS	22°	14°
NUEVO LAREDO	18°	13°

Fuente: Accu-Weather

PROCURADURIA GENERAL DE JUSTICIA DEL DISTRITO FEDERAL

Vocabulario para conversar   229

3 Questions and answers will vary, but encourage students to use the full range of chapter vocabulary. Look for interrogatives such as *¿adónde?* and *¿con quién?*

Answers: ¿Qué sabes ahora?
- Answers will vary.
- pienso
- Answers will vary.
- *Answers will vary, but may include:* Llueve or Hace . . . .

Using Realia
Using the conversion guide given below, have students compare the temperatures in the weather chart. For example: 18°C = 64.4°F and 5°C = 41°F. Have them convert the temperatures for the remaining cities.

Celsius = 5/9 (F - 32)
Fahrenheit = 9/5 C + 32

 Audio Activity 7.3

 Writing Activity 7-D

Cultural Notes

Cooperative Learning
Have groups of three or four students write their names and birthdays (day and month only) on a sheet of paper. Next, have them pass their papers to the right. Students then write a sentence to describe what the weather is like during that month. Students pass their papers to the right again. This time, they are to list one or two items that might be useful to have or wear during that month. Papers are now passed to owners. Call on individuals to read their papers, discussing other items that may not have been included.

(p. 229, left realia)
Newspaper weather forecast for Monterrey, Mexico. This northern city has a climate much like that of Texas: hot summers and frost or occasional snow in the winter. The capital of the state of Nuevo León, Monterrey is Mexico's second-largest industrial center and, with a population of around two million, its third-largest city.

Present & Apply

Multicultural Perspectives

The tourist bureaus in Spain and many Latin American countries advertise in the U.S. and Europe to attract visitors to their countries. Spain, for example, entices Scandinavians and other people living in cold winter climates through advertisements that feature its many beaches. The Dominican Republic and Puerto Rico use similar strategies to appeal to potential tourists in the northern sections of the U.S. Mexico also attracts many people with its advertisements of ancient ruins and beautiful beaches. Invite students to identify print or television ads directed at potential tourists. What methods do they use to attract people?

Perspectiva cultural

En el verano, muchas personas van de vacaciones. A muchos jóvenes les gusta ir a la playa. A otros les gusta ir a las montañas. Y a ti, ¿qué te gusta hacer?

The large photo was taken in Chile. In which months might the activities be taking place? Would that be during the school year or vacation time?

January and February are summer months in Chile. Because of Chile's long coastline along the Pacific Ocean, going to the beach is very popular.

A Chilean teen reports, "I like to go to Viña del Mar with my family. In the daytime, we swim in the ocean or in a pool, and we sunbathe. We rest in the afternoon, and in the evening we can play tennis, go to a movie, or go dancing. There are a lot of people my age there."

In July, Chilean students have a short winter vacation. Some may go to a ski resort in the Andes, but it is much more common for them to visit relatives and friends.

In Chile, most high-school students do not get a summer job. However, some may bag groceries at a supermarket or work at one of the growing number of fast-food restaurants.

La cultura desde tu perspectiva

1 How is your vacation similar to or different from that of Chilean teens?

2 How does the geography affect vacation options for Chilean students? How does the geography of your area affect your vacation options?

Esquiando en Le Grand Mur, Valle Nevado, Chile

230   Capítulo 7

Options

Strategies for Reaching All Students

Spanish-Speaking Students
Ask Spanish-speaking students:
¿Qué haces durante las vacaciones? ¿Trabajas? ¿Practicas deportes? ¿Sales de viaje? ¿Qué tipos de trabajo puede tener un(a) joven en este país durante las vacaciones? ¿Te gustaría ir a la playa en enero? ¿Por qué? ¿Te gustaría pasar las vacaciones en otro país? ¿En cuál?

Un paso más Ex. 7-E

Students Needing Extra Help
Discuss the equator and how climates change as you move away from it in either direction. On a map or globe, explain the difference in seasons for the month of December, for example, in Chile and in the northern section of the U.S.

Trabajando durante las vacaciones

En una playa de Chile

Answers
Answers will vary for inductive questions. / Most students will say December, January, and February. However, as they read further on in the text, they'll discover that the seasons are reversed. When it's summer in the U.S., it's winter in Chile. / Answers will vary, but students will know later that it's during winter vacation in July.

Answers: La cultura desde tu perspectiva
1 Answers will vary, but encourage student discussion by asking for reasons whenever possible.

2 Answers will vary, but might include the proximity to a beach or the mountains. / Answers will vary depending on what part of the country students live in.

Preview

Answers

Answers will vary for inductive questions, but may include: travel brochures, ads, promotional programs, etc.

A *puede* (you can) / *pueden* (they can), *quiere* (you want) / *queremos* (we want), *piensa* (you plan) / *pensamos* (we plan) / *Pensamos* doesn't contain *ie* in the stem of the verb.

B The infinitive follows *para.*

C The direct objects are *la familia* and *un suéter o su abrigo.* / The direct object is a thing in the second question; it is people in the first question. / The word before the direct object referring to people is *a.*

Gramática en contexto

Look at this ad for a travel agency. How does a travel agency attract new clients?

¿Qué piensa hacer Ud. este invierno?

¿Adónde puede ir Ud. para hacer todo esto y mucho más?

¡A la República Dominicana, el paraíso de las vacaciones!

¿Piensa llevar a la familia? Pues, debe ir a Puerto Plata, donde hay muchas actividades que sus hijos pueden hacer. ¿Piensa llevar un suéter o su abrigo? Pues, nos los necesita. En Puerto Plata nunca hace frío. Hace buen tiempo todo el año.

Aquí en la Agencia de Viajes Cristal estamos para ayudar a nuestros clientes. Queremos y pensamos hacer de sus vacaciones algo fabuloso. Visite nuestra oficina en la Quinta Avenida 578, o llame al número 1-555-523-3493.

La República Dominicana, donde el verano nunca termina...

¿Quiere tomar el sol?

¿Quiere jugar tenis?

¿Quiere pasear en bote?

A Can you find in the ad at least one other form of each of these verbs: *puedo / puedes, quiero / quieres,* and *pienso / piensas?* What do these verb forms mean? How is the *nosotros* form of *pensar* different from its other forms?

B Look at the first question in the ad and the first sentence of paragraph 4. What form of the verb follows *para?*

C In paragraph 3, look at the two questions that begin, *¿Piensa llevar . . . ?* What are the direct objects? In which question is the direct object a thing? In which question is the direct object people? What word comes before the direct object that refers to people?

232   Capítulo 7

Options

Strategies for Reaching All Students

Students Needing Extra Help
Have students write out this section so that they can highlight the words.
Have them start to fill in the grammar portion of their Organizers.
B: Remind students that infinitives end in -ar, -er, and -ir.
C: Review direct object pronouns and how they replace a noun.

Write the complete sentences on the chalkboard, underlining the direct objects so that students can focus on them.
El verbo poder: Stem-changing verbs can be referred to as "boot" verbs. (If you outline the four forms that change, it resembles a boot and creates a memorable visual for the students. Or you can color-code the stems on a transparency.) Review -er endings.

El verbo *poder*

Puedo and *puedes* come from the infinitive *poder,* "can, to be able to."

(yo)	**puedo**	(nosotros) (nosotras)	**podemos**
(tú)	**puedes**	(vosotros) (vosotras)	**podéis**
Ud. (él) (ella)	**puede**	Uds. (ellos) (ellas)	**pueden**

- When we drop the *-er* of the infinitive, the part that remains is called the stem. Notice that in four forms of *poder*, the *o* of the stem changes to *ue*. We call *poder* an *o → ue* stem-changing verb.

- The endings follow the pattern of regular *-er* verbs.

- When the forms of *poder* are followed by another verb, the second verb is always in the infinitive. For example:

    No **puedo ir** al cine contigo el viernes.

Artesanía maya

Gramática en contexto   233

Teaching Suggestions
By introducing the *Gramática en contexto* section from the previous page, students will learn about stem-changing verbs in context. As they work through the exercises, they will formulate for themselves the rules given on the following pages. Remind them that they already know examples of stem-changing verbs from previous chapters: *puedo / puedes* and *quiero / quieres* (Chap. 3); *prefiero / prefieres* (Chap. 4).

Present & Practice

Re-enter / Recycle
Exs. 1 and 4: activities from Chaps. 1 and 3
Ex. 2: activities from Chap. 1

1 Answers
a. Felipe no puede subir la pirámide porque llueve.
b. Alejandro y María Teresa no pueden nadar porque hace frío.
c. Margarita no puede pasear en bote porque hace viento.
d. Pablo y tú no pueden jugar básquetbol porque nieva.
e. Esteban y yo no podemos bucear porque hace frío.
f. Ud. no puede ir de compras porque hace mal tiempo.

2 ESTUDIANTE A
a. ¿Puedes ir a sacar fotos conmigo?
b. . . . esquiar . . .
c. . . . tomar el sol . . .
d. . . . una fiesta . . .
e. Questions will vary.

ESTUDIANTE B
a.–e. No, no puedo. No tengo . . . (*Answers will vary. Possible endings include:* a. cámara, b. botas, c. traje de baño, d. ropa buena.)

 Practice Wkbk. 7-5

 Writing Activity 7-E

 Prueba 7-5

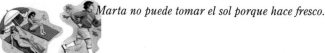

¿Adónde vas a ir de vacaciones?

1 With a partner, take turns telling what these people cannot do and why.

Marta no puede tomar el sol porque hace fresco.

Marta

a. Felipe   b. Alejandro y María Teresa   c. Margarita

d. Pablo y tú   e. Esteban y yo   f. Ud.

2 While you are on vacation your friend asks if you can do these activities together. Tell your friend you can't because you don't have the necessary items.

A — *¿Puedes ir a nadar conmigo?*
B — *No, no puedo. No tengo traje de baño.*

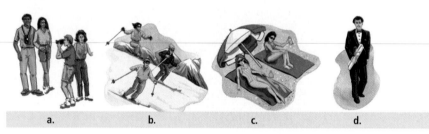

a.   b.   c.   d.   e.

234   Capítulo 7

Options

Strategies for Reaching All Students

Students Needing Extra Help
Ex. 1: Review compound subjects and how the verb form changes when answering a question. For example, questions with *tú* are answered with *yo,* and so on. Remind students that they saw *puedo / puedes* in Chap. 3.
Ex. 2: Students may find it helpful to think of possible responses that correspond to each item before beginning the exercise. Have students use their Organizers.

Ex. 3: If students need more practice with this structure, adapt the exercise in the following way: *Para estudiar, necesitamos un cuaderno.*
Ex. 4: Point out that *la casa de Felipe* becomes *allí.* Review compound subjects.

Enrichment
Ex. 1: As one student tells what the people can't do, have the other student name an activity he or she *can* do. For example: *Hace fresco y Marta no puede tomar el sol. Pero puede ir al cine.*
Ex. 3: To expand this exercise as homework, tell students to name five more items and explain why they need them.

234

Para + infinitivo

You know that *para* means "for" or "in order to." Whenever *para* is followed by a verb, the verb is in the infinitive form. For example:

Vamos a México **para bucear** y **tomar** el sol.

3 With a partner, take turns telling what you need these things for.

cuaderno   *Necesitamos un cuaderno para estudiar.*

a. piscina	d. papas	cocinar	leer
b. hoja de papel	e. cámara	sacar fotos	dibujar
c. libro	f.	nadar	

4 With a partner, take turns telling why these young people are going to a friend's house.

A —*Antonio va a la casa de Felipe, ¿verdad?*
B —*Sí, va allí para escuchar música.*

Antonio / Felipe

Estudiante A

a. Marisol / Yolanda

b. Eduardo y Raúl / David

c. Tú / Manuel

d. Lourdes / Andrea

e. Armando y tú / Sergio

Estudiante B

Gramática en contexto   235

Present & Practice

On the day following initial presentation of *querer* and *pensar,* you might begin the class by having students complete this sentence:

Voy al (a la) ___ (place) para ___ (activity).

On subsequent days, have them complete this sentence:

Voy al (a la) ___ (place), porque quiero (pienso) ___.

Ask follow-up questions, such as:

¿Quién quiere (piensa) ___?

Los verbos *querer* y *pensar*

You know that we use *quiero* and *quieres* to tell what we want to do, and we use *pienso* and *piensas* to tell what we plan to do. These verb forms come from the infinitives *querer* and *pensar.* Here are their present-tense forms:

(yo)	pienso quiero	(nosotros) (nosotras)	pensamos queremos
(tú)	piensas quieres	(vosotros) (vosotras)	pensáis queréis
Ud. (él) (ella)	piensa quiere	Uds. (ellos) (ellas)	piensan quieren

• Notice that there is a stem change from *e* to *ie* in all except the *nosotros* and *vosotros* forms. *Querer* and *pensar* are called *e → ie* stem-changing verbs.

• The endings follow the pattern of regular *-ar* and *-er* verbs.

• When the forms of *querer* and *pensar* are followed by another verb, the second verb is always in the infinitive. For example:
  — ¿Quieres **estudiar** conmigo?
  — No, pienso **ver** la tele.

236   Capítulo 7

Options

Strategies for Reaching All Students

Students Needing Extra Help
Ex. 5: Review compound subjects and the "boot" or color-coding for the verbs.
La a personal: Give students an example of an inanimate object that is used as a direct object. For example: *Quiero visitar el museo.*

Enrichment
To reinforce *querer* and *pensar,* give students an assignment in which they write two sentences for each verb—one in which the verbs are used alone, and the other in which they are used with another verb. For example: *Quiero ese libro. Lo quiero comprar hoy. Pienso que esa blusa es muy cara. No la pienso comprar.*

5 Take turns asking and answering what these tourists plan to do tomorrow.

A — *¿Qué quiere hacer Javier mañana?*
B — *Piensa sacar fotos.*

Javier

Estudiante A

a. Mariana

b. Enrique y tú

c. Miguel y Julia

d. Ud.

e. Juan Carlos

f. tú

g. Clara y Teresa

Estudiante B

La *a* personal

You know that the direct object is the person or thing that receives the action of a verb. In Spanish, when the direct object is a specific person or group of people, we use *a* before it. That's why it's called the personal *a*.

Quiero visitar **a** mis abuelos.
Quiero visitar **al** señor López.

• To ask who receives the action of a verb, we use *¿A quién?*

— **¿A quién** quieres visitar?
— Quiero visitar **a** mis primos.

• We can also use the personal *a* when the direct object is an animal, especially a pet.
Busco **a mi perro**.

• We usually do not use the personal *a* after the verb *tener.*
Tengo muchos tíos.

Gramática en contexto   237

Re-enter / Recycle
Ex. 5: activities from Chap. 3

Answers

5 ESTUDIANTE A
a. ¿Qué quiere hacer Mariana mañana?
b. . . . quieren hacer Enrique y tú . . .
c. . . . quieren hacer Miguel y Julia . . .
d. . . . quiere hacer Ud. . . .
e. . . . quiere hacer Juan Carlos . . .
f. . . . quieres hacer tú . . .
g. . . . quieren hacer Clara y Teresa . . .

ESTUDIANTE B
Answers will vary, but look for correct forms of *pensar.*
Suggested activities include: *ir de compras, bucear, tomar el sol, subir la pirámide, pasear en bote, visitar la catedral.*
a. Piensa. . . .
b. Pensamos. . . .
c. Piensan. . . .
d. Pienso. . . .
e. Piensa. . . .
f. Pienso. . . .
g. Piensan. . . .

 Practice Wkbk. 7-7, 7-8

 Writing Activity 7-G

 Pruebas 7-7, 7-8

 Comm. Act. BLM 7-2

Practice

Re-enter / Recycle

Ex. 6: family and friends from Chap. 5
Ex. 7: places and buildings from Chap. 3, family and friends from Chap. 5

Answers

6 ESTUDIANTE A

a. ¿A quién quieren visitar Anita y Claudia?
b. ...quieren visitar Armando y Andrea?
c. ...quieren visitar Paco y Marta?
d. ...quiere visitar Paco?
e. ...quiere visitar Graciela?
f. ...quiere visitar Ernesto?

ESTUDIANTE B

a. Quieren visitar a sus abuelos.
b. Quieren visitar a su hijo.
c. Quieren visitar a sus primas.
d. Quiere visitar a sus tíos.
e. Quiere visitar a sus padres.
f. Quiere visitar a su hermana.

---

6 Imagine that the members of the Ramírez family live in different parts of the country. They all want to visit each other. Ask your partner which family member each person wants to visit. Your partner's answers will be based on the family tree.

Andrea y Armando

Graciela y Gustavo

Dolores y Ernesto

Anita y Claudia

Marta y Paco

Claudia / Marta y Paco

A — *¿A quién quiere visitar Claudia?*
B — *Quiere visitar a sus primos.*

a. Anita y Claudia / Armando y Andrea
b. Armando y Andrea / Ernesto
c. Paco y Marta / Anita y Claudia
d. Paco / Gustavo y Graciela
e. Graciela / Armando y Andrea
f. Ernesto / Graciela

Options

Strategies for Reaching All Students

Students Needing Extra Help
Ex. 6: Review how to read a family tree. Do this as a whole-class activity, going step by step.
Ahora lo sabes: Have students write out this section so that they can track their progress.

7 Find out what or whom each of these tourists is looking for.

Pedro / Elena

    A —*¿A quién busca Pedro?*
    B —*Busca a Elena.*
        o:

Pedro / el paraguas

    A —*¿Qué busca Pedro?*
    B —*Busca el paraguas.*

a. Ana María / sus hijos   e. Eugenio y Cristóbal / Diana
b. Juan y Enrique / la catedral   f. Clara y Bárbara / las ruinas
c. Carmen / la maleta   g. Ud. / el museo
d. Pablo / su hermana   h. Elisa y tú /

Ahora lo sabes

Can you:

■ tell what someone can do, plans to do, and wants to do?

    —Yo ___ nadar.
    —Julio ___ visitar la selva tropical.
    —Ellas ___ subir la pirámide.

■ tell the reason for doing something?

    —Luz va a la playa para ___.

■ use the personal *a* correctly?

    —¿___ quién ves?
    —Veo ___ Antonio.

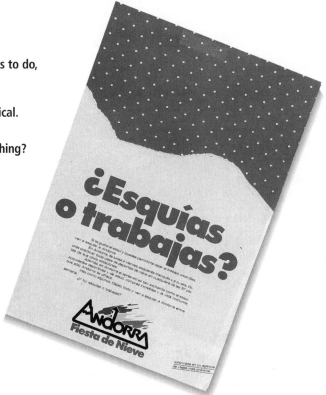

¿Esquías o trabajas?

Gramática en contexto   239

Apply

 ¡A conversar!

Play

Step

Using the Video
Video segment 3: See the Video Teacher's Guide.

 Video Activity C

Re-enter / Recycle
Ex. 1: calendar expressions from *El primer paso*, activities from Chap. 1, leisure-time activities from Chap. 3
Ex. 2: calendar expressions from *El primer paso*
Ex. 3: family and friends from Chap. 5

Answers: Actividades
1–3 Dialogues will vary, but encourage students to use the full range of chapter vocabulary.

Para decir más

Here is some additional vocabulary that you might find useful for activities in this section.

Está nublado.
It's cloudy.

el cielo
sky

las manoplas
mittens

el esquí acuático
waterskiing

dar una caminata
go hiking

ir de camping
go camping

visitar a los parientes
visit relatives

Actividades

Here's an opportunity for you to expand your use of Spanish by putting together the material you learned in this chapter with what you learned earlier.

Find out where your partner plans to go on Saturday and what he or she plans to do. Also find out with whom your partner is going.

A — *Jaime, ¿adónde piensas ir el sábado y qué piensas hacer?*
B — *Pienso ir al gimnasio para practicar deportes.*
A — *¿Con quién vas a ir?*
B — *Voy a ir con Federico.*

When you finish, report the results to another classmate.

♪ *El sábado, Jaime piensa ir al gimnasio para practicar deportes. Va a ir con su amigo Federico.*

Options

Strategies for Reaching All Students

Spanish-Speaking Students
Ask Spanish-speaking students to answer in writing: *¿Cuáles son tus actividades favoritas al aire libre? ¿En qué estación o estaciones puedes participar en actividades al aire libre? ¿En qué estación o estaciones prefieres estar (o quedarte) en casa? ¿Cuáles son tus actividades favoritas en casa?*

Students Needing Extra Help
Ex. 1: Show students how in reporting, the verb changes to the third person singular.
Ex. 2: Have students make a chart with columns for places, activities, time, and necessities. Have them refer to maps and use the information from the photos on pp. 218–219 for suggested places.
Ex. 3: Have students make a grid or chart with names of family members on the vertical line and time expressions going horizontally. Review object pronouns.

Enrichment
Ex. 3: You may want to have students write their findings as a homework assignment in addition to reporting them to a classmate.

2 With your partner, role-play an interview with a travel agent and discuss a place your family can visit, activities you can do there, when you plan to go, and anything you might need to take along. For example:

A — *Queremos ir de pesca en el mar.*
B — *Pues, Uds. pueden ir a Puerto Rico.*
A — *¿También podemos bucear allí?*
B — *Sí, pueden bucear y nadar.*
    ¿Cuándo quieren ir Uds.?
A — *Pensamos ir en julio. Queremos salir*
    el dos de julio y regresar el veinticinco.
    ¿Qué necesitamos llevar?
B — *Pues, necesitan ropa de verano, traje de baño*
    y una cámara. En julio hace sol y hace calor
    en Puerto Rico.

3 In a group, find out when and how frequently your classmates visit family members on their vacations. Ask about *primos, abuelos, tíos,* and other family members. On a piece of paper make tally marks under the following headings: *Muchas veces, A veces, Nunca.* When you finish, report the results to your class.

A — *En las vacaciones, ¿visitas a tus abuelos?*
B — *Sí, los visito muchas veces.*

El Aeropuerto Internacional Luis Muñoz Marín en San Juan, Puerto Rico

Con la familia en Xochimilco, México

Actividades   241

Cultural Notes

Cooperative Learning
Divide the class into groups of four. Have students answer the following questions on a sheet of paper. After each answer, have them pass their papers to the left. Ask: *¿Adónde quieres ir de vacaciones este verano?* The answers to the next questions depend on the first answer: *¿Qué vas a llevar? ¿Con quién o con quiénes? ¿Qué piensas hacer?* Call on students to read their answers. Ask them how they would have replied differently.

(p. 241, top photo)
The Luis Muñoz Marín International Airport is located on the eastern outskirts of San Juan. It bears the name of one of Puerto Rico's political leaders during the twentieth century. The son of Luis Muñoz Rivera, also an illustrious political leader, Muñoz Marín was a poet and a writer of political commentary, and in 1948, became the first governor to be elected by the people of Puerto Rico.

(p. 241, bottom photo)
Along with el Parque de Chapultepec, the floating gardens at Xochimilco have traditionally been a favorite spot for Mexico City's families to gather on Sundays. Riders on the colorful *trajineras* may bring their own food and drinks, or buy them from vendors. Mariachi bands, photographers, and souvenir vendors also navigate the canals, offering their wares and services to the Sunday crowds.

Apply

Process Reading
For a description of process reading, see p. 48.

Teaching Suggestions
Tell students that you will answer questions about word meanings only after they have applied coping strategies. Make sure there are dictionaries available.

Answers
Antes de leer
Answers will vary, but may include information about things to see and places to go. Activities that you might expect to find may include visiting cultural or archaeological sites, festivals, etc.

Mira la lectura
Mexico / archaeological sites and beaches / The aspect mentioned is hospitality. / You would receive more information.

¡Vamos a leer!

Antes de leer

STRATEGY Using prior knowledge

Advertisements can give us lots of ideas about things to do in unknown locales. What kinds of information might you expect to find in this travel advertisement? Name three or four different kinds of activities that you would expect to find.

Mira la lectura

Look at the title, photograph, and coupon.
- What country is advertised?
- What two tourist attractions does the photograph suggest it offers?
- What aspect of Mexico is mentioned in the coupon heading?
- What would you receive if you sent the coupon?

DEJA DE SOÑAR Y HAZ LA MALETA.

México.

México, un tesoro de 3,000 años de antiguas civilizaciones. Olmecas, Aztecas, Mixtecas y Mayas. Sus monumentos se encuentran por todas partes: Pirámides y templos, murales y frisos e, incluso, ciudades totalmente amuralladas. Todo en México es increíble.

Ven a México, tendrás mucho que recordar. Sus nobles ciudades coloniales, 10,000kms. de soleadas playas. Sus alegres mariachis. Su arte y escultura. Sus fiestas y folklore.

Tiendas de piel, plata, laca, tejidos. Y sus gentes que te reciben cordialmente, dándote siempre la bienvenida para que te sientas como en casa.

En México, vas a encontrar lo más moderno, elegante, lujoso y confortable. Con todo su pasado milenario a tu alrededor, México todavía sigue siendo México. Todavía sigue siendo mágico.

Visita México este año. Vas a tener las vacaciones que tú siempre has deseado. Ahora está a tu alcance, 14 días desde 123,050. pts.

Infórmate en tu agencia de viajes o envía este cupón a: Oficina de Turismo de México en España. Velázquez, 126. 28006 Madrid. Tel:261.18.27.

VENGA. VIVA LA HOSPITALIDAD DE MÉXICO.

Sírvase enviarme más información.   HO.2
Nombre _____
Dirección _____

_____ Código postal _____
SECRETARÍA DE TURISMO DE MÉXICO.

Chac-Mool, Yucatán Peninsula.

242   Capítulo 7

Options

Strategies for Reaching All Students

Spanish-Speaking Students
Have Spanish-speaking students make a similar brochure. *Haz un anuncio o un folleto para un lugar de vacaciones en tu estado que atrae a los turistas. ¿Cómo se llama? ¿Dónde está? ¿En qué estación es más popular con los turistas? ¿Cuáles son algunas de las atracciones principales? ¿Cómo pueden recibir más información?*

 Un paso más Ex. 7-F

Students Needing Extra Help
Infórmate: Have students write out this exercise so they can number the items.

Enrichment
As an in-class assignment, have students work in pairs to list the cognates in this reading selection. Then have the entire class compare lists, discussing how they recognized the cognates and what the sentences in which they appear might mean.
As a homework assignment, ask students to create an ad for their hometown, region, or the U.S. in general. Ask them to think of the aspects of this country they would promote to appeal to foreign visitors.

Infórmate

STRATEGIES▶ Identifying main ideas
Coping with unknown words

If you run across a word you don't know, there are several things you can do. You can keep reading and discover that you don't need to know its meaning. You may discover that you can figure out its meaning from the surrounding words or the following sentence. Or you may find out that you *do* need to know its meaning and must either look it up or ask someone. Use this strategy when you run across a word you don't understand.

1 Look at each paragraph to find the main idea, then tell in which paragraph (1–6) each of the following ideas is featured.

- Affordable vacation package
- Monuments of ancient civilizations
- Modern and traditional features
- Places and things to see
- How to get more information
- Opportunities for shopping

2 Which of the first four paragraphs describes the attractions that you find most appealing? Why do they appeal to you?

3 Scan the last paragraph to discover the country where this advertisement appeared.

Aplicación

List at least three words you did not know or need to know in order to understand this ad.

Mapa del mundo de 1589

Montando en bicicleta en el Zócalo de la Ciudad de México

Infórmate

1 1 = Monuments of ancient civilizations, 2 = Places and things to see, 3 = Opportunities for shopping, 4 = Modern and traditional features, 5 = Affordable vacation package, 6 = How to get more information

2 Answers will vary. Encourage student discussion and ask for reasons whenever possible.

3 Spain

Aplicación

Lists will vary.

Cultural Notes ☼

(p. 242, realia)
As this ad from Spain indicates, the Mexican tourist office promotes the country as actually "three Mexicos," the archaeological, colonial, and resort. Every year, about seven million tourists visit Mexico (over 85 percent of them from the U.S.). The government, through various projects such as the one that transformed the fishing village of Cancún into a thriving tourist center, hopes to increase this number in the future.

(p. 243, photo)
Mexico City's main square, which stands on the site of what was once the central square of the magnificent Aztec city of Tenochtitlán, is officially named la Plaza de la Constitución. More commonly called el Zócalo (literally the "base" or "pedestal," but in Mexico the word refers to the central *plaza),* the area is today the site of events such as this bicycle race, religious ceremonies, and dance performances.

Apply

Process Writing
For information regarding developing a writing portfolio, see p. 50.

¡Vamos a escribir!

Imagine that the government of Puerto Rico is offering a free vacation in San Juan to the student who writes the best short essay in Spanish on vacationing in Puerto Rico. Write an entry for this contest. Follow these steps.

1 First, think about what you want to say. Use the postcards to help you brainstorm some ideas. You may want to list your ideas under the headings Weather, Sights, Recreation, and Clothing.

2 Write a first draft of your essay. Focus on communicating your ideas clearly.

San Juan

El Capitolio, San Juan

El Parque Nacional de Luquillo, Puerto Rico

Options

Strategies for Reaching All Students

Students Needing Extra Help
Step 1: Have students use their Organizers.
Step 2: Help students with the first two or three sentences. Since students have just worked with ads (using incomplete sentences and single words), they might have to be encouraged to write in complete sentences.

Enrichment
As a twist on this activity, have students write postcards from one of the places listed in the *Vocabulario para conversar* on pp. 220–221, explaining the weather and their activities, but without revealing the place. Students read their postcards aloud and classmates guess what places are being described.

Cultural Notes ☀

(p. 244, left photo)
Puerto Rico's capitol, located in the section of San Juan known as Puerta de Tierra, was constructed in the 1920s under the direction of architect Rafael Carmoega. Inside the capitol dome are four murals representing scenes from Puerto Rican history. The original constitution, ratified in 1952 when the island became a U.S. commonwealth, is contained in an urn that stands at the center of the rotunda.

3 Show your first draft to a partner. Ask what he or she likes about it and what should be changed. Think about any changes that you want to make, then revise it.

4 Check your work for spelling, accents, and question and exclamation marks at the beginning and end of sentences.

5 Make a clean copy. You can file your work in your writing portfolio, or you can share it with your classmates, who can vote on the most interesting, the most complete, and the one that most makes them want to visit Puerto Rico.

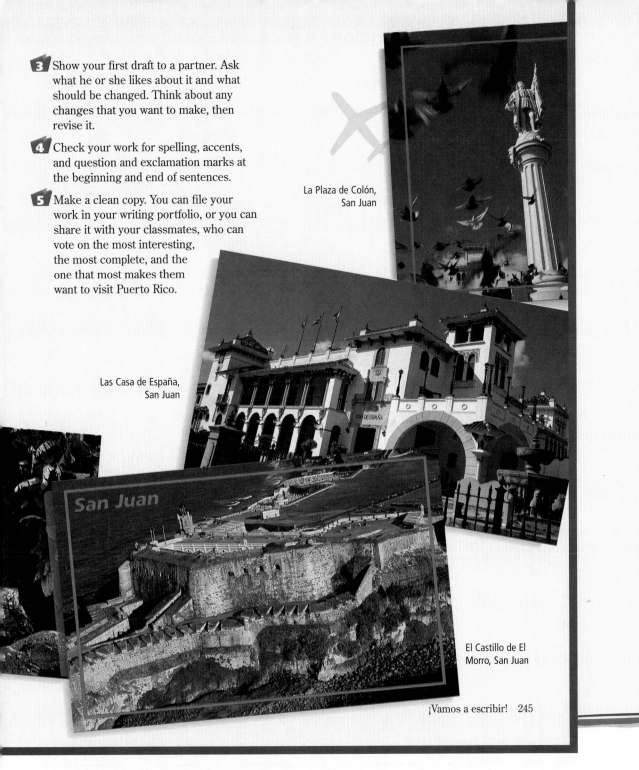

La Plaza de Colón, San Juan

Las Casa de España, San Juan

San Juan

El Castillo de El Morro, San Juan

¡Vamos a escribir! 245

(p. 244, right photo)
The Luquillo Division of the Caribbean National Forest, more commonly known as El Yunque (the Anvil) lies high in the mountains of northeastern Puerto Rico. The last remnant of a much larger rain forest, El Yunque covers 28,000 acres of mountain area and is the habitat for 240 species of plants and trees. The rain forest serves as a bird sanctuary and is protected by the U.S. National Forest Service.

(p. 245, center photo)
The Casa de España in San Juan is one example of Spanish colonial architecture in the crowded old section of the city. Viejo San Juan is a historic landmark district with many of its buildings restored to their appearance in the sixteenth and seventeenth centuries. This section covers an area of several square blocks and lies on the tip of a long peninsula.

(p. 245, bottom photo)
The massive Castillo de San Felipe del Morro, known as El Morro, was built by the Spaniards over more than two centuries beginning in 1539. El Morro is one of three fortresses built to protect San Juan, and it is said to be the strongest Spanish fortress in the Americas. Its walls are 20 feet thick in certain places and contain a network of stairways and ramps that were designed to facilitate quick movement of troops and artillery should the fort come under attack.

Assess & Summarize

Test Preparation

You may want to assign parts of this section as written homework or as an in-class writing activity prior to administering the *Examen de habilidades*.

Reteach / Review: Vocabulary

Speaking: Ask pairs of students to take turns naming various real or imaginary family members, describing their personalities, and then suggesting vacation destinations and activities they might enjoy. For example: *Mi hermana es deportista. Puede ir a Puerto Rico para bucear.*

Answers

Listening: *Llueve y quisiera visitar el museo. Menos mal que ayer fui a la catedral y a pasear en bote en el parque. Mañana, si hace buen tiempo, puedo ir a las cataratas.* Tomás may need the following: *las botas, el impermeable, el paraguas.* The weather was nice yesterday. Tomás will go to the waterfalls only if it's nice out.

Reading: The main idea is to attract people to Isla Mujeres in Mexico, because its beaches, the sea, and the weather all seem appealing.

¿Lo sabes bien?

This section will help you organize your studying for the proficiency test, where you will be asked to do similar, though not identical, tasks. There will not be any models on the test.

Listening

Can you understand when people talk about their vacation activities? Listen as your teacher reads a sample similar to what you will hear on the test. Can you name, in Spanish, at least two items that Tomás may need today? What do you think the weather was like yesterday? Is Tomás definitely going to the waterfalls tomorrow?

Reading

Can you scan this travel ad and identify its author's main idea?

En Isla Mujeres en México

El mar es azul y las playas son blancas. En diciembre hace calor, hace sol y nunca llueve. Si no le gusta un invierno frío, venga a Isla Mujeres. Sólo necesita llevar su traje de baño, sus anteojos de sol y su pasaporte.

246   Capítulo 7

Writing

Can you write a postcard telling about your vacation at a ski resort? Here is an example:

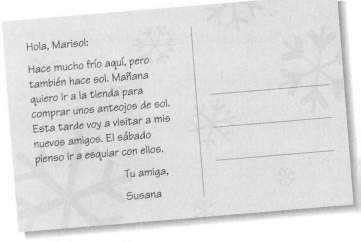

Hola, Marisol:

Hace mucho frío aquí, pero también hace sol. Mañana quiero ir a la tienda para comprar unos anteojos de sol. Esta tarde voy a visitar a mis nuevos amigos. El sábado pienso ir a esquiar con ellos.

Tu amiga,

Susana

Culture

Based on what you know about vacation time in Chile, how would that affect the time of year you would visit that country?

Speaking

Can you discuss vacation choices and activities with a partner? For example:

A — *¿Adónde te gustaría ir este verano?*
B — *A mí me gustaría visitar las ruinas en Guatemala. ¿Y a ti?*
A — *Yo prefiero ir a una ciudad grande. Me gusta mucho visitar museos y comprar recuerdos. ¿Con quién piensas ir a Guatemala?*
B — *Con mi familia. Mi padre es de Guatemala. Y tú, ¿con quién piensas ir?*
A — *Con mi madre. A ella le gustan las ciudades grandes también.*

Options

Students Needing Extra Help
Listening: Have students write their answers.
Do an example in English, pointing out that they don't have to hear the words raincoat or umbrella, but because they hear the word rain, they know those items will be needed.

Writing: Have students use their Organizers to help them with their postcards.
Culture: Review the *Perspectiva cultural.*
Speaking: Do in smaller segments: A–B–A and then B–A. Give more examples.

Resumen del capítulo 7

Use the vocabulary from this chapter to help you:
- describe vacation choices and activities
- talk about the weather
- discuss what to take on a trip

to talk about vacation
las vacaciones (pl.)
ir de vacaciones

to talk about places to visit on vacation
las cataratas
la catedral
la ciudad
el lago
los lugares de interés
el mar
las montañas
el museo
el país
la pirámide
las ruinas
la selva tropical

to talk about things to do on vacation
bucear
los recuerdos
descansar
esquiar
explorar (la selva)
llevar
pasear (en bote)
el bote
sacar fotos
la foto (f.)
subir (la pirámide)
tomar el sol
visitar

to talk about planning a vacation
pensar (e → ie) + inf.
regresar
salir

to name items to take on vacation
el abrigo
los anteojos de sol
las botas
el bronceador
la bufanda
la cámara
el gorro
los guantes
el impermeable
la maleta
el paraguas (sing.)
el pasaporte
el traje de baño

to ask about or describe weather
¿Qué tiempo hace?
fantástico, -a
Hace buen tiempo.
Hace calor.
Hace fresco.
Hace frío.
Hace mal tiempo.
Hace sol.
Hace viento.

la lluvia
la nieve
el sol
el viento
Llueve.
Nieva.

to say that you want or would like something
querer (e → ie)
quisiera

to say where you went
ir: (yo) fui
    (tú) fuiste
ninguna parte

to say when events occur
cuando
pasado, -a

to indicate use or purpose
para + inf.

to express amazement
¡Vaya!

to express satisfaction
menos mal que

to express ability or permission
poder (o → ue)

Resumen   247

CAPÍTULO 8

THEME: HOME

SCOPE AND SEQUENCE   Pages 248–281

COMMUNICATION

Topics

Rooms in the house

Furniture

Household appliances

Household chores

Objectives

To talk about homes in Spanish-speaking countries

To talk about where someone lives

To talk about houses or apartments

To indicate possession

To name household chores

To indicate obligation

To name and describe household items

To indicate that someone is right or wrong

To indicate whether you agree with someone or something

CULTURE

Architecture and the home

GRAMMAR

Los verbos poner *y* hacer

El verbo vivir

El verbo preferir

Los adjetivos posesivos: su *y* nuestro

Ancillaries available for use with Chapter 8

Multisensory/Technology

 Overhead Transparencies, 41–45

 Audio Tapes and CDs

 Vocabulary Art Blackline Masters for Hands-On Learning, pp. 43–47

 Classroom Crossword

 Video

CD-ROM

Print

 Practice Workbook, pp. 84–93

 Writing, Audio & Video Activities, pp. 47–52, 114–116, 166–167

 Communicative Activity Blackline Masters

Pair and Small Group Activities, pp. 57–62

Situation Cards, p. 63

Un paso más: Actividades para ampliar tu español, pp. 44–49

Assessment

 Assessment Program

Pruebas, pp. 111–121

Examen de habilidades, pp. 122–125

 Test Generator

Video still from Chap. 8

Architectural Influences

If you were to travel from the southwestern U.S. to the southern tip of South America, you would sense a certain familiarity in almost every place you visited. Although regional differences would quickly become apparent, you would still be conscious of a certain look shared by many southwestern U.S. and South American communities. This look in large part can be traced to the architecture of Moorish Spain. The Moors ruled most of the Iberian Peninsula from the early eighth century until the early thirteenth century.

Many elements common to Latin American architecture were first introduced in Moorish Spain. Patios, for example, became common in places such as Sevilla and Córdoba beginning in the early eleventh century. Because of widespread political and social upheaval during this time, houses were built with heavy doors and thick, fortresslike walls. Patios, positioned in the center of the house and accessible from all first-floor rooms, often had tiled floors. In the center, surrounded by lemon trees and flowers, was often a large clay pot filled with cool water. Patios were possibly the first naturally "air-conditioned" rooms of the house. Throughout Latin America today, as well as in Spain, they are still a popular feature in many commercial buildings as well as homes.

Another predominant element of Latin American architecture is the *balcón,* or *mirador.* In Moorish Spain, typical homes had balconies off of the second-floor sleeping areas. These balconies, which often included intricately fashioned iron railings and grates, overlooked the patio. During the colonial period, balconies became commonplace in Latin America as well. However, most of them did not face the patio as they did in Spain. Instead, they faced the street to facilitate the observation of street life.

Homes and other buildings in Moorish Spain stood apart from those in northern Europe in other ways. In traditional Spanish construction, thick walls helped shield inner rooms from the sun's heat. Although wood was used for ceiling beams, doors, and windows, it was not used as commonly as in northern Europe. Instead, adobe, stone, and brick were the popular building materials.

Today, builders in Latin America and the southwestern U.S. employ many of these same materials and techniques. In addition, they utilize many of the same building techniques and materials used for centuries by American Indians.

Introduce

Planning

Cross-Curricular Connections

Design Connection *(pp. 252–253)*
Have students create drawings of their ideal room, labeling all the items with descriptions including color, size, etc. Then divide the class into pairs. Have students describe their drawings without showing them to their partners. As one student describes a room, the other draws it. Students then switch roles. Display the drawings that are most alike.

Architecture Connection *(pp. 256–257)*
Using magazine cutouts or by drawing, have students create the house of a famous person. The house should have a cutaway view so that the interior is visible. (Provide an example.) Students should include items and a decor that characterize the person. Have them write a paragraph describing the house by means of a brief interview with the celebrity. When finished, students can display their houses, and the class can try to guess the owner.

Spanish in Your Community
See if students have ever noticed any houses or other structures in their community built in the Spanish architectural style. Ask: What are the characteristics of this style? Where are the buildings located?

CAPÍTULO 8

¿Qué haces en tu casa?

OBJECTIVES

At the end of this chapter you will be able to:

- tell where you live
- describe your home
- name household chores
- compare and contrast the use of outdoor space in a home in Spain and in the United States

Una casa en Maracaibo, Venezuela

249

¿Qué haces en tu casa?

Play

 Video Activity A

Using the Video

This chapter's video focuses on the home. Students will visit the Madrid homes of each of our hosts and tour the El Escorial palace and monastery outside Madrid.

To prepare students for the video, first ask them to predict what this chapter's tape will be about. Then have students watch the segment several times. After the first time, you may wish to have them brainstorm possible vocabulary and expressions they will need to talk about what they saw on the video. Ask students to identify: a) things they saw that were familiar to them, and b) things they saw that they probably would not see where they live.

Video segment 1: For more teaching suggestions, see the Video Teacher's Guide.

¡Piénsalo bien!

Look at the photographs.

Una casa de Segovia, España

In what ways is this house similar to and different from homes that you know?

250   Capítulo 8

Options

Strategies for Reaching All Students

Spanish-Speaking Students
Ask Spanish-speaking students: *Describe la casa que ves en la foto. ¿Es como las casas en tu comunidad? Y el dormitorio, ¿es como el tuyo? ¿Cómo es diferente? ¿En qué se parece? ¿Se parece la cocina a la de tu casa o apartamento?*

 Un paso más Ex. 8-A

Enrichment
If possible, bring to class a collection of photographs of homes in Spanish-speaking countries. Strive for a sampling that includes homes representative of those from all socioeconomic groups. Students will be particularly interested in viewing the insides of homes, especially the bedrooms of teenagers.

Students Needing Extra Help
Relate *dormir* to *dormitorio* and *cocinar* to *cocina*. In talking about families, be sensitive to issues involving single-parent households, disadvantaged families, etc.

In the captions, find the Spanish names for the rooms shown in the photographs. What do you think *dormitorio* might mean? What Spanish word do you know that is related to *la cocina*?

En Caracas, Venezuela

"Nuestro dormitorio no es muy grande, pero hay espacio para todo."

"Me gustan las cocinas modernas. ¡Puedo preparar de todo!"

251

Multicultural Perspectives

In many countries in Latin America, adobe is the preferred building material for homes. Made of mud and / or clay, it is not only extremely strong, but also energy efficient, keeping houses cool in hot months and warm in cold ones. Ask students what types of materials are used to build houses in their neighborhoods.

Answers: ¡Piénsalo bien!

(p. 250) Answers will vary.

(p. 251) dormitorio, cocina / See if students can guess from visual clues that *dormitorio* means "bedroom." You may wish to point out that this word is a false cognate and doesn't mean "dormitory" *(una residencia estudiantil)*. / *cocinar*

Using Photos

(p. 251, top and bottom photos) Ask: ¿Qué hace el muchacho? ¿Y la muchacha?

Cultural Notes ☀

(p. 250, photo)
A typical old house in Spain, like this one in Segovia, shows a strong Arabic influence in its use of intricately designed ceramic tiles. The Moors brought tile production to Spain when they ruled the country and developed it to a true artistic peak. An outstanding example of decorative tile work by Moorish artisans is in the Alhambra in Granada.

Present

Chapter Theme
Home: Rooms of a house and household chores

Communicative Objectives
- To talk about where someone lives
- To talk about houses or apartments
- To indicate possession
- To name household chores
- To indicate obligation

 Transparencies 41–42

 Vocabulary Art BLMs

 Pronunciation Tape 8-1

 Vocabulario para conversar A

Play

Using the Video
Video segment 2: See the Video Teacher's Guide.

 Video Activity B

Vocabulario para conversar

¿Cómo es tu casa?

Aquí tienes palabras y expresiones necesarias para hablar sobre dónde vives, cómo es tu casa y algunas cosas que tienes que hacer en casa. Léelas varias veces y practícalas con un(a) compañero(a) en las páginas siguientes.

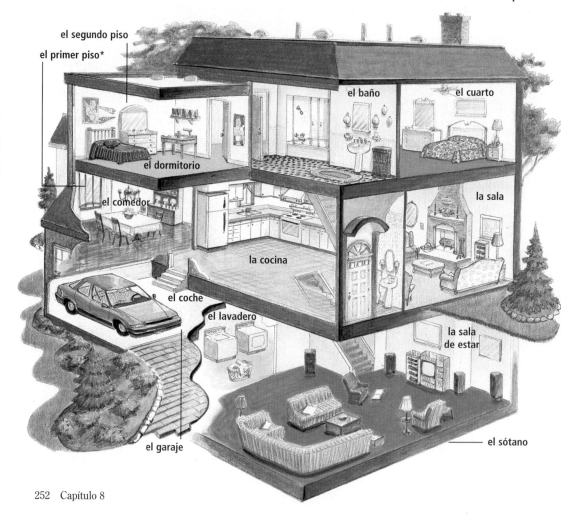

una casa de dos pisos
el segundo piso
el primer piso*
el baño
el cuarto
el dormitorio
el comedor
la sala
la cocina
el coche
el lavadero
la sala de estar
el garaje
el sótano

252 Capítulo 8

Options

Strategies for Reaching All Students

Students Needing Extra Help
Have students begin to fill in their Organizers.
To facilitate learning, present the rooms and chores separately.
También necesitas . . . : To help reinforce meaning, give some examples of *tener que* using activities vocabulary from Chap. 1.

Learning Spanish Through Action
STAGING VOCABULARY: *Señalen* and the commands for household chores listed in the *Vocabulario para conversar*
1) MATERIALS: none
DIRECTIONS: Tell students that they are going to help you clean your house on Saturday. Direct them to act out the chores that you mention.

2) MATERIALS: transparency of the *Vocabulario para conversar* or an enlarged photocopy of the page
DIRECTIONS: Direct students to point to rooms as you tell where people in your family are. Be sure to include pets.

hacer la cama

sacudir los muebles

lavar los platos

quitar la mesa

pasar la aspiradora

limpiar el baño

arreglar el cuarto

lavar la ropa

poner la mesa

cortar el césped

sacar la basura

el apartamento

También necesitas . . .

cerca (de)	*near*	hacer: (yo) hago	*to do, to make:*
lejos (de)	*far (from)*	(tú) haces	*I do / make,*
vivir: (yo) vivo	*to live: I live,*		*you do / make*
(tú) vives	*you live*	el quehacer	*(household) chore*
el piso	*floor*	(de la casa)	
bastante	*rather, quite*	tener que + *inf.*	*to have to ___*
nuestro, -a	*our*	más	*here: else*

* In a multistory building, we usually call the ground floor *la planta baja,* the second floor *el primer piso,* the third floor *el segundo piso,* the fourth floor *el tercer piso,* and so on. Note that for "first" and "third," we use *primer* and *tercer* in front of a masculine singular noun.

Vocabulario para conversar 253

Grammar Preview
Hago / haces, vivo / vives and *nuestro(a)* are presented lexically. The explanation appears later in the grammar section.

Teaching Suggestions
Preparing students to speak: Use one or two options from each of the categories of Comprehensible Input, Physical Response, or Limited Verbal Response. For a complete explanation of these categories and some sample activities, see the front section of this Teacher's Edition.

Note that from this point on, exercise directions are in Spanish. Words that would be difficult to understand are translated for the first few times. Help students see this as part of the reading process. Encourage them to use strategies that they are developing in *¡Vamos a leer!*

Remind students of the expression *ayudar en casa* from Chap. 1.

Class Starter Review
On the day following initial presentation, you might begin the class with one of these activities:
1) Have students list the rooms in their homes.
2) Have students form pairs. One describes the layout of his or her home while the other draws it. Switch roles and repeat on a subsequent day. (Allow students the option of describing their dream house or that of a friend or relative.)

Practice & Apply

Re-enter / Recycle

Ex. 2: places from Chap. 3
Ex. 4: numbers 0–31 from *El primer paso*
Ex. 5: activities from Chaps. 1 and 3
Ex. 6: *gustar* expressions from Chap. 1

Reteach / Review: Vocabulary

Ex. 3: Students can extend this dialogue by having *Estudiante A* say that he or she can't do the chore because he or she has something else to do, somewhere to go, or doesn't feel well.

Answers: Empecemos a conversar

1 ESTUDIANTE A
a. ¿Dónde está el coche?
b. . . . el dormitorio?
c. . . . la sala?
d. . . . el comedor?
e. . . . el baño?
f. . . . la sala de estar?
g. . . . el lavadero?

ESTUDIANTE B
a. Está en el garaje.
b. . . . el segundo piso.
c. . . . el primer piso.
d. . . . el primer piso.
e. . . . el segundo piso.
f. . . . el sótano.
g. . . . el sótano.

Empecemos a conversar

Túrnate con un compañero(a) para ser *Estudiante A* y *Estudiante B*. Reemplacen las palabras subrayadas con las palabras representadas o escritas en los recuadros. 💡 quiere decir que puedes escoger tu propia respuesta. Para el Ejercicio 1, ve *(see)* el dibujo de la casa en la página 252.

1
   A —¿Dónde está *la cocina*?
   B —*Está en el primer piso.*
      Y ahora Uds.

Estudiante A   Estudiante B

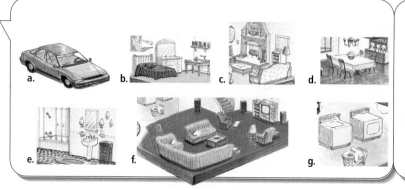

el garaje

el primer piso

el segundo piso

el sótano

2
   A —¿Vives cerca de *un almacén*?
   B —*Sí, bastante cerca.*
      o: *No, vivo lejos.*
      Y ahora Uds.

Estudiante A   Estudiante B

254   Capítulo 8

Options

Strategies for Reaching All Students

Spanish-Speaking Students
Ex. 7: Ask Spanish-speaking students: *En tu familia, ¿tienen todos quehaceres? ¿Deben todos ayudar en casa? ¿Por qué? ¿Qué hacen?*

 Un paso más Exs. 8-B, 8-C

Students Needing Extra Help
Ex. 1: Point out that the answers are not in order and will be used more than once.
Ex. 2: Explain the choice of answers. Define "near" and "far" in terms of distance for this exercise.
Ex. 3: Remind students that *hacer* in a question usually is answered with a different action word. Have them use their Organizers for *Estudiante B*'s responses.

Ex. 4: Remind students of when to use *nuestro* or *nuestra*.
Ex. 7: *¿Qué quehaceres . . . ?* may be confusing. Show students the correct pronunciation by modeling. Review *ir a* + inf. from Chap. 3.

3

A —*¿Qué más tengo que hacer hoy? ¿Tengo que* <u>*lavar los platos*</u>*?*

B —*Sí, y también tienes que* <u>*sacar la basura*</u>*.*

Y ahora Uds.

Estudiante A   **Estudiante B**

a.

b.

c.

d.

e.

Empecemos a escribir

Escribe tus respuestas en español.

4 ¿Cuántos pisos y cuántos cuartos hay en tu casa o apartamento?

Nuestra casa / Nuestro apartamento tiene . . .

5 ¿En qué cuarto de la casa prefieres . . .

jugar videojuegos?
ver la tele?
leer?
estudiar?
escuchar música?

6 ¿Te gusta más cortar el césped, pasar la aspiradora o sacudir los muebles? ¿Por qué?

7 ¿Qué quehaceres tienes para este fin de semana? ¿Qué más vas a hacer?

También se dice

el living

la recámara
la habitación (de dormir)
la alcoba
la pieza
el cuarto

el carro
el auto
la máquina

el zacate
la hierba
el pasto
la grama

Present

Chapter Theme
Home: Household items

Communicative Objectives
- To name and describe household items
- To indicate that someone is right or wrong
- To indicate whether you agree with someone or something

 Transparencies 43–44

 Vocabulary Art BLMs

 Pronunciation Tape 8-2

 Vocabulario para conversar B

Play

Using the Video
Video segment 2: See the Video Teacher's Guide.

 Video Activity B

Grammar Preview
The verb forms *pongo / pones* are presented lexically. The complete paradigm appears on p. 267.

Vocabulario para conversar

¿Cómo es tu dormitorio?

Aquí tienes el resto del vocabulario necesario para hablar sobre las cosas que hay en una casa.

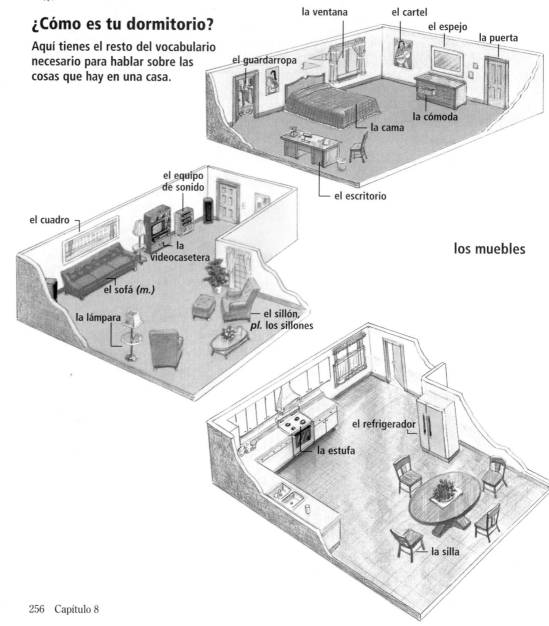

los muebles

256   Capítulo 8

Options

Strategies for Reaching All Students

Learning Spanish Through Action
STAGING VOCABULARY: *Pongan*
MATERIALS: floor plan with room labels drawn on the chalkboard; pictures of furniture cut out from magazines or newspapers, tape
DIRECTIONS: Tell students that they are helping you move into a new house. Give them the furniture pictures. As you tell what item goes in which room, students go to the chalkboard and place the furniture in the appropriate room.

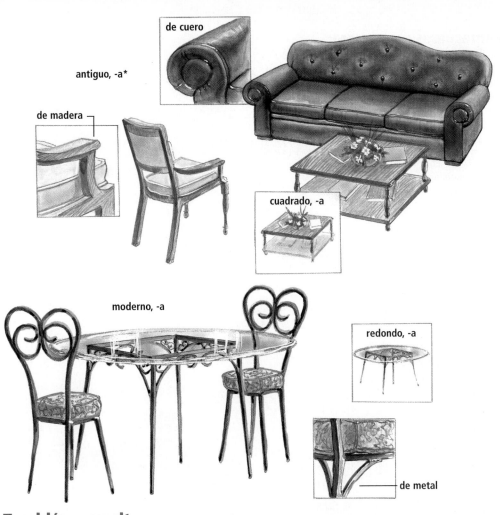

de cuero

antiguo, -a*

de madera

cuadrado, -a

moderno, -a

redondo, -a

de metal

También necesitas . . .

las cosas	*things*	poner: (yo) pongo	*to put (I put, you put),*
cómodo, -a	*comfortable*	(tú) pones	*to place, to set*
incómodo, -a	*uncomfortable*	(no) tener razón	*to be right (wrong)*
limpio, -a	*clean*	(no) estar de acuerdo	*to (dis)agree*
sucio, -a	*dirty*		

* In general, we use the adjective *antiguo, -a* for things, whereas we can use *viejo, -a* for either people or things. *Antiguo, -a* can imply value, as in *muebles antiguos.*

Vocabulario para conversar   257

Practice

Re-enter / Recycle
Exs. 9–11: adjective agreement
from Chaps. 1 and 4
Ex. 10: direct object pronouns
from Chap. 6
Ex. 11: expressing likes and preferences from Chap. 4

Answers: Empecemos a conversar

8 ESTUDIANTE A

a. ¿Qué hay en el dormitorio de tu
casa (apartamento)?

b. ...la sala...

c. ...la sala de estar...

d. ...el comedor...

ESTUDIANTE B

a.–d. A ver...hay.... *(Answers
will vary.)*

9 ESTUDIANTE A

a. ¿Qué vas a poner en el dormitorio?

b. ...la sala de estar?

c. ...la cocina?

d. ...la sala?

ESTUDIANTE B

Answers will vary. Look for logical
responses.

a. Voy a poner una cómoda.

b. ...tres sillones azules.

c. ...una estufa blanca.

d. ...un equipo de sonido.

Empecemos a conversar

8 la cocina   A —¿*Qué hay en* <u>*la cocina*</u> *de tu casa (apartamento)?*

B —*A ver...hay* <u>*una estufa y un refrigerador*</u>.

Y ahora Uds.

Estudiante A

a. el dormitorio
b. la sala
c. la sala de estar
d. el comedor

Estudiante B

9   A —¿*Qué vas a poner en* <u>*la sala*</u>?

B —*Voy a poner* <u>*un sofá muy cómodo*</u>.

Y ahora Uds.

Estudiante A

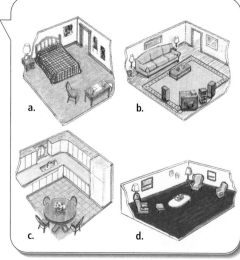

a.

b.

c.

d.

Estudiante B

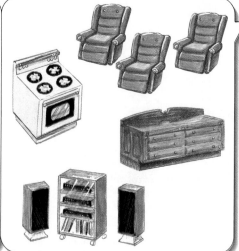

Options

Strategies for Reaching All Students

Students Needing Extra Help
Ex. 8: Use the Organizer along with
Transparency 43.
Exs. 9–10: Remind students that the
responses depicted by art for *Estudiante B*
are not in sequential order and they must
choose.

Ex. 10: Remind students of placement of
object pronouns and adjective agreement.
Model a feminine noun.
Ex. 11: Remind students of adjective agreement and that *Estudiante B* has to listen
carefully for his or her choices.

Enrichment
Ex. 8: To extend this dialogue, *Estudiante A*
can ask whether he or she likes the furniture
named and, once *Estudiante B* has
answered, ask for reasons for that answer.
Estudiante B's answer should include
descriptions of the furniture named.
Ex. 9: Extend this dialogue by having
Estudiante A ask where he or she plans to
buy the items named, and how much he or
she wants to pay.

10

A —*El refrigerador está sucio.*
B —*¿Sucio? ¡Pero está limpio!*
   o: *Tienes razón. Lo tengo que limpiar.*

   Y ahora Uds.

¡NO OLVIDES!

Remember that the adjective agrees with the noun in gender and number.

Estudiante A

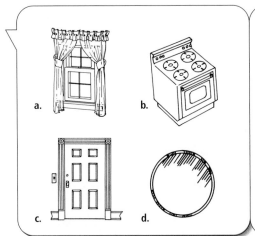

a. b.

c. d.

Estudiante B

11

A —*¿Prefieres un escritorio de madera o de metal?*
B —*Prefiero un escritorio de metal.*

   Y ahora Uds.

Estudiante A

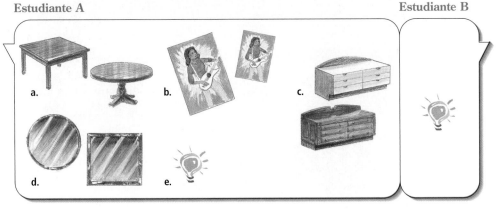

a. b. c.

d. e.

Estudiante B

10 ESTUDIANTE A

a. La ventana está sucia.
b. La estufa está sucia.
c. La puerta está sucia.
d. El espejo está sucio.

ESTUDIANTE B

a. ¿Sucia? ¡Pero está limpia!
b. Tienes razón. La tengo que limpiar.
c. Tienes razón. La tengo que limpiar.
d. ¿Sucio? ¡Pero está limpio!

11 ESTUDIANTE A

a. ¿Prefieres una mesa cuadrada o una mesa redonda?
b. ...un cartel grande o un cartel pequeño?
c. ...una cómoda moderna o una cómoda antigua?
d. ...un espejo redondo o un espejo cuadrado?
e. Questions will vary.

ESTUDIANTE B

a.–e. Answers will vary depending on *Estudiante B*'s preferences.

Apply

Re-enter / Recycle
Ex. 12: numbers 0–31 from *El primer paso*, adjectives describing physical characteristics from Chap. 5, colors from Chap. 6

Answers: Empecemos a escribir y a leer

(In Exs. 12–13, give students the option of writing about a friend's house or an imaginary house.)

12–14 Answers will vary, but encourage students to use the full range of chapter vocabulary.

15 Drawings will vary, but should contain these features: The house has two stories with no basement. The first (ground) floor has a kitchen, a small bathroom, a large living room, a dining room, and a family room. The second floor has a bathroom and three bedrooms: two rather large ones and one very small one. The first floor also has a modern laundry room and a two-car garage.

 Practice Wkbk. 8-3, 8-4

 Audio Activity 8.2

 Writing Activity 8-C

 Pruebas 8-3, 8-4

Empecemos a escribir y a leer

Escribe tus respuestas en español.

12 Describe los muebles de un cuarto en tu casa. Di *(tell)* de qué colores son y si *(if)* son cómodos o incómodos.

En nuestra sala de estar hay dos sofás. Son . . .

13 ¿Cómo es tu dormitorio? ¿Hay muchas ventanas? ¿Cuadros? ¿Qué más hay?

14 ¿Estás de acuerdo con que todos tienen que ayudar con los quehaceres de la casa? ¿Por qué?

15 Lee este párrafo y dibuja la casa descrita aquí.

Nuestra casa tiene dos pisos, pero no tiene sótano. En el primer piso hay una cocina, un baño pequeño, una sala grande, un comedor y una sala de estar. En el segundo piso hay otro baño y tres dormitorios: dos bastante grandes y uno muy pequeño. También tenemos en el primer piso un lavadero moderno y muy práctico y un garaje para dos coches. Los muebles que más me gustan son un sofá antiguo pero cómodo, y ¡la videocasetera!

En el patio de una casa en la Ciudad de México

260 Capítulo 8

Options

Strategies for Reaching All Students

Spanish-Speaking Students
Ex. 12: Ask Spanish-speaking students: *¿En qué cuarto te gusta más estar? ¿Por qué? ¿Cómo te sientes ahí?*

 Un paso más Exs. 8-D, 8-E

Students Needing Extra Help
Ex. 12: Give students time to think through the exercise. You may wish to give a complete model. Have them use their Organizers and assign different rooms to groups or pairs.
Ex. 13: Give a model in which all the questions are answered.

Enrichment
Ex. 12: Students can also make a chart with three columns: *De metal, De madera,* and *De cuero.* Have them list items in their home that belong in each category.
For additional practice, students can also write a dialogue with *Estudiante A* saying that he or she wants to buy new furniture and *Estudiante B* asking why. After *Estudiante A* gives reasons, *Estudiante B* can say whether or not *Estudiante A* is right or wrong.

Usando el lavaplatos en Zaragoza

Cortando el césped en la Ciudad de México

el gavetero
el buró

el afiche
el póster

la refrigeradora
la nevera
el frigorífico
la heladera

la cocina

el armario
el clóset
el ropero
el placard

Vocabulario para conversar   261

Cultural Notes ☼

(p. 261, top photo)
Young woman loading a dishwasher in Aragón, Spain. Traditionally, many Spanish middle-class families hired servants to do their housework. Today, however, this is much less true. In addition, modern conveniences such as the dishwasher have made household chores easier for everyone.

Practice

Re-enter / Recycle

Ex. 1: time-telling from Chap. 2, places and buildings from Chap. 3
Ex. 2: direct object pronouns from Chap. 6

Answers:
¡Comuniquemos!

1 Dialogues will vary and may include: *el centro comercial, la playa, el parque de diversiones, el parque, la piscina, el gimnasio, cortar el césped, lavar la ropa, sacudir los muebles, arreglar el cuarto, lavar los platos, pasar la aspiradora.*

¡Comuniquemos!

Aquí tienes otra oportunidad para usar el vocabulario de este capítulo.

1 Antes de *(before)* hacer planes con tus amigos, tienes que hacer otras cosas. Usa los dibujos y túrnate *(take turns)* con un(a) compañero(a) para hacer y aceptar invitaciones.

A — *¿Por qué no vamos al cine?*
B — *¿A qué hora? Tengo que limpiar el baño primero.*
A — *¿Puedes ir a las dos?*
B — *No, pero puedo ir a las cuatro.*

Estudiante A

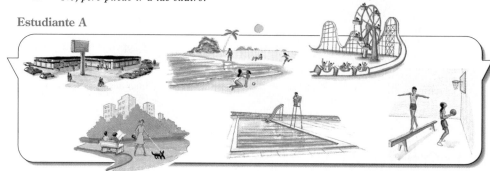

Estudiante B

262   Capítulo 8

Options

Strategies for Reaching All Students

Spanish-Speaking Students

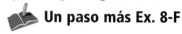 **Un paso más Ex. 8-F**

Students Needing Extra Help
Ex. 1: Review time-telling and *al (a la)*, and show what changes in the dialogue.
Ex. 2: Have students use their Organizers. Have each pair choose four different things and make a chart listing "object" and "object location."
¿Qué sabes ahora?: Have students write out this section so they can check off what they have mastered.

Enrichment
Ex. 2: As an in-class assignment, have students describe the home in which he or she would like to live. Tell students to begin their descriptions: *Quisiera vivir en una casa (un apartamento) con . . . .* They could also begin: *En mi casa (apartamento) perfecta(o) hay . . . .*

2 Tu familia acaba de mudarse *(has just moved)* a una casa nueva. Con un(a) compañero(a), di dónde están los muebles y los aparatos *(appliances)* y dónde quieres ponerlos. Después, tu compañero(a) va a decir *(say)* si *(if)* está de acuerdo o no.

A — *¿Dónde está la videocasetera?*
B — *Creo que está en el dormitorio de mamá.*
A — *Sí, aquí está. La pongo en la sala de estar.*
B — *No estoy de acuerdo. Debemos ponerla en el dormitorio.*

¿Qué sabes ahora?

Can you:

■ tell where you live?

—Vivo en un(a) ___ cerca de ___.

■ name the rooms in your house?

—Mi casa tiene una cocina, ___, ___ y ___.

■ describe some furnishings?

—Las sillas que están en el comedor son ___.

■ name some household chores?

—Yo tengo que ___ y mis hermanos tienen que ___.

Vocabulario para conversar   263

2 Dialogues will vary. Suggested items include: *la videocasetera, el sofá (de cuero), el cartel, el cuadro, el sillón.*

Answers: ¿Qué sabes ahora?

• apartamento (casa) / *Answers will vary.*
• Answers will vary.
• Answers will vary. Look for correct adjective agreement.
• Answers will vary.

Audio Activity 8.3

Cooperative Learning
Divide the class into groups of three or four students. Tell them they are to prepare an advertisement for a house for sale. The ad should feature a picture, a written description, the price, and possibly a floor plan. Assign tasks within each group: writer, artist, proofreader, presenter. Students should discuss the features of their house before work begins. Have presenters show and read the ads to the whole class. Display the ads on bulletin boards. Prior to assigning the exercise, you might want to have students clip ads from newspapers to use as models.

Cultural Objective
- To compare and contrast the use of outdoor space in a home in Spain and in the U.S.

Teaching Suggestions
Have students compare the home here with the one shown in the photo on p. 250.

Multicultural Perspectives
In Granada, a *carmen* (from the Arabic word *karmat,* meaning garden) is a lush garden surrounded by walls. The same architectural concept was employed in the Spanish missions of the American Southwest and can still be seen today in the mission-style houses of California and other states in that region. Ask students if they know of architectural influences from other countries that have had a similar lasting impact.

Perspectiva cultural

En España hay casas y apartamentos muy diferentes. También hay diversos tipos de patios.

What family members might use the part of the house pictured, and for what purpose? What might some people call it in English?

In the large cities of Spain, neighbors often visit each other's apartments in the same building. In small towns, you might see neighbors talking to each other through the windows that open onto the *patio.*

When you hear the English word "patio" you probably think of a small patch of concrete in a backyard. In Spanish, however, it can mean different things. For example, in a modern apartment building in a large city like Madrid, the *patio* is an air shaft in the center of the building. The kitchen may have a window that opens onto it.

However, in the south, in towns such as Sevilla and Córdoba, some *patios* are gardens with flowers, chairs, and perhaps caged birds. Some *patios* in Sevilla are in the front of the house and lead visitors in. More often, they are in the middle of the house, with big doors leading into the rooms. A *patio* in Sevilla is a place for friends and family to gather and talk.

Even though a *patio* in an apartment building in Madrid looks very different from a traditional one in Sevilla, they still have similar functions. A *patio* is a space that opens to the sky where friends and neighbors can spend time together chatting.

264   Capítulo 8

La cultura desde tu perspectiva

1   Many houses in the United States have patios in back. They are usually made of concrete. In what ways is the design and function of a patio in the United States similar to and different from one in Spain?

2   In the United States, most open spaces are in front or in back of the house, while in Spain you might find them in the middle. What advantages do you see to having an open space in the middle of a house? If you were building a home, would you include a Spanish-style patio in your plans? Why or why not?

Un patio en Córdoba, España

Options

Strategies for Reaching All Students

Spanish-Speaking Students
Ask Spanish-speaking students: *¿Qué actividades son comunes en los patios? ¿Tienes patio donde vives? ¿Es fácil o difícil encontrar casas con patios en tu comunidad?*

 Un paso más Ex. 8-G

Students Needing Extra Help
Discuss patios, decks, porches, outside entertainment areas, and so on.
Ex. 2: Explain that there is no roof on a *patio* in the middle of a house. Ask students if they would like this type of outdoor space.

Enrichment
Find photos of traditional homes in Spain or Latin America that have balconies and shuttered windows. After students have looked at these photos, conduct a brief class discussion. Ask: How are balconies and windows in these photos different from those you see in the U.S.?

Una familia en su patio, Santiago de Chile

Cultural Notes ☼

(p. 265, inset photo)
This family relaxes on their *patio* in Santiago, Chile. The *patio* has always been a special family place in Spanish-speaking countries, functioning as an "inner room outside" where the entire family can gather for refreshments, games, reading, and conversation.

(p. 265, photo)
This *patio* in Córdoba, Spain, clearly shows an Arabic influence in its layout and decoration. The *patio* is open from above, and can be entered or viewed from several rooms in the house. The archways, tile decoration on the floors and lower walls, and fountain are all distinctly Arabic, as is the tendency to decorate with an abundance of potted plants and shrubs.

Preview

 Transparency 45

Teaching Suggestions

Remind students that they saw *la alberca* in the *También se dice* section of Chap. 3 as another way of saying *la piscina.*

Answers

Answers will vary, but may include the family members, their home, etc.

A The word that follows determines whether *nuestra* or *nuestros* is used.

B It belongs to the grandparents.

Gramática en contexto

Look at this page out of a student's photo album made during her trip to Cuernavaca, Mexico. From the photographs you see here, what do you think she will remember as she looks at this page?

Aquí estamos Marcia y yo con nuestra familia mexicana. Los señores Ortiz y sus hijos, Julia y Ramón.

Nuestra mamá mexicana cocina y pone la mesa. Al señor Ortiz también le gusta cocinar. Nosotros arreglamos nuestros cuartos y hacemos las camas.

Los abuelos Ortiz viven cerca. Su casa es muy grande y tienen un patio con alberca.

Yo prefiero tomar el sol por la mañana, pero Marcia prefiere tomar el sol por la tarde. ¡Qué buena vida!

A In the photo captions, you find *nuestra* and *nuestros*. What words determine whether *-a* or *-os* is used at the end?

B In the sentence *"Su casa es muy grande . . . ,"* the word *su* indicates the house belongs to someone. Whom do you believe it belongs to?

266 Capítulo 8

Options

Strategies for Reaching All Students

Spanish-Speaking Students
Ex. 1: Have Spanish-speaking students write out this exercise.

Students Needing Extra Help
Have students begin their Organizers for the grammar portion.
Los verbos poner *y* hacer: Review *-er* verb endings from Chap. 4. Show students that these two verbs are presented together because of the *-go* in the *yo* form. Ask if they remember another verb that has *-go* in the *yo* form *(tengo).*
Ex. 1: Review compound subjects.

Los verbos *poner* y *hacer*

The forms of *poner* ("to put, to place, to set") and *hacer* ("to make, to do") follow the pattern of other *-er* verbs in all except the *yo* forms, *pongo* and *hago*.

Here are all the present-tense forms of *poner* and *hacer*.

(yo)	pon**go** ha**go**	(nosotros) (nosotras)	pon**emos** hac**emos**
(tú)	pon**es** hac**es**	(vosotros) (vosotras)	pon**éis** hac**éis**
Ud. (él) (ella)	pon**e** hac**e**	Uds. (ellos) (ellas)	pon**en** hac**en**

1 Estas personas ayudan a una amiga a mudarse. Di en qué cuarto ponen las cosas.

 Teresa pone el espejo en el baño.

Teresa

a. Ud.   b. Elena y tú   c. tú

d. yo   e. Roberto y Paco   f. Enrique y yo

Gramática en contexto 267

Class Starter Review
On the day following the initial presentation of *hacer*, you might begin by asking students for which classes they always do homework.

1 Answers
a. Ud. pone el sillón en la sala de estar.
b. Elena y tú ponen la cama en el dormitorio.
c. Tú pones el sofá en la sala.
d. Yo pongo la silla en el comedor.
e. Roberto y Paco ponen la estufa en la cocina.
f. Enrique y yo ponemos la mesa en el comedor.

Present & Practice

Re-enter / Recycle

Ex. 2: school subjects from Chap. 2
Ex. 3: places and buildings from Chaps. 3 and 6

Answers

2 **ESTUDIANTE A**

a. ¿Qué tarea hace Felipe todos los días?
b. ...hacen Fabiola y tú ...
c. ...hacen Irene y Bárbara ...
d. ...hace Ud....
e. ...hacen Lupe y Raúl ...
f. ...haces tú ...

ESTUDIANTE B

a. Generalmente hace la tarea de ciencias.
b. ...hacemos ...español.
c. ...hacen ...ciencias de la salud.
d. ...hago ...inglés.
e. ...hacen ...ciencias sociales.
f. ...hago ... *(Answers will vary.)*

 Practice Wkbk. 8-5

 Writing Activity 8-D

 Prueba 8-5

---

2 ¿Qué tareas tienen que hacer estos estudiantes todos los días?

A —¿Qué tarea hacen Carlos y Javier todos los días?
B —Generalmente hacen la tarea de matemáticas.

Carlos y Javier

a. Felipe

b. Fabiola y tú

c. Irene y Bárbara

d. Ud.

e. Lupe y Raúl

f. tú

El verbo *vivir*

You already know the pattern of endings of present-tense *-ar* and *-er* verbs. There is one other group of regular verbs, those that end in *-ir*. *Vivir* ("to live") is a regular *-ir* verb. Here are all its present-tense forms.

(yo)	viv**o**	(nosotros) (nosotras)	viv**imos**
(tú)	viv**es**	(vosotros) (vosotras)	viv**ís**
Ud. (él) (ella)	viv**e**	Uds. (ellos) (ellas)	viv**en**

• Notice that the pattern of endings for -ir verbs is identical to that of -er verbs, except for the nosotros and vosotros forms.

• Notice that *salir* is a regular *-ir* verb in the present tense except for its *yo* form: *(yo) salgo.*

268   Capítulo 8

Options

Strategies for Reaching All Students

Students Needing Extra Help
Ex. 2: Review compound subjects.
El verbo vivir: Show similarities with *-er* and *-ir* endings. Tell students they practiced the *yo / tú* forms of *vivir* in Ex. 2 in the *Empecemos a conversar.*
Ex. 3: Remind students that when a question is asked with the *Uds.* form, the answer will be in the *nosotros* form. Therefore, students should be looking for *nosotros* on the drawing.

3 Mira *(look at)* el dibujo de este pueblo *(town)*. Di a tu compañero(a) si estas personas viven cerca o lejos de ciertos lugares *(places)*.

David y Agustín

A — *¿Dónde viven David y Agustín?*
B — *Viven cerca del centro comercial.*
    o: *Viven lejos de la escuela.*

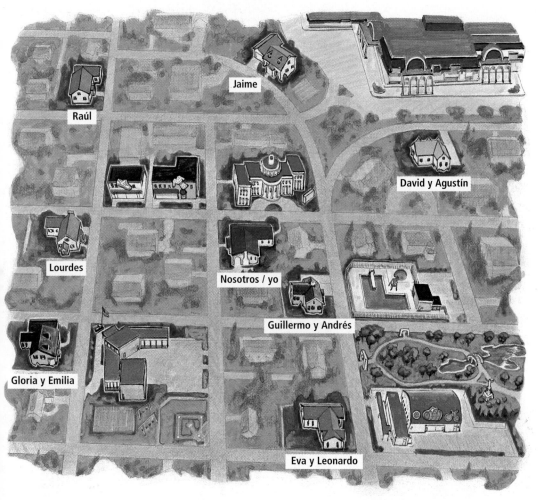

a. Gloria y Emilia
b. Uds.
c. Eva y Leonardo
d. Raúl
e. tú
f. Jaime
g. Lourdes
h. Guillermo y Andrés

Gramática en contexto   269

3 This exercise requires the contraction *del (de + el)*. Ask students to notice what happens to the definite article in the expression *cerca del centro comercial,* as contrasted with the expression *cerca de la escuela.*

ESTUDIANTE A
a. ¿Dónde viven Gloria y Emilia?
b. ...viven Uds.?
c. ...viven Eva y Leonardo?
d. ...vive Raúl?
e. ...vives tú?
f. ...vive Jaime?
g. ...vive Lourdes?
h. ...viven Guillermo y Andrés?

ESTUDIANTE B
Answers may vary depending on students' perception of distance.
a. Viven cerca de la escuela (lejos del centro comercial).
b. Vivimos cerca de (lejos de) ...
c. Viven cerca de (lejos de) ...
d. Vive cerca de (lejos de) ...
e. Vivo cerca de (lejos de) ...
f. Vive cerca de (lejos de) ...
g. Vive cerca de (lejos de) ...
h. Viven cerca de (lejos de) ...

 Practice Wkbk. 8-6

 Prueba 8-6

Present & Practice

Re-enter / Recycle
Ex. 4: activities from Chap. 1, expressing likes and preferences from Chap. 4, family and friends from Chap. 5
Ex. 5: activities from Chaps. 1 and 3, adjective agreement from Chaps. 1 and 4

Answers

4 ESTUDIANTE A
a. ¿Qué prefiere tu abuelo / abuela, ir de pesca o ver la tele(visión)?
b. ¿Qué prefiere tu papá / mamá, cocinar o lavar los platos?
c. ¿Qué prefieren tus hermanos(as) / amigos(as), tomar el sol o nadar?
d. ¿Qué prefieren tus primos / tíos, ir de compras o pasar la aspiradora?
e. ¿Qué prefiere tu profesor(a) / prefieren tus compañeros, ir a una fiesta o ir al cine?
f. ¿Qué prefiere tu amigo(a), leer o jugar videojuegos?

ESTUDIANTE B
Answers will vary.
a. Mi abuelo / abuela prefiere . . .
b. Mi papá / mamá prefiere . . .
c. Mis hermanos(as) / amigos(as) prefieren . . .
d. Mis primos / tíos prefieren . . .
e. Mi profesor(a) prefiere . . . / mis compañeros prefieren . . .
f. Mi amigo(a) prefiere . . .

El verbo *preferir*

Preferir "to prefer" is an *e → ie* stem-changing verb, similar to *querer* and *pensar*. Here are all its present-tense forms.

(yo)	prefiero	(nosotros) (nosotras)	preferimos
(tú)	prefieres	(vosotros) (vosotras)	preferís
Ud. (él) (ella)	prefiere	Uds. (ellos) (ellas)	prefieren

- Notice that the endings of *preferir* follow the pattern of regular *-ir* verbs, like *vivir*.

4 Con un(a) compañero(a), túrnate para preguntar y contestar *(asking and answering)* sobre las preferencias de estas personas. Escoge sólo una de las opciones para cada letra *(letter)*.

A —*¿Qué prefiere tu hermano, jugar fútbol o tenis?*
B —*Mi hermano prefiere jugar tenis.*

tu hermano / tu hermana

a. tu abuelo / tu abuela   b. tu papá / tu mamá   c. tus hermanos(as) / tus amigos(as)

d. tus primos / tus tíos   e. tu profesor(a) / tus compañeros   f. tu amigo / tu amiga

270   Capítulo 8

Options

Strategies for Reaching All Students

Spanish-Speaking Students
Ex. 4: Ask Spanish-speaking students: *¿En qué actividades prefieres participar en el verano? ¿Durante el año escolar?*

Students Needing Extra Help
El verbo preferir: Review stem-changing verbs from Chap. 7. Remind students that they practiced the *yo / tú* forms in Ex. 11 in the *Empecemos a conversar.* Using the Organizer, brainstorm examples of *preferir, querer,* and *pensar* + inf.
Ex. 5: Have students use their Organizers from Chap. 1.
Los adjetivos posesivos: Have students review their Chap. 5 Organizers with *mi, tu,* and *su.*

5 Di que las personas prefieren hacer estos pasatiempos y por qué.

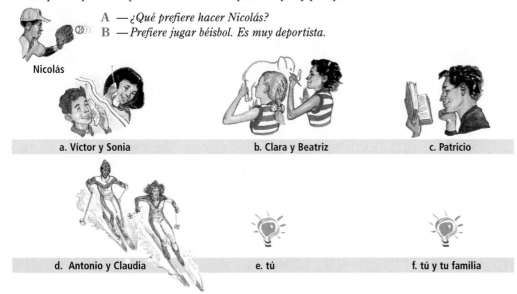

A — *¿Qué prefiere hacer Nicolás?*
B — *Prefiere jugar béisbol. Es muy deportista.*

Nicolás

a. Víctor y Sonia   b. Clara y Beatriz   c. Patricio

d. Antonio y Claudia   e. tú   f. tú y tu familia

Los adjetivos posesivos: *Su* y *nuestro*

You already know that when we want to tell what belongs to
someone and to show relationships, we can use *mi(s)*, *tu(s)*, and
su(s). Here are the other possessive adjectives.

nuestro primo	**nuestra** prima
nuestros primos	**nuestras** primas
*****vuestro** tío	**vuestra** tía
vuestros tíos	**vuestras** tías
su hermano	**su** hermana
sus hermanos	**sus** hermanas

Vuestro, -a, -os, -as is used mainly in Spain. We will use it occasionally and you
should learn to recognize it.

• Like other adjectives, the possessive adjectives agree in number
with the nouns that follow them. Only *nuestro* and *vuestro* have
different masculine and feminine endings.

Gramática en contexto   271

Practice

Re-enter / Recycle

Exs. 6–7: adjectives describing physical characteristics from Chap. 5, colors from Chap. 6

Answers

6 Remind students that they may describe their own home or someone else's. If an item does not apply to their family situation, they may respond *No tenemos* . . . .
a. Nuestra mesa (no) es de metal.
b. Nuestras sillas (no) son de madera.
c. Nuestros sillones (no) son antiguos.
d. Nuestro sofá (no) es de cuero.
e. Nuestro equipo de sonido (no) es moderno.
f. Nuestros cuadros (no) son bonitos.
g. Nuestro garaje (no) es para dos coches.
h. Nuestra sala de estar (no) es cómoda.
i. Statements will vary.

7 a.–i. Statements will vary. Make sure students use correct possessive adjective forms.

6 Describe parte de tu casa o de otra casa. Usa las palabras *(words)* de abajo *(below)*.

casa / azul
Nuestra casa (no) es azul.
dormitorios / grandes
Nuestros dormitorios (no) son grandes.

    a. mesa / de metal
    b. sillas / de madera
    c. sillones / antiguos
    d. sofá / de cuero
    e. equipo de sonido / moderno
    f. cuadros / bonitos
    g. garaje / para dos coches
    h. sala de estar / cómoda
    i. 💡

7 Intercambia *(exchange)* tu hoja del Ejercicio 6 con un(a) compañero(a). Usa esta información para describir su casa a otro(a) estudiante.

La casa de los Johnson es azul. Sus dormitorios son muy grandes.

Una casa típica en Ushuaia, Tierra del Fuego, Argentina

272

Options

Strategies for Reaching All Students

Students Needing Extra Help

Ex. 6: Show students that they will use *es* or *son*, depending on how many objects are discussed.
Ex. 7: Remind students that *su(s)* does not reflect gender. Give examples.

Ahora lo sabes

Can you:

■ tell where someone puts something?

—Generalmente (yo) ___ mis papeles en mi carpeta.

■ say what someone makes or does?

—Ana María y yo ___ las camas todos los días.

■ tell where a person lives?

—Mis abuelos ___ en Los Ángeles.

■ tell what someone prefers?

—Mis hermanos y yo ___ ir al cine el sábado.

■ describe possession using *su* and *nuestra?*

—___ mesa es redonda pero ___ mesa es cuadrada.

Answers: Ahora lo sabes
- pongo
- hacemos
- viven
- preferimos
- Su, nuestra

 Practice Wkbk. 8-8, 8-9

 Audio Activities 8.4, 8.5

 Writing Activity 8-F

 Prueba 8-8

 Comm. Act. BLM 8-2

Unas casas en La Boca, una zona de Buenos Aires

Una casa en Bolivia

Cultural Notes

(p. 272, photo)
This modest house is in the town of Ushuaia, on the Argentine side of Tierra del Fuego, the archipelago at the southernmost tip of South America. Formerly little more than an outpost, Ushuaia (population 35,000) is becoming an important industrial and tourist center, with housing construction growing at a rapid pace.

(p. 273, right photo)
The vivid colors of this house in the La Boca suburb of Buenos Aires fit in perfectly with the neighboring homes, all of which are painted in similar bright colors. This working-class neighborhood, known for its colorful, corrugated iron houses, is also home to many artists. In the early twentieth century, the Argentine painter, Benito Quinquela Martín, was a driving force behind La Boca's use of exterior home colors.

Apply

Using the Video
Video segment 3: See the Video
Teacher's Guide.

 Video Activity C

Para decir más

Aquí tienes vocabulario adicional que te puede ayudar para hacer las actividades de esta sección.

la mecedora
rocking chair

la alfombra
rug

la escalera
stairway

el pasillo
hallway

el balcón
balcony

el jardín
garden, yard

el patio
patio, yard

el garaje para dos coches
two-car garage

el tocadiscos de discos compacto
CD player

el walkman
personal stereo

274   Capítulo 8

Actividades

Esta sección te ofrece la oportunidad de aumentar tus conocimientos de español al integrar lo que aprendiste en este capítulo con lo que aprendiste en capítulos anteriores.

1 Usando el dibujo de la página 269, escoge una casa e imagina que vives allí. Tu compañero(a) va a adivinar *(guess)* dónde vives con preguntas como las siguientes.

¿Vives cerca o lejos del centro comercial?
¿Es amarilla tu casa?

2 ¿Qué prefieren hacer tu compañero(a) y sus amigos cuando hace frío o calor? Pregunta y contesta según *(according to)* el modelo y luego anota *(then note)* las actividades más populares.

A — *¿Qué prefieren hacer Uds. cuando hace fresco?*
B — *Preferimos practicar deportes.*

Options

Strategies for Reaching All Students

Spanish-Speaking Students
Ex. 3: Have Spanish-speaking students summarize : *Escucha bien lo que dicen en clase de los quehaceres. ¿Cuáles son los quehaceres más comunes para los estudiantes en tu clase? ¿Tienes tú estos mismos quehaceres u otros?*

Students Needing Extra Help
Ex. 1: Give students time to organize and formulate questions. Suggest that each pair formulate four or five questions.
Ex. 2: Review weather from Chap. 7. Have students use their Organizers from Chaps. 1, 3, and 7.
Ex. 3: Have students use their Organizers. Do a complete model and review *también* and *tampoco*. Keep track of the information on a chart for reporting purposes.

Enrichment
Ex. 3: As a homework assignment, students can tell which family member does which household chore, how often or when, and whether or not that person likes doing the chore.

3 Con un(a) compañero(a), haz *(make)* una lista de algunos quehaceres. Pregunta y contesta cuáles Uds. tienen que hacer.

A — ¿*Tienes que* . . . ?

B — *Sí. ¿Y tú?*

    o: *No. ¿Y tú?*

A — *Yo también.*

    o: *Yo no.*

    o: *Yo tampoco.*

Luego haz un informe *(report)* para la clase.

A — *Yo tengo que* . . . , *pero Mateo no.*

    o: *Mateo y yo tenemos que* . . .

    o: *Ni Mateo ni yo tenemos que* . . .

Tus compañeros van a preguntar qué quehaceres prefieren Uds.

Clase — ¿*Prefieres (Prefieren)* . . . *o* . . . ?

A o B — *Prefiero (Preferimos)* . . .

4 Con un(a) compañero(a) inventa este diálogo:

• pregunta si tu compañero(a) quiere hacer algo

• él (ella) no puede y explica *(explains)* lo que *(what)* tiene que hacer en casa

• tú tienes que sugerir *(suggest)* otro plan

• tu compañero(a) dice si está de acuerdo o no

Re-enter / Recycle

Ex. 1: places and buildings from Chaps. 3, 6, and 7

Ex. 2: activities from Chaps. 1, 3, and 7; expressing likes and preferences from Chap. 4; weather expressions from Chap. 7.

Ex. 3: *también, tampoco, ni . . . ni* from Chap. 1

Answers: Actividades

1 Questions will vary.

2 ESTUDIANTE A

Questions may include: ¿*Qué prefieren hacer Uds. cuando . . . hace sol / hace calor / hace frío / hace fresco / hace viento / llueve / nieva?*

ESTUDIANTE B

Answers will vary depending on *Estudiante B*'s preferences.

3 Lists of chores will vary. Make sure students use correct verb forms when reporting to the class.

4 Answers will vary, but encourage students to use chapter vocabulary. Look for use of *tener que* + inf.

 Writing Activities 8-G, 8-H

 Comm. Act. BLMs 8-3, 8-4, 8-5

Cooperative Learning

Divide the class into groups of three or four students. Tell them that as owners of an apartment building, they are responsible for the upkeep and maintenance, with a budget of $199 per day. On the chalkboard, list the prices charged by a maintenance or cleaning company. For example: *cortar el césped:* *$35; limpiar el baño: $20; lavar el piso: $20; limpiar las ventanas: $10 por ventana; limpiar la estufa: $35,* etc. They must decide what the company will do and what they themselves will do: *Yo prefiero no limpiar las ventanas; tengo que cortar el césped.* Have students keep a tally and then present it to the class.

Apply

Process Reading
For a description of process reading, see p. 48.

Answers
Antes de leer
Answers will vary.

Mira la lectura
Answers will vary.

Todo junto

¡Vamos a leer!

Antes de leer

STRATEGY ➤ Using prior knowledge

Remember the story of Cinderella? Did you ever wonder what it would be like to be in her shoes? In this reading, a young man is about to find out. Use the pictures and what you know about Cinderella to predict what this reading might be about.

Mira la lectura

STRATEGY ➤ Skimming

Skim through the story. Is it what you expected?

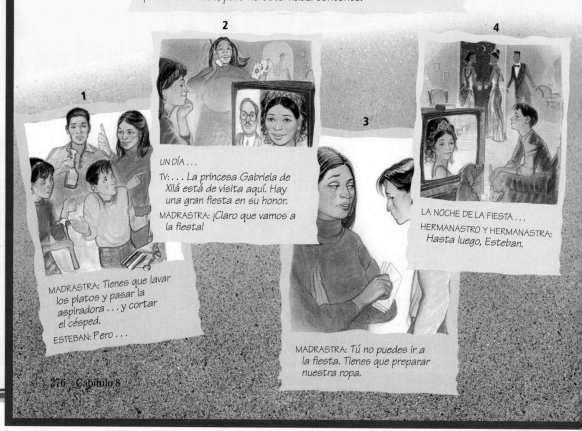

Esteban es un muchacho de 18 años. Vive en una casa más o menos grande con su padre, su madrastra y un hermanastro y una hermanastra. Pero su padre está frecuentemente fuera del país. ¿Y quién hace todos los quehaceres de la casa? Esteban, ¡claro! Los hace, pero no está nada contento.

MADRASTRA: Tienes que lavar los platos y pasar la aspiradora . . . y cortar el césped.
ESTEBAN: Pero . . .

UN DÍA . . .
TV: . . . La princesa Gabriela de Xilá está de visita aquí. Hay una gran fiesta en su honor.
MADRASTRA: ¡Claro que vamos a la fiesta!

MADRASTRA: Tú no puedes ir a la fiesta. Tienes que preparar nuestra ropa.

LA NOCHE DE LA FIESTA . . .
HERMANASTRO Y HERMANASTRA: Hasta luego, Esteban.

276 Capítulo 8

Options

Strategies for Reaching All Students

Spanish-Speaking Students
Have Spanish-speaking students rewrite the last four panels of the story.

 Un paso más Ex. 8-H

Students Needing Extra Help
Antes de leer: Ask for a volunteer to summarize the Cinderella story.
Infórmate 1: Be aware of students' sensitivity to family issues.
Infórmate 2: Review the term "turning point."

Enrichment
Explain that *Xilá* is a Nahuatl word that is actually the name of a princess in a Nicaraguan legend.
Aplicación: Have students work in pairs and propose a different solution to Esteban's situation. Ask: Instead of having the fairy godmother appear, what would you suggest Esteban do? How would you end the story?

Infórmate

STRATEGIES▶ Using prior knowledge
Recognizing word families

Often you can use Spanish words you know to figure out the meaning of new words. For example: *madrastra, hermanastra,* and *hermanastro.* What names for family members do you recognize as parts of these words? Then think about the characters in Cinderella. Use this information to figure out the meaning of the three words. What do you think *madrina* means?

1 Compare the story with Cinderella. How are they alike and how are they different?

2 What is the turning point in the story? What happens?

3 Do you agree with the way the story ends? Why or why not?

Aplicación

What do you think *padrastro* means?

6

Pero ¿quién es?
¡Qué guapo!
¡Debe ser un príncipe! ¡Mira los zapatos de vidrio!

5

MADRINA: Hola, Esteban. Soy la madrina de la Cenicienta. Y tú también vas a ir a la fiesta. A ver, ¿dónde están tu perro y la aspiradora? Los voy a convertir en un chófer y una limosina.

7

HERMANASTRA: Mamá . . . ¡Es Esteban!
HERMANASTRO: Pero ¿qué hace aquí?
MADRASTRA: No sé, hijo . . .

8

UNA SEMANA MÁS TARDE . . .
ESTEBAN: Voy a ser el asistente personal de la princesa. Y ¡no voy a hacer nunca más los quehaceres!

¡Vamos a leer! 277

Infórmate

madre, hermana, and *hermano* / stepmother, stepsister, and stepbrother / godmother

1 Answers will vary, but similarities may include the stepmother and the glass shoes. Differences may include the father and stepbrother; a dog and vacuum cleaner (instead of mice and a pumpkin); and Esteban as the personal assistant at the end of the story.

2 The fairy godmother appears to change Esteban's life. He goes to the party and eventually becomes the personal assistant to the princess.

3 Answers will vary.

Aplicación
Students should be able to figure out the meaning (stepfather) from *padre.*

Apply

Process Writing

For information regarding developing a writing portfolio, see p. 50.

Multicultural Perspectives

Mud is used to keep houses looking new and clean in some countries in Central America. The color of the soil used varies from region to region. In some areas it is gray; in others, peach-colored or white. The soil is mixed with water to form a paste and then applied to the walls to make them smooth and new. Ask students what they and their family members do for home maintenance and upkeep.

Using Photos

Ask: *Describe las casas en las fotos. ¿Te gustaría vivir en una de estas casas? ¿Por qué o por qué no?*

Todo junto

¡Vamos a escribir!

Everyone can picture an ideal home—the perfect dream house. How would you describe your dream house? Write an ad in Spanish for a dream house for sale.

1 First, think about the house plan and list the rooms. Is it a one- or two-story house? Name three or four special features.

2 Then write at least five sentences describing the house as if you were trying to sell it. You can start with the phrase *Se vende casa* (House for sale).

3 Show your description to a partner. Then revise and edit it. Recopy your corrected description. You might want to add a sketch of the floor plan with the rooms labeled.

4 Now you are ready to share your work. You can:
- collect all the ads into a book called *Se venden casas* and exchange books with another class
- display the ads on a bulletin board for each student to choose the house he or she would like to buy
- keep your ad in your writing portfolio

Casa moderna en Los Ángeles

278 Capítulo 8

Options

Strategies for Reaching All Students

Students Needing Extra Help
Step 1: Students may not be familiar with the term "special features"; give them some examples.
Step 2: Have students use their Organizers, emphasizing adjectives. Brainstorm and model some sentences. You may wish to use real newspaper ads as a possible source.

Enrichment
Step 2: To give students ideas about sales pitches, bring in real estate magazines or newspaper sections in English and study the language used in them. The properties are often described as having qualities that go well with buyers' personalities, or as themselves having "personalities." Encourage students to write their ads along these lines (as well as listing house size, location, and price).

Follow-up activity: If students choose a house they would like to buy, have them state the reasons. This can then become another speaking or writing activity.

En la zona de Chapultepec,
Ciudad de México

Una casa al estilo
de Gaudí en
Los Ángeles

Cultural Notes 🌀

(p. 278, photo)
House in Los Angeles, California. The territorial limits of Nueva España included a large part of the U.S. west and southwest. For this reason, many homes in the area were built, and continue to be built, in the Spanish style. Stucco walls, tile roofs, long front balconies, and arched doorways are very typical.

(p. 279, top photo)
This sprawling, luxurious house is in one of Mexico City's wealthiest residential areas, Las Lomas de Chapultepec. The stucco walls, tiled roof, arches, and grillwork are all in the traditional Spanish style. Within the walls of most of the homes in this neighborhood are such amenities as pools, tennis courts, and elaborate gardens.

(p. 279, bottom photo)
House in Los Angeles, California, built in the Gaudí style. The Spanish architect, Antonio Gaudí y Cornet (1852–1926), is famous for his unique style, which blends elements of Gothic art and *art nouveau* to produce an undulating, flowing form. Gaudí spent most of his adult life in Barcelona, building residences for rich patrons and, most importantly, la Iglesia de la Sagrada Familia, which was left unfinished after his death.

Assess & Summarize

Test Preparation

You may want to assign parts of this section as written homework or as an in-class writing activity prior to administering the *Examen de habilidades*.

Answers

Listening: *Sí, puedes ir al cine con tu amiga, pero primero tienes que limpiar el refrigerador, sacar la basura, sacudir los muebles, lavar los platos y arreglar tu cuarto.* Answers will vary, but students should choose from among these chores to help Marina: clean the refrigerator, take out the garbage, dust the furniture, wash the dishes, and pick up her room. Answers will vary for the time it takes to perform two of the chores. When they finish, they'll go to the movies.

Reading: Answers will vary.

Writing: Writing samples will vary, but students should use chapter vocabulary.

Culture: Answers will vary. Students should make reference to the *Perspectiva cultural:* In Sevilla, a patio is more like a garden or courtyard in the middle of the house. In Madrid, it is an air shaft in an apartment building. Both let air and light in and offer a space for people to talk.

¿Lo sabes bien?

This section will help you organize your studying for the proficiency test, where you will be asked to do similar, though not identical, tasks. There will not be any models on the test.

Listening

Can you understand when people talk about their household chores? Listen as your teacher reads a sample similar to what you will hear on the test. This is a note from Marina's mother explaining what Marina has to do on Saturday. What could you do to help Marina? How long do you think it would take you to do two of these chores? What are you going to do when you finish?

Reading

Can you understand a description of a dream house? Read the text that follows. Do you agree with some of the things María Elena wants?

"Quiero tener una casa no muy grande y amueblarla con cosas que me gustan— prácticas pero bonitas. Y me gusta vivir cómodamente. Quiero un equipo de sonido, una videocasetera, una piscina, una cancha de tenis, . . . ¡y otra persona para hacer todos los quehaceres!"

Writing

Can you write a letter to a friend describing the new house or apartment you've just moved into? Here is a sample:

> Querido Ernesto:
>
> Vivo con mi madre en un apartamento de Manhattan. Tenemos dos dormitorios, un baño, una cocina y una sala. Nuestro apartamento es pequeño, pero tenemos muchos muebles. En la sala hay una mesa con ocho sillas, un sofá con dos sillones, tres mesitas, un escritorio, tres lámparas, diez cuadros y dos espejos. Menos mal que en mi cuarto no hay muchas cosas. Tengo sólo una cama y una cómoda. Me gusta donde vivo, pero quisiera tener una casa más grande.
>
> Tu amiga,
> Magdalena

Culture

Can you describe a patio in Sevilla and in Madrid and its uses?

Speaking

Can you talk about household chores? Create a dialogue with your partner. Do you and your friend like and dislike the same chores? Here is a sample dialogue:

A —*¿Tienes quehaceres de la casa para el sábado?*
B —*Sí. Por la mañana tengo que cortar el césped, lavar los platos y sacar la basura.*
A —*A mí no me gusta ni sacar la basura ni limpiar el baño, pero lo hago todos los sábados. Prefiero hacer las camas.*

Options

Strategies for Reaching All Students

Students Needing Extra Help
Listening: Model the answers to the questions.
Writing: Have students practice writing another letter. Tell them what you will be expecting from them in this exercise.
Culture: Review the *Perspectiva cultural.*
Speaking: Be sure that responses are appropriate to the questions. In both this and the writing section, give students time to prepare. You may want to give them the assignment in advance.

Resumen del capítulo 8

Use the vocabulary from this chapter to help you:

- tell where you live
- describe your home
- name household chores

to talk about where someone lives
cerca (de)
lejos (de)
vivir: (yo) vivo
     (tú) vives

to talk about houses or apartments
el apartamento
el baño
la casa (de ... pisos)
el césped
la cocina
el comedor
el cuarto
el dormitorio
el garaje
el lavadero
el (primer) piso
la sala
la sala de estar
el sótano

to name household items
la cama
el cartel
el coche
la cómoda
las cosas
el cuadro
el equipo de sonido
el escritorio
el espejo

la estufa
el guardarropa
la lámpara
los muebles
la puerta
el refrigerador
la silla
el sillón, *pl.* los sillones
el sofá *(m.)*
la ventana
la videocasetera

to describe household items
antiguo, -a
bastante
cómodo, -a
cuadrado, -a
de cuero
de madera
de metal
incómodo, -a
limpio, -a
moderno, -a
redondo, -a
sucio, -a

to indicate possession
nuestro, -a
su, -s (here: *their*)

to name chores around a home
arreglar
cortar (el césped)

hacer: (yo) hago
    (tú) haces
hacer la cama
lavar la ropa / los platos
limpiar el baño
pasar la aspiradora
poner: (yo) pongo
    (tú) pones
poner / quitar la mesa
el quehacer (de la casa)
sacar la basura
sacudir los muebles

to indicate preferences
preferir (e → ie)

to indicate obligation
tener que + *inf.*

to indicate that someone is right or wrong
(no) tener razón

to indicate whether you agree with someone or something
(no) estar de acuerdo

other useful expressions
más (here: *else*)

Resumen   281

CAPÍTULO 9
THEME: HEALTH

SCOPE AND SEQUENCE   Pages 282–311

COMMUNICATION

Topics

Parts of the body

Health

Physical sensations

Objectives

To talk about health and health practices in the Spanish-speaking world

To name parts of the body

To ask or describe how someone is feeling

To name ways to maintain good health

To name medical professions

To indicate how long something has been going on

To express and ask for an opinion

To name places to go or things to do when you are sick

CULTURE

Health and health practices

GRAMMAR

El verbo dormir

El complemento indirecto: Los pronombres me, te, le

La expresión hace . . . que

La sustantivación de adjetivos

Ancillaries available for use with Chapter 9

Multisensory/Technology

 Overhead Transparencies, 46–50

 Audio Tapes and CDs

 Vocabulary Art Blackline Masters for Hands-On Learning, pp. 48–52

 Classroom Crossword

 Video

 CD-ROM

Print

 Practice Workbook, pp. 94–103

 Writing, Audio & Video Activities, pp. 53–58, 117–119, 168–169

 Communicative Activity Blackline Masters

Pair and Small Group Activities, pp. 64–69

Situation Cards, p. 70

 Un paso más: Actividades para ampliar tu español, pp. 50–55

Assessment

 Assessment Program

Pruebas, pp. 127–137

Examen de habilidades, pp. 138–141

 Test Generator

Video still from Chap. 9

Health-Care Practices

Mexico addresses the medical needs of its rural populations through a compulsory service program for medical students. Upon completion of medical school, interns and residents must work for at least one year in the Instituto Mexicano de Seguro Social (IMSS) clinics in rural areas. Local clinics have a permanent nursing staff in addition to the medical residents. These clinics often have three or four beds for women in labor or for the very ill. In addition, the IMSS system has a network of hospitals that support the clinics. Ambulances are available to transport people needing hospitalization from outlying clinics to hospitals in larger towns.

Latin American doctors are more likely to practice from offices in their homes. Health care can thus have a less institutionalized feeling. Physicians throughout Latin America, especially in smaller cities and towns, may still make house calls.

Pharmacies are another important component of the health-care system. They are often small, family-run businesses rather than large chain stores. When walking into a typical large pharmacy in the U.S., the consumer is presented with aisle upon aisle of colorfully packaged products. In contrast, a traditional *farmacia* will usually not carry the many items we are accustomed to seeing. The only products available at a *farmacia* are medicinal drugs and specific health-care related items. In a family-run pharmacy, the owner often greets customers at the door. Customers may purchase a single bandage or a single dose of a medicine. Prepackaged quantities are not as common as in the U.S.

Pharmacists play an important role in health care because they are legally able to dispense many medications that are only available through a doctor's prescription in the U.S. Thus, customers often rely on the pharmacist's medical expertise to recommend treatments and medications when they are unable to visit a doctor or do not feel that such a visit is necessary.

In addition to traditional Western medicine, *yerberos* are sometimes consulted for health problems. These folk healers use the medicinal qualities of plants for healing. *Curanderos* are also healers who treat both physical and spiritual ailments. Herb shops called *yerberías* or *botánicas* sell a variety of products for both physical and spiritual healing.

Introduce

Re-entry of Concepts

The following list represents words, expressions, and grammar topics re-entered from *El primer paso* to Chap. 7.

El primer paso
Numbers 0–31
Calendar expressions

Chapter 1
Activities
Gustar expressions
Adjective agreement

Chapter 3
Activities
Places and buildings

Chapter 4
Foods

Chapter 6
Colors
Clothes
Direct object pronouns
Places and buildings

Chapter 7
Activities
Places and buildings

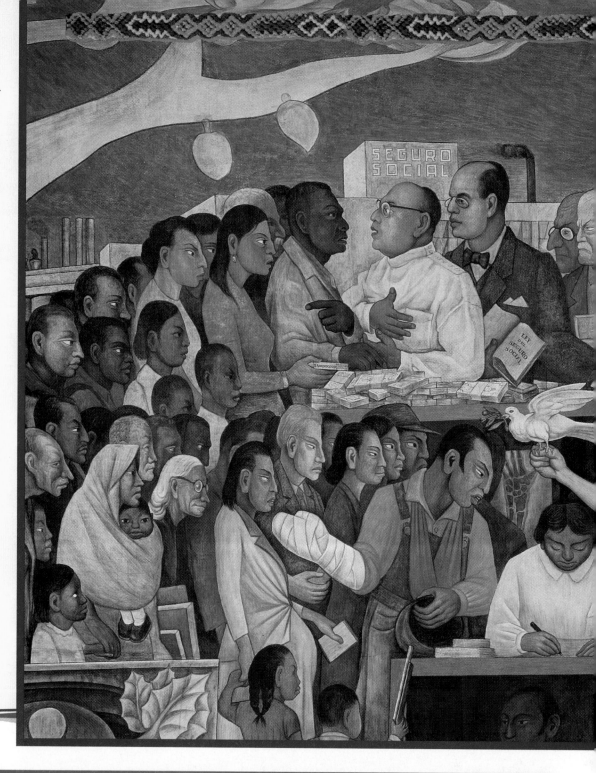

Planning

Cross-Curricular Connections

Art / Language Arts Connection (pp. 286–287)
Have each student secretly choose a well-known character or famous personality, write the person's name on a sheet of paper, and give it to you. For homework, each student prepares a drawing of the person chosen. On the bottom of the paper, they should write a short physical description and personality profile. To prepare for the next day, make copies of a list of all the names in alphabetical order with a blank next to each name. At the beginning of class, have students display the pictures and number them. Each student is then given a copy of the list and tries to match the names and numbers.

Health Connection (p. 308)
In small groups or pairs, have students prepare a poster advertising a new health product. Students should create a name, give a price, and a write a list that describes what the product does.

CAPÍTULO 9

¿Cómo te sientes?

OBJECTIVES

At the end of this chapter, you will be able to:

■ describe how you are feeling

■ tell what parts of your body hurt

■ suggest things you or others can do to feel better

■ discuss attitudes toward health and health practices in the Spanish-speaking world

La medicina antigua y la moderna (1953), Diego Rivera

283

Cultural Objective
• To talk about health and health practices

¿Cómo te sientes?

Play

 Video Activity A

Using the Video
This chapter's video focuses on health. Students will accompany one of our hosts in Madrid to the doctor's office and then to a class in flamenco dance.

To prepare students for the video, first ask them to predict what this chapter's tape will be about. Then have students watch the segment several times. After the first time, you may wish to have them brainstorm possible vocabulary and expressions they will need to talk about what they saw on the video. Ask students to identify: a) things they saw that were familiar to them, and b) things they saw that they probably would not see where they live.

Video segment 1: For more teaching suggestions, see the Video Teacher's Guide.

¡Piénsalo bien!

Look at the pictures and read the captions.

"Me duele la garganta. ¿Qué puedo tomar?"

In the photo, what do you think this person is saying to the pharmacist?

En una farmacia en Chile

"Pero mamá, no me gusta ir al médico."

What do you think a *Centro Pediátrico* is? What are the specialties of the doctors in this medical center?

Clínica del Centro Pediátrico de Isla Verde, Puerto Rico

284 Capítulo 9

Options

Strategies for Reaching All Students

Spanish-Speaking Students
Ask Spanish-speaking students to describe the photos in the chapter introduction.
In addition, ask: *¿Qué haces tú cuando no te sientes bien?*

Students Needing Extra Help
Discuss some of the terminology we use to discuss health: fever, headache, and so on.

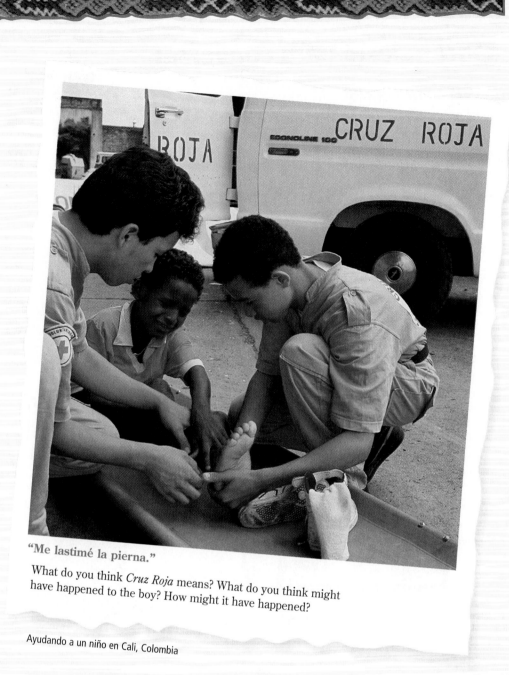

"Me lastimé la pierna."

What do you think *Cruz Roja* means? What do you think might have happened to the boy? How might it have happened?

Ayudando a un niño en Cali, Colombia

285

285

Critical Thinking: Synthesizing

Students probably have already had experience filling out medical profile forms. Ask: What type of information is usually asked for? (name, age, past illnesses, types of exercises / sports that are played, etc.) Based partly on student responses, devise a simple profile form in Spanish for students to fill out using known vocabulary.

Answers: ¡Piénsalo bien!

(p. 284, top photo) Have students brainstorm to figure out the meaning of the photo caption. If they need help, preview the vocabulary on pp. 286–287.

(p. 284, bottom photo) Students should be able to figure out the meaning: Pediatric Center. / *psicólogo:* psychologist (psychology), *pediatría:* pediatrics, *especialista de los pies:* foot specialist (podiatry), *psiquiatra:* psychiatrist (psychiatry), *patóloga del habla lenguaje:* speech pathologist (speech pathology).

(p. 285, photo) Since students already know *rojo(a)*, they should be able to guess the meaning: Red Cross. / The boy seems to have hurt his leg or foot. / Answers will vary.

Cultural Notes

(p. 284, top photo)
Self-service drugstores and large drugstore chains are not as common in Spain and Latin America as they are in the U.S. The customer must ask the pharmacist for most items, even common over-the-counter ones such as aspirin or cough syrup. The pharmacist in Spanish-speaking countries also plays more of a medical practitioner role, offering advice on ailments and their remedies that usually would be given by physicians or nurses in the U.S.

Present

Chapter Theme
Parts of the body and health

Communicative Objectives
- To name parts of the body
- To ask or describe how someone is feeling
- To name ways to maintain good health
- To name medical professions
- To indicate how long something has been going on
- To express and ask for an opinion
- To name places to go or things to do when you are sick

 Transparencies 46–47

 Vocabulary Art BLMs

 Pronunciation Tape 9-1

 Vocabulario para conversar A

Play

Using the Video
Video segment 2: See the Video Teacher's Guide.

 Video Activity B

Vocabulario para conversar

¡Ay! ¡Me duele el pie!

Aquí tienes palabras y expresiones necesarias para hablar sobre las partes del cuerpo que te duelen y para sugerir *(suggest)* qué puedes hacer para sentirte mejor. Léelas varias veces y practícalas con un(a) compañero(a) en las páginas siguientes.

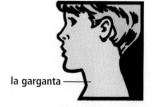

El cuerpo

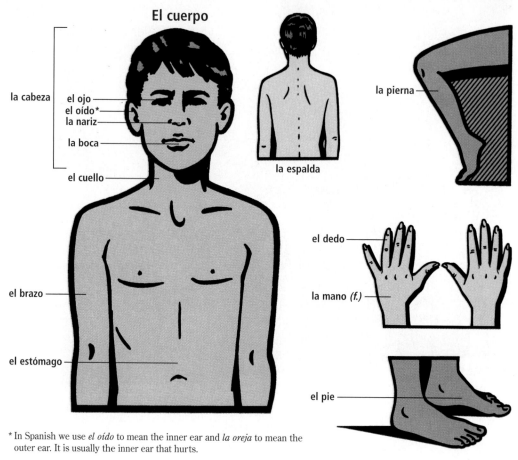

la garganta

la pierna

la cabeza
el ojo
el oído*
la nariz
la boca
el cuello
el brazo
el estómago

la espalda

el dedo
la mano *(f.)*
el pie

* In Spanish we use *el oído* to mean the inner ear and *la oreja* to mean the outer ear. It is usually the inner ear that hurts.

286   Capítulo 9

Options

Strategies for Reaching All Students

Spanish-Speaking Students

 Un paso más Exs. 9-A, 9-B, 9-C, 9-D

Students Needing Extra Help
Have students start their Organizers. Emphasize the difference between *médico(a)* and *doctor(a)*.
Show the connection between *doler, el dolor,* and *duele(n).*
If necessary, tell students that *hace* + time expression + *que* will be explained in the grammar section.

Emphasize the second footnote on p. 287. Since students hear "my," "your," etc. in the translation, they will be tempted to use *mi, tu,* etc. They will probably need frequent reminders.

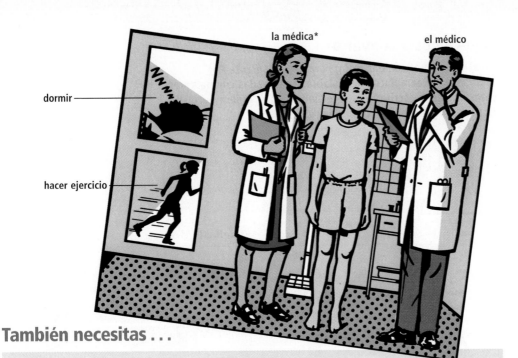

la médica*
el médico
dormir
hacer ejercicio

También necesitas . . .

¡Ay!	*Ouch!*
Me siento bien / mal.	*I feel well / ill.*
¿Qué pasa?	*What's the matter?*
doler (o → ue)	*to hurt, to ache*
¿Qué te duele?	*Where does it hurt?*
†(A mí / ti) me / te duele(n) ___.	*My / your ___ hurts (hurt).*
(No me duele) nada.	*Nothing (hurts me).*
derecho, -a	*right*
izquierdo, -a	*left*
¿Cuánto (tiempo) hace que ___?	*How long has it been since ___? /*
	(For) how long ___?
Hace + *time expression* + que ___.	*It's been + time expression + since ___. /*
	___ for + time expression
(Yo) creo que ___.	*I think that ___.*
Debes quedarte en la cama.	*You should stay in bed.*
llamar	*here: to call*

> **¿Y qué quiere decir . . . ?**
> el dedo del pie
> el dolor

* To refer to or address a physician, we use the term *doctor(a)*.
  —*Doctor, me duele mucho la cabeza.*

† With expressions like *me / te duele(n)*, we usually use the definite article when talking about body parts: *Me duele **el** brazo.*

Vocabulario para conversar   287

Grammar Preview
Use of *me / te* with *doler* and the expression *hace . . . que* are presented lexically. Their explanation appears in the grammar section.

Teaching Suggestions
Preparing students to speak: Use one or two options from each of the categories of Comprehensible Input, Physical Response, or Limited Verbal Response. For a complete explanation of these categories and some sample activities, see the front section of this Teacher's Edition.

Bring in one or more children's dolls for teaching the vocabulary in this section. In advance, prepare stick-on labels with the names of the parts of the body taught in this chapter.

Class Starter Review
On the day following initial presentation, you might begin the class with this activity:
Play *Simón dice* with you leading the class. Ask students to point to various parts of the body. Have students play the role of Simón on subsequent days.

Learning Spanish Through Action
STAGING VOCABULARY: *Dibujen*
MATERIALS: large sheets of plain paper; colored pencils or markers
DIRECTIONS: Tell students that they are going to draw an extraterrestrial. Describe an alien creature using vocabulary for various parts of the body, colors, and sizes. (As an option, have individuals go to the chalkboard and draw one part of the body. Continue until you have completed the whole creature.)

Practice & Apply

Re-enter / Recycle
Ex. 3: calendar expressions from *El primer paso*
Ex. 6: activities from Chaps. 1, 3, and 7

Grammar Preview
Ex. 4 previews nominalization of adjectives. The explanation of this grammar point is on p. 302.

Answers: Empecemos a conversar

1 ESTUDIANTE A
a. ¿Qué pasa? ¿Te duele el pie?
b. ...¿Te duele el brazo?
c. ...¿Te duele la pierna?
d. ...¿Te duele la garganta?

ESTUDIANTE B
a.–d. No, me duele(n) .... *(Endings will vary, but may include:* las manos, los dedos, los pies, el cuello.*)*

2 ESTUDIANTE A
a. Hoy no puedo hacer ejercicio. Me siento mal; me duele la cabeza.
b. ... la espalda.
c. ... la garganta.
d. ... el estómago.
e. ... el cuello.

ESTUDIANTE B
a.–e. Creo que debes ....
(Endings will vary. Remind students to transpose no *before* debes *in the fourth and fifth possible response for* Estudiante B.*)*

Empecemos a conversar

Túrnate con un(a) compañero(a) para ser *Estudiante A* y *Estudiante B*. Reemplacen las palabras subrayadas con palabras representadas o escritas en los recuadros. 💡 quiere decir que puedes escoger *(choose)* tu propia respuesta.

1
A — ¿Qué pasa? ¿Te duele <u>la cabeza</u>?
B — No, me duelen <u>los ojos</u>.
  o: *No, no me duele nada. Me siento bien.*
  Y ahora Uds.

Estudiante A   Estudiante B

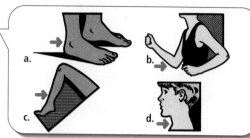   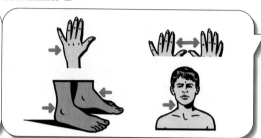

2
A — *Hoy no puedo hacer ejercicio. Me siento mal; me duele <u>el oído</u>.*
B — *Creo que debes <u>llamar al médico</u>.*
  Y ahora Uds.

Estudiante A   Estudiante B

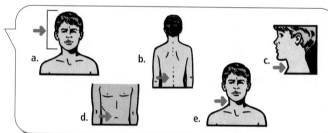

descansar
dormir
llamar al médico
no hacer ejercicio
no practicar deportes
quedarte en la cama

Options

Strategies for Reaching All Students

Spanish-Speaking Students
Ex. 5: Ask: *¿Qué debes hacer si estás enfermo(a) y no puedes ir a la escuela? Menciona tres cosas.*

 Un paso más Ex. 9-E

Students Needing Extra Help
Ex. 1: Allow students to use the second response with *nada* only once.
Ex. 2: Encourage *Estudiante B* to use all the responses, not just one.
Ex. 6: Have students use their Organizers.
Ex. 7: Be specific if students have difficulty answering. Ask questions such as: *¿Te duele el brazo?* Have students refer back to Ex. 1.

Enrichment
Ex. 2: To vary this dialogue, have pairs of students take turns telling each other what other activities they can't do because a certain part of their body hurts. Students should give each other advice on how to get rid of the pain. For example: *No puedo leer. Me duelen los ojos. (Debes dormir) / No puedo hablar. Me duele la garganta. (Debes ir al médico.)*
Ex. 4: As a homework assignment, ask students to create a dialogue between two

3 A —¿*Cuánto tiempo hace que te duele la espalda?*
    B —*Hace una semana que me duele.*

      Y ahora Uds.

Estudiante A   Estudiante B

4 A —¿*Qué pasa? ¿Te duele el oído?*
    B —*Sí, el derecho.*
        o: *No, no me duele.*

      Y ahora Uds.

Estudiante A   Estudiante B

Empecemos a escribir

Escribe tus respuestas en español.

5 Dale *(give him / her)* dos consejos *(pieces of advice)* a un(a) amigo(a) que tiene dolor de garganta.

6 ¿Qué te duele cuando . . .

participas en un maratón? *Me duelen los pies.*

   a. estudias toda la noche para un examen?
   b. comes demasiado?
   c. lanzas la pelota *(pitch)* en un partido de béisbol?
   d. animas *(cheer)* mucho en un partido de básquetbol?
   e. tocas el piano por tres horas?

7 ¿Te duele algo? ¿Qué?

3 ESTUDIANTE A
¿Cuánto tiempo hace que te duele(n) . . .? *(Questions will vary. Look for correct verb agreement.)*
ESTUDIANTE B
Hace . . . que me duele(n). *(Answers will vary. Make sure students say* hace, *even with plural time periods:* Hace dos días . . . .)

4 ESTUDIANTE A
¿Qué pasa? ¿Te duele . . .? *(Questions will vary.)*
ESTUDIANTE B
Sí, ... (No, no me duele.) *(Answers will vary, but see if students correctly omit the noun in their responses.)*

Answers: Empecemos a escribir

5–7 Answers will vary. Possible responses for Ex. 6:
a. Me duele(n) la cabeza (los ojos).
b. Me duele el estómago.
c. Me duele el brazo.
d. Me duele la garganta.
e. Me duelen los dedos (las manos).

 Practice Wkbk. 9-1, 9-2

 Audio Activity 9.1

 Writing Activities 9-A, 9-B

 Pruebas 9-1, 9-2

 Comm. Act. BLM 9-1

hypochondriacs in a doctor's waiting room who are asking each other what hurts and vying with one another to be the sicker one. The dialogue can progress from the more or less normal inquiries and responses to exaggerations. Encourage students to be creative and to use as much of their vocabulary as possible. For example: *¿Qué te duele? Me duele la mano. / Pues a mí me duele el brazo. / ¡Pues a mí me duelen los dos brazos!*

Present

Chapter Theme
Health

Communicative Objectives
- To ask or describe how someone is feeling
- To name medical professions
- To indicate how long something has been going on
- To express and ask for an opinion
- To name places to go or things to do when you are sick

 Transparencies 48–49

 Vocabulary Art BLMs

 Pronunciation Tape 9-2

 Vocabulario para conversar B

Play

Using the Video
Video segment 2: See the Video Teacher's Guide.

 Video Activity B

Vocabulario para conversar

¿Qué tienes?

Aquí tienes el resto del vocabulario necesario para describir cómo te sientes.

La enfermería

Tengo dolor de cabeza.

Tengo dolor de garganta.

Tengo dolor de oído.

Tengo dolor de muelas.

Tengo dolor de estómago.

290   Capítulo 9

Options

Strategies for Reaching All Students

Spanish-Speaking Students

 Un paso más Ex. 9-F

Students Needing Extra Help
También necesitas . . . : Practice *me lastimé* with other parts of the body.

Learning Spanish Through Action
STAGING VOCABULARY: *Finjan que tienen . . . .*
MATERIALS: none
DIRECTIONS: Ask students to act out ailments or illnesses from this vocabulary section. For example: *Finjan que tienen un resfriado.*

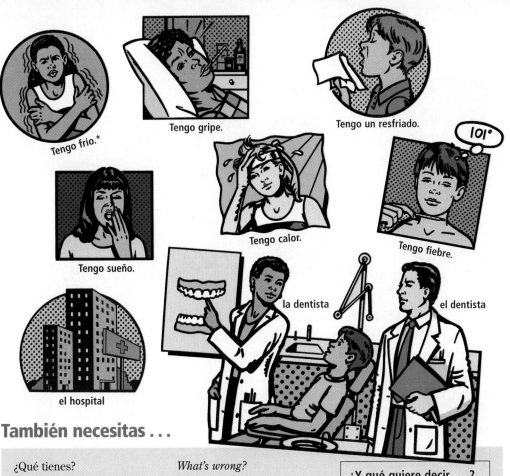

Tengo frío.*

Tengo gripe.

Tengo un resfriado.

Tengo sueño.

Tengo calor.

Tengo fiebre.

101°

la dentista

el dentista

el hospital

También necesitas . . .

¿Qué tienes?	*What's wrong?*
(Yo) me lastimé (la pierna).	*I hurt my (leg).*
¿Cómo te sientes?	*How do you feel?*
mejor	*better*
peor	*worse*
Debo quedarme en la cama.	*I should stay in bed.*
tomar	here: *to take*
ahora	*now*
todavía	*still*
ya no	*no longer, not anymore*
¿no?	*don't you? aren't I . . .*

> ¿Y qué quiere decir . . . ?
> la clínica
> la fiebre
> terrible

* If we want to say "very," we use *mucho* with *sueño, frío,* and *calor,* but *mucha* with *hambre* and *sed: Tengo mucho sueño,* but *Tengo mucha sed.*

Teaching Suggestions
Preparing students to speak: Use one or two options from each of the categories of Comprehensible Input, Physical Response, or Limited Verbal Response. For a complete explanation of these categories and some sample activities, see the front section of this Teacher's Edition.

Class Starter Review
On the day following initial presentation, you might begin the class with this activity:
Ask students: *¿Cómo te sientes hoy? (¿Qué tienes?) ¿Tienes dolor de . . . ?* etc. Then have them turn to a partner and ask how he or she is feeling today.

Practice & Apply

Re-enter / Recycle

Ex. 10: activities from Chaps. 1, 3, and 7

Answers: Empecemos a conversar

8 ESTUDIANTE A

a. ¿Todavía tienes frío?

b. . . . fiebre?

c. . . . calor?

d. . . . un resfriado?

e. Questions will vary.

ESTUDIANTE B

a.–e. Sí, todavía tengo. . . . (No, ya no tengo. . . .) *(Answers will vary.)*

9 Explain to students that in talking about parts of the body, we usually use the definite article. The use of the possessive adjective in this exercise is an exception.

ESTUDIANTE A

a. ¿Cómo te sientes? ¿Está mejor tu oído?

b. . . . pie?

c. . . . espalda?

d. . . . dolor de muelas?

e. . . . cuello?

f. . . . pierna?

ESTUDIANTE B

a.–f. No, ahora está peor. Creo que debo . . . . *(Endings may vary, depending on* Estudiante B*'s choices.)*

Empecemos a conversar

8
A — *¿Todavía tienes <u>sueño</u>?*
B — *Sí, todavía tengo <u>sueño</u>.*
o: *No, ya no tengo <u>sueño</u>.*
Y ahora Uds.

Estudiante A

Estudiante B

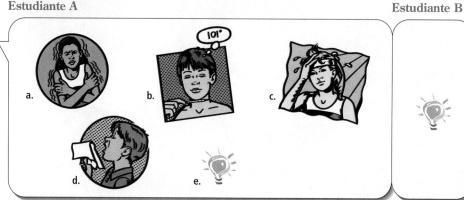

a.   b.   c.

d.   e.

9
A — *¿Cómo te sientes? ¿Está mejor <u>tu brazo</u>?*
B — *No, ahora está peor. Creo que debo <u>ir a la enfermería</u>.*
Y ahora Uds.

Estudiante A

Estudiante B

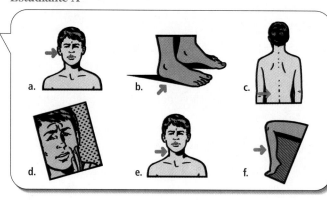

a.   b.   c.

d.   e.   f.

ir al hospital

ir a la enfermería

llamar al médico / al dentista

quedarme en la cama

tomar algo

descansar

Options

Strategies for Reaching All Students

Spanish-Speaking Students

Ex. 11: Ask: *¿Qué remedios recomiendan en tu familia si tienes un resfriado o gripe?*
Ex. 13: Ask: *¿Hay un remedio especial para el dolor de estómago? ¿Cuál es?*

 Un paso más Exs. 9-G, 9-H

Students Needing Extra Help

Ex. 10: If necessary, explain the difference between *me lastimé* and *¡qué lástima!* Brainstorm possible answers and have students use their Organizers.
Ex. 11: Have students use their Organizers.
Ex. 12: Refer students back to the *También necesitas . . .* on pp. 287 and 291.

Enrichment

Ex. 10: To expand this dialogue, have *Estudiante A* suggest a place for *Estudiante B* to go to get medical attention: *la enfermería, la clínica, el hospital, el (la) médico(a), el (la) dentista.*

10

A — *Vamos a <u>hacer ejercicio</u> el viernes, ¿no?*
B — *Lo siento, pero no puedo. <u>Me lastimé</u> <u>la pierna</u> y me duele mucho.*
A — *¡Qué lástima!*

  Y ahora Uds.

Estudiante A   **Estudiante B**

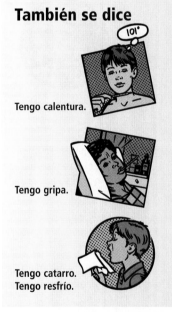

a.   b.   c.   d.

Empecemos a escribir y a leer

Escribe tus respuestas en español.

11 ¿Cómo te sientes?

12 Escribe otras dos formas diferentes para decir *¿Cómo te sientes?*

13 Cuando tienes dolor de estómago, ¿qué debes hacer?

14 Marta dice: "Carolina, lo siento, pero hoy no puedo ir al cine contigo. Me siento mal. Tengo mucho frío y me duele la garganta. Tengo un terrible dolor de cabeza también. Creo que debo quedarme en la cama."

a. ¿Qué crees que tiene Marta?
b. ¿Qué más debe hacer?

También se dice

Tengo calentura.

Tengo gripa.

Tengo catarro.
Tengo resfrío.

Vocabulario para conversar   293

Grammar Preview

Exs. 10 and 14 preview the use of *me* + *doler*. Its explanation appears in the grammar section on pp. 299–300.

10 ESTUDIANTE A
a. Vamos a ir de pesca el viernes, ¿no? / ¡Qué lástima!
b. ...jugar básquetbol .../...
c. ...ir de compras .../...
d. ...ir al cine .../...

ESTUDIANTE B
a.–d. Lo siento, pero no puedo. Me lastimé ... y me duele(n) mucho. *(Statements will vary.)*

Answers: Empecemos a escribir y a leer

11 Answers will vary.

12 ¿Cómo estás? ¿Qué tienes? ¿Te duele algo? ¿Qué pasa?

13 Answers will vary.

14 a. Marta tiene gripe (un resfriado).
   b. Debe descansar (llamar al médico).

Practice Wkbk. 9-3, 9-4

Audio Activities 9.2, 9.3

Writing Activity 9-C

Pruebas 9-3, 9-4

Comm. Act. BLM 9-2

Practice

Re-enter / Recycle

Exs. 2–3: activities from Chaps. 1, 3, and 7
Ex. 2: places and buildings from Chaps. 3, 6, and 7

Answers:
¡Comuniquemos!

1 ESTUDIANTE A

¿Cómo te sientes? ¿Todavía tienes sed?

. . .dolor de estómago?

. . .hambre?

. . .dolor de cabeza?

. . .dolor de oído?

. . .dolor de garganta?

ESTUDIANTE B

Ya no. Ahora tengo . . . . *(Answers will vary.)*

2 For the first three dialogues, the endings are not logical. Possible solutions will vary. Dialogue 4 is logical.

¡Comuniquemos!

Aquí tienes otra oportunidad para usar el vocabulario de este capítulo.

1 Tu hermana menor no se siente bien. Cada vez *(each time)* que le preguntas le duele algo diferente. Túrnate con un(a) compañero(a) para preguntar y contestar.

> A —*¿Cómo te sientes? ¿Todavía tienes fiebre?*
> B —*Ya no. Ahora tengo dolor de cabeza.*

2 ¿Es lógica la tercera línea? Si no, escribe una solución lógica. Después, escribe un diálogo semejante *(similar)*. Un(a) compañero(a) va a escribir una buena solución.

A —*¿Por qué no quieres ir a nadar?*
B —*Porque llueve.*
A —*Ah, podemos ir a tomar el sol.*

A —*¿Por qué no vamos al cine?*
B —*Porque me duelen mucho los ojos.*
A —*Pero, bueno, podemos ver la tele aquí en tu casa.*

A —*¿Por qué no vamos al gimnasio?*
B —*Porque me lastimé la espalda.*
A —*Entonces, ¿prefieres jugar golf?*

A —*¿Por qué no comes algo?*
B —*Todavía tengo este terrible dolor de estómago.*
A —*Yo creo que debes llamar al médico.*

294   Capítulo 9

Options

Strategies for Reaching All Students

Spanish-Speaking Students
Ex. 2: Ask students to write a logical ending for the first three dialogues.

Students Needing Extra Help
Ex. 1: Review *tener hambre / tener sed.*
Ex. 2: Guide students through this exercise. Model a possible response. You may wish to act out the dialogues for the class.
Ex. 3: Have students use their Organizers. Point out the difference in the grammar structure in the choices *(me duelen* and *tengo).*
¿Qué sabes ahora?: Have students write out this section so they can track their progress.

Cooperative Learning
Have groups of three or four students jointly create drawings of the human body. One student names a part of the body while another draws it and passes the drawing to the person on his or her right, allowing everyone an opportunity to name a part of the body. The group continues until the drawing is complete. Tell students that parts do not have to be named in any particular order. When completed, one member from each group describes the drawing.

3 Túrnate con un(a) compañero(a) para representar a una turista entusiasta y a su amiga que nunca se siente bien.

A —*¡Qué bonito está el día! ¿Quieres ir a hacer ejercicio?*

B —*Lo siento, pero me duelen mucho las piernas.*
    o: *Pues, no. Tengo un terrible dolor de cabeza.*

¿Qué sabes ahora?

Can you:

■ name some parts of your body?

—Tengo dos ___, dos ___ y diez ___.

■ tell how you feel or describe your symptoms?

—¿Cómo te sientes?

— ___.

■ tell how long you have been feeling that way?

—¿Cuánto tiempo hace que te duele el oído?

— ___ dos días ___ me duele el oído.

■ make a suggestion to someone who is feeling ill?

—Me duele la garganta.
—Creo que debes ___.

Vocabulario para conversar   295

Present & Apply

Cultural Objective
• To discuss attitudes toward health and health practices in the Spanish-speaking world

Teaching Suggestions
Prior to assigning the *Perspectiva cultural*, gather additional information and photographs about folk healers and remedies in Spanish-speaking countries to share with students after they have read the material.

Critical Thinking: Synthesizing
Have small groups of students prepare lists of adjectives that could be used to describe what they consider to be the ideal doctor or other health-care giver. Examples: *inteligente, simpático(a), paciente.* Afterward, the same groups could compile lists of adjectives that describe attributes they would *not* want their ideal health-care giver to have. For example: *cansado(a), impaciente, perezoso(a).* Record students' lists on the chalkboard and compare the results.

Perspectiva cultural

Algunas veces, cuando no me siento bien, voy a la farmacia para comprar una medicina. Otras veces tomo algunas hierbas medicinales.

Options

Strategies for Reaching All Students

Spanish-Speaking Students
Ask Spanish-speaking students: *¿Hay curanderos(as) en tu comunidad? ¿Va mucha gente a consultarlos(las)? ¿A quién prefieres ver cuando te sientes mal, a un(a) médico(a) o a un(a) curandero(a)? ¿Por qué?*

 Un paso más Ex. 9-I

Students Needing Extra Help
Ask students if their parents, grandparents, or other relatives have a home remedy that they use. Remind them of popular home remedy books with which they may be familiar because of television advertisements.

Enrichment
This rhyme is used to comfort a child when he or she is hurt: *Sana, sana, colita de rana / Si no sana hoy, sanará mañana.* It is used for scrapes and bruises, and the person reciting it waves a hand over the injury or caresses it. Although the rhyme makes little sense and has no real healing power, it often stops the child's crying by getting him or her to stop thinking of the pain. Discuss the power of positive thinking and its role in folk healing and standard medicine.

Why do you think these two photos are shown? Why might someone who is sick choose to go sometimes to one of these two places and sometimes to the other?

Imagine this. You aren't feeling well. Your mother talks to some friends, but they can't agree on what your illness is or how to treat it. There is a woman in your community who is not a doctor, but who is known to be able to help people who are sick. You go to see her. She asks about your recent activities. After a while she decides which of her remedies is best for your situation.

In many Hispanic communities, folk remedies have been passed down from generation to generation, largely due to the availability of plants with medicinal value. For example, a tea made from mint (known in Mexico as *yerbabuena*) may be given to someone with a stomachache. A little piece of camphor *(alcanfor)* or the herb rue *(ruda)* wrapped in cotton and put in the ear is said to cure an earache. Other home remedies, such as quinine, have found their way into modern medicine.

Una farmacia en Chetumal, México

Members of many ethnic groups treat an illness in this way. They may consult a doctor, or they may decide the illness can be more easily cured by a long-used folk remedy.

Today scientists are investigating new sources of medicine by consulting ethnic groups that have long used remedies made from local plants.

La cultura desde tu perspectiva

1 What folk remedies are you familiar with? Why might someone choose to go to a folk healer instead of a doctor?

2 If you were living in a different country and your friends and neighbors went to folk healers, would you do the same? Why or why not?

Las hierbas medicinales son importantes en la medicina moderna.

UNIDAD MEDICA DE ESPECIALISTAS

✛ DR. JESUS MANUEL LOZANO G.
PEDIATRA
-ENFERMEDADES DE LOS NIÑOS Y ADOLESCENTES

✛ DR. JUAN MANUEL VILLASEÑOR
TRAUMATOLOGO Y ORTOPEDISTA
-FRACTURAS Y DEFORMACIONES DE LOS HUESOS
-ORTOPEDIA PEDIATRICA

✛ DR. JULIAN GARCIA VILLEGAS
MEDICINA GENERAL

CONTAMOS CON SERVICIO DE LABORATORIO Y BANCO DE SANGRE

CITAS AL
☎ 2-12-33 ☎
CALLE NOGAL No. 40
(A UNA CUADRA DE LA IGLESIA CATOLICA)

Perspectiva cultural 297

Cultural Notes ☀

(p. 296, photo)
Pharmacy clerk in Chetumal, capital of the state of Quintana Roo, Mexico. As in the U.S., the fields of nursing and teaching in Mexico have traditionally been dominated by women, with medical and legal careers more often pursued by men. A notable difference between the two countries, however, is that in Mexico, pharmaceutical careers attract many more women than men.

(p. 297, photo)
Medicinal herbs at a market in Tenancingo, Mexico. Traditional indigenous methods of healing, which often employ herbs in combination with special prayers, are still practiced throughout Latin America. So established and respected are the *curanderos(as)* that every year they meet for several days in Catemaco, Veracruz, to share their knowledge.

(p. 297, realia)
Newspaper ad for private medical specialists. In Mexico, many citizens employed by the government or private companies receive benefits from the IMSS (Instituto Mexicano de Seguro Social). However, people not under this coverage must rely on certain government-run hospitals or pay cash at private hospitals for their medical needs.

Preview

 Transparency 50

Answers

Answers will vary, but may include a description of the illness, how to detect the illness, possible remedies, advice on treatment, etc.

A *Le* is used because it refers to a person other than the speaker. In this case it refers to *su hijo.*

B *Duele* is used when the object to which it refers is singular; *duelen,* when the object is plural. The other verb is *gustan.*

C It tells how long something has been going on (a week).

Gramática en contexto

Look at this article from a health magazine that tells parents how to detect an illness in their children. What kind of information would you expect to find?

¿Cómo puede saber si su hijo tiene mononucleosis?

Ud. debe prestar atención si:

• a su hijo le duele la garganta
• le duelen los ojos y la cabeza
• tiene un resfriado o tiene gripe, y no se mejora
• está siempre cansado o duerme muchas horas
• hace una semana que no puede ir a la escuela
• no tiene energía para hacer ejercicio, aunque le gustan los deportes

Éstos pueden ser síntomas de mononucleosis. Por eso, Ud. debe llevar a su hijo a una clínica para hacerle un examen completo. Mientras tanto, su hijo debe descansar y beber mucho líquido.

A In the article, find the expressions *le duele(n)* and *le gusta(n).* Why do you think *le* is used instead of *me?*

B Compare the two sentences that use *duele* and *duelen.* When do we use each of these? Find another verb in the article that follows this pattern.

C Look at the sentence *Hace una semana que no puede ir a la escuela. Que* connects two parts of this sentence. The second part tells what the person cannot do. What information does the first part of the sentence give?

298   Capítulo 9

Options

Strategies for Reaching All Students

Students Needing Extra Help
A: Students may understand this concept but they might not be able to express it.
C: Write the sentence on the chalkboard. Highlight it and separate the parts.
Have students start to fill in the grammar portion of their Organizers.
El verbo dormir: Emphasize the *nosotros* ending, since *dormir* is an *-ir* verb. Review *poder* and its verb forms.
Ex. 1: Review *-ir* verb endings.

El verbo *dormir*

Like *poder*, *dormir* is an *o → ue* stem-changing verb. Here are all its present-tense forms:

(yo)	d**ue**rmo	(nosotros) (nosotras)	d**o**rmimos
(tú)	d**ue**rmes	(vosotros) (vosotras)	d**o**rmís
Ud. (él) (ella)	d**ue**rme	Uds. (ellos) (ellas)	d**ue**rmen

1 Pregunta a un(a) compañero(a) si estas personas duermen bien.

A — *¿Duerme bien Marta?*
B — *No, duerme mal porque todavía tiene dolor de oído.*

Marta

a. Antonio y Pedro   b. Rosita   c. Juanito y Miguel   d. tú   e. Uds.

El complemento indirecto: Los pronombres *me, te, le*

Indirect object pronouns replace indirect object nouns. We use indirect object pronouns with *doler* (*o → ue*).

• In Spanish, the part of the body that hurts is the subject of the sentence and the verb agrees with it. The indirect object pronoun tells who hurts:

Me duele **la pierna.** / **Me** duele**n** **las piernas.**

Gramática en contexto   299

Present & Practice

Class Starter Review
For the day after the presentation of *dormir*, have pairs of students ask and answer how long they sleep on weekdays or weekends. Ask volunteers to report to the class on the information they found out.

Answers
1 ESTUDIANTE A
a. ¿Duermen bien Antonio y Pedro?
b. ¿Duermes bien?
c. ¿Duermen bien Juanito y Miguel?
d. ¿Duerme bien Rosita?
e. ¿Duermen bien Uds.?
ESTUDIANTE B
a. No, duermen mal porque todavía tienen fiebre.
b. No, duermo mal porque todavía tengo gripe.
c. No, duermen mal porque todavía tienen dolor de estómago.
d. No, duerme mal porque todavía tiene dolor de muelas.
e. No, dormimos mal porque todavía tenemos un resfriado.

 Practice Wkbk. 9-5

 Prueba 9-5

Present & Practice

Re-enter / Recycle
Ex. 4: *gustar* expressions from Chap. 1, foods from Chap. 4

Reteach / Review: Verbs like *gustar*
Ex. 2: Remind students that *duele(n)* is used the same way as *gusta(n), encanta(n),* and *queda(n).*

Answers
2 ESTUDIANTE A
¿Qué te duele?

ESTUDIANTE B
(Order of responses will vary.)
Me duele la mano izquierda.
. . . el brazo izquierdo.
. . . el estómago.
. . . la espalda.
. . . la pierna izquierda.
. . . la pierna derecha.

(yo)	**me**	(tú)	**te**	(Ud.) (él) (ella)	**le**

- We also use indirect object pronouns with *gustar* and *encantar:*

    Le encanta tocar la guitarra.

- Sometimes we use *a* + a pronoun or a person's name for emphasis or to make it clear who we are referring to.

    Me duelen los pies. Y **a ti,** ¿qué **te** duele?
    A Pablo le duelen los pies.
    A Ud. le duelen los pies, ¿no?

2 Después de hacer ejercicio durante mucho tiempo, te duele todo el cuerpo. Túrnate con un(a) compañero(a) para preguntar y decir qué te duele.

A — *¿Qué te duele?*
B — *Me duele el cuello.*

300   Capítulo 9

Options

Strategies for Reaching All Students

Spanish-Speaking Students
Ex. 4: Ask Spanish-speaking students: *¿Qué comidas te encantan a ti? ¿Cuáles no te gustan nada?*

Students Needing Extra Help
Ex. 2: To simplify the use of *duele(n)*, tell students that when one thing hurts, use *duele.* When two (or more) things hurt, use *duelen.*
Ex. 3: Emphasize the necessary change of *cansado* to *cansada* in some items.

Ask what will happen to *cansado* with *Maricarmen,* as students may see it as two names.
Remind students to use *duelen* when two things hurt.
Ex. 4: Have students use their Organizers from Chap. 4.

3 Después de un examen difícil de historia estos estudiantes están cansados. Habla con un(a) compañero(a) y di cómo se sienten.

José

A —*Veo que José está cansado.*
B —*Sí, y también le duele mucho la cabeza.*

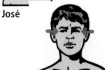

a. Felipe

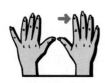

b. Maricarmen

c. Tomás

d. Fernando

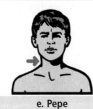

e. Pepe

d. Sarita

4 Pregunta a tus compañeros de clase qué comidas les gustan o no les gustan.

A —*¿A ti te gustan las uvas?*
B —*Sí, a mí me gustan.*
    o: *Sí, a mí me encantan.*
    o: *No, a mí no me gustan.*

Ahora di qué comidas les gustan o no les gustan a tus compañeros de clase.

A Verónica le encantan las uvas.

La expresión *hace ... que*

To tell how long something has been going on, we use *Hace* + period of time + *que* + present-tense verb.

Hace tres días **que estoy** enfermo.

If we want to ask how long something has been going on, we can use *¿Cuánto (tiempo) hace que* + present-tense verb?

¿Cuánto tiempo hace que Elena **está** enferma?

Gramática en contexto   301

Reteach / Review:
También and tampoco
Ex. 4: To practice *también / tampoco,* have students continue this dialogue by having *Estudiante A* agree with *Estudiante B*'s tastes.

Class Starter Review
For the day after the presentation of *hace ... que,* ask students *¿Cuánto tiempo hace que ___?* Possible expressions: *estudiar español, practicar deportes, tener un resfriado,* etc.

Answers
3 ESTUDIANTE A
a. Veo que Felipe está cansado.
b. ...Maricarmen está cansada.
c. ...Tomás está cansado.
d. ...Fernando está cansado.
e. ...Pepe está cansado.
f. ...Sarita está cansada.
ESTUDIANTE B
a. Sí, y también le duelen mucho los ojos.
b. ...le duele mucho el dedo.
c. ...le duele mucho la espalda.
d. ...le duelen mucho las manos.
e. ...le duele mucho el cuello.
f. ...le duele mucho el brazo derecho.

4 Questions and answers will vary, but encourage students to use previously learned vocabulary.

Practice Wkbk. 9-6, 9-7

¿? Prueba 9-6

Present & Practice

Re-enter / Recycle

Ex. 5: numbers 0–31 from *El primer paso,* calendar expressions from Chap. 1

Answers

5 ESTUDIANTE A

a. ¿Cuánto hace que María tiene dolor de oído?

b. ...Susana tiene gripe?

c. ...Alejandra tiene dolor de garganta?

d. ...José tiene un resfriado?

e. ...Andrés tiene dolor de estómago?

f. ...Cecilia tiene fiebre?

ESTUDIANTE B

a. Pues, hace dos días que tiene dolor de oído.

b. ...una semana que tiene gripe.

c. ...tres días que tiene dolor de garganta.

d. ...seis días que tiene un resfriado.

e. ...dos días que tiene dolor de estómago.

f. ...cinco días que tiene fiebre.

 Practice Wkbk. 9-8

 Writing Activities 9-F, 9-G

 Prueba 9-7

---

5 Pregunta a un(a) compañero(a) cuánto tiempo hace que estas personas están enfermas.

A — *¿Cuánto hace que Rodolfo tiene dolor de muelas?*
B — *Pues, hace seis días que tiene dolor de muelas.*

Rodolfo / 6 días

a. María / 2 días

b. Susana / 1 semana

c. Alejandra / 3 días

d. José / 4 días

e. Andrés / 2 días

f. Cecilia / 5 días

La sustantivación de adjetivos

Look at how we can avoid repeating the noun in these instances:

¿Te duele **la pierna derecha** o **la izquierda?**

¿Qué prefieres, **un gorro azul** o **uno amarillo?**

To avoid repetition we drop the noun in the second part of the sentence and put the definite or indefinite article right before the second adjective. Note that the adjective must agree in gender and number just as if the noun were still there. Also note that *un* becomes *uno(a)* when it is not followed by a noun.

We can do the same thing with what we call a "prepositional phrase," or a description that begins with *de, para,* etc.

¿Qué haces, **la tarea de matemáticas** o **la de ciencias?**

¿Necesitas marcadores **para la clase de inglés** o **para la de arte?**

302   Capítulo 9

Options

Strategies for Reaching All Students

Students Needing Extra Help
Ex. 5: Give other examples of time: hours, weeks, months, years.
Have students use their Organizers and point out that this exercise is using *tener* expressions.
Sustantivación de adjetivos: Give students further examples. Show how *clase* and *tarea* are removed, but *la de* + subject remain in the examples given.
Ahora lo sabes: Have students write out this section so they can track their progress.

Enrichment
Ex. 5: As a homework assignment, have students create other dialogues in which *Estudiante A* asks *Estudiante B* how long someone has been doing an activity. Encourage them to use plural as well as singular subjects. For example: *¿Cuánto hace que los muchachos patinan? Hace cuarenta y cinco minutos que patinan.*

6 ¿Qué le duele a tu compañero(a)?

A — *¿Qué tienes?*
B — *Me duele el ojo.*
A — *¿El derecho o el izquierdo?*
B — *El derecho.*

a.

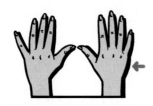

b.

c.

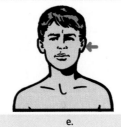

d.

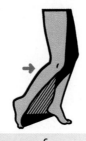

e.

Ahora lo sabes

Can you:

■ recommend a way to maintain good health?
—Debes dormir más. Estás enfermo porque no ___ bien.

■ say that a part of the body hurts?
—___ María ___ la mano derecha.

■ tell how long something has been going on?
—___ tres días ___ Rafael tiene un resfriado.

■ avoid repeating a noun?
—¿Te duele el oído derecho o ___?

Apply

Pronunciation Tape 9-3

¡A conversar!

Play

Step

Using the Video

Video segment 3: See the Video Teacher's Guide.

 Video Activity C

Re-enter / Recycle

Ex. 1: activities from Chaps. 1, 3, and 7
Ex. 2: colors, clothes, and direct object pronouns from Chap. 6
Ex. 3: *gustar* expressions from Chap. 1, activities from Chaps. 1, 3, and 7

Answers: Actividades

1 Statements will vary, but look for correct use of *duele(n)*.

Para decir más

Aquí tienes vocabulario adicional que te puede ayudar para hacer las actividades de esta sección.

**el enfermero,
la enfermera**
nurse

tener mareos
to have dizzy spells

tener escalofríos
to have chills

tener tos
to have a cough

Me duele todo el cuerpo.
My whole body aches.

Me siento débil.
I feel weak.

tomar vitaminas
to take vitamins

el consultorio
the doctor's (dentist's) office

304   Capítulo 9

Actividades

Esta sección te ofrece la oportunidad de aumentar tus conocimientos de español al integrar lo que aprendiste en este capítulo con lo que aprendiste en capítulos anteriores.

1 Cada estudiante debe escribir en una ficha *(index card)* un problema de salud imaginario. El profesor recogerá *(will collect)* las fichas y dará *(will give)* una a cada estudiante. Ahora representa *(act out)* el problema de tu ficha. La clase debe identificar el problema y hacer una recomendación.

A Juan le duele el brazo (izquierdo).
No debe jugar béisbol hoy.
o: *Debe descansar esta tarde.*

Options

Strategies for Reaching All Students

Students Needing Extra Help
Ex. 1: Brainstorm responses. Have students use their Organizers.
Ex. 2: Bring in extra items in case some students forget to bring theirs. Review *ni. . . ni.*
Ex. 3: Review *hace* + time expression + *que* formula.

Enrichment
As an in-class writing assignment, have students create a dialogue between an overworked, sleepy doctor and a patient. Tell students that the basic situation to be dramatized here is a reversal of roles between doctor and patient, with the patient gradually realizing that the doctor needs care and advice.

Cooperative Learning
In groups of three or four, have students brainstorm and compile a list of activities that they all do. Have them then list how long they have been doing these activities. Give them a time limit of approximately five minutes, and then ask one member from each group to summarize their information.

2 Trae (*bring*) a la clase dos cosas iguales (*two similar things*) pero de color diferente; por ejemplo, una camisa roja y otra amarilla. Inventa un diálogo con un vendedor (*salesperson*) y su cliente. Por ejemplo:

A — *¿Qué desea señor (señorita)?*
B — *Me encanta esa camisa roja. ¿La tiene en amarillo?*
A — *Sí, aquí la tiene.*
B — *Me queda bien. ¿Cuánto cuesta?*
A — *Treinta y cuatro dólares.*
B — *¡Muy bien! La compro.*

3 Escribe cuatro actividades que te gusta hacer o cuatro cosas que tienes. Puedes usar los verbos y expresiones de la lista u otros. Lee tus frases a un(a) compañero(a). Tu compañero(a) debe averiguar (*find out*) cuánto tiempo hace que haces esas actividades.

A —*A mí me gusta patinar.*
   o: *Yo patino.*
B —*¿Cuánto tiempo hace que patinas?*
A —*Hace seis años (que patino).*

Nadando en la piscina de la
Universidad de Caracas, Venezuela

nadar
patinar
esquiar
tocar la guitarra
tener un perro
tener un gato
practicar deportes

2 Dialogues will vary, but should include correct agreement of adjective (color) and article.

3 Dialogues will vary, but remind students to use *hace* + period of time + *que* when talking about duration. (You can expand on Ex. 3 by having students report to the class the information they obtained from their partners.)

Comm. Act. BLMs 9-3, 9-4, 9-5

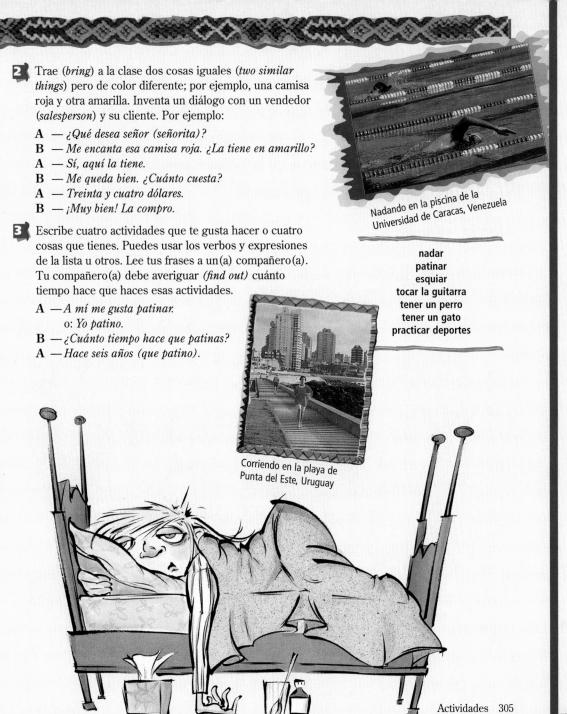

Corriendo en la playa de
Punta del Este, Uruguay

Actividades   305

Cultural Notes

(p. 305, bottom photo)
Vacationers at Punta del Este, Uruguay, one of South America's most exclusive beach resorts, can choose from a wide range of activities. In addition to jogging along the beach, one can enjoy fishing, surfing, water skiing, tennis, golf, and polo.

Apply

Process Reading
For a description of process reading, see p. 48.

Teaching Suggestions
Remind students of some of the reading strategies that they have already practiced and that they can now apply to everything they read to help their comprehension: for example, prediction, skimming, scanning, using context clues, using prior knowledge, and identifying the main idea.

¡Vamos a leer!

Antes de leer

STRATEGY ➤ Using prior knowledge

Look at the pictures. What do you think this article will be about? In two or three sentences, try to summarize what you know about the topic. What new information do you think you might find out?

Mira la lectura

STRATEGY ➤ Using titles and photos to predict

Find the title and the name of the section in the magazine where it appears. Look at the photo and the caption, and read the boldface headings. What cause of headaches do you think will be discussed?

TU SALUD

CAUSAS DEL DOLOR DE CABEZA

El dolor de cabeza tiene diferentes causas. La mala postura puede ser una de ellas. Diversos doctores y terapistas han hablado sobre la importancia de comprobar la postura de nuestro cuerpo cada vez que nos sentamos. Para eso, hay que considerar varios aspectos:

- **Los pies** deben apoyarse totalmente sobre el suelo mientras estamos sentados.
- **La espalda baja** debe apoyarse contra el respaldo de la silla.
- **La cabeza** debe estar colocada correctamente sobre los hombros.
- **Los hombros** no deben estar tensos.

Sin duda, una buena postura puede evitar que nos duela la espalda, el cuello, los hombros y, por supuesto, la cabeza.

Cabeza
Hombros
Espalda baja
Pies

Siéntate derecho y di adiós al dolor de cabeza

306   Capítulo 9

Options

Strategies for Reaching All Students

Students Needing Extra Help
Antes de leer: Have students write a list of the cognates.

Enrichment
Extended activity: Think of another common health problem and recommend several things you can do to avoid it.

Infórmate

STRATEGY ➤ Coping with unknown words

Remember that you should keep reading when you come across an unknown word. You may find that you do not need to know its meaning, that you can use the surrounding words to figure it out, or that you may have to look it up or ask someone the meaning.

1 Read the entire article several times, without stopping to puzzle over words you do not know. What general body behavior does the author recommend to avoid headaches?

2 Now read the article carefully, paying attention to words you don't know. Can you identify instances where the exact meaning of unknown words isn't important for getting the gist of the sentence?

Use context clues and the diagram to figure out the meaning of each underlined word.

hombros . . . estar <u>tensos</u>
pies . . . sobre *(on)* el <u>suelo</u>
cabeza . . . está <u>colocada</u> . . . sobre <u>los hombros</u>

Para no tener dolor de cabeza, visita al dentista regularmente

Una visita al dentista

Aplicación

Look at yourself and your classmates right now. Are you following the article's recommendations? If not, try doing the four things that the author advises. Do they feel comfortable or uncomfortable, natural or unnatural? Evaluate the article's recommendations on a scale of 1 to 5 (1 = not at all useful; 5 = extremely useful).

¡Vamos a leer! 307

Apply

Process Writing
For information regarding developing a writing portfolio, see p. 50.

Multicultural Perspectives
In many Latin American countries, government health agencies use educational radio programs to transmit health information to the people in rural areas. Poster campaigns to encourage vaccination of children are common. Traveling nurses and other health practitioners make rounds to remote areas that don't have clinics or hospitals. Discuss health-related advertisements, public service announcements, and / or commercials that students have seen or heard in Spanish. Could they figure out what messages these ads and announcements were trying to get across?

Answers: ¡Vamos a escribir!
Look for correct use of adjectives and verbs, and encourage students to use the chapter vocabulary.

¡Vamos a escribir!

Make a poster in Spanish that might be displayed in a nurse's office or other medical facility. The poster should give information about how to prevent illness or how to take care of yourself when you are sick.

1 First, decide on your theme. Do you want to give suggestions for staying healthy *(Ideas para mantener la salud)*, such as eating healthful foods, exercising, and getting enough sleep? Or do you want to make suggestions for someone who isn't feeling well *(Ideas para sentirte mejor)*, such as staying in bed, drinking a lot of water, and resting?

2 Write the suggestions that you will put on your poster. You may want to use the verbs *debes* or *necesitas*.

3 Show the text of your poster to a partner. Then revise and edit it. Recopy the corrected sentences on your poster. You may want to add a drawing or a picture from a magazine to illustrate your suggestions.

4 Now you are ready to share your work. Here are some ways you can do this:
- Display your posters in the classroom, the hallway, or the nurse's office.
- With your teacher's help, organize a school health fair, and make your posters the main display.
- With your teacher's help, find out if some nearby elementary school or health facility would like to display your posters.

308   Capítulo 9

Options

Strategies for Reaching All Students

Spanish-Speaking Students
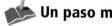 **Un paso más Ex. 9-J**

Students Needing Extra Help
Step 1: Emphasize that you are asking students to make a choice between maintaining health or feeling better. Brainstorm ideas with the class. Have students use their Organizers from other chapters.

"Me encanta caminar para hacer ejercicio."

Assess & Summarize

Test Preparation

You may want to assign parts of this section as written homework or as an in-class writing activity prior to administering the *Examen de habilidades*.

Answers

Listening:
—Señor Donoso, tengo un terrible dolor de cabeza. Tengo un resfriado, tengo fiebre y me duele la garganta. Debo quedarme en la cama. Si necesita hablar conmigo, puede llamar a mi casa.
—Pero, Justino, hace una semana que te sientes mal. ¡Debes llamar al médico!
Justino is feeling bad. Justino's problems include: He has a terrible headache, a cold, a fever, and a sore throat. His boss suggests that he call the doctor.

Reading: The prescription is probably for a toothache. / No, it should be taken with food or milk.

Writing: Encourage students to use the chapter vocabulary. Look for logical sentences.

Culture: Answers will vary. Students may include references to the *Perspectiva cultural*, such as taking *yerbabuena* or consulting a doctor.

¿Lo sabes bien?

This section will help you organize your studying for the proficiency test, where you will be asked to do similar, though not identical, tasks. There will not be any models on the test.

Listening

Can you understand this telephone conversation between Justino and his boss, Señor Donoso? Listen as your teacher reads a sample similar to what you will hear on the test. How is Justino feeling? Mention at least two problems he has. What does his boss suggest?

Reading

Can you read the label on this prescription bottle and use cognates, context, or any other strategy to understand the gist of it? What is the prescription for? Should this medicine be taken on an empty stomach?

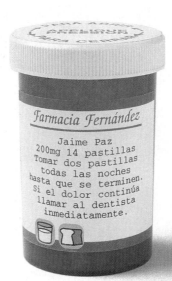

Writing

Can you write a letter to a friend explaining how you are feeling after an accident you have just had? Here is a sample:

> Querida María Marta:
>
> Hace una semana que estoy en la cama. Me lastimé la pierna derecha, los brazos y la espalda. Me siento muy mal. Todavía me duelen mucho los brazos. Pero creo que voy a estar mejor en unos días y voy a poder ir a la escuela.
>
> Tu amiga,
> Maribel

Culture

Can you explain some options for what you could do if you had a stomachache while visiting México?

Speaking

Can you work with a partner to play the roles of a doctor and a patient? Here is a sample dialogue:

A —*Doctor, me siento muy mal. Me duele mucho el estómago.*
B —*¿Cuánto tiempo hace que te duele el estómago?*
A —*Hace sólo unas horas, doctor.*
B —*Pues, creo que comes mucho. Pero, bueno, ahora debes ir a tu casa, quedarte en la cama y no comer nada esta noche.*

Options

Strategies for Reaching All Students

Students Needing Extra Help

Listening: Make a three-column chart with headings "feelings," "problems," and "suggestions."
To indicate two people speaking, put on a hat, move to a new spot, alter your voice, etc.
Writing: Brainstorm other possibilities, such as a specific number of days until you are better, other activities you might be returning to such as skating, playing the guitar, and so on. Go sentence by sentence. Have students use their Organizers from this and other chapters.
Culture: Review the *Perspectiva cultural*.
Speaking: Make up some other possibilities. Have students use their Organizers.

Enrichment

Writing: Students can also write instructions for a pet-sitter taking care of a sick dog or cat. Remind students to name or describe the ailment and its symptoms as well as to list instructions for giving the animal what it needs to get better (food, water, rest, etc.).

Resumen del capítulo 9

Use the vocabulary from this chapter to help you:

- describe how you are feeling
- tell what parts of your body hurt
- suggest things you or others can do to feel better

to name parts of the body
la boca
el brazo
la cabeza
el cuello
el cuerpo
el dedo
el dedo del pie
derecho, -a
la espalda
el estómago
la garganta
izquierdo, -a
la mano (f.)
la nariz
el oído
el ojo
el pie
la pierna

to ask how someone is feeling
¿Cómo te sientes?
¿Qué pasa?
¿Qué te duele?
¿Qué tienes?

to describe how someone is feeling
¡Ay!
el dolor
doler (o → ue)
(A mí / ti) me / te duele(n) ___.

(No me duele) nada.
la fiebre
Me siento bien / mal.
Tengo dolor de cabeza.
⠀⠀⠀⠀⠀⠀⠀⠀⠀⠀⠀⠀estómago.
⠀⠀⠀⠀⠀⠀⠀⠀⠀⠀⠀⠀garganta.
⠀⠀⠀⠀⠀⠀⠀⠀⠀⠀⠀⠀muelas.
⠀⠀⠀⠀⠀⠀⠀⠀⠀⠀⠀⠀oído.

Tengo calor.
⠀⠀⠀⠀⠀⠀fiebre.
⠀⠀⠀⠀⠀⠀frío.
⠀⠀⠀⠀⠀⠀gripe.
⠀⠀⠀⠀⠀⠀sueño.
⠀⠀⠀⠀⠀⠀un resfriado.

(Yo) me lastimé ___.
mejor
peor
terrible

to name places to go or things to do when you are sick
la clínica
la enfermería
el hospital
Debo quedarme en la cama.
Debes quedarte en la cama.
llamar
tomar

to name ways to maintain good health
dormir (o → ue)
hacer ejercicio

to name medical professions
el / la dentista
el médico, la médica

to indicate how long something has been going on
¿Cuánto (tiempo) hace que ___?
Hace + *time expression* + que ___.
ahora
todavía
ya no

to express and ask for an opinion
(Yo) creo que ___.
¿no?

 Prueba cumulativa

 Examen de habilidades

 Test Generator

Speaking: Dialogues will vary, but students should use chapter vocabulary. Look for correct use of *me / te duele(n)* and *hace* + time expression + *que*. Encourage use of vocabulary from previous chapters.

Resumen 311

CAPÍTULo 10
THEME: COMMUNITY

COMMUNICATION

Topics

Places in the community

Activities and errands

Transportation

Numbers 200–1,000

Objectives

To talk about Hispanic communities in the U.S.

To talk about places

To talk about activities or errands in a community

To talk about things you buy

To talk about money

To talk about mailing things

To ask and give directions

To talk about transportation

To talk about past activities

To indicate when an event occurred

To say you don't / didn't know something

CULTURE

Hispanic communities in the U.S.

GRAMMAR

La preposición de + el

El pretérito de los verbos que terminan en -ar

El pretérito del verbo ir

Ancillaries available for use with Chapter 10

Multisensory/Technology

 Overhead Transparencies, 51–55

 Audio Tapes and CDs

 Vocabulary Art Blackline Masters for Hands-On Learning, pp. 53–57

 Classroom Crossword

 Video

 CD-ROM

Print

 Practice Workbook, pp. 104–113

 Writing, Audio & Video Activities, pp. 59–64, 120–122, 170–171

 Communicative Activity Blackline Masters

    Pair and Small Group Activities, pp. 71–76

    Situation Cards, p. 77

 Un paso más: Actividades para ampliar tu español, pp. 56–61

Assessment

 Assessment Program

    Pruebas, pp. 143–153

    Examen de habilidades, pp. 154–157

 Test Generator

Video still from Chap. 10

Hispanic Communities in the U.S.

Hispanic culture is evident in most parts of the U.S. But who are Hispanic Americans?

The meaning of the word Hispanic is somewhat elusive. Contrary to popular notions, not all U.S. Hispanics speak Spanish, are Roman Catholics, or are recent immigrants, even though these characteristics do describe many Hispanics. Virtually all, however, can trace their lineage to Latin America or to Spain. The most common places of origin are Mexico, Puerto Rico, and Cuba.

Much of the southwestern U.S. was Mexican territory before the Mexican-American War (1846–1848), and many Mexican American families have resided in the region for generations. In this century, immigration from Mexico to the U.S. was spurred by the revolution of 1910–1917. This northward migration established large Mexican communities in such places as Kansas City and Chicago.

During the 1940s, Puerto Rican immigration to the U.S. mainland became substantial. Fueled by an expanding job market, as well as the availability of regular airline flights between San Juan and New York City, large Puerto Rican communities were established in New York, Connecticut, Rhode Island, and Illinois. Since the passage of the 1917 Jones Act, Puerto Ricans have been U.S. citizens by birth. This status facilitates their movement between the mainland and the island. Puerto Rican migration has been described as a "revolving door," as there is frequent travel back and forth, often for long periods of time. This provides a regular infusion of Puerto Rican culture in the U.S. and U.S. culture in the island.

Economic, social, and political conditions have sparked four large waves of immigration from Cuba to the U.S. in the last 35 years. The first wave began in 1959, shortly after Fidel Castro gained power; the second one in 1965. The third, one in which approximately 125,000 Cubans arrived in the U.S. during the Mariel boat lift, occurred during a five-month period in 1980. In 1994 thousands of Cubans once again sought refuge in the U.S. Because of a U.S. policy limiting Cuban visas to about 2,700 a year, however, most were taken to refugee camps in Guantánamo Bay. There they awaited results of negotiations between the U.S. and Cuban governments that would tell them if they would be allowed to immigrate to the U.S. or be forced to return to Cuba. Many Cuban immigrants have now settled in the Miami area. However, smaller, but vital communities also exist in New Jersey, Illinois, and elsewhere.

Introduce

Re-entry of Concepts

The following list represents words, expressions, and grammar topics re-entered from *El primer paso* to Chap. 9:

El primer paso
Numbers 0–31
Calendar expressions

Chapter 1
Activities

Chapter 2
Time-telling
School supplies
School subjects

Chapter 3
Leisure-time activities
Places and buildings
Ir a + infinitive

Chapter 4
Food
Expressing likes and preferences

Chapter 6
Places and buildings
Direct object pronouns
Clothing

Chapter 7
Vacation activities
Para + inf.

Chapter 8
Household chores

Chapter 9
Places and buildings
Hace . . . que

Planning

Cross-Curricular Connections

Geography Connection *(pp. 316–317)*
Have students choose a Spanish-speaking country and create a stamp or monetary note. This might feature a famous historical figure, landmark, or place. They should draw it large enough for the whole class to see.

Math Connection *(pp. 316–317)*
Using census data for your community, have students make a bar graph to illustrate the distribution of ethnic communities in your city, town, or state.

Spanish in Your Community
Have students investigate where in their community they could go to exchange U.S. money for foreign currency. Have them determine how much money can be exchanged and what foreign currencies are available. Ask them to find the exchange rate tables in the newspaper.

CAPÍTULO 10

¿Qué hiciste ayer?

OBJECTIVES

At the end of this chapter you will be able to:

- **name various places in your community**
- **name activities you do or did in your community**
- **identify different means of transportation available in your area**
- **compare and contrast a Hispanic community with a community you are familiar with**

Volcán en Puerto Varas, Chile

313

(pp. 312–313, photo)
The town of Puerto Varas (population 23,000) on the shore of Lake Llanquihue is one of Chile's most picturesque spots. Easily accessible by rail and road, Puerto Varas was founded as a German settlement, and, in its mountain setting, has much the look of a village in the Swiss Alps. The Osorno and Calbuco volcanoes tower over the town, which is made even more scenic by its streets lined with rose bushes.

Preview

Cultural Objective
- To compare errands and activities in Spanish-speaking countries with those in the U.S.

 ¿Qué hiciste ayer?

Play

 Video Activity A

Using the Video
This chapter's video focuses on community. Our host takes students on a tour of the area of Miami known as Little Havana. To prepare students for the video, first ask them to predict what this chapter's tape will be about. Then have students watch the segment several times. After the first time, you may wish to have them brainstorm possible vocabulary and expressions they will need to talk about what they saw on the video. Ask students to identify: a) things they saw that were familiar to them, and b) things they saw that they probably would not see where they live.
Video segment 1: For more teaching suggestions, see the Video Teacher's Guide.

¡Piénsalo bien!

Look at the pictures and read the captions.

Think about the many different errands and activities you normally do in your community. Which of the activities in these photos have you done most recently? When?

"Yo fui a ver un partido de béisbol."

Here's a baseball stadium in the Dominican Republic, which has produced many major league baseball players. Do you know the names of any of them?

314   Capítulo 10

Options

Strategies for Reaching All Students

Spanish-Speaking Students
Ask: *¿Haces las mismas cosas que las personas en las fotos? ¿Cuándo fue la última vez que fuiste a la biblioteca, que fuiste al correo o que fuiste a un partido? ¿Te gusta el béisbol? ¿Lo juegas? ¿Qué posición juegas? Si no lo juegas, ¿te gusta verlo? ¿Qué deportes juegas?*

 Un paso más Exs. 10-A, 10-B

Students Needing Extra Help
(p. 315, top photo): Some students may not be familiar with the idea of a rural post office as compared to large urban ones.

Enrichment
(p. 314, photo): Ask students if they know of any Hispanic players in other sports. (Mary Jo Fernández, Aranxta Sánchez-Vicario, and Conchita Martínez, tennis; Julio César Chavez, boxing; Lee Treviño and Chi Chi Rodríguez, golf; Jorge Campos and Tab Ramos, soccer)

"Envié una carta a mis tíos."

How is this post office similar to and different from the one in your community?

En Madrid

"¿Y a ti te gusta ir a la biblioteca?"

Estudiantes en la Universidad de Caracas

315

Cultural Notes

315

Present

Chapter Theme
Errands and activities

Communicative Objectives
- To talk about places
- To talk about activities or errands in a community
- To talk about money
- To talk about mailing things
- To talk about past activities
- To indicate when an event occurred
- To say you didn't know something
- To express a condition

 Transparencies 51–52

 Vocabulary Art BLMs

 Pronunciation Tape 10-1

 Vocabulario para conversar A

Play

Using the Video
Video segment 2: See the Video Teacher's Guide.

 Video Activity B

Vocabulario para conversar

¿Adónde vas?

Aquí tienes palabras y expresiones necesarias para hablar de las cosas que puedes hacer en tu comunidad. Léelas varias veces y practícalas con un(a) compañero(a) en las páginas siguientes.

el supermercado
la librería
la biblioteca
sacar un libro
los comestibles
las pastillas (para la garganta)
devolver (o → ue) un libro
la farmacia
el champú
la tarjeta de cumpleaños
el regalo
el jabón
la pasta dentífrica
ir a pasear
ver un partido de béisbol
la tienda de regalos
la tarjeta postal
el banco
el sello
depositar dinero
sacar dinero
el correo
enviar una carta
la carta
el dinero

316   Capítulo 10

Options

Strategies for Reaching All Students

Students Needing Extra Help
Have students begin to fill in their Organizers.
También necesitas . . . : Some of these words can be taught as opposites. For example: *abrir* and *cerrar, sacar* and *devolver, temprano* and *tarde.*
Teach the preterite verbs as vocabulary, not grammar.
Write out the complete present-tense *cerrar* chart.

Learning Spanish Through Action
STAGING VOCABULARY: *Borren, Escriban, Pasen*
MATERIALS: a dozen index cards, with any number from 200 to 1,000 written on each one
DIRECTIONS: Call on a group of three or four students to go to the chalkboard. Select a card and show it to the class but not to the group at the board. Now read the num-
ber and have students at the board write out the number. Continue with new groups until all numbers have been written. For extra practice, call out selected numbers from the board, having volunteers erase them as you call them out.

316

doscientos*

trescientos

cuatrocientos

seiscientos

quinientos

setecientos

mil

ochocientos

novecientos

También necesitas . . .

abrir	to open	anoche	last night
cerrar (e → ie)	to close	ayer	yesterday
llegar	to arrive, to get to	luego	afterward, later, then
devolver:	to return (an object):	temprano	early
(yo) devolví	I returned	tarde†	late
(tú) devolviste	you returned	ya	already
enviar: (yo) envié	to send: I sent	(Yo) no lo sabía.	I didn't know that.
hacer:	to do, to make:	si	if, whether
(yo) hice	I did / made		
(tú) hiciste	you did / made		
sacar: (yo) saqué	to take out: I took out		
ver: (yo) vi	to see: I saw		
(tú) viste	you saw		

> **¿Y qué quiere decir . . . ?**
> ¿Me compras ___?
> (yo) deposité

* Note that when a number ending in *-ientos* is followed by a feminine noun, we use *-ientas* instead: *doscientas personas, trescientas cincuenta cartas.*
† Remember that *la tarde* means "afternoon" or "evening."

Vocabulario para conversar   317

Grammar Preview
Envié and *saqué* are presented lexically. The explanation of the preterite of *-ar* verbs appears in the grammar section on p. 333.

Teaching Suggestions
Preparing students to speak: Use one or two options from each of the categories of Comprehensible Input, Physical Response, or Limited Verbal Response. For a complete explanation of these categories and some sample activities, see the front section of this Teacher's Edition.

Point out that *mil* is a false cognate (often referred to as an *amigo falso*). It means "thousand," but it may be confused with "million." A million is *un millón*.

Class Starter Review
On the day following initial vocabulary presentation, you might begin the class with one of these activities:
1) Call out specific activities related to places shown in the *Vocabulario para conversar.* Have students name the places. Then reverse the activity.
2) Have students name three places where they might run errands.

Practice

Reteach / Review: ¿Por qué? / porque

Ex. 1: To extend this dialogue, *Estudiante A* can ask *Estudiante B* why he or she has to go to the second place mentioned.

Re-enter / Recycle

Ex. 1: places and buildings from Chap. 3
Ex. 2: school supplies from Chap. 2, food from Chap. 4, direct object pronouns from Chap. 6, places and buildings from Chap. 9
Ex. 3: places and buildings from Chap. 3
Ex. 4: calendar expressions from *El primer paso*, time-telling from Chap. 2

Answers: Empecemos a conversar

1 ESTUDIANTE A
a. ¿Adónde vas? ¿A la biblioteca?
b. ...¿Al supermercado?
c. ...¿Al correo?
d. ...¿Al parque?
e. ...¿A la tienda de regalos?

ESTUDIANTE B
a. Sí, y luego tengo que ir a la farmacia.
b. ...al gimnasio.
c. ...al almacén.
d. ...a la piscina.
e. ...a la tienda de descuentos.

Empecemos a conversar

Túrnate con un(a) compañero(a) para ser *Estudiante A* y *Estudiante B*. Reemplacen las palabras subrayadas con palabras representadas o escritas en los recuadros.
 quiere decir que puedes escoger *(choose)* tu propia respuesta.

1
A — ¿Adónde vas? ¿Al banco?
B — Sí, y luego tengo que ir al parque.
Y ahora Uds.

Estudiante A   Estudiante B

2

A — Si vas a la farmacia, ¿me compras pastillas para la garganta?
B — Pero ya las compré ayer.
A — ¡Ah! No lo sabía.
Y ahora Uds.

¡NO OLVIDES!
Remember that the direct object pronouns are *lo, la, los,* and *las.*

Estudiante A   Estudiante B

318   Capítulo 10

Options

Strategies for Reaching All Students

Spanish-Speaking Students
Exs. 1–4: Pair bilingual and non-bilingual students whenever possible.

Un paso más Exs. 10-C, 10-D

Students Needing Extra Help
Ex. 1: Review *al* and *a la* from Chap. 3.
Ex. 2: Show students how *pastillas para la garganta* becomes *las* in the response. Write it on the chalkboard and then do another example.
Ex. 3: Write *fui, fuiste, llevé, compré, pagué, envié,* and other preterite forms on the chalkboard for possible responses.

Otherwise students may be tempted to use just one response. Show students that the places and associated activities from p. 316 are grouped together. They will need to know this to do the activity.
Ex. 4: Review *tarde* and *temprano*. Review time-telling from Chap. 2.

3

A — ¿Qué hiciste ayer? ¿Fuiste <u>al banco</u>?
B — Sí, fui y <u>saqué (deposité) dinero (doscientos dólares)</u>.
   o: No, fui <u>al parque de diversiones</u>.

   Y ahora Uds.

Estudiante A   Estudiante B

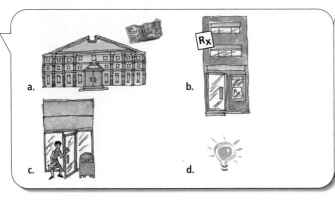

4

A — ¿<u>La biblioteca</u> abre tarde los sábados?
B — <u>Sí, abre a las diez y cierra temprano por la noche</u>.
   o: No, abre temprano y cierra temprano por la tarde.

   Y ahora Uds.

Estudiante A   Estudiante B

Vocabulario para conversar   319

---

2 ESTUDIANTE A
a. Si vas al correo, ¿me compras sellos? / ¡Ah! No lo sabía.
b. . . . al supermercado, . . . papas? / . . .
c. . . . a la librería, . . . lápices? / . . .
d. . . . al supermercado, . . . refrescos? / . . .
e. . . . a la farmacia, . . . *(Endings will vary.)*

ESTUDIANTE B
a. Pero ya los compré ayer.
b. . . . las . . .
c. . . . los . . .
d. . . . los . . .
e. Answers will vary. Look for correct use of direct object pronouns.

3 ESTUDIANTE A
a. ¿Qué hiciste ayer? ¿Fuiste a la farmacia?
b. . . . a la librería?
c. . . . al correo?
d. . . . al parque?
e. . . . a la biblioteca?
f. . . . al supermercado?

ESTUDIANTE B
a.–f. Answers will vary. Encourage students to use vocabulary from previous chapters.

4 ESTUDIANTE A
a. ¿El banco abre tarde los sábados?
b. ¿La farmacia . . .
c. ¿El correo . . .
d. Questions will vary.

ESTUDIANTE B
a.–d. Answers will vary.

Enrichment
Ex. 3: This exercise can be done with the entire class with you playing the role of *Estudiante A* and eliciting various answers for each place named. Vary the initial question. Examples: *Y tú, ¿qué hiciste ayer? Y tú, ¿fuiste al banco también? Y tú, ¿adónde fuiste ayer?*

Apply

Re-enter / Recycle

Ex. 5: places and buildings from Chaps. 3 and 6, expressing likes and preferences from Chap. 4
Ex. 6: direct object pronouns from Chap. 6
Ex. 8: *ir a* + inf. from Chap. 3

Answers: Empecemos a escribir

5 Answers will vary, but look for *prefiero* + inf. and use of the contraction *al*.

6 Answers will vary, but look for use of *hice / hago* and the pronoun *las*.

7 Answers will vary, but make sure students use the preterite form. Encourage use of new vocabulary.

8 Answers will vary, but look for *ir a* + inf.

Empecemos a escribir

Escribe tus respuestas en español.

5 ¿Prefieres llegar tarde o temprano a una fiesta? ¿A un partido? ¿Al cine?

6 ¿Ya hiciste todas las tareas para hoy? ¿Las hiciste anoche? Generalmente, ¿las haces por la tarde o por la noche?

7 ¿Adónde fuiste ayer? ¿Y el fin de semana pasado? ¿A quién viste?

8 ¿Qué vas a hacer si recibes *(receive)* mil dólares? ¿Vas a depositarlos en el banco o vas a comprar cosas? ¿Qué vas a comprar?

Options

Strategies for Reaching All Students

Spanish-Speaking Students

Have Spanish-speaking students write a paragraph about the last time they went shopping for a gift. *Escribe sobre la última vez que saliste a comprar un regalo. ¿Adónde fuiste? ¿Qué compraste? ¿Para quién lo compraste? ¿Por qué le compraste un regalo? ¿Fue fácil encontrar lo que querías?*

Students Needing Extra Help

Ex. 7: Have students make a three-column chart before writing sentences if this exercise is done in groups. Remind students of the *a personal*.
Ex. 8: Have students make a columned chart to help them get organized.

Enrichment

Empecemos a escribir: Additional writing assignments: 1) Students can write a sentence telling three things they saw on their last vacation. 2) Students can tell when and where they last bought three school supplies or items of clothing.

**Practice Wkbk.
10-1, 10-2**

Audio Activity 10.1

**Writing Activities
10-A, 10-B**

Pruebas 10-1, 10-2

También se dice

la estampilla
el timbre

la postal

el hipermercado

los correos
la oficina de correos

la botica
la droguería

La Plaza de la
Cibeles en Madrid

Delante del Correo
Central en Madrid

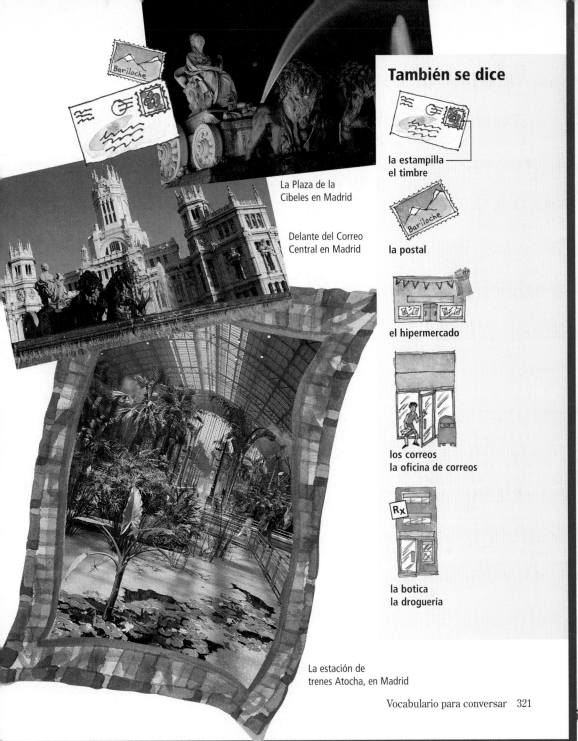

La estación de
trenes Atocha, en Madrid

Vocabulario para conversar   321

Cultural Notes

(p. 321, top and center photos)
Cibeles fountain, a landmark in Madrid, dates from the 1700s and represents Cibeles (Cybele), the Greek goddess of fertility, riding her chariot amid cascading water. The fountain stands in the center of a major traffic circle, la Plaza de la Cibeles. The building in the background is the city's main post office, el Palacio de Comunicaciones, built in the early 1900s.

(p. 321, bottom photo)
The Spanish government owns and operates Spain's rail network, RENFE *(Red Nacional de los Ferrocarriles Españoles)*. In 1992, Spain improved its already efficient service by launching its first high-speed train, the AVE *(Alta Velocidad Española),* to make the run between Madrid and Expo '92 in Sevilla. Traveling at speeds of up to 186 miles per hour, the AVE cuts the travel time between these two cities from six hours to two hours and forty-five minutes.

Present

Chapter Theme
Transportation

Communicative Objectives
- To talk about places
- To ask and give directions
- To talk about transportation
- To express agreement
- To say you don't know something

 Transparencies 53–54

 Vocabulary Art BLMs

 Pronunciation Tape 10-2

 Vocabulario para conversar B

Play

Using the Video
Video segment 2: See the Video Teacher's Guide.

 Video Activity B

Grammar Preview
Del appears here lexically. The explanation of the preposition *de + el* appears in the grammar section on p. 331.

Vocabulario para conversar

¿Dónde queda el banco?

Aquí tienes el resto del vocabulario necesario para hablar de tu comunidad.

322   Capítulo 10

Options

Strategies for Reaching All Students

Students Needing Extra Help
También necesitas . . . : Illustrate the location words with hand and / or body motions. Explain *en* + vehicle by giving examples with the new vocabulary.

Enrichment
También necesitas . . . : Review *lejos de / cerca de* and practice the new prepositions by asking questions about the location of classroom objects and where students are sitting. You may want to preview *del* with *lejos de / cerca de* and the new prepositions by modeling a complete sentence: *El bolígrafo está cerca (a la izquierda) del cuaderno.*

Learning Spanish Through Action
STAGING VOCABULARY: *Señalen, Toquen*
MATERIALS: photocopies of this vocabulary section from the Vocabulary Art BLMs
DIRECTIONS: Tell students where you went last week. Have them touch or point to the locations on the map. Ask follow-up questions such as: *¿Dónde está el (la) ____? ¿Está a la derecha (izquierda) del (de la) ____?*

322

el teatro

el zoológico

el estadio

LA REFORMA

METRO

la avenida

el autobús

la parada del autobús

CALLE DEL SOL

el metro

la estación del metro

la biblioteca

la iglesia

la calle

También necesitas...

trabajar	*to work*	enfrente (de)	*facing, opposite, in front (of)*
¿A cuántas cuadras (de ___)?	*How many blocks (from ___)?*	entre	*between, among*
A (cinco) cuadras (de ___).	*(Five) blocks (from ___).*	¿Cómo?	*How?*
queda(n)	*is (are) located*	en + *vehicle*	*by* + vehicle
a la derecha (de)	*to the right (of)*	Bueno	here: *OK, fine, all right*
a la izquierda (de)	*to the left (of)*		
al lado (de)	*next to, beside*		
detrás (de)	*behind*		

¿Y qué quiere decir...?
la comunidad
el templo
(Yo) no sé.

Teaching Suggestions
Preparing students to speak: Use one or two options from each of the categories of Comprehensible Input, Physical Response, or Limited Verbal Response. For a complete explanation of these categories and some sample activities, see the front section of this Teacher's Edition.

Note: Only boldface labels are new vocabulary items. The others were introduced earlier in this chapter.

Class Starter Review
Following initial vocabulary presentation, you might begin the class with this activity:
Mark a specific spot on the overhead transparency of the town. Ask pairs of students to write down as many ways as they can to say where that place is. Provide a time limit. Do one place per day for several days. (As an alternative, bring in authentic city maps of your area or one from a Spanish-speaking country so students can practice asking for and giving directions.)

Practice & Apply

Re-enter / Recycle

Ex. 14: numbers 0–31 from *El primer paso*

Answers: Empecemos a conversar

9 ESTUDIANTE A

a. ¿Cómo vamos al zoológico? / Bueno.

b. ...al hotel? / ...

c. ...al restaurante? / ...

d. ...al estadio? / ...

e. ...a la iglesia? / ...

ESTUDIANTE B

a. Pues, no sé. ¿Porqué no vamos a pie?

b. ...en taxi?

c. ...en metro?

d. ...en autobús?

e. Answers will vary.

10 ESTUDIANTE A

a. Perdón, señora (señor / joven / señorita). ¿Dónde queda la estación de policía?

b ...el zoológico?

c. ...la estación del metro?

d. ...la estación de servicio?

e. ...el correo?

f. ...la plaza?

ESTUDIANTE B

a.–f. Answers will vary.

Empecemos a conversar

Para los ejercicios 10–11, usa el mapa en las páginas 322–323.

9

A — ¿Cómo vamos *al teatro*?

B — Pues, no sé. ¿Por qué no vamos *en coche*?

A — Bueno.

Y ahora Uds.

Estudiante A   Estudiante B

10

A — *Perdón, señora (señor / joven / señorita). ¿Dónde queda el banco?*

B — *Está en la calle Rivera, entre el restaurante y la estación de servicio.*

Y ahora Uds.

Estudiante A   Estudiante B

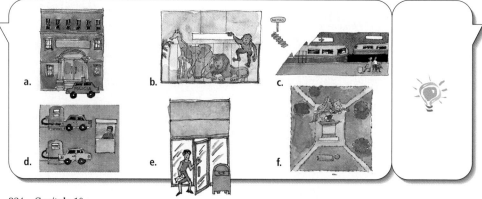

324   Capítulo 10

Options

Strategies for Reaching All Students

Spanish-Speaking Students

Exs. 9–10: Pair bilingual with non-bilingual students whenever possible.

Ex. 14: After this exercise, ask Spanish-speaking students: *¿Cómo se llega a tu casa o apartamento desde la escuela? Escribe direcciones específicas.*

Ex. 15: Have students create a similar letter and ask non-bilingual students to help find the sentences that don't make sense.

Students Needing Extra Help

Ex. 10: Remind students to use the map. Have students repeat the activity using location words in preparation for Ex. 11.

Ex. 11: Point out the entrances to the buildings on the map.

Ex. 12: Have students use their Organizers. Brainstorm possible responses by using the map. Start with a list of location words.

Ex. 14: Students in rural areas may not be familiar with the term "block." Provide an example.

Enrichment

Ex. 10: Encourage students to give a variety of answers. For instance, *el banco queda al lado del restaurante.*

Ex. 12: To extend this assignment, students can make and label a map of their neighborhood that includes as many of the places as possible from both vocabulary sections.

Ex. 15: In pairs, have students create their own illogical letters. Post the letters and have them select the funniest ones.

324

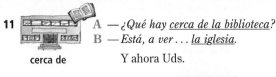

11
A — ¿Qué hay *cerca de la biblioteca*?
B — Está, a ver . . . *la iglesia*.

cerca de

Y ahora Uds.

Estudiante A

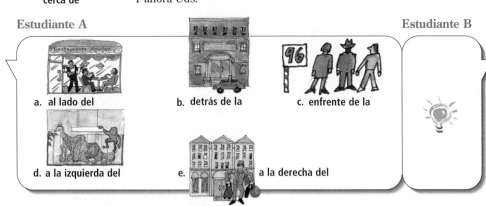

a. al lado del   b. detrás de la   c. enfrente de la

d. a la izquierda del   e.   a la derecha del

Estudiante B

Empecemos a escribir y a leer

Escribe tus respuestas en español.

12 ¿Qué hay en tu comunidad? Por ejemplo:

En mi comunidad hay un monumento en una plaza, un templo, una iglesia, dos bancos, . . .

13 ¿Dónde trabajan tus padres? ¿Trabajan en tu comunidad o en otra comunidad? ¿Y los padres de tu compañero(a)?

14 ¿Dónde queda la estación de policía de tu comunidad? ¿Queda cerca o lejos de tu casa? ¿A cuántas cuadras?

15 Lee la carta y luego cambia *(change)* las palabras *(words)* o frases que no tienen sentido *(make sense)*.

> Querida mamá:
> Ayer estuve muy ocupada todo el día. Primero fui al correo y compré unas pastillas para la garganta. Luego fui al teatro y vi un partido de vóleibol. Por la tarde fui al supermercado, donde compré unas tarjetas postales deliciosas. Luego, fui al zoológico para comprar zapatos nuevos. Hoy tengo que ir a la biblioteca porque necesito comprar un regalo para papá.
>
> Tu hija,
> Teresa

También se dice

la gasolinera

el subterráneo (el subte)

el bus
el camión
el colectivo
la guagua
el micro
el ómnibus

Vocabulario para conversar   325

Practice

Re-enter / Recycle

Ex. 1: school supplies from Chap. 2, food from Chap. 4, clothing from Chap. 6, vacation items from Chap. 7
Ex. 2: school subjects and numbers 32–59 from Chap. 2, numbers 60–100 from Chap. 5

Answers:
¡Comuniquemos!

1 ESTUDIANTE A

Dialogues will vary since students may use different verbs. Look for logical statements and encourage maximum use of vocabulary.
a. comprar un sello / buscar una tarjeta de cumpleaños
b. comprar una tarjeta postal / buscar un regalo
c. comprar pastillas para la garganta / enviar una carta
d. comprar un suéter / buscar un marcador
e. comprar leche / sacar dinero
f. comprar zapatos / buscar unos anteojos de sol

ESTUDIANTE B

Questions will vary. Places may include:
a. el correo / la librería
b. el correo / la tienda de regalos
c. la farmacia / el correo
d. la tienda de ropa / la librería
e. el supermercado / el banco
f. la zapatería / el almacén

¡Comuniquemos!

Aquí tienes otra oportunidad para usar el vocabulario de este capítulo.

1 Con un(a) compañero(a), imaginen que Uds. van a ir de compras. Primero tienen que decidir qué van a hacer y luego adónde van a ir.

A —*Necesito comprar comestibles y buscar un regalo también.*
B —*¿Por qué no vamos primero a la tienda de regalos y luego al supermercado?*

a.

b.

c.
d.

e.

f.

Options

Strategies for Reaching All Students

Spanish-Speaking Students

Exs: 1–2: Have Spanish-speaking students work together and present one of these to the whole class.

 Un paso más Ex. 10-E

Students Needing Extra Help

Ex. 1: Discuss when *comprar* and *buscar* would be used. Otherwise students might just repeat them indiscriminately.
Use a map and generate a list of stores using Chap. 6 vocabulary.
¿Qué sabes ahora?: Have students write out this section so that they can check off what they have mastered.

Cooperative Learning

Divide the class into groups of three or four. Using the map on pp. 322–323 of their texts, have them write clear instructions in how to get from one place to another. Assign each group a different set of start and end points. After they have written their sentences, call on individuals to read them, but without revealing the destination. Have other groups try to guess the final destination.

2 Los padres van a visitar tu escuela esta noche, y tú tienes que trabajar de guía *(guide)*. Con un(a) compañero(a), ayuda a los padres a llegar a los lugares correctos.

A —*¿Quién es tu profesor de ciencias?*
B —*Es el señor/la señora ____.*
A —*¿Dónde queda su sala de clases?*
B —*Queda cerca de ____. Es la sala número ____.*

¿Qué sabes ahora?

Can you:

■ **name places in your community?**
  —**En mi comunidad hay ____.**
■ **ask about and give the location of a place?**
  —**¿Dónde ____ la estación de policía?**
  —**Está ____ la librería.**
■ **tell where you go to run errands?**
  —**Voy ____ para enviar unas cartas.**

Plaza Morazán en Tegucigalpa
(1969), José Antonio Velásquez

Vocabulario para conversar   327

Answers: ¿Qué sabes ahora?
• Answers will vary.
• *queda;* Answers will vary, but look for a variety of prepositions.
• Answers will vary. Look for *al* or *a la* + noun.

Multicultural Perspectives
Ancient civilizations such as those of the Mayas in Central America and the Incas in South America organized their cities around a *plaza*. The site was selected for religious or for practical reasons, such as its being a source of water. Temples and palaces were built around the *plaza*. Ask students to think about how towns and cities are designed and organized. Ask them what the central area or areas of their own towns are. How do they attract people?

 Audio Activity 10.3

Cultural Notes ☼

(p. 327, photo)
The Honduran artist, José Antonio Velázquez, was born in La Caridad in 1906. He worked as a telegraph operator and barber before devoting himself to his art in 1930. Today he is one of the most renowned painters in Latin America.

Present & Apply

Cultural Objective
• To compare and contrast a Hispanic community with a community you are familiar with

Critical Thinking: Identifying Stereotypes
Help students understand that Hispanics are not the only group that has established neighborhoods such as Pilsen. Discuss immigrant groups, past and present, that have developed similar neighborhoods in towns and cities throughout the country. Ask students why they believe people decide to move to areas that are heavily populated with people of their own ethnicity or cultural background. Identify and discuss stereotypes that sometimes cloud people's perceptions of ethnic neighborhoods and why people choose to live in them.

Perspectiva cultural

En esta ciudad hay muchos productos hispanos y servicios en español.

Do you think these photographs were taken in the United States? Why do you think so? Looking at the signs on the right in English and Spanish, which language do you think predominates? Why? What do the signs tell you about the community and the people who live there?

Yrma is fourteen and lives in Chicago with her family. When she wants to see a Spanish-language movie at a local theater, she can find the information she needs in any of several Spanish-language papers published in the city. These are the papers that almost one million Hispanic residents in Chicago can read to keep informed, look for a job, or find weekly sales on groceries.

Yrma's neighborhood is called Pilsen. It's one of several large Hispanic communities in Chicago. Most residents of Pilsen are Mexican-American. The Pilsen community offers its residents and the rest of the city a large variety of products and services. Within walking distance of Yrma's home, you can find several small tortilla factories; offices of bilingual doctors, lawyers, and dentists; grocery stores with products from the United States and Mexico; bookstores and record stores with Spanish-language titles; restaurants; and several travel agencies.

328   Capítulo 10

Options

Strategies for Reaching All Students

Spanish-Speaking Students
Ask: ¿Hay muchos hispanos en tu comunidad? ¿Puedes comprar periódicos y revistas en español? ¿Hay tiendas y comidas especiales? ¿Qué otros idiomas se hablan donde vives? ¿Has visitado otras partes de tu pueblo o ciudad donde viven personas de otras partes del mundo? ¿Qué puedes ver o hacer allí?

 Un paso más Ex. 10-F

Students Needing Extra Help
Have students take notes on important information to use as a review later in ¿Lo sabes bien?
Discuss the Spanish-speaking community in your area. Ask students which Spanish-speaking culture predominates in your area.
Exs. 1–2: Be aware that some students may not be familiar with any culture other than their own.

Enrichment
Tell students that in Spanish the name of the Mexican Fine Arts Center Museum is El Centro Museo de Bellas Artes Mexicanas and that it is the largest facility of its kind in the country. It not only presents exhibits on the visual arts, but also offers film, theater, music festivals, and art education programs and materials. Among other goods and services in Pilsen are newspapers and magazines from Mexico and clothing stores featuring Western or vaquero fashions.

328

(De izquierda a derecha) Del Centro Museo de Bellas Artes Mexicanas en Chicago: la entrada del Museo; un árbol de la muerte en la tienda de regalos; tápiz de madera hecha por una joven mexicana

Tienda de productos latinoamericanos en Nueva Jersey

A few blocks from Yrma's home is the Mexican Fine Arts Center Museum, where works by Mexican and Mexican-American artists are always on view.

People from other areas of Chicago come to Pilsen looking for the special products and services it offers. Where else would you buy the freshest tortillas in town? Or the latest pop hits from Mexico?

Yrma's neighborhood is a good example of how the many Hispanic communities throughout the United States provide unique goods and services to the entire population of the city. Pilsen is part of the diverse mosaic of cultures that make the United States a multicultural society.

La cultura desde tu perspectiva

1 How is Pilsen similar to your own community?

2 Are there communities in your city where the primary language is something other than English? Have you visited them? What products and services do they provide?

Perspectiva cultural   329

Cultural Notes ☼

(pp. 328–329, photo)
Stores like this one in Union City, New Jersey, cater to large communities of Hispanics. They carry products that can be found in American grocery stores, in addition to foods, spices, newspapers, and magazines from Latin America. The sign in the window, *Paleticas de cerdo* (ham hocks), uses the Cuban form of the diminutive for *paletas (-icas* instead of *-itas),* indicating that it is either Cuban-owned or serves a primarily Cuban clientele.

(p. 329, top photos)
The Mexican Fine Arts Center Museum (founded 1982) is located in Pilsen, a Chicago neighborhood that has been predominantly Mexican for several decades. It is the Midwest's first Mexican cultural center and the largest of its kind in the U.S. Every year more than 75,000 visitors view its exhibits or enjoy performing arts events.

Preview

 Transparency 55

Answers

A *Llegaron* means "they arrived"; *llevaron* "they took"; *enviaron,* "they mailed (sent)"; and *regresaron,* "they returned."

B *Escuchó* means "he listened"; *habló,* "he talked."

C *Fueron / fue*

Gramática en contexto

Read this story about a reporter and some visiting aliens.

Hoy dos individuos muy extraños llegaron a nuestra ciudad. Creemos que son agentes secretos de otro planeta.

Los dos agentes fueron a diferentes partes de la ciudad. Uno de ellos fue a ver un desfile y sacó fotos.

El otro agente fue al estadio a escuchar un concierto del grupo Los Tigres. El agente escuchó la música rock y grabó el concierto. También habló con varias personas.

Options

Strategies for Reaching All Students

Students Needing Extra Help
C: Have students start filling in the grammar portion of their Organizers. Have them refer to the verb chart on p. 336 if necessary.

Creemos que los agentes llevaron las fotos y otras cosas a su nave espacial y las enviaron a su líder.

No sabemos dónde están en este momento, pero creemos que los agentes ya regresaron a su planeta.

A In the story, the verb forms *llegaron, llevaron, enviaron,* and *regresaron* are used. What do you think they mean? (Remember you already know the meaning of *llegar, llevar, enviar,* and *regresar.*)

B The verbs *escuchó* and *habló* are used to talk about what one of the secret agents did. Can you figure out what these words mean?

C In the second paragraph, find two verb forms that tell where both secret agents went and then where one secret agent went.

La preposición *de + el*

When we use the preposition *a + el*, we form the contraction *al*. In the same way, when we use the preposition *de + el*, we form the contraction *del* ("of the," "from the").

Luisa está enfrente **del** cine.

Gramática en contexto   331

Present & Practice

Re-enter / Recycle

Ex. 1: numbers 0–31 from *El primer paso,* places and buildings from Chaps. 3 and 6

Answers

1 Answers will vary, but should be based on the accompanying map. Look for contractions *al* and *del.*

 Practice Wkbk. 10-6

 Prueba 10-5

---

1 Mira el mapa de abajo. Imagina que buscas varios lugares y tu compañero(a) es un(a) agente de policía. Pregunta y contesta según *(according to)* el modelo. Puedes usar las palabras *(words)* de la lista a la derecha.

A —*¿Dónde está la farmacia? ¿Queda lejos?*
B —*No, no queda lejos. Está al lado del hotel.*
A —*¿A cuántas cuadras de aquí?*
B —*Pues, queda a una (dos) cuadra(s) de aquí.*

cerca (de)
lejos (de)
a la izquierda (de)
a la derecha (de)
detrás (de)
enfrente (de)
al lado (de)
entre

ESTÁS AQUÍ

Options

Strategies for Reaching All Students

Spanish-Speaking Students

Exs. 1–6: For this grammar section, have Spanish-speaking students work together when possible.

Students Needing Extra Help

Ex. 1: Review *a + el* with examples from earlier chapters, using all forms *(al, a la, a los, a las).*
Point out that *entre* is the only one that does not require *de.*
Generate a list of places; students have only a list of location words.
El pretérito de los verbos que terminan en -ar: First review the present-tense endings with a chart. Then use preterite endings. Emphasize the need for the accent *(o* without the accent is the present-tense *yo* form; with the accent it's the preterite tense *Ud. / él / ella* form.). Practice pronunciation with examples.
Write out a complete chart for all the irregular verbs, color-coding or highlighting the stem-changing or irregular parts.
Show *cerrar* in both tenses to illustrate that there is no stem change in the preterite.

El pretérito de los verbos que terminan en *-ar*

Up to now you have seen verbs in the present tense and a few in the past tense. This past tense is called the preterite. Here are all the forms of *comprar* in the preterite.

(yo)	compré	(nosotros) (nosotras)	compramos
(tú)	compraste	(vosotros) (vosotras)	comprasteis
Ud. (él) (ella)	compró	Uds. (ellos) (ellas)	compraron

• You have already learned that the verb endings tell you who does an action. They also tell you when an action is done (in the present, in the past, or in the future). In the same way that *-o, -as, -a, -amos, -áis, -an* tell you that the action takes place in the present, *-é, -aste, -ó, -amos, -asteis, -aron* tell you that the action took place in the past.

• Notice the accent marks on the endings *-é* and *-ó*.

• Verbs that end in *-gar*, like *pagar, jugar,* and *llegar,* end in *-gué* in the *yo* form. For example:
> —¿Cuándo lle**gaste** al teatro?
> —Lle**gué** a las ocho.

• Verbs that end in *-car*, like *buscar, tocar,* and *sacar,* end in *-qué* in the *yo* form. For example:
> —¿Cuántos libros sa**caste** de la biblioteca ayer?
> —Sa**qué** dos.

• Verbs that have a stem change in the present do *not* have a stem change in the preterite. For example:
> Generalmente la tienda c**ie**rra a las diez,
> pero anoche c**e**rró a las ocho.

Gramática en contexto   333

Practice

Re-enter / Recycle

Ex. 2: time-telling from Chap. 2
Ex. 3: activities from Chap. 1,
leisure-time activities from
Chap. 3, vacation activities from
Chap. 7
Ex. 4: activities from Chap. 1,
household chores from Chap. 8

2 ESTUDIANTE A

a. ¿A qué hora llegaron Alejandro
y Carmen al banco?
b. ... llegó Catalina ...
c. ... llegó Agustín ...
d. ... llegaron Soledad y
Victoria ...
e. ... llegaste tú ...

ESTUDIANTE B

a. Llegaron temprano: a las ocho
y treinta y cinco.
b. Llegó muy tarde: a las nueve y
treinta y cinco.
c. Llegó muy tarde: a las nueve y
cuarenta y cinco.
d. Llegaron temprano: a las ocho
y cuarenta y cinco.
e. Llegué temprano: a las ocho y
media (treinta).

3 Dialogues will vary. Possible
exchanges may include these verb
forms: *escuché (escuchaste)
música, dibujé (dibujaste), prac-
tiqué (practicaste) deportes, saqué
(sacaste) fotos, paseé (paseaste)
en bote, esquié (esquiaste), tomé
(tomaste) el sol, toqué (tocaste) la
guitarra.*

2 Los empleados de este banco tienen que llegar a las 9:00 de la
mañana. ¿A qué hora llegaron ayer?

A —¿A qué hora llegó Carlos al banco?
B —*Llegó muy tarde: a las nueve y veinticinco.*

Carlos

a. Alejandro y Carmen   b. Catalina   c. Agustín

d. Soledad y Victoria   e. tú

3 Escoge *(choose)* cinco de las actividades y di cuándo las hiciste
la última vez *(last time).* Tu compañero(a) va a preguntar con
quién las hiciste.

A —*Hace dos días que escuché música.*
B —*¿Con quién escuchaste música?*
A —*Con mi amiga Isabel.*
    o: *Lo hice solo(a).*

Options

Strategies for Reaching All Students

Students Needing Extra Help
Ex. 2: Review time-telling.
Point out that early and late are based on a
9:00 A.M. opening.
Write a *llegar* chart (in the preterite) on the
chalkboard.
Ex. 3: Review *hace* + time period.
Have students make three columns, indicat-
ing *what* you did, *when* you did it, and *with
whom* you did it.

Review the *yo* and *tú* forms of each of the
possible verb choices.
Ex. 4: Remind students that the responses
depicted by art for *Estudiante B* are not in
sequential order with the questions for
Estudiante A.

4 Josefina sabe *(knows)* que todos tuvieron *(had)* cosas que hacer ayer. Pero no tiene la información correcta. Con un(a) compañero(a), pregunta y contesta según el modelo.

Teresa y Julia

A — *Teresa y Julia cocinaron ayer, ¿verdad?*
B — *Creo que no. Ellas escucharon música.*

Estudiante A

a. Clara

b. Guillermo y Miguel

c. Laura y Mario

d. Marcos y Jesús

e. Manolo

f. Ricardo

Estudiante B

Gramática en contexto   335

4 **ESTUDIANTE A**
a. Clara estudió ayer, ¿verdad?
b. Guillermo y Miguel limpiaron el baño . . .
c. Laura y Mario sacaron dinero . . .
d. Marcos y Jesús pasaron la aspiradora . . .
e. Manolo ayudó en casa . . .
f. Ricardo envió una carta . . .
ESTUDIANTE B
a.–f. Creo que no. . . . *(Answers will vary, but may include:* escuchar música, cortar el césped, lavar los platos, depositar dinero, sacar un libro. *Make sure students use the correct verb form.)*

 Practice Wkbk. 10-7, 10-8

 Writing Activity 10-E

 Pruebas 10-6, 10-7

 Comm. Act. BLM 10-2

Present & Practice

Class Starter Review

After the initial presentation of the preterite of *ir,* you might begin the class with this activity:
Hang signs labeled with the countries from *El primer paso.* Have volunteers (individually or in pairs) stand beneath the signs. Ask students where their classmates went: *¿Adónde fue Miguel? (Fue a Bolivia.) ¿Adónde fueron Ana y Alex? (Fueron a España.)* Continue until all preterite forms of *ir* have been used.

Re-enter / Recycle

Ex. 5: places and buildings from Chap. 3
Ex. 6: activities from Chap. 1, leisure-time activities from Chap. 3, vacation activities from Chap. 7, places and buildings from Chaps. 3 and 6

5 ESTUDIANTE A

a. ¿Adónde fue Jorge? / ¿Cómo fue?
b. ¿Adónde fueron los Sánchez? / ¿Cómo fueron?
c. ¿Adónde fueron Adela y Nicolás? / ¿Cómo fueron?
d. ¿Adónde fue la Sra. Ochoa? / ¿Cómo fue?
e. ¿Adónde fue Pilar? / ¿Cómo fue?
f. ¿Adónde fueron tú y tu hermano(a)? / ¿Cómo fueron?

El pretérito del verbo *ir*

You know that we use *fui* and *fuiste* to say that "I went" and "you went" somewhere. They are preterite-tense forms of *ir.* Here are all the forms of *ir* in the preterite.

(yo)	**fui**	(nosotros) (nosotras)	**fuimos**
(tú)	**fuiste**	(vosotros) (vosotras)	**fuisteis**
Ud. (él) (ella)	**fue**	Uds. (ellos) (ellas)	**fueron**

Notice that, unlike regular *-ar* verbs in the preterite, the forms of *ir* do not have accent marks.

5 Con un(a) compañero(a), di adónde y cómo fueron estas personas.

A —*¿Adónde fueron Federico y Esteban?*
B —*Fueron al centro comercial.*
A —*¿Cómo fueron?*
B —*En taxi.*

Federico y Esteban

a. Jorge   b. los Sánchez   c. Adela y Nicolás

d. la Sra. Ochoa   e. Pilar   f. tú y tu hermano(a)

336   Capítulo 10

Options

Strategies for Reaching All Students

Students Needing Extra Help

El pretérito del verbo ir: Remind students that *fui* and *fuiste* were taught in Chap. 7.
Ex. 6: Allow students enough time to make their lists of destinations, talk with their classmates, and record their answers.
Ahora lo sabes: Have students write out this section so that they can check off what they have mastered.

6 Di adónde fueron tú y otras personas, cuándo fueron y qué hicieron *(what you did)* allí.

Mis amigos y yo fuimos al parque ayer y jugamos básquetbol.

a. mis amigos y yo
b. mis padres
c. yo
d. (nombre de un amigo)
e. (nombres de dos amigos)

Ahora lo sabes

Can you:

■ indicate where one person or place is in relation to another?
—El restaurante está al lado ___ hotel. Está ___ la biblioteca.

■ talk about an errand someone ran?
—Mi mamá ___ al banco para ___ dinero.

■ tell where someone went?
—Anoche mis hermanos ___ a la farmacia y nosotros ___ al supermercado.

La estación del metro Universidad, Ciudad de México

ESTUDIANTE B
a. Fue al estadio. / A pie.
b. Fueron a la farmacia. / En autobús.
c. Fueron al parque de diversiones. / En coche.
d. Fue a la estación de policía. / En taxi.
e. Fue al banco. / En metro.
f. Fuimos . . . *(Answers will vary.)*

6 Answers will vary. Look for the correct form of *ir* and of the *-ar* verbs in the preterite. Make sure that there is logic in the place, activity, and time expression chosen. Students should answer in the following manner:
a. Mis amigos y yo fuimos a la piscina el sábado pasado y nadamos.
b. Mis padres fueron . . .
c. Yo fui . . .
d. (nombre de un amigo) fue . . .
e. (nombres de dos amigos) fueron . . .

Answers: Ahora lo sabes
• del / *Answers will vary.*
• fue / depositar (sacar)
• fueron / fuimos

 Practice Wkbk. 10-9

 Audio Activity 10.4

 Writing Activity 10-F

 Prueba 10-8

 Comm. Act. BLM 10-3

Cultural Notes

(p. 337, photo)
Several stations in Mexico City's *metro* feature murals such as this one. Others display archaeological artifacts unearthed while the system was being constructed. The *metro* opened in 1969 and transports around five million passengers every day. Miraculously, its efficient, inexpensive service was not interrupted during the devastating earthquakes that struck Mexico City in September 1985.

¡A conversar!

Play

Step

Using the Video
Video segment 3: See the Video Teacher's Guide.

 Video Activity C

Critical Thinking: Synthesizing
Using vocabulary from this chapter and previous ones, have groups develop planning guides for a trip that they will be taking to a destination of their choice. Planning guides may vary, but should include: 1) a list of items to buy or things to do before the trip, 2) a list of things to pack, and 3) an itinerary. Illustrations are optional. Groups should divide work evenly. Have them be prepared to present their planning guides to the whole class.

Para decir más
Aquí tienes vocabulario adicional que te puede ayudar para hacer las actividades de esta sección.

el maquillaje
makeup

ir de viaje
to take a trip

la estación de bomberos
fire station

Actividades

Esta sección te ofrece la oportunidad de aumentar tus conocimientos de español al integrar lo que aprendiste en este capítulo con lo que aprendiste en capítulos anteriores.

 Trabaja en un grupo de cuatro personas. En una hoja de papel, cada estudiante debe escribir tres cosas que él (ella) hizo el mes pasado.

> *Compré champú y pasta dentífrica.*
> *Fui al parque de diversiones.*
> *Trabajé en la farmacia.*

Junten *(put together)* las hojas de papel. Luego deben sacar los papeles y preguntar quién hizo qué cosa.

> *¿Quién compró champú y pasta dentífrica?*
> *¿Quién fue al parque de diversiones?*
> *¿Quién trabajó en la farmacia?*

¿Cuántas personas hicieron la misma *(same)* cosa?

> *¿Cuántas personas compraron champú y pasta dentífrica?*
> *¿Cuántas fueron a un parque de diversiones... ?*

¿Qué actividades hizo la mayoría de las personas?

338　Capítulo 10

Options

Strategies for Reaching All Students

Spanish-Speaking Students
Ex. 2: After doing this exercise, have Spanish-speaking students write a paragraph: *Escribe un párrafo acerca del viaje de tu compañero(a) y su familia.*

Students Needing Extra Help
Actividades: If you have time constraints, choose the activity most appropriate for your group. Ex. 2 may be the easiest.
Ex. 1: Have students use the Organizers from all chapters and review preterite endings.
Ex. 2: Review *hace* + time expressions. Be sensitive to the idea of family trips, as some families can't afford them. A fantasy trip would be a good alternative.

Compile a list of activities done on vacation to help students begin the exercise.
Ex. 3: Simplify the sentences if your class is having difficulty.
Point out how the verb changes when you are reporting the information (*fui* to *fue*).
Write out the formula on the chalkboard:
Fue + place + *para* + action.

Chiles en un campo en Santa Fe

La Catedral de San Francisco, Santa Fe

2 En una tarjeta, escribe una frase sobre cuándo y adónde fueron de viaje tú y tu familia.

> *Hace tres años que mi familia y yo fuimos a Santa Fe, Nuevo México.*

Intercambia *(exchange)* tarjetas con tu compañero(a). En una hoja de papel, escribe cinco preguntas sobre lo que hicieron tu compañero(a) y su familia.

> *¿Qué hiciste en Santa Fe?*
> *¿Compraron muchos recuerdos?*
> *¿Sacaron muchas fotos?*

Luego, di a otro grupo lo que hizo tu compañero(a) y su familia cuando fueron de viaje.

3 Trabaja en grupos de tres personas. Una persona piensa en un lugar de tu comunidad y dice lo que hizo allí. Otra persona debe repetir esto y añadir *(add)* adónde él (ella) fue y lo que hizo. Sigue *(Continue)* hasta que *(until)* alguien se olvide de lo que dijeron las otras personas.

A — *Fui a la farmacia para comprar jabón.*
B — *Tomás fue a la farmacia para comprar jabón.*
    Yo fui al correo para enviar unas cartas.
C — *Tomás fue a la farmacia ... Rosa fue al correo ...*
    Yo fui ...

El Museo de Bellas Artes en Santa Fe

Actividades 339

Re-enter / Recycle
Ex. 2: *hace ... que* from Chap. 9
Ex. 3: *para* + inf.

Answers:
Actividades

1 Answers will vary. Look for the use of *al* and the correct form of the preterite: *Fui al cine; nadé; saqué fotos (¿Quién fue al cine? ¿Quién nadó? ¿Quién sacó fotos?)*

2 Answers will vary. Students should answer the first part in the following manner:
Hace + time expression + *que* + *mi familia y yo fuimos a* + place.
Or: *Mi familia y yo fuimos a* + place + *hace* + time expression. Answers will vary in the second part, but look for the correct forms of the preterite.

3 Answers will vary. Look for the correct forms of the preterite and the use of *para* + inf.

 Writing Activities 10-G, 10-H

 Comm. Act. BLMs 10-4, 10-5

Enrichment
Ex. 2: As an extension, you could do the exercise using your own family. Students could then ask you questions: *¿Subió Ud. la pirámide? ¿Visitó Ud. la catedral?* etc.

Cooperative Learning
Divide the class into groups of three. Have each student write a preterite-tense form of *ir.* Papers are passed to the right and students then write a destination (place). Papers are passed to the right once again, with students writing a reason *(para* + inf.) for going somewhere. Ask one member of each group to read the three sentences. Poll the class to see if they make sense. If the sentences seem illogical, ask what changes should be made to make them logical.

Cultural Notes

(p. 339, right photo)
La catedral de San Francisco in Santa Fe, New Mexico, is a fine example of the city's Spanish colonial architecture. Santa Fe was founded in 1609 and is the oldest capital in the U.S.

(p. 339, bottom photo)
Santa Fe's Museum of Fine Arts includes in its collection several works by Georgia O'Keeffe, Edward Weston, and many twentieth-century Native American artists.

339

Apply

Process Reading
For a description of process reading, see p. 48.

Answers
Antes de leer
Answers will vary. / Explain that folk tales are stories circulated by word of mouth. They tend to be traditional in theme, and may be anonymous, timeless, and even placeless.

Mira la lectura
They are never able to finish filling the holes in their town.

¡Vamos a leer!

Antes de leer

STRATEGY > Using prior knowledge

Think of a folktale that you know. Who are the characters? What problems do they have? How is it resolved? How are folktales different from other stories?

Mira la lectura

STRATEGY > Skimming

Skim the reading. What seems to be the problem facing the Tolencianos?

EL PUEBLO DE TONTOS

Hay muchos tontos en la Tierra, pero en el pueblo de Tolencia todos son tontos. Un día don Hortensio Hortalecio, el alcalde de Tolencia, fue a su oficina y vio un hoyo enorme en el camino. "¿Qué pasa?" dijo don Hortensio. "¡Vamos a arreglar este hoyo ahora!"

Don Hortensio llamó a los tolencianos. "¡Tienen que arreglar el hoyo del camino!" Y lo arreglaron.

Después de trabajar don Hortensio fue a su casa. ¿Qué vio en el camino? ¡Otro hoyo! Llamó a los tolencianos y ellos arreglaron ese hoyo también.

Un día después don Hortensio salió de casa. ¿Qué vio delante de su puerta? ¡Sí! ¡OTRO HOYO! El alcalde llamó a los tolencianos y ellos arreglaron ese hoyo también. "¡Ya estamos cansados de arreglar hoyos!" dijeron. Pero esta cosa de los

340   Capítulo 10

Options

Strategies for Reaching All Students

Students Needing Extra Help
Antes de leer: Explain what a folk tale is and elicit some examples. You may want to check with the English department in your school to find out what kinds of literature students are familiar with.
Infórmate: Students may be discouraged if they can't find the word as it's spelled here. Help them come up with the dictionary form before they start to look for it.

Aplicación: Have the class brainstorm possible endings and use the Organizer to rewrite the ending. Show the exact place in the text where the new ending would begin. Give students a definite minimum or maximum number of words or sentences that you expect them to write for the new ending.

Infórmate

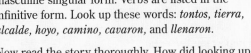 Using the dictionary
Scanning

In a dictionary, adjectives and nouns that have masculine and feminine forms are listed under the masculine singular form. Verbs are listed in the infinitive form. Look up these words: *tontos, tierra, alcalde, hoyo, camino, cavaron,* and *llenaron.*

Now read the story thoroughly. How did looking up the words help you?

1 How did the Tolencianos' problem worsen?

2 How was it solved?

3 Do you think the Tolencianos learned from their mistake?

Aplicación

If you had written this folk tale, how would your ending have differed? Get together with a partner and write your own ending for this tale.

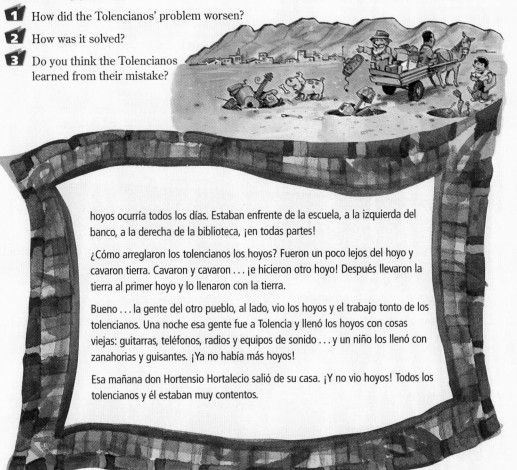

hoyos ocurría todos los días. Estaban enfrente de la escuela, a la izquierda del banco, a la derecha de la biblioteca, ¡en todas partes!

¿Cómo arreglaron los tolencianos los hoyos? Fueron un poco lejos del hoyo y cavaron tierra. Cavaron y cavaron . . . ¡e hicieron otro hoyo! Después llevaron la tierra al primer hoyo y lo llenaron con la tierra.

Bueno . . . la gente del otro pueblo, al lado, vio los hoyos y el trabajo tonto de los tolencianos. Una noche esa gente fue a Tolencia y llenó los hoyos con cosas viejas: guitarras, teléfonos, radios y equipos de sonido . . . y un niño los llenó con zanahorias y guisantes. ¡Ya no había más hoyos!

Esa mañana don Hortensio Hortalecio salió de su casa. ¡Y no vio hoyos! Todos los tolencianos y él estaban muy contentos.

¡Vamos a leer! 341

Infórmate

tontos: silly, dumb, foolish; *tierra:* earth; *alcalde:* mayor; *hoyo:* hole; *camino:* path; *cavaron:* they dug; *llenaron:* they filled / Remind students that they should look up the masculine, singular form *tonto,* and the infinitives *cavar* and *llenar.* / Answers will vary.

1. They kept digging new holes to fill the old ones.

2. People from another town filled the holes with old things.

3. Answers will vary.

Aplicación
Story endings will vary.

Apply

Process Writing
For information regarding developing a writing portfolio, see p. 50.

Multicultural Perspectives
The growth of settlements on the outskirts of many Latin American cities is attributed in large part to people moving from rural to urban areas in search of jobs. These settlements, known as *barrios*, or *pueblos jóvenes*, are common in many large cities in Latin America. The houses of these *pueblos jóvenes* are usually made of cardboard, adobe, or any material people can find. Some of the older *pueblos* have formed committees to obtain water and electrical services and to start schools. Have students compile a list of reasons that people migrate from rural areas to urban ones.

Todo junto

¡Vamos a escribir!

Every community has places or programs that depend on volunteers. Think about the programs in your community. What kinds of help do they need, and who can help? Make a poster that encourages people to volunteer. Follow these steps.

1 First, think about why community service is important. *(¿Por qué es importante trabajar como voluntario?)* List three reasons. Who can help? *(¿Quién puede ayudar?)*

2 Use your list and the answers to the questions to design your poster.

3 Show the draft of your poster to a partner. Then revise, edit, and make a final copy.

4 Now you are ready to show your poster. In addition to sending it to a Spanish-language newspaper or magazine, you can:

- post your work in the classroom
- submit it to your school newspaper
- include it in a newsletter or other publication that the school sends home
- add it to your writing portfolio

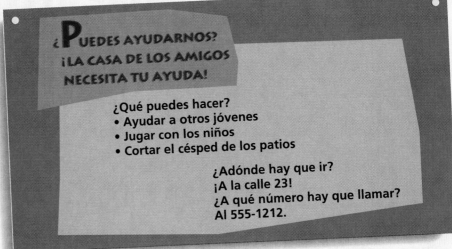

¿**P**UEDES AYUDARNOS?
¡LA CASA DE LOS AMIGOS NECESITA TU AYUDA!

¿Qué puedes hacer?
- Ayudar a otros jóvenes
- Jugar con los niños
- Cortar el césped de los patios

¿Adónde hay que ir?
¡A la calle 23!
¿A qué número hay que llamar?
Al 555-1212.

Jóvenes guatemaltecos hacen trabajo comunitario.

Options

Strategies for Reaching All Students

Spanish-Speaking Students
Step 1: Ask Spanish-speaking students: *¿Benefician al (a la) voluntario(a) los servicios a la comunidad?*

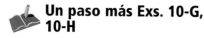
Un paso más Exs. 10-G, 10-H

Students Needing Extra Help
Brainstorm places, help needed, who can help, and the benefits. The local newspaper might be a good resource.

"¡Hola! Soy Jorge y trabajo en un proyecto escolar en Tegucigalpa."

Using Photos
Ask: *¿Cómo ayudan estos jóvenes en la comunidad?*

Assess & Summarize

Test Preparation

You may want to assign parts of this section as written homework or as an in-class writing activity prior to administering the *Examen de habilidades*.

Answers

Listening: *Ayer por la tarde fui al banco y deposité dinero. Luego fui al correo que está al lado del banco y envié una carta a mis tíos. También compré una tarjeta postal.*

The person speaking went to the bank and then to the post office.

Culture: Answers will vary. Students may include references to the *Perspectiva cultural.* For example: grocery stores, theaters, doctor's offices, newspapers, books, etc.

Reading: Remind students to look up the infinitive form of verbs and the masculine, singular form of adjectives.

Writing: Encourage students to use most of the vocabulary from this chapter and from Chaps. 1 and 3.

Speaking: Answers will vary. Students may use actual places in their community, or they may refer to the map on pp. 322–323.

¿Lo sabes bien?

This section will help you organize your studying for the proficiency test, where you will be asked to do similar, though not identical, tasks. There will not be any models on the test.

Listening

Can you understand when someone talks about what he or she did in different places in the community? Listen as your teacher reads a sample similar to what you will hear on the test. Can you mention two places the person making the statement went to run these errands?

Culture

Can you name some services or products especially offered to meet the needs of the Hispanic community?

Reading

Can you read a passage and know how to look up unknown words in the dictionary?

Ayer vi a Ana en el centro. Ella fue al banco y después a la biblioteca, donde sacó varios libros. Después tomó el autobús y la vi luego cerca del estadio. Por la tarde la vi entrando en una tienda de regalos. Entonces recordé que va a ser el cumpleaños de su esposo dentro de dos semanas. Me gustaría saber qué le compró . . . .

Writing

Can you write a letter about various places in your community and the activities that you did there? There is a sample letter on the right.

Speaking

Can you tell someone the location of a place? Here is a sample:

— *Ud. tiene que tomar el metro porque el correo no está muy cerca de aquí. Queda cerca de la farmacia, en la esquina de la Calle Ocho y Valencia. Enfrente del correo hay un banco y una tienda de ropa. Debe ir rápido; es tarde. El correo cierra a las dos y ya es la una y media.*

Querida Luisa:

Este fin de semana hice muchas cosas. Por la mañana, fui a la librería para comprar un regalo para mi tía, y luego fui al correo para enviarlo. Luego, fui a pasear en el parque y al supermercado para comprar comestibles. Por la tarde, vi un partido de béisbol en la tele.

Cariños,

Rebeca

Una tienda hispana en San Francisco

344   Capítulo 10

Options

Strategies for Reaching All Students

Students Needing Extra Help

Have students write out this section so that they can check off what they have mastered.
Listening: Have students first review their Organizers for possible words they will hear in the sample.
Reading: Remind students how to look up unknown words in a dictionary.
Writing: Have students use their Organizers. Give some guidelines as to the number of places and activities you want included.

Culture: Have students review any notes they might have taken during their reading of the *Perspectiva cultural.*
Speaking: Give this assignment a few days ahead of time so students can prepare. Have students use their Organizers. Emphasize what needs to be included: a place, transportation, and a landmark. Show students how *no está muy cerca de aquí* is the same as *está lejos de aquí.*

The principal's office might be a good place for which to provide directions.
Give students a visual, such as a map, to use while speaking.

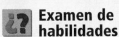
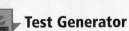
Resumen del capítulo 10

Use the vocabulary from this chapter to help you:

- name various places in your community
- name activities you do or did
- identify different means of transportation

to talk about places
la avenida
el banco
la biblioteca
la calle
el correo
la cuadra
la esquina
la estación (de policía / etc.)
el estadio
la farmacia
el hotel
la iglesia
la librería
el monumento
la parada
   del autobús
la plaza
el restaurante
el supermercado
el teatro
el templo
la tienda de regalos
el zoológico

to talk about activities or errands in a community
abrir
cerrar
la comunidad
el partido
devolver (o → ue) un libro
ir a pasear

llegar
sacar un libro
trabajar

to talk about things you buy
¿Me compras ___?
los comestibles
el champú
el jabón
la pasta dentífrica
las pastillas (para la garganta)
el regalo

to talk about money
el dinero: depositar / sacar
doscientos ...
quinientos ...
setecientos ...
novecientos
mil

to talk about mailing things
la carta
enviar
el sello
la tarjeta de cumpleaños
la tarjeta postal

to ask and give directions
¿A cuántas cuadras (de ___)?
A (cinco) cuadras (de ___).
queda(n)
del

a la derecha / izquierda (de)
al lado (de) / detrás (de) /
   enfrente (de)
entre

to talk about transportation
el autobús   ¿Cómo?
el metro   a pie
el taxi   en + *vehicle*

to talk about past activities
(yo) devolví, (tú) devolviste
(yo) hice, (tú) hiciste
(yo) vi, (tú) viste

to indicate when an event occurred
anoche / ayer
luego
temprano / tarde
ya

to say you don't / didn't know something
(Yo) no sé. / (Yo) no lo sabía.

to express a condition
si

to express agreement
Bueno.

Resumen   345

Cultural Notes ☼

(p. 344, photo)
The sign on this market in San Francisco's Mission District reflects the presence of Central and South American immigrants to this established Mexican American community. A well-organized network of agencies exists there to help newly arrived people adapt to ways of life in the U.S.

CAPÍTULO 11

THEME: MOVIES AND TV SHOWS

SCOPE AND SEQUENCE Pages 346–379

COMMUNICATION

Topics

TV shows

Movies

Objectives

To discuss television in the Spanish-speaking world

To name types of movies

To talk about TV and TV shows

To describe a movie or TV show

To indicate time or duration

To express opinions or reactions

To indicate a reason

CULTURE

Spanish-language television

GRAMMAR

Los comparativos y los superlativos

Los pronombres y el infinitivo

El pretérito del verbo ver

Los pronombres nos *y* les

Ancillaries available for use with Chapter 11

Multisensory/Technology

 Overhead Transparencies, 56–60

 Audio Tapes and CDs

 Vocabulary Art Blackline Masters for Hands-On Learning, pp. 58–62

 Classroom Crossword

 Video

 CD-ROM

Print

 Practice Workbook, pp. 114–124

 Writing, Audio & Video Activities, pp. 65–70, 123–125, 172–173

 Communicative Activity Blackline Masters

Pair and Small Group Activities, pp. 78–83

Situation Cards, p. 84

 Un paso más: Actividades para ampliar tu español, pp. 62–67

Assessment

 Assessment Program

Pruebas, pp. 159–170

Examen de habilidades, pp. 171–174

 Test Generator

Video still from Chap. 11

Spanish-Language Television

Spanish-language television was first broadcast in San Antonio and New York in the mid-1940s. Programs were aired in time slots purchased from English-language stations. In 1955, the first Spanish-language station, KCOR-TV in San Antonio, was born. One early program was called *Buscando estrellas,* a talent search and entertainment show that brought young entertainers from Mexico to Texas.

In the early 1970s the Spanish International Communications Corporation (SICC) was formed by U.S. and Mexican partners. This corporation was organized to provide programming to stations around the country. Many of the programs distributed through SICC were produced by Telesistema (now Televisa) in Mexico.

Today there is a well-established audience for Spanish-language broadcasting. Viewers can enjoy *telenovelas* and other entertainment shows from Mexico, Argentina, Venezuela, and Spain. International sports events are beamed from around the globe, accompanied by commentary and play-by-play coverage in Spanish.

Because Hispanic populations in the U.S. represent many different cultures, one challenge has been to create programs that appeal to the very diverse market. One major success was a *telenovela* entitled *Angélica, mi vida,* produced in Puerto Rico in the 1980s. The subplots dealt with love, tragedy, passion, and power struggles involving families of Puerto Rican, Cuban, and Mexican origin.

Popular shows today include *Cristina,* a talk show hosted by Cuban-born Cristina Saralegui, and the game show *Sábado gigante.* Cristina engages her guests and audiences in debates on lively topics. *Sábado gigante* features celebrity guest appearances, contests, games, and comedy. Other shows originating outside the U.S. include *El show de Chespirito* (Mexico), *Informe semanal* (Spain), and *Sábados felices* (Colombia).

Introduce

Re-entry of Concepts

The following list represents words, expressions, and grammar points re-entered from *El primer paso* to Chap. 8:

El primer paso
Calendar expressions

Chapter 1
Activities
Gustar expressions
Adjectives describing personality

Chapter 2
Time-telling

Chapter 3
Ir a + inf.
Leisure-time activities

Chapter 4
Foods
Expressing likes and preferences

Chapter 5
Adjectives describing physical characteristics

Chapter 6
Demonstrative adjectives

Chapter 8
Household chores
Tener que + inf.

Planning

Cross-Curricular Connections

Journalism Connection *(pp. 350–351)*
Have pairs of students write or orally present a critique of their favorite TV show from the current week. They should describe the key elements of the plot and give it a rating of 1–5 *estrellas*. Have them tell why they gave that rating.

Speech and Debate Connection *(pp. 366–367)*
Divide the class in half. Name two TV programs, movies, or songs. Then have both groups discuss which one is better and why. A spokesperson from each group can then present the views to the class.

Drama Connection *(pp. 372–373)*
In groups of three or four, have students plan and act out a scene from a TV program or movie. For homework, they can follow up with a written script.

CAPÍTULO 11

¿Qué te gustaría ver?

OBJECTIVES

At the end of this chapter you will be able to:

■ talk about a TV show or movie

■ tell when events begin and end, and how long they last

■ express and defend an opinion

■ compare and contrast Spanish-language TV shows with the TV shows you usually see

Uno de los muchos cines de Madrid

347

Cultural Notes ☀

Spanish in Your Community
Have students look at television guides to find out what types of Spanish-language movies are available in their community. Have them select three types of movies (dramas, mysteries, comedies, etc.) and compare them with similar movies in English.

(pp. 346–347, photo)
This movie theater in Madrid is showing the Spanish-language version of the box-office hit *The Joy Luck Club.* The Spanish title, *El club de la buena estrella,* only approximates the spirit of the unusual English title. Sometimes, even the most translatable titles are not literally rendered into Spanish. Rather, they are often worded to better describe the content of the film and capture the imagination of the Spanish-speaking audience.

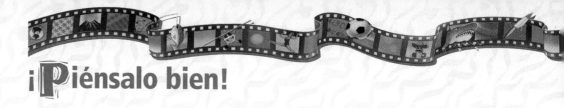

Preview

- To talk about Spanish-language television shows and movies

 ¿Qué te gustaría ver?

Play

 Video Activity A

Using the Video

This chapter's video focuses on communication and entertainment. Host Alexander Ruiz and his friends go to a movie at CocoWalk Mall in Miami and discuss their opinions. Afterwards Alexander interviews moviegoers about their own entertainment preferences. To prepare students for the video, ask them to predict what this chapter's tape will be about. Then have students watch the segment several times. Ask them to identify: a) how the movie theater in Little Havana resembles their favorite theater, and b) what was new to them about the Little Havana theater.

Video segment 1: For more teaching suggestions, see the Video Teacher's Guide.

¡Piénsalo bien!

Look at the photos and read the captions.

"Dos entradas, por favor."

Does this movie theater look like the ones you go to? What kind of information do you think appears on the window?

Comprando entradas en un cine en Barcelona

348 Capítulo 11

Options

Strategies for Reaching All Students

Spanish-Speaking Students
Ask: *¿Ves películas en español? ¿Dónde? ¿Qué te gusta más, ver la tele(visión) o ir al cine? ¿Qué clase de programa te gusta ver en la tele(visión)?*

 Un paso más Ex. 11-A

Students Needing Extra Help
(p. 349, bottom photo): Since not all of your students may watch the news, review the format with them. Assign students to watch the news the night before beginning this chapter.

Mexican movies—from the comedies of Cantinflas to the dramas of
Jorge Negrete—continue to be
favorites with Spanish-speaking
communities in the U.S. and
throughout Latin America.
Cantinflas (1911–1993) has been
compared to Charlie Chaplin. His
characters poked fun at distinguished members of society.
Invite students familiar with other
cultures to share their knowledge
of popular film and television personalities.

La cantante
Gloria Estefan

"Desde la oscuridad . . . "

Gloria Estefan and the Miami Sound Machine have
contributed to the popularity of music with a Latin beat.
How many of their songs can you name? What different
types of Latin music do you know?

Answers: ¡Piénsalo bien!
(p. 348, photo) Answers will vary.
/ Ticket prices and show times of
the movie are listed.

(p. 349, top photo) Answers will
vary. Some song titles include:
"Conga," "Anything for You,"
"Can't Stay Away from You," and
"Rhythm is Gonna Get You." /
Students may mention *salsa,*
tango, or *cha-cha-cha.*

(p. 349, bottom photo) Answers
will vary.

Un grupo de jóvenes ve
la televisión en
Caracas, Venezuela.

"Pero Javier . . . ¿qué nos va a pasar?"

These teens are watching a *telenovela,* a Spanish soap opera.
Can you name any *telenovelas* shown on Spanish-language
television in your community?

349

Cultural Notes ☼

(p. 348, photo)
The Spanish film industry suffered severe
censorship during the 36-year rule of
Francisco Franco. Since Franco's death in
1975, however, a new Spanish cinema has
flourished. Much of the credit for this success can be given to the Ministry of Culture,
which was founded in 1977. This govern-
mental agency provides subsidies for films
showing artistic merit.

(p. 349, top photo)
Gloria Estefan made her mark on the inter-
national popular music scene in the late
1980s as lead singer for Miami Sound
Machine, a band whose music is a mix of
Afro-Cuban, jazz, and rock 'n' roll rhythms.
In 1994 she released her first solo album,
Mi tierra, which featured original composi-
tions strongly influenced by traditional
Cuban music.

Present

Chapter Theme
Television

Communicative Objectives
- To talk about TV and TV shows
- To describe a movie or TV show
- To express opinions or reactions
- To indicate a reason

 Transparencies 56–57

 Vocabulary Art BLMs

 Pronunciation Tape 11-1

 Vocabulario para conversar A

Play

Using the Video
Video segment 2: See the Video Teacher's Guide.

 Video Activity B

Grammar Preview
El / la / los / las mejor(es) / peor(es) are presented lexically. The explanation of superlatives is in the grammar section on p. 366.

Vocabulario para conversar

¿Cuál es tu programa favorito?

Aquí tienes palabras y expresiones necesarias para hablar sobre la televisión y para expresar o defender una opinión. Léelas varias veces y practícalas con un(a) compañero(a) en las páginas siguientes.

Televisión
un concierto
el programa musical
cómico, -a
la comedia
el canal
el programa de detectives
la actriz
el actor
la telenovela
el programa deportivo
el anuncio
las noticias
interesante
el programa educativo

350   Capítulo 11

Options

Strategies for Reaching All Students

Students Needing Extra Help
Have students begin to fill in the Organizer. *También necesitas . . . :* Explain how the word "here" is not part of the definition, but means "in this chapter."
Emphasize that the asterisk for *aburrir, dar miedo, fascinar,* and *interesar* is not part of the spelling. Give examples.

Give examples of *dar* + movie or program. Write out *¿cuál?* and *¿cuáles?* Students may have difficulty with the parentheses and fail to see these as two different questions. Remind students that they already know *pensar* (Chap. 7). Review the forms and explain the slight change in meaning when *que* is added.

Learning Spanish Through Action
STAGING VOCABULARY: *Apunten, Marquen, Señalen*
MATERIALS: *Vocabulario para conversar* transparency or Vocabulary Art BLMs
DIRECTIONS: Direct students to mark appropriate shows using plus and minus as you give your opinion. For example: *Los dibujos animados son muy divertidos.* (plus) / *Los programas de entrevistas son aburridos.* (minus)

divertido, -a

los dibujos animados

realista

el programa de hechos
de la vida real

el pronóstico del tiempo

el documental

el programa de
entrevistas

aburrido, -a

También necesitas . . .

dar + *movie or TV program*	*to show*	el / la / los / las peor(es)	here: *worst*
la clase (de)	here: *kind / type (of)*	aburrir*	*to bore*
sobre	*about*	dar miedo*	*to scare*
pensar (e → ie) (que)	here: *to think (that)*	fascinar*	*to fascinate*
por eso	*that's why, for that reason, therefore*	interesar*	*to interest*
¿Cuál(es)?	*Which? Which one(s)?*		
demasiado	*too*		
emocionante	*exciting, touching*		
tonto, -a	*silly, dumb*		
más	here: *more*		
el / la / los / las mejor(es)	here: *best*		

> **¿Y qué quiere decir . . . ?**
> en blanco y negro
> en colores
> fascinante

* With the verbs *aburrir, dar miedo, fascinar,* and *interesar* we use the indirect object pronouns *me* and *te,* as we do with *gustar* and *encantar: **Me fascinan** las películas de terror.*

Vocabulario para conversar   351

Practice & Apply

Re-enter / Recycle

Ex. 1: *gustar* expressions from Chap. 1, demonstrative adjectives from Chap. 6

Ex. 3: demonstrative adjectives from Chap. 6

Ex. 7: calendar expressions from *El primer paso,* time-telling from Chap. 2

Answers: Empecemos a conversar

1 ESTUDIANTE A

a. ¿Te gustaría ver un programa educativo?

b. ...un programa musical?

c. ...un documental?

d. Questions will vary.

ESTUDIANTE B

a.–d. Answers will vary.

2 ESTUDIANTE A

a. ¿Quién es el mejor actor de televisión?

b. ...la mejor actriz de televisión?

c. ...el peor actor de televisión?

d. ...la peor actriz de televisión?

ESTUDIANTE B

a.–d. Answers will vary.

Empecemos a conversar

Túrnate con un(a) compañero(a) para ser *Estudiante A* y *Estudiante B*. Reemplacen las palabras subrayadas con palabras representadas o escritas en los recuadros. quiere decir que puedes escoger tu propia respuesta.

1
A —¿Te gustaría ver *un programa de entrevistas*?
B —*Sí, me gustaría mucho.*
   o: *No, esa clase de programas me aburre.*
   Y ahora Uds.

Estudiante A   **Estudiante B**

a.   b.   c.   d.

2   la mejor actriz de televisión
A —¿Quién es *la mejor actriz de televisión*?
B —*Para mí, (nombre) es la mejor. Me fascina.*
   Y ahora Uds.

Estudiante A   **Estudiante B**

a. el mejor actor de televisión   c. el peor actor de televisión

b. la mejor actriz de televisión   d. la peor actriz de televisión

352   Capítulo 11

Options

Strategies for Reaching All Students

Spanish-Speaking Students

Exs: 1–3: Pair bilingual with non-bilingual students if possible.

Ex. 7: After this exercise, ask Spanish-speaking students: *¿Cuál es tu telenovela favorita? ¿De qué se trata?*

 Un paso más Exs. 11-B, 11-C, 11-D

Students Needing Extra Help

Ex. 1: Review *Me dan miedo.* Brainstorm other possibilities using *aburrir, fascinar,* and *interesar.* Regardless of whether *Estudiante B* answers in the negative or the affirmative, have him or her give a reason.

Ex. 6: Explain that *¿por qué?* refers to each question.

Exs. 6–7: Encourage complete sentences.

3

A — *Pienso que deben dar <u>más (menos)</u> <u>programas de detectives</u>. Y tú, ¿qué piensas?*

B — <u>*(No) Estoy de acuerdo. Esos programas (no) son muy interesantes.*</u>

Y ahora Uds.

Estudiante A   **Estudiante B**

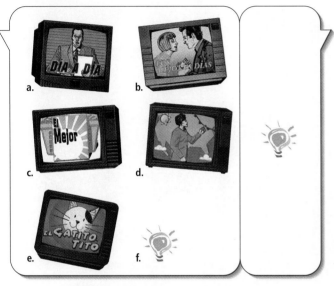

a.   b.

c.   d.

e.   f.

Empecemos a escribir

Escribe tus respuestas en español.

4 ¿Ves la televisión después de la escuela? ¿Qué programas de televisión te interesan? ¿Por qué?

5 ¿Qué piensas tú? ¿Crees que deben dar más o menos programas de hechos de la vida real en la tele? ¿Más o menos programas de entrevistas? ¿Por qué?

6 ¿Te interesan las noticias o te aburren? ¿Y los dibujos animados? ¿Y las telenovelas? ¿Por qué?

7 ¿Cuál es tu programa favorito? ¿A qué hora empieza? ¿Qué día de la semana lo dan? ¿En qué canal?

También se dice

la artista   el artista

el programa policial
el programa policíaco
el programa de misterio

el comercial
la propaganda

el noticiero
el informativo

3 ESTUDIANTE A

a. Pienso que deben dar más (menos) noticias. Y tú, ¿qué piensas?

b. ... telenovelas ...

c. ... anuncios ...

d. ... pronósticos del tiempo ...

e. ... dibujos animados ...

f. Questions will vary.

ESTUDIANTE B

a.–f. Answers will vary.

Answers: Empecemos a escribir

4 Answers will vary.

5 Answers will vary, but should begin with *Deben dar más (menos) programas ... porque ....*

6 Answers will vary and may include *Me interesan ... porque ....*

7 Answers will vary.

Practice Wkbk. 11-1, 11-2

Audio Activity 11.1

Writing Activity 11-A

Pruebas 11-1, 11-2

Present

Chapter Theme
Movies

Communicative Objectives
- To name types of movies
- To indicate time or duration

 Transparencies 58–59

 Vocabulary Art BLMs

 Pronunciation Tape 11-2

 Vocabulario para conversar B

Play

Using the Video
Video segment 2: See the Video Teacher's Guide.

 Video Activity B

Grammar Preview
Más is presented here lexically. The explanation of comparatives is in the grammar section on p. 363.

Vocabulario para conversar

¿Quién es la mejor actriz de cine?

Aquí tienes el resto del vocabulario necesario para hablar sobre el cine y para decir cuándo algo empieza y termina, y cuánto dura.

Cine

la película romántica

la película de terror

la película de ciencia ficción

la película del oeste

354   Capítulo 11

Options

Strategies for Reaching All Students

Students Needing Extra Help
Vocabulario para conversar: Have students continue to fill in their Organizers. Have them review their Organizers for Chap. 2 (time-telling).

Enrichment
Help students expand their use of new vocabulary by pointing out that they can apply the same descriptive words to both movies and TV programs. For example, talk about *películas de dibujos animados, películas musicales, películas cómicas,* and ask students to name movies that fit in those categories. Include *programas de ciencia ficción, programas del oeste,* and *programas románticos* and ask students to name TV shows of those kinds.

Learning Spanish Through Action
STAGING VOCABULARY: *Dibujen, Muestren*
MATERIALS: sheets of paper with blank clock faces or individual toy clocks
DIRECTIONS: Ask students to draw or move the clock hands to the times you announce. Remember to include *en punto* and *de la mañana (tarde, noche).* If you elect to have your students draw, have them also put in a sun *(el sol)* or a moon *(la luna)* to show morning, afternoon, or evening.

la película de aventuras

la película musical

También necesitas . . .

en punto	*sharp, on the dot*	largo, -a	here: *long* (duration)
de la mañana	*in the morning, A.M.*	corto, -a	here: *short* (duration)
de la tarde	*in the afternoon, early evening; P.M.*	más tarde	*later*
		más temprano	*earlier*
de la noche	*in the evening, at night; P.M.*		
medianoche	*midnight*		
mediodía	*noon*		
casi	*almost*		
durar	*to last*		
hasta	*until*		
el tiempo	here: *time*		
un poco	*a little*		

> **¿Y qué quiere decir . . . ?**
> media hora
> el minuto
> puntualmente
> todavía no

Vocabulario para conversar   355

Teaching Suggestions
Preparing students to speak: Use one or two options from each of the categories of Comprehensible Input, Physical Response, or Limited Verbal Response. For a complete explanation of these categories and some sample activities, see the front section of this Teacher's Edition.

También necesitas . . . : Explain that *de la tarde* is usually used until 6:00 P.M. *(las seis de la tarde).* From 7:00 P.M. and on, *de la noche (las siete de la noche)* is used, although in certain regions of the Spanish-speaking world 7:00 P.M. is still considered *la tarde* and 8:00 P.M. is the start of *la noche.*

Class Starter Review
On the day following initial vocabulary presentation, you might begin the class with this activity: Ask students to name their favorite movie (in English) or one they've recently seen. Ask them what kind of movie it is and who the actors are.

Reteach / Review: Time-telling
To review time-telling, write several times of the day on the chalkboard. Ask: *¿Qué hora es?* or *¿Son las . . . ?* (Say a time different from the one shown to get students to respond in the negative.) Encourage them to use *en punto, casi,* and *todavía no.*

Practice & Apply

Re-enter / Recycle
Ex. 8: *gustar* expressions from Chap. 1
Exs. 9–10, 12: time-telling from Chap. 2
Ex. 13: expressing likes and preferences from Chap. 4
Ex. 14: calendar expressions from *El primer paso,* time-telling from Chap. 2

Answers: Empecemos a conversar

8 ESTUDIANTE A

a. ¿Qué piensas sobre las películas de terror?

b. ... las películas de aventuras?

c. ... las películas del oeste?

d. ... las películas románticas?

ESTUDIANTE B

a.–d. Answers will vary.

9 ESTUDIANTE A

a. ¿Hoy dan una película de ciencia ficción en el cine?

b. ... una comedia ...

c. ... una película musical ...

d. ... una película de aventuras ...

e. Questions will vary.

ESTUDIANTE B

a. Sí, pero empezó a las cinco y ya son casi las seis.

b. ... a las diez ... las diez y media.

c. ... a las siete y media (... a las siete y treinta) ... las ocho.

d. ... a las seis ... las siete.

e. Answers will vary.

Empecemos a conversar

8

A — ¿Qué piensas sobre las películas <u>de ciencia ficción</u>?

B — *Pienso que son <u>interesantes y divertidas</u>. Por eso <u>me gustan</u>.*

Y ahora Uds.

Estudiante A

a.   b.   c.   d.

Estudiante B

9

A — ¿Hoy dan <u>una película de terror</u> en el cine?

B — *Sí, pero empezó a <u>las nueve</u> y ya son casi <u>las nueve y media</u>.*

Y ahora Uds.

¡NO OLVIDES!

You know the word *empezar.* It is an *e → ie* verb.

Estudiante A

a.   b.   c.

d.   e.

Estudiante B

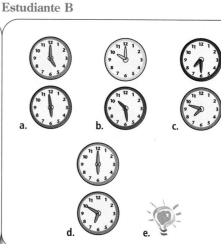

a.   b.   c.

d.   e.

356   Capítulo 11

Options

Strategies for Reaching All Students

Spanish-Speaking Students
Exs. 8–10: Pair bilingual with non-bilingual students if possible.

 Un paso más Ex. 11-E

Students Needing Extra Help
Ex. 10: Do the last response *(Solamente dura ...)* on the chalkboard.

Enrichment
Ex. 9: As a homework assignment, have students do this exercise twice: first, using the *menos* form of telling time, and then using the digital way: *doce y cincuenta y cinco, diez y cuarenta y cinco,* and so on.
Empecemos a escribir y a leer: Additional topics to write and read about:
1) Ask students to list three of their favorite movies or TV programs and to tell why they like them. Remind them that they can name

10

A — *¿Va a ser largo el documental?*
B — *Sí. Dura una hora y media.*
   o: *No, es corto. Solamente dura . . .*
   Y ahora Uds.

Estudiante A

a.
b.
c.
d.
e.

Estudiante B

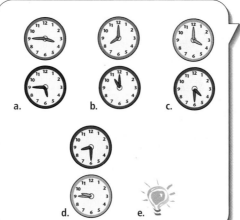

a.
b.
c.
d.
e.

Empecemos a escribir y a leer

Escribe tus respuestas en español.

11 ¿Qué clases de películas te interesan? ¿Por qué? ¿Cómo se llama tu película favorita?

12 ¿Cuánto tiempo dura tu programa favorito? ¿Lo dan tarde o temprano? ¿De qué hora a qué hora?

13 ¿Qué prefieres, las películas en blanco y negro o en colores? ¿Por qué?

14 Mariana dice: "El domingo, a las nueve de la noche, dan una presentación especial en el cine Elíseos. Dura tres horas y media. Quiero llegar puntualmente. ¿Quieres venir conmigo?"

¿Termina la película antes de la medianoche?

También se dice

la película de vaqueros

Practice

Re-enter / Recycle

Ex. 1: calendar expressions from *El primer paso,* time-telling from Chap. 2

Ex. 2: *gustar* expressions from Chap. 1, time-telling from Chap. 2, *ir a* + inf. from Chap. 3

Ex. 3: adjectives describing personality from Chap. 1, adjectives describing physical characteristics from Chap. 5

Answers: ¡Comuniquemos!

1 a. A —Ya son las ocho. ¿Qué podemos hacer? / *(Answers will vary for* Estudiante A*'s second response.)*

　B —En media hora hay un concierto de música folklórica de Honduras. ¿Quieres ir?

b. A —Ya son las tres y cuarto . . .

　B —. . . hay un partido de fútbol . . . (. . . hay una película de aventuras . . .)

c. A —Ya son las nueve . . .

　B —. . . hay un concierto de la orquesta nacional . . .

d. A —Ya son las cuatro y media . . .

　B —. . . hay un partido de béisbol . . . (. . . hay un concierto de la guitarra de Paco Argollas . . . / . . . hay una exposición internacional . . .)

¡Comuniquemos!

Aquí tienes otra oportunidad para usar el vocabulario de este capítulo.

1 Tu amigo(a) y tú están aburridos. Uds. buscan actividades que les gustaría hacer media hora después de la hora indicada *(given)*. Deben usar este calendario.

7:20

A — *Ya son las siete y veinte. ¿Qué podemos hacer?*

B — *En media hora hay una película de ciencia ficción. ¿Quieres ir?*

A — *Sí, vamos.*
　o: *Hoy no. A mí me aburre esa clase de películas.*

a. 8:00	d. 4:30
b. 3:15	e. 7:20
c. 9:00	f. 3:30

Este sábado en nuestra comunidad

Deportes
Béisbol: Tigres contra Leones
Fútbol: Cachorros contra Medias Blancas
　　　　5:00
　　　　3:45

Cine
El detective perezoso
La conquista del Sol
Aventura en la selva
　　　　4:00 y 7:50
　　　　7:50
　　　　3:45

Teatro
Festival nacional de teatro
La casa de Teresa
　　　　7:45
　　　　4:15 y 8:45

Conciertos
La guitarra de Paco Argollas
Orquesta Nacional
Música folklórica de Honduras
　　　　5:00
　　　　9:30
　　　　8:30

Museos
Exposición internacional
Impresionismo mexicano
　　　　4:00 y 5:00
　　　　7:15

Options

Strategies for Reaching All Students

Spanish-Speaking Students

Exs. 2–3: Have Spanish-speaking students write out these exercises.

Students Needing Extra Help

Ex. 1: Encourage students playing *Estudiante A* to vary the reasons they give whenever they disagree with *Estudiante B*'s suggestion: chores to do, not feeling well, and so on.

Ex. 3: To prepare for this exercise, you may want to have students do a written homework assignment the night before in which they describe their favorite actor or actress (both their personality and physical appearance). Have them use their Organizers.

¿Qué sabes ahora?: Have students write out this section so they can check off what they have mastered.

2 ¿Te gustaría ir al cine? Con un(a) compañero(a) haz *(make)* planes para ver una película este sábado.

3 En una hoja de papel, escribe una descripción corta de tu actor o actriz favorito(a). ¿Es alto(a)? / ¿Bajo(a)? ¿Es joven? / ¿Viejo(a)? ¿Cuál es el nombre de una película o del programa de televisión en el que aparece? No escribas su nombre. En grupos de cuatro, cada *(each)* estudiante lee su descripción. El resto del grupo debe adivinar *(guess)* quién es.

¿Qué sabes ahora?

Can you:

- tell what kind of television programs and movies you are interested in?
  —Los programas ___ me ___.
- say why you like or dislike certain programs or movies?
  —Las telenovelas (no) me gustan porque ___.
- tell how long something lasts?
  —Este programa dura ___; de la(s) ___ hasta la(s) ___ de la ___.

Vocabulario para conversar   359

e. A —Ya son las siete y veinte . . .
   B —. . . hay una película de detectives (de ciencia ficción) . . .

f. A —Ya son las tres y media . . .
   B —. . . hay una película de detectives . . . (. . . hay una exposición internacional . . .)

2–3 Answers will vary.

Answers: ¿Qué sabes ahora?
- Answers will vary / *interesan*
- Answers will vary.
- Answers will vary.

Using Realia
Ask students if they can guess the meaning of *el mando a distancia* (remote control). What comparison is made in the ad? *(Teleprograma* is compared to a remote control.)

Audio Activity 11.4

Cultural Notes

Cooperative Learning
Divide students into groups of three or four. Prepare or have students prepare index cards with the names (in English) of popular movies or television shows. Students then select a card and, in Spanish, give the category to which it corresponds. Compile complete lists and see which group has the most categories.

(p. 359, realia)
Teleprograma, a Spanish television guide, is presented in this ad as *el mando a distancia inteligente* (the smart remote control) that can turn even *la caja tonta* (slang for the TV set) into something intelligent. The television industry in Spain has grown tremendously in the past few decades. Today, programming originates from state, private, and regional networks, with regional ones broadcasting in their native language, such as *catalán* or *vasco.*

Present & Apply

Cultural Objective

• To compare and contrast Spanish-language TV shows with the TV shows you usually watch

Critical Thinking: Drawing Conclusions

After reading the *Perspectiva cultural,* have students identify valid and invalid conclusions. Write these sentences on the chalkboard:
1) All Venezuelan teenagers like soap operas.
2) Most Venezuelan teenagers do not have TVs in their bedrooms. (Sentence 2 is valid.) Formulate additional statements if time permits.

Using Realia

Ask students to look at the *Venevisión* section of the TV guide. Using their knowledge of Spanish and certain clues, such as the program's time, ask them to figure out what *Cine para noctámbulos* and *Cine al amanecer* mean (movie for "night owls" and movie to dawn).

Perspectiva cultural

En estos canales dan programas divertidos. ¿Qué clases de programas son más populares en América del Sur? ¿Son como los que ven tus amigos y tú?

Look at the picture of a Venezuelan household. What does the information in the photo tell you about what room the TV is usually located in and who would you find watching it?

Imagine this: You're an exchange student living in Caracas, Venezuela. You're staying with a family that has two children: Jaime,

who is fourteen, and Mariana, sixteen. On your first night there, you sit down with them to watch television and ... surprise! Bill Cosby pops up speaking perfect Spanish!

What you're watching is the dubbed version *El Show de Bill Cosby.*

Although Jaime and Mariana can also watch other dubbed imports from the United States, those programs are the exception. Venezuela has one of the largest television industries in Latin America.

Some weekend variety shows in Venezuela last several hours. For instance, *Super Sábado Sensacional.* It features performers from all over the world, combining entertainment with mini-interviews. *Super Sábado Sensacional* competes with similar shows from other countries that are also shown in Venezuela, such as Mexico's *Siempre en domingo* and *Sábado gigante,* produced by a Spanish-language station in Miami.

In most of the Spanish-speaking world, teenagers rarely have their own TV, even if the family can afford it. So at night, Jaime and Mariana sit down with the rest of the family to watch TV in the living room. They usually tune in to one of several *culebras.* The word means "snake," which is how Venezuelans jokingly

360 Capítulo 11

Options

Strategies for Reaching All Students

Spanish-Speaking Students
Ask Spanish-speaking students: *¿Has visto "Siempre en domingo" o "Sábado gigante"? ¿Qué te gusta más de estos programas? ¿Prefieres ver los programas en inglés o en español? ¿Por qué?*

 Un paso más Ex. 11-F

Students Needing Extra Help
Discuss the Spanish TV stations in your viewing area. Assign students to watch a program or find a listing in the paper. Have them take notes from the text to use later when reviewing for the test.

refer to their soap operas, because they're long and winding. Venezuela, Mexico, Argentina, and Spain produce many popular soap operas. They usually last several months, then new shows begin, with new characters.

If Jaime and Mariana could watch Spanish-language TV in other countries, they would be surprised to see how many shows from Venezuela are broadcast there. This would give them a sense of how Venezuelan television plays an important role in world communications.

La cultura desde tu perspectiva

1 If there is a Spanish-language TV channel in your area, watch a program for at least ten minutes. Make sure you see a commercial break. Write down everything you understood. Which was easier to understand, the program or the commercials? How might watching TV in Spanish benefit you beyond learning the language?

2 If you don't have access to a Spanish-language broadcast, imagine that you are living in Venezuela for an extended period of time. What would be the advantages of watching TV? What could you learn from a Venezuelan program that you could not learn from a dubbed imported program? How might you benefit from watching a dubbed imported program?

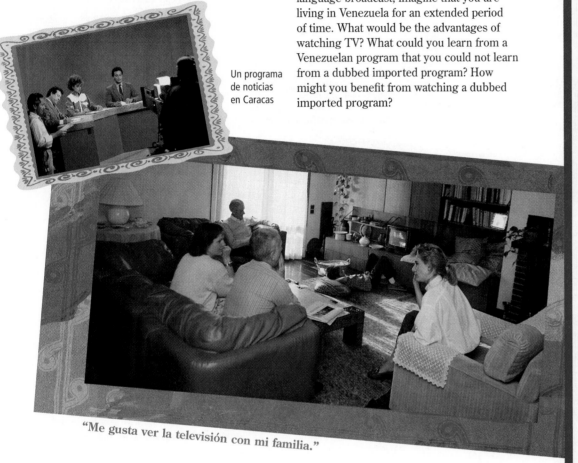

Un programa de noticias en Caracas

"Me gusta ver la televisión con mi familia."

Perspectiva cultural   361

Cultural Notes

(p. 361, photo)
Since 1980, television programs in Venezuela are subject to government approval. Private and government-run stations must submit their programs to the Ministry of Communications 48 hours before airtime to ensure that their content meets educational or cultural standards.

361

Preview

Transparency 60

Critical Thinking: Distinguishing Between Fact and Opinion

Advertisements often rely upon opinions rather than facts to try to sell products. Have students read the advertisement once again. Ask: What are some of the adjectives that are used to describe the food? *(deliciosa, sabrosas,* etc.) Are these descriptions based on facts or are they just the opinions of the restaurant's owners?

Answers

Answers will vary. Students may say they are showing customers' testimonies, the commercial is trying to reach a large audience, etc.

A The expressions are: *nos gustan* and *les encanta. Nos* refers to us and *les,* to them *(a nuestros hijos).*

B The foods being compared are *pollo al horno* and *las ensaladas.* The words that make the comparison are *menos, más,* and *que.* The two comparisons have the word *que* in common.

Gramática en contexto

Look at the story boards for this TV commercial for a restaurant delivery service. How is the restaurant using TV to advertise?

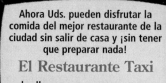

Ahora Uds. pueden disfrutar la comida del mejor restaurante de la ciudad sin salir de casa y ¡sin tener que preparar nada!
El Restaurante Taxi
les lleva a sus casas una cena deliciosa. Aquí tienen Uds. los comentarios de algunos de nuestros clientes:

A nosotros nos gustan mucho las enchiladas. Por eso, siempre llamamos al Restaurante Taxi, donde hacen las más sabrosas enchiladas.

Las ensaladas del Restaurante Taxi son más sabrosas y baratas que las ensaladas de otros restaurantes.

El pollo al horno del Restaurante Taxi tiene menos grasa que el pollo frito de los otros restaurantes. A nuestros hijos les encanta.

A You know that we use *me gusta(n)* and *me encanta(n)* when we talk about things we "like" or "love." In the ad, there are similar expressions, but *nos* and *les* are used instead of *me.* Find these expressions. To whom do you think *nos* refers? To whom do you think *les* refers?

B Find the sentence that begins *El pollo al horno del Restaurante Taxi tiene . . .* and the one that begins *Las ensaladas del Restaurante Taxi son . . . .* In each sentence, what foods are being compared? Which words make the comparison? What word do the two comparisons have in common?

362   Capítulo 11

Options

Strategies for Reaching All Students

Students Needing Extra Help
A: Students might have trouble with the pronoun "we" associated with just one thing. Make a chart that indicates to students that one person can like one thing, one person can like two things, two people can like one thing, and two people can like two things. Model with several sentences.
B: If students have difficulty, remind them of their first introduction to *más* in *Me gusta más . . .* and build from there.

Los comparativos: Write the formula on the chalkboard.
Show students how the adjectives agree. The irregular forms can be difficult for some students. Comparing to the English "good, better, best" helps them understand the irregular forms in Spanish. Give some examples, both with regular and irregular forms.

Enrichment
A–B: To help students answer these questions, you may want to first have individuals take turns reading this passage aloud. (This will also give you a chance to check pronunciation and overall comprehension.) Have students look at the expressions *gusta(n)* and *encanta(n).* Then ask: Which nouns determine whether the singular or plural form is used in these expressions? Which noun determines the form of the verb: the person who likes the food or the food itself?

Los comparativos

You have learned *más* and *menos* in certain expressions.
> Me gusta el tenis pero me gusta **más** el fútbol.
> ¿Te gustan las manzanas? Sí, **más o menos**.

- We also use *más / menos* + adjective + *que* ("than") to make comparisons.
  > Las películas de aventuras son **más emocionantes que** las películas del oeste.
  > Una telenovela es **menos realista que** un programa de hechos de la vida real.

- The adjectives agree with the nouns they refer to.

- The adjectives *bueno, -a, malo, -a, grande,* and *pequeño, -a* have irregular comparative forms. We do not use *más* with them.

ADJETIVO	COMPARATIVO
bueno, -a	**mejor (que)**
malo, -a	**peor (que)**
grande	**mayor (que)**
pequeño, -a	**menor (que)**

- *Mejor, peor, mayor,* and *menor* have plural forms ending in *-es*. However, they don't have a different feminine form:
  > **Las hermanas** de Pedro son **menores** que las de Juan.

- *Mejor* ("better") is also the comparative form of *bien* ("well"), and *peor* ("worse") is also the comparative form of *mal* ("badly"). When used in this sense, *mejor* and *peor* have only one form.
  > Graciela y Fabián son **mejores que** Susana y Gustavo en tenis.
  > Graciela y Fabián juegan tenis **mejor que** Susana y Gustavo.

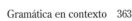

Gramática en contexto 363

Present

Class Starter Review
On the day following the presentation of comparatives, you might begin the class with this activity: Arrange pictures of three famous people on the chalkboard. Students then give a comparative sentence saying who is more or less intelligent, beautiful, interesting, etc.

Los comparativos: Have students work in pairs to create more sets of sentences such as that at the bottom of the box: *Graciela y Fabián son <u>mejores</u> que Susana y Gustavo en tenis. Graciela y Fabián juegan tenis <u>mejor</u> que Susana y Gustavo.* Make sure students understand that in each set one sentence has *mejor* or *peor* referring to nouns, and therefore changing (in number only) as required, and the other sentence has *mejor* or *peor* referring to verbs and remaining unchanged.

Practice

Re-enter / Recycle

Ex. 2: activities from Chaps. 1, 3, and 7; adjectives describing physical characteristics from Chap. 5

Answers

1 (Statements will vary.)

a. Las telenovelas son más tristes que las comedias. (Las comedias son menos tristes que las telenovelas.)

b. Los programas educativos son más interesantes que las películas musicales. (Las películas musicales son menos interesantes que los programas educativos.)

c. Las películas del oeste son más realistas que las películas de ciencia ficción. (Las películas de ciencia ficción son menos realistas que las películas del oeste.)

d. Los programas de entrevistas son más aburridos que los programas musicales. (Los programas musicales son menos aburridos que los programas de entrevistas.)

e. Las comedias son más cómicas que los programas de entrevistas. (Los programas de entrevistas son menos cómicos que las comedias.)

f. Los dibujos animados son más divertidos que las noticias. (Las noticias son menos divertidas que los dibujos animados.)

1 Túrnate con un(a) compañero(a) para comparar estos programas y películas:

Las películas de detectives son más emocionantes que las películas románticas.

o: Las películas románticas son menos emocionantes que las películas de detectives.

a. triste   b. interesante   c. realista

d. aburrido   e. cómico   f. divertido

Options

Strategies for Reaching All Students

Spanish-Speaking Students
Ex. 1: Have Spanish-speaking students write out this exercise.
Ex. 2: Pair Spanish-speaking students if possible.

Students Needing Extra Help
Ex. 2: Review irregular forms and when to use them.

Enrichment
Ex. 2: You may want to extend the practice of *mejor* and *peor* having students compare movies and TV programs: *Pienso que* Aladino *es mejor (peor) que . . .* , etc.

2 Haz una afirmación *(statement)* falsa sobre cada una de estas personas. Tu compañero(a) te va a dar la información correcta.

Rebeca

Luisa

A — *Rebeca patina peor que Luisa.*
B — *¡Claro que no! Rebeca patina mejor que Luisa.*
  o: *Luisa patina peor que Rebeca.*

A — *Adela y Natalia son mayores que Gabriel y Timoteo.*
B — *¡Claro que no! Adela y Natalia son menores
   que Gabriel y Timoteo.*
  o: *Gabriel y Timoteo son mayores que Adela y Natalia.*

Adela y Natalia / Gabriel y Timoteo

a. Adán / Gerardo   b. Elena / Julio   c. Diana y tú / Fabiola y yo

d. Pepe / Beto   e. yo / Laura   f. Cristóbal / Mateo

365

Present & Practice

Re-enter / Recycle
Ex. 4: calendar expressions from *El primer paso*
Ex. 5: *gustar* expressions from Chap. 1

Class Starter Review
After the presentation of superlatives, you might begin the class with this activity:
Ask: *¿Quién es la actriz de cine más bonita? ¿Cuál es el programa de televisión más divertido? ¿Cuál es la peor película del año?* etc. Encourage students to explain their answers.

Answers
3 Answers will vary, but look for the following construction: *El programa más . . . es . . .*

4 Answers will vary, but look for the definite article in the superlative construction.

 Practice Wkbk. 11-6

 Writing Activity 11-E

 Prueba 11-6

 Comm. Act. BLM 11-2

Los superlativos

- To say that someone or something is "the most" of a group, we use the definite article + (noun) + *más* + adjective.
  Para mí, *Los tres perezosos* es **el programa más divertido**.

- To say that someone or something is "the best" or "the worst," we use *el / la mejor* and *el / la peor*. These come before the noun.
  Pienso que Gonzalo Ochoa es **el mejor actor**.

- When we say that someone or something is "the most," "the best," or "the worst" in a group or category, we use *de* to refer to that group or category.
  Para mí, *El día del terror* es **la peor película de todas**.
  Mis amigos los perros es **el mejor programa del domingo**.
  Clara Vega es **la mejor actriz de las telenovelas**.

3 Con un(a) compañero(a), contesta las preguntas.

interesante

A —*¿Cuál es el programa más interesante?*
B —*El programa más interesante es . . .*

a. aburrido
b. divertido
c. emocionante
d. tonto
e. 💡

4 En grupos de cinco o seis, hagan una encuesta *(survey)* para averiguar *(find out)* el / la mejor y el / la peor de estas categorías y por qué. Luego, escribe los resultados de la encuesta.

mes del año

A —*Para ti, ¿cuál es el mejor mes del año?*
B —*Creo que el mejor mes del año es . . . porque . . .*
A —*¿Y cuál es el peor mes del año?*
B —*El peor mes del año es . . . porque . . .*

a. programa de televisión
b. anuncio de televisión
c. grupo musical
d. película del año
e. restaurante de la ciudad
f. tienda de la ciudad

Ahora, informa a la clase sobre los resultados de la encuesta.
Tres personas creen que . . . es el mejor mes del año porque . . .
Cuatro estudiantes creen que . . . es el peor mes del año porque . . .

Options

Strategies for Reaching All Students

Students Needing Extra Help
Los superlativos: Write the formula on the chalkboard, replacing the words "definite article" with *el, la, los,* and *las.* Have students generate examples.
Ex. 4: Remind students that a.–f. need a "best" and "worst."
El complemento directo: Los pronombres y el infinitivo: Give more examples of how to use the pronouns attached to the infinitive or before the main verb: *¿Vas a hacer la tarea? (Sí, la voy a hacer. / Sí, voy a hacerla.) ¿Vas a comprar estos libros? (Sí, los voy a comprar. / Sí, voy a comprarlos.)* Give each of three students a card: one reads *Voy,* one reads *a ver,* and one reads *las noticias.* On the back of *las noticias,* it reads *las.* Line the students up so that the sentence makes sense. Then have the last student flip his or her card over to *las* and move in front of the student holding *Voy.* This visual makes an impression on stu-dents. Do the same for attaching *las* to *a ver.* Students can do the same with cards on their desks.
Ex. 5: Have students note that when using a direct object pronoun with *me gustaría* + infinitive, the pronoun is always attached to the infinitive.

El complemento directo:
Los pronombres y el infinitivo

You know that we use direct object pronouns (*lo, la, los, las*) to avoid repeating a noun.

- When we use direct object pronouns with infinitives, we can either put them before the verb or attach them to the end of the infinitive. For example:
  — ¿Vas a ver **las noticias**?
  — Sí, **las** voy a ver.
    o: Sí, voy a ver**las.**

5   Escribe los nombres de cuatro películas y de qué clase es cada una de ellas. Después pregunta a otros(as) compañeros(as) si quieren verlas.

A — *¿Quieres ver la película* Terror en la noche?
B — *Sí, me gustaría verla. Me encantan las películas de terror.*
    o: *No, no quiero verla. A mí me aburren las películas de terror.*

Answers
5 (Questions and answers will vary.)
ESTUDIANTE A
¿Quieres ver la película *La hora de la comedia*?
. . . *Un gran detective*?
. . . *Aventuras del oeste*?
. . . *La conquista del espacio*?
ESTUDIANTE B
Sí, me gustaría verla. Me encantan las comedias. (No, no quiero verla. A mí me aburren las comedias.)
. . . las películas de detectives.
. . . las películas del oeste.
. . . las películas de ciencia ficción.

Enrichment
Ex. 4: As an in-class assignment, have students work in pairs or groups to survey all of their classmates on just one of the items in a.–f. In that way, information about the opinions of the entire class on a given topic can be gathered and presented later.

El complemento directo: Los pronombres y el infinitivo: Do a quick review with students in which they answer these questions in one or another of the ways indicated in the example in the box: *¿Vas a hacer la tarea? ¿Vas a visitar a tus primas? ¿Vas a comprar estos libros? ¿Vas a comer ese flan?*

Present & Practice

Re-enter / Recycle

Ex. 6: household chores and *tener que* + inf. from Chap. 8

Answers

6 ESTUDIANTE A

a. ¿Tengo que arreglar el cuarto?
b. . . . sacudir los muebles?
c. . . . cortar el césped?
d. . . . limpiar el baño?
e. . . . hacer la cama?
f. . . . poner la mesa?

ESTUDIANTE B

a. Sí, tienes que arreglarlo. Hay ropa en la cama, en la silla y en el escritorio.
b. . . . sacudirlos. Puedes empezar con la sala.
c. . . . cortarlo. El césped está demasiado alto.
d. . . . limpiarlo. Está sucio.
e. . . . hacerla. ¡Ya son las once y no vas a dormir más!
f. . . . ponerla. Vamos a comer en cinco minutos.

 Practice Wkbk. 11-7

 Prueba 11-7

---

6 Pregúntale a un(a) compañero(a) si tienes que hacer estos quehaceres en la casa y por qué.

A — ¿Tengo que lavar la ropa?
B — Sí, tienes que lavarla. Está sucia.

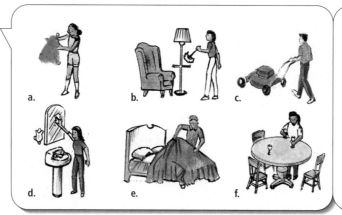

a.
b.
c.
d.
e.
f.

El césped está demasiado alto.

Vamos a comer en cinco minutos.

Hay ropa en la cama, en la silla y en el escritorio.

¡Ya son las once y no vas a dormir más!

Puedes empezar con la sala.

Está sucio.

El pretérito del verbo *ver*

We use *vi* and *viste* to talk about things that we saw. Here are all the preterite-tense forms of the verb *ver*.

(yo)	vi	(nosotros) (nosotras)	vimos
(tú)	viste	(vosotros) (vosotras)	visteis
Ud. (él) (ella)	vio	Uds. (ellos) (ellas)	vieron

Options

Strategies for Reaching All Students

Students Needing Extra Help

Ex. 6: Remind students to attach the *lo, la, los,* or *las* to the first part of *Estudiante B's* answer before choosing the second part from the list on the right.
El pretérito de ver: Remind students that preterite means "past" and of the clue words *ayer, anoche, la semana pasada,* etc.

Ex. 7: Remind students of the change in the verb form when *tú* or a *tú* verb form is in the question.
Ex. 8: Make a chart with columns for "movie" and "place." Do the exercise using TV programs if students haven't seen a movie recently. Remind them to use the third person when reporting.

Enrichment

Ex. 8: As a homework assignment, students can tell which they like better—seeing movies at the theater or on a VCR at home. Have them give reasons for their preferences and name the advantages and disadvantages of each kind of viewing.

7 ¿Qué clase de programa vieron estas personas anoche?

A — *¿Qué clase de programa vieron Rolando y Julia anoche?*
B — *Vieron una comedia.*

Rolando y Julia

a. Juan

b. tú

c. Carmen y Raquel

d. Teresa y tú

e. Carlitos

f. tus padres

8 ¿Qué películas vieron tus compañeros(as) el mes pasado? ¿Dónde? Haz una encuesta para averiguarlo. Escribe la información y comparte *(share)* tus resultados con la clase.

A — *¿Qué película viste el mes pasado?*
B — *Vi Aladino.*
A — *¿Dónde la viste?*
B — *La vi en mi casa.*
   o: *La vi en el cine.*

¿Qué películas vieron tus compañeros(as)?

Dos estudiantes vieron la película Aladino el mes pasado.
La vieron en sus casas.

Gramática en contexto   369

Answers
7 ESTUDIANTE A
a. ¿Qué clase de programa vio Juan anoche?
b. . . . viste (tú) . . .
c. . . . vieron Carmen y Raquel . . .
d. . . . vieron Teresa y tú . . .
e. . . . vio Carlitos . . .
f. . . . vieron tus padres . . .
ESTUDIANTE B
a. Vio un programa de hechos de la vida real.
b. Vi una telenovela.
c. Vieron un programa de entrevistas.
d. Vimos un programa musical.
e. Vio dibujos animados.
f. Vieron un documental.

8 Answers will vary. Look for correct use of *ver* in the preterite.

Practice Wkbk. 11-8

Writing Activity 11-F

Prueba 11-8

Present & Practice

Re-enter / Recycle

Ex. 9: *gustar* expressions from Chap. 1, *ir a* + inf. from Chap. 3

Reteach / Review: Vocabulary

Ex. 9: To review time-telling, have *Estudiante A* ask *Estudiante B* when the person named will be watching the particular program.

Answers

9 *Estudiante B*'s last part will vary.

a. A —¿Qué programa va a ver el profesor?

B —*Día a día.*

A —¿De veras? ¿A él le gustan las noticias?

B —Sí, le gustan (encantan / fascinan / interesan) mucho.

b. A —... van a ver Mario y Eva?

B —*Misterio sin solución.*

A —...¿A ellos les gustan los programas de detectives?

B —... les ...

c. A —... van a ver Uds.?

B —*Hablando con Olivia.*

A —...¿A Uds. les gustan los programas de entrevistas?

B —... nos ...

d. A —... va a ver Luisita?

B —*El gatito Tito.*

A —...¿A ella le gustan los dibujos animados?

B —... le ...

El complemento indirecto: Los pronombres *nos* y *les*

We use the indirect object pronouns *me, te,* and *le* with verbs like *dar, doler, encantar, fascinar, gustar,* and *interesar.* Here are all the indirect object pronouns.

me	*(to / for) me*	**nos**	*(to / for) us*
te	*(to / for) you*	**os***	*(to / for) you*
le	*(to / for) you him her it*	**les**	*(to / for) you them*

* The pronoun *os* is used mainly in Spain. We will use it occasionally and you should learn to recognize it.

¡NO OLVIDES!

Sometimes we use *a* + noun or name to clarify who the indirect object pronoun refers to.
A mis padres les encantan los programas musicales.

9 Habla con un compañero(a) sobre los programas de televisión que van a ver estas personas.

Ricardo

A —*¿Qué programa va a ver Ricardo?*
B —*Nuestros amigos los delfines.*
A —*¿De veras? ¿A él le gustan los programas educativos?*
B —*Sí, le gustan mucho.*
   o: *Sí, le encantan / fascinan / interesan mucho.*

a. el profesor   b. Mario y Eva   c. Uds.   d. Luisita

e. tú   f. Inés y Vicente   g. Santiago y tú

370   Capítulo 11

Options

Strategies for Reaching All Students

Students Needing Extra Help

Ahora lo sabes: Have students write out this section so they can check off what they have mastered.

Ahora lo sabes

Can you:

■ compare people and things?

—Las películas de aventuras son ___ emocionantes ___ las románticas.

■ tell what is the best or worst in a group or category?

—(No) me gusta ese programa. Es _____ programa de televisión.

■ avoid repeating a noun?

—¿Cuándo vas a ver la película? Voy a ___ esta tarde.

■ tell what you saw?

—La semana pasada, mis hermanos y yo ___ una película del oeste.

■ tell what you and others are interested in?

—A nosotros _____ las ciencias.

e. A —...vas a ver?
   B —*Julio en concierto.*
   A —...¿A ti te gustan los programas musicales?
   B —...me...

f. A —...van a ver Inés y Vicente?
   B —*El tío Pepito.*
   A —...¿A ellos les gustan las comedias?
   B —...les...

g. A —...van a ver Santiago y tú?
   B —*Los mejores días.*
   A —...¿A Uds. les gustan las telenovelas?
   B —...nos...

Answers: Ahora lo sabes

• más (menos) / que
• el mejor (peor)
• verla
• vimos
• nos interesan

 Practice Wkbk. 11-9

 Audio Activity 11.5

 Writing Activity 11-G

 Prueba 11-9

Apply

**Pronunciation Tape
11-3**

¡A conversar!

Play

Step

Using the Video
Video segment 3: See the Video
Teacher's Guide.

 Video Activity C

Para decir más

Aquí tienes vocabulario
adicional que te puede ayudar
para hacer las actividades de
esta sección.

el concurso
contest

el cable
cable

religioso, -a
religious

alegre
merry, lively

infantil
childish

mediocre
mediocre

(yo) recomiendo
I recommend

parecido, -a (a)
similar (to)

la última vez que . . . fue
the last time . . . was

la actuación
acting, performance

la calidad
quality

372   Capítulo 11

Actividades

Esta sección te ofrece la oportunidad de aumentar
tus conocimientos de español al integrar lo que
aprendiste en este capítulo con lo que aprendiste
en capítulos anteriores.

 Prepara una crítica *(review)* de una película. En tu
crítica puedes hablar sobre:

• qué película viste y cuándo
• qué clase de película es
• quiénes son los actores y qué piensas de ellos
• algo que uno de los actores hizo *(did)* en la película
• dónde dan la película y a qué hora
• qué piensas de la película

Options

Strategies for Reaching All Students

Students Needing Extra Help
Ex. 2: Designate one corner of the room as
programas de terror, another corner as *programas musicales,* another as *programas
educativos,* and so on.
With an index card, block off certain lines of
the dialogue and ask students what they
learned from the line. Then go back to the
bullets and start each sentence for the class.
Ex. 3: Create the dialogue as a class.

Enrichment
Ex. 1: Students may benefit from hearing
you model a movie review. They can then
prepare their reviews orally or in writing.
They can present orally in front of the entire
class or in small groups. If presentations
are done in small groups, students can
respond by saying whether they also saw
the movie, what they think of it, what
movies are comparable, and so on.

Ex. 2: This activity allows students to
express and defend opinions about TV programs. Encourage them to agree or disagree
with other groups' comments. To generate
discussion, you might repeat the opinions of
one group and then ask what others think of
these opinions: *A ellos les interesan los programas de detectives. ¿Qué piensan Uds.?*

2 ¿Qué programas de televisión te interesan más? Para esta actividad, diferentes lugares de la clase representan clases de programas diferentes. Tu profesor(a) te va a decir el lugar adonde debes ir. En grupo, digan *(tell)* a la clase:

- qué clase de programa de televisión les gusta y por qué
- cuál es el mejor ejemplo de esta clase de programa
- cuándo lo vieron

A — *¿Qué clase de programas les gusta a Uds.?*
B — *A nosotros nos gustan los programas de detectives porque son emocionantes. Son más interesantes que los programas educativos. Rafael Sánchez, detective es el mejor programa de detectives. Lo vimos el martes a las nueve de la noche en el canal 15.*

El cómico mexicano Cantinflas

3 Para esta actividad, necesitas la sección de pasatiempos del periódico. Haz planes con otro(a) estudiante para ir al cine este fin de semana. Necesitas:

La cantante Celia
Cruz en concierto

- averiguar qué clase de películas le gusta a tu compañero(a)
- buscar en el periódico una película que le va a interesar
- invitarle a ir al cine
- decidir qué día van a ir y a qué hora
- decidir cómo van a ir

Actividades   373

Critical Thinking: Synthesizing

Tell groups of three or four students to imagine that they are television producers developing a new half-hour show. Have each group prepare a newspaper advertisement for the show that will include: type of show (comedy, drama, talk show, sports, etc.), main characters (with a brief description of each), and when it can be seen (channel, time, day). Encourage students to add other information and to be as creative as they can. Display ads on the bulletin board.

Re-enter / Recycle

Ex. 2: *gustar* expressions from Chap. 1
Ex. 3: *gustar* expressions from Chap. 1, *ir a* + inf. from Chap. 3

Answers: Actividades

1–3 Answers will vary, but encourage the use of new chapter vocabulary as well as comparatives and superlatives, *ver* in the preterite, and indirect object pronouns.

 Practice Wkbk. 11-10

 Writing Activities 11-H, 11-I

 Comm. Act. BLMs 11-3, 11-4, 11-5

Cultural Notes ☼

Cooperative Learning
Tell students that they are going to develop a show similar to the People's Choice Awards. Help the class develop categories for awards and then assign a specific category, such as sports, television, music, etc., to each group. Instruct each group to develop four questions, using comparatives / superlatives, and a tally sheet for their category. Collect the questions to compile a whole-class list.

(p. 373, top photo)
Mexican movie star Cantinflas (b. Mario Moreno) appears here in a scene from the 1956 film *Around the World in 80 Days*. Born in Mexico City, Cantinflas was beloved by audiences for the quick, confounding word play that was the trademark of his comedy. He died at age 81 in 1993, leaving a legacy of 49 films as well as a new verb for the Spanish language—*cantinflear,* which means talking a great deal but saying nothing.

(p. 373, bottom photo)
The "Queen of Salsa," Celia Cruz, shown here in concert, was born the youngest of 14 children in Havana. She began her singing career performing Afro-Cuban religious music. In the 1950s she sang with popular *salsa* orchestras, and today continues to tour worldwide. Long enjoying widespread popularity in Spanish-speaking countries, Celia Cruz recently has begun to gain many fans in the U.S.

Apply

Process Reading
For a description of process reading, see p. 48.

Multicultural Perspectives
A wide variety of children's television programs are available in Puerto Rico. One of the most popular is *El show de Don Pacheco.* Children in Puerto Rico dream of having their birthday acknowledged or of winning a contest on this after-school program that features games, contests, and *muñequitos.* Dressed in a suit, a bow tie, and a Panama straw hat (his trademark) Don Pacheco has been entertaining children for years with his comforting voice and grandfatherly image. Invite students to share information about programs that they watched when they were children. Encourage comparisons with children's programs that younger brothers or sisters watch today.

Answers
Antes de leer
Answers will vary, but may include: day, time, and channel listings; a review or description of the movies; etc. / The information would probably be presented in order of day, time, and then channel. / Students' movie listings will vary.

¡Vamos a leer!

Antes de leer

STRATEGY ➤ Using prior knowledge

What kind of information would you expect to find in a page of movie listings? How would you expect it to be presented? Think of a movie you know well and write a movie listing for it.

Mira la lectura

Look at this selection from the Puerto Rican magazine *Vea.* What is the topic of this page? How is the information organized? (Alphabetically? By time sequence? By location?)

Infórmate

STRATEGY ➤ Using cognates

One of the most useful strategies for dealing with unfamiliar words is using cognates. Here are some patterns that might help you recognize them.

- Frequently a double consonant in an English word is represented by a single consonant in the Spanish cognate: *clase, inocente, aceptar.*
- Often words ending in *-y* in English end in *-ia* or *-ía* in Spanish: *historia, geografía, infancia.*
- Many English adjectives ending in *-ed* end in *-ado(a)* or *-ido(a)* in Spanish: *aceptado, -a; permitidos, -as.*

374   Capítulo 11

Puerto Rico/televisión
el cine en la tv

11 AM ⑪⑨㉒ "Alice in Wonderland" con las voces de Kathryn Beaumont y Ed Wynn (1951). Versión animada del clásico de Disney sobre la famosa historia de Lewis Carroll de una niña que al caer en una cueva de conejo entra a un mundo mágico poblado por extrañas criaturas. ★★★

12 PM ② "First Blood" con Sylvester Stallone y Brian Dennehy (1982). Después de ser arrestado por vagancia, un Boinas Verde veterano de Vietnam escapa a las junglas y emplea la guerrilla en contra de la Policía y de la Guardia Nacional. ★★★

1 PM ⑪⑨㉒ "The Towering Inferno" con Steve McQueen y Paul Newman (1974). Dramático rescate que comienza justo en el momento en que unos invitados a la inauguración de un rascacielos quedan atrapados en el piso 138 cuando el edificio se enciende en llamas. ★★★

2 PM ② "Black And White".

3 PM ⑦ "Caña Brava".

1 PM ⑥③ Película.

7 PM ⑪⑦⑨㉒ "The Amy Fisher Story".

8 PM ④⑫ "V.I. Warshawski" con Kathleen Turner y Jay O. Sanders (1991). Una atractiva pero ruda mujer policía trata de resolver un caso en el que tiene un interés personal. ★★★

9 PM ⑪⑦⑨㉒ "The Kansas City Massacre" con Dale Robertson y Bo

DOMINGO 15
con Braulio Castillo.

5 PM ②⑤ "Romancing The Stone" con Michael Douglas y Kathleen Turner (1984). Una solitaria y romántica novelista pasa su tiempo escribiendo y soñando con el hombre perfecto. Pero su vida toma un giro drástico y comienza a parecerse a una de sus novelas cuando vuela a Sudamérica para rescatar a su hermana secuestrada y se encuentra a sí misma buscando un misterioso tesoro con su sueño del hombre perfecto hecho realidad. ★★★

6 PM ④⑫ "Oscar" con Sylvester Stallone y Peter Riegert (1991). Un hampón trata de enderezarse y conseguirle esposo a su hija en el Chicago de 1920. ★★

7 PM ②⑤ "Teenage Mutant Ninja Turtles" con Judith Hoag y Elias Koteas (1990). Las adorables máquinas de batalla verdes hacen su debut cinematográfico como amantes del bien, de la gente buena y de las pizzas de pepperoni. ★★★

LUNES 16
agente a cargo de la oficina del FBI en el medio oeste en los 1930, transporta a un notorio gángster por tren a la ciudad de Kansas y después por auto hasta la prisión de Levinworth. La movida es la señal para una emboscada en la que los gángsteres rivales tratan de secuestrar al prisionero de la Policía y del FBI. ★★★

11⑦⑨㉒ "Father of The Bride" con Steve Martin y Diane Keaton (1991). Un padre no puede lidiar con el anuncio de su hija de que piensa comprometerse y menos con los preparativos para su boda. ★★★

10 PM ②⑤ "Black Magic" con Bud Spenser y Philip Michael Thomas. La misteriosa muerte de una joven causa un sinnúmero de problemas a su novio quien, sin embargo, se canta inocente. Pero la Policía no le cree. Se unen dos detectives para investigar el crimen. ★★

11:30 ④⑫ "Things Change" con Don Ameche y Joe Mantegna (1989). Un sencillo zapatero italiano acepta, a cambio de dinero, pagar los platos rotos por un maleante de Chicago. Pero el hombre asignado a vigilarlo por un fin de semana decide lo imprevisto. ★★

12 AM ⑦ "La Devoradora" con María Félix y Luis Aldas.

⑪⑨㉒ "Dos Esposas".

William Shatner (1982). Una periodista de televisión resulta brutalmente atacada en su hogar después de transmitir un editorial a favor de los derechos de la mujer. En el hospital descubre a su asaltante, cuyo torturante pasado le ha transformado en un criminal sicópata masivo que anhela terminar su trabajo. ★★★

⑥③ Película. (WIPR-

los películas
OPCIONES:
Excelente
Buena
Regular
Mala

Semana
(Cualquier de
responsab

MAR

go "P
politic
vertirs
prime
suade
que e
traici
bles e
much

11 PM
(WIP

MIC

II"
Billy
unid
la M
una
con
noa
★★

9 PM
Ene
11 P
Co
★★

"Dios Los Cría"
Tan.

⑪③ Película.
TV no sabía el tí-
Crime", "Lori" es
de citas que tie-
oportunidad de
su vida cuando
ciante, y su ami-

⑨⑫ "To Sa-
Child" con Marita
y Peter Kowan-
El recién naci-
mujer le es se-
por su esposo
de brujos. La
pone en efecto un
rescate para
bebé. ★★

⑫ Delta Force

⑧ "Caperucita y
Tres Amigos" con
Gracia y Manuel
Valdez.

⑪⑨㉒ "The
Purple" con Who-
dberg y Danny
(1985). La historia
or de dos herma-
1909 a 1949, quie-
ron separadas al
to de su nacimien-
nidas después.

⑥③ Película.
TV no sabía el tí-

⑪⑦⑨㉒ "Live!
Death Row" con
Cassidy y Bruce

JL
Ba
na
ze
★

11 P
ze
vi
F
L

Options

Strategies for Reaching All Students

Spanish-Speaking Students
 Un paso más Exs. 11-G, 11-H

Students Needing Extra Help
Infórmate 1: Make a chart with columns to help students organize the information.
Infórmate 3: Have students pick words that tell what is important.
Show how adding a negative or *más / menos* could easily change the description.
Aplicación: Ex. 1: Have students use their Organizers from previous chapters.

Enrichment
Aplicación: As a homework assignment, students can pretend that they have seen two of the movies listed and tell what happened, using the brief description from the movie listings. Remind students that to recount the action in the past, they must use the preterite.

1 Look at the bold-faced headings in the reading.

- When are the most movies shown, in the morning, afternoon, or evening?
- How many channels show movies?
- Read the titles, then classify the movies according to type. See the list on the right. Which category seems to be the most popular?

2 Choose a movie that sounds interesting and read its description several times to get an idea about the plot. Pick out a few cognates that help you understand the description.

3 After reading the description, do you still think the movie belongs to the category suggested by its title? If you have already seen the movie, do you think the description tells what is most important about the plot? Would you change the description? How?

película de detectives
comedia
película musical
película del oeste
película romántica
película de aventuras
dibujos animados

"**En busca del arca perdida** (Raiders of the Lost Ark) **es una película emocionante.**"

Aplicación

1 Which of these movies would you prefer to see? Why?

2 On a piece of paper, list at least ten new words that you learned from this reading selection and ten cognates that you found.

Mira la lectura
The topic of the page is TV listings of movies. The information is organized by day and time.

Infórmate
1 Most movies are shown in the evening. / Eight channels show movies: 2, 4, 5, 7, 9, 11, 12, 22. / *película de detectives:* Black Magic, V.I. Warshawski, The Kansas City Massacre; *comedia:* Father of the Bride; *película romántica:* Oscar; *película de aventuras:* First Blood, The Towering Inferno, Romancing the Stone, Teenage Mutant Ninja Turtles, Things Change, Visiting Hours; *dibujos animados:* Alice in Wonderland. The category *película de aventuras* has the most titles.

2–3 Answers will vary.

Aplicación
1 Answers will vary.

2 New words that students have learned will vary. Possible cognates found may include: *versión, clásico, famosa, mágico, veterano, escapa,* etc.

Cultural Notes

(p. 374, realia)
The strong U.S. influence on Puerto Rican culture is clear in the many listings of films in this television guide. Although many of these films may be dubbed or subtitled in Spanish, English is widely used, as it is a required subject in all school grades. About 97 percent of Puerto Rican homes have a TV set, with approximately one out of four having a VCR.

Apply

Process Writing
For information regarding developing a writing portfolio, see p. 50.

Answers: ¡Vamos a escribir!
Students' reviews will vary.

Todo junto

¡Vamos a escribir!

Choose a recent TV show that you enjoyed and write a review of it.

1 First, write out the answers to these questions about the program.

- ¿Cómo se llama el programa?
- ¿Qué clase de programa es?
- ¿Qué día viste el programa? ¿En qué canal? ¿Cuánto tiempo duró?
- ¿Qué artistas participaron? ¿Cómo son?
- ¿Te gustó el programa? ¿Por qué?
- ¿Lo recomiendas? ¿A quién lo recomiendas? (a los niños, a los jóvenes . . .)

2 Now write the review using your answers to the preceding questions as a guide. Show your review to a partner. Ask if there is any other information he or she would want to have or if you should change or rearrange any of your information to make it more helpful to the reader.

3 Decide about the changes you might like to make, and rewrite your review.

La miniserie "Vida de mi Vida," de Radio Caracas Televisión

El actor Franklin Virguez en una escena de una telenovela

376 Capítulo 11

Options

Strategies for Reaching All Students

Students Needing Extra Help
Have students use their Organizers.
Step 1: Tell students to first answer with phrases, then put in complete sentences.

Enrichment
For an alternate writing assignment, students can pretend to be television or movie writers trying to sell their new show or movie to entertainment industry executives. Students should describe their TV show or movie by giving its title, genre, length, and intended audience. They can also suggest actors to play the roles and, if their creation is a TV show, the best time slot.

4 Check for spelling and accents. Did you use the correct forms of the verbs and adjectives? If necessary, rewrite your review.

5 Now you are ready to share your work. You can:

* collect all the reviews into a class program guide called *Guía de televisión: Los mejores programas,* or
* include it in your writing portfolio

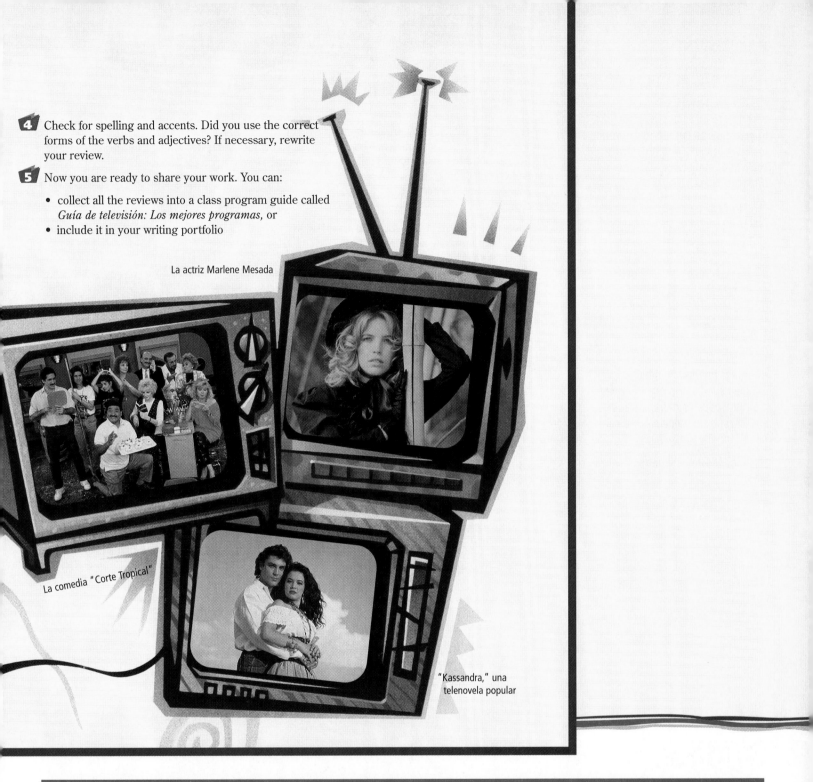

La actriz Marlene Mesada

La comedia "Corte Tropical"

"Kassandra," una telenovela popular

Cultural Notes

(pp. 376–377, photos)
The situation comedy *Corte Tropical* is broadcast by Univisión, one of the leading Spanish networks in the U.S. Univisión, which is headquartered in Dade County, Florida, also carries the variety game show *Sábado gigante,* which is popular in the U.S. and throughout Latin America. Miniseries from Venezuela, such as *Vida de mi vida,* are favorites with family viewers.

Telenovelas such as *Kassandra* and *Pobre Negro* also enjoy a wide viewership in the U.S. and Latin America. Many are filmed in Caracas; others come mainly from Mexico, Argentina, and Puerto Rico. Several *telenovelas,* such as *El Magnate,* are filmed in the U.S. with Miami as their setting.

Assess & Summarize

Test Preparation

You may want to assign parts of this section as written homework or as an in-class writing activity prior to administering the *Examen de habilidades*.

Answers

Listening: *Esta noche dan una comedia divertida en el canal doce. En la comedia van a estar los mejores actores de cine de Puerto Rico. La comedia empieza a las nueve menos cuarto y termina a las diez.* More than one hour. The person would be watching at home.

Reading: By using cognates and phrases such as *no hay ni fantasmas ni vampiros ni monstruos* and *el robo de un banco,* we can tell it's an adventure film.

Writing: Movie descriptions will vary.

Culture: Answers will vary. Students may cite some variety shows, such as *Sábado sensacional* or *Siempre en domingo.* Other programming includes soap operas and dubbed imports from the U.S. / Answers will vary for program choices.

Speaking: Answers will vary.

¿Lo sabes bien?

This section will help you organize your studying for the proficiency test, where you will be asked to do similar, though not identical, tasks. There will not be any models on the test.

Listening

Can you understand when someone talks about how long an event will last? Listen as your teacher reads a sample similar to what you will hear on the test. According to the person making the statement, how much time would someone spend watching this, one hour or more than an hour? Would the person watching be at home or at a movie theater?

Reading

Can you read this movie review and use the cognates that appear in it to find out what kind of movie it is?

> Con *Tren expreso,* Ud. no puede aburrirse.
> *Tren expreso* es una película divertida, con mucho humor, donde no hay ni fantasmas ni vampiros ni monstruos. Todo es real. Es una emocionante aventura que empieza con el robo de un banco. Los críticos dicen que es la mejor película del año. Véala en el Cine Acuario.
>
> ★ ★ ★ ★

378 Capítulo 11

Writing

Can you write a letter describing a movie you saw recently? Here is a sample letter:

> Hola, Carmelo:
>
> La semana pasada, mi hermano y yo vimos una película bastante buena. Es muy realista. Nos fascinó. En la película hay una familia que no tiene dinero: el padre no tiene trabajo y la hija está enferma. Una persona generosa los ayuda. No es la mejor película del verano, pero es muy interesante.
>
> Saludos, Ana

Culture

Can you explain what is shown on TV in Venezuela, what programs would you choose to watch, and why?

El programa de entrevistas *Cristina*

Speaking

Can you express and defend an opinion about a television program?

—*Para mí, el mejor programa del canal 9 es el programa educativo, Ambiente. Es un programa fascinante. Los dibujos animados son demasiado tontos y aburridos. No me interesan. Yo creo que deben dar más programas educativos.*

Options

Strategies for Reaching All Students

Students Needing Extra Help
Have students write out this section so they can check off what they have mastered.
Listening: Ask students what words they should be listening for, given the topic (numbers, time expressions).
Reading: Ask students for words that might be found in a description of different types of movies. Put them in columns.

Remind students to watch for these words. Remind them that a negative word changes the meaning of the phrase.
Writing: Break this into parts. What information is given in each sentence?
Have them write a letter as a class.
Culture: Have students review any notes they took earlier.

Resumen del capítulo 11

Use the vocabulary from this chapter to help you:

- talk about a TV show or movie
- tell when events begin and end, and how long they last
- express and defend an opinion

to name types of movies
la clase (de)
la película de aventuras
la película de ciencia ficción
la película musical
la película del oeste
la película romántica
la película de terror

to talk about TV and TV shows
el actor
la actriz
el anuncio (de televisión)
el canal
la comedia
el concierto
dar + *movie or TV program*
los dibujos animados
el documental
las noticias
el programa deportivo
el programa de detectives
el programa educativo
el programa de entrevistas
el programa de hechos de la vida real
el programa musical
el pronóstico del tiempo
la telenovela

to describe a movie or TV show
aburrido, -a
cómico, -a
¿Cuál(es)?
demasiado
divertido, -a
emocionante
en blanco y negro
en colores
fascinante
interesante
más (here: *more*)
el / la / los / las mejor(es) (here: *best*)
el / la / los / las peor(es) (here: *worst*)
realista
tonto, -a
triste
un poco

to indicate time or duration
casi
corto, -a
de la mañana
de la noche
de la tarde
durar
en punto
hasta
largo, -a
más tarde

más temprano
media hora (*f.*)
mediodía
medianoche
el minuto
puntualmente
el tiempo
todavía no

to express opinions or reactions
aburrir
dar miedo
fascinar
interesar
pensar (e → ie) (que)
sobre

to indicate a reason
por eso

Resumen 379

(p. 378, photo)
Cuban-born Cristina Saralegui hosts *El Show de Cristina,* the most popular talk show on Spanish-language television. The program is similar in style and content to English-language talk shows in the U.S.

CAPÍTULO 12

THEME: RESTAURANTS

SCOPE AND SEQUENCE Pages 380–413

COMMUNICATION

Topics

Restaurants

Mexican food

Table settings

Objectives

To discuss Mexican food and restaurants

To name and discuss foods

To talk about food

To describe table settings

To talk about eating out

To express needs

To indicate time or frequency

To indicate position

CULTURE

Mexican food and restaurants

GRAMMAR

Verbos con el cambio e → i

El verbo traer

El complemento indirecto: Los pronombres

El pretérito de los verbos que terminan en -er *e* -ir

Ancillaries available for use with Chapter 12

Multisensory/Technology

 Overhead Transparencies, 61–65

 Audio Tapes and CDs

 Vocabulary Art Blackline Masters for Hands-On Learning, pp. 63–67

 Classroom Crossword

 Video

 CD-ROM

Print

 Practice Workbook, pp. 125–135

 Writing, Audio & Video Activities, pp. 71–76, 126–128, 174–175

 Communicative Activity Blackline Masters

Pair and Small Group Activities, pp. 85–90

Situation Cards, p. 91

 Un paso más: Actividades para ampliar tu español, pp. 68–73

Assessment

 Assessment Program

Pruebas, pp. 175–185

Examen de habilidades, pp. 186–189

 Test Generator

Video still from Chap. 12

The Versatile Tortilla

When the Spaniards first arrived in Tenochtitlán, the site that is now Mexico City, they arrived with barrels of wheat. Within 25 years, according to some sources, Mexican bakers could produce bread as well as any baker in Spain. This legacy continues.

In spite of the popularity of bread, tortillas are considered staples in Mexican cooking. They are used to prepare such dishes as *tacos, enchiladas, tostadas, chilaquiles,* and *sopa de tortilla.* They serve as thickeners in soups, *moles,* and stews and are used to scoop beans, eggs, and salsas.

Tortillas can be found throughout Mexico, and preparation techniques vary little from region to region. They can be made by hand at home or by mechanized press and conveyor belt in a *tortillería.* Corn tortillas *(tortillas de maíz)* are prepared the same way as they were in the days of the Aztec empire. Flour tortillas *(tortillas de harina)* are an innovation developed after the Spaniards introduced wheat to the American continent.

Corn tortillas are made with white corn, slaked lime (a white powder obtained by exposing calcium hydroxide to moist air or water), and water. The washed corn is boiled in water with dissolved lime for about five minutes. After standing for several hours, it is rinsed, ground, and kneaded into dough *(masa).* (Prepackaged *masa* mixes are now available in supermarkets.) Then the tortillas are shaped.

To shape a tortilla by hand, a small ball of *masa* is clapped back and forth from hand to hand to form a thin, flat circle. (When making tortillas at home, many people use a special press that flattens the dough to a uniform thickness and diameter.) After the tortilla has been formed, it is baked on a griddle until it puffs in the center and acquires a golden brown color.

Flour tortillas are prepared with flour, lard or vegetable shortening, salt, and water. The shortening produces a slightly more elastic tortilla with a chewy texture. As with corn tortillas, a small ball of *masa* is pinched off. Flour tortillas, on the other hand, when prepared at home, are usually rolled out with a lightly floured rolling pin and then baked over a low flame on a griddle for a only few seconds.

Introduce

Re-entry of Concepts

The following list represents words, expressions, and grammar topics re-entered from *El primer paso* to Chap. 9:

El primer paso
Calendar expressions

Chapter 1
Gustar expressions

Chapter 2
Time-telling

Chapter 3
Ir a + inf.
Seasons

Chapter 4
Foods
Expressing likes and preferences

Chapter 5
Family members

Chapter 6
Clothing
Places in a community
Direct object pronouns

Chapter 7
Para + inf.
Querer + inf.
Items brought on vacation

Chapter 9
Health-care items

Planning

Cross-Curricular Connections

Health Connection (pp. 384–385)
Tell students that, as nutrition consultants, they are to plan a lunch for the following clients:
1) A group of vegetarians
2) A sports team that needs to maintain their weight
3) A weight-loss group

Math Connection (pp. 388–389)
Assign prices to the food items in the *Vocabulario para conversar* on pp. 384–385. Have students order a meal, complete with beverage and dessert. Have them add up the bill and then calculate a 20 percent tip for the waiter.

Visual Arts Connection (pp. 388–389)
Have students create a poster for a place setting of a restaurant of their choice. Students should pay attention to balance and scale, color, texture, and pattern. They might use a sheet of colored construction paper as the tablecloth and then add cutouts to represent the silverware, glassware, plates, and condiments. Then have them label the components of their place setting. Display the posters around the classroom.

CAPÍTULO 12

¡Vamos a un restaurante mexicano!

OBJECTIVES

At the end of this chapter, you will be able to:

■ ask politely to have something brought to you

■ order a meal

■ say what you ate or drank

■ compare family dinners in the Spanish-speaking world and in the United States

Haciendo tortillas en el mercado de Chichicastenango, Guatemala

381

Cultural Notes

Spanish in Your Community
Have students visit a local Mexican restaurant where the waiters speak Spanish. Have the students order in Spanish. If this is not possible, have them visit a Mexican fast-food restaurant. They might want to follow up their visit by writing a review of the establishment in the style used by restaurant critics.

(pp. 380–381, photo)
Corn meal tortillas have been a staple at mealtimes in Mexico and Central America since ancient times. Today, some people continue to make tortillas the traditional way—by hand—as this woman is doing at the Sunday market in Chichicastenango, Guatemala. Others, however, now save themselves several hours of work by taking their corn to the *tortillería,* where it is ground and then made into tortillas by machine.

Preview

Cultural Objective
• To talk about Mexican food and restaurants

 ¡Vamos a un restaurante mexicano!

Play

 Video Activity A

Using the Video
This chapter's video focuses on restaurants. Students will visit two restaurants in Guadalajara to see typical Mexican food being prepared and eaten.

To prepare students for the video, first ask them to predict what this chapter's tape will be about. Then have students watch this segment several times. After the first time, you may wish to have them brainstorm possible vocabulary and expressions they will need to talk about what they saw on the video. Ask students to identify: a) things they saw that were familiar to them, and b) things they saw that they probably would not see where they live.

For more teaching suggestions, see the Video Teacher's Guide.

¡Piénsalo bien!

Look at the photos and read the captions.

Think about the Mexican restaurants you're familiar with. What are their names? Are they fast-food places, diners, or fancy restaurants? Which of the restaurants shown in these photos is most similar to those in your community?

"¿Me pasas la sal, por favor?"

En el centro comercial Plaza Flamingo de Cancún

"Este es mi restaurante favorito. Se especializan en enchiladas de toda clase."

Restaurante hispano en Albuquerque, Nuevo México

The people of Mexico eat as wide a variety of foods as we do.

382   Capítulo 12

Options

Strategies for Reaching All Students

Spanish-Speaking Students
Ask: *¿Te gusta la comida mexicana? ¿Te gusta la comida de otras culturas? ¿Cuáles? ¿Cuál es tu plato favorito? ¿Quién lo prepara en tu casa?*

 Un paso más Exs. 12-A, 12-B

Students Needing Extra Help
If there are no Mexican restaurants in your community, ask students if they have heard about one that they would like to see in their town.

Enrichment
Invite a chef from a local Mexican restaurant to speak about food preparation. If possible, have him or her prepare a dish for your class.

"¿Y qué van a pedir?"

En el patio del restaurante Casa de Pico en San Diego

Multicultural Perspectives
In Mexico many people begin the day with a *desayuno* consisting of *café* and *pan dulce.* In some regions, people might have a second breakfast in mid-morning. This might include eggs, beans, tortillas, and a beverage. The *comida,* usually the heaviest and most important meal of the day, often occurs in early afternoon. Later in the day, some people have a *merienda* of fruit or something sweet. Ask students to share their meal patterns. Can they describe the meal patterns of any other cultures?

Answers: ¡Piénsalo bien!
Answers will vary for inductive questions.

Cultural Notes ☀

(p. 382, top photo)
Fast-food area in Cancún's Plaza Flamingo mall. Like other Mexican resort areas, Cancún has an abundance of American-style restaurants. These restaurants offering table service are usually more expensive, serving mainly seafood and steak, with only a few traditional Mexican dishes on the menu.

(p. 382, bottom photo)
Not all of the so-called "Tex-Mex" dishes that are popular in the U.S. have been adapted from Mexican recipes. Original Tex-Mex foods include *chile con carne, nachos,* and *burritos.* These distinctly U.S. dishes are now appearing in Mexico, particularly in tourist-oriented cities.

(p. 383, photo)
Mexican-style restaurants abound in the U.S., with Los Angeles having the highest number. Americans are also serving more Mexican-style foods in their own homes. In some cases, traditional American food staples have been replaced by them. For example, more and more Americans now use *salsa* than catsup, and an increasing number prefer corn chips to potato chips.

Present

Chapter Theme
Mexican food: Ingredients

Communicative Objectives
- To name and discuss foods
- To talk about food
- To indicate time or frequency

 Transparencies 61–62

 Vocabulary Art BLMs

 Pronunciation Tape 12-1

 Vocabulario para conversar A

Play

Using the Video
Video segment 2: See the Video Teacher's Guide.

 Video Activity B

Grammar Preview
Pedir is presented here lexically. The complete paradigm is in the grammar section on p. 397.

Vocabulario para conversar

¿Con qué se hacen las enchiladas?

Aquí tienes palabras y expresiones necesarias para hablar sobre algunas comidas mexicanas y con qué se hacen. Léelas varias veces y practícalas con un(a) compañero(a) en las páginas siguientes.

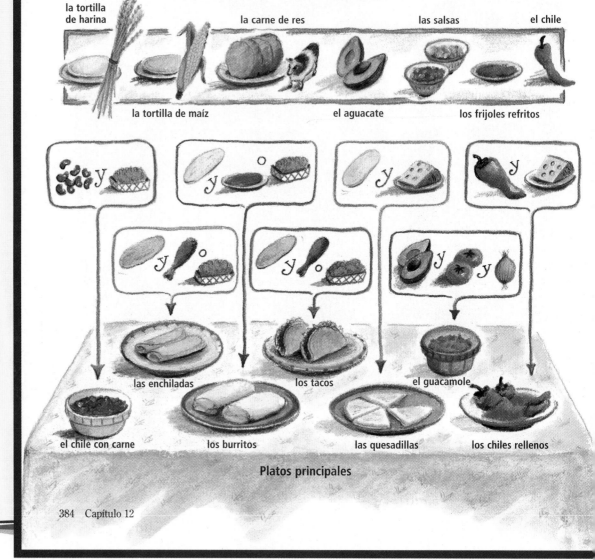

la tortilla de harina

la carne de res

las salsas

el chile

la tortilla de maíz

el aguacate

los frijoles refritos

las enchiladas

los tacos

el guacamole

el chile con carne

los burritos

las quesadillas

los chiles rellenos

Platos principales

384   Capítulo 12

Options

Strategies for Reaching All Students

Students Needing Extra Help
Vocabulario para conversar: Have students start their Organizers.
También necesitas . . . : Give examples of *¿con qué se hace(n) ___?* and *se hace(n) con ___.*
Model *probar* if necessary.

Learning Spanish Through Action
STAGING VOCABULARY: *Tráiganme*
MATERIALS: index cards with pictures of the food items from the Vocabulary Art BLMs or cut out of magazines
DIRECTIONS: Distribute the index cards at random. Tell students you are going to pre-

pare a main dish from the vocabulary list: *Voy a preparar quesadillas. Tráiganme el queso y las tortillas.* The students with the corresponding cards should then pass them to you and say *Aquí está(n).* Redistribute the cards and continue until all main dishes have been covered.

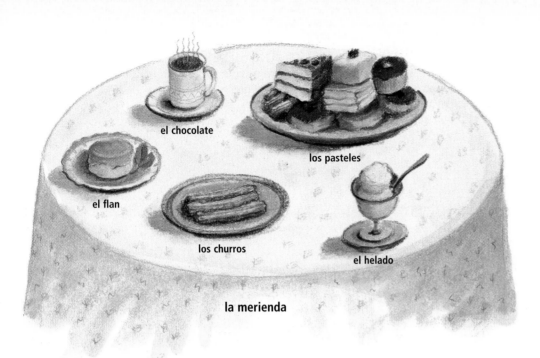

el chocolate

los pasteles

el flan

los churros

el helado

la merienda

También necesitas . . .

¿Con qué se hace(n) ___?	*What is / are ___ made with?*
Se hace(n) con ___.	*It's (they're) made with . . .*
pedir (e → i)	*to ask for; to order*
probar (o → ue)	*to try; to taste*
¿Has probado ___?	*Have you tried ___?*
he probado	*I've tried*
una vez	*once*
alguna vez	*ever*
¿Algo más?	here: *Anything else?*
el postre*	*dessert*
de postre	*for dessert*
picante	*spicy, peppery, hot (flavor)*
no picante	*mild (flavor)*
a menudo	*often*
vender	*to sell*

> **¿Y qué quiere decir . . . ?**
> de merienda
> muchas veces

* It's not typical in Spanish-speaking countries to have ice cream or cake for dessert. When dining at home, the usual dessert is *queso y fruta*. For your late-afternoon *merienda* you might have sandwiches, pastries, rolls, and *té* or *café con leche*, or *chocolate con churros*.

Vocabulario para conversar   385

Teaching Suggestions
Preparing students to speak: Use one or two options from each of the categories of Comprehensible Input, Physical Response, or Limited Verbal Response. For a complete explanation of these categories and some sample activities, see the front section of this Teacher's Edition.

Class Starter Review
On the day following initial vocabulary presentation, have students tell a partner what they are going to order for dinner and dessert tonight at a Mexican restaurant.

Reteach / Review: Vocabulary
Vocabulario para conversar: To complement the presentation of new vocabulary, review foods and the *Perspectiva cultural* information *(la merienda)* from Chap. 4.

Practice & Apply

Re-enter / Recycle

Ex. 1: foods from Chap. 4
Ex. 2: *gustar* expressions from Chap. 1
Ex. 3: *gustar* expressions from Chap. 1, *ir a* + inf. from Chap. 3, *querer* + inf. from Chap. 7
Ex. 5: *gustar* expressions from Chap. 1
Ex. 6: expressing likes and preferences from Chap. 4
Ex. 8: foods from Chap. 4

Answers: Empecemos a conversar

1 ESTUDIANTE A
a. ¿Qué vas a pedir de postre?
b. . . . de merienda?
c. . . . para el almuerzo?
d. . . . para la cena?

ESTUDIANTE B
a.–d. Answers will vary, but encourage a wide selection of foods.

2 ESTUDIANTE A
a. ¿Has probado aguacate alguna vez?
b. . . . frijoles refritos. . .
c. . . . churros. . .
d. . . . sopa de tomate. . .
e. Questions will vary.

ESTUDIANTE B
a.–e. Answers will vary, but look for the correct use of *gustar*.

Empecemos a conversar

Túrnate con un(a) compañero(a) para ser *Estudiante A* y *Estudiante B*. Reemplacen las palabras subrayadas con palabras representadas o escritas en los recuadros. quiere decir que puedes escoger *(choose)* tu propia respuesta.

1 plato principal
A — *¿Qué vas a pedir de plato principal?*
B — *Quisiera probar las quesadillas.*
Y ahora Uds.

Estudiante A   Estudiante B

a. de postre   b. de merienda

c. para el almuerzo   d. para la cena

2
A — *¿Has probado chiles rellenos alguna vez?*
B — *Sí, una vez. (Sí, muchas veces.)*
o: *No, nunca. (No me gustan los chiles rellenos.)*
Y ahora Uds.

Estudiante A   Estudiante B

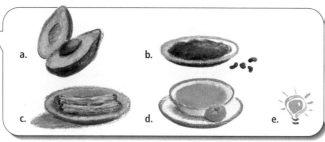

a.   b.   c.   d.   e.

386   Capítulo 12

Options

Strategies for Reaching All Students

Spanish-Speaking Students
Ex. 7: Add: *¿Cómo se prepara ___? Escribe la receta.*

 Un paso más Ex. 12-C

Students Needing Extra Help
Ex. 1: Remind *Estudiante B* to use the Organizer.
Ex. 2: Explain the meanings of the possible responses. Encourage students to vary their responses.

Ex. 3: Have students use their Organizers from Chap. 4.
Ex. 5: Remind students of *has probado* and *he probado* from *También necesitas . . . .*
Ex. 7: Have students use their Organizers and model *¿con qué se hace ___?*

3

A — *¿Quieres probar el flan?*
B — *Sí, voy a pedirlo(s).*
  o: *No, no me gusta(n).*
  Y ahora Uds.

Estudiante A   Estudiante B

a.
b.
c.
d.

4 A — *¿Con qué se hacen las enchiladas?*
B — *Con tortillas de maíz y pollo o carne de res.*

  Y ahora Uds.

Estudiante A   Estudiante B

Empecemos a escribir

Escribe tus respuestas en español.

5 ¿Cuáles de las comidas de la página 384 has probado? ¿Cuáles te gustaron? ¿Dónde las probaste?

6 ¿Prefieres la comida picante o no picante? ¿Qué restaurantes de tu comunidad sirven comida picante?

7 ¿Cuál es tu comida mexicana favorita? ¿Con qué se hace? ¿Hay tiendas en tu comunidad donde venden los ingredientes necesarios?

8 ¿Qué comes de postre más a menudo? ¿Pasteles, helado o frutas? ¿Cuál es tu favorito?

¡NO OLVIDES!

Remember that you can attach the pronouns *lo, la, los,* or *las* to an infinitive.

También se dice

las masas

el ají

los porotos

la palta

Vocabulario para conversar 387

3 ESTUDIANTE A
a. ¿Quieres probar los churros?
b. ...el chocolate?
c. ...el helado?
d. ...los pasteles?

ESTUDIANTE B
a.–d. Answers will vary, but look for correct use of pronouns.

4 Dialogues will vary.

Answers: Empecemos a escribir

5 Answers will vary, but look for *He probado, Me gustó (gustaron),* and *lo, la, los, las + probé.*

6–8 Answers will vary.

Practice Wkbk.
12-1, 12-2

Audio Activity 12.1

Writing Activities
12-A, 12-B

Pruebas 12-1, 12-2

387

Present

Chapter Theme
Restaurants: Eating out

Communicative Objectives
- To describe table settings
- To talk about food
- To talk about eating out
- To express needs
- To indicate position

 Transparencies 63–64

 Vocabulary Art BLMs

 Pronunciation Tape 12-2

 Vocabulario para conversar B

Play

Using the Video
Video segment 2: See the Video Teacher's Guide.

 Video Activity B

Vocabulario para conversar

¡Me falta una cuchara!

Aquí tienes el resto del vocabulario necesario para pedir algo, para pedir una comida y para decir lo que comiste o bebiste.

el camarero — la camarera —

el menú

la cuenta

el plato

el vaso

la taza
el platillo — la mantequilla

el tazón

la sal

la pimienta

el tenedor

el cuchillo

el azúcar

la cuchara

la servilleta

el mantel

388 Capítulo 12

Options

Strategies for Reaching All Students

Students Needing Extra Help
Vocabulario para conversar: Bring in some old dishes and silverware, paper / plastic plates, etc. from home. When students have learned the vocabulary, have them set the table, naming each item as they go along. *También necesitas . . . :* Give examples of *me falta, me faltan, me pasas, me trae,* and *lo mismo.* To review *la merienda,* refer to the *Perspectiva cultural* from Chap. 4.

Learning Spanish Through Action
STAGING VOCABULARY: ¿Me trae ___?
MATERIALS: paper goods (paper cups, plates, etc.) for table settings, index cards with pictures of food items from the Vocabulary Art BLMs or cut out from magazines

DIRECTIONS: Pass out the materials to groups of students. Sit at a table set for dinner. State that an item is missing. Ask a student to bring it to you. Repeat two or three times. Then pretend to get your food. State that you ordered an item and do not have it. Ask if a student will bring it to you. This can be continued until asking for the check.

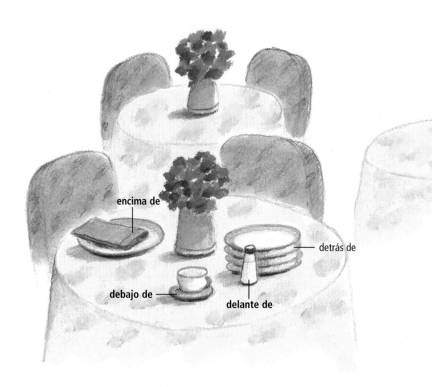

encima de

detrás de

debajo de

delante de

También necesitas . . .

Me falta(n)	*I need; I am lacking*
¿Me pasas ___?	*Will you pass me ___?*
¿Me trae ___?	*Will you bring me ___?*
(Le) traigo	*I'm bringing (you)*
beber: (yo) bebí	*to drink: I drank*
(tú) bebiste	*you drank*
comer: (yo) comí	*to eat: I ate*
(tú) comiste	*you ate*
pedir: (yo) pedí	*to order: I ordered*
(tú) pediste	*you ordered*
lo mismo	*the same thing*
en seguida	*right away*

¿Y qué quiere decir . . . ?
a la carta
la especialidad de la casa
el plato del día

Grammar Preview
Traigo / trae are presented lexically. The complete paradigm is on p. 398. *Bebí / bebiste, comí / comiste,* and *pedí / pediste* are presented lexically. The explanation of the preterite of *-er* and *-ir* verbs is on p. 403.

Teaching Suggestions
Preparing students to speak: Use one or two options from each of the categories of Comprehensible Input, Physical Response, or Limited Verbal Response. For a complete explanation of these categories and some sample activities, see the front section of this Teacher's Edition.

Note: Only boldface labels are new vocabulary items. The others were introduced in earlier chapters.

Class Starter Review
On the day following initial vocabulary presentation, you might begin the class with this activity: Arrange table settings on a table in the classroom. Have students close their eyes as you hide one or two items. When students open their eyes, ask: *¿Qué te (nos) falta?*
As an alternate activity, have students place the items on a table, telling you where each item goes as they set the table.

Practice & Apply

Re-enter / Recycle
Ex. 11: direct object pronouns from Chap. 6
Exs. 11–12: foods from Chap. 4
Ex. 13: expressing likes and preferences from Chap. 4

Answers: Empecemos a conversar

9 ESTUDIANTE A
a. Camarero, me falta una taza. ¿Me trae una, por favor?
b. ...un menú. ...uno...
c. ...un tazón. ...uno...
d. ...una servilleta. ...una...
e. ...un tenedor. ...uno...
f. Questions will vary, but look for correct use of *uno(a)*.

ESTUDIANTE B
a. Sí, le traigo una taza en seguida.
b. ...un menú...
c. ...un tazón...
d. ...una servilleta...
e. ...un tenedor...
f. Answers will vary, but look for correct use of indefinite articles.

10 ESTUDIANTE A
a. No veo el vaso. ¿Dónde está?
b. ...la sal. ...está?
c. ...el azúcar. ...está?
d. ...los platos. ...están?
e. ...las servilletas. ...están?
f. ...la cuenta. ...está?

Empecemos a conversar

9

A — *Camarero, me falta un vaso. ¿Me trae uno, por favor?*
B — *Sí, le traigo un vaso en seguida.*

Y ahora Uds.

Estudiante A   Estudiante B

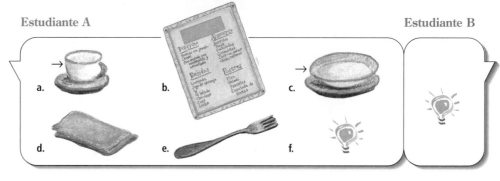

a.   b.   c.   d.   e.   f.

10

A — *No veo la(s) cuchara(s). ¿Dónde está(n)?*
B — *Está(n) delante de los vasos.*

Y ahora Uds.

Estudiante A   Estudiante B

a.   b.   c.   d.   e.   f.

390   Capítulo 12

Options

Strategies for Reaching All Students

Spanish-Speaking Students
Ex. 12: Add: *¿Por qué es bueno desayunar todos los días?*

Students Needing Extra Help
Ex. 9: Remind students that *una* refers to feminine nouns.
Ex. 10: Review prepositions of place from Chap. 10.
Write a singular and a plural example separately on the chalkboard. Students might find the parentheses confusing.

Ex. 11: Review direct object pronouns *lo, la, los,* and *las.*
Exs. 12–13: Have students use their Organizers from Chap. 4.
Ex. 14: Clarify the question by adding: *¿Te falta algo para escribir tus respuestas?*

11 A —¿Me pasas _la sal_, por favor?

B —Sí, aquí _la_ tienes. ¿Necesitas algo más?

A —Ahora no, gracias.

Y ahora Uds.

Estudiante A   Estudiante B

Empecemos a escribir y a leer

Escribe tus respuestas en español.

12 ¿Qué bebiste en el desayuno esta mañana? ¿Y ayer?

13 Cuando vas a un restaurante, ¿qué prefieres, el plato del día o la especialidad de la casa? ¿Por qué?

14 ¿Te falta algo ahora? ¿Qué te falta?

15 ¿Es lógico o no? Si no, escribe frases lógicas.

— ¿Con qué se hacen las quesadillas?
— Con tortillas de maíz y queso. Son muy picantes. ¡Me encantan!

— ...Y de plato principal pedí chiles rellenos y quesadillas. ¡Me encanta la comida española!

— Javier, ¿me pasas la mantequilla, por favor?
— Sí, en seguida. Está debajo del tenedor.

¡NO OLVIDES!

Remember that the pronouns _lo, la, los,_ and _las_ are placed before the conjugated verb.

También se dice

el mesero, la mesera
el mozo, la moza

la carta
la minuta
la lista

Vocabulario para conversar 391

ESTUDIANTE B

(Answers may vary.)

a. Está detrás de la sal (delante del azúcar).

b. Está delante del vaso (al lado de la pimienta).

c. Está detrás del vaso.

d. Están debajo de las servilletas.

e. Están encima de los platos.

f. Está debajo (detrás) del tenedor.

11 Dialogues will vary, but look for correct use of pronouns.

Answers: Empecemos a escribir y a leer

12–14 Answers will vary, but look for correct use of verb forms.

15 None of the exchanges are logical. Possible changes to make them logical include: 1: _No son picantes,_ 2: ¡_Me encanta la comida mexicana!,_ and 3: ¿_Me pasas la cuenta?_ or ¿_Me pasas la servilleta?_

 Practice Wkbk. 12-3, 12-4

 Audio Activity 12.2

 Writing Activity 12-C

 Pruebas 12-3, 12-4

 Comm. Act. BLM 12-1

Enrichment

Ex. 10: To extend this exercise, have pairs of students find other ways of giving the locations of objects by using location words from Chap. 10: _entre, a la izquierda (de), a la derecha (de), al lado (de)._

391

Practice

Re-enter / Recycle
Ex. 1: *ir a* + inf. from Chap. 3, foods from Chap. 4
Ex. 2: foods from Chap. 4, *querer* + inf. from Chap. 7

Reteach / Review: Vocabulary
Ex. 3: Before doing this exercise, review location words from Chap. 10. Ask the location of students and classroom objects, encouraging as many answers as possible to describe a location.

Answers:
¡Comuniquemos!
1 Dialogues will vary.

2 Questions may vary:
a. ¿Me trae una cuchara, por favor?
b. ¿Con qué se hace el guacamole...
c. ¿Me trae la mantequilla, ...
d. ¿Me trae más agua, ...
e. ¿Me trae otro tenedor, ...
f. ¿Me trae la cuenta, ...
g. ¿Me trae algo para beber, ...

¡Comuniquemos!

Aquí tienes otra oportunidad para usar el vocabulario de este capítulo.

1 Usa el menú para pedir una comida completa. Con tu compañero(a) representen *(play the role)* al (a la) camarero(a) y al (a la) cliente.

MENÚ

Desayuno
Huevos con jamón
Cereal
Pan tostado con mantequilla y mermelada

Bebidas
Limonada
Jugo de naranja
Té
Té helado
Chocolate
Café
Leche

Almuerzo
Burritos
Tacos
Enchiladas
Quesadillas
Chile con carne
Chiles rellenos

Postres
Flan
Helado
Pasteles
Ensalada de frutas

A — ¿*Qué desea, señor?*
o: ¿*Qué va a comer?*
(¿*Y para beber? ¿Y de postre?*)
B — *Pan tostado con queso.*

2 ¿Qué dirías *(would you say)* en estas situaciones?

Pediste el bistec pero sólo tienes un tenedor y una cuchara.
¿Me trae un cuchillo, por favor?

a. Pediste sopa pero sólo tienes un tenedor y un cuchillo.
b. Te gustaría pedir guacamole pero no sabes con qué se hace.
c. Hay pan pero no hay nada más en la mesa.
d. Pediste agua pero ya la bebiste.
e. Tu tenedor está sucio.
f. Quieres salir del restaurante pero no sabes cuánto tienes que pagar.
g. Las enchiladas que comes están demasiado picantes. Necesitas beber algo.

392   Capítulo 12

Options

Strategies for Reaching All Students

Spanish-Speaking Students

 **Un paso más Exs. 12-D, 12-E, 12-F**

Students Needing Extra Help
Ex. 1: Tell students if they will be ordering breakfast or lunch.
Remind them that they must address each other as *señor* or *señorita*.
Ex. 2: Have students brainstorm as many ways as possible to answer: *necesito, no tengo, me falta(n), quisiera, ¿me trae?,* etc.

Ex. 3: Review food from Chap. 4 and prepositions of place from Chap. 10.
¿Qué sabes ahora?: Have students write out this section so they can check off what they have mastered.

3 En este dibujo hay siete errores. ¿Cuántos puedes encontrar? Trabaja en grupos pequeños para encontrarlos. Después, compartan *(share)* con otros grupos los errores que encontraron.

El vaso está debajo del plato.

¿Qué sabes ahora?

Can you:

■ describe the ingredients in certain dishes?

—Los burritos se hacen con ___ y con ___.

■ make polite requests to have something brought or passed to you?

¿ ___ la salsa, por favor?

■ order a meal?

—Voy a comer ___, y de ___ quisiera un helado.

■ tell what you ate or drank?

—Ayer yo ___ chile con carne y ___ una limonada.

3 *(Answers will vary.)* Las frutas están encima del tazón. La cuchara está debajo del plato. El plato está encima del vaso. La zanahoria está debajo del vaso. El sandwich está en el tazón. La ensalada está en la mesa. El tomate está en el vaso.

Answers: ¿Qué sabes ahora?

• tortillas de harina / frijoles refritos o carne de res
• Me trae
• *Answers will vary.* / postre
• comí / bebí

 Audio Activity 12.3

Cooperative Learning
Divide the class into groups of three. Prepare copies of the Vocabulary Art BLMs from the second *Vocabulario para conversar* (p. 388) for each group, with different table items "missing" from each table setting. Have one person in each group be responsible for recording what's missing. Have another person report the findings to the class.

393

Present & Apply

Cultural Objective

• To compare family dinners in Spanish-speaking countries and in the U.S.

Critical Thinking: Identifying Stereotypes

Clear up any misconceptions students may still have about what is considered Mexican food. Stress that cuisine varies tremendously from region to region, as it does in the U.S. Draw a comparison between Mexican food with Chinese food in the U.S.

Perspectiva cultural

¿Vas a restaurantes con frecuencia? ¿Te gusta ir con tu familia? ¿Con tus amigos? Generalmente, ¿con quién vas?

What words would you use to describe this restaurant and the people in it? How often do you eat the foods shown on the plate?

The large photo gives you a glimpse of what a family dinner might be like in a restaurant in Mexico. If you lived there, you'd probably be looking forward to seeing your favorite aunt and uncle at the next dinner, because a restaurant meal usually implies a Sunday afternoon dinner, which is an important family event. It is generally a long, leisurely meal that can last for two or three hours. It is an occasion for the whole extended family to get together: brothers, sisters, parents, aunts, uncles, and godparents. Unlike in the United States, where children are often left at home with a baby-sitter, in Mexico even infants are an important presence during a family dinner.

A restaurant dinner can also take place very late at night, especially in a bustling metropolis such as Mexico City. It is common to see an entire family arrive at a restaurant at 10 or 11 in the evening. On Friday and Saturday nights, restaurants often stay open until 2 or 3 in the morning. Some restaurants have entertainment, such as a band.

Many late-night restaurants are inexpensive and the food is very good. They attract people from all walks of life. A man in a work shirt might end up having dinner with his family next to a table of people dressed in suits and expensive fur coats who have just come from the theater.

La cultura desde tu perspectiva

1 What are the similarities and differences between dining out in Mexico and in the United States?

2 You have read about a typical Saturday night and Sunday afternoon in a Mexican restaurant. What values do you think these customs reflect?

Cenando en la Ciudad de México

394   Capítulo 12

Options

Strategies for Reaching All Students

Spanish-Speaking Students

Ask Spanish-speaking students: *¿Te gusta la comida típica mexicana como las tortillas, los chiles y los frijoles? ¿Qué clase de comida se prepara en tu casa? ¿Es como los platos que se describen aquí o es diferente?*

 Un paso más Ex. 12-G

Enrichment

Have students bring in various food items for a class *fiesta*. Ask Spanish-speaking students to bring in a dish that they frequently prepare at home.

Un plato típico mexicano: camarones rancheros, arroz, guacamole y salsa

Cultural Notes

(p. 395, photo)
Mexico City's Sanborn's restaurants serve inexpensive Mexican and international food. They are most often located within department stores of the same name. The most famous Sanborn's restaurant is housed in the glass-roofed courtyard of a seventeenth-century mansion known as the *Casa de los azulejos,* so named because of the beautiful tile work on its outer walls.

(p. 395, inset photo)
This dish of *camarones rancheros* (jumbo prawns sautéed in tomato sauce) illustrates the blend of indigenous and Spanish foods that characterizes Mexican cuisine. Shown here in different preparations are beans, rice, and guacamole.

Transparency 65

Teaching Suggestions

A Remind students that *-ir* verbs use the present-tense ending *-imos* for *nosotros*. Ask whether the present-tense ending is different from or the same as the preterite-tense ending.

B Remind students that in the preterite the *yo* forms of *comer* and *beber* are *comí* and *bebí*. Ask them to look at the captions to find the *yo* form of an *-ir* verb in the preterite. Then ask whether the ending of this form is the same as or different from the ending of the *yo* form of the *-er* verbs.

Answers

A *bebieron;* this ends in *-ron* like the ending for *-ar* verbs; it uses *e* rather than *a* before the *-ron*.

B *describió:* he described; *vendió:* he sold / Both verbs are third-person singular and end in *-ió*.

C The guide described the plan of the city to us. / *nos*

Gramática en contexto

Look at this page from a student's travel album and read the captions that she wrote.

El segundo día fuimos a visitar las pirámides de Teotihuacán, cerca de la Ciudad de México.

Nuestro guía nos describió el plano de la ciudad antigua.

Luego, todos subimos la Pirámide del Sol. Yo subí primero y les saqué esta foto a mis amigos en las escaleras.

Cuando bajamos, un vendedor les vendió refrescos a mis amigos. Ellos bebieron los refrescos de unas bolsas de plástico.

A You know that *-aron* is the ending for the *ellos / Uds.* form of *-ar* verbs in the preterite. In the captions, find an *-er* verb that has the *ellos / Uds.* ending in the preterite. How is it similar to the ending for *-ar* verbs? How is it different?

B There are two verbs used in the captions that may be new to you: *describió* and *vendió*. Can you guess their meanings? What do these preterite verb forms have in common?

C Find the sentence that begins *Nuestro guía ....* To whom did the guide describe the plan of the city? What word gives you this information?

396   Capítulo 12

Options

Strategies for Reaching All Students

Students Needing Extra Help
B: Remind students of cognates.
C: Give more examples of indirect object pronouns in the selection: 1) In the sentence that begins *Yo subí primero ...,* whose picture did the girl take? (her friends') What words give you this information? *(les ... a mis amigos)* 2) In the sentence that begins *Cuando bajamos ...,* to whom did the vendor sell soft drinks? (the girl's friends) What words give you this information? *(les ... a mis amigos)*

Verbos con el cambio e → i: To review *pensar* and *poder,* refer students to the Chap. 7 Organizer.
Remind them of the "boot" verb construction.
Ex. 1: Remind students of the stem change in *pedir.*

Enrichment
Ex. 1: Personalize the model dialogue by telling students what you actually order. Encourage students to use appropriate expressions of frequency in the *Estudiante B* response.

Verbos con el cambio *e → i*

You know two types of stem-changing verbs: those like *poder (o → ue)* and those like *pensar (e → ie)*. There is a third type in which the *e* in the stem changes to *i* in some of the present-tense forms. *Pedir* is an example of this type. Here are all of its present-tense forms.

(yo)	pido	(nosotros) (nosotras)	pedimos
(tú)	pides	(vosotros) (vosotras)	pedís
Ud. (él) (ella)	pide	Uds. (ellos) (ellas)	piden

• The infinitives of all *e → i* verbs end in *-ir*. Notice that the endings follow the pattern of regular *-ir* verbs.

• Another verb of this type that you know is *servir*.
  En ese restaurante siempre **sirven** arroz con pollo.

1 Dile a un(a) compañero(a) qué piden de postre o de merienda las siguientes personas en un restaurante.

tu profesor A — *En un restaurante, ¿qué pide de postre tu profesor?*
             B — *Generalmente pide flan.*

a. tú
b. tus amigos
c. tu papá / tu mamá
d. Uds.
e. tu hermano / tu hermana
f. tus abuelos

En la Zona Rosa, Ciudad de México

Gramática en contexto   397

Answers
1 Answers will vary, but should include the correct forms of *pedir*.
a. pides tú
b. piden tus amigos
c. pide tu papá (mamá)
d. piden Uds.
e. pide tu hermano (hermana)
f. piden tus abuelos

Cultural Notes ☼

(p. 397, photo)
A café in Mexico City's Zona Rosa, whose streets are lined with art galleries, shops, discotheques, and restaurants. Although many visitors and residents now prefer to do their shopping in malls, la Zona Rosa continues to thrive as a shopping and entertainment center.

Present & Practice

Class Starter Review
After the initial presentation of present-tense *traer,* you might begin the class with this activity: Have students write a sentence listing five things they bring to school every day.

Re-enter / Recycle
Ex. 2: calendar expressions from *El primer paso,* seasons from Chap. 3, family from Chap. 5
Ex. 3: foods from Chap. 4, items brought on vacation from Chap. 7

Answers
2 Answers will vary, but should include the correct forms of *servir.* Suggested foods include: *jamón, pescado, helado, burritos, pasteles, hamburguesas, guacamole, enchiladas.*
a. Mis amigos sirven
b. Mi restaurante favorito sirve
c. Mi mamá (papá) sirve
d. (Yo) sirvo
e. Mis amigos y yo servimos
f. La cafetería de la escuela sirve

 Practice Wkbk. 12-5

 Prueba 12-5

---

2 Escribe frases para decir qué comida sirven en diferentes ocasiones.

Mis amigos y yo servimos sandwiches y guacamole en la cena.

a. mis amigos
b. mi restaurante favorito
c. mi mamá / mi papá
d. (yo)
e. mis amigos y yo
f. la cafetería de la escuela

en el verano
en el invierno
los domingos
los fines de semana
en las fiestas
todos los días
en la cena
de postre
el 4 de julio

El verbo *traer*

Here are all of the present-tense forms of *traer* (to bring).

(yo)	**traigo**	(nosotros) (nosotras)	**traemos**
(tú)	**traes**	(vosotros) (vosotras)	**traéis**
Ud. (él) (ella)	**trae**	Uds. (ellos) (ellas)	**traen**

- Like *poner* and *hacer, traer* has only one irregular present-tense form: *traigo.* All other forms follow the pattern of regular *-er* verbs.

398   Capítulo 12

Options

Strategies for Reaching All Students

Students Needing Extra Help
Ex. 2: Remind students that they are to formulate their answers in the present tense.
El verbo traer: Do a quick review of *poner* and *hacer* for the *yo* form ending *(-go).* Or present *traer* and then ask students for other words they know that have a similar *yo* form.
Ex. 3: Remind students of how *Uds.* changes to *nosotros* in the answer. Give more examples so that students can see that *creo que* does not change.

3 Estás en la playa con un(a) amigo(a). Pregúntale a tu amigo(a)
qué trae al picnic cada *(each)* una de estas personas.

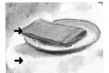

A — ¿*Qué trae Marta?*
B — *Creo que trae los platos y los vasos.*

Marta

a. Alejandro y Federico   b. Uds.   c. Paquita

d. Elena y Joaquín   e. tú   f. Diego

399

Reteach / Review:
Ir a + inf.
Ex. 3: Have students redo this
exercise by using *ir a* + inf.: *¿Qué
va a traer Marta? Creo que va a
traer los platos y los vasos.*

Answers
3 **ESTUDIANTE A**
a. ¿Qué traen Alejandro y
Federico?
b. . . . traen Uds.?
c. . . . trae Paquita?
d. . . . traen Elena y Joaquín?
e. . . . traes tú?
f. . . . trae Diego?
ESTUDIANTE B
a. Creo que traen los refrescos.
b. . . . traemos el bronceador y la
cámara.
c. . . . trae las cucharas y los
cuchillos.
d. . . . traen el mantel.
e. . . . traigo los sandwiches de
jamón y queso.
f. . . . trae la ensalada de fruta.

**Practice Wkbk.
12-6, 12-7**

Prueba 12-6

**Comm. Act. BLM
12-2**

Present & Practice

Re-enter / Recycle

Ex. 4: foods from Chap. 4, *querer* + inf. from Chap. 7
Ex. 5: foods from Chap. 4

Answers

4 ESTUDIANTE A

a. Quiero hacer enchiladas. ¿Me traes . . . ? *(Ingredients will vary.)* / Sí, por favor. (No, gracias.)
b. . . . burritos . . . / . . .
c. . . . tacos . . . / . . .
d. . . . quesadillas . . . / . . .
e. . . . chiles rellenos . . . / . . .
f. . . . flan . . . / . . .
g. Questions will vary, but make sure students use correct ingredients from p. 384 or recipes brought from outside of class.

ESTUDIANTE B

a.–g. Answers will vary, but encourage students to use vocabulary from this chapter and Chap. 4.

El complemento indirecto: Los pronombres

An indirect object tells to whom or for whom an action is performed. You already know the indirect object pronouns *me, te, le, nos,* and *les.* They are used to replace an indirect object noun.

El camarero **nos** sirve enchiladas de queso. — *The waiter serves **us** cheese enchiladas.*
Me trae un refresco. — *He's bringing **me** a soft drink.*
¿**Te** trae el postre ahora? — *Is he bringing **you** dessert now?*

- Because *le* and *les* can have more than one meaning, we can make the meaning clear by adding *a* + pronoun.

Rafael **le** trae el postre **a ella**. — *Rafael is bringing dessert **to her**.*
Les servimos tacos **a ellos**. — *We serve **them** tacos.*

- When we use an indirect object noun, we usually use the indirect object pronoun too.

Le compro naranjas a **mi mamá**. — *I'm buying oranges **for my mom**.*
Les sirvo burritos **a mis amigos**. — *I serve burritos **to my friends**.*

- We can attach an indirect object pronoun to an infinitive or put it before the main verb.

Voy a traer**les** guacamole.
Les voy a traer guacamole. } *I'm going to bring **them** guacamole.*

- Remember that we use indirect object pronouns with verbs like *doler, gustar, encantar,* and *interesar.* This is also true of *faltar.*

400   Capítulo 12

Options

Strategies for Reaching All Students

Students Needing Extra Help
El complemento indirecto: Los pronombres: Students may look for the "to" because of the "to whom, for whom" explanation. Show them how in English we drop the "to": We say "bring me" rather than "bring to me." Explain why we can attach the pronoun to the infinitive, but give students the option of using whichever way is more comfortable to them.

Give examples using *duele(n)* and other verbs listed here.
Ex. 4: Have students refer to the first vocabulary section to identify which ingredients are in each dish.
Explain that flan is a baked custard dessert. Have students take note of the change in verb form from question to answer and the change in the pronoun.

Ex. 5: Make a chart of corresponding subject pronouns and object pronouns: *yo (me), tú (te),* and so on.
Show that *pedir* and the object pronoun change; the *servir* verb form does not. Categorize main meal, vegetables, and desserts so that students will use related foods.

400

4 Tu compañero(a) y tú van a preparar las siguientes comidas. Pídele algo que necesitas. Luego continúa la conversación.

A — *Quiero hacer guacamole. ¿Me traes una cebolla?*
B — *Sí, ¿y te traigo tomates también?*
A — *Sí, por favor.*
    o: *No, gracias.*

a.   b.   c.

d.   e.   f.   g.

5 El camarero nunca les sirve a Uds. lo que *(what)* piden. Explica la situación con un(a) compañero(a).

Cuando ella pide pollo, el camarero le sirve pescado.

a.   b.

c.

d.   e.   f.

Gramática en contexto   401

Re-enter / Recycle

Ex. 6: places in a community, clothing from Chap. 6, health-care items from Chap. 9

Ex. 7: foods from Chap. 4, family members from Chap. 5

Reteach / Review:
Para + inf.

Ex. 6: Encourage students to use *para* + inf. with the indirect object pronoun attached to tell why they are going to the place named: *Para comprarle un regalo a mi mamá.*

Answers

6 ESTUDIANTE A

a.–f. ¡Hola!, ¿adónde vas? / ¿Por qué?

ESTUDIANTE B

Second part of *Estudiante B*'s response will vary.

a. Voy a la librería. / Necesito comprarle un libro a mi amiga.

b. Voy al correo. / . . . comprarles sellos a mis abuelos.

c. Voy al supermercado. / . . . comprarles comestibles a mis padres.

d. Voy a la tienda de ropa. / . . . comprarle un suéter (calcetines) a mi hermano.

e. Voy al almacén. / . . . comprarle un suéter (calcetines) a mi amigo.

f. Voy a la farmacia. / . . . comprarles pastillas a mis primos.

---

6 Vas al centro *(downtown)* para comprar diferentes cosas. Tu compañero(a) te pregunta adónde vas y por qué vas allí.

a mi mamá

A —*¡Hola!, ¿adónde vas?*
B —*Voy a la tienda de regalos.*
A —*¿Por qué?*
B —*Necesito comprarle un regalo a mi mamá.*

a. a mi amiga

b. a mis abuelos

c. a mis padres

d. a mi hermano

e. a mi amigo

f. a mis primos

7 Vas a invitar a estas personas a tu casa. Dile a tu compañero(a) qué vas a servirles.

tus abuelos

A —*¿Qué vas a servirles a tus abuelos?*
B —*Voy a servirles arroz con pollo, ensalada, zanahorias y pan.*

a. tu mejor amigo(a)
b. tus primos
c. el Presidente de los Estados Unidos
d. tu profesor(a) de español
e. (nombre de un actor o una actriz)
f. (nombre de un grupo musical)

Options

Strategies for Reaching All Students

Students Needing Extra Help

Ex. 6: Remind students that *le* can mean a variety of things. Give them a minute to associate stamps with post office, lozenges with pharmacy, and so on.

Ex. 7: Have students use their Organizers from this chapter and Chap. 4.

Before starting Ex. 7, ask students if they can figure out what *mejor amigo(a)* in item *a* means.

El pretérito de los verbos que terminan en -er e -ir: Model an *-ar* verb in the preterite. Then, when the *-er* and *-ir* verb endings are presented, students can see similarities with what they have already learned.

¡No olvides!: Write out *ver* in chart form.

El pretérito de los verbos que terminan en *-er* e *-ir*

As you know, we use the preterite tense to tell what happened in the past. For *-ar* verbs, we use this pattern of endings: *-é, -aste, -ó, -amos, -asteis, -aron*. The preterite endings for regular *-er* and *-ir* verbs are alike: *-í, -iste, -ió, -imos, -isteis, -ieron*.

Here are all of the preterite forms of *comer* and *salir*:

(yo)	com**í** sal**í**	(nosotros) (nosotras)	com**imos** sal**imos**
(tú)	com**iste** sal**iste**	(vosotros) (vosotras)	com**isteis** sal**isteis**
Ud. (él) (ella)	com**ió** sal**ió**	Uds. (ellos) (ellas)	com**ieron** sal**ieron**

• Notice the accent marks on the endings *-í* and *-ió*. These must be included as a part of the spelling.

¡NO OLVIDES!

As you learned in Chapter 11, *ver* does not have accent marks on any of its preterite forms: *vi, viste, vio, vimos, vieron.*

7 ESTUDIANTE A

a. ¿Qué vas a servirle a tu mejor amigo(a)?
b. ...servirles a tus primos?
c. ...servirle al Presidente de los Estados Unidos?
d. ...servirle a tu profesor(a) de español?
e.–f. *(Questions will vary.)*
...servirle a ___?

ESTUDIANTE B
Answers will vary according to students' choices.
a. Voy a servirle...
b. Voy a servirles...
c. Voy a servirle...
d. Voy a servirle...
e. Voy a servirle...
f. Voy a servirle...

 Practice Wkbk. 12-8

 Writing Activities 12-D, 12-E

 Prueba 12-7

Gramática en contexto   403

Practice

Re-enter / Recycle
Ex. 8: time-telling from Chap. 2
Ex. 9: foods from Chap. 4

Answers

8 ESTUDIANTE A

a. ¿A qué hora comieron Eduardo y Santiago? / ¿Y luego salieron?

b. ...comió Benjamín? / ...salió?

c. ...comieron Uds.? / ...salieron?

d. ...comieron Claudia y Soledad? / ...salieron?

e. ...comió María Eugenia? / ...salió?

f. ...comiste tú? / ...saliste?

ESTUDIANTE B

a. Comieron a las siete y cuarto (quince). / Sí, salieron a las siete y cuarenta y cinco (a las ocho menos cuarto / quince).

b. Comió a las ocho y veinte. / ...salió a las ocho y cincuenta (nueve menos diez).

c. Comimos a las ocho y cuarenta y cinco (nueve menos cuarto / quince). / ...salimos a las nueve y cuarto (quince).

d. Comieron a las seis y cuarenta (siete menos veinte). / ...salieron a las siete y diez.

e. Comió a las siete y media. / ...salió a las ocho.

f. *Answers will vary, but should include:* Comí a la(s) ... *and* Salí a la(s) ....

---

8 Estas personas salieron de sus casas treinta minutos después de comer. Dile a tu compañero(a) a qué hora comieron y a qué hora salieron.

Pablo / 6:30

A —*¿A qué hora comió Pablo?*
B —*Comió a las seis y media.*
A —*¿Y luego salió?*
B —*Sí, salió a las siete.*

a. Eduardo y Santiago / 7:15
b. Benjamín / 8:20
c. Uds. / 8:45
d. Claudia y Soledad / 6:40
e. María Eugenia / 7:30
f. tú / 💡

9 En cuatro hojas de papel escribe cuatro cosas diferentes que comiste o bebiste la semana pasada. Mezcla *(mix)* tus papeles con los de otros(as) tres compañeros(as). Una persona del grupo va a escoger un papel y preguntar quién comió o bebió esas cosas.

A —*¿Quién comió tacos la semana pasada?*
B —*Yo comí tacos.*
C —*Yo también.*

Lleva un registro *(keep a tally)* de las respuestas de tus compañeros(as) para informar a la clase qué comieron y bebieron las personas de tu grupo.

> *Miguel y yo comimos tacos la semana pasada.*
> o: *Miguel y Sara comieron tacos la semana pasada.*
> o: *Ricardo no comió tacos la semana pasada.*

Options

Strategies for Reaching All Students

Spanish-Speaking Students
Ex. 9: Have Spanish-speaking students write sentences: *Escribe oraciones que dicen qué comieron y bebieron tus compañeros(as).*

Students Needing Extra Help
Ex. 8: Review time-telling from Chap. 2. Go through the exercise, having students add the half hour to each example beforehand so they can concentrate their efforts on forming the preterite.
Ahora lo sabes: Have students write out this section so they can check off what they have mastered.

Ahora lo sabes

Can you:

- tell what people order and serve?

  —Mis padres siempre ___ pescado cuando van al restaurante.

  —La cafetería de mi escuela ___ hamburguesas a menudo.

- tell what someone brings to a place or to another person?

  —(Yo) le ___ una cuchara a mi hermana.

- tell what someone does or did for you or for someone else?

  —Mis padres no tienen servilletas. Por eso, la camarera ___ trae servilletas.

- tell what someone ate?

  —Federico ___ chile con carne anoche.

Con la familia a la hora de la cena en Madrid

Gramática en contexto   405

Apply

Play

Step

Using the Video
Video segment 3: See the Video Teacher's Guide.

 Video Activity C

Critical Thinking: Synthesizing Information
Have students make columns with the headings *siempre, nunca,* and *a veces* to generate a list of how often they eat the foods from both *Vocabulario para conversar* sections. Tally the lists and post the results.

Answers: Actividades
1 Answers will vary, but look for correct use of *comer* and *beber* in the preterite and encourage a wide range of food choices.

Para decir más

Aquí tienes vocabulario adicional que te puede ayudar para hacer las actividades de esta sección.

ahumado, -a
smoked

el ajo
garlic

a la parrilla
barbecued

a la plancha
grilled

asado, -a
roasted

salteado, -a
sautéed

la ternera
veal

muy condimentado
spicy

Actividades

Esta sección te ofrece la oportunidad de aumentar tus conocimientos de español al integrar lo que aprendiste en este capítulo con lo que aprendiste en capítulos anteriores.

1 Haz una lista de lo que comiste y bebiste durante los últimos tres días. Si comiste o bebiste algo más de una vez, indica cuántas veces. Con un(a) compañero(a) habla de lo que Uds. comieron y bebieron y escríbanlo en una hoja de papel. Luego informen a la clase o a otro grupo sobre lo que comieron. Pueden hablar sobre:
- lo que comiste y bebiste y cuántas veces
- lo que tu compañero(a) comió y bebió
- si sus dietas tienen algo en común o no
- si comieron y bebieron cosas buenas o malas para la salud

406   Capítulo 12

Options

Strategies for Reaching All Students

Spanish-Speaking Students
Ex. 3: After completing this exercise, have Spanish-speaking students write a letter to a friend who missed the party. *Escríbele una carta a un(a) amigo(a) que se perdió la fiesta. Dile cómo estuvo la fiesta, quiénes fueron, qué comieron, etc.*
Have students give a demonstration on how to make a dish which can be easily prepared in the classroom.

Students Needing Extra Help
Exs. 1–2: Have students use their Organizers to help them develop statements. Remind students to change the verb form when reporting to the class.

Enrichment
Ex. 2: Have students design posters about their favorite restaurants. The description of a favorite restaurant can be written as a short composition and included on the poster. They can then give a presentation about their favorite restaurant, using the poster as an aid. Encourage other students to follow up each presentation with questions and comments.
Ex. 3: Additional topics pairs of students might discuss: 1) how much to expect to

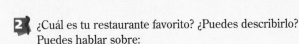

2 ¿Cuál es tu restaurante favorito? ¿Puedes describirlo? Puedes hablar sobre:

- dónde está
- la clase de comidas que sirve
- qué pides generalmente cuando vas allí
- si el restaurante es caro o barato
- cuándo fuiste allí por última vez y qué comiste

3 Con un(a) compañero(a) prepara una comida para una fiesta de la escuela. Deben:

- decidir qué comida van a preparar
- hacer una lista de los ingredientes que van a necesitar
- y cuánto van a necesitar de cada uno

Luego, digan a la clase qué comida piensan traer a la fiesta. También pueden decidir quiénes van a:

- poner la mesa
- lavar los platos
- ser los camareros y las camareras
- sacar la basura

15 tortillas de maíz

carne de res

5 aguacates

4 tomates

2 cebollas

15 pasteles

"Aquí venden los ingredientes que necesito."

Dos jóvenes de compras en la Ciudad de México

Actividades   407

2 Answers will vary, but look for correct use of *servir, pedir,* and preterite of *comer.*

3 Answers will vary, but look for a wide selection of food choices and the correct use of *ir a* + inf.

 **Writing Activities
12-G, 12-H**

 **Comm. Act. BLMs
12-3, 12-4, 12-5**

---

spend on ingredients; 2) how long the dish will take to make (students may discuss what time to start preparing the dish and what can be prepared ahead of time); 3) where to keep the dish at school.

Cooperative Learning
Divide the class into groups of three. Tell students that, as owners of a Mexican restaurant, they are to design a menu. Each person in every group will be responsible for creating one of these categories: *carne, postres,* and *bebidas.* The menus should include food items, prices, name and location of the restaurant, etc. When completed, have the class pass around their menus to see which one represents the most popular restaurant.

Cultural Notes ☀

(p. 407, photo)
Although modern supermarkets are now common in Mexico's large cities, small neighborhood grocery stores such as this continue to attract customers. In these establishments most of the food products are stored behind a counter. Grocers weigh and price customers' purchases individually.

Apply

Process Reading
For a description of process reading, see p. 48.

Multicultural Perspectives
Mole, which is a thick sauce commonly served with poultry, was created by the Aztecs well before the arrival of the Spanish. *Mole* comes from the Nahuatl word *molli,* meaning "mixture." The Spanish then adapted the sauce with ingredients from Europe. In addition to various blends of herbs and spices, many *moles* include poultry broth, tomatoes or tomatillos, chiles, pumpkin seeds or sesame seeds, and ground tortillas. In some *moles,* chocolate is a key ingredient. Students familiar with other cultures can share information about other traditional dishes.

Answers
Antes de leer
Answers will vary, but students may say that the menu in a restaurant in Mexico might be more varied and feature more authentic food.

Mira la lectura
Veracruz, Jalisco, and Nuevo León / Most students would say yes, that American cooking also varies from one region to another.

Todo junto

¡Vamos a leer!

Antes de leer

STRATEGY ➤ Using prior knowledge

How familiar are you with Mexican food? Do you suppose the menu in a restaurant in Mexico might be different from one found in a Mexican restaurant in the United States? How do you think it might be different?

Mira la lectura

STRATEGY ➤ Scanning

This article compares Mexican food found in Mexico with that found in the United States. It also points out the variety of dishes in three different states in Mexico. What states do the menus come from? Does American cooking vary from one region to another?

EN LA VARIEDAD ESTÁ EL GUSTO

¿Con qué frecuencia comes en restaurantes mexicanos? ¿Te gustan los burritos o el chile con carne? ¿Crees que estas comidas son auténticas? La comida mexicana en los Estados Unidos es diferente a la que se come en México. Los inmigrantes y los mexico-americanos han creado un nuevo mundo de la cocina mexicana. Los burritos y el chile con carne son populares en las ciudades norteamericanas, pero en México son casi desconocidos.

La comida de México es más variada y sustancial. Tiene sus orígenes en las diferentes culturas precolombinas y en España. El chile, el maíz y el tomate son de origen americano, pero la pimienta, la cebolla y el trigo fueron traídos por los españoles. La comida mexicana de hoy usa todos estos ingredientes.

En cada región de México se pueden encontrar diferentes tipos de comidas o platillos. Imagina que haces un viaje por tres estados de México y que en cada estado comes algo distinto. Mira los menús a la derecha.

PLATILLOS DE VERACRUZ,
EN EL SURESTE DE MÉXICO

ensalada tropical
pescado a la veracruzana
arroz verde
dulce de guayaba
café

408   Capítulo 12

Options

Strategies for Reaching All Students

Students Needing Extra Help
Mira la lectura: Students may not be aware that there are states in Mexico. Show them a map that has all the states clearly labeled. *Infórmate:* In No. 1, tell students that certain beverages can also be food ingredients; as in this case, *leche.* In No. 3, have students list the similarities and differences.

Infórmate

STRATEGY> Using illustrations to guess the meaning of unknown words

1 Were you able to figure out some of the items in each menu by looking at the pictures? What drinks are offered with each meal?

2 Are there any ingredients you did not expect to find in a Mexican dish? What are they?

3 After reading these menus, explain how the food served in Mexico compares with that served in the United States.

Aplicación

A Mexican exchange student in your class wants to eat at a Mexican restaurant this weekend. What would you tell him about the Mexican food found in the United States? What do you think will surprise him the most?

PLATILLOS DE NUEVO LEÓN,
AL NORTE DE MÉXICO

guacamole con enchiladas
huevos con carne de res
dulce de leche
té helado

¿Te gustaría probar alguna de estas tres variedades de comida? ¿Cuál te parece más interesante? ¡Las tres son deliciosas!

PLATILLOS DE JALISCO,
EN EL CENTRO DEL PAÍS

ensalada de nopales
carne asada
arroz con leche
agua de horchata

¡Vamos a leer! 409

Infórmate

1 Answers will vary. / coffee (Veracruz), a type of rice drink (Jalisco), iced tea (Nuevo León)

2 Answers will vary, but students may say eggs with beef.

3 Answers will vary, but students may say that some foods, such as guacamole and enchiladas, are also served in the U.S.

Aplicación

Answers will vary, but students may say that the Mexican food found in the U.S. will probably be different from that found in Mexico. The exchange student would probably be surprised to find that *chile con carne* is not what the name implies, or that food he or she has never heard of is considered Mexican food in the U.S.

Apply

Process Writing
For information regarding developing a writing portfolio, see p. 50.

¡Vamos a escribir!

Everyone enjoys going out to eat, but it's not always easy to decide where to go. Write a review of a restaurant that you would recommend to your classmates.

1 Think about a restaurant you go to. It can be a fast-food restaurant, a coffee shop, or even the school cafeteria.

- ¿Cómo se llama el restaurante?
- ¿Dónde está?
- ¿A qué hora abre y a qué hora cierra?
- ¿Qué clase de comida sirve?
- ¿Cuáles son sus platos especiales?
- ¿Qué plato te gusta más? ¿Por qué?
- ¿Es caro o barato? ¿Aceptan tarjetas de crédito?
- ¿Es accesible para personas incapacitadas?

2 Use the answers to the questions to write a review of the restaurant. Show your review to a partner. Does he or she think you should change anything? Is there some other information your partner would suggest adding?

3 Rewrite your review, taking into consideration the changes suggested by your partner and any others you might like to make. Check for spelling, accents, verb forms, and adjective agreement. If necessary, write your review again.

4 Now your review is ready to be published. You can:

- submit it to the school paper or Spanish club
- include it in a pamphlet about local restaurants called *Buenos restaurantes*
- add it to your writing portfolio

Buenos Restaurantes

En la Fonda Refugio se cocina la mejor comida mexicana de la ciudad. Allí puede probar la especialidad de la casa: chiles con queso. Son sabrosos, nutritivos y no son muy picantes. Además, en la Fonda Refugio hay una variedad de enchiladas, tacos, quesadillas y burritos.

El restaurante está en la calle Independencia, 4. Abren de 8:00 de la mañana a 11:00 de la noche. ¡Debe visitarlo!

410   Capítulo 12

Options

Strategies for Reaching All Students

Students Needing Extra Help
Show the class a typical review from a newspaper or magazine.
Have students use their Organizers.

"Y para la merienda, ¿te gustaría pedir unos pasteles?"

Café al aire libre en la Ciudad de México

Cultural Notes ☼

(p. 411, photo)
This outdoor café is located in Coyoacán, a suburb of Mexico City, where some of the city's most beautiful colonial mansions are located. Many of them house art and antique dealers, galleries, and museums.

Assess & Summarize

Test Preparation

You may want to assign parts of this section as written homework or as an in-class writing activity prior to administering the *Examen de habilidades.*

Answers

Listening: *Después de comer un chile relleno y dos enchiladas con salsa picante, voy a pedir un flan. ¡Nunca lo he probado!* The speaker is planning to eat a main meal with dessert.

Culture: Answers will vary. Similarities may include conversation and live entertainment. Differences may include the length and time of the meal and the participation of the entire family.

Reading: This dish is prepared by grilling skirt steak over a charcoal grill. *Asar* means to grill. The dish is called *carne al carbón* because of the way it's cooked over coals.

Writing: Letters will vary.

Speaking: Dialogues will vary.

¿Lo sabes bien?

This section will help you organize your studying for the proficiency test, where you will be asked to do similar, though not identical, tasks. There will not be any models on the test.

Listening

Can you understand when someone talks about a meal? Listen as your teacher reads a sample similar to what you will hear on the test. Is the person planning to eat a snack, a main meal, or a dessert?

Culture

Can you name two similarities and two differences between dining out in Mexico and in the United States?

"El domingo voy al restaurante con mi familia."

Reading

Using the illustration on this recipe, can you figure out how to prepare this dish? What do you think *asar* means? Why is the dish called *carne al carbón?*

CARNE AL CARBÓN

Ingredientes:

carne de res
1 limón verde
sal y pimienta

Diez minutos antes de servirla, pon el jugo de limón verde, la sal y la pimienta sobre la carne. Debes asar la carne tres minutos por cada lado.

Writing

Can you write a letter to a friend describing a meal you ate recently? Here is a sample letter:

Querido Carlos,

Ayer fui a un restaurante que te gustaría mucho.
Pedí dos tazas de chocolate con churros. ¿Has probado los churros? Se hacen con harina, agua y azúcar. ¡Me encantan! ¡Te traigo churros para tu fiesta de cumpleaños el sábado!

Tu amigo,
Berto

Speaking

Can you and a partner play the roles of a waiter and a customer?

A — *Aquí le traigo el menú.*
B — *Gracias. ¿Cuál es el plato del día?*
A — *Enchiladas de pollo, pero no son muy picantes.*
B — *¡Genial! Pero, camarero, me faltan una servilleta y un tenedor.*
A — *¿De veras? ¡Los traigo en seguida!*

Options

Strategies for Reaching All Students

Students Needing Extra Help

Have students write out this section so they can check off what they have mastered. Reading: Remind students to use picture and word clues to help them read the recipe.

Resumen del capítulo 12

Use the vocabulary from this chapter to help you:
- ask politely to have something brought to you
- order a meal
- say what you ate or drank

to name and discuss foods

el aguacate
el azúcar
los burritos
la carne de res
el chile
el chile con carne
los chiles rellenos
el chocolate
los churros
las enchiladas
el flan
los frijoles refritos
el guacamole
el helado
la mantequilla
los pasteles
la pimienta
las quesadillas
la sal
las salsas
los tacos
la tortilla de harina / de maíz

to talk about food
a la carta
la especialidad
  de la casa
la merienda

de merienda
(no) picante
el plato del día
los platos principales
el postre
de postre
beber: (yo) bebí
          (tú) bebiste
comer: (yo) comí
          (tú) comiste
¿Con qué se hace(n) ___?
Se hace(n) con ___.
pedir (e → i)
probar (o → ue):
  (yo) he probado
  (tú) has probado
vender

to describe table settings
la cuchara
el cuchillo
el mantel
el platillo
el plato
la servilleta
la taza
el tazón
el tenedor
el vaso

to talk about eating out
el camarero, la camarera
la cuenta
el menú

to express needs
Me falta(n) ___.
¿Me pasas ___?
¿Me trae ___?
Le traigo ___.
traer: (yo) traigo
       (tú) traes

to indicate time or frequency
alguna vez
a menudo
en seguida
muchas veces
una vez

to indicate position
debajo de
delante de
encima de

other useful expressions
¿Algo más?
lo mismo

CAPÍTULO 13
THEME: THE ENVIRONMENT

SCOPE AND SEQUENCE   Pages 414–445

COMMUNICATION

Topics

Environmental conservation

Environmental dangers

Endangered species

Objectives

To discuss endangered species in the U.S. and the Spanish-speaking world

To talk about conservation

To name items that can be recycled

To talk about animals

To talk about nature and the environment

To describe environmental dangers

To talk about transportation

To talk about everyday activities

To give an opinion

CULTURE

Endangered species in the Spanish-speaking world

GRAMMAR

El verbo decir

El mandato afirmativo (tú)

El verbo saber

Ancillaries available for use with Chapter 13

Multisensory/Technology

 Overhead Transparencies, 66–70

 Audio Tapes and CDs

 Vocabulary Art Blackline Masters for Hands-On Learning, pp. 68–72

 Classroom Crossword

 Video

 CD-ROM

Print

 Practice Workbook, pp. 136–146

 Writing, Audio & Video Activities, pp. 77–82, 129–131, 176–177

 Communicative Activity Blackline Masters

  Pair and Small Group Activities, pp. 92–97

  Situation Cards, p. 98

 Un paso más: Actividades para ampliar tu español, pp. 74–79

Assessment

 Assessment Program

  Pruebas, pp. 191–200

  Examen de habilidades, pp. 201–204

 Test Generator

Video still from Chap. 13

Environmental Problems and Solutions

Population growth coupled with efficient transportation have contributed to an extraordinary migration in the latter half of the twentieth century. In Latin America, as in much of the world, urban locales have become the destination for millions of people. Mexico City's population grew from 2.9 million in 1950 to 20.5 million in 1990. Buenos Aires had a population of 5.1 million in 1950. Today, it is home to 11.6 million. In Peru, the Lima-Callao area has grown from 1 million in 1950 to 6.5 million in 1990.

Such rapid growth inevitably places a strain on the availability of resources and the quality of the environment. Mexico City, for example, lacks an adequate supply of drinking water. To fill its needs, the metropolis draws water from surrounding areas which, in turn experience water shortages. Many areas of Mexico City lack a developed infrastructure of services and utilities. The Netzahualcóyotl landfill, for example, presents a problem because it is growing too rapidly. Although entrepreneurs collect and sell recyclable items from the landfill, they cannot keep up with the steadily increasing volume of material.

The destruction of Latin America's rain forests has captured the attention of many people in the U.S. In Central American countries and in the Amazon Basin of South America, rain forests have been destroyed for grazing land, farms, and roads. They have also been cut for the tropical hardwoods that are sold at high prices in the world market. In addition, forested lands are sometimes destroyed as the by-product of other projects, such as hydroelectric dams, which can flood hundreds of thousands of forest acres. Often the trees are not cut before flooding, and as the vegetation decomposes in the water, it emits a toxic hydrogen sulfide gas.

Environmentalists are searching for solutions to these problems. Mexico City has devised a system of "non-driving" days *(días de "no circula")* for motorists. License plates are color-coded to indicate one day a week on which that car may not be driven within the city, and anyone who breaks the law is issued a stiff fine. This system has helped somewhat to reduce traffic congestion and air pollution.

Introduce

Re-entry of Concepts

The following list represents words, expressions, and grammar topics re-entered from Chap. 1 to Chap. 11:

Chapter 1
Activities

Chapter 3
Leisure-time activities

Chapter 4
Obligation

Chapter 5
Family members

Chapter 6
Demonstrative adjectives
Direct object promouns

Chapter 7
Vacation activities
Vacation destinations
Pensar + inf.

Chapter 8
Tener que + inf.
Household chores

Chapter 11
Comparatives

Planning

Cross-Curricular Connections

Math Connection *(pp. 430–431)*
Provide students with census data on the size of major cities in Latin America in 1950 and today. Have them compute the percentage of growth which has taken place in the intervening decades, and compare the rate of growth for these cities.

Science Connection *(pp. 434–435)*
Have pairs of students write and present a recycling plan, using commands, that the school can use on a class-by-class basis. Tell students to illustrate their ideas with drawings or pictures.

Communications Connection
(pp. 438–439)
Have pairs of students create and perform a public service ad in which they assume the roles of endangered plants or animals. They may enhance their presentations with posters or by wearing costumes. Some students might like to videotape their ad.

CAPÍTULO 13

Para proteger la Tierra

OBJECTIVES

At the end of this chapter, you will be able to:

- describe the natural environment
- list actions to protect the environment
- discuss environmental dangers
- name species in danger of extinction in the United States and the Spanish-speaking world and say what can be done to protect them

Las cataratas de Iguazú, Argentina

Spanish in Your Community
Help students contact local utilities or waste disposal companies to obtain energy conservation or recycling information in Spanish. Ask them to share the brochures and other information with the class.

(pp. 414–415, photo)
On the border of Argentina and Brazil, Iguazú Falls consist of about 275 waterfalls two miles wide that plunge over 200 feet. In the early 1900s the Argentine government made this area a national park in order to preserve the vegetation, wildlife, and scenic beauty. Examples of fauna here include the jaguar, puma, coati, ocelot, capybara, heron, toucan, and at least 500 species of butterflies.

Preview

Cultural Objective

- To discuss conservation efforts in Spanish-speaking countries and in the U.S.

 Para proteger la Tierra

Play

 **Video Activity A**

Using the Video

This chapter's video focuses on the environment. Host Karina Romera visits a recycling center to see how Guadalajarans are working to clean up the environment. She also visits the Guadalajara Zoo, where she learns about endangered species.

To prepare students for the video, first ask them to predict what this chapter's tape will be about. Then have students watch the segment several times. After the first viewing, have them brainstorm possible vocabulary words and phrases they will need to discuss environmental issues in Spanish. After subsequent viewings, ask students to identify: a) ways in which residents of Guadalajara help keep the environment clean and safe, and

¡Piénsalo bien!

Look at this photograph. What do you see that is similar to the environmental efforts in your community?

"Es importante reciclar para proteger la Tierra."

Jóvenes en un centro de reciclaje en Puerto Rico

What do you think the words *reciclar* and *proteger* mean?
What does *centro de reciclaje* mean?

416   Capítulo 13

Options

Strategies for Reaching All Students

Spanish-Speaking Students
Ask: *¿Por qué es importante reciclar? ¿Qué reciclan tú y tus amigos(as)? ¿Qué podemos hacer para proteger la Tierra? ¿Qué haces tú?*

 Un paso más Ex. 13-A

Students Needing Extra Help
(p. 417, photo) Check with the science department of your school for pictures and information about endangered species.

En América Central el jaguar está en peligro de extinción.

What other animals do you know of that are endangered?

b) ways in which they can work to protect the environment where they live.

Video segment 1: For more teaching suggestions, see the Video Teacher's Guide.

Multicultural Perspectives

The *quetzal,* the national bird of Guatemala, is an exotic animal in danger of extinction. The male has green feathers, a red breast, and white tail feathers as long as 60 centimeters (24 in.). Legend tells how the *quetzal* was the spiritual protector of the Maya. When Pedro de Alvarado, the Spanish *conquistador,* defeated Tecun Uman, the Mayan chief, the *quetzal* fell on the chest of Uman. The bird watched over the body, and when it flew away, its breast was covered with blood. This is why the *quetzal* has a blood-red breast. Ask students to share any animal legends or myths from other cultures that they might know.

Answers: ¡Piénsalo bien!

(p. 416, photo) Answers will vary, but students may mention recycling efforts. / *Reciclar:* to recycle; *proteger:* to protect; *centro de reciclaje:* recycling center

(p. 417) Answers will vary, but may include the California condor, American crocodile, red wolf, black-footed ferret, and panda.

417

Cultural Notes

(p. 416, photo)
The work of these teenagers at a recycling center in San Juan reflects an island-wide concern with environmental problems directly linked to Puerto Rico's growing population, estimated in 1991 at 3,551,000, and expected to reach 1,200 people per square mile in the near future.

(p. 417, top photo)
The jaguar, native to tropical forests in the Americas, is now one of many animals that have become endangered through hunting or destruction of their habitat. In Guatemala, destruction of the forests—the jaguar's home—has proceeded at a devastating rate: great areas of the country's original forest cover have been destroyed over the last three to four decades.

(p. 417, stamps)
Equatorial Guinea, a small country with provinces on the west coast of Africa and five offshore islands, was under Spanish rule from 1778 until 1968, when it declared its independence. It has a total land area approximately the size of the state of Maryland, most of which is covered by dense tropical rain forests.

417

Present

Chapter Theme
Environmental conservation

Communicative Objectives
- To talk about conservation
- To name items that can be recycled
- To talk about transportation
- To give an opinion
- To talk about everyday activities

 Transparencies 66–67

 Vocabulary Art BLMs

 Pronunciation Tape 13-1

 Vocabulario para conversar A

Play

Using the Video
Video segment 2: See the Video Teacher's Guide.

 Video Activity B

Grammar Preview
Saber is presented here lexically. The complete present-tense paradigm is on p. 436.

Vocabulario para conversar

¿Cómo podemos conservar energía?

Aquí tienes palabras y expresiones necesarias para discutir peligros del medio ambiente y para hablar sobre qué podemos hacer para protegerlo. Léelas varias veces y practícalas con un(a) compañero(a) en las páginas siguientes.

la luz, *pl.* las luces

la botella

la madera

el plástico

la piel

el cartón

la lata*

el aluminio

el vidrio

418   Capítulo 13

Options

Strategies for Reaching All Students

Spanish-Speaking Students

 Un paso más Exs. 13-B, 13-C, 13-D

Students Needing Extra Help
Remind students that they saw *de* + material (*de madera* and *de metal*) in Chap. 8. Likewise, they can also say *de aluminio, de plástico,* and *de vidrio* to describe something: *una lata de aluminio, un vaso de plástico, una botella de vidrio.*
También necesitas . . . : Give examples of *hay que* and *no hay que.* Explain *vale la pena* and *no vale la pena.*

Learning Spanish Through Action
STAGING VOCABULARY: *Pon*
MATERIALS: Vocabulary Art BLMs or magazine cutouts, index cards
DIRECTIONS: Mount photocopies of the following pictures on index cards: *hoja de papel (El primer paso), vaso* (Chap. 12), and recyclable items from this chapter. On sepa-

Teaching Suggestions
Preparing students to speak: Use one or two options from each of the categories of Comprehensible Input, Physical Response, or Limited Verbal Response. For a complete explanation of these categories and some sample activities, see the front section of this Teacher's Edition.

Class Starter Review
On the day following initial vocabulary presentation, you might begin the class by asking students to list four or five recyclable products.

montar en bicicleta

la bicicleta

la revista

el periódico

la guía telefónica

También necesitas . . .

apagar	*to turn off*	
proteger*	*to protect*	**¿Y qué quiere decir . . . ?**
la gente	*people*	conservar
saber: (yo) sé	*to know: I know*	la energía
(tú) sabes	* you know*	reciclar
(No) hay que ___ .	*It's (not) necessary to___.*	reducir†
(No) vale la pena.	*It's (not) worth it.*	separar
a la vez	*at the same time*	usar

* Note that to talk about a tin can, a glass bottle, a cardboard folder, a metal table, etc., we use noun + *de* + material.
  For example: *lata de aluminio, botella de vidrio.*
* *Proteger* is a regular *-er* verb with a spelling change in the *yo* form of the present tense: *protejo.*
† *Reducir* is a regular *-ir* verb in the present tense, except for the *yo* form: *reduzco.*

rate index cards, mount pictures of glass, paper, plastic, and aluminum, and post them in a row on the chalkboard. (Use real items, if possible.) Distribute the first set of index cards. Ask: *¿Quién tiene el vaso? Ponlo en la categoría correcta, por favor.* Continue in this manner until all items have been sorted under the proper category.

Practice & Apply

Re-enter / Recycle

Ex. 2: household chores from
Chap. 8
Ex. 3: direct object pronouns from
Chap. 6, *tener que* + inf. from
Chap. 8

Answers: Empecemos a conversar

1 ESTUDIANTE A
a. ¿Vale la pena reciclar el plástico?
b. ... el vidrio?
c. ... el cartón?
d. ... el periódico (el papel)?
e. ... la madera?
ESTUDIANTE B
a.–e. Answers will vary.

2 ESTUDIANTE A
a. ¿Cómo puedo reducir la basura?
b. ... conservar agua?
c. ... proteger el medio ambiente?
d. Questions will vary.
ESTUDIANTE B
a.–d. Answers will vary, but look for a logical response that follows this format: *Puedes* + inf. phrase.

3 ESTUDIANTE A
a. ¿Sabes si tenemos que reciclar las latas?
b. ... las guías telefónicas?
c. ... el periódico (el papel)?
d. ... las revistas?
e. ... las botellas?
f. Questions will vary.

Empecemos a conversar

Túrnate con un(a) compañero(a) para ser *Estudiante A* y *Estudiante B*. Reemplacen las palabras subrayadas con palabras representadas o escritas en los recuadros.
🔆 quiere decir que puedes escoger *(choose)* tu propia respuesta.

¡NO OLVIDES!

In *El primer paso* you learned *hoja de papel* for "a sheet of paper." *Papel* is the term for "paper" in general.

1 A — ¿Vale la pena reciclar <u>el aluminio</u>?
B — ¡Claro que sí (o: no)!
   Y ahora Uds.

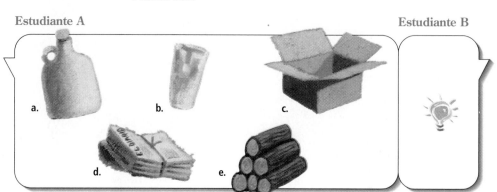

Estudiante A
a. b. c. d. e.

Estudiante B

2 conservar energía A — ¿Cómo puedo <u>conservar energía</u>?
B — Puedes <u>usar menos luz</u>.
   Y ahora Uds.

Estudiante A
a. reducir la basura
b. conservar agua
c. proteger el medio ambiente
d. 🔆

Estudiante B
reciclar latas y botellas
montar más en bicicleta
usar menos agua en el baño
lavar mucha ropa a la vez
lavar muchos platos a la vez
usar menos el coche
apagar las luces

420   Capítulo 13

Options

Strategies for Reaching All Students

Spanish-Speaking Students
Ex. 7: Add: *¿Cómo podemos tener la comida y los productos como el cuero que necesitamos y, a la vez, proteger a los animales de la Tierra?*

 Un paso más Exs. 13-E, 13-F, 13-G

Students Needing Extra Help
Ex. 2: Remind students of the spelling change from *luz* to *luces*.
Ex. 3: Point out how the object pronoun moves in *Estudiante B*'s answer. Refer to the grammar section in Chap. 12.
Remind students that the object pronoun may be *lo, la, los,* or *las*.
Ex. 6: Ask the same question with regard to your school.

Enrichment
As a homework assignment, have students make lists with the following headings: *Cosas que puedo apagar, Cosas que puedo conservar,* and *Cosas que puedo reciclar.*

3

A — ¿Sabes si tenemos que reciclar <u>las botellas de plástico</u>?

B — Sí, las tenemos que reciclar.
  o: No. No hay que reciclarlas.

  Y ahora Uds.

Estudiante A   Estudiante B

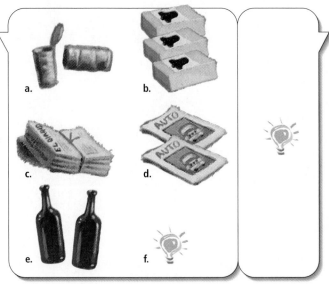

a.

b.

c.

d.

e.

f.

Empecemos a escribir

Escribe tus respuestas en español.

4 ¿Qué puedes hacer con libros que ya no usas? ¿Con ropa que ya no te queda bien?

5 ¿Cómo vas a la escuela? ¿En bicicleta? ¿En autobús? ¿A pie? ¿Por qué?

6 En tu comunidad, ¿qué pueden reciclar que no reciclan ahora?

7 ¿Piensas que la gente debe comprar abrigos u otra ropa de piel o no? ¿Por qué?

¡NO OLVIDES!

When we use direct object pronouns with infinitives, we can either attach them to the end of the infinitive or put them before the main verb. When we use *hay que* they must be attached to the infinitive.

También se dice

andar en bicicleta

el directorio
la guía de teléfonos
el listín

Vocabulario para conversar   421

ESTUDIANTE B

a. Sí, las tenemos que reciclar.
(No. no hay que reciclarlas.)
b. Sí, las . . . (. . . reciclarlas.)
c. Sí, lo . . . (. . . reciclarlo.)
d. Sí, las . . . (. . . reciclarlas.)
e. Sí, las . . . (. . . reciclarlas.)
f. Answers will vary.

Answers: Empecemos a escribir

4 Answers will vary, but will probably include the verb *reciclar*: *Puedo reciclarlos(la).*

5 Answers will vary, but should follow this pattern: *Voy a la escuela en* + mode of transportation, or *a pie.*

6 Answers will vary, but should follow this construction: *Podemos reciclar . . . porque . . . .*

7 Answers will vary. Help students with additional vocabulary as necessary.

Practice Wkbk. 13-1, 13-2

Audio Activity 13.1

Writing Activity 13-A

Pruebas 13-1, 13-2

Comm. Act. BLM 31-1

Present

Chapter Theme
The natural environment

Communicative Objectives
- To talk about animals
- To talk about nature and the environment
- To talk about transportation
- To describe environmental dangers
- To talk about everyday activities

 Transparencies 68–69

 Vocabulary Art BLMs

 Pronunciation Tape 13-2

 Vocabulario para conversar B

Play

Using the Video
Video segment 2: See the Video Teacher's Guide.

 Video Activity B

Grammar Preview
Decir is presented lexically. The complete present-tense paradigm is presented on p. 433.

Vocabulario para conversar

¿La Tierra forma parte del medio ambiente?

Aquí tienes el resto del vocabulario necesario para hablar sobre el medio ambiente y sus peligros.

Los animales

el jaguar

la vaca

el caballo

el lobo

el oso

el gorila

la ballena

el océano

el elefante

la serpiente

el tigre

Options

Strategies for Reaching All Students

Students Needing Extra Help
También necesitas . . . : Some students may need to see the complete paradigm of *decir.*

Learning Spanish Through Action
STAGING VOCABULARY: *Nombren, Señalen*
MATERIALS: transparency of the *Vocabulario para conversar*
DIRECTIONS: Project the transparency and direct students to point to animals as you describe them.

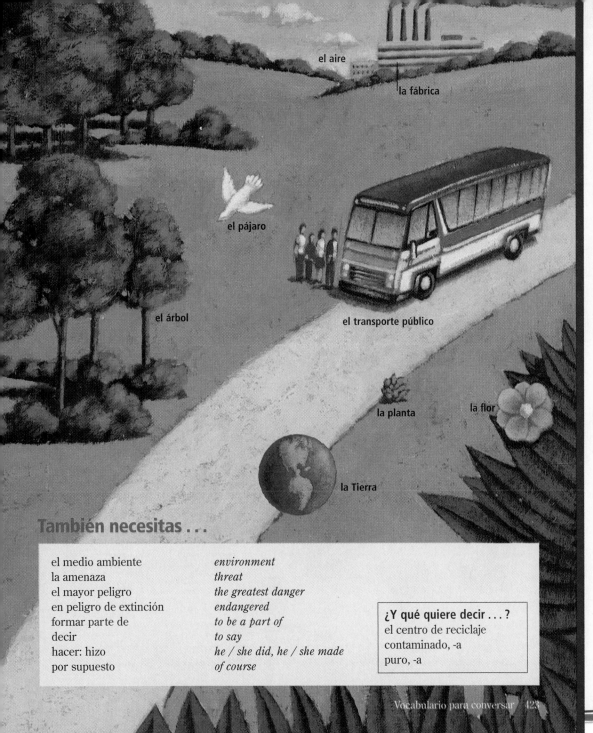

el aire

la fábrica

el pájaro

el árbol

el transporte público

la planta

la flor

la Tierra

También necesitas ...

el medio ambiente	*environment*
la amenaza	*threat*
el mayor peligro	*the greatest danger*
en peligro de extinción	*endangered*
formar parte de	*to be a part of*
decir	*to say*
hacer: hizo	*he / she did, he / she made*
por supuesto	*of course*

¿Y qué quiere decir ... ?
el centro de reciclaje
contaminado, -a
puro, -a

Vocabulario para conversar 423

Teaching Suggestions
Preparing students to speak: Use one or two options from each of the categories of Comprehensible Input, Physical Response, or Limited Verbal Response. For a complete explanation of these categories and some sample activities, see the front section of this Teacher's Edition.

Class Starter Review
On the day following initial vocabulary presentation, you might begin the class with this activity: Write two categories on the board: *En peligro de extinción* and *No en peligro de extinción.* Have pairs of students put the animals listed in the chapter vocabulary into the categories. Compile a class consensus.

Practice

Re-enter / Recycle

Ex. 8: direct object pronouns from Chap. 6

Answers: Empecemos a conversar

8 Point out the structure of the answer in the model: direct object pronoun *(Las)*, verb *(hizo)*, subject *(el hombre)*.

ESTUDIANTE A

a. ¿Los árboles forman parte del medio ambiente?

b. ¿El aire forma . . .

c. ¿Las flores forman . . .

d. ¿El océano forma . . .

e. ¿Los coches forman . . .

f. ¿La selva tropical forma . . .

ESTUDIANTE B

a.–d., f. Sí, por supuesto.

e. No. Los hizo el hombre.

9 ESTUDIANTE A

a. ¿Qué es una amenaza para los animales?

b. . . . para los árboles?

c. . . . para la Tierra?

d. . . . para la selva tropical?

e. . . . para las ruinas?

ESTUDIANTE B

a.–e. Answers will vary and may include more than one option.

Empecemos a conversar

8

A — *¿La Tierra forma parte del medio ambiente?*
B — *Sí, por supuesto.*
   o:
A — *¿Las fábricas forman parte del medio ambiente?*
B — *No. Las hizo el hombre.*
   Y ahora Uds.

Estudiante A   **Estudiante B**

9

A — *¿Qué es una amenaza para el aire puro?*
B — *Los coches.*
   Y ahora Uds.

Estudiante A   **Estudiante B**

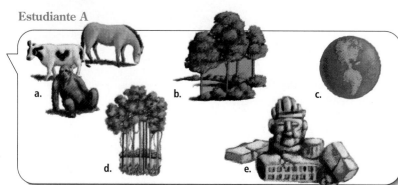

las fábricas
las ciudades
la gente
el aire
   contaminado
el agua
   contaminada

Options

Strategies for Reaching All Students

Students Needing Extra Help
Ex. 9: Students may need some background information regarding the effects of the environment on ruins and the rain forest.

10

A —¿*Están en peligro de extinción los jaguares?*
B —*Creo que sí.*
　　o: *No, creo que no.*
　　Y ahora Uds.

Estudiante A

Estudiante B

a.
b.
c.
d.
e.
f.
g.

El último retorno del salmón (1988), Alfredo Arreguín

Vocabulario para conversar　425

10 ESTUDIANTE A
a. ¿Están en peligro de extinción los lobos?
b. . . . los osos?
c. . . . los caballos?
d. . . . los gorilas?
e. . . . los perros?
f. . . . las vacas?
g. Questions will vary, but should follow the same format.
ESTUDIANTE B
a.–g.　Answers will vary.

Practice & Apply

Re-enter / Recycle
Ex. 11: comparatives from
Chap. 11

Answers: Empecemos a conversar

11 ESTUDIANTE A

a. ¿Qué es más importante para
la comunidad, el aire puro o las
fábricas?

b. ...los coches o el transporte
público?

c. ...las ciudades o la selva
tropical?

d. ...los parques o...?
(Questions will vary.)

ESTUDIANTE B

a.–d. Answers will vary, but look
for a logical choice. Encourage
class discussion.

11

A — *¿Qué es más importante para la comunidad, los árboles*
o los centros comerciales?

B — *Los árboles.*

o: *No sé. Las dos cosas son importantes.*

Y ahora Uds.

Estudiante A   Estudiante B

a.   b.

c.   d.

Ricky

Si mantienes presente estas tres palabras:

CORRESPONSABILIDAD, CODEPENDENCIA
Y COEVOLUCION

podrás conservar mejor nuestro medio ambiente
y nuestros recursos naturales. ¡Recuerda que tu
comportamiento es importante para que todos
vivan mejor!

RR

"UNETE A LA CAMPAÑA DE:
RICKY EL RECICLADOR

426   Capítulo 13

Options

Strategies for Reaching All Students

Spanish-Speaking Students
Ex. 12: Add: *¿Qué podemos hacer para*
mantenerlos limpios o limpiarlos?

Students Needing Extra Help
Exs. 14–15: Have students use their
Organizers from Chaps. 3 and 10 for
places, location words, and means of
transportation.
Ex. 15: Ask *¿te gustaría usar el transporte*
público? if there is no public transportation
in your area.

Empecemos a escribir y a leer

Escribe tus respuestas en español.

12 ¿El agua de tu comunidad está contaminada o es pura? ¿Y el aire?

13 ¿Trabaja alguien que conoces en un centro de reciclaje? ¿Quién? ¿Qué hace?

14 ¿Cuántos parques con muchos árboles y flores hay en tu comunidad? ¿Dónde están?

15 En tu opinión, ¿hay suficiente transporte público en tu comunidad? ¿De qué clase? ¿Usa la gente de tu comunidad el transporte público?

16 Lee este párrafo ¿En qué recipiente debemos poner las botellas? ¿Y los periódicos?

Debemos reciclar latas, botellas, plásticos, revistas, periódicos, cartón, vidrio. No olvide que debe poner las revistas, los periódicos y el cartón en el recipiente amarillo. El aluminio, el vidrio y el plástico deben ponerse en el rojo.

También se dice

la culebra
la víbora

YO PROTEJO EL MEDIO AMBIENTE

EN MI CASA USAMOS ENERGIA LIMPIA DE GASCO'

Practice

Re-enter / Recycle

Ex. 1: obligation from Chap. 4
Ex. 3: demonstrative adjectives
and direct object pronouns from
Chap. 6, *pensar* + inf. from
Chap. 7

Answers:
¡Comuniquemos!

1 *(Answers will vary.)* La señora debe apagar las luces y la calculadora. Debe reciclar las cosas en la basura.

2 Statements will vary. Animals pictured include: *el elefante, el oso, la serpiente, el jaguar.*

¡Comuniquemos!

Aquí tienes otra oportunidad para usar el vocabulario de este capítulo.

1 ¿Qué debe hacer la señora para proteger el medio ambiente? Observa bien este dibujo. Trabaja con un(a) compañero(a).

Debe reciclar las latas.

2 ¿Están estos animales en peligro de extinción? Si lo están, di por qué. Tu compañero(a) debe decir qué podemos hacer para protegerlos.

A —*Las ballenas están en peligro de extinción porque los océanos están contaminados.*
B —*Debemos mantener el agua de los océanos limpia.*

Estudiante A   Estudiante B

a.   b.   c.

d.   e.

428   Capítulo 13

Options

Strategies for Reaching All Students

Spanish-Speaking Students
Ex. 1: Have Spanish-speaking students write out this exercise.

Students Needing Extra Help
Ex. 3: Students may have difficulty deciding which verb to use in the response. Brainstorm with them.
Review *este / ese* from the Chap. 6 Organizer.
Remind students of the direct object pronouns *lo, la, los,* and *las.*
¿Qué sabes ahora?: Have students write out this section so they can check off what they have mastered.

Cooperative Learning
Divide the class into groups of four. Tell students that they are going to develop some new home products made out of recycled materials: paper, wood, glass, and aluminum. Assign the four materials to each group and ask students to brainstorm ideas

3 Dile (*tell*) a tu compañero(a) cómo piensas reciclar estas cosas viejas.

A —*¿Qué piensas hacer con ese vaso viejo?*
B —*Voy a usarlo para poner lápices.*

Estudiante A   **Estudiante B**

¿Qué sabes ahora?

Can you:

■ **describe the natural environment?**

— ___, ___ y ___ forman parte del medio ambiente.

■ **describe our responsibilities to the environment?**

—Hay que ___ el medio ambiente.

—Debemos ___ energía y ___ la basura.

■ **state ways to protect the environment?**

—Hay que apagar ___, ___ transporte público y ___ las latas y las botellas.

3 **ESTUDIANTE A**

¿Qué piensas hacer con ese papel viejo?

. . . con esa revista vieja?

. . . con esa camiseta vieja?

. . . con esa taza vieja?

. . . con esa botella vieja?

. . . con esa puerta vieja?

ESTUDIANTE B

(Answers will vary.)

Voy a usarlo para dibujar.

. . . usarla para hacer un cartel.

. . . usarla para sacudir los muebles.

. . . usarla para poner flores.

. . . usarla para (hacer) una lámpara.

. . . usarla para (hacer) un escritorio / una mesa.

Answers: ¿Qué sabes ahora?

• Answers will vary.
• proteger / conservar / separar (reducir)
• las luces / usar / reciclar

Audio Activity 13.3

Writing Activity 13-C

for the products. Set a time limit for the activity. After they have written down their ideas, you may want to have students create drawings of their products. Ask the groups to share their drawings and to explain them to the class. You may then wish to display the artwork on posterboard.

Present & Apply

Cultural Objective
• To discuss endangered species in Cuba and the U.S.

Multicultural Perspectives
Anthropologists, other scientists, and traditional healers are collaborating to collect and document species of plants from tropical rain forests throughout Latin America. Scientists are learning from traditional healers about the medicinal value of plants virtually unknown to the scientific community. Documenting this valuable knowledge is extremely important, especially in light of the fact that the rain forests are disappearing at an alarming rate. In Costa Rica alone, 1,500 species of orchids have been recorded. The possible existence of plants with curative properties is a major reason for the collaboration between scientists and traditional healers. Ask students to research information about plants from other areas of the world that are used for medicinal purposes.

Perspectiva cultural

Muchas especies de plantas y animales están en peligro de extinción. Otras ya han desaparecido.

Options

Strategies for Reaching All Students

Spanish-Speaking Students
Ask: *¿Por qué es importante proteger a estos animales? ¿Por qué crees que los científicos del mundo se interesan tanto en estos animales? ¿Qué animales quisieras tú proteger? ¿Por qué?*

 Un paso más Ex. 13-H

Students Needing Extra Help
Ex. 1: Make this an interdisciplinary unit with science. Invite your school's Life science teacher to speak to the class.
Ex. 2: Students should realize that there is no simple answer to this question. Discuss why solutions for one country might not necessarily work for another.

Enrichment
Have students research one of these environmental problems facing Latin America: 1) Pollution and other environmental problems caused by factories in Mexico. 2) The hunt for sea turtles and their eggs in the Gulf of Mexico and what's being done to curb it. 3) Pollution in Mexico City and how residents and the government are trying to deal with it.

Does anything seem unusual about the animals in these photographs? Explain. What clues do the captions give you about the part of the world they live in?

Can you imagine a three-foot-tall owl or a bird as small as a bee? The giant owl is long extinct, but the *zunzún*, the smallest bird in the world, still lives in Cuba, although it is endangered.

The *Greta cubana* is a very beautiful butterfly with transparent wings. Like the *zunzún*, it lives only in Cuba, and, like so many other species around the world, it is also endangered.

Another very unusual animal from Cuba is the *almiquí*. It has furry feet like a rabbit, the tail of a mouse, and a long snout like an opossum. It's an insect-eating animal about the size of a cat, and one of the few remaining native mammals of Cuba. Catching sight of an *almiquí* is really difficult, because there are so few of them left.

El zunzún, el pájaro más pequeño del mundo

Greta cubana

Why are these species disappearing? It's a long process that started with the first human settlements in Cuba about 7,000 years ago. In recent years, more species have become endangered because of population growth and the redevelopment of the tourist industry, which has again become an important aspect of the Cuban economy.

Learning about these species has been a group effort. A team of Cuban scientists from the Museo Nacional de Historia Natural and U.S. scientists from the American Museum of Natural History in New York, among others, have been researching Cuban animal and plant life. This project is an example of how people around the world are pooling their efforts to study ecology and preserve its biological wonders. The Cuban–U.S. scientific team is also a good example of cooperation between the people of Latin America and the people of the United States.

Este animal, de casi 3 pies de alto, está extinto desde hace más de 7.000 años.

La cultura desde tu perspectiva

1 What endangered species in the United States do you know about? How are the threats facing these animals similar to those facing endangered species in Cuba? How do the threats differ, if they do?

2 How might knowing each other's languages and cultures help experts in Latin America and the United States solve problems more effectively? What problems besides endangered species do you think could be solved by cooperation between the United States and Latin America?

Solenodon cubano

Perspectiva cultural 431

Cultural Notes

(pp. 430–431, photos)
Other endangered animals that are native to Cuba are two mammals: a member of the rodent family, the dwarf hutia *(hutía enana)* and the manatee, or sea cow *(manatí)*. The manatee was on the brink of extinction in the mid-1950s. Thanks to a very strict endangered species program, however, it was saved and is now thriving in marshes and on riverbanks.

Teaching Suggestions
Point out the form *pide* to students. Then ask them what they think happens with a command form of a stem-changing verb. Tell them to notice Luis's last statement. Ask them how they have used *sé* before and what its meaning in Luis's statement might be.

Answers
Answers will vary, but students may mention rules or regulations regarding use of the park.

A Answers will vary.

B *Dice* means "he / she says." The *ellos / ellas* form of *decir* is *dicen*. The *nosotros* form is *decimos*.

C These verb forms resemble the *Ud. / él / ella* form in the present tense. *Pon* differs from the others because it is not like the *Ud. / él / ella* form of *poner*.

Gramática en contexto

You might see a poster like this at the entrance to a national park. What information would you expect to find there?

A Did the poster contain the type of information you expected?

B You have seen the word *dice* many times in this book. What does it mean? The infinitive is *decir*. Like *pedir* and *servir*, *decir* has an e → i stem change. What would be the *ellos / ellas* form of *decir*? And the *nosotros* form?

C In the poster you can see the following commands: *protege, usa, pide, apaga, lleva, pon*. Do these verb forms look more like present or preterite-tense forms? How does *pon* differ from the others?

432   Capítulo 13

Options

Strategies for Reaching All Students

Students Needing Extra Help
A–C: Elicit from students that this kind of poster often has commands for readers to follow. Give an example.
Have students start to fill in the grammar portion of their Organizers.
El verbo decir: Emphasize that the *yo* form is spelled with a *g: digo*.
Ex. 1: Point out that some responses are specific; others are general and could be said by any of the people.

432

El verbo *decir*

The verb *decir* means "to say" or "to tell." Here are all its present-tense forms:

(yo)	**digo**	(nosotros) (nosotras)	**decimos**
(tú)	**dices**	(vosotros) (vosotras)	**decís**
Ud. (él) (ella)	**dice**	Uds. (ellos) (ellas)	**dicen**

• Notice the *e* of the stem changes to *i* in all forms except *nosotros* and *vosotros*.

1 ¿De quién son las opiniones de la lista de la derecha? Túrnate con un(a) compañero(a) para decirlo.

La gente dice que las fábricas no son buenas para el medio ambiente.

a. Los padres
b. Mis amigos(as)
c. Los profesores
d. Nosotros, los estudiantes
e. La gente
f. Muchas personas
g. Nadie
h. Yo

Es importante conservar energía.
Debemos estudiar siempre.
Hay que conservar agua contaminada.
La tarea es una amenaza para la salud.
Las fábricas no son buenas para el medio ambiente.
Vale la pena proteger los árboles.
No hay que estudiar nunca.
El aire contaminado es el mayor peligro de las ciudades.

¡NO OLVIDES!

Remember that we must use *que* after *decir: Dice que . . ., dicen que . . . .*

Teaching Suggestions
Ex. 1: Point out that *gente* and *nadie* use the singular verb form.

Answers
1 Statement endings will vary.
a. Los padres dicen que . . .
b. Mis amigos(as) dicen que . . .
c. Los profesores dicen que . . .
d. Nosotros, los estudiantes, decimos que . . .
e. La gente dice que . . .
f. Muchas personas dicen que . . .
g. Nadie dice que . . .
h. Yo digo que . . .

 Practice Wkbk. 13-5, 13-6

 Writing Activity 13-D

 Prueba 13-5

Gramática en contexto   433

Present & Practice

Re-enter / Recycle
Ex. 3: household chores from Chap. 8

Class Starter Review
On the day following the presentation of commands, you might begin the class with this activity: In pairs, have students list three commands aimed at helping the environment, their community, school, etc.

Answers
2 Statements will vary, as more than one logical choice exists.
a. Pues, bebe jugo de naranja.
b. ...descansa.
c. ...compra unas pastillas.
d. ...llama a la clínica.
e. ...haz ejercicio.

3 Clara, arregla tu cuarto.
Estela, limpia el baño.
Paco, lava los platos.
Beto, pasa la aspiradora.
Beatriz, saca la basura.
Queta, pon la mesa.
Marta, sacude los muebles.
Ramón, haz tu cama.

El mandato afirmativo *(tú)*

When you tell someone to do something, you are giving an affirmative command. Here are some affirmative commands you might give to a person you address as *tú*.

> Pablo, **apaga** las luces por favor.
> Linda, **recoge** la basura.
> Cristóbal, **sirve** la cena ahora.

- Notice that command forms are usually the same forms that we use for *él / ella / Ud.* in the present tense.

- Certain verbs, like *poner, hacer,* and *decir,* have irregular command forms.

> Isabel, **pon** los libros en la mesa.
> Miguel, **haz** tu cama.
> Elena, **di** lo que piensas.

- Object pronouns are attached to the end of affirmative commands. When a pronoun is attached to a command that has two or more syllables, an accent mark is added to the stressed vowel.

> —¿Qué debo hacer con las botellas y latas?
> —**Sepáralas**, por favor.

2 Tus amigos tienen un problema y te piden un consejo *(advice)*. Contéstales usando el mandato del verbo de la lista.

A — *Tengo mucho sueño.*
B — *Pues, duerme un poco.*

a. Tengo catarro.
b. Me lastimé la pierna ayer.
c. Me duele mucho la garganta.
d. Tengo gripe y quiero ver al médico.
e. Quiero ser mejor deportista.

Llamar a la clínica
Comprar unas pastillas
Descansar
Hacer ejercicio
Beber jugo de naranja

Options

Strategies for Reaching All Students

Students Needing Extra Help
El mandato afirmativo (tú): Emphasize the irregular forms and have students develop commands using them.
Give more examples of attaching the object pronoun to the command.
Write examples of another *-ar* verb and two for *-er* and *-ir* verbs.

3 Túrnate con un(a) compañero(a) para decirles a estas personas lo que (what) deben hacer en la casa.

Daniel, corta el césped.

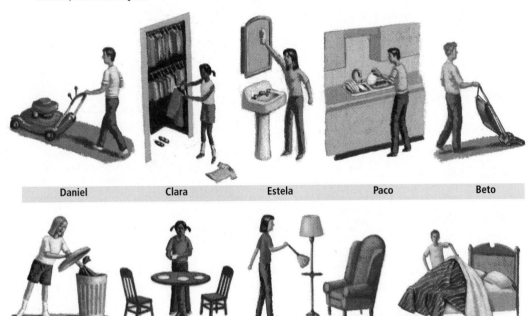

| Daniel | Clara | Estela | Paco | Beto |

| Beatriz | Queta | Marta | Ramón |

4 Túrnate con un(a) compañero(a) para leer estas ideas sobre el medio ambiente. Uno(a) de Uds. lee, agregando *(adding) Dicen que . . ..* El (la) otro(a) responde usando el mandato.

Debemos sacar   **A** — *Dicen que debemos sacar la basura.*
la basura   **B** — *Pues, sácala.*

a. Hay que apagar las luces.
b. Debemos conservar energía.
c. Vale la pena proteger el medio ambiente.
d. Tenemos que usar el transporte público.
e. Necesitamos conservar agua.
f. Hay que separar la basura.

Cultural Notes ☼

(p. 434, photo)
El último retorno del salmón (The Last Salmon Run), a 1988 painting by Alfredo Arreguín. A Mexican American artist, sculptor, and educator, Arreguín is known for his realistic depictions of nature. Besides having his works displayed at many U.S. galleries, he has also designed greeting cards for UNICEF.

Present & Practice

Re-enter / Recycle
Ex. 7: activities from Chap. 1, leisure-time activities from Chap. 3, family members from Chap. 5, vacation activities from Chap. 7

Class Starter Review
On the day following the presentation of *saber*, you might begin the class with this activity:
Ask students what they know how to do: *Mónica, ¿sabes cocinar? Enrique y Lucía, ¿saben esquiar?*

Answers
5 Answers will vary, but look for correct command forms.

 Practice Wkbk. 13-7, 13-8

 Writing Activities 13-E, 13-F

 Prueba 13-6

 Comm. Act. BLM 13-2

6 Questions will vary. Remind students that they still need to use *cómo* in the questions, since the infinitive doesn't immediately follow the *saber* form.

---

5 Pregúntale a tu compañero(a) qué puedes hacer tú para proteger el medio ambiente. Él(ella) deberá decirte tres cosas que puedes hacer.

A —*¿Qué debo hacer para proteger el medio ambiente?*
B —*Primero, recicla las botellas y las latas.*
Segundo, conserva agua.
Tercero, apaga las luces si no las necesitas.

El verbo *saber*

We use the verb *saber* ("to know") to talk about knowing facts or information. Here are all of its present-tense forms.

(yo)	sé	(nosotros) (nosotras)	sabemos
(tú)	sabes	(vosotros) (vosotras)	sabéis
Ud. (él) (ella)	sabe	Uds. (ellos) (ellas)	saben

- *Saber* follows the pattern of regular *-er* verbs except for the *yo* form: *sé.*

- When saber is immediately followed by the infinitive, it means "to know how to."
  Mis amigos **saben esquiar** muy bien.

6 Pregúntale a un(a) compañero(a) si sabe cómo podemos proteger la Tierra. Pregunta y contesta con elementos de las tres columnas.

A —*¿Sabes cómo podemos reciclar las latas y las botellas?*
B —*Sí, lo sé. Debemos llevarlas a un centro de reciclaje.*

a. reciclar	el aire contaminado	apagar las luces cuando no las usamos
b. conservar	los jaguares	reciclar revistas y periódicos
c. proteger	las latas y las botellas	usar menos papel
d. reducir	la basura	montar en bicicleta o usar transporte
	energía	público
	los árboles de la selva	llevar(las) a un centro de reciclaje

436   Capítulo 13

Options

Strategies for Reaching All Students

Students Needing Extra Help
Ex. 5: Have the whole class brainstorm possibilities, using their Organizers. Then divide the class into groups, assigning two or three verbs to each group.
El verbo saber: Emphasize *sé.* Some students will want to use *sabo.*
Have students develop examples of *saber* + inf. Emphasize that there isn't a direct translation for the "how."

¡No olvides!: Have students develop sentences using *que.* Tell them that the two verbs must be separated.
Ex. 6: Match the three columns before conjugating the verbs and making other necessary changes.
Model at least one more example.
Point out that *Sí, lo sé* means "I know (it)" and does not refer to cans and bottles.
Remind students that the purpose of the exercise is to practice using *saber.*
Do a model using *proteger.*

Ex. 7: Unlike other activities, students will need to draw upon their own experiences for answers. Have them make up an answer if necessary.
Elicit a *nosotros* answer by asking a student directly if he or she and a friend know how to do something.
Ahora lo sabes: Have students write out this section so they can check off what they have mastered.

7 Pregúntale a tu compañero(a) si él(ella), su familia o sus amigos saben hacer estas cosas.

A — ¿Sabes esquiar?
B — Sí, sé esquiar bien. Mi amigo Miguel también sabe.
   o: No, yo no sé esquiar, pero mis hermanas sí saben.

a.   b.   c.   d.

e.   f.   g.

Ahora lo sabes

Can you:

■ report what people say or tell?

—Ellos ___ que debemos separar el vidrio y el aluminio.
¿Qué ___ tú?

■ Tell a friend, a family member, or a child what to do?

—¿Debo apagar la luz?

—Sí. No la necesitas ahora. _____

■ say what people know?

—Mis padres ___ que es importante reciclar.

Apply

Using the Video
Video segment 3: See the Video Teacher's Guide

Video Activity C

Answers: Actividades
1 Answers will vary, but look for the correct forms of *saber, decir,* and commands.

Para decir más

Aquí tienes vocabulario adicional que te puede ayudar para hacer las actividades de esta sección.

ensuciar
to dirty

purificar
to purify

mantener
to keep, to maintain

lograr
to achieve

la capa de ozono
ozone layer

la mejor manera
the best way

las sustancias químicas
chemicals

talar
to fell, to cut down

la electricidad
electricity

dañar
to harm

438   Capítulo 13

Actividades

Esta sección te ofrece la oportunidad de aumentar tus conocimientos de español al integrar lo que aprendiste en este capítulo con lo que aprendiste en capítulos anteriores.

1 En un grupo pequeño, haz un anuncio de radio o de televisión sobre el transporte público de tu comunidad. Estas ideas te pueden ayudar:

> La gente que sabe usa el metro.
> Dicen los pasajeros: ¡El metro es muy rápido!
> ¡Qué cómodo es!
> Úsalo todos los días.
> Es la mejor manera de ir a trabajar y a la escuela.

Presenta tu anuncio al resto de la clase.

Una estación del metro en Buenos Aires

Options

Strategies for Reaching All Students

Students Needing Extra Help
Ex. 1: If there is no city-run public transportation in your town, use a taxi or walking as your means of transportation.
Use Organizers from earlier chapters.
Because *metro* has already been done, do the other three modes of transportation (taxi, bus, walking) as a class activity. Show students that the greatest number of changes will be for walking.

Ex. 2: Have travel brochures on hand. Use Organizers from earlier chapters.
Ex. 3: Model an example and use Organizers from earlier chapters to brainstorm commands with the whole class; for example, *cocinar: cocina esta noche.* Then have students give possible excuses. Finally, assign three students per group to put the exercise together.

Cooperative Learning
Divide the class into groups of three or four. Help students develop a list of situations where one might encounter written rules and another list where one might encounter unwritten rules; for example, in school or at home. Instruct groups to select a topic from among those discussed and develop eight to ten laws, or affirmative commands, for that topic. Groups should read their commands to another group. Afterward, they could make a poster of their commands.

2 Prepara un cartel turístico con fotografías o dibujos de un lugar que te gustaría visitar. Usa el mandato para decirle al turista lo que debe hacer. Puedes incluir esta información:

- qué lugar visitar y cuándo
- cómo llegar
- qué hacer en ese lugar
- qué comprar
- de qué sacar fotos
- qué llevar

Prepara una presentación oral sobre tu cartel para la clase.

3 En grupos pequeños, escriban cada verbo de la lista en un pedazo *(piece)* de papel. Luego debes escoger un pedazo de papel y dar un mandato a otra persona del grupo. Esa persona debe dar una excusa y no hacer lo que dices. Cada uno debe dar tres mandatos y tres excusas.

—Come una ensalada de frutas.
—Pero no tengo ni uvas
  ni manzanas.

—Limpia el baño.
—Pero no está sucio.

"Mirar los pájaros es un buen pasatiempo."

ayudar	decir	hacer	practicar
beber	depositar	lavar	probar (o → ue)
buscar	dormir (o → ue)	leer	sacar
cerrar (e → ie)	empezar (e → ie)	limpiar	sacudir
cocinar	enviar	llegar	servir (e → i)
comer	escuchar	llevar	terminar
comprar	estudiar	pedir (e → i)	traer
cortar	hablar	poner	ver

2–3 Answers will vary, but look for correct command forms.

Critical Thinking: Synthesizing
Refer students back to the poster on p. 432. Using the commands *protege, usa, pide, apaga, lleva,* and *pon,* have small groups write slogans that would be appropriate for each of the following people: babysitter, school bus driver, police officer, firefighter. Collect the slogans and read the best ones to the class.

 Writing Activity 13-H

 Comm. Act. BLMs 13-4, 13-5

Cultural Notes

(p. 438, photo)
The subway system in Buenos Aires has long offered an efficient alternative to commuting along the city's traffic-congested boulevards. It was built by the French in 1913 and is the oldest mass transit system in South America. It consists of five lines identified by the letters A–E. Street entrances to the stations are marked *subte* (for *subterráneo)* and show the letter of the line.

Apply

Process Reading
For a description of process reading, see p. 48.

Teaching Suggestions
Encourage students to use the reading strategies they have practiced in previous lessons—especially prediction and context clues—to get the meaning of this reading selection. Tell them to rely, too, on their prior knowledge of the subject and on what they have learned in this chapter.

Answers
Antes de leer
Answers will vary.

Mira la lectura
The title of the article is *Cuide el mundo desde casa.* The girl in the picture is prepared to clean up the environment beginning at home. The purpose of the introductory statement is to let the reader know what the article is about.

¡Vamos a leer!

Antes de leer

STRATEGY ➤ Using prior knowledge

How can you help protect the environment? Make a list of five things you can do.

Muchacha recogiendo basura en Honduras

Mira la lectura

Look over the reading to get an idea about how it is organized. What is the title? What does the picture tell you? What is the purpose of the introductory statement?

Cuide el mundo desde casa

¡Ud. puede hacer mucho para proteger el mundo!

Unidos podemos mantener el mundo más limpio y mejor. Cada uno de nosotros debe hacer algo diariamente para protegerlo. Con la ayuda de todos, ensuciando menos el planeta y ayudando a purificar el medio ambiente, lograremos crear verdaderamente un mundo mejor para nosotros y para nuestra familia. ¡No olvide que su participación es muy importante!

¿Qué puede hacer desde su propia casa?

- Ahorre energía. No use innecesariamente electricidad ni gasolina.
- No desperdicie agua.
- Compre alimentos o productos envasados en materiales reciclables.
- No use atomizadores, o cualquier otro producto que pueda dañar la capa de ozono.

- Consuma productos naturales que no contengan demasiadas sustancias químicas alterantes.
- Revise la salida de gas de su vehículo periódicamente.
- Conserve limpios los lugares públicos y privados: calles, parques, plazas, playas, etc.
- No tale árboles innecesariamente.
- Infórmese sobre campañas ecológicas en su comunidad.
- Lea artículos o vea programas de televisión sobre el medio ambiente.

Como ve, hay muchas cosas que puede hacer para ayudar y cuidar el mundo en que vivimos. No se desanime si otras personas no contribuyen. ¡Contribuya Ud. con su ejemplo!

440   Capítulo 13

Options

Strategies for Reaching All Students

Students Needing Extra Help
Antes de leer: This may be a challenging reading. Have students first read silently, then read aloud while students follow along.
Mira la lectura: If students are having difficulty with the last question, ask them: "What information do you get from the introductory statement?"
Infórmate: Caution students that they are not looking for cognates, but rather for families of related words.

Infórmate

STRATEGY ➤ Recognizing word families

Word families are groups of related words that are used in different ways as nouns, verbs, adjectives, and so on. Often if you know one word in a family you can figure out the meaning of others. Here are some examples from the article:

el día   diariamente

la verdad   verdaderamente

la ayuda   ayudar   ayudando

"Todos debemos ayudar a reciclar."

1 Now read the article carefully. Were any of the suggestions the same as those on your list? Check off on your list the ones they did mention.

2 Find three or four words whose meaning you can figure out because you know the word family they belong to. For example: *sucio / ensuciando*.

3 Divide the suggestions into two groups: those that you do or could easily do and those that don't apply to you.

Una niña reciclando latas en Buenos Aires, Argentina

Aplicación

Make new words out of the following by adding the ending *–mente*. Then use one of the words in a sentence about how you protect the environment. For example: *Reciclo cartón regularmente.*

frecuente
general
rara
regular

¡Vamos a leer!   441

Apply

Process Writing

For information regarding developing a writing portfolio, see p. 50.

Teaching Suggestions

Point out to students that they can also write free-form or concrete poetry: poetry in the form of the person, animal, or object being described.

¡Vamos a escribir!

How can we express our concern about the environment? One way is through our writing. Write a poem, on your own or in groups, about an animal or a place that you think needs to be protected. Remember, a poem does not need to rhyme. You can follow a pattern of a diamond poem. For example:

```
           Ballena
      grande      buena
  bucea      nada      juega
      triste      gris
           ballena
```

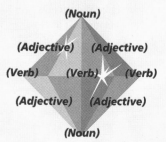

```
              (Noun)
     (Adjective)     (Adjective)
  (Verb)     (Verb)     (Verb)
     (Adjective)     (Adjective)
              (Noun)
```

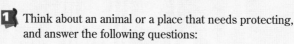

Una ballena gris frente a Baja California, México

1 Think about an animal or a place that needs protecting, and answer the following questions:

- ¿Cómo te sientes cuando piensas en ese animal o ese lugar?
- ¿Qué vocabulario puedes usar en una descripción del animal o del lugar?
- ¿Por qué debemos cuidarlo?
- ¿Cómo podemos protegerlo?

2 Use your answers to the questions to write your poem. Organize your ideas in the way you think will be most powerful and effective.

442   Capítulo 13

Options

Strategies for Reaching All Students

Students Needing Extra Help

Step 1: Students may be more successful with something more concrete than free verse. Give them a line or two of some poems in English with which they are familiar. Then they can finish them. You might consult with your colleagues in the English department for selections that could be easily translated and / or adapted.

Post pictures of endangered species or natural settings to inspire students.

Step 3: Poetry can be very personal, and students may prefer to work alone. On the other hand, students who are apprehensive about taking ownership of a creative work may be more comfortable working in a group.

Step 4: Have students use their Organizers.

3 Show your poem to a partner. Does your partner understand how you feel about the animal or place? Does he or she think you should change, reorganize, or correct anything? Rewrite your poem.

4 Check for accuracy in spelling and the use of accent marks. Did you use the correct forms of the adjectives and verbs? Did you try to use a varied vocabulary? If necessary, rewrite your poem. You may want to add an illustration to make it more eye-catching.

5 Share your poem by:
- submitting it to the school literary magazine or newspaper
- including it in a collection of class poems called *Vamos a proteger nuestra Tierra*
- posting it on a bulletin board in the school library during Earth Day celebration
- adding it to your writing portfolio

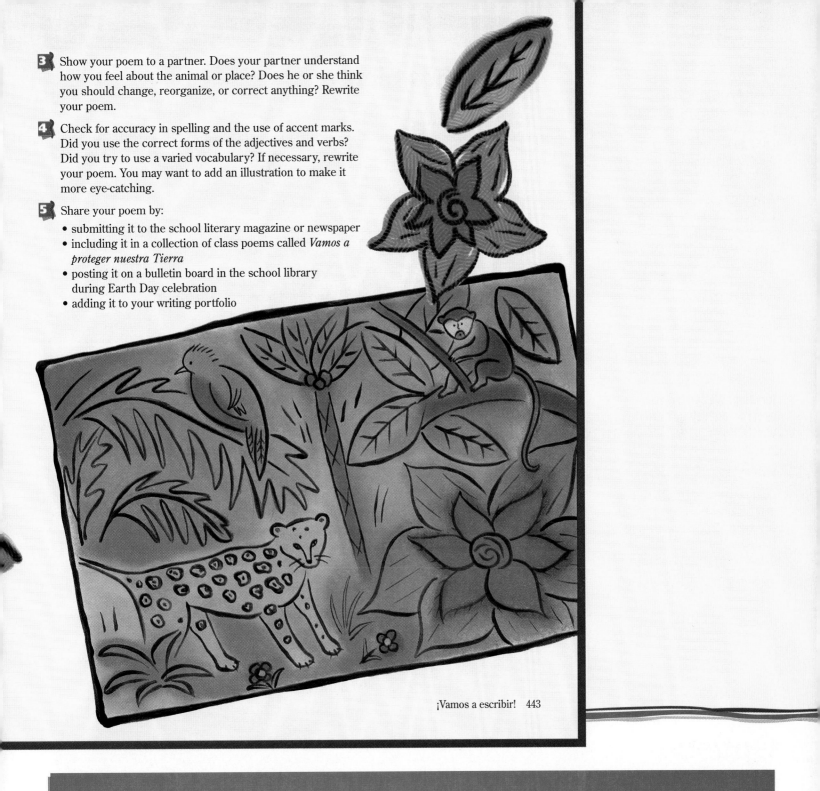

¡Vamos a escribir! 443

Assess & Summarize

Test Preparation

You may want to assign parts of this section as written homework or as an in-class writing activity prior to administering the *Examen de habilidades*.

Answers

Listening: *El medio ambiente está en peligro. Para ayudar a resolver este problema, debemos usar menos papel, conservar agua y reciclar. También vale la pena apagar las luces que no necesitamos.* The environment is in danger. Some suggestions for saving it are to use less paper, conserve water, recycle, and turn off lights when not in use.

Reading: We can have a better world by not cutting down trees unnecessarily, by not littering the streets, and by recycling.

Writing: Letters will vary.

Culture: Answers will vary, but may include: Population growth and industrial development have contributed to the disappearance of some species of animals.

Speaking: Dialogues will vary.

¿Lo sabes bien?

This section will help you organize your studying for the proficiency test, where you will be asked to do similar, though not identical, tasks. There will not be any models on the test.

Listening

Can you understand when someone talks about the environment? Listen as your teacher reads a sample similar to what you will hear on the test. According to the person making the statement, what is the problem and what are some suggestions for solving it?

Reading

Can you understand an environmental ad by using word families to guess the meaning of the words you might not know? According to this ad, how can we have a better world?

> No tale árboles innecesariamente. No tire papeles en las calles. Recicle. Ayudándonos y trabajando juntos lograremos un mundo mejor.

Writing

Can you write a letter to a friend in which you describe a place you visited while on vacation and what the people there do to protect the environment? Here is a sample letter:

> Querida Luisa,
>
> ¡Qué puro está el aire aquí! La gente de esta ciudad sabe que tiene que trabajar mucho para proteger el medio ambiente. Muchas personas montan en bicicleta o usan el transporte público. Por toda la ciudad hay carteles que dicen: Separa la basura, las revistas, las botellas y las latas. La ciudad tiene un parque grande donde hay flores y animales en peligro de extinción.
>
> Tu amiga,
> Rebeca

Culture

Can you name two reasons for the gradual disappearence of some species of animals living in the Caribbean region and compare this with other parts of the planet?

Estas ranitas doradas de Costa Rica están casi extintas.

Speaking

Can you and a partner play the roles of a park ranger and a camper in a national park? Here is a sample dialogue:

A —*¿Qué puedo hacer para proteger el medio ambiente del parque?*

B —*Separa la basura para poder reciclarla después y conserva el agua. También puedes proteger las flores y las plantas del parque.*

A —*¿Y si monto en bicicleta . . . ?*

B —*¡Claro que sí! Necesitamos aire puro. No queremos contaminarlo con los coches.*

444 Capítulo 13

Options

Strategies for Reaching All Students

Students Needing Extra Help

Have students write out this section so they can check off what they have mastered.

Resumen del capítulo 13

Use the vocabulary from this chapter to help you:
- describe the natural environment
- list actions to protect the environment
- discuss environmental dangers

to talk about conservation
el centro de reciclaje
la luz, *pl.* las luces
apagar
conservar
proteger
reciclar
reducir
separar
usar

to name items that can be recycled
el aluminio
la botella
el cartón
la energía
la guía telefónica
la lata
la madera
el periódico
el plástico
la revista
el vidrio

to talk about animals
los animales, *sing.* el animal
la ballena
el caballo
el elefante
el gorila

el jaguar
el lobo
el oso
el pájaro
la serpiente
el tigre
la vaca
la piel

to talk about nature and the environment
el aire
el árbol
la flor
el medio ambiente
el océano
la planta
la Tierra

to describe environmental dangers
la amenaza
contaminado, -a
la fábrica
el mayor peligro
en peligro de extinción
puro, -a

to talk about transportation
la bicicleta: montar en bicicleta
el transporte público

to talk about everyday activities
decir
hacer: (Ud., él, ella) hizo
saber: (yo) sé
         (tú) sabes

to give an opinion
(No) hay que ___.
(No) vale la pena ___.

other useful terms and expressions
a la vez
formar parte de
la gente
por supuesto

Cultural Notes

(p. 444, photo)
Endangered golden toads in Costa Rica. Although Costa Rica is a relatively small country in area, it is home to an abundance of flora and fauna. Aware of its rich natural life, the government has placed nearly one third of its land under protection, giving the country 34 national parks, wildlife refuges, and reserves.

CAPÍTULO 14

THEME: PARTIES AND CELEBRATIONS

SCOPE AND SEQUENCE Pages 446–475

COMMUNICATION

Topics

Parties

Gift-giving

Introductions

Objectives

To discuss teenage parties in Spanish-speaking countries

To talk about parties

To introduce people

To talk about what to wear to a party

To talk about gift-giving

CULTURE

Teenage parties / celebrations

Los quince años

GRAMMAR

Construcciones negativas

El presente progresivo

El verbo dar

Ancillaries available for use with Chapter 14

Multisensory/Technology

 Overhead Transparencies, 71–75

 Audio Tapes and CDs

 Vocabulary Art Blackline Masters for Hands-On Learning, pp. 73–77

 Classroom Crossword

 Video

 CD-ROM

Print

 Practice Workbook, pp. 147–156

 Writing, Audio & Video Activities, pp. 83–88, 132–134, 178–179

 Communicative Activity Blackline Masters

Pair and Small Group Activities, pp. 99–104

Situation Cards, p. 105

 Un paso más: Actividades para ampliar tu español, pp. 80–85

Assessment

 Assessment Program

Pruebas, pp. 205–214

Examen de habilidades, pp. 215–218

 Test Generator

Video still from Chap. 14

Fiestas

Celebrations and parties all over the world often include festive decorations. In Mexico, party decorations are usually made by hand. They may consist of long strips of crepe paper folded over each other at right angles and stretched open, or elaborate papier-mâché flowers that are shaped around a wire core.

Piñatas are common at young people's parties. Although *piñatas* are available in stores and markets throughout Mexico and the U.S., they are often constructed by hand of cardboard, papier-mâché, and layers of colored paper. Traditionally, the *piñata* is filled with candy and suspended by a rope. Blindfolded contestants take turns trying to break the *piñata* with a stick to gain access to the contents.

Many celebrations in northern Mexican and Mexican American homes include *mariachis.* These bands usually include eight or nine members who wear outfits derived from the traditional attire of Mexican cowboys, or *charros.* The hat is a large, embroidered *sombrero* made of velvet. The entire *traje de charro* is very expensive.

Mariachis usually consist of two trumpets, four violins, a small guitar called the *vihuela,* and a standard-sized guitar. The *guitarrón,* a large guitar with its back shaped like a bow, provides the bass. *Mariachis* play a traditional form of the *son,* which is native to the state of Jalisco. Most, however, also play other Mexican music, such as *rancheras, boleros, huapangos,* and *corridos,* or ballads. At parties, they may also play dance music *(cumbias, merengues, salsa, tangos,* waltzes, and polkas).

Although formal social affairs include elaborate decorations, formal dress, and live music, social life in Mexico and Mexican American communities in the U.S. mostly revolves around informal gatherings at friends' homes.

Introduce

Re-entry of Concepts
The following list represents words, expressions, and grammar topics re-entered from *El primer paso* to Chap. 13:

El primer paso
Numbers 0–31
Greetings
Calendar expressions

Chapter 1
Adjectives describing personality
Activities
Gustar expressions

Chapter 2
School subjects
School supplies
Time-telling

Chapter 3
Ir a + inf.
Leisure-time activities

Chapter 4
Food

Chapter 5
Family members
Physical characteristics

Chapter 6
Clothing
Colors
Direct object pronouns

Chapter 7
Vacation activities

Chapter 9
Health-related activities

Planning

Cross-Curricular Connections

Math Connection *(pp. 454–455)*
Have pairs of students imagine they are exchange students in Mexico and are planning an end-of-semester party. Have them prepare a list of what they need, along with prices in dollars; add up the total. Then have each pair figure their totals in *pesos*, using current exchange rates.

Social Studies Connection *(pp. 460–461)*
Assign pairs of students a Spanish-speaking country. Have them make a chart for a festival or celebration particular to that country. Ask them to present to the class: the time of year it takes place, the cultural / historical significance of the celebration, and any special clothing, food, crafts, games or ceremonies associated with it.

Journalism Connection *(pp. 464–465)*
Have students take turns playing the role of a reporter who arrives at a Hollywood premiere party. The reporter's job is to describe the guests as they get out of their limousines and enter the party. Students can try to guess the names of celebrities as they are described by the reporters. Encourage them to write out their reports the night before their presentations. Tell them that they must use the present progressive and, if possible, negative expressions.

CAPÍTULO 14

¡Vamos a una fiesta!

OBJECTIVES

At the end of this chapter, you will be able to:

- make plans for giving or attending a party
- describe gift-giving
- make and acknowledge introductions
- compare parties that Spanish-speaking teenagers go to with those you usually attend

Bailando en la calle durante la feria de Málaga

447

Cultural Notes ☀

Spanish in Your Community
Obtain (if available) a local Spanish newspaper. Ask students to look through it for the announcement of a *quinceañera*. What information is presented in the announcement? How does it compare with the U.S. custom of "Sweet Sixteen"? Look for *quinceañera* cards. If available locally, purchase one and share it with the class.

(pp. 446–447, photo)
Las ferias are a spectacular part of Spanish life. Most towns celebrate these gatherings with processions, fireworks, and dancing. For example, *la feria de Málaga* is held between the second and third Saturdays of August with flamenco dancing, bullfights, theater, music, and food.

Preview

Cultural Objective
• To discuss teenage parties in Spanish-speaking countries

¡Vamos a una fiesta!

Play

 Video Activity A

Using the Video
In this chapter's video, host Karina Romera attends a *quince años* party in Guadalajara. After shopping for a gift and choosing her party attire, Karina joins the hosting family for this special celebration.

To prepare students further for the video, ask them to predict what this chapter's tape will be about. Then have students watch the segment several times. After the first time, you may wish to have them brainstorm possible vocabulary and expressions they will need to talk about what they saw on the video. Ask students to identify: a) activities they saw which reminded them of parties they have attended, and b) activities they saw which are unique to the *quince años* celebration. Video segment 1: For more teaching suggestions, see the Video Teacher's Guide.

¡Piénsalo bien!

Look at the pictures and read the captions.

If you were purchasing a birthday gift for a friend, how would you answer the question?

En una tienda de regalos, España

"¿Qué regalo quieres comprar, algo práctico o algo más personal?"

"¿Qué ropa debo comprar para ir a la fiesta?"

En una tienda en la Ciudad de México

At what types of occasions might you need to wear clothes like these?

448   Capítulo 14

Options

Strategies for Reaching All Students

Spanish-Speaking Students
Ask: *¿Te gusta recibir regalos? ¿Cuáles prefieres, los prácticos o los personales? ¿Te gustan las fiestas y los bailes? ¿Prefieres fiestas grandes o íntimas (con sólo la familia)? ¿Vas a bailes formales?*

 Un paso más Ex. 14-A

"Pasamos toda la noche bailando."

En una discoteca en Buenos Aires

Teenagers in the Spanish-speaking world usually attend a wide variety of parties, from family occasions like weddings and baptisms to *quinceañeras* and school dances. What kinds of parties do you usually attend? Are they family occasions, school dances, or get-togethers with friends?

449

Cultural Notes

Present

Chapter Theme
Celebrations: Introductions

Communicative Objectives
• To talk about parties
• To introduce people
• To talk about gift-giving

 Transparencies 71–72

 Vocabulary Art BLMs

 Pronunciation Tape 14-1

 Vocabulario para conversar A

Play

Using the Video
Video segment 2: See the Video Teacher's Guide.

 Video Activity B

Grammar Preview
Dar is presented here lexically. The complete paradigm is on p. 466.

Vocabulario para conversar

¿A quién vas a invitar?

Aquí tienes palabras y expresiones necesarias para hablar sobre las fiestas. Léelas varias veces y practícalas con un(a) compañero(a) en las páginas siguientes.

la fiesta de la escuela

la novia, el novio

bailar

el baile

la fiesta de fin de año

Options

Strategies for Reaching All Students

Students Needing Extra Help
Show how *baile* comes from *bailar*. *También necesitas . . . :* Present the entire *conocer* and *dar* paradigms if necessary. Remind students that they saw some expressions using *dar* in Chap. 11. Give some examples of the use of *soler*. Continue discussion of word families: *regalar* from *regalo* and *encantado* from *encantar*.
Students may think that *parientes* means "parents." Remind them of *los padres*.

Learning Spanish Through Action
STAGING VOCABULARY: *Señalen*
MATERIALS: transparency of the *Vocabulario para conversar*
DIRECTIONS: Direct students to point to the type of party as you give descriptions such as those on p. 457, Ex. 15.

450

¡Feliz Cumpleaños!

cantar

la fiesta de cumpleaños

la fiesta de sorpresa

la fiesta de disfraces

También necesitas . . .

la reunión	*get-together*
alguien	*someone, somebody*
algunos, algunas	*some*
conocer: (yo) conozco*	*to know, to be acquainted with:*
(tú) conoces	*I know, you know*
Encantado, -a.	*Delighted.*
el pariente, la parienta	*relative*
Te presento a ___.	*I'd like you to meet ___.*
dar: (yo) doy	*to give: I give, you give*
(tú) das	
recibir	*to receive*
hecho, -a a mano	*handmade*
Depende.	*It depends.*
soler (o → ue) + *inf.*	*to be in the habit of*

¿Y qué quiere decir . . . ?
elegante
¡Feliz cumpleaños!
invitar
el / la joven, *pl.* los / las jóvenes
personal
práctico, -a
regalar

* *Conocer* is a regular *-er* verb in the present tense except for the *yo* form: *conozco.*

Vocabulario para conversar   451

Practice & Apply

Re-enter / Recycle

Ex. 1: *ir a* + inf. from Chap. 3, family from Chap. 5
Exs. 2–3: family from Chap. 5
Ex. 4: family from Chap. 5, direct object pronouns from Chap. 6
Exs. 5–6: *gustar* expressions from Chap. 1
Ex. 7: clothing from Chap. 6
Ex. 8: physical characteristics from Chap. 5

Answers: Empecemos a conversar

1 ESTUDIANTE A
a. ¿A quiénes vas a invitar a tu baile?
b. ... fiesta de la escuela?
c. ... fiesta de fin de año?
d. ... fiesta de sorpresa?
e. ... fiesta de disfraces?
f. Questions will vary.

ESTUDIANTE B
a.–f. Answers will vary, but look for use of the personal *a*.

2 ESTUDIANTE A
a. ¿Qué sueles regalarle a tu madre para su cumpleaños?
b. ... hermano(a) ...
c. ... primo(a) ...
d. ... abuelo(a) ...
e. ... amigo(a) ...
f. ... novio(a) ...
g. Questions will vary, but look for the correct use of the personal *a*.

Empecemos a conversar

Túrnate con un(a) compañero(a) para ser *Estudiante A* y *Estudiante B.* Reemplacen las palabras subrayadas con palabras representadas o escritas en los recuadros. quiere decir que puedes escoger tu propia respuesta.

1 A —¿A quiénes vas a invitar a *tu fiesta de cumpleaños?*
    B —*Voy a invitar a quince amigos y a algunos parientes.*
         Y ahora Uds.

Estudiante A   **Estudiante B**

a.   b.   c.   d.   e.   f.

2 padre   A —¿Qué sueles regalarle a tu *padre* para su cumpleaños?
    B —*Depende, pero suelo darle algo práctico.*
         o: *Pues, a veces le doy sólo una tarjeta de cumpleaños.*
         Y ahora Uds.

Estudiante A   **Estudiante B**

Estudiante A		Estudiante B
a. madre	d. abuelo(a)	elegante
		serio(a) / cómico(a)
		romántico(a)
b. hermano(a)	e. amigo(a) g.	barato(a) / caro(a)
		personal
c. primo(a)	f. novio(a)	hecho(a) a mano

452   Capítulo 14

Options

Strategies for Reaching All Students

Spanish-Speaking Students
Ex. 7: After this exercise, ask: *¿Cuándo fue la última vez que fuiste a un baile? ¿Con quién fuiste? ¿Fue tu familia también? ¿Cómo ibas vestido(a), formal o informalmente? ¿Cómo estuvo la música? ¿Bailaste mucho?*

 Un paso más Ex. 14-B

Students Needing Extra Help
Ex. 1: Remind students of the *a personal*. Insist that students vary answers so that they don't repeat *quince* and *algunos*.
Ex. 4: Review *lo, la*. Give a feminine model.
Ex. 7: Have students use their Organizers from Chap. 6.
Ex. 8: Have students use their Organizers from Chaps. 1 and 5 for descriptive words.

Enrichment
Ex. 1: To extend this exercise, review vocabulary for dates by asking the birthdates of individual students.
Ex. 2: As a homework assignment, have students make a table with three columns headed *Pariente / amigo(a), Personalidad / apariencia,* and *Por eso, suelo regalarle.* In the first column, students should list five family members or friends. In the second, they should describe the personalities and physical characteristics of the people they

452

3 a mi amiga

A — *Te presento a mi amiga Juanita.*
B — *Encantado(a).*

Y ahora Uds.

Estudiante A

a. a mi tía, ___

b. a mi madre, ___

c. a mi abuelo, ___

d. a mi profesor, el señor ___

e. a mi profesora,
la señora (señorita) ___

Estudiante B

Encantado(a).

Mucho gusto.

4 mi primo

A — *¿Conoces a mi primo Alberto?*
B — *No, no lo (la) conozco.*
o: *Sí, lo (la) conozco.*

Y ahora Uds.

Estudiante A

Estudiante B

También se dice

For *regalar,* we can also say
hacer un regalo.

Empecemos a escribir

Escribe tus respuestas en español.

5 ¿Qué regalos sueles hacer? ¿Qué regalo te gustaría recibir?

6 ¿Te gustaría dar una fiesta grande? ¿A quiénes te gustaría invitar?
¿A toda la familia? ¿A muchos jóvenes? ¿O prefieres las reuniones
pequeñas?

7 Cuando vas a un baile, ¿qué ropa sueles llevar?

8 ¿Conoces a alguien famoso? ¿A alguien muy viejo? ¿A alguien
fascinante? ¿Quiénes son? ¿Cómo se llaman? ¿Cómo son?

Vocabulario para conversar   453

ESTUDIANTE B

a.–g. Answers will vary, but look
for a variety of adjectives and the
correct placement of the indirect
object pronoun.

3 ESTUDIANTE A

a. Te presento a mi tía, ___.
b. . . .a mi madre, ___.
c. . . .a mi abuelo, ___.
d. . . .a mi profesor, el señor ___.
e. . . .a mi profesora, la señora
(señorita) ___.

ESTUDIANTE B

a.–e. Statements may vary.

4 ESTUDIANTE A

Questions will vary. Suggest that
students use names of friends or
famous people.

ESTUDIANTE B

Answers will vary. Look for the
correct use of the direct object
pronoun.

Answers: Empecemos a escribir

5–8 Answers will vary.
Encourage a wide range of
vocabulary.

 **Practice Wkbk.
14-1, 14-2**

 Audio Activity 14.1

 **Writing Activities
14-A, 14-B**

 Pruebas 14-1, 14-2

named. In the third column, they should
name the gifts they usually buy for each of
these people.
Exs. 3–4: Encourage students to use *Hola,
¿cómo estás?* and any other greetings from
El primer paso.
Ex. 3: Have students role play this exercise.

Empecemos a escribir: Students can also
write about these topics: 1) the kind of gift
they prefer: personal, handmade, elegant,
etc.; 2) where they usually *(soler)* buy gifts;
3) the kinds of parties they like best and
why.

Present

Chapter Theme
Celebrations: Clothes and activities

Communicative Objectives
- To talk about parties
- To talk about what to wear to a party

 Transparencies 73–74

 Vocabulary Art BLMs

 Pronunciation Tape 14-2

 Vocabulario para conversar B

Play

Using the Video
Video segment 2: See the Video Teacher's Guide.

 Video Activity B

Grammar Preview
Bailando / cantando / comiendo / hablando / viendo are presented here lexically. The explanation of the present progressive is on pp. 464–465.

Vocabulario para conversar

En la fiesta

Aquí tienes el resto del vocabulario necesario para hablar sobre las fiestas y los regalos.

el traje

el vestido de fiesta

los zapatos de tacón alto

la corbata

las joyas

el collar

el reloj pulsera

los aretes (m.)

la pulsera

el lugar: *Virrey Arredondo 2553*
la hora: *7:00 de la tarde*
la fecha: *viernes, 2 de julio*

la invitación

454 Capítulo 14

Options

Strategies for Reaching All Students

Spanish-Speaking Students

 Un paso más Ex. 14-C

Students Needing Extra Help
También necesitas . . . : Present the entire *escoger* paradigm if necessary.
Separate *pasarlo bien* from *pasarlo mal.*
Explain the difference between *el ambiente* and *el medio ambiente.*

Learning Spanish Through Action
STAGING VOCABULARY: *Dibujen*
MATERIALS: none
DIRECTIONS: Describe a party from preparation to cleanup. At each stage, direct students to draw the activities on the chalkboard: *Primero hay que escribir las invitaciones, luego hay que preparar la comida, luego hay que decorar,* and so on, up to *¿Quién va a sacar la basura?*

la invitada

el invitado

las decoraciones (pl.)

la entrada

decorar

Teaching Suggestions
Preparing students to speak: Use one or two options from each of the categories of Comprehensible Input, Physical Response, or Limited Verbal Response. For a complete explanation of these categories and some sample activities, see the front section of this Teacher's Edition.

Class Starter Review
On the day following initial vocabulary presentation, you might begin the class with this activity: Following the example given in this *Vocabulario para conversar,* have students write a very short invitation to their next birthday party, including address, day, date, and time.

También necesitas . . .

el ambiente	*atmosphere*
bailar: bailando	*dancing*
cantar: cantando	*singing*
comer: comiendo	*eating*
hablar: hablando	*talking*
pasarlo bien / mal	*to have a good / bad time*
ver: viendo	*looking*
escoger: (yo) escojo*	*to choose: I choose, you choose*
(tú) escoges	
De ninguna manera.	*Not at all.*

¿Y qué quiere decir . . . ?
la fecha
la hora
el lugar
escribir
escuchar (la radio, el disco compacto)
tocar música

* *Escoger* is a regular -er verb with a spelling change in the *yo* form of the present tense: *escojo.*

Vocabulario para conversar   455

Practice & Apply

Re-enter / Recycle

Ex. 9: *gustar* expressions from Chap. 1
Ex. 10: clothing from Chap. 6
Ex. 11: calendar expressions from *El primer paso,* time-telling from Chap. 2, *ir a* + inf. from Chap. 3
Ex. 14: *gustar* expressions from Chap. 1

Answers: Empecemos a conversar

9 ESTUDIANTE A
a. ¡Qué fiesta tan aburrida! ¡Nadie está hablando!
b. ...comiendo!
c. ...cantando!
d. ...pasándolo bien!

ESTUDIANTE B
a.–d. Creo que no les gusta(n) ... *(Answers will vary, and should include the correct use of* gustar.*)*

10 ESTUDIANTE A
a. ¿Necesitas comprar algo para llevar con tu traje?
b. ...tu collar?
c. ...tu vestido?
d. ...tu falda?
e. ...tus pantalones?
f. ...tu chaqueta?

ESTUDIANTE B
a.–f. Answers will vary, but may include: *unos zapatos de tacón alto, una camiseta, una corbata, un reloj pulsera, una blusa, unos aretes.*

Empecemos a conversar

9 bailando

A — *¡Qué fiesta tan aburrida! ¡Nadie está <u>bailando</u>!*
B — *Creo que no les gusta <u>la música</u>.*
Y ahora Uds.

Estudiante A

a. hablando
b. comiendo
c. cantando
d. pasándolo bien

Estudiante B

la comida
la música
el ambiente

10

A — *¿Necesitas comprar algo para llevar con tu <u>vestido de fiesta</u>?*
B — *Sí, <u>un collar</u>.*
Y ahora Uds.

Estudiante A

a. b. c. d. e. f.

Estudiante B

456   Capítulo 14

Options

Strategies for Reaching All Students

Spanish-Speaking Students
Ex. 15: After this exercise, ask: *Vas a una fiesta de disfraces. ¿Qué disfraz te gustaría llevar? ¿Por qué?*

 Un paso más Ex. 14-D

Students Needing Extra Help
Ex. 9: Discuss word families: *comer, comida.*
Some of these items have only one logical answer; others have a choice.
Exs. 9–10: Remind students that the responses for *Estudiante B* are not in sequential order with the statements or questions for *Estudiante A.*
Ex. 11: Remind students that dates are presented in a different order (4 of July as opposed to July 4).

Imagina que vas a dar una fiesta el 2 de junio.

11 decorar
el lugar

A —¿*Cuándo vas a* <u>*decorar el lugar*</u> *para la fiesta?*
B —<u>*El 1° de junio*</u>.

Y ahora Uds.

Estudiante A

a. escoger la hora y la fecha

b. escribir las invitaciones

c. escoger la música

d. preparar la comida

e. escoger la ropa que vas a llevar

Estudiante B

Empecemos a escribir y a leer

Escribe tus respuestas en español.

12 ¿Llevas aretes? ¿Y reloj pulsera? ¿Cuándo los llevas?

13 ¿Para qué fiestas necesitas comprar entradas?

14 Para dar una fiesta, ¿qué necesitas hacer? ¿Qué música te gusta tocar?

15 ¿Qué clase de fiesta es? Lee las descripciones y contesta las preguntas.

a. Alejandro le compró un collar a Anita. Llegó a su casa temprano con los otros invitados. Cuando Anita entró en la casa, todos dijeron: "¡Feliz cumpleaños!"

b. María llevaba un vestido elegante y zapatos de tacón alto. Su novio, un traje gris con una corbata azul. La música era muy bonita y les gustó mucho la fiesta. Pero hoy les duelen mucho los pies.

c. Adela no sabía qué llevar a la fiesta. ¿Jeans, botas y un sombrero vaquero? ¿Un traje de baño, una toalla, anteojos de sol y sandalias? Al final, decidió irse de detective.

¿A qué clase de fiesta fue Alejandro? ¿Y María? ¿Y Adela?

También se dice

los aros
los pendientes
los zarcillos

el brazalete

el vestido de gala
el vestido de etiqueta

457

Practice

Re-enter / Recycle

Ex. 1: clothing and colors from Chap. 6

Ex. 2: school subjects from Chap. 2, physical characteristics from Chap. 5, direct object pronouns from Chap. 6

Ex. 3: calendar expressions and numbers 0–31 from *El primer paso,* family members from Chap. 5, clothing from Chap. 6

Using Realia

Tell students to scan the ad for *la joyería Talia* and find the date mentioned. For what occasion is this ad appearing? (Valentine's Day)

Answers:
¡Comuniquemos!

1 Dialogues will vary, but should include a wide variety of chapter vocabulary.

2 Dialogues will vary, but should include the correct forms of *conocer (conoces, conozco)* and adjective agreement.

¡Comuniquemos!

Aquí tienes otra oportunidad para usar el vocabulario de este capítulo.

1 Escoge cinco de tus compañeros(as). ¿Qué ropa llevan hoy? Toma notas en español para no olvidarlo. Después, describe a un(a) estudiante. Tu compañero(a) debe adivinar *(guess)* a quién describes.

A — *Lleva aretes azules, un suéter y jeans. ¿Quién es?*
B — *¿Son blancos los jeans?*
A — *Sí.*
B — *Es Sara.*

2 ¿Conoce tu compañero(a) a las personas de quienes hablas?

A — *¿Conoces a Mike Smith?*
B — *Sí, lo conozco. Es un estudiante de mi clase de matemáticas. Es muy simpático.*
    o:
B — *No, no lo conozco. ¿Quién es?*
A — *Es un estudiante de mi clase de arte.*
B — *¿Cómo es?*
A — *Es alto y rubio.*

458   Capítulo 14

Options

Strategies for Reaching All Students

Spanish-Speaking Students

 Un paso más Exs. 14-E, 14-F

Students Needing Extra Help

Ex. 1: Follow this procedure: 1) Choose a student; 2) identify some articles of clothing or accessories; 3) develop questions using color words or other descriptives; 4) have students use their Organizers.

Ex. 2: Have students use their Organizers from Chaps. 1 and 5.

Encourage students to vary descriptions.

Ex. 3: Have students review the vocabulary for different kinds of gifts before doing this exercise.

¿Qué sabes ahora?: Have students write out this section so that they can check off what they have mastered.

3 ¡Cuántos regalos! Tu compañero(a) va a comprar regalos para su familia y sus amigos. Ayúdalo(la) a decidir qué comprar.

A — *El cumpleaños de (mi hermano) es (el 10 de junio).*
  ¿Qué le regalo?
B — *¿Por qué no le compras (un reloj pulsera)?*

¿Qué sabes ahora?

Can you:

■ discuss preparations for a party?

—Tengo que preparar ___, escoger ___ y escribir ___.

■ tell what kinds of gifts you like to give and receive?

—Me gusta hacer regalos ___. Me gusta recibir regalos ___.

■ tell what you wear to a party?

—Cuando voy a una fiesta de cumpleaños, llevo ___ y ___.

■ introduce people and acknowledge introductions?

—Te ___ a mi amigo Andrés.

—___.

---

3 Dialogues will vary, but should follow the pattern of the model. Encourage use of chapter vocabulary. Suggested gifts include: *un collar, una pulsera, unos tenis, un suéter, unos zapatos, una corbata, unos aretes, un reloj pulsera, una chequeta, una camiseta.*

Answers: ¿Qué sabes ahora?

• las decoraciones / la fecha / (las) invitaciones
• Answers will vary, but look for correct adjective agreement.
• Answers will vary.
• presento / Encantado(a)

 Audio Activity 14.3

Cooperative Learning
Assign groups of four students different types of parties or gatherings listed in the first *Vocabulario para conversar.* Then ask each group to list what they would bring to celebrate it. After they have prepared their lists, have one person in each group summarize. As each group reports, have all other students check off the items that also appeared on their lists.

Present & Apply

Cultural Objective

- To compare teenage parties in Spanish-speaking countries and the U.S.

Critical Thinking: Identifying Stereotypes

Help students understand that although *quinceañera* parties are common in many Spanish-speaking countries, the amount of importance given to them varies from country to country. The celebrations themselves also differ greatly, depending upon socioeconomic level and regional or local customs and traditions.

Perspectiva cultural

¿Qué fiestas especiales hay en tu familia? ¿Y en tu comunidad?

Based on these photographs, what do you think the people are celebrating? What tells you that this is a very special party?

It's 4 o'clock on a Saturday afternoon in Camuy, a town on the northern coast of Puerto Rico. You can hear the approaching sounds of a ten-car caravan blowing their horns. When the caravan arrives in front of the church, Tamaris, a young woman in a white dress, steps out of the first car with her mother and father. Inside the church, Tamaris will receive a blessing from the priest while her mother places a crown on her head.

What might look like a wedding party is actually Tamaris's *quince años*, her fifteenth birthday celebration. It marks the girl's entrance into adulthood.

A *quince años* party can be very lavish or very simple. But one thing they all have in common is that family and friends of all ages join together to make it a memorable success. In Tamaris's case, the caravan was driven by her father's closest friends. They all own similar cars and have formed a car club that meets regularly for fun and to serve as escorts for local parties and celebrations, such as a *quince años*.

The white dress Tamaris is wearing was made by her mother, and her grandparents contributed the crown and white high-heeled shoes. Other family members and friends prepared food and refreshments for the party at her home, where a friend from school will act as deejay. Traditionally, the *quinceañera* starts the first dance with her father and then moves on to her escort. Then other couples will join them. The party will continue late into the night.

Guadalupe Velasco fue Presentada en Sociedad

Options

Strategies for Reaching All Students

Spanish-Speaking Students

Ask: ¿Has participado en una quinceañera? ¿Has ido a una quinceañera? ¿Fue muy elegante? ¿Dónde tuvo lugar? ¿Fue mucha gente? ¿Fueron muchos de tus amigos? ¿Te divertiste? ¿Qué piensas de las fiestas de quinceañeras?

 Un paso más Exs. 14-G, 14-H

Students Needing Extra Help

Talk about the cultural significance of a fifteenth birthday party. Note the difference in the degree of formality and the close relationship with the Church.
Explain that the word *quinceañera* can refer both to the girl celebrating her fifteenth birthday and to the party in her honor.

Dos quinceañeras celebran su día especial en Austin, Texas.

Another tradition has the girls at the party gathering around the cake to pull ribbons from it. The one who pulls the ribbon with a ring on it will presumably be the first one to get married.

However, not all young girls are interested in having a quince años party. Some might ask for a trip or a special gift instead of a formal party and a white dress. Tamaris's friend Loida has asked for a plane

ticket so she can spend her summer vacation with her cousins in New Jersey and visit New York City. Loida is looking forward to her first long trip alone. That will really make her feel like an adult.

La cultura desde tu perspectiva

1 Is the party described here similar to any parties you have ever attended? How were they alike or different?

2 What events in the United States are similar to a *quince años?* In what ways are they similar?

Answers
Answers will vary for inductive questions in Spanish. / Students may mention that the people are celebrating a special occasion. A birthday party or even a wedding might be suggested. / Answers will vary, but may include: The party seems special because of the way the people are dressed.

Answers: La cultura desde tu perspectiva
1 Answers will vary.

2 Answers will vary, but students may mention a "Sweet 16" party or a Bar (Bat) Mitzvah. / These celebrations usually mark a person's passage into adulthood and often include the gathering of family and friends.

Multicultural Perspectives
In Puerto Rico today, at a *quince años* party, a deejay is often hired to play the popular hits from the island and the mainland. *Salsa* or *merengue* are among the popular choices of dance music. Perhaps at the request of the father of the *quinceañera*, a traditional *danza* might be played. *La danza puertorriqueña* dates to the eighteenth century and has elements from the French *contredances*. Ask students familiar with other cultures to share their knowledge of popular and traditional dance music.

Cultural Notes ☼

(p. 460, realia)
Among many Spanish-speaking families, *quinceañera* celebrations often are very formal affairs, rivaling weddings in preparation and expense. For young women from these families, their fifteenth birthday marks not only the end of childhood, but also their "formal presentation to society," as illustrated by this newspaper announcement.

(p. 461, photo)
Los quince años, the rite of passage into adulthood for young women in many Spanish-speaking countries, is also celebrated in many Hispanic communities in the U.S.

Preview

Transparency 75

Answers

A The ending used on -ar verbs is -ando, and the ending used on -er verbs is -iendo. The meaning of *están saliendo* is "they are leaving."

B *nadie; no, ni . . . ni; nada;* and *nunca. / No, nunca,* and *ni . . . ni* come before the verb; *nadie* comes either before or after the verb; *nada* comes after the verb.

C The sentences in captions 2, 3, and 5 have more than one negative word. When the negative word comes before the verb, *no* is not included. When the negative word comes after the verb, another negative word such as *no* is included.

Gramática en contexto

¡La peor fiesta de cumpleaños! ¡Pobre Eugenia! ¡Lo está pasando horrible! ¿Por qué?

Nadie está bailando.

Los invitados no están ni comiendo ni bebiendo.

Mi novio no está hablando con nadie.

Algunos invitados están viendo . . . ¡la tele!

Muchas personas ya están saliendo, pero nadie me regaló nada.

¡Nunca voy a tener otra fiesta de cumpleaños!

A The verbs in the first four captions are made up of two words. What ending is used on the -ar verbs when they follow *estar*? And on the -er verbs? What is the meaning of *están saliendo* in the fifth caption?

B Find all the negative words that Eugenia uses to express her feelings (such as *no* and

nadie). Do these words come before or after the verbs?

C In which sentences do you find more than one negative word? What word is used before the verb in these sentences?

462   Capítulo 14

Options

Strategies for Reaching All Students

Students Needing Extra Help
A: As students identify the tense made up of two verbs, write out the use of *estar* + a verb form ending in -ando or -iendo to express an action that's happening right now. Ask students from what infinitive *pasando* comes. Go through each present participle. Then ask for the difference in endings for verbs ending in -ar and those ending in -er or -ir.

B: As students use negative words and note their position, elicit the idea that when the negative word comes before the verb, *no* is not included. When the negative word comes after the verb, *no* is included. Students probably won't recognize anything but *no* as a negative. Point out other negative words: *nada, nadie, nunca,* etc. Tell them that in English, double negatives are incorrect, but in Spanish they are correct.

Give some examples with and without the *no*.
Remind students of the *a personal* with *nadie*.
Stress opposites: *algo–nada; alguien–nadie; nunca–siempre.*

Construcciones negativas

To make a sentence negative, we put *no* in front of the verb. Some other negative words that you know are: *nada* ("nothing"), *nunca* ("never"), *nadie* ("nobody"), *tampoco* ("neither"), and *ni... ni* ("neither ... nor"). Recall how we use them:

> **Nunca** saco fotos.
> **Nadie** va a ayudarme con las decoraciones.
> **No** me gusta bailar **tampoco.**
> **No** hay **ni** sandwiches **ni** refrescos.
> **No** quiero comer **nada.**

- Sometimes we can put the negative word before the verb and leave out the *no*. However, if the negative word comes after the verb, we must use *no* or another negative word.

> Antonio **nunca** estudia con **nadie.**
> **No** conozco a **nadie** en esta fiesta.

---

1 Pregúntale a tu compañero(a) qué va a hacer. Usa una palabra *(word)* o una frase de cada columna.

leer

A —*¿Vas a leer algo esta tarde?*
B —*Sí, voy a leer una revista.*
 o: *No, no voy a leer nada.*

a. comer   hoy
b. jugar   esta tarde
c. ver   esta noche
d. beber   mañana
e. escuchar   este fin de semana
f. hacer
g. comprar

Gramática en contexto   463

Present & Practice

Re-enter / Recycle

Ex. 2: leisure-time activities and *ir a* + inf. from Chap. 3, food from Chap. 4

Ex. 3: direct object pronouns from Chap. 6, TV and movies from Chap. 11, recycling from Chap. 13

Ex. 4: leisure-time activities from Chap. 3, vacation activities from Chap. 7, health-related activities from Chap. 9

Answers

2 ESTUDIANTE A

a. ¿Alguien va a traer una grabadora?

b. ...revistas?

c. ...sandwiches de jamón y queso?

d. ...vasos?

e. ...videojuegos?

ESTUDIANTE B

a. No, nadie va a traer una grabadora. ¡No vamos a escuchar nada!

b. ...revistas. ...leer nada!

c. ...sandwiches (de jamón y queso). ...comer nada!

d. ...vasos. ...beber nada!

e. ...videojuegos. ...jugar nada!

---

2 Quieres hacer una reunión pero nadie quiere llevar nada. Explícale a tu compañero(a) qué problemas van a tener.

A — *¿Alguien va a traer refrescos?*
B — *No, nadie va a traer refrescos. ¡No vamos a beber nada!*

a.　　b.　　c.　　d.　　e.

3 ¿Cuáles son algunas cosas que no haces nunca? Con un(a) compañero(a), di *(tell)* si siempre, a veces, o nunca haces estas cosas.

llevar aretes

A — *Yo nunca llevo aretes. ¿Y tú?*
B — *Yo tampoco.*
　　o: *Yo los llevo siempre.*

a. llevar un vestido de fiesta / una corbata
b. escribir cartas / tarjetas postales
c. pasarlo mal en una fiesta
d. regalar algo hecho a mano

e. dar fiestas de sorpresa
f. reciclar botellas de plástico
g. montar en bicicleta
h. ver dibujos animados

El presente progresivo

We use the present tense to talk about an action that always or often takes place or that is happening now.

Ellos **comen** hamburguesas.

They eat hamburgers. (always / usually)
They're eating hamburgers. (now)

We use the present progressive tense when we want to emphasize that something is happening right now.

Ellos **están comiendo** hamburguesas.

They're eating hamburgers. (right now)

464　Capítulo 14

Options

Strategies for Reaching All Students

Spanish-Speaking Students
Ex. 3: Have students write out this exercise.
Ex. 4: For Spanish-speaking students, replace Ex. 4 with: *Escribe un párrafo explicando lo que está haciendo cada persona.*

Students Needing Extra Help
Ex. 2: Have students match the artwork with a corresponding verb; for example, sandwiches with *comer*, video games with *jugar*. Stress that *algo* and *nada* are used with things and that *alguien* and *nadie* are used with people.
Brainstorm with students the new verb that will be used in the second statement of the *Estudiante B* response.

El presente progresivo: Go through a list of verbs from earlier chapters, changing them to the present participle.
Ex. 4: Have students use their Organizers from Chap. 7. Remind them that the form of *estar* changes with the subject while the participle remains the same.

The present progressive uses a present-tense form of *estar* + the present participle of another verb. To form the present participle, we drop the ending of the infinitive and add *-ando* to the stem of *-ar* verbs and *-iendo* to the stem of *-er* and *-ir* verbs.

(yo)	**estoy**	bail**ando** com**iendo** escrib**iendo**	(nosotros) (nosotras)	**estamos**	bail**ando** com**iendo** escrib**iendo**
(tú)	**estás**	bail**ando** com**iendo** escrib**iendo**	(vosotros) (vosotras)	**estáis**	bail**ando** com**iendo** escrib**iendo**
Ud. (él) (ella)	**está**	bail**ando** com**iendo** escrib**iendo**	Uds. (ellos) (ellas)	**están**	bail**ando** com**iendo** escrib**iendo**

4 Tienes unas fotos de tus vacaciones en Yucatán. Túrnate con un(a) compañero(a) para explicar qué están haciendo las personas en cada foto.

Aquí nosotros estamos explorando la selva.

nosotros

a. mi papá   b. mi hermana   c. mis padres

d. mi familia y yo   e. unos amigos mexicanos   f. yo

Gramática en contexto   465

a. Yo (siempre / a veces / nunca) llevo un vestido de fiesta / una corbata. ¿Y tú?
b. . . . escribo cartas / tarjetas postales. . . .
c. . . . lo paso mal en una fiesta. . . .
d. . . . regalo algo hecho a mano. . . .
e. . . . doy fiestas de sorpresa. . . .
f. . . . reciclo botellas de plástico. . . .
g. . . . monto en bicicleta. . . .
h. . . . veo dibujos animados. . . .
ESTUDIANTE B
a.–h. Answers will vary.

 Practice Wkbk. 14-5

 Writing Activity 14-D

 Prueba 14-5

 Comm. Act. BLM 14-2

4 Answers
a. Aquí mi papá está haciendo ejercicio.
b. . . . mi hermana está tomando el sol.
c. . . . mis padres están buceando.
d. . . . mi familia y yo estamos subiendo una pirámide.
e. . . . unos amigos mexicanos están jugando fútbol.
f. . . . yo estoy bailando y cantando.

Enrichment
Ex. 4: To extend this exercise, you may want to have students bring their own vacation photos (or those from a magazine for a "pretend" vacation) and take turns presenting one or two of them to the class. Encourage students to be as detailed as possible in their descriptions of the photos, naming people, place, and time (season, month) as well as what's happening.

Present & Practice

Re-enter / Recycle

Ex. 5: activities from Chap. 1, leisure-time activities from Chap. 3, vacation activities from Chap. 7

Ex. 6: *gustar* expressions from Chap. 1, school subjects and school supplies from Chap. 2, clothing from Chap. 6

Ex. 7: family members from Chap. 5

Answers

5 ESTUDIANTE A

a. ¿Qué están haciendo Paco y Jorge?

b. ...están haciendo Uds.?

c. ...estás haciendo tú?

d. ...está haciendo Julia?

e. ...está haciendo Carlos?

ESTUDIANTE B

a. Están comiendo tacos.

b. Estamos escuchando música.

c. Estoy hablando por teléfono.

d. Está tocando la guitarra.

e. Está sacando fotos.

 Practice Wkbk. 14-6, 14-7

 Writing Activity 14-E

 Prueba 14-6

 Comm. Act. BLM 14-3

---

5 Tu amigo(a) está enfermo(a) y no puede ir a la fiesta de fin de año. Por eso, te llama por teléfono para preguntar qué están haciendo todos los invitados.

A —¿*Qué están haciendo Raquel y Fernando?*

B —*Están bailando.*

Raquel y Fernando

| a. Paco y Jorge | b. Uds. | c. tú | d. Julia | e. Carlos |

El verbo *dar*

The verb *dar* means "to give." Here are all its present-tense forms.

(yo)	**doy**	(nosotros) (nosotras)	**damos**
(tú)	**das**	(vosotros) (vosotras)	**dais**
Ud. (él) (ella)	**da**	Uds. (ellos) (ellas)	**dan**

- Except for the *yo* form, *dar* takes the same present-tense endings as regular -*ar* verbs.

- Because we often say to whom we give something, *dar* is usually used with the indirect object pronouns *me, te, le, nos,* and *les.*

  Nuestro profesor **nos da** mucha tarea.
  Nunca **les doy** nada a mis primos.
  Mis abuelos van a **darme** un libro para mi cumpleaños.

466 Capítulo 14

Options

Strategies for Reaching All Students

Students Needing Extra Help

El verbo dar: Do students remember other verbs that have a similar *yo* form? *(soy, voy)*

Have them review their Organizers from Chaps. 9 and 11 for indirect object pronouns.

Point out the position of the pronoun when there are two verbs.

Show that in English we drop the "to" in the statement "to give to someone." ("I gave Mary a gift" as opposed to "I gave to Mary a gift.")

Ex. 6: Because the indirect objects are all singular, you may want to add some plural ones.

Ex. 7: Do the exercise using the first response, then again using the second.

Ahora lo sabes: Have students write out this section so that they can check off what they have mastered.

Enrichment

Ex. 7: As a homework assignment, have students do this exercise with plural names for the people named as "givers." As another assignment, students can list other people (singular and plural) who give them other things.

6 ¿Qué les regalas a las siguientes personas? Trabaja con un(a) compañero(a) para escoger el regalo apropiado.

un amigo que
juega béisbol

A — *¿Qué le das a un amigo que juega béisbol?*
B — *Le doy algunas entradas a un partido.*

a. un amigo a quien le gusta dibujar
b. una amiga a quien le gusta esquiar
c. una amiga que estudia álgebra
d. un amigo que escribe mucho
e. una amiga que ve muchas películas
f. un amigo que va a menudo a la playa
g. una amiga a quien le gusta la ropa

7 Dile a tu compañero(a) quién te da estas cosas.

dinero

A — *¿Quién te da dinero?*
B — *Mi padre me da dinero.*
   o: *Nadie me da dinero.*

a. ropa nueva
b. poca tarea
c. regalos hechos a mano
d. los exámenes más difíciles
e. regalos prácticos
f. tarjetas de cumpleaños

Ahora lo sabes

Can you:

■ express a negative statement?
—No tengo hambre. ___ voy a comer ___ ahora.

■ tell what is happening right now?
—Marta y Rosa ___ unas enchiladas porque tienen hambre.

■ tell what someone gives to someone else?
—Yo siempre les ___ regalos a mis amigos.

6 ESTUDIANTE A
a. ¿Qué le das a un amigo a quien le gusta dibujar?
b. ...una amiga a quien le gusta esquiar?
c. ...una amiga que estudia álgebra?
d. ...un amigo que escribe mucho?
e. ...una amiga que ve muchas películas?
f. ...un amigo que va a menudo a la playa?
g. ...una amiga a quien le gusta la ropa?
ESTUDIANTE B
a.–g. Answers will vary.

7 ESTUDIANTE A
a. ¿Quién te da ropa nueva?
b. ...poca tarea?
c. ...regalos hechos a mano?
d. ...los exámenes más difíciles?
e. ...regalos prácticos?
f. ...tarjetas de cumpleaños?
ESTUDIANTE B
a.–f. Answers will vary.

Answers: Ahora lo sabes
• No / nada
• están comiendo
• doy

 **Practice Wkbk.
14-8, 14-9**

 Audio Activity 14.4

 **Writing Activity
14-F**

 Prueba 14-7

Apply

Pronunciation Tape 14-3

¡A conversar!

Play

Step

Using the Video
Video segment 3: See the Video Teacher's Guide.

 Video Activity C

Para decir más

Aquí tienes vocabulario adicional que te puede ayudar para hacer las actividades de esta sección.

el casco
helmet

el certificado de regalo
gift certificate

el dulce
sweet, candy

el pañuelo
handkerchief, scarf

el perfume
perfume

el sombrero
hat

los esquís
skis

los patines
roller skates

468   Capítulo 14

Actividades

Esta sección te ofrece la oportunidad de aumentar tus conocimientos de español al integrar lo que aprendiste en este capítulo con lo que aprendiste en capítulos anteriores.

1 Quieres dar una fiesta. Con un(a) compañero(a), decidan:

- qué clase de fiesta va a ser
- cuándo la quieren dar
- dónde
- a quiénes van a invitar
- qué van a servir
- qué ropa llevar
- qué música tocar

Luego escriban una invitación para la fiesta y compártanla *(share it)* con los miembros de la clase.

Options

Strategies for Reaching All Students

Spanish-Speaking Students
Ex. 3: Pair bilingual students with non-bilingual students if possible.

 Un paso más Ex. 14-I

Students Needing Extra Help
Ex. 1: To keep the comments appropriate, you should decide on the kind of party. Perhaps you can suggest the anniversary of grandparents, a party honoring a local celebrity, etc.
Bring in a sample invitation.
Have students use their Organizers from Chaps. 4, 6, and 12 (food and clothing).
Brainstorm additional questions.

Ex. 2: If possible, bring in an ad aimed at gift-giving from a Spanish-language newspaper or magazine to serve as a model.
Ex. 3: Remind students that they will pantomime the sentences for their classmates. Be aware that some students may feel reluctant to act or perform in front of a group.

2 Trabaja con un(a) compañero(a) para crear un anuncio para un regalo. Si quieren, pueden incluir esta información:

- descripción del regalo
- para qué tipo de persona es
- precio
- por qué es el regalo perfecto
- dónde comprarlo

Luego compartan el anuncio con sus compañeros de clase.

3 Escribe en diferentes hojas de papel cuatro cosas que quisieras estar haciendo en este momento.

Estoy tocando el piano.
Estoy bebiendo un refresco.

Pon tus papeles con los de otros tres estudiantes. Después, túrnense para representar lo que dicen los papeles. Los otros estudiantes deben adivinar qué estás haciendo.

¿Estás tocando el piano?
¿Estás bebiendo un refresco?

Luego escojan las mejores representaciones. Háganlas para otro grupo. Ellos deben adivinar lo que están haciendo.

¿Están tocando el piano?
¿Están bebiendo refrescos?

Una muchacha celebra el fin del año escolar en Cuernavaca, México.

Answers: Actividades
1 Invitations will vary, but look for logical responses and a wide variety of chapter vocabulary.

2 Ads will vary, but should contain a wide variety of vocabulary.

3 Sentences will vary, but should include correct use of the present progressive.

 Writing Activities 14-G, 14-H

 Comm. Act. BLMs 14-4, 14-5

Cooperative Learning
Have each student bring to class a small item that relates to an interest, hobby, personality trait, etc. For example, a tennis ball represents someone good at tennis, sheet music indicates interest in singing or playing an instrument, and so on. The next day, divide the class into groups of three or four. Have students put the items in a bag so that classmates cannot see them. Place all of the items in a larger bag. Now tell students that they will be going shopping for a gift for someone in the class. One by one, have them select an item from the bag. Groups then discuss to whom the item should be given. Set a time limit. After they have chosen the person, a representative gives the item to him or her. As the item is given, the student uses a form of the verb *dar,* an indirect object pronoun, and a reason for giving the object. Afterward, check to see how many objects were "correctly" given as gifts.

Cultural Notes ☼

(p. 469, photo)
Girl at her sixth-grade graduation party with her mother. The bond between children and their parents is generally very strong in Spanish-speaking cultures, even when the children are grown and have families of their own. Respect for and devotion to one's parents are highly valued. For example, in many families children still use the formal *usted* address, no matter how familiar the conversation.

Apply

Process Reading

For a description of process reading, see p. 48.

Answers

Antes de leer

Students may say that the story is about two boys and a girl, and that the setting might be a dance held somewhere, possibly involving a contest of some kind.

Mira la lectura

Answers will vary.

¡Vamos a leer!

Antes de leer

STRATEGY ➤ Using titles and pictures to predict

Look at the title of the story and the pictures to predict who the characters are and what the setting might be.

Uno, dos, tres, ¡rumba!

Roberto es un muchacho cubano que acaba de llegar a Chicago. No sabe una palabra de inglés. Los primeros meses yo le ayudo con las clases y las tareas. También le ayudo con otras cosas. Cada viernes por la tarde, los muchachos tienen que llevar pantalones negros, camisa blanca y una corbata negra para ir a las clases de baile. Nos reunimos en el gimnasio de la escuela por una hora. El primer viernes, Roberto me dice: "Antonio, ¡no sé bailar! ¿Qué voy a hacer? ¡No voy a entender a la profesora y no puedo hablar con las muchachas!"

470   Capítulo 14

Mira la lectura

STRATEGY ➤ Skimming

Remember that you can get an overview of a story by skimming it. Skim the story now. Were your predictions correct?

Le digo a Roberto que sólo tiene que observar lo que hacen los otros. Y eso es lo que hace. Cuando baila con las muchachas no puede decirles nada. Pero no importa, porque debe pensar en lo que hace.

Un día la profesora anuncia que va a regalar un disco compacto a la mejor pareja de la clase. Entonces una muchacha llamada Susan le dice: *"Come on, Roberto, we have to win!"*

Options

Strategies for Reaching All Students

Students Needing Extra Help

Infórmate: On the chalkboard or overhead, write out the entire sentence that contains the phrase *lo que hacen los otros* (second panel) so that students can understand the context.

Aplicación: If necessary, help students with writing an ending for the story.

Infórmate

STRATEGY ➤ Using cognates

Remember that you can use what you know about cognates to figure out the meaning of new words. For example, if you think *observar* means "observe," two facts support that guess. First, if you don't know how to dance, observing the other dancers is something you might do. Second, the phrase *lo que hacen los otros* makes sense after the word *observar*. So *observar* probably means "observe."

1 What do you think *interpreto* means? What information helps you figure it out?

2 Which word makes sense in this sentence?

Roberto no sabe ___ sus ideas en inglés.

a. imitar
b. expresar
c. solucionar

3 How did Roberto solve his problem in the dance class?

"Pero ¿qué me dice?" me pregunta el pobre Roberto. Cuando le explico que la profesora va a dar un regalo a los mejores bailarines y que Susan quiere bailar con él, Roberto está un poco nervioso. "No te preocupes," le digo. "Estás bailando muy bien."

Aplicación

Write an ending for this story in one or two sentences. Compare your ending with that of a partner.

La profesora toca una rumba—¡un baile cubano!—y Roberto empieza a bailar bien. Todos lo miran con sorpresa. ¡Roberto y Susan ganan el disco compacto! Después, Susan dice algo y yo interpreto: "Está preguntando si quieres escuchar el disco compacto con ella después de la clase." Y de esta manera Roberto y Susan se hicieron novios. Él aprendió un poco de inglés y ella un poco de español, y los dos aprendieron a bailar.

Infórmate

1 It means "I interpret." First, it is a cognate, and second, we know from the story that Roberto doesn't know English. His friend helps him out when Susan asks if he wants to listen to the CD with her.

2 The word that makes sense is *expresar.*

3 Roberto and Susan became boyfriend and girlfriend. He learned a little English from her and learned to dance.

Aplicación
Story endings will vary.

Apply

Process Writing

For information regarding developing a writing portfolio, see p. 50.

Multicultural Perspectives

People celebrate festivals throughout the Spanish-speaking world. One important festival is *las fallas* in Valencia, Spain. *Las fallas* is a carnival held from March 12–19 that honors the patron saint of the carpenter, San José. In addition to bullfights, processions, and street vendors, there is a contest that consists of each neighborhood teaming up weeks before the start of the festival to build decorative, elaborately made statues of wood, cardboard, and papier-mâché. Each team bases its statue on a different current social or political theme. At the beginning of *las fallas,* each team exhibits its statue. Judges go from neighborhood to neighborhood to evaluate and select the best one. On the last night, *las fallas* culminates in the burning of the statues, all-night dancing, a tremendous fireworks show, and orchestras playing music. Ask students: What are some popular festivals or celebrations held in your community? What kinds of *fiestas* are popular in other cultures?

¡Vamos a escribir!

You have just been to a party or a prom *(un baile de graduación).* What do you want to remember about it? Write a diary entry about the party. Follow these steps.

1 First, think about the dance and answer these questions.

- ¿Dónde fue la fiesta? ¿A qué hora empezó? ¿A qué hora terminó?
- ¿Con quién fuiste?
- ¿Qué ropa llevaron?
- ¿Viste a muchos amigos en la fiesta? ¿A quiénes viste?
- ¿Qué comieron?
- ¿Qué tipo de música tocaron? ¿Bailaron?
- ¿Qué te gustó más: la música, la comida, las decoraciones?
- ¿Cómo lo pasaste?

2 Use the answers to these questions to write in your diary. You can start your entry with the words *Querido diario*.

3 Show your entry to a partner. Does he or she think you should add or change anything? Using your partner's recommendations and your own ideas, make the necessary changes and rewrite your entry.

4 Check carefully for accuracy in spelling, the use of written accents, the form and placement of adjectives, and the form of verbs. Rewrite if necessary.

5 Share your entry by

- including it in a collection of writings called *Las fiestas de este año*
- posting it on the bulletin board in your classroom
- adding it to your writing portfolio

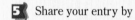

Estudiantes mexicanos en el Instituto Tecnológico en Nuevo Laredo

Options

Strategies for Reaching All Students

Students Needing Extra Help
Have students use their Organizers to help answer the questions.

Enrichment
Have students write about the same party from two opposite points of view. In each case, they can begin writing by telling who they are and describing their tastes or themselves in a way that would explain their viewpoint. For instance, what would a younger sibling have to say about the party? What would a snobby or envious guest say? What would a true friend say?

Una celebración en Montevideo, Uruguay

Cultural Notes

(pp. 472–473, photos)
Gatherings of friends and family members are an important part of life in Spanish-speaking countries. Close relationships provide not only companionship, but often emotional support during difficult times.

Assess & Summarize

Test Preparation
You may want to assign parts of this section as written homework or as an in-class writing activity prior to administering the *Examen de habilidades*.

Answers
Listening: *Voy a invitar a algunos amigos para el cumpleaños de Vanesa, la nueva estudiante en la clase de inglés. De ninguna manera debes llegar después de las siete y media. ¡Es una sorpresa! ¿Darle un regalo? Pues sí, pero nada elegante ni caro, por favor. Algo barato o hecho a mano.*
As a guest, you should not arrive after 7:30 because it's a surprise party. You shouldn't buy an elegant or expensive gift, either.

Reading: A costume party is described. The words or phrases that tell you this are *traje de disfraz* and *fiestas de ambiente informal*.

Writing: Letters will vary, but should include logical steps for planning a party.

¿Lo sabes bien?

This section will help you organize your studying for the proficiency test, where you will be asked to do similar, though not identical, tasks. There will not be any models on this test.

Listening
Can you understand when someone talks about a party he or she is planning to give? Listen as your teacher reads a sample similar to what you will hear on the test. As a guest invited to this party, what two things should you do and why?

Reading
Can you understand a written description of a party? Here's a written transcription from a radio announcer. What kind of party is described here? Which words or phrases tell you that?

> Todos lo están pasando bien y nadie está aburrido. La actriz Manuela lleva zapatos de tacón alto para su traje de disfraz y Kati Rojas lleva joyas y un vestido de fiesta. Está bailando con Enrique Salas, que nunca lleva corbata ni traje. ¡Me encantan las fiestas de ambiente informal!

Writing
Can you write a letter describing the arrangements you need to make for a special occasion? Here is a sample letter:

> Querida Susana:
>
> Me gustaría tener una fiesta para nuestra abuelita, una reunión con toda la familia. No me gusta preparar las fiestas grandes. Nunca lo hago. Pero mi mamá dice que tengo que hacerlo. Mi hermana puede ayudar con las decoraciones. (Ella está decorando su cuarto otra vez, pero suele hacerlo bien.) ¿Qué piensas? ¿Me puedes ayudar?
>
> Tu prima, Lina

Culture
Can you describe the way many girls in Spanish-speaking countries celebrate their fifteenth birthday?

Una muchacha celebrando sus quince años

Speaking
Can you and your partners play the roles of teenagers introducing one another at a party? Here is a sample dialogue:

A —*Laura, ¿conoces al novio de mi hermana?*
B —*No, no lo conozco.*
A —*Pues, Laura, te presento a Jaime Fernández.*
B —*Encantada, Jaime.*
C —*Mucho gusto, Laura.*

474 Capítulo 14

Options

Strategies for Reaching All Students

Students Needing Extra Help
Have students write out this section so that they can check off what they have mastered.

Resumen del capítulo 14

Use the vocabulary from this chapter to help you:

- make plans for giving or attending a party
- describe gift-giving
- make and acknowledge introductions

to talk about parties
el ambiente
bailar
el baile
cantar
las decoraciones *(pl.)*
escribir
la fecha
¡Feliz cumpleaños!
la fiesta
    de cumpleaños
    de disfraces
    de fin de año
    de la escuela
    de sorpresa
la hora
la invitación
el invitado, la invitada
invitar
el / la joven, *pl.* los /
    las jóvenes
el lugar
pasarlo bien / mal
preparar
la reunión

to introduce people
alguien
conocer: (yo) conozco
         (tú) conoces
Encantado, -a.
el novio, la novia
el pariente, la parienta
Te presento a ___.

**to talk about what to wear
to a party**
los aretes *(m.)*
el collar
la corbata
las joyas
la pulsera
el reloj pulsera
el traje
el vestido de fiesta
los zapatos de tacón alto

to talk about gift-giving
dar: (yo) doy
    (tú) das
escoger: (yo) escojo
      (tú) escoges
recibir
regalar
el regalo
    elegante
    hecho, -a a mano
    personal
    práctico, -a

**other useful terms and
expressions**
algunos, algunas
De ninguna manera.
Depende.
la entrada
soler (o → ue) + *inf.*

Culture: Answers will vary. Students may mention that a *quince años* party is usually given where family and friends attend. Instead of a formal party, some girls may ask for a special gift.

Speaking: Dialogues will vary.

 Prueba cumulativa

 Examen de habilidades

 Test Generator

Cultural Notes

(p. 474, photo)
Young girl with her parents at her *quinceañera* celebration, Novato, California. There are many similarities between *quinceañera* celebrations and weddings. For both events, announcements are usually made in the society pages, formal invitations are sent, a formal dress is required, and a mass is held, followed by a banquet with a fancy cake and a band.

Verbos

INFINITIVE	PRESENT		PRETERITE	

Regular Verbs

estudiar	estudio	estudiamos	estudié	estudiamos
	estudias	estudiáis	estudiaste	estudiasteis
	estudia	estudian	estudió	estudiaron
comer	como	comemos	comí	comimos
	comes	coméis	comiste	comisteis
	come	comen	comió	comieron
vivir	vivo	vivimos	viví	vivimos
	vives	vivís	viviste	vivisteis
	vive	viven	vivió	vivieron

Stem-changing Verbs

(You will learn the verb forms that are in italic type next year.)

cerrar (e → ie)	cierro	cerramos	cerré	cerramos
	cierras	cerráis	cerraste	cerrasteis
	cierra	cierran	cerró	cerraron
costar (o → ue)	cuesta	cuestan	costó	costaron
doler (o → ue)	duele	duelen	dolió	dolieron
dormir (o → ue)	duermo	dormimos	dormí	dormimos
	duermes	dormís	dormiste	dormisteis
	duerme	duermen	*durmió*	*durmieron*
empezar (e → ie)	See *cerrar.*		*empecé*	empezamos
			empezaste	empezasteis
			empezó	empezaron
jugar (u → ue)	juego	jugamos	jugué	jugamos
	juegas	jugáis	jugaste	jugasteis
	juega	juegan	jugó	jugaron
llover (o → ue)	llueve		llovió	
nevar (e → ie)	nieva		nevó	
pedir (e → i)	pido	pedimos	*pedí*	*pedimos*
	pides	pedís	*pediste*	*pedisteis*
	pide	piden	*pidió*	*pidieron*
pensar (e → ie)	See *cerrar.*			

INFINITIVE	PRESENT	PRETERITE	

poder (o → ue)   See *Irregular Verbs.*

preferir (e → ie)

prefiero	preferimos	*preferí*	*preferimos*
prefieres	preferís	*preferiste*	*preferisteis*
prefiere	prefieren	*prefirió*	*prefirieron*

probar (o → ue)

pruebo	probamos	probé	probamos
pruebas	probáis	probaste	probasteis
prueba	prueban	probó	probaron

querer (e → ie)   See *Irregular Verbs.*

servir (e → i)   See *pedir.*

soler (o → ue)

suelo	solemos
sueles	soléis
suele	suelen

Verbs with Spelling Changes

(You will learn the verb forms that are in italic type next year.)

apagar

apago	apagamos	apagué	apagamos
apagas	apagáis	apagaste	apagasteis
apaga	apagan	apagó	apagaron

buscar

busco	buscamos	busqué	buscamos
buscas	buscáis	buscaste	buscasteis
busca	buscan	buscó	buscaron

conocer

conozco	conocemos	conocí	conocimos
conoces	conocéis	conociste	conocisteis
conoce	conocen	conoció	conocieron

creer

creo	creemos	creí	creímos
crees	creéis	creíste	creísteis
cree	creen	*creyó*	*creyeron*

empezar   See *Stem-changing Verbs.*

escoger

escojo	escogemos	escogí	escogimos
escoges	escogéis	escogiste	escogisteis
escoge	escogen	escogió	escogieron

jugar   See *Stem-changing Verbs.*

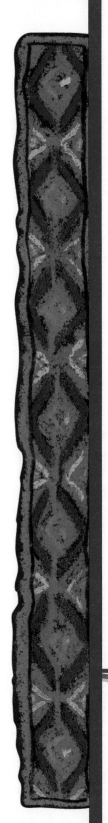

Verbos   477

leer	See *creer.*
llegar	See *apagar.*
pagar	See *apagar.*
practicar	See *buscar.*
proteger	See *escoger.*
reducir	See *conocer.*
sacar	See *buscar.*
tocar	See *buscar.*

Irregular Verbs

(You will learn the verb forms that are in italic type next year.)

Infinitive	Present		Preterite	
dar	doy	damos	*di*	*dimos*
	das	dais	*diste*	*disteis*
	da	dan	*dio*	*dieron*
decir	digo	decimos	*dije*	*dijimos*
	dices	decís	*dijiste*	*dijisteis*
	dice	dicen	*dijo*	*dijeron*
estar	estoy	estamos	*estuve*	*estuvimos*
	estás	estáis	*estuviste*	*estuvisteis*
	está	están	*estuvo*	*estuvieron*
hacer	hago	hacemos	hice	*hicimos*
	haces	hacéis	hiciste	*hicisteis*
	hace	hacen	hizo	*hicieron*
ir	voy	vamos	fui	fuimos
	vas	vais	fuiste	fuisteis
	va	van	fue	fueron
poder	puedo	podemos	*pude*	*pudimos*
	puedes	podéis	*pudiste*	*pudisteis*
	puede	pueden	*pudo*	*pudieron*
poner	pongo	ponemos	*puse*	*pusimos*
	pones	ponéis	*pusiste*	*pusisteis*
	pone	ponen	*puso*	*pusieron*

478 Verbos

INFINITIVE	PRESENT		PRETERITE	
querer	quiero	queremos	*quise*	*quisimos*
	quieres	queréis	*quisiste*	*quisisteis*
	quiere	quieren	*quiso*	*quisieron*
saber	sé	sabemos	*supe*	*supimos*
	sabes	sabéis	*supiste*	*supisteis*
	sabe	saben	*supo*	*supieron*
salir	salgo	salimos	salí	salimos
	sales	salís	saliste	salisteis
	sale	salen	salió	salieron
ser	soy	somos	*fui*	*fuimos*
	eres	sois	*fuiste*	*fuisteis*
	es	son	*fue*	*fueron*
tener	tengo	tenemos	*tuve*	*tuvimos*
	tienes	tenéis	*tuviste*	*tuvisteis*
	tiene	tienen	*tuvo*	*tuvieron*
traer	traigo	traemos	traje	trajimos
	traes	traéis	trajiste	trajisteis
	trae	traen	trajo	trajeron
ver	veo	vemos	vi	vimos
	ves	veis	viste	visteis
	ve	ven	vio	vieron

VOCABULARIO ESPAÑOL-INGLÉS

The *Vocabulario español-inglés* contains all active vocabulary from the text, including vocabulary presented in the grammar sections.

A dash (—) represents the main entry word. For example, **pasar la** — after **la aspiradora** means **pasar la aspiradora.**

The number following each entry indicates the chapter in which the word or expression is presented. The letter *P* following an entry refers to *El primer paso.*

The following abbreviations are used: *adj.* (adjective), *dir. obj.* (direct object), *f.* (feminine), *fam.* (familiar), *ind. obj.* (indirect object), *inf.* (infinitive), *m.* (masculine), *pl.* (plural), *prep.* (preposition), *pron.* (pronoun), *sing.* (singular).

a at (2); to (3)
  a la, al *(a + el)* to the (3)
el **abrigo** coat (7)
abril April (P)
abrir to open (10)
el **abuelo, la abuela** grandfather, grandmother (5)
los **abuelos** grandparents (5)
aburrido, -a boring (11)
aburrir to bore (11)
el **actor, la actriz** actor, actress (11)
acuerdo: estar de — to agree (8)
adiós good-by (P)
¿adónde? (to) where? (3)
agosto August (P)
el **agua** *f.* water (4)
el **aguacate** avocado (12)
ahora now (9)
el **aire** air (13)
algo something (4)
  — **más** something else (12)
alguien someone, somebody (14)
alguna vez ever (12)
algunos, -as some (14)
allí there (2)

  — **está** there it is (2)
el **almacén,** *pl.* los **almacenes** department store (6)
el **almuerzo** lunch (2)
  en el — for lunch (4)
alto, -a tall (5)
el **aluminio** aluminum (13)
amable kind, nice (1)
amarillo, -a yellow (6)
el **ambiente** atmosphere (14)
  el medio — environment (13)
la **amenaza** threat (13)
el **amigo, la amiga** friend (3)
anaranjado, -a orange *(color)* (6)
el **animal,** *pl.* **los animales** animal (13)
anoche last night (10)
los **anteojos (de sol)** (sun)glasses (7)
antiguo, -a old, traditional (8)
antipático, -a unfriendly, unpleasant (5)
el **anuncio (de televisión)** ad, commercial (11)
el **año** year (P)
  la fiesta de fin de —

  New Year's Eve party (14)
  tener . . . —s to be . . . years old (P, 5)
apagar to turn off (13)
el **apartamento** apartment (8)
aquí here (2)
  — **está** here it is (2)
  por — around here (6)
el **árbol** tree (13)
el **arete** earring (14)
arreglar to clean up (8)
el **arroz** rice (4)
el **arte** art (2)
artístico, -a artistic (1)
asco: ¡qué —! yuck! that's disgusting! (4)
así, así so-so, fair (P)
la **aspiradora** vacuum cleaner (3)
  pasar la — to vacuum (8)
atractivo, -a attractive (5)
atrevido, -a bold, daring (1)
el **autobús** *pl.* **los autobuses** bus (10)
  la parada del — bus stop (10)

la **avenida** avenue (10)
aventura: la película de —s adventure film (11)
¡ay! ouch! (9)
ayer yesterday (10)
ayudar to help (1)
el **azúcar** sugar (12)
azul, *pl.* **azules** blue (6)

bailar to dance (14)
el **baile** dance (14)
bajo, -a short *(height)* (5)
la **ballena** whale (13)
el **banco** bank (10)
el **baño** bathroom (8)
  el **traje de —** bathing suit (7)
barato, -a cheap, inexpensive (6)
básquetbol: jugar — to play basketball (3)
bastante rather (8)
la **basura** garbage (8)
beber to drink (4, 12)
la **bebida** beverage (4)
el **béisbol** baseball (3)
la **biblioteca** library (10)
la **bicicleta** bicycle (13)
  montar en — to ride a bike (13)
bien well (P)
el **bistec** steak (4)
blanco, -a white (6)
la **blusa** blouse (6)
la **boca** mouth (9)
el **bolígrafo** pen (P)
bonito, -a pretty (5)
la **bota** boot (7)
el **bote** rowboat (7)
  pasear en — to row (7)
la **botella** bottle (13)
el **brazo** arm (9)
el **bronceador** suntan lotion (7)
bucear to skin-dive (7)

bueno (buen), -a good (P)
bueno OK, fine, all right (10)
la **bufanda** winter scarf (7)
el **burrito** burrito (12)
buscar to look for (6)

el **caballo** horse (13)
la **cabeza** head (9)
  tener dolor de — to have a headache (9)
el **café** coffee (4)
el **calcetín,** *pl.* **los calcetines** sock (6)
la **calculadora** calculator (2)
callado, -a quiet (1)
la **calle** street (10)
calor:
  hace — it's hot (out) (7)
  tener — to be hot *(person)* (9)
la **cama** bed (8)
la **cámara** camera (7)
el **camarero, la camarera** waiter, waitress (12)
la **camisa** shirt (6)
la **camiseta** T-shirt (6)
el **campo** countryside (3)
el **canal** (TV) channel (11)
canoso: pelo — gray hair (5)
cansado, -a tired (3)
cantar to sing (14)
cariñoso, -a affectionate, loving (5)
la **carne (de res)** beef (12)
caro, -a expensive (6)
la **carpeta** pocket folder (2)
  la — de argollas three-ring binder (2)
la **carta** letter (10)
  a la — a la carte (12)
el **cartel** poster (8)
el **cartón** cardboard (13)
la **casa** house (8)

el **quehacer (de la —)** household chore (8)
en — at home (1)
la **especialidad de la —** house specialty (12)
casi almost (11)
castaño: pelo — brown (chestnut) hair (5)
las **cataratas** waterfall (7)
la **catedral** cathedral (7)
catorce fourteen (P)
la **cebolla** onion (4)
la **cena** dinner (4)
el **centro** center (13)
  el **— comercial** mall (3)
  el **— de reciclaje** recycling center (13)
cerca (de) near (8)
el **cereal** cereal (4)
cero zero (P)
cerrar (e → ie) to close (10)
el **césped** lawn (8)
el **champú** shampoo (10)
la **chaqueta** jacket (6)
el **chile** chili pepper (12)
  el **— con carne** beef with beans (12)
  el **— relleno** stuffed pepper (12)
el **chocolate** hot chocolate (12)
el **churro** churro (12)
cien one hundred (5)
la **ciencia ficción** science fiction (11)
las **ciencias** science (2)
  — de la salud health (science) (2)
  — sociales social studies (2)
ciento uno, -a; ciento dos; etc. 101, 102, etc. (6)
cinco five (P)
cincuenta fifty (2)
el **cine** movie theater (1)

ir al — to go to the movies (1)

la **ciudad** city (7)

claro:

¡**— que sí!** of course! (3)

¡**— que no!** of course not! (3)

la **clase (de)** class (2); kind, type (11)

después de las —s after school (3)

la sala de —s classroom (P)

la **clínica** clinic (9)

el **coche** car (8)

la **cocina** kitchen (8)

cocinar to cook (1)

el **collar** necklace (14)

el **color** color (6)

¿**de qué —?** what color? (6)

en —es in color (11)

la **comedia** comedy, sitcom (11)

el **comedor** dining room (8)

comer to eat (4, 12)

los **comestibles** groceries (10)

cómico comical (11)

la **comida** meal, food (4)

¿**cómo?** how? (10)

¿**— eres?** what are you like? (1)

¿**— está (usted)?** how are you? *formal* (P)

¿**— estás?** how are you? *fam.* (P)

¡**— no!** certainly! (12)

¿**— se dice . . . ?** how do you say . . . ? (P)

¿**— se llama(n)?** what is his/her/their name? (5)

¿**— te llamas?** what's your name? (P)

la **cómoda** dresser (8)

cómodo, -a comfortable (8)

el **compañero, la compañera**

classmate (P)

comprar to buy (6)

¿**me compras . . . ?** can you buy me . . . ? (10)

compras: ir de — to go shopping (3)

la **comunidad** community (10)

con with (3)

el **concierto** concert (11)

conmigo with me (3)

conocer to know (14)

conservar to conserve, save *(energy)* (13)

contaminado, -a contaminated, polluted (13)

contigo with you (3)

la **corbata** tie (14)

el **correo** post office (10)

cortar to cut, to mow (8)

corto, -a short *(length)* (11)

la **cosa** thing (8)

costar (o → ue) to cost (6)

creer to think, to believe (4, 9)

creo que no I don't think so (4)

creo que sí I think so (4)

el **cuaderno** spiral notebook (2)

la **cuadra** block (10)

cuadrado, -a square (8)

el **cuadro** picture (8)

¿**cuál(es)?** what? which? which one(s)? (11)

¿**cuándo?** when (P)

cuando when (7)

¿**cuánto?** how much? (6)

¿**— (tiempo) hace que . . . ?** how long has it been since . . . ? (9)

¿**cuántos, -as?** how many? (5)

¿**— años tiene . . . ?** how old is . . . ? (5)

¿**— años tienes?** how old are you? (P)

cuarenta forty (2)

cuarto, -a quarter (2); fourth (2, 8)

y — *(time)* quarter after, quarter past (2)

el **cuarto** room (8)

cuatro four (P)

cuatrocientos four hundred (10)

la **cuchara** spoon (12)

el **cuchillo** knife (12)

el **cuello** neck (9)

la **cuenta** bill *(in restaurant)* (12)

el **cuero** leather (8)

de — (made) of leather (8)

el **cuerpo** body (9)

el **cumpleaños** birthday (P)

¡**feliz —!** happy birthday! (14)

la fiesta de — birthday party (14)

la tarjeta de — birthday card (10)

dar to give (14)

— + *movie* or *TV program* to show (11)

— miedo a to scare (11)

de from (P); of **— 's, — s'** (5)

de la, del *(de + el)* of the, from the (10)

— la mañana / la tarde / la noche in the morning / afternoon / evening (11)

— + *material* made of (8)

— nada you're welcome (3)

— postre for dessert (12)

¿**— veras?** really? (1)

debajo de under(neath) (12)

deber ought to, should (4)

decir to say (13)

  ¿cómo se dice . . . ? how do you say . . . ? (P)

  ¡no me digas! really?, you don't say! (3)

  ¿qué quiere — . . . ? what does . . . mean? (P)

  se dice . . . it is said . . . (P)

la **decoración** *pl.* **las decoraciones** decoration (14)

el **dedo** finger (9)

  — del pie toe (9)

delante de in front of (12)

demasiado too (11)

el/la **dentista** dentist (9)

depende it depends (14)

los **deportes** sports (1)

deportista athletic (1)

deportivo: el programa — sports program (11)

depositar to deposit (10)

derecha: a la — (de) to the right (of) (10)

derecho, -a right (9)

el **desayuno** breakfast (4)

descansar to rest (7)

el **descuento: la tienda de —s** discount store (6)

desear: ¿qué desea Ud? may I help you? (6)

desordenado, -a messy (1)

después de after (3)

detective: el programa de —s detective show (11)

detrás (de) behind (10)

devolver (o → ue) to return *(something)* (10)

el **día** day (P)

  buenos —s good morning (P)

  el plato del — daily special (12)

  ¿qué — es hoy? what day is it? (P)

  todos los —s every day (3)

dibujar to draw (1)

el **dibujo: los —s animados** cartoons (11)

el **diccionario** dictionary (2)

dice: ¿cómo se — . . . ? how do you say . . . ? (P)

diciembre December (P)

diecinueve nineteen (P)

dieciocho eighteen (P)

dieciséis sixteen (P)

diecisiete seventeen (P)

diez ten (P)

difícil difficult, hard (2)

digas: ¡no me —! really?, you don't say! (3)

el **dinero** money (10)

disfraces: la fiesta de — costume party (14)

la **diversión: el parque de diversiones** amusement park (3)

divertido, -a amusing, funny (11)

doce twelve (P)

el **documental** documentary (11)

el **dólar** dollar (6)

doler (o → ue) to hurt, to ache (9)

dolor: tener — de . . . to have a . . . ache (9) *see also* **cabeza, estómago, garganta, muelas, oído**

domingo Sunday (P)

  el — on Sunday (3)

¿dónde? where? (3)

  ¿de — eres? where are you from? (P)

dormir (o → ue) to sleep (9)

el **dormitorio** bedroom (8)

dos two (P)

doscientos two hundred (10)

durar to last (11)

educativo: el programa — educational show (11)

ejercicio: hacer — to exercise (9)

el **the** *m. sing.* (P, 2) **—** *number* + de + *month* (P)

él he (2); him *after prep.* (3)

el **elefante** elephant (13)

elegante elegant (14)

ella she (2); her *after prep.* (3)

ellos, ellas they (2); them *after prep.* (3)

emocionante exciting, funny (11)

empezar (e → ie) to begin, to start (2)

en in, at, on (P) **—** + *vehicle* by (10)

encantado, -a delighted (14)

encantar to love (5)

  le encanta(n) he/she loves (5)

  me encanta(n) I love (4)

la **enchilada** enchilada (12)

encima (de) on, on top of (12)

la **energía** energy (13)

enero January (P)

la **enfermería** nurse's office (9)

enfermo, -a ill, sick (3)

enfrente (de) facing, opposite, in front of (10)

la **ensalada** salad (4)

enseñar to teach (2)

entre between (10)

entrevista: el programa de —s talk show (11)
enviar to send, to mail (10)
el **equipo de sonido** stereo (8)
eres you *fam.* are (1)
es it is (P); he/she is (2)
escoger to choose (14)
escribir to write (14)
  ¿cómo se escribe . . . ? how do you spell . . . ? (P)
el **escritorio** desk (8)
escuchar to listen to (1)
la **escuela** school (1)
ese, -a; -os, -as that; those (6)
eso: por — that's why, therefore (11)
la **espalda** back (9)
el **español** Spanish *(language)* (2)
la **especialidad de la casa** house specialty (12)
el **espejo** mirror (8)
esquiar to ski (7)
la **esquina** corner (10)
la **estación,** *pl.* las **estaciones** season (3); station (10)
el **estadio** stadium (10)
estar to be (3)
  ¿cómo estás? how are you? (P)
  la **sala de —** family room (8)
este, -a; -os, -as this; these (6)
el **estómago** stomach (9)
  tener dolor de — to have a stomachache (9)
el/la **estudiante** student (P)
estudiar to study (1)
la **estufa** stove (8)
explorar to explore (7)
extinción: en peligro de — endangered (13)

la **fábrica** factory (13)
fácil easy (2)
la **falda** skirt (6)
faltar to be lacking, to be missing (12)
la **familia** family (3)
fantástico, -a fantastic (7)
la **farmacia** drugstore (10)
fascinante fascinating (11)
fascinar to fascinate (11)
febrero February (P)
la **fecha** date (P)
¡feliz cumpleaños! happy birthday! (14)
feo, -a ugly (5)
la **fiebre** fever (9)
  tener — to have a fever (9)
la **fiesta** party (3)
  el vestido de — party dress (14)
el **fin:**
  el — de semana the weekend (3)
  la fiesta de — de año New Year's Eve party (14)
físico, -a: la educación — a physical education (2)
el **flan** flan (12)
la **flor** flower (13)
formar: — parte de to be a part of (13)
la **foto** photo (7)
  sacar —s to take pictures (7)
fresco: hace — it's cool outside (7)
el **frijol** bean (12)
  los —es refritos refried beans (12)
frío:
  hace — it's cold outside (7)
  tener — to be cold *(person)* (9)
la **fruta** fruit (4)

fui, fuiste I went, you went (7)
el **fútbol** soccer (3)
  el — americano football (3)

la **ganga** bargain (6)
el **garaje** garage (8)
la **garganta** throat (9)
  las pastillas para la — throat lozenges (10)
  tener dolor de — to have a sore throat (9)
el **gato** cat (5)
el **gemelo, la gemela** twin (5)
generalmente usually, generally (3)
generoso, -a generous (1)
¡genial! great! wonderful! (3)
la **gente** people (13)
el **gimnasio** gymnasium (3)
el **gorila** gorilla (13)
el **gorro** ski cap (7)
la **grabadora** tape recorder (2)
gracias thank you (P)
gracioso, -a funny (1)
grande big (5)
la **gripe** flu (9)
  tener — to have the flu (9)
gris *pl.* **grises** gray (6)
el **guacamole** avocado dip (12)
el **guante** glove (7)
guapo, -a handsome, good-looking (5)
el **guardarropa** closet (8)
la **guía telefónica** phone book (13)
el **guisante** pea (4)
la **guitarra** guitar (1)
gustar to like (1)
  le gusta(n) he/she

likes (5)

me, te gusta I like, you like (1)

me gusta más I prefer (1)

(A mí) me gustaría I'd like . . . (3)

¿(A ti) te gustaría? would you like . . .? (3)

hablar to talk (1)
— **por teléfono** to talk on the phone (1)
hablando talking (14)
hacer to do, to make (8)
hace + *(time)* . . . ago (6)
hace + *(time)* **+ que** it's been *(time)* since (9)
— **ejercicio** to exercise (9)
se hace(n) con . . . it's (they're) made with . . . (12)
hice/hiciste/hizo did/made (10, 13) *see also* **calor, fresco, frío, sol, tiempo, viento**
hambre: tener — to be hungry (4)

la **hamburguesa** hamburger (4)

la **harina** flour (12)
la tortilla de — flour tortilla (12)
hasta until (11)
— **luego** see you later (P)
hay there is, there are (P)
¿cuántos(as) . . . —? how many . . . are there? (P)
— **que** it's necessary to (13)
hecho, -a made (14)
— **a mano** handmade (14)

el **hecho** fact (11)
helado: el té — iced tea (4)

el **helado** ice cream (12)

el **hermano, la hermana** brother, sister (5)

los **hermanos** brothers; brother(s) and sister(s) (5)

el **hijo, la hija** son, daughter (5)

los **hijos** sons; sons and daughters (5)

la **hoja de papel** sheet of paper (P)
¡hola! hi!, hello! (P)

el **hombre** man (5)

la **hora** period (2); time (2, 14)
¿a qué —? at what time? (2)
¿qué — es? what time is it? (2)

el **horario** schedule (2)
horrible horrible (4)

el **hospital** hospital (9)

el **hotel** hotel (10)
hoy today (P)
— **no** not today (3)

el **huevo** egg (4)

la **iglesia** church (10)
igualmente likewise (P)
impaciente impatient (1)

el **impermeable** raincoat (7)
incómodo, -a uncomfortable (8)

el **inglés** English *(language)* (2)

el **ingrediente** ingredient (12)
inteligente intelligent (5)

el **interés: el lugar de —** place of interest (7)
interesante interesting (11)
interesar to interest (11)

el **invierno** winter (3)

la **invitación** *pl.* **las**

invitaciones invitation (14)

el **invitado, la invitada** guest (14)
invitar to invite (14)
ir to go (3)
— **a +** *inf.* to be going to + *verb* (3)
— **a la escuela** to go to school (1)
— **a pasear** to take a walk (10)
— **de compras** to go shopping (3)
— **de pesca** to go fishing (3)
izquierda: a la — (de) to the left of (10)
izquierdo, -a left (9)

el **jabón** soap (10)

el **jaguar** jaguar (13)

el **jamón** ham (4)

los **jeans** jeans (6)
joven *adj.* young (5)

el **joven** young man, sir (6)

la **joven** young lady (6)

los **jóvenes** young people (14)

las **joyas** jewelry (14)

las **judías verdes** green beans (4)
jueves Thursday (P)
el — on Thursday (3)
jugar (u → ue) to play (3)

el **jugo** juice (4)
— **de naranja** orange juice (4)
julio July (P)
junio June (P)

la **the** *f. sing.* (P, 2); her, it, you *dir. obj. pron.* (6)
lado: al — de next to,

beside (10)

el **lago** lake (7)

la **lámpara** lamp (8)

el **lápiz,** *pl.* **los lápices** pencil (2)

largo, -a long (11)

las the *f. pl.* (2); them, you *dir. obj. pron.* (6)

lástima: ¡qué —! that's too bad! what a shame! (3)

lastimar to hurt (9)

la **lata** can (13)

el **lavadero** laundry room (8)

lavar to wash (8)

le (to) him, her, it, you *ind. obj. pron.* (9)

la **leche** milk (4)

la **lechuga** lettuce (4)

leer to read (1)

lejos (de) far (from) (8)

les (to) them *ind. obj.* (11)

la **librería** bookstore (10)

el **libro** book (P)

la **limonada** lemonade (4)

limpiar to clean (8)

limpio, -a clean (8)

llamar to call (9)

¿cómo se llama(n)? what is his /her /their name? (5)

¿cómo te llamas? what's your name? (P)

me llamo my name is (P)

se llama(n) his / her /their name is (5)

llegar to arrive (10)

llevar to wear (6); to take, to carry along (7)

llover: llueve it rains, it's raining (7)

la **lluvia** rain (7)

lo him, it, you *dir. obj. pron.* (6)

— siento I'm sorry (2)

el **lobo** wolf (13)

los the *m. pl.* (P, 4); them *dir. obj. pron.* (6)

— + *day of week* on + *day of week* (3)

luego then, if (10)

el **lugar** place (14)

— de interés place of interest (7)

lunes Monday (P)

el — on Monday (3)

la **luz,** *pl.* **las luces** light (13)

la **madera** wood (13)

de — (made of) wood (8)

la **madre** mother (5)

el **maíz** corn (12)

mal:

menos — que . . . it's a good thing that . . . (7)

me siento — I feel ill (9)

la **maleta** suitcase (7)

malo, -a bad (4)

manera: de ninguna — not at all (14)

la **mano** *f.* hand (9)

hecho, -a a — handmade (14)

el **mantel** tablecloth (12)

la **mantequilla** butter (12)

la **manzana** apple (4)

mañana tomorrow (P, 3)

la **mañana** morning (3)

por la — in the morning (3)

el **mar** sea (7)

el **marcador** marker (2)

marrón, *pl.* **marrones** brown (5, 6)

martes Tuesday (P)

el — on Tuesday (3)

marzo March (P)

más else (8, 12) more, *adj.* + -er (11)

el / la / los / las — + *adj.* the most + *adj.,* the + *adj.* + -est (11)

— o menos more or

less (4)

— tarde later (11)

— temprano earlier (11)

las **matemáticas** mathematics (2)

mayo May (P)

mayor older (5); bigger (11)

el — peligro greatest danger (13)

me me *obj. pron.* (9)

media:

— hora *f.* half an hour (11)

una hora y — an hour and a half (11)

y — half-past (2)

la **medianoche** midnight (11)

el **médico, la médica** doctor (9)

el **medio ambiente** environment (13)

el **mediodía** noon (11)

mejor better (9)

el / la (los / las) — (es) the best (11)

menor *pl.,* **menores** younger (5); smaller (11)

menos less (4, 11)

el / la / los / las — + *adj.* the least + *adj.* (11)

más o — more or less (4)

— mal que . . . it's a good thing that . . . (7)

el **menú** menu (12)

menudo: a — often (12)

la **merienda** afternoon snack (12)

de — for a snack (12)

el **mes** month (P)

la **mesa** table (P)

metal: de — (made of) metal (8)

el **metro** subway (10)

mi, mis my (3)

mí me *after prep.* (12)

miércoles Wednesday (P)

el — on Wednesday (3)

mil one thousand (10)

el **minuto** minute (11)

mismo: lo — the same thing (12)

la **mochila** backpack (2)

moderno, -a modern (8)

la **montaña** mountain (7)

montar en bicicleta to ride a bike (13)

el **monumento** monument (10)

morado, -a purple (6)

el **muchacho, la muchacha** boy, girl (5)

mucho, -a a lot of, much (2)

muchas veces many times (12)

— gusto pleased / nice to meet you (P)

los **muebles** furniture (8)

las **muelas: tener dolor de —** to have a toothache (9)

la **mujer** woman (5)

el **museo** museum (7)

la **música** music (2)

musical musical (11)

el programa — music program (11)

muy very (1)

nada nothing (9)

de — you're welcome (3)

no me duele — nothing hurts (9)

no me gusta — . . . I don't like . . . at all (1)

nadar to swim (1)

nadie nobody (5)

la **naranja** orange (4)

la **nariz** nose (9)

necesitar to need (2)

negro, -a black (6)

en blanco y — in black and white (11)

nevar: nieva it snows, it's snowing (7)

ni . . . ni neither . . . nor, not . . . or (1)

la **nieve** snow (7)

ninguna parte nowhere, not anywhere (7)

no no, not (P)

creo que — I don't think so (4)

¿no? don't you?, aren't I . . . ? (9)

la **noche** evening (P)

buenas — s good evening, good night (P)

de la — at night (11)

por la — in the evening (3)

el **nombre** name (5)

nos us *obj. pron.* (11)

nosotros, -as we (2); us *after prep.* (3)

las **noticias** news (11)

novecientos nine hundred (10)

noventa ninety (5)

noviembre November (P)

el **novio, la novia** boyfriend, girlfriend (14)

nuestro, -a our (8)

nueve nine (P)

nuevo, -a new (6)

el **número** number (P)

nunca never (4)

o or (P)

el **océano** ocean (13)

ochenta eighty (5)

ocho eight (P)

ochocientos eight hundred (10)

octavo, -a eighth (2)

octubre October (P)

ocupado, -a busy (3)

el **oeste: la película del —** western (11)

el **oído** ear (9)

tener dolor de — to have an earache (9)

el **ojo** eye (9)

once eleven (P)

ordenado, -a neat, tidy (1)

el **oso** bear (13)

el **otoño** fall, autumn (3)

otro, -a another, other (6)

paciente patient *adj.* (1)

el **padre** father (5)

los **padres** parents (5)

pagar to pay (6)

el **país** country (7)

el **pájaro** bird (13)

el **pan** bread (4)

el — tostado toast (4)

los **pantalones** pants (6)

las **pantimedias** pantyhose (6)

la **papa** potato (4)

la — al horno baked potato (4)

la — frita French fry (4)

el **papel** paper (P)

la hoja de — sheet of paper (P)

para for (2)

— + *inf.* to, in order to (7)

la **parada del autobús** bus stop (10)

el **paraguas** umbrella (7)

el **pariente, la parienta** relative (14)

el **parque** park (3)

el — de diversiones amusement park (3)

el **partido** game, match (10)

pasado, -a last, past (7)

el **pasaporte** passport (7)
pasar to pass (12)
— **la aspiradora** to vacuum (8)
—**lo bien (mal)** to have a good (bad) time (14)
¿qué pasa? what's the matter? (9)
el **pasatiempo** pastime, hobby (3)
pasear:
ir a — to take a walk (10)
— **en bote** to row (7)
la **pasta dentífrica** toothpaste (10)
el **pastel** cake, pastry (12)
la **pastilla** tablet, lozenge (10)
patinar to skate (1)
pedir (e → i) to order, to ask for (12)
la **película** film, movie (11)
el **peligro** danger (13)
en — de extinción endangered (13)
pelirrojo, -a red-haired (5)
el **pelo** hair (5)
pensar (e → ie) to think (11)
— + inf. to plan (7)
peor worse (9)
el / la (los / las) —(es) the worst (11)
pequeño, -a small, little (5)
perdón excuse me (6)
perezoso, -a lazy (1)
el **periódico** newspaper (13)
pero but (1)
el **perro** dog (5)
la **persona** person (5)
personal personal (14)
pesca: ir de — to go fishing (3)
el **pescado** fish (4)
picante spicy, peppery, hot *(flavor)* (12)
no — mild *(flavor)* (12)
el **pie** foot (9)

a — walking, on foot (10)
el dedo del — toe (9)
la **piel** fur (13)
la **pierna** leg (9)
la **pimienta** pepper (12)
la **pirámide** pyramid (7)
la **piscina** pool (3)
el **piso** story, floor (8)
la **pizarra** chalkboard (P)
la **planta** plant (13)
el **plástico** plastic (13)
de — (made of) plastic (13)
el **plátano** banana (4)
el **platillo** saucer (12)
el **plato** dish, plate (12)
el — del día daily special (12)
los —s principales main dishes (12)
la **playa** beach (3)
la **plaza** town square (10)
poco: un — (de) a little (11)
poder (o → ue) can, to be able to (3, 7)
la **policía** police (10)
el **pollo** chicken (4)
poner to put, to place, to set (8)
— **la mesa** to set the table (8)
por for (6)
— **aquí** around here (6)
— **eso** that's why, therefore (11)
— **la mañana / la tarde / la noche** in the morning / afternoon / evening (3)
¿— qué? why? (4)
— **supuesto** of course (13)
porque because (4)
el **postre** dessert (12)
de — for dessert (12)
practicar to practice (1)

práctico, -a practical (14)
preferir (e → ie) to prefer (4, 8)
preparar to prepare (14)
presentar to introduce (14)
te presento a . . . I'd like you to meet . . . (14)
la **primavera** spring (3)
primero (primer), -a first (P, 2, 8)
el **primo, la prima** cousin (5)
probar (o → ue) to try, to taste (12)
el **profesor, la profesora** teacher (P)
el **programa** program, show (11)
el **pronóstico del tiempo** weather forecast (11)
proteger to protect (13)
prudente cautious (1)
puedo, puedes *see* **poder**
la **puerta** door (8)
pues well *(to indicate pause)* (1)
la **pulsera** bracelet (14)
el reloj — wristwatch (14)
punto: en — sharp, on the dot (11)
puntualmente on time (11)
el **pupitre** student desk (P)
puro, -a pure, clean (13)

que that, who (5)
qué what (2)
¡— + *adj.*! how + *adj.*! (6)
¿— tal? how's it going? (P)
quedar to fit (6); to be located (10)
me queda(n) bien it fits (they fit) me well (6)
—**se (en la cama)** to stay (in bed) (9)

el **quehacer (de la casa)**
    household chore (8)
querer (e → ie) to
    want (3, 7)
    ¿qué quiere decir ...?
        what does ... mean? (P)
    (yo) quisiera I'd like (7)
la **quesadilla** quesadilla (12)
el **queso** cheese (4)
¿quién(es)? who? whom?
    (2)
quince fifteen (P)
quinientos five hundred
    (10)
quinto, -a fifth (2)
quisiera *see* **querer**
quitar la mesa to clear the
    table (8)

razón: (no) tener — to be
    right (wrong) (8)
real real (11)
realista realistic (11)
recibir to receive (14)
el **reciclaje: el centro de —**
    recycling center (13)
reciclar to recycle (13)
recoger to pick up (13)
el **recuerdo** souvenir (7)
redondo, -a round (8)
reducir to reduce (13)
el **refresco** soft drink (4)
el **refrigerador** refrigerator
    (8)
regalar to give (a gift) (14)
el **regalo** gift (10)
    la tienda de —s gift
        shop (10)
la **regla** ruler (2)
regresar to come back, to
    return (7)
regular so-so, fair (P)
el **reloj pulsera** wristwatch
    (14)
el **resfriado** cold (9)

el **restaurante** restaurant (10)
la **reunión,** *pl.* **las reuniones**
    get-together (14)
la **revista** magazine (13)
rojo, -a red (6)
romántico, -a romantic
    (11)
la **ropa** clothes (6)
rosado, -a pink (6)
rubio, -a blonde (5)
las **ruinas** ruins (7)

sábado Saturday (P)
    el — on Saturday (3)
saber to know (13)
    (yo) no sabía I didn't
        know (10)
sabroso, -a delicious, tasty
    (4)
sacar to take out (8)
    — dinero to withdraw
        money (10)
    — fotos to take pictures
        (7)
    — un libro to check out
        a book (10)
sacudir to dust (8)
la **sal** salt (12)
la **sala** living room (8)
    la — de clases
        classroom (P)
    la — de estar family
        room (8)
salir to leave (7)
la **salsa** sauce (12)
la **salud** health (4)
el **sandwich** sandwich (4)
sed: tener — to be thirsty
    (4)
seguida: en — right away
    (12)
segundo, -a second (2, 8)
seis six (P)
seiscientos six hundred
    (10)

el **sello** stamp (10)
la **selva** forest (7)
    la — tropical rain
        forest (7)
la **semana** week (P)
    el fin de — on the
        weekend (3)
el **semestre** semester (2)
sentir:
    ¿cómo te sientes? how
        do you feel? (9)
    lo siento I'm sorry (2)
    me siento bien / mal I
        feel well / ill (9)
señor Mr. (P); sir (6)
señora Mrs. (P); ma'am (6)
señorita Miss (P); miss (6)
separar to separate, to sort
    (13)
septiembre September (P)
séptimo, -a seventh (2)
ser to be (5)
serio, -a serious (1)
la **serpiente** snake (13)
el **servicio: la estación de**
    — gas station (10)
la **servilleta** napkin (12)
servir (e → i) to serve (12)
sesenta sixty (5)
setecientos seven hundred
    (10)
setenta seventy (5)
sexto, -a sixth (2)
si if, whether (10)
sí yes (P); do *(emphatic)*
    (1)
siempre always (4)
siento, sientes *see* **sentir**
siete seven (P)
la **silla** chair (8)
el **sillón,** *pl.* **los sillones**
    armchair (8)
simpático, -a nice, friendly
    (5)
sobre about (11); on (12)
sociable outgoing (1)
el **sofá** *m.* sofa (8)

el sol sun (7)

    los anteojos de — sunglasses (7)

    hace — it's sunny (7)

    tomar el — to sunbathe (7)

soler (o → ue) + *inf.* to be in the habit of (14)

solo, -a alone (3)

sólo only (5)

son (they) are (4)

    — las it is ... *(in telling time)* (2)

sonido: el equipo de — stereo (8)

la sopa soup (4)

la sorpresa: la fiesta de — surprise party (14)

el sótano basement (8)

soy I am (1)

su, sus his, her (5); your *formal* their (8)

subir to climb (7)

sucio, -a dirty (8)

la sudadera sweatshirt (6)

sueño: tener — to be sleepy (9)

el suéter sweater (6)

el supermercado supermarket (10)

supuesto: por — of course (13)

tacaño, -a stingy (1)

el taco taco (12)

tal: ¿qué —? how's it going? (P)

también also, too (1)

    a mí — me too (1)

tampoco either (1)

tarde late (10)

la tarde afternoon (P)

    buenas —s good afternoon, good evening (P)

    por la — in the afternoon (3)

la tarea homework (2)

la tarjeta card (10)

    la — postal post card (10)

el taxi taxi (10)

la taza cup (12)

el tazón, *pl.* **los tazones** bowl (12)

te you *fam. obj. pron.* (9)

el té tea (4)

    el — helado iced tea (4)

el teatro theater (10)

el teléfono telephone (1)

    hablar por — to talk on the telephone (1)

    el número de — phone number (P)

la telenovela soap opera (11)

la tele(visión) television (1)

    ver la — to watch television (1)

el templo temple (10)

temprano early (10)

el tenedor fork (12)

tener to have (2, 5)

    ¿qué tienes? what's wrong? (9)

    — que + *inf.* to have to (8) *see also* **año, calor, dolor, fiebre, frío, gripe, hambre, sed, sueño**

el tenis tennis (3)

los tenis sneakers (6)

tercer, tercera third (8)

terminar to end (2)

terrible terrible (9)

terror: la película de — horror film (11)

ti you *fam. after prep.* (12)

el tiempo weather (7); time (11)

    hace buen, mal — the weather is nice, bad (7)

    el pronóstico del — weather forecast (11)

    ¿qué — hace? what's the weather like? (7)

la tienda store (6)

    la — de ropa clothing store (6)

la Tierra Earth (13)

el tigre tiger (13)

el tío, la tía uncle, aunt (5)

    los tíos uncles; aunts and uncles (5)

típico, -a typical (12)

tocar to play (1)

todavía still (9)

    — no not yet (11)

todos, -as all; everyone (5)

    — los días every day (3)

tomar to take (9)

    — el sol to sunbathe (7)

el tomate tomato (4)

tonto, -a silly, dumb (11)

la tortilla (de harina, de maíz) (flour, corn) tortilla (12)

tostado: el pan — toast (4)

trabajador, -a hard-working (1)

trabajar to work (10)

traer to bring (12)

el traje suit (14)

    el — de baño bathing suit (7)

el transporte público public transportation (13)

trece thirteen (P)

treinta thirty (P, 2)

el tren train (10)

    la estación del — train station (10)

tres three (P)

trescientos three hundred (10)

triste sad (11)

tu, tus your *fam.* (2, 3)

tú you *fam.* (2)

un, una a, an, one (P, 2)
  es la una it's one o'clock (2)
único, -a only (5)
unos, -as a few, some (4)
usar to use (13)
usted (Ud.) you *formal sing.* (2)
ustedes (Uds.) you *formal pl.* (2)
la **uva** grape (4)

la **vaca** cow (13)
las **vacaciones** vacation (7)
  ir de — to go on vacation (7)
  valer: (no) vale la pena it's (not) worthwhile (13)
el **vaso** glass (12)
  ¡vaya! my goodness! gee! wow! (7)
veinte twenty (P)
veintiuno (veintiún) twenty-one (P)
vender to sell (12)
la **ventana** window (8)
  ver to see, to watch (1)
    a — let's see (2)

el **verano** summer (3)
  veras: ¿de — ? really? (1)
  ¿verdad? isn't that so?, right? (4)
verde green (6)
las **verduras** vegetables (4)
  sopa de — vegetable soup (4)
el **vestido** dress (6)
  el — de fiesta party dress (14)
  vez, *pl.* **veces:**
    a la — at the same time (13)
    alguna — ever (12)
    a veces at times, sometimes (1)
    dos veces two times (twice) (12)
    muchas veces many times (12)
    una — one time (once) (12)
  vi, viste *see* **ver**
la **vida** life
  el programa de hechos de la — real fact-based program (11)
la **videocasetera** VCR (8)

el **videojuego** video game (3)
el **vidrio** glass *(material)* (13)
  de — (made of) glass (13)
viejo, -a old (5)
el **viento** wind (7)
  hace — it's windy (7)
viernes Friday (P)
  el — on Friday (3)
visitar to visit (7)
vivir to live (8)
el **vóleibol** volleyball (3)
  vosotros(as) you *pl.* (2)

y and (1)
ya already (10)
  — no no longer, not anymore (9)
yo I (2)

la **zanahoria** carrot (4)
la **zapatería** shoe store (6)
el **zapato** shoe (6)
  los —s de tacón alto high-heeled shoes (14)
el **zoológico** zoo (10)

ENGLISH-SPANISH VOCABULARY

The *English-Spanish Vocabulary* contains all active vocabulary from the text, including vocabulary presented in the grammar sections.

A dash (—) represents the main entry word. For example, — **party** following **birthday** means **birthday party.**

The number following each entry indicates the chapter in which the word or expression is presented. The letter *P* following an entry refers to the *El primer paso.*

The following abbreviations are used: *adj.* (adjective), *dir. obj.* (direct object), *f.* (feminine), *fam.* (familiar), *ind. obj.* (indirect object), *inf.* (infinitive), *m.* (masculine), *pl.* (plural), *prep.* (preposition), *pron.* (pronoun), *sing.* (singular).

a, an un, una (2)
able: to be — poder
  (o → ue) (3, 7)
about sobre (11)
ache el dolor (9)
actor, actress el actor, la
  actriz (11)
ad el anuncio (de televisión)
  (11)
adventure film la película de
  aventuras (11)
affectionate cariñoso, -a (5)
after después (de) (3)
  — **school** después de las
  clases (3)
afternoon la tarde (P)
  — **snack** la merienda (12)
  good — buenas tardes (P)
  in the — por la tarde (3)
ago hace + *(time)* . . . (6)
to **agree** estar de acuerdo (8)
air el aire (13)
all todo, -a (5)
  — **right** bueno (10)
almost casi (11)
alone solo, -a (3)
already ya (10)
also también (1)
aluminum el aluminio (13)
always siempre (4)

amusement park el parque
  de diversiones (3)
amusing divertido, -a (11)
and y (1)
animal el animal, *pl.* los
  animales (13)
another otro, -a (6)
anywhere: not — ninguna
  parte (7)
apartment el apartamento
  (8)
apple la manzana (4)
April abril (P)
arm el brazo (9)
armchair el sillón, *pl.* los
  sillones (8)
around here por aquí (6)
to **arrive** llegar (10)
art el arte (2)
artistic artístico, -a (1)
to **ask for** pedir (e → i) (12)
at en (P); a (2)
athletic deportista (1)
atmosphere el ambiente (14)
attractive atractivo, -a (5)
August agosto (P)
aunt la tía (5)
  —**s and uncles** los tíos (5)
autumn el otoño (3)
avenue la avenida (10)

avocado el aguacate (12)
  — **dip** el guacamole (12)

back la espalda (9)
backpack la mochila (2)
banana el plátano (4)
bank el banco (10)
bargain la ganga (6)
baseball el béisbol (3)
basement el sótano (8)
basketball el básquetbol (3)
bathing suit el traje de baño
  (7)
bathroom el baño (8)
to **be** estar (3); ser (5)
  — **from** ser de (P)
  to — **able to** poder
  (o → ue) (7)
beach la playa (3)
beans los frijoles (12)
  green — las judías verdes
  (4)
  refried —**s** los frijoles
  refritos (12)
bear el oso (13)
because porque (4)
bed la cama (8)
bedroom el dormitorio (8)

beef la carne (de res) (12)

to **begin** empezar (e → ie) (2)

behind detrás (de) (10)

to **believe** creer (4)

beside al lado (de) (10)

best el / la mejor (11)

better mejor (9)

between entre (10)

beverage la bebida (4)

bicycle la bicicleta (13)

   to ride a — montar en bicicleta (13)

big grande (5)

bigger mayor (11)

bill (*in restaurant*) la cuenta (12)

binder (3-ring) la carpeta de argollas (2)

bird el pájaro (13)

birthday el cumpleaños (P)

   — card la tarjeta de cumpleaños (10)

   — party la fiesta de cumpleaños (4)

   happy —! ¡feliz cumpleaños! (14)

black negro, -a (6)

   in — and white en blanco y negro (11)

block la cuadra (10)

   how many —s (from . . .)? ¿a cuántas cuadras (de . . .)? (10)

blond rubio, -a (5)

blouse la blusa (6)

blue azul, *pl.* azules (6)

body el cuerpo (9)

bold atrevido, -a (1)

book el libro (P)

bookstore la librería (10)

boot la bota (7)

to **bore** aburrir (11)

boring aburrido, -a (11)

bottle la botella (13)

bowl el tazón, *pl.* los tazones (12)

boy el muchacho (5)

boyfriend el novio (14)

bracelet la pulsera (14)

bread el pan (4)

breakfast el desayuno (4)

   for — en el desayuno (4)

to **bring** traer (12)

brother el hermano (5)

   —(s) and sister(s) los hermanos (5)

brown marrón, *pl.* marrones (6); *(hair)* castaño (5)

burrito el burrito (12)

bus el autobús, *pl.* los autobuses (10)

   — stop la parada del autobús (10)

busy ocupado, -a (3)

but pero (1)

butter la mantequilla (12)

to **buy** comprar (6)

by por (6)

   — + *vehicle* en + *vehicle* (10)

calculator la calculadora (2)

to **call** llamar (9)

camera la cámara (7)

can poder (o → ue) (7); la lata (13)

cap el gorro (7)

car el coche (8)

card la tarjeta (10)

cardboard el cartón (13)

carrot la zanahoria (4)

carte: a la — a la carta (12)

cartoons los dibujos animados (11)

cat el gato (5)

cathedral la catedral (7)

cautious prudente (1)

center:

   recycling — el centro de reciclaje (13)

   shopping — el centro comercial (3)

cereal el cereal (4)

chair la silla (8)

chalkboard la pizarra (P)

channel el canal (11)

cheap barato, -a (6)

to **check out a book** sacar un libro (10)

cheese el queso (4)

chestnut(-colored) castaño, -a (5)

chicken el pollo (4)

   — soup la sopa de pollo (4)

chili pepper el chile (12)

chocolate: hot — el chocolate (12)

to **choose** escoger (14)

chore: household — el quehacer (de la casa) (8)

church la iglesia (10)

churro el churro (12)

city la ciudad (7)

class la clase (de) (2, 11)

classmate el compañero, la compañera (P)

classroom la sala de clases (P)

clean limpio, -a (8); puro, -a (13)

to **clean** limpiar (8)

   — up arreglar (8)

to **clear the table** quitar la mesa (8)

to **climb** subir (7)

clinic la clínica (9)

to **close** cerrar (e → ie) (10)

closet el guardarropa (8)

clothes la ropa (6)

coat el abrigo (7)

coffee el café (4)

cold frío, -a (7)

   it's — out hace frío (7)

   to be (very) — tener (mucho) frío (9)

   to have a — tener (un) resfriado (9)

color el color (6)

   in — en colores (11)

   what —? ¿de qué color? (6)

comedy la comedia (11)

comfortable cómodo (8)

comical cómico -a (11)

commercial el anuncio (de televisión) (11)

community la comunidad (10)

concert el concierto (11)

to **conserve** *(energy)* conservar (13)

contaminated contaminado, -a (13)

to **cook** cocinar (1)

cool: it's — out hace fresco (7)

corn el maíz (12)

   — tortilla la tortilla de maíz (12)

corner la esquina (10)

to **cost** costar (o → ue) (6)

costume party la fiesta de disfraces (14)

country el país (7)

countryside el campo (3)

course: of — por supuesto (13)

cousin el primo, la prima (5)

cow la vaca (13)

cup la taza (12)

to **cut** cortar (8)

daily special el plato del día (12)

dance el baile (14)

to **dance** bailar (14)

danger el peligro (13)

daring atrevido, -a (1)

date la fecha (P, 14)

   what's today's —? ¿cuál es la fecha de hoy? (P)

daughter la hija (5)

day el día (P)

   every — todos los días (3)

December diciembre (P)

decoration la decoración *pl.* las decoraciones (14)

delicious sabroso, -a (4)

delighted encantado, -a (14)

dentist el / la dentista (9)

department store el almacén, *pl.* los almacenes (6)

to **depend** depender (14)

to **deposit** depositar (10)

desk el escritorio (8); *(student)* (P)

dessert el postre

   for — de postre (12)

detective show el programa de detectives (11)

dictionary el diccionario (2)

difficult difícil (2)

dining room el comedor (8)

dinner la cena (4)

   for — en la cena (4)

to **disagree** no estar de acuerdo (8)

disgusting: that's — ! ¡qué asco! (4)

dish el plato (12)

to **do** hacer (8)

documentary el documental (11)

dog el perro (5)

dollar el dólar (6)

door la puerta (8)

dot: on the — en punto (11)

to **draw** dibujar (1)

dress el vestido (6)

   party — el vestido de fiesta (14)

dresser la cómoda (8)

to **drink** beber (4, 12)

drugstore la farmacia (10)

dumb tonto, -a (11)

to **dust** sacudir (8)

ear el oído (9)

   —ache el dolor de oído (9)

early temprano (10)

earring el arete (14)

Earth la Tierra (13)

easy fácil (2)

to **eat** comer (4, 12)

educational show el programa educativo (11)

egg el huevo (4)

eight ocho (P)

eighteen dieciocho (P)

eighth octavo, -a (2, 8)

eight hundred ochocientos (10)

eighty ochenta (5)

either tampoco (1)

elephant el elefante (13)

eleven once (P)

else más (8)

   anything — algo más (12)

enchilada la enchilada (12)

to **end** terminar (2)

endangered en peligro de extinción (13)

energy la energía (13)

English *(language)* inglés (2)

environment el medio ambiente (13)

evening la noche (P)

   good — buenas noches, buenas tardes (P)

   in the — por la noche, por la tarde (3)

ever alguna vez (12)

every day todos los días (3)

everyone todos, -as (5)

exciting emocionante (11)

excuse me perdón (6)

to **exercise** hacer ejercicio (9)

expensive caro, -a (6)

to **explore** explorar (7)

eye el ojo (9)

facing enfrente (de) (10)

fact el hecho (11)

   — -based program el programa de hechos de la vida real (11)

factory la fábrica (13)

fair regular, así, así (P)

fall el otoño (3)

family la familia (3)

   — room la sala de estar (8)

fantastic fantástico, -a (7)

far (from) lejos (de) (8)

to **fascinate** fascinar (11)

fascinating fascinante (11)

father el padre (5)

February febrero (P)

to **feel** sentir

   how do you —? ¿cómo te sientes? (9)

   I — well / ill me siento bien / mal (9)

fever la fiebre (9)

   to have a — tener fiebre (9)

few: a — unos, unas (4)

fifteen quince (P)

fifth quinto, -a (2, 8)

fifty cincuenta (2)

film la película (11)

finger el dedo (9)

first primero (primer), -a (P, 2, 8)

fish el pescado (4)

   to go —ing ir de pesca (3)

to **fit** quedar (6)

five cinco (P)

five hundred quinientos (10)

flan el flan (12)

floor el piso (8)

flour la harina (12)

   — tortilla la tortilla de harina (12)

flower la flor (13)

flu la gripe (9)

   to have the — tener gripe (9)

folder la carpeta (2)

foot el pie (9)

   on — a pie (10)

football el fútbol americano (3)

for para (2); por (6)

forest la selva (17)

   rain — la selva tropical (7)

fork el tenedor (12)

forty cuarenta (2)

four cuatro (P)

four hundred cuatrocientos (10)

fourteen catorce (P)

French fries las papas fritas (4)

Friday viernes (P)

   on — el viernes (3)

friend el amigo, la amiga (3)

friendly simpático, -a (5)

front: in — of enfrente de (10); delante de (12)

fruit la fruta (4)

funny gracioso, -a (1); emocionante (11); divertido, -a (11)

fur la piel (13)

furniture los muebles (8)

game el partido (10)

garage el garaje (8)

garbage la basura (8)

gas station la estación de servicio (10)

gee! ¡vaya! (7)

generally generalmente (3)

generous generoso, -a (1)

get-together la reunión (14)

gift el regalo (10)

   — shop la tienda de regalos (10)

girl la muchacha (5)

girlfriend la novia (5)

to **give** dar (14)

   to — a gift regalar (14)

glass el vaso (12); *(material)* el vidrio (13)

   (made of) — de vidrio (13)

glasses los anteojos (7)

glove el guante (7)

to **go** ir (3)

   — on! ¡vaya! (7)

   to be —ing to + *verb* ir a + *inf.* (3)

   to — fishing ir de pesca (3)

   to — on vacation ir de vacaciones (7)

   to — shopping ir de compras (3)

   to — to school ir a la escuela (1)

good bueno (buen), -a (P)

   — afternoon buenas tardes (P)

   — evening buenas noches (P)

   — morning buenos días (P)

   — night buenas noches (P)

   it's a — thing that . . . menos mal que . . . (7)

good-by adiós (P)

good-looking guapo, -a (5)

goodness: my —! ¡vaya! (7)

gorilla el gorila (13)

grandfather el abuelo (5)

grandmother la abuela (5)

grandparents los abuelos (5)

grape la uva (4)

gray gris, *pl.* grises (6)

— **hair** pelo canoso (5)

great! ¡genial! (3)

green verde (6)

— **beans** las judías verdes (4)

groceries los comestibles (10)

guest el invitado, la invitada (14)

guitar la guitarra (1)

gymnasium el gimnasio (3)

habit: to be in the — of soler (o → ue) + *inf.* (14)

hair el pelo (5)

half:

— **an hour** media hora (11)

— **-past** y media (2)

ham el jamón (4)

hamburger la hamburguesa (4)

hand la mano (9)

—**made** hecho, -a a mano (14)

handsome guapo, -a (5)

hard difícil (2)

hard-working trabajador, -a (1)

to **have** tener (2, 5)

to — a good (bad) time pasarlo bien (mal) (14)

to — to tener que + *inf.* (8)

he él (2)

head la cabeza (9)

—**ache** dolor de cabeza (9)

health la salud (4); *(class)* las ciencias de la salud (2)

hello! ¡hola! (P)

to **help** ayudar (1)

may I — you? ¿qué desea (Ud.)? (6)

her su, sus (5); *dir. obj. pron.* la (6); *ind. obj. pron.* le (9)

here aquí (2)

around — por aquí (6)

— **it is** aquí está (2)

hi! ¡hola! (P)

high-heeled shoes los zapatos de tacón alto (14)

him *dir. obj. pron.* lo (6); *ind. obj. pron.* le (9)

his su, sus (5)

hobby el pasatiempo (3)

homework la tarea (2)

horrible horrible (4)

horror movie la película de terror (11)

horse el caballo (13)

hospital el hospital (9)

hot *(flavor)* picante (12)

it's — out hace calor (7)

to be — *(person)* tener calor (9)

hotel el hotel (10)

house la casa (8)

— **special** la especialidad de la casa (12)

household chore el quehacer (de la casa) (8)

¡how! qué + *adj.* (6)

how? ¿cómo? (10)

— **are you?** ¿cómo está (usted)? ¿cómo estás (tú)? (P)

— **long has it been since** …¿cuánto (tiempo) hace que…? (9)

— **many?** ¿cuántos, -as? (5)

— **much?** ¿cuánto? (6)

— **old are you?** ¿cuántos años tienes? (P)

— **old is …?** cuántos años tiene …? (5)

—**'s it going?** ¿qué tal? (P)

hundred cien (5); ciento (6)

hungry: to be — tener hambre (4)

to **hurt** doler (o → ue) (9); lastimarse + *part of body* (9)

I yo (2)

ice cream el helado (12)

iced tea el té helado (4)

if si (10)

ill enfermo, -a (3)

I feel — me siento mal (9)

impatient impaciente (1)

in en (P)

— **order to** para + *inf.* (7)

inexpensive barato, -a (6)

ingredient el ingrediente (12)

intelligent inteligente (5)

interest: place of — el lugar de interés (7)

to **interest** interesar (11)

interesting interesante (11)

to **introduce** presentar (14)

invitation la invitación *pl.* las invitaciones (14)

to **invite** invitar (14)

it *dir. obj.* lo (6)

jacket la chaqueta (6)

jaguar el jaguar (13)

January enero (P)

jeans los jeans (6)

jewelry las joyas (14)

juice el jugo (4)

orange — el jugo de naranja (4)

July julio (P)

June junio (P)

kind amable (1); la clase (11)
kitchen la cocina (8)
knife el cuchillo (12)
to **know** saber (13); conocer (14)

lacking: to be — faltar a (12)
lake el lago (7)
lamp la lámpara (8)
to **last** durar (11)
last pasado, -a (7)
  — night anoche (10)
late tarde (10)
  see you —r hasta luego (P)
laundry room el lavadero (8)
lawn el césped (8)
  to mow the — cortar el césped (8)
lazy perezoso, -a (1)
to **learn** aprender (2)
least el / la / los / las menos + *adj.* (11)
leather el cuero (8)
  (made of) — de cuero (8)
to **leave** salir (7)
left izquierdo, -a (9)
  to the — (of) a la izquierda (de) (10)
leg la pierna (9)
lemonade la limonada (4)
less menos (4, 11)
  more or — más o menos (4)
letter la carta (10)
lettuce la lechuga (4)
library la biblioteca (10)
life la vida (11)
light la luz, *pl.* las luces (13)
to **like** gustar a (5)
  he / she —s le gusta(n) (5)

I / you — (a mí) me / (a ti) te gusta(n) (1)
I'd — quisiera (7)
likewise igualmente (P)
to **listen** escuchar (1)
little pequeño, -a (5)
  a — un poco (de) (11)
to **live** vivir (8)
living room la sala (8)
located: to be — quedar (10)
long largo, -a (11)
to **look for** buscar (6)
lot: a — of mucho, -a (2)
to **love** encantar (5)
  he / she —s le encanta(n) (5)
  I— me encanta(n) (4)
loving cariñoso, -a (5)
lunch el almuerzo (2)
  for — en el almuerzo (4)

ma'am señora (6)
made hecho, -a (14)
  — of de + *material* (8)
magazine la revista (13)
to **mail** enviar (10)
to **make** hacer (8)
mall el centro comercial (3)
man el hombre (5)
March marzo (P)
marker el marcador (2)
match el partido (10)
mathematics las matemáticas (2)
matter: what's the —? ¿qué pasa? (9)
May mayo (P)
me *obj. pron.* me (9); *after prep.* mí (1, 12)
meal la comida (4)
to **meet:**
  I'd like you to — te presento a… (14)

pleased to — you mucho gusto (P); encantado, -a (14)
menu el menú (12)
messy desordenado, -a (1)
metal el metal (8)
  (made of) — de metal (8)
midnight medianoche (11)
mild *(flavor)* no picante (12)
milk la leche (4)
minute el minuto (11)
mirror el espejo (8)
miss la señorita (P, 6)
miss: to be —ing faltar a (12)
modern moderno, -a (8)
Monday lunes (P)
  on — el lunes (3)
money el dinero (10)
month el mes (P)
monument el monumento (10)
more más (4, 11)
  — or less más o menos (4)
morning la mañana (3)
  good — buenos días (P)
  in the — por la mañana (3)
most: the — el / la / los / las más + *adj.* (11)
mother la madre (5)
mountain la montaña (7)
mouth la boca (9)
movie la película (11)
  — theater el cine (1)
  to go to the —s ir al cine (1)
  to show a — dar una película (11)
to **mow the lawn** cortar el césped (8)
Mr. (el) señor (P)
Mrs. (la) señora (P)
much mucho, -a (2)
  how —? ¿cuánto? (6)

museum el museo (7)
music la música (2)
   — program el programa musical (11)
musical film la película musical (11)
my mi, mis (3)

name el nombre (5)
   his / her / their — is se llama(n) (5)
   my — is me llamo (P)
   what's your —? ¿cómo te llamas? (P)
napkin la servilleta (12)
near cerca (de) (8)
neat ordenado, -a (1)
necessary: it's — to hay que (13)
neck el cuello (9)
necklace el collar (14)
necktie la corbata (14)
to **need** necesitar (2)
neither . . . nor ni . . . ni (1)
never nunca (4)
new nuevo, -a (6)
news las noticias (11)
newspaper el periódico (13)
next to al lado (de) (10)
nice amable (1); simpático, -a (5)
night noche
   at — de la noche (11)
   good — buenas noches (P)
   last — anoche (10)
nine nueve (P)
nine hundred novecientos (10)
nineteen diecinueve (P)
ninety noventa (5)
no no (P)
   — longer ya no (9)
nobody nadie (5)
noon el mediodía (11)

nor: neither . . . — ni . . . ni (1)
nose la nariz (9)
not no (P)
   — anymore ya no (9)
   — at all de ninguna manera (14)
   — yet todavía no (11)
notebook el cuaderno (2)
nothing nada (9)
November noviembre (P)
now ahora (9)
nowhere ninguna parte (7)
number el número (P)
   phone — el número de teléfono (P)
nurse's office la enfermería (9)

ocean el océano (13)
October octubre (P)
of de (5)
   — course por supuesto (13)
often a menudo (12)
ok bueno (10)
old viejo -a (5); antiguo, -a (8)
   how — are you? ¿cuántos años tienes? (P)
   how — is . . . ? ¿cuántos años tiene . . . ? (5)
older mayor (5)
on en (P); sobre (12)
   — the dot en punto (11)
   — time puntualmente (11)
   — top (of) encima (de) (12)
once una vez (12)
one uno, -a (P)
   it's — o'clock es la una (2)
onion la cebolla (4)
only sólo (5)
   — child el hijo único, la

hija única (5)
to **open** abrir (10)
opposite enfrente (de) (10)
or o (P)
   not . . . — ni . . . ni (1)
orange *(color)* anaranjado, -a (6)
orange la naranja (4)
   — juice el jugo de naranja (4)
to **order** pedir (e → i) (12)
other otro, -a (6)
ouch! ¡ay! (9)
ought to deber (4)
our nuestro, -a (8)
outgoing sociable (1)

pants los pantalones (6)
pantyhose las pantimedias (6)
paper el papel (P)
   sheet of — la hoja de papel (P)
parents los padres (5)
park el parque (3)
   amusement — el parque de diversiones (3)
part: to be a — of formar parte de (13)
party la fiesta (14)
to **pass** pasar (12)
passport el pasaporte (7)
past:
   half- — y media (2)
   quarter — y cuarto (2)
pastime el pasatiempo (3)
pastry el pastel (12)
patient *adj.* paciente (1)
to **pay** pagar (6)
pea el guisante (4)
pen el bolígrafo (P)
pencil el lápiz, *pl.* los lápices (2)
people la gente (13)

pepper la pimienta (12)
  stuffed — el chile relleno (12)
peppery picante (12)
period la hora (2)
person la persona (5)
personal personal (14)
phone el teléfono (1)
  — book la guía telefónica (13)
  — number el número de teléfono (P)
photo la foto (7)
physical education la educación física (2)
physician el médico, la médica (9)
to **pick up** recoger (13)
picture el cuadro (8)
pink rosado, -a (6)
place el lugar (14)
  — of interest el lugar de interés (7)
to **place** poner (8)
to **plan** pensar + *inf.* (7)
plant la planta (13)
plastic el plástico (13)
  (made of) — de plástico (13)
plate el plato (12)
to **play** jugar (u → ue) (3)
pleased to meet you mucho gusto (P); encantado, -a (14)
pocket folder la carpeta (2)
police la policía (10)
  — station la estación de policía (10)
polluted contaminado, -a (13)
pool la piscina (3)
post card la tarjeta postal (10)
post office el correo (10)
poster el cartel (8)
potato la papa (4)

baked — la papa al horno (4)
French-fried — la papa frita (4)
practical práctico, -a (14)
to **practice** practicar (1)
to **prefer** preferir (e → ie) (4, 8)
  I — me gusta más (1); prefiero (4)
to **prepare** preparar (14)
pretty bonito, -a (5)
program el programa (11)
to **protect** proteger (13)
public transportation el transporte público (13)
pure puro, -a (13)
purple morado, -a (6)
to **put** poner (8)
pyramid la pirámide (7)

quarter cuarto, -a (2)
  — past y cuarto (2)
quesadilla la quesadilla (12)
quiet callado, -a (1)

rain la lluvia (7)
to **rain** llover (o → ue) (7)
  it's —ing llueve (7)
raincoat el impermeable (7)
rain forest la selva tropical (7)
rather bastante (9)
to **read** leer (1)
real real (11)
realistic realista (11)
really? ¿de veras? (1); ¡no me digas! (3)
to **receive** recibir (14)
to **recycle** reciclar (13)
recycling center el centro de reciclaje (13)
red rojo, -a (6)

— -haired pelirrojo, -a (5)
to **reduce** reducir (13)
refrigerator el refrigerador (8)
relative el pariente, la parienta (14)
to **rest** descansar (7)
restaurant el restaurante (10)
to **return** regresar (7); devolver (o → ue) (10)
rice el arroz (4)
right? ¿verdad? (4)
right derecho, -a (9)
  — away en seguida (12)
  to be — tener razón (8)
  to the — (of) a la derecha (de) (10)
romantic movie la película romántica (11)
room el cuarto (8)
round redondo, -a (8)
to **row** pasear en bote (7)
rowboat el bote (7)
ruins las ruinas (7)
ruler la regla (2)

sad triste (11)
salad la ensalada (4)
salt la sal (12)
same: the — thing lo mismo (12)
sandwich el sandwich (4)
Saturday sábado (P)
  on — el sábado (3)
sauce la salsa (12)
saucer el platillo (12)
to **save** *(energy)* conservar (13)
to **say** decir (13)
  how do you — . . . ? ¿cómo se dice . . . ? (P)
  it is said . . . se dice . . . (P)
  you don't — ! ¡no me digas! (3)

English-Spanish Vocabulary 499

to scare dar miedo a (11)
schedule el horario (2)
school la escuela (1)
  after — después de las clases (3)
science las ciencias (2)
science fiction la ciencia ficción (11)
sea el mar (7)
season la estación, *pl.* las estaciones (3)
second segundo, -a (2, 8)
to see ver (1)
  let's — a ver (2)
to sell vender (12)
semester el semestre (2)
to send enviar (10)
to separate separar (13)
September septiembre (P)
serious serio, -a (1)
to serve servir (e → i) (12)
to set poner (8)
  — the table poner la mesa (8)
seven siete (P)
seven hundred setecientos (10)
seventeen diecisiete (P)
seventh séptimo, -a (2)
seventy setenta (5)
shampoo el champú (10)
sharp en punto (11)
she ella (2)
shirt la camisa (6)
  T- — la camiseta (6)
shoe el zapato (6)
  high-heeled —s los zapatos de tacón alto (14)
  — store la zapatería (6)
shopping:
  — center el centro comercial (3)
  to go — ir de compras (3)
short *(height)* bajo, -a (5)
  — *(length)* corto, -a (11)

shorts los pantalones cortos (6)
should deber + *inf.* (4)
show el programa (11)
to show *movie or TV program* dar (11)
sick enfermo, -a (3)
  I feel — me siento mal (9)
silly tonto, -a (11)
since: it's been *(time)* **—** hace + *(time)* + que (9)
to sing cantar (14)
sir señor (6)
sister la hermana (5)
sitcom la comedia (11)
six seis (P)
six hundred seiscientos (10)
sixteen dieciséis (P)
sixth sexto, -a (2, 8)
sixty sesenta (5)
to skate patinar (1)
to ski esquiar (7)
ski cap el gorro (7)
to skin-dive bucear (7)
skirt la falda (6)
to sleep dormir (o → ue) (9)
sleepy: to be — tener sueño (9)
small pequeño, -a (5)
  —er menor *pl.,* menores (11)
snack *(afternoon)* la merienda (12)
  for a — de merienda (12)
snake la serpiente (13)
sneakers los tenis (6)
snow la nieve (7)
to snow nevar (e → ie) (7)
  it's —ing nieva (7)
soap el jabón (10)
  — opera la telenovela (11)
soccer el fútbol (3)
sock el calcetín, *pl.* los calcetines (6)
social studies las ciencias

sociales (2)
sofa el sofá (8)
soft drink el refresco (4)
some unos, unas (4); algunos, -as (14)
someone, somebody alguien (14)
something algo (4)
  — else algo más (12)
sometimes a veces (1)
son el hijo (5)
  —s; —s and daughters los hijos (5)
sorry: I'm — lo siento (2)
to sort separar (13)
so-so así, así, regular (P)
soup la sopa (4)
souvenir el recuerdo (7)
Spanish *(language)* el español (2)
special: daily — el plato del día (12)
spell: how do you — . . . ? ¿Cómo se escribe . . . ? (P)
spicy picante (12)
spoon la cuchara (12)
sports los deportes (1)
  — program el programa deportivo (11)
spring la primavera (3)
square cuadrado, -a (8)
stadium el estadio (10)
stamp el sello (10)
to start empezar (e → ie) (2)
station la estación, *pl.* las estaciones (10)
to stay (in bed) quedarse (en la cama) (9)
steak el bistec (4)
stereo el equipo de sonido (8)
still todavía (9)
stingy tacaño, -a (1)
stomach el estómago (9)
  —ache el dolor de

estómago (9)
store la tienda (6)
  clothing — la tienda de
    ropa (6)
  department — el
    almacén, *pl.* los
    almacenes (6)
  discount — la tienda de
    descuentos (6)
story *(of a building)* el piso
  (8)
stove la estufa (8)
street la calle (10)
student el / la estudiante (P)
to **study** estudiar (1)
subway el metro (10)
  — **station** la estación del
    metro (10)
sugar el azúcar (12)
suit el traje (14)
  bathing — el traje de baño
    (7)
suitcase la maleta (7)
summer el verano (3)
sun el sol (7)
to **sunbathe** tomar el sol (7)
Sunday domingo (P)
  on — el domingo (3)
sunglasses los anteojos de
  sol (7)
sunny: it's — hace sol (7)
suntan lotion el bronceador
  (7)
supermarket el
  supermercado (10)
surprise party la fiesta de
  sorpresa (14)
sweater el suéter (6)
sweatshirt la sudadera (6)
to **swim** nadar (1)
  swimming pool la piscina
    (3)

table la mesa (P)
  to clear the — quitar la
    mesa (8)
  to set the — poner la
    mesa (8)
tablecloth el mantel (12)
taco el taco (12)
to **take** llevar (7); sacar, tomar
  (9)
  to — **out** sacar (8)
  to — **pictures** sacar fotos
    (7)
  to — **a walk** ir a pasear
    (10)
to **talk** hablar (1)
  to — **on the phone** hablar
    por teléfono (1)
  — **show** el programa de
    entrevistas (11)
tall alto, -a (5)
tape recorder la grabadora
  (2)
to **taste** probar (o → ue) (12)
tasty sabroso, -a (4)
taxi el taxi (10)
tea el té (4)
  iced — el té helado (4)
to **teach** enseñar (2)
teacher el profesor, la
  profesora (P)
teeth las muelas (9)
telephone el teléfono (1); *see
  also* **phone**
television la tele(visión) (1)
  to watch — ver la
    tele(visión) (1)
temple el templo (10)
ten diez (P)
tennis el tenis (3)
terrible terrible (9)
thank you gracias (P)
that ese, esa; (6); que (5)
  isn't — **so?** ¿verdad? (4)
  —**'s too bad!** ¡qué lástima!
    (3)
  —**'s why** por eso (11)

the el, la, los, las (P, 2)
theater *(movie)* el cine (1);
  el teatro (10)
their su, sus (8)
them *after prep.* ellos, ellas
  (3); los, las *dir. obj. pron.*
  (6); les *ind. obj. pron.*
  (11)
then luego (10)
there allí (2)
  — **is / are** hay (P)
  — **it is** allí está (2)
therefore por eso (11)
these estos, estas (6)
they ellos, ellas (2)
thing la cosa (8)
to **think** creer (4); pensar
  (e → ie) (11)
  I don't — **so** creo que no
    (4)
  I — **so** creo que sí (4)
  to — **about** pensar en (11)
third tercer, -a (2, 8)
thirsty: to be — tener sed
  (4)
thirteen trece (P)
thirty treinta (P)
this este, esta (6)
those esos, esas (6)
thousand mil (10)
threat la amenaza (13)
three tres (P)
three hundred trescientos
  (10)
three-ring binder la carpeta
  de argollas (2)
throat la garganta (9)
  sore — el dolor de
    garganta (9)
  — **lozenges** las pastillas
    para la garganta (10)
Thursday jueves (P)
  on — el jueves (3)
tidy ordenado, -a (1)
tie la corbata (14)
tiger el tigre (13)

time la hora (2, 14); el tiempo (11); la vez (13)

  at the same — a la vez (13)

  at —s a veces (1)

  at what — ¿a qué hora ? (2)

  many —s muchas veces (12)

  on — puntualmente (11)

  what — is it? ¿qué hora es? (2)

tired cansado, -a (3)

to a (3)

  in order — para + *inf.* (7)

toast el pan tostado (4)

today hoy (P)

  not — hoy no (3)

toe el dedo del pie (9)

tomato el tomate (4)

  — soup la sopa de tomate (4)

tomorrow mañana (P, 3)

too también (1); demasiado (11)

  me — a mí también (1)

toothache el dolor de muelas (9)

toothpaste la pasta dentífrica (10)

tortilla la tortilla (12)

town square la plaza (10)

train el tren (10)

  — station la estación del tren (10)

tree el árbol (13)

to try probar (o → ue) (12)

Tuesday martes (P, 3)

  on — el martes (3)

to turn off apagar (13)

twelve doce (P)

twenty veinte (P)

twice dos veces (12)

twin el gemelo, la gemela (5)

two dos (P)

two hundred doscientos (10)

type la clase (11)

typical típico, -a (12)

ugly feo, -a (5)

umbrella el paraguas (7)

uncle el tío (5)

uncomfortable incómodo, -a (8)

under(neath) debajo de (12)

unfriendly antipático, -a (5)

unpleasant antipático, -a (5)

until hasta (11)

us *after prep.* nosotros, -as (3); *obj. pron.* nos (11)

to use usar (13)

usually generalmente (3)

vacation las vacaciones (7)

  to go on — ir de vacaciones (7)

to vacuum pasar la aspiradora (8)

vacuum cleaner la aspiradora (8)

VCR la videocasetera (8)

vegetable la verdura (4)

  — soup la sopa de verduras (4)

very muy (P, 1)

video game el videojuego (3)

to visit visitar (7)

volleyball el vóleibol (3)

waiter, waitress el camarero, la camarera (12)

walking a pie (10)

to want querer (e → ie) (7)

to wash lavar (8)

to watch ver (1)

water el agua (4)

waterfall las cataratas (7)

we nosotros, -as (2)

to wear llevar (6)

weather el tiempo (7)

  the — is nice (bad) hace buen (mal) tiempo (7)

  — forecast el pronóstico del tiempo (11)

  what's the — like? ¿qué tiempo hace? (7)

Wednesday miércoles (P)

  on — el miércoles (3)

week la semana (P)

weekend el fin de semana (3)

welcome: you're — de nada (3)

well bien (P); *(to indicate pause)* pues (1)

went fui, fuiste (7, 10)

western la película del oeste (11)

whale la ballena (13)

what qué (2)

when ¿cuándo? (P); cuando (7)

where? ¿dónde? (3); donde (7)

  from —? ¿de dónde? (P)

  (to) —? ¿adónde? (3)

whether si (10)

white blanco, -a (6)

  in black and — en blanco y negro (11)

who? whom? ¿quién(es)? (2)

why ¿por qué? (4)

  that's — por eso (11)

wind el viento (7)

window la ventana (8)

winter el invierno (3)

  — scarf la bufanda (7)

with con (3)

  — me conmigo (3)

  — you contigo (3)

to **withdraw** *(money)* sacar (10)
  wolf el lobo (13)
  woman la mujer (5)
  wonderful fantástico (7);
    ¡genial! (3)
  wood la madera (13)
    (made of) — de madera
    (8)
to **work** trabajar (10)
  worse peor (9)
  worst el / la (los / las)
    peor(es) (11)
  worthwhile: it's (not) —
    (no) vale la pena (13)
  wow! ¡vaya! (7)
  wristwatch el reloj pulsera
    (14)
to **write** escribir (14)

wrong:
  to be — no tener razón (8)
  what's —? ¿qué tienes? (9)

year el año (P)
  New —**'s Eve party** la
    fiesta de fin de año (14)
  to be . . . —**s old** tener . . .
    años (P, 5)
yellow amarillo, -a (6)
yes sí (P)
yesterday ayer (10)
you *fam.* tú *; formal* usted
    (Ud.), *pl.* ustedes (Uds.)
    (2); lo, la, los, las *dir. obj.*
    pron. (6); te *fam. dir. obj.*

pron. (8); le, les *ind. obj.*
    pron. (9, 11); ti *fam. after*
    prep. (1, 12)
young *adj.* joven (5)
  —**er** menor *pl.* menores (5)
  — **lady** la joven (6)
  — **man, sir** el joven (6)
  — **people** los jóvenes (14)
your tu (2); tus (3); su, sus
    (8)
yuck! ¡qué asco! (4)

zero cero (P)
zoo el zoológico (10)

Índice

In almost all cases, structures are first presented in the *Vocabulario para conversar,* where they are practiced lexically in conversational contexts. They are explained later, usually in the *Gramática en contexto* section of that chapter. Light-face numbers refer to pages where structures are initially presented or, after explanation, where student reminders occur. **Bold-face numbers** refer to pages where structures are explained or otherwise highlighted.

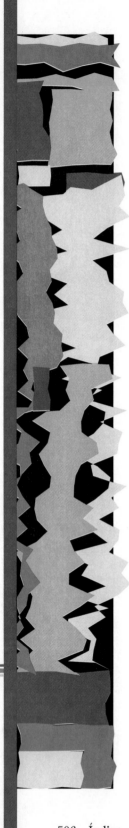

ACKNOWLEDGMENTS

Illustrations   Kaz Aizawa: pp. **346-347, 439;**   Andrea Baruffi: pp. **90-101, 104-108;**   Mark Bender: pp **470-471;**   Jennifer Bolten: pp. **148, 397;**   Margaret Carsello: pp. **63, 343;**   Mark Charlier: pp. **67, 77, 147;**   Rick Clubb: pp. **30-44, 210-211, 252-259, 261-271, 276-277, 281;**   Tim Foley: pp. **340-341;**   Joe Fournier: pp. **304-305;**   Elissé Jo Goldstein: pp. **316-326, 330-332, 334-336, 345;**   Chuck Gonzales: pp. **150-151;**   David Gothard: pp. **274-275;**   Patti Green: pp. **78, 142, 144-145;**   Donna Ingemanson: pp. **40, 46, 51;**   Iskra Lettering Design: Hand lettering on cover and pp.**I-XIII, 1, 3, 27, 55, 87, 119, 151, 181, 217, 249, 283, 313, 347, 381, 415, 447;**   Paul Jermann: pp. **118-119;**   Mike Kasun: pp. **376-377;**   Hiro Kimura: pp. **350-357, 362-371;**   Mapping Specialists Limited: pp. **XIV-XVII, 11;**   James Mellett: pp. **58-62, 64, 66-67, 71-72, 74-76, 85, 210-218, 224-227;**   Susan Melrath: pp. **408-409;**   Jane Mjolsness: p. **443;**   Lori Osiecki: pp. **184-193, 195-196, 201-203, 205-207, 215;**   Donna Perrone: pp. **49, 69, 243;**   Rob Porazinski: pp. **173, 307, 308;**   Karen Pritchett: pp. **154-163, 167-170;**   Mike Reed: pp. **418-429, 432-437;**   Javier Romero Design: p. **46;**   Sandra Shap: pp. **286-295, 299-303;**   Scott Snow: pp. **7-23, 450-459, 462-467;**   Mark Stearney: pp. **414-415;**   Stephen Sweeny: pp. **468-469;**   Susan Williams: pp. **175, 240;**   Elizabeth Wolf: pp. **122-130, 135-137, 139, 141; 149, 384-396, 398-405, 413.**

Photographs   **Front and back covers, II, XVIII-1:** Suzanne L. Murphy/FPG. All rights reserved.;   **IV:** Otis Imboden ©National Geographic Society;   **VI, 19:** David Ryan/DDB Stock Photo;   **VII(t), 28, 54-55, 63, 71, 219(t), 251(t):** ©Peter Menzel;   **VII(b), 57(b), 77, 133, 152, 165(b), 173(tl), 189(b), 361(b):** ©Ulrike Welsch;   **VIII(t), 89(t):** James K. Hackett/Leo de Wys, Inc.;   **VIII(b), 40, 48(b), 51, 56, 136, 148, 182, 188(r), 238(br), 241(t), 244(l), 245(b), 284(t):** David R. Frazier Photolibrary;   **XI(t),57(t), 79, 81, 86-87, 89(b), 102, 125, 131, 133(t), 175, 177(b), 183(t), 183(b), 189(b), 216-217, 231(r), 238(cr), 250, 260, 279(t), 321(t), 321(c), 380-381, 446-447, 448(b):** Frerck/Odyssey/Chicago;   **IX(b), XI(b), 189(t), 189(c), 194, 265, 315(t), 328-329, 346-347, 397, 407, 416, 438, 441(t), 473:** ©Beryl Goldberg Photographer;   **X(t), 230-231:** ©1989 Glenn Randall;   **X(bl), 50(bl), 173(br), 273(l):** Owen Franken/Stock Boston;   **X(br):** M. Díaz Vélez/DDB Stock Photo;   **XI(t), 343:** ©K. Preuss/The Image Works;   **5(t):** Gerardo Ramírez/Photography by Vicki Lee Ragan;   **6(tl):** Tom McCarthy/PhotoEdit;   **6(tr), 166, 307:** Tony Freeman/PhotoEdit;   **6(bl):** Richard Hutchings/PhotoEdit;   **6(br), 26-27, 29(b), 47(t), 48(t), 50(br), 52, 80, 120(b), 173(bl), 188(l), 198(l), 232(t), 232(c), 238(t), 238(cl), 238(bl), 241(b), 305(b), 337, 395:** Chip & Rosa Maria de la Cueva Peterson;   **14:** Otis Imboden ©National Geographic Society;   **18:** ©David Lavender;   **29(t), 348, 449:** ©Owen Franken;   **41, 47(b), 265(inset), 361(t):** Stuart Cohen/Comstock;   **42:** ©Carl Toth;   **46:** ©Sven Martson/Comstock;   **50(t), 339:** ©Jack Parsons;   **69, 120(t):** ©Nancy D'Antonio   **81(t),199(t), 261(t), 279(b), 349(b), 405:** Joe Viesti/Viesti Associates;   **86-87(t), 88-89(t):** Adamsmith Productions/Westlight;   **88:** ©Diane Joy Schmidt;   **103(t), 118-119, 180-181, 219(c):** ©Wolfgang Kaehler;   **103(b), 111(b), 116, 411:** ©D. Donne Bryant;   **104:** Pete Seaward/Tony Stone Images;   **109:** ©M. Algaze/The Images Works;   **110:** ©Jack Vartoogian. All rights reserved.;   **111(t), 382(t):** Robert Fried/Stock Boston;   **112:** Courtesy Paramount Pictures/United International; Pictures, Madrid;   **121:** ©Martha Cooper/Viesti Associates;   **133(c):** Steve Vidler/Leo de Wys, Inc.;   **138:** Focus On Sports;   **150-151:** Viesti Associates;   **152:** Bohdan Hrynewych/Stock Boston;   **165(t):** Randall Hyman/Stock Boston;   **171:** Museo Nacional de Historia, Castillo de Chapultepec, Mexico City;   **174(l):** David Young Wolff/PhotoEdit;   **174(r):** Mary Kate Denny/PhotoEdit;   **176(t):** Ilene Perlman/Stock Boston;   **176(b), 343, 460, 469:** Bob Daemmrich/Stock Boston;   **177(t):** ©R.S. Wagner;   **177(c):** Spencer Grant/Stock Boston;   **199(b):** Courtesy the Puerto Rican Tourism Company;   **200:** Superstock;   **214:** Peter Menzel/Stock Boston;   **218:** Eric Lessing/Art Resource;   **219(b):** Max & Bea Hunn/DDB Stock Photo;   **231(l),232(b):** ©David Wells/The Image Works;   **243(t):** The Bettmann Archive;   **243(b):** Randy G. Taylo/Leo de Wys, Inc.;   **244(r):** Ray Pfortner/Peter Arnold, Inc.;   **245(t), 245(c):** Comstock;   **248-249:** Chris R. Sharp/DDB Stock Photo;   **251(b):** Rhoda Sidney/PhotoEdit;   **261(b):** Vince Dewitt/DDB Stock Photo;   **272:** Cahlus Goldin/DDB Stock Photo;   **273(r):** M. Díaz Vélez/DDB Stock Photo;   **278:** Ken Ross/Viesti Associates;   **282-283:** Schalkwijk/Art Resource;   **284(b):** Jeff Greenberg/PhotoEdit;   **285:** ©Victor Englebert;   **296:** Jeff Greenberg/The Image Works;   **297:** Alyx Kellington/DDB Stock Photo;   **305(t), 315(b):** M. Antman/The Image Works;   **309:** Bob Daemmrich/The Image Works;   **312-313:** Rob Crandall/Stock Boston;   **314:** Algaze/The Image Works;   **321(b):** Charles Kennard/Stock Boston;   **327:** Art Museum of the Americas/Organization of American States;   **329:** Alan Landau for ScottForesman;   **343(inset), 440, 472:** Bob Daemmrich Photography;   **349(t):** ©Maler/Retna Ltd., NY;   **373(t), 375:** Kobal Collection;   **373(b):** Imapress/Archive Photos;   **376-377:** Courtesy Coral Picture Corporation/Radio Caracas Televisión, Venezuela;   **378:** Jack Demuth for ScottForesman;   **382(b):** ©1990 Chase/PhotoBank, Inc.;   **383:** ©Billy E. Barnes/PhotoEdit;   **395(inset):** Robert Fried/DDB Stock Photo;   **412:** ©Gary A. Conner/PhotoEdit;   **415:** ©Wayne Lynch/DRK Photo;   **417:** Gerard Lacz/Animals, Animals;   **430:** ©Robert A. Tyrrell/Animals, Animals;   **430(inset):** Richard La Val/Animals, Animals;   **431(r):** American Museum of Natural History/Courtesy Eduardo Aparicio;   **431(l):** J.A. Hancock/Photo Researchers;   **434:** ©Alfredo Arreguín;   **439:** Gerry Ellis Nature Photography;   **441(b):** Courtesy Waste Management, Inc.;   **442:** ©Betsy Blass/Photo Researchers, Inc.;   **444:** ©Michael Fogden/DRK Photo;   **448(t):** David Simpson/Stock Boston;   **474:** ©Robert Fried.

Realia   Page 112: Excerpt, "Calendario" from *El Diario de Juárez,* July 16, 1993, p. 7.

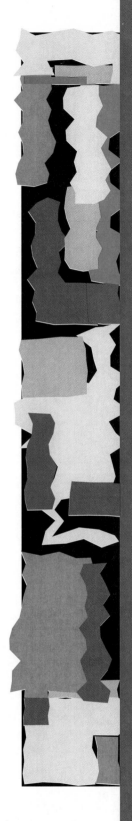

Acknowledgments   507

507